Community Builders Handbook Series

RESIDENTIAL DEVELOPMENT HANDBOOK
Second Edition

Sponsored by the
Members
of the
Residential Development Councils
of
ULI–the Urban Land Institute
1990

ULI–the Urban Land Institute, Washington, D.C.

About ULI–the Urban Land Institute

ULI–the Urban Land Institute is a nonprofit education and research organization that fosters and encourages high standards of land use planning and development. To this end, the Institute sponsors a wide range of education programs, conducts research, interprets current land use trends, and disseminates pertinent information.

Established in 1936, ULI is recognized as one of America's most respected and widely quoted sources of objective information on urban planning, growth, and development. Members of the Washington, D.C.–based Institute include land developers, builders, architects, city planners, investors, planning and renewal agencies, financial institutions, and others interested in land use.

ULI Staff for *Residential Development Handbook*

Staff Vice President, Research and Education	J. Thomas Black
Staff Vice President, Publications	Frank H. Spink, Jr.
Director, Housing and Community Development Research	Diane R. Suchman
Project Director	Lloyd W. Bookout, Jr.
Managing Editor	Nancy H. Stewart
Manuscript Editor	Barbara M. Fishel/Editech
Manager, Computer-Assisted Publishing	Helene Y. Redmond
Art Director	M. Elizabeth Van Buskirk
Artist	Jeffrey Urbancic
Production Manager	Diann Stanley-Austin
Word Processor	Laurie Nicholson

This handbook is part of a series of publications based on the philosophy of *The Community Builders Handbook*, first published in 1947 and last published in the Fifth or Anniversary Edition, 1968.

Community Builders Handbook Series:
Industrial Development Handbook, 1975 (out of print)
Shopping Center Development Handbook, 1977; Second Edition, 1985
Residential Development Handbook, 1978
Downtown Development Handbook, 1980
Recreational Development Handbook, 1981
Office Development Handbook, 1982
Mixed-Use Development Handbook, 1987
Business and Industrial Park Development Handbook, 1988

Community Builders Handbook Supplement Series:
Working with the Community: A Developer's Guide, 1985
Project Infrastructure Development Handbook, 1989

Recommended bibliographic listing:
Lloyd W. Bookout, Jr., et al. *Residential Development Handbook*.
Washington, D.C.: ULI–Urban Land Institute, 1990
ULI Catalog Number R22

International Standard Book Number 0-87420-705-3
Library of Congress Catalog Card Number 90-70875
Printed in the United States of America

Principal Author

Lloyd W. Bookout, Jr., Senior Associate
Housing and Community Development Research
ULI–the Urban Land Institute

Contributing Authors

Kenneth Leventhal & Company, Los Angeles, California
The William E. Becker Organization, Hackensack, New Jersey
W. Paul O'Mara, Principal, Economics Research Associates, Vienna, Virginia
D. Scott Middleton, Senior Associate, Housing and Community Development Research,
ULI–the Urban Land Institute

With a Steering Committee
composed of the following
Urban Land Institute members

James M. DeFrancia,
Steering Committee Chair
President
Lowe Enterprises Mid-Atlantic, Inc.
Sterling, Virginia

William E. Becker
President
The William E. Becker Organization
Hackensack, New Jersey

Richard L. Michaux
National Partner
Trammell Crow Company
Alexandria, Virginia

C. Lewis Christensen
President
Vintage Communities, Inc.
Colorado Springs, Colorado

Gary M. Ryan
President
Gary M. Ryan Real Estate
San Diego, California

David R. Jensen
President
David Jensen Associates, Inc.
Denver, Colorado

Bruce T. Yoder
Vice President
Greenhorne & O'Mara, Inc.
Greenbelt, Maryland

With special review
provided by the following
Urban Land Institute members

Wayne S. Hyatt
Attorney
Hyatt & Rhoads, P.C.
Atlanta, Georgia

Judith H. Reagan
President
Community Consultants, Inc.
Deerfield Beach, Florida

Gadi Kaufmann
Managing Partner
Robert Charles Lesser & Company
Beverly Hills, California

Paul Z. "Pete" Rose
President
The Klingbeil Company
San Francisco, California

Acknowledgments

The ULI handbooks result from the collective efforts of many organizations and professionals over a long period. I would like to thank all those who participated in the three-year process of preparing this book.

First, thanks must be extended to the four individuals and organizations who contributed directly to the text. Under the direction of Stan Ross and the daily management of James Carberry, Kenneth Leventhal & Company (Los Angeles) is responsible for Chapter 3 on financing. The William E. Becker Organization (Hackensack, New Jersey) provided much of the material on market analysis and on marketing contained in Chapters 2 and 6, respectively. Under the direction of W. Paul O'Mara, Economics Research Associates (Vienna, Virginia) drafted a major part of the text for Chapter 8 on rehabilitation and adaptive use. Thanks also go to D. Scott Middleton for his contributions to Chapters 5 and 7 and for frequently serving as a sounding board.

Special credit must be given to the members of the steering committee who helped to develop the book's scope and who provided comments and suggestions on each chapter as it was completed. James M. DeFrancia, Lowe Enterprises Mid-Atlantic, Inc., as chair of the steering committee, made himself available to help resolve issues as they arose. Other steering committee members deserving recognition include William E. Becker, The William E. Becker Organization; C. Lewis Christensen, Vintage Communities, Inc.; David R. Jensen, David Jensen Associates, Inc.; Richard L. Michaux, Trammell Crow Company; Gary M. Ryan, Gary M. Ryan Real Estate; and Bruce T. Yoder, Greenhorne & O'Mara, Inc.

Four other ULI council members provided review of topical areas and chapters. Paul Z. (Pete) Rose, The Klingbeil Company, reviewed the chapter on rehabilitation and adaptive use. Gadi Kaufmann, Robert Charles Lesser & Company, reviewed the text pertaining to market analysis issues. And special thanks are due to Wayne S. Hyatt, Hyatt & Rhoads, P.C., and Judith H. Reagan, Community Consultants, Inc., who expertly assisted in the drafting of the community governance chapter and who contributed much of the material contained in that chapter's text and supplements.

At least several dozen other ULI members offered invaluable insights and experiences that appear as quotes throughout the text. And appreciation is extended to the approximately 20 council members who made themselves available for information-gathering interviews during ULI's Spring 1989 meeting in New Orleans.

As the primary author of the first edition of this handbook, W. Paul O'Mara, formerly ULI's director of Housing and Community Development Research and now a vice president with Economics Research Associates, provided an excellent base on which to begin the update.

Thanks to Michael Brandman Associates, and especially to Joan Kelly in the Los Angeles office, for submitting extensive materials and information on site analysis and development regulations for use in Chapter 2. And thanks go to the many individuals and organizations contributing feature boxes, graphics, photographs, and other supplemental materials used throughout the book.

Several ULI staff members must be noted for their hard work and dedication to the production of this book. Nancy Stewart oversaw the editing of the text and assumed much of the responsibility for the production schedule. Barbara Fishel, Editech, edited the manuscript, making many valuable suggestions along the way. Assisted by a computer, Helene Y. Redmond expertly laid out the text and its hundreds of photos, graphics, and feature boxes. Betsy Van Buskirk and Jeff Urbancic produced the dozens of graphics and other artwork that help to bring the text to life. Diann Stanley-Austin arranged for and managed printing and photo processing, and Laurie Nicholson gave strong word-processing support. Also appreciated are the efforts of several interns and part-time and temporary staff who helped gather research: Maria Brisbane, Kelley Roark, Elaine Vaudreuill, Lisa Mendleson, and Cynthia Angell.

I would also like to extend special thanks to Diane R. Suchman, Tom Black, and Frank Spink of ULI for their patience and support during the long research, writing, and production process.

To those named above and to the others who have contributed to this book, thank you.

Lloyd W. Bookout, Jr.

About ULI Councils

Within the Urban Land Institute, there are 25 councils representing the land use disciplines: Community Development Councils—Blue Flight, Gold Flight; Commercial and Retail Development Councils—Blue Flight, Gold Flight, Silver Flight, Green Flight; Development Regulations Council; Development Infrastructure and Services Council; Industrial and Office Park Development Councils—Blue Flight, Gold Flight, Silver Flight, Green Flight; National Policy Council; Residential Development Councils—Blue Flight, Gold Flight, Silver Flight; Recreational Development Council; Small-Scale Development Councils—Blue Flight, Gold Flight, Silver Flight; Urban Development/Mixed-Use Councils—Blue Flight, Gold Flight, Silver Flight, Green Flight; International Council. Each council is composed of active members drawn from the ULI membership. Council appointment is based on knowledge, experience, and a willingness to share. Developers, consultants, financial institutions, public officials, and academics are all represented on each council to provide a broad perspective and to encourage interaction among various disciplines.

Residential Development Councils
1988–1989

RESIDENTIAL DEVELOPMENT (BLUE FLIGHT) COUNCIL MEMBERS

Chair

D. Michael Crow
Area Partner
Trammell Crow Company
Irving, TX

Assistant Chair

Michael S. Blum
Vice Chair
Heller Financial, Inc.
Chicago, IL

Stephen P. Beinke
Executive Vice President
Blackhawk Corporation
Danville, CA

William M. Bell
Vice Chair
The Liberty National Bank and
  Trust Company of Oklahoma City
Oklahoma City, OK

Yehuda Ben-Arieh
President
Lansbrook Group, Inc.
Chicago, IL

Joan S. Betts
Vice President
The Fidelity Mutual Group
Atlanta, GA

Thomas E. Black
Dallas, TX

Fred H. Burnstead
President
Burnstead Construction Company
Bellevue, WA

Richard A. Carnaghi
Senior Vice President
Heritage Development Group, Inc.
Southbury, CT

George E. Casey, Jr.
Senior Vice President
Toll Brothers, Inc.
New Hope, PA

Kathleen M. Connell
President
Connell & Associates
Los Angeles, CA

William A. Estes, Jr.
President
The Estes Company
Tucson, AZ

Don Fleming
President
The Equity Development Group, Inc.
Toronto, Ontario, Canada

Lewis M. Goodkin
President
Goodkin Research Corporation
Lauderdale-by-the-Sea, FL

James D. Harper, Jr.
President
JDH Realty Company
Chicago, IL

James B. Harvie III
President
James Harvie & Partners
Purchase, NY

Alvin Hayman
Chair
The Hayman Companies
San Francisco, CA

Thomas L. Hodges
President
Greenbelt Companies
Dallas, TX

Liza Hogan
Owner
Liza Hogan Real Estate Investments
Boulder, CO

Arnold M. Kronstadt
Partner
Collins & Kronstadt—Leahy, Hogan, Collins, Draper
Architects & Planners
Silver Spring, MD

Timothy F. Mobley
President
Mobley Homes of Florida
Tampa, FL

David Robert Nelson
President
The Nelson/Ross Companies
Farmington, MI

Dudley Omura
President
Omura Casey, Inc.
North Palm Beach, FL

Jonathan C.K. Peake
Partner
Kagan/Peake Associates
Farmington, CT

Peter B. Perrin
President
Bramalea California, Inc.
Irvine, CA

Clarence L. Roeder
Vice President
J.C. Nichols Company
Kansas City, MO

Eugene I. Ross
President
The Ross Group, Inc.
Chicago, IL

Stephen M. Ross
President
The Related Companies, Inc.
New York, NY

Louis L. Rozenfeld
President
The Desco Group, Inc.
Lafayette, CA

Peter M. Ryan
Senior Vice President
Chase Manhattan Bank
New York, NY

Thomas L. Safran
President
Thomas Safran & Associates
Los Angeles, CA

Robert R. Short
President
The Genesee Company
Golden, CO

Perry J. Snyderman
Partner
Rudnick & Wolfe
Chicago, IL

Alice Larkin Steiner
Senior Vice President
Wallace Associates Consulting Group
Salt Lake City, UT

Jerome D. Stone
President
Residential Planning Corporation
Chicago, IL

Gary E. Stout
President
Public Private Ventures, Inc.
Edina, MN

Charlotte Ann Temple
Principal
Temple Spencer Company
San Francisco, CA

Louis J. Timchak, Jr.
President
Timchak Real Estate Group II, Inc.
North Palm Beach, FL

Gordon E. Tippell
President
Taylor Woodrow Homes California Limited
Newport Beach, CA

Marilyn Kramer Weitzman
President
The Weitzman Group, Inc.
New York, NY

Bruce T. Yoder
Vice President
Greenhorne & O'Mara, Inc.
Greenbelt, MD

Richard D. Zipes
Chair
Omni Funding Corporation
New York, NY

RESIDENTIAL DEVELOPMENT (GOLD FLIGHT) COUNCIL MEMBERS

Chair

J. Ronald Terwilliger
Managing Partner
Trammell Crow Residential
Atlanta, GA

Assistant Chair

Gary W. Fenchuk
President
East West Partners of Virginia
Midlothian, VA

Allen J. Anderson
Principal
Anderson Capital Advisors, Inc.
Dallas, TX

Garland S. Anderson, Jr.
Partner
The Linpro Company
Southbury, CT

Jeffry B. Baldwin
Executive Vice President
The Artery Organization, Inc.
Bethesda, MD

James T. Bisesi
Vice President
Gene B. Glick Company, Inc.
Indianapolis, IN

Peter J. Blampied
President
The Boston Five Cents Savings Bank FSB
Boston, MA

Jack Bloodgood
President
Bloodgood Architects & Planners, Inc.
Des Moines, IA

George M. Brady, Jr.
Washington, DC

Alan M. Connor
Senior Vice President
AEtna Realty Investors, Inc.
Hartford, CT

James B. Digney
Senior Vice President
Metropolitan Life Insurance Company
New York, NY

Darla Totusek Flanagan
Senior Vice President
JMB Realty Corporation
San Francisco, CA

Robert Freed
President
Bedford Properties
Lafayette, CA

Vern R. Halter
President
Secured Communities
Atlanta, GA

John W. Hancock
Executive Vice President
Security Pacific National Bank
Costa Mesa, CA

Christopher W. E. Hovey
President
Mackenzie, Hovey & Associates
Denver, CO

Michael L. Ives
President
Michael L. Ives & Associates, Inc.
Scottsdale, AZ

Peter E. Jarvis
Principal
Bennett-Ringrose-Wolsfeld-Jarvis-Gardner, Inc.
Minneapolis, MN

Steven A. Karpf
Vice President
New England Development and Management
Newton Centre, MA

Edwin L. Kelly
Senior Vice President
Interstate General Company L.P.
Waldorf, MD

Edwin R. Kimsey, Jr.
Vice President
Niles Bolton Associates, Inc.
Atlanta, GA

Warren B. Lane
Managing Director
Dean Witter Realty, Inc.
New York, NY

Paul M. Lehner
National Partner–Finance
Trammell Crow Residential
Dallas, TX

David R. Lewis
President
Osprey Investment Company
Greenbelt, MD

Thomas E. Lewis
President
Lewis Property investors, Inc.
Tampa, FL

William B. McGuire, Jr.
Partner
The McGuire Group
Charlotte, NC

J. Steven Manolis
Managing Director
Salomon Brothers, Inc.
New York, NY

Melvin A. Mister
Vice President
Chase Manhattan
New York, NY

James C. Niver
President
Century Land Company
Houston, TX

Peter S. O'Neill
President
River Run Development Company
Boise, ID
Columbia Willamette Development Company
Portland, OR

R. Craig Overturf
President
Cal Fed Enterprises/Cal Fed Investment Management
  Corp.
Los Angeles, CA

Sarah E. Peck
President
Rouse/Chamberlin, Inc.
Exton, PA

William H. Possiel
Partner
Ralph Edgar Group Inc.
Marietta, GA

Renay Regardie
President
Housing Data Reports, Inc./Housing Strategies, Inc.
Washington, DC

Randhir Sahni
President
Llewelyn-Davies Sahni, Inc.
Houston, TX

Milton Schneiderman
President
The Milton Company
McLean, VA

Jeffrey A. Scott
Owner
Scott Realty Company
Tulsa, OK

Bruce E. Smith
President
Arvida Company—South Atlantic Division
Atlanta, GA

Lamar E. Smith
Senior Vice President
Citizens Federal Savings & Loan
Dayton, OH

Robert J. Thiebaut
President
Sterling Trust
Atlanta, GA

Frederic J. VanderKloot
Managing Director
Southport Financial Corp.
Southport, CT

M.A. Warren
Manger–Land Development
Estate of James Campbell
Honolulu, HI

Leon N. Weiner
President
Leon N. Weiner & Associates, Inc.
Wilmington, DE

John Wieland
President
John Wieland Homes, Inc.
Atlanta, GA

G. Ronald Witten
President
M/PF Research, Inc.
Dallas, TX

Joseph L. Zehr
President
North Eastern Companies
Fort Wayne, IN

RESIDENTIAL DEVELOPMENT (SILVER FLIGHT) COUNCIL MEMBERS

Chair

Ronald C. Nahas
Vice President
R.T. Nahas Company
Castro Valley, CA

Assistant Chair

Frank A. Passadore
President
The Grupe Company
Stockton, CA

Lark M. Anderson
Vice President
Prudential Property Company
Newark, NJ

William E. Becker
President
The William E. Becker Organization
Hackensack, NJ

George R. Bosworth, Jr.
Vice President
Evans Withycombe, Inc.
Phoenix, AZ

Coleman D. Boylan, Jr.
Partner
The Maneely Group
Collingswood, NJ

Patricia M. Burke
Managing Director
Nationwide Capital Corporation
Arlington, VA

Thomas M. Coleman
President
Coleman Company
Bakersfield, CA

Allen M. Condon
President
Calmark Homes
Los Angeles, CA

James M. DeFrancia
President
Lowe Enterprises Mid-Atlantic, Inc.
Sterling, VA

Stephen B. Drogin
President
The Drogin Company
San Diego, CA

W. Joseph Duckworth
President
Realen Homes
Berwyn, PA

Winston E. Folkers
President
Folkers Associates
Cincinnati, OH

John Gehan
President
Gehan Investments, Inc.
Irving, TX

James C. Ghielmetti
Chief Executive Officer
Signature Properties, Inc.
Pleasanton, CA

Donald L. Goetz
Senior Vice President
The Fidelity Mutual Life Insurance Company
Radnor, PA

Karl H. Grabbe
President
Interhomes KG
Bremen, West Germany

James B. Grant
President
LJ Melody and Company
Irvine, CA

James D. Hemphill
President
Home by Hemphill, Inc.
Northfield, IL

Philip M. Hove
Principal
Berkus Group Architects
Irvine, CA

Donovan D. Huennekens
President
The Lusk Company
Irvine, CA

Thomas A. Hunter, III
Senior Vice President
Charter Properties, Inc.
Charlotte, NC

John F. Hyer
Principal
The Hyer Group
Dublin, OH

David R. Jensen
President
David Jensen Associates, Inc.
Denver, CO

Bruce E. Karatz
President
Kaufman and Broad Home Corporation
Los Angeles, CA

Robert L. Karnell
President
The Karnell Group
Piscataway, NJ

Walter A. Koelbel, Jr.
President
Koelbel and Company
Denver, CO

Gary J. Kopff
President
Heritage Management Ltd.
Washington, DC

Robert A. Lawson, Jr.
President
Lawson-Essex, Inc.
Norfolk, VA

Christopher Lee
Senior Vice President
Kibel, Green, Inc.
Santa Monica, CA

Randall W. Lewis
Executive Vice President/
  Director of Marketing
Lewis Homes
Upland, CA

Thomas J. Maher
President
Thomas J. Maher & Company, Inc.
Philadelphia, PA

Richard L. Michaux
National Partner
Trammell Crow Company
Alexandria, VA

W. Ross Mollard
President
Ross Company
Newport Beach, CA

Raymond L. Morgan
Executive Vice President
The Travelers Realty Investment Company
Hartford, CT

Emmanuel D. Paradeses
President
Citizens Savings Corporation of Stark County
Canton, OH

Jay Parker
President
HOH Associates, Inc.
Alexandria, VA

Roger Postlethwaite
President
Taylor Woodrow Homes Florida, Inc.
Sarasota, FL

Paul C. Robertson, Jr.
President
Robertson Brothers
Bloomfield Hills, MI

Paul Z. Rose
President
The Klingbeil Company
San Francisco, CA

Gary M. Ryan
Owner
Gary M. Ryan Real Estate
San Diego, CA

John B. Slidell
Executive Vice President
Bozzuto and Associates
Greenbelt, MD

Peter Steil
Principal
The RREEF Funds
New York, NY

Anthony J. Trella
President
Markborough Communities, Inc.
Coral Gables, FL

Dale R. Walker
Executive Vice President
Wells Fargo Bank
San Francisco, CA

James W. Wentling
Principal
James Wentling/Architects
Philadelphia, PA

Leonard W. Wood
Regional Partner
Trammell Crow Residential
Atlanta, GA

AFFILIATED RESIDENTIAL DEVELOPMENT COUNCIL MEMBERS

viii

Contents

List of Illustrations

A Brief History of the Community Builders Handbook Series

The Community Builders Handbook Series came into being when the *Industrial Development Handbook* was published in 1975. This series replaced *The Community Builders Handbook*, first published in 1947.

The original handbook was intended as a medium through which to share the experience and knowledge of developers and to encourage the improvement of land use and development practices. The handbook was sponsored by the Community Builders Council (now the Residential Development Council), which had been formed in 1944. Although the first edition contained only 205 pages and was sparsely illustrated, it represented a major achievement: for the first time, a book was available that described the development of residential communities and shopping centers.

The second edition, the J.C. Nichols Memorial Edition, published in 1950, was a modest revision and update of the original text. In 1954, the third or Members Edition, with 315 pages, significantly expanded the scope of the work. The fourth or Executive Edition, published in 1960, continued this expansion in response to the increasing complexity of development practices. With this edition, the handbook had grown to 476 pages, but it had continued to focus on residential and shopping center development.

The fifth or Anniversary Edition was published in 1968. The handbook had jumped to 526 pages, and its coverage had once more been broadened. In addition to sections on residential and shopping center development, new material discussing a variety of special types of land development was included. Also added was a section on industrial development, drawing on the experience of ULI's Industrial Council, which had been formed in 1951. This was to be the last single volume of *The Community Builders Handbook*.

By 1970, the Institute had decided to publish future editions of *The Community Builders Handbook* in separate volumes, in order to provide expanded and more comprehensive coverage of each topic. Following the publication of the *Industrial Development Handbook* in 1975, successive volumes were added through 1982 on shopping center, residential, downtown, recreational, and office development. In 1985, the second edition of the *Shopping Center Development Handbook* was published, and in 1987, the *Mixed-Use Development Handbook* became the seventh volume in the series. The *Business and Industrial Park Development Handbook*, published in 1988, replaced the *Industrial Development Handbook*, which went out of print in 1987.

The need to deal with topics that crossed the boundaries of the development types covered in each of the handbooks resulted in the creation of a supplement series. Two volumes thus far have been published in the Community Builders Handbook Supplement Series: *Working with the Community: A Developer's Guide* in 1985 and the *Project Infrastructure Development Handbook* in 1989. This series is intended to be an adjunct to all seven of the development types covered in the main handbook series.

This second edition of the *Residential Development Handbook*, which is larger by one-third than its predecessor, reflects the growth in both knowledge and complexity of residential development. The traditional family, the principal occupants of single-family detached housing, has given way to an ever-changing mix of household profiles, and residential development has responded to this changing market with new housing and community concepts.

The handbook series, with the supplement series, now totals more than 2,600 pages, as compared with the 205 pages of the first single-volume edition. The three councils that were the sponsors of the early editions now number 25. While not encyclopedic in organization, these works are the closest of their kind to a complete body of knowledge on the private sector's practice of land use and development. It is the Institute's hope that this distinctive compilation of learning and experience from ULI's members can be shared with both the knowledgeable and the novices in land use and development.

Frank H. Spink, Jr.
Managing Editor
Community Builders Handbook Series
Staff Vice President
Publications

Foreword

The first edition of the *Residential Development Handbook* was published in 1978—when America's baby boom population was entering the housing market full force, creating a seemingly endless demand for new housing. In the decade that followed, the handbook provided residential developers with a comprehensive manual of principles and practices to guide their work.

But during the 1980s, a number of new realities began to take shape that challenged the practices of the residential development industry: market demands shifted as baby boomers moved through life stages and new immigrant populations emerged; changing tax laws and a crisis in the savings and loan industry sent developers searching for new debt and equity sources; land and housing prices skyrocketed in some markets and collapsed in others; new types of residential products emerged that reflected the nation's rapidly increasing diversity of lifestyles, income, and needs for shelter; and regulations and impact fees became increasingly important factors in the development process.

By 1986, it became clear that the *Residential Development Handbook* would need to be updated to illustrate fully the many new forces influencing residential development practices. The update was funded by ULI's Research Committee with the support of ULI's three Residential Development Councils. A steering committee composed of seven members of the councils was formed to review the first edition and suggest the scope of the revision. Work began on redrafting the handbook in April 1987; as chapters were completed, the steering committee reviewed and revised them to assimilate committee members' comments and ideas.

Members of other ULI councils were brought into the review process to critique portions of the manuscript related to their areas of expertise. Interviews were held with over 20 of ULI's council members at the Spring 1989 meeting in New Orleans to solicit opinions about trends in residential development and the prospect for developers in the 1990s. A draft manuscript for each of the nine chapters was completed in late 1989.

The same basic precepts have been followed in this revision that led to the popular acceptance of the original handbook as a standard working manual on development principles and practices. The text and illustrations are intended to reflect trends in residential development and current practices of members of the Residential Development Councils.

On behalf of the Institute and the approximately 150 members of the Residential Development Councils, we offer this contribution to the residential development industry with the hope that it will provide all developers, public officials, and students involved in the industry with a better understanding of today's issues and practices.

D. Michael Crow
J. Ronald Terwilliger
Ronald C. Nahas

Chairs, 1987–1989
Residential Councils

1.
Introduction to the Development Process

Historical Perspective

At one time, residential land development consisted merely of acquiring a tract, filing a plat of its division into blocks and lots, and then selling those lots to buyers. New subdivisions were usually extensions of already built-up areas. But a series of social, economic, and physical factors brought about significant changes: zoning ordinances and subdivision regulations were instituted as land use controls to protect public health, safety, and welfare; an economic depression brought construction to a halt; and World War II created a further shortage of housing. When conditions returned to normal after the war, building boomed. People had money to spend and the demand for housing was high. New households formed, and the high marriage rate and demand for separate households that had been postponed because of the depression and the war spurred the increase.

Inexpensive land was available on the urban fringe, and public investment in infrastructure, such as sewer and water extensions and roads, was significant. The strong demand for housing shifted development to the open land outside cities, often bypassing land closer in with one or more perceived constraints on development—varied topography or higher land costs, for example. Before long, the creation of lots merged with the building of houses, and merchant builders provided a finished single-family house on

an improved lot—the "tract" house. With rapid growth of the suburbs, the pattern of residential development changed forever.

Since World War II, residential development has tended to grow horizontally, outward from central cities. Private investment in the United States has generally supported and nurtured this pattern of growth. During the 1960s and 1970s, however, concern about the ill effects of urban sprawl began to take root, necessitating a new, more efficient pattern of development. What emerged was the principle of community—a commitment to the community, its long-term value, and its relationship with its surroundings. The concept includes not only living accommodations—houses and apartments—but also shopping centers, schools, open space, recreational and cultural facilities, and places of worship and employment—all in relation to the circulation system that ties the elements into the community. The principle of community—driven by a need to respond to every form of lifestyle—is still a major factor influencing residential land development.

ULI's *Community Builders Handbook,* first published in 1947, sought to document the steps necessary for sound residential development. When the first edition of the handbook was published, this country had just begun to experience massive suburban development, and the principles of community planning were not well defined. The editions of the

1

1-1   Single-family housing mass-produced by merchant builders satisfied the surge in housing demand after World War II.

handbook published in the 1950s and 1960s sought to explore these and other issues to help postwar housing builders improve the quality of emerging residential neighborhoods. The first separate edition of the *Residential Development Handbook,* published in 1978, helped residential developers cope with new problems—shortages of energy, the environment, and rising costs of housing.

As development has changed, so has the handbook. This edition follows the original *Community Builders Handbook* by over 40 years and the first edition of the *Residential Development Handbook* by a dozen. The basic philosophy expressed in the first edition remains the same, however: to provide a forum whereby the practices and knowledge of community builders can be exchanged, analyzed, and reevaluated in light of long and intimate experience and to make this knowledge and experience available to those in the field, whether newcomers or long-time practitioners.

Developers cannot and should not employ the cookie-cutter approach to residential building, simply applying yesterday's products on new locations and to new markets. The circumstances facing residential developers in the 1990s present new challenges that will require fresh ideas and approaches:

- *Housing costs.* Increased costs for land, development, and financing have driven the cost of market-priced housing beyond the reach of virtually all low- and many middle-income families.
- *Regulations.* In response to concerns about the deteriorating environment, pressures from growth, and quality of design, federal, state, and local governments have vastly expanded the regulatory framework within which residential projects are considered. In many communities, increased regulations have resulted in two,

RESIDENTIAL DEVELOPMENT COST COMPONENTS AS A PERCENTAGE
OF TOTAL DEVELOPMENT COST: 1984/1988

COMPONENT	1984 (PERCENTAGE)	1988 (PERCENTAGE)	CHANGE (PERCENTAGE POINTS)
Raw Land	17	19.3	+ 2.3
Land Improvements	7	12.6	+ 5.6
Financing	6	4.4	- 1.6
Labor	18	17.4	- 0.6
Marketing/Sales	4	4.3	+ 0.3
Materials	29	24.1	- 4.9
Overhead	7	6.5	- 0.5
Profit	9	8.1	- 0.9
Advertising	2	1.2	- 0.8
Other	2	0.4	- 1.6

Note: Numbers may not add to 100 percent because of rounding.
Source: "Consumer Builders Survey," *Professional Builder & Remodeler,* September 1988, p. 144.

three, or more years required for approvals from zoning to building permits, compounding the risks of development.

- *Decreased public funding.* The federal government has cut back sharply on its funding of housing and community development programs, leaving state and local governments and the private sector to try to fill the void. The decreased federal role has in part contributed to the national crisis of homelessness. The number of homeless Americans increased dramatically during the 1980s, bringing public attention to the need for housing. But without public subsidies, the residential development industry is hard-pressed to contribute substantially to a solution.

- *Shortages of infrastructure.* As a result of inadequate public resources, the nation's basic infrastructure—transportation systems and public services—has not kept pace with new development. Residential developers are being required to fund major improvements to infrastructure through increased development fees and exactions, which historically were funded by the public sector through taxes. Indeed, costs associated with land and land improvements have increased more than any other component of the total cost of a house.

- *Changing demographics.* The baby boom continues to leave its mark on the housing industry as it ages. The generally aging population means fewer young families (the staple of many resi-

dential developers) entering the market. Changing household characteristics—delayed marriages, two-worker families, single-parent households, decreased household size—influence preferences for housing type. The effects of recent immigration and a soaring elderly population are still to be felt.

- *Increased densities.* Rising land costs and changing locational preferences and lifestyles are driving suburban residential densities higher than ever before in major metropolitan areas. The pressures to build at higher densities are bringing about new types of housing that are not familiar to either residential developers or homebuyers. Yet despite all obstacles, the overwhelming choice of maturing baby boomers—today's primary market force—remains the traditional single-family house.

- *Growth management.* Many municipalities and states have responded to the tremendous housing boom of the 1980s and the disproportionate funding of infrastructure and public services with ordinances designed to control growth, to slow or halt new residential construction. The attitude, which has come to be known as "NIMBY" (Not In My Back Yard), presents a new obstacle for developers—one based on emotional rather than planning or financial considerations.

- *Financing.* The demise of a large segment of the nation's savings and loan industry has further complicated residential development through new banking regulations and a more varied array of possible sources of funding developers must understand. Locating short- and long-term funds is increasingly challenging.

These new challenges require today's developers to find ways to stimulate interest in their developments, to set them apart from the competition. The developer's role is therefore more than just builder:

RESIDENTIAL LOT PRICES AND PERCENTAGE CHANGES
FOR SELECTED METROPOLITAN AREAS: 1975–1990

	YEAR				PERCENTAGE CHANGE			
	1975	1980	1985	1990	1975–1980	1980–1985	1985–1990	1975–1990
NORTHEAST/ MIDWEST								
Boston	$18,176	$23,750	$45,000	$90,000	30.7%	89.5%	100.0%	395.2%
Cincinnati	8,700	15,000	17,500	18,000	72.4	16.7	2.9	106.9
Hartford	12,000	20,000	25,000	35,000	66.7	25.0	40.0	191.7
Indianapolis	7,000	12,000	16,500	21,000	71.4	37.5	27.3	200.0
Kansas City	10,000	14,000	15,000	26,500	40.0	7.1	76.7	165.0
Minneapolis	9,500	20,000	22,000	25,000	110.5	10.0	13.6	163.2
Pittsburgh	10,000	16,900	20,000	29,500	69.0	18.3	47.5	195.0
St. Louis	10,500	15,000	20,000	25,000	42.9	33.3	25.0	138.1
SOUTH								
Atlanta	8,000	13,250	16,000	18,000	65.6	20.8	12.5	125.0
Charlotte	6,000	9,500	14,250	16,000	58.3	50.0	12.3	166.7
Chattanooga	4,500	7,500	8,750	10,150	66.7	16.7	16.0	125.6
Dallas	9,500	16,000	30,000	32,500	68.4	87.5	8.3	242.1
Ft. Lauderdale	13,875	21,250	25,000	48,000	53.2	17.6	92.0	245.9
Houston	7,850	12,000	20,000	18,000	52.9	66.7	(10.0)	129.3
Jacksonville	8,500	12,000	17,250	30,000	41.2	43.8	73.9	252.9
Lexington	10,000	14,000	25,000	31,000	40.0	78.6	24.0	210.0
Louisville	9,900	15,125	25,000	23,000	52.8	65.3	(8.0)	132.3
Miami	11,750	25,000	30,000	37,500	112.8	20.0	25.0	219.1
New Orleans	13,500	21,000	35,000	32,000	55.6	66.7	(8.6)	137.0
Oklahoma City	7,300	13,000	15,000	15,000	78.1	15.4	–	105.5
Raleigh	8,580	14,500	25,000	30,000	69.0	72.4	20.0	249.7
WEST								
Albuquerque	11,650	21,250	28,500	37,500	82.4	34.1	31.6	221.9
Boulder	11,500	25,000	35,000	43,000	117.4	40.0	22.9	273.9
Phoenix	10,000	20,000	30,000	30,000	100.0	50.0	–	200.0
Portland	10,000	22,000	22,000	31,250	120.0	–	42.0	212.5
Salt Lake City	8,375	16,625	19,750	25,500	98.5	18.8	29.1	204.5
San Diego	15,000	40,000	50,000	150,000	166.7	25.0	200.0	900.0
San Jose	14,500	40,000	70,000	230,000	175.9	75.0	228.6	1,486.2
Seattle	8,000	20,000	31,000	77,500	150.0	55.0	150.0	868.8
Tacoma	7,500	16,500	21,000	23,000	120.0	27.3	9.5	206.7

Source: ULI–the Urban Land Institute Residential Land Price Inflation Survey, 1990. Based on the price of a standard 10,000-square-foot lot with standard characteristics.

1-4   In many fast-growing markets, rising land costs have contributed to a trend toward higher-density housing in the suburbs.

residential development has become an educational process for municipalities, special interest groups, citizens, and consumers. This edition of the *Residential Development Handbook* addresses the effects of these and other issues influencing residential development today.

Elements of the Process

ULI Fellow Shirley Weiss notes that "the residential development process involves a complex set of decisions over time by a group of key and supporting participants or decision agents—landowners, developers, and consumers in key roles, realtors, financiers, and public officials in supporting ones." Once begun, the process continues only through positive decision making by one or more of the actors involved.

The transition of a parcel of land to residential use occurs in a series of discernible stages guided by decisions based on certain identifiable incentives: consumers, for example, by issues of everyday life and lifestyle; developers by profit and other motives; and professional planners by the public interest. The sequence of events usually follows a pattern: 1) in anticipation of urban use, speculation occurs on land at the urban fringe where ownership may change several times and where large parcels may be broken into smaller increments for development, 2) land then acquires a market-based—not speculation-based—potential for urban use, 3) it is actively considered for purchase and subsequent development, 4) a developer has a definite idea about the character of development and the specific timing involved based on market and feasibility studies, 5) formal plans are submitted to the municipality and appropriate agencies for review and approval, 6) active development begins, and 7) a consumer purchases or leases a housing unit.

A rapid turnover in the ownership of land on the urban fringe does not always indicate that the land is being programmed for development. Speculation may occur in anticipation of the land's potential for conversion to urban use. The initial state of urban potential is achieved merely when one of the decision makers considers it so. It can occur when a landowner decides that the relative value he receives from land in its current state is far outweighed by the value he can receive from selling the parcel, or it can occur when a planning agency considers a parcel to be a part of the future growth pattern of a metropolitan area.

For land to pass from possible to actual urban use, the developer, as key decision maker, must make a judgment about the market. This step is crucial, because if the site and price do not meet the developer's requirements, he decides not to purchase the site and the land returns to "potential" urban use.

5

1-5 The emergence of large commercial and employment centers in the suburbs (such as the City Post Oak area of Houston, pictured above) is indicative of the strong growth pressure that faced the suburbs during the 1980s. Nonresidential suburban growth fueled demand for housing in even more distant suburban locations where houses could be built at more affordable prices.

Developers might also decide to purchase land and hold (or "warehouse") it until the market makes development feasible. When developers buy and hold land, they become real estate speculators, not necessarily developers. They are speculating that their carrying costs will be less than the increased value of the land at the time that development is feasible. During the 1980s, many developers made more money speculating in land than they did actually developing residential properties. But according to ULI council member Dale R. Walker, the risks can be high: "Many developers are buying large parcels of land at high prices, relying on sustained price inflation. If land prices drop, they could be in financial trouble."

These decisions early in the development process—to wait, to buy, to develop—are not made in a vacuum. Developers must weigh all of the variables that relate to the context of development, the property itself, and the decision makers. For example, developers must consider the economic structure of the community and its climate for future growth, the local housing market, the level of current activity, what portion of the market they might be able to capture, the community's past and future policies regarding capital improvements, services relating to transportation, education, and utility systems, the community's

annexation policies and tax structure, and its mechanisms for enacting ordinances—building codes, zoning and subdivision regulations, and time frames for obtaining approvals. In short, developers must evaluate the business opportunity produced by the interplay of supply and demand and the regulatory environment.

Developers often sense intuitively that a parcel of land has the potential for development. By analyzing the market, developers can determine actual housing needs and the proper timing of development, and the analysis either tempers or confirms their intuition. Asking "What can I do with my land?" is unwise, as the question often results in unrealistic answers and contrived development schemes. The better course is to ask what kind of development the market will absorb, whether the land can be developed to meet that market, or, if not, where the developer can find land that can. A site should fit the market, not vice versa.

The analysis of a particular parcel under consideration for development includes physical, locational, and institutional characteristics: a physical analysis to determine, among other things, topography, soil and water conditions, underlying geology, and any environmental hazards; a study of the parcel's location within surrounding land uses to determine its accessibility; and a survey of characteristics like zoning classifications and subdivision ordinances that are imposed upon the site rather than inherent to it. In addition, each decision maker's individual characteristics play a vital role. For example, a local government that has adopted policies to limit or curtail growth will probably negatively affect the timeliness of development but could also lengthen the supply pipeline so that each development finds reduced competition. Further, a developer's conception of the project will be tempered by the size and type of his firm. Conversely, a consumer's decision to buy or rent is generally based on family status, stage in life, education, income, and the cost and availability of mortgage financing.

Next, the developer should compare alternative sites, analyze the principal features of the selected site, and develop preliminary plans and sketches. Close behind site selection and analysis are the method of acquiring the parcel, financing development, and seeking required public approvals. The developer must remain flexible in the approach to development to account for changes in the local market and methods of financing, however. Some developers, according to ULI council member Richard Michaux, seek to address these market risks by entering a joint venture with partners having a strong financial base.

Developers might install streets, utilities, or other infrastructure and some or all of the amenities necessary for the development, and they must initiate a phasing schedule consistent with their cash flow. If the project involves land sales, developers sell parcels to merchant builders; otherwise, they can begin to construct the units themselves. As the first units near completion, sales and marketing and the establishment of some entity for maintaining the development (such as a community association) begin. And an evaluation upon completion of development is vital if developers wish to learn from their mistakes. Questions developers ask themselves and residents of the project will help program future projects or subsequent phases of the same project.

Each factor—the context of development, the property itself, and the decision makers—can change over time, thus changing its relative weight as a variable. For example, a developer might decide to build a shopping center as well as the residential project to nullify the effect of being farther away from existing centers than preferred. Or based on an updated comprehensive plan, a community might change a parcel's zoning and its resultant land use or permitted density.

It is possible to begin describing the residential development process at any point, because, like a flow chart, all its actions are interrelated. This book attempts to proceed chronologically (and perhaps idealistically), beginning with the developer's willingness to undertake some sort of residential project, and proceeds through feasibility evaluations (Chapter 2), financing (Chapter 3), design (Chapter 4), plans and regulatory approvals (Chapter 5), marketing and merchandising (Chapter 6), and postdevelopment community governance (Chapter 7). The final two chapters address issues concerning rehabilitation and adaptive use (Chapter 8) and emerging trends likely to affect the residential development industry into the next century (Chapter 9).

The Developer's Role

Developers are the central actors in the development process, because their actions determine the what, when, and for whom of residential development: what land will be considered for development, when improvements will begin, and for whom the project will be developed. To be sure, developers need the help of others—site planners, architects, marketing specialists, the related technical and service specialists—but it is developers who ultimately take the risks. They are also subject to the limits imposed by private decision makers (e.g., lenders) and public participants (e.g., zoning officials) in the process. But much of a project's success depends upon developers' managerial ability and business sense. "A basic consideration, always to be kept firmly in mind, is that private housing development for a private market is first, last, and all the time a business operation, conducted for profit, and the merit of decisions is always judged by their effect upon profit."[1] The interrelationship of all the factors involved offers a challenge to developers, a challenge that is even more pronounced when the profit margin is small or the strength of the market questionable.

Before beginning any residential project, developers must assess the need for various forms of housing in the particular location. It might be a highly sophisticated analysis involving various market elements, or it can be highly impressionistic and personal. Typically, developers consider demand for several years (depending on the size of the development and time frame for approvals) so as to anticipate continued future demand for the project.

Those who develop land and houses are interested in providing a product that will attract potential buy-

[1] Marion Clawson, *Suburban Land Conversion in the United States* (Baltimore: Johns Hopkins Press, 1971), p. 59.

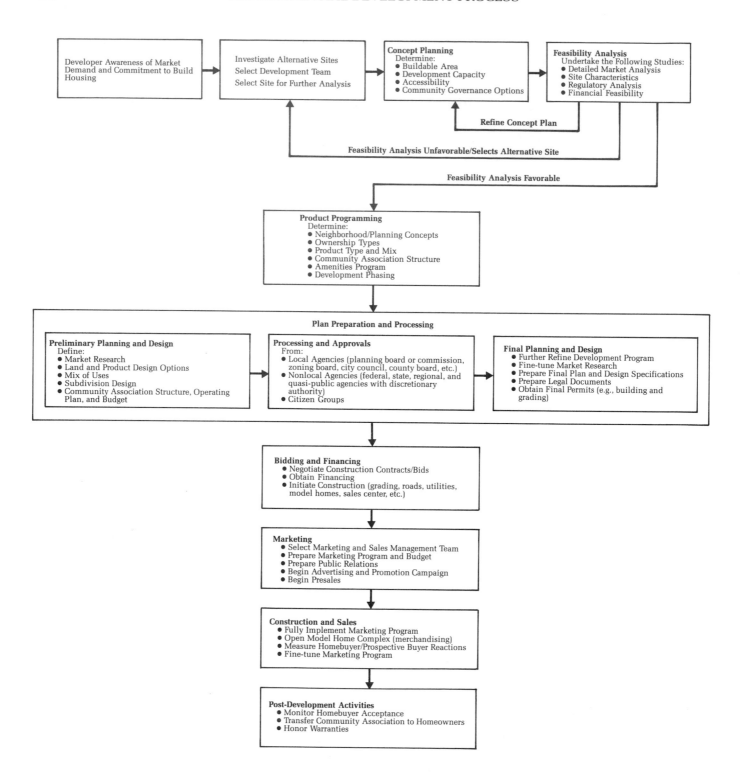

Note: This chart depicts the sequence of activities typical to a residential development; however, there are many variations. This chart emphasizes planning and design factors—many other items that are part of the development process are not shown. Residential development is an iterative process and it may be necessary to return to and repeat some steps in the process several times. Options to purchase a site usually occur after the concept is planned and the site is purchased after approvals have been received.

ers immediately—that is, a short-term interest. Many allied professions, however, have a longer-term interest. Financial institutions and other investors almost always consider their interests to be long term, as borrowed funds are generally paid back over a long period of time. Comprehensive planning implemented by public officials envisions the long term.

Developers of residential property must continue to lengthen their scope of concern, for subdividing land, building houses, and installing streets bear on the type of community that ultimately results. And how these subdivided properties serve the intended residents has a long-term effect on developers' financial success. As creators of residential neighborhoods or communities, developers must be sensitive to long-range needs and expectations, in a sense being responsible for the judicious long-term management of land. Raymond L. Watson, former president of The Irvine Company, observed in 1975, "Regardless of ownership, land is looked at by a large portion of society as belonging to all of the people, with the owner's role being that of caretaker."[2] This belief is even more pronounced today. According to ULI council member Frank A. Passadore, "During the 1980s, the number of groups working to take land out of development increased tremendously. Issues like wetlands, endangered species, traffic congestion, and hazardous wastes stimulated an increase in the number of lawsuits and local growth management. As a result of these and other important issues, developers must invest more time and more money to obtain development approvals.

In all likelihood, residential developers will witness the increasing involvement of municipalities and citizen groups in the development process in the 1990s. Developers must acknowledge that society has changed—and will continue to change. Remaining flexible and responsive to community concerns will be essential for developers' continued success. Council member Passadore notes, "Successful developers in the 1990s will be those who understand how to structure a development organization and team to get past regulatory roadblocks. A cooperative spirit must exist between the private and public sectors."

The Development Team

In the past, the development process was often viewed as a linear set of operations rather than as an ongoing process requiring constant analysis. Roles were narrowly defined, and development stages were segregated into neat chronological sections. This traditional method no longer works because none of the elements of today's development can be considered

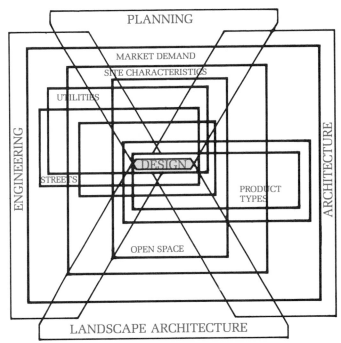

1-7   Finding the design solution by combining the overlapping disciplines of the design team and the factors influencing a site's development. *Source:* Adapted from Robert Engstrom and Marc Putnam, *Planning and Design of Townhouses and Condominiums* (Washington, D.C.: ULI–the Urban Land Institute, 1979), p. 24.

apart from the others. The increased complexity and size of development plus the greater participation of the public and government at all levels necessarily complicate the task of building. Consequently, each step has to be weighed and incorporated into the framework of the entire process.

Thus, it is imperative for the experts in various disciplines to participate in all phases of decision making. Developers cannot assume they know everything themselves. They need a team. While economic, political, financial, aesthetic, environmental, and legal experts were once considered necessary only for large-scale projects, today they have become increasingly important for any development beyond simply splitting a lot. The team approach has been used in one form or another in most development projects considered models of responsible land planning.

The scope of such experts' contributions to a development project is difficult to generalize. The team's extent and nature depend on the type of project, the characteristics of the site, and the local political climate. Nevertheless, the project's developer, by

    [2] Raymond L. Watson, "The Private Developer et al.: Changing Roles," in *Management and Control of Growth*, vol. 3 (Washington, D.C.: ULI–the Urban Land Institute, 1975), p. 487.

reason of the position of risk, is the leader, first and final arbiter, and ultimate decision maker. The developer decides whether to proceed or not, based on the realities of the marketplace. But the decisions are based on the qualified input of experts—the development team.

Timing—when to assemble a development team—has changed. The frequent requirement for an environmental impact assessment for private development (whether legally mandated or merely as part of good practice) has brought with it the necessity of accurately measuring the environmental constraints that may dictate the ultimate land use—constraints that must be recognized before the purchase of the site is negotiated. This early environmental assessment will further require some preliminary definitions of the size of development, concepts of grading and drainage, alternative site uses, traffic to be generated, and mitigating circumstances.

Much of the conceptualization that will be carried into project design must now be generated in this initial evaluation of the project's feasibility. The increased front-end costs attributable to specialists in land planning, geology, civil and traffic engineering, and the social and biological sciences represent a protective investment—or "insurance"—for the developer. The value of this investment is most evident when alternative land purchases are screened. Without this early evaluation, a developer could purchase land with physical, social, or political constraints fatal to residential development. More positively put, however, these expenses for physical, economic, and environmental evaluations can significantly shorten the project's design time.

Depending on a particular project's complexity, the following team members might be involved: attorneys, planners, market researchers, engineers/geologists, environmental specialists, architects, landscape architects, financiers, contractors, and sales managers or real estate agents. The preparation and execution of a business plan includes all these functional pieces—the expertise to determine demand, response, and profitability. The input is not necessarily provided by individual experts or specialists at each stage, however. Project analysis is a repetitive process of increasing refinement, each time weighing all the elements and passing the economic test. While developers could initially perform all or most of these functions themselves, depending on in-house expertise, eventually they will need expert help for most of the functions, because development is a multidiscipline business. The developer's role is to identify and coordinate the disciplines rather than try to perform each of them.

It is not necessary—in some cases not even possible—for all of the technical talents to be on the developer's staff throughout the entire process. Retaining a large, highly specialized staff substantially increases the developer's financial risk. Council member David Sunderland concurs: "A developer cannot afford to retain really good professionals on staff unless his company is big and diversified. What a developer needs is people who can manage these professional activities, not perform them." The developer should temper need with economic restraint.

Individuals or multifaceted consulting firms offer consulting services pertaining to almost every issue relating to residential development. Competent, experienced team members can help to maximize the site's potential for development, decrease construction and maintenance costs, and add tremendously to the project's appeal and marketability. Developers should not try to pinch pennies here: if they take the attitude that good planning makes money, not costs money, they will be more willing to call in the experts. Council member Gary Ryan agrees: "Good planning does not add costs; it adds value."

In seeking consultants, developers should inspect other projects in which prospective consultants have participated and review their qualifications and experience with other developers. Developers must also be certain that the most competent individuals of the consultant's staff are assigned to their projects. Council member James M. DeFrancia believes this point cannot be overstressed: "A professional *firm* is only as good as the *individual* assigned to one's project." Before retaining a firm, developers should meet with the proposed project manager to gauge the individual's as well as the firm's qualifications.

Each development team must be structured to meet the needs of a given project, but the following team players will be included on most project teams.

Land Developers/Builders

Land developers are investors who commit their equity, expertise, labor force, and management talent to the conversion of land from one use to another. Developers must be familiar with costs and procedures for estimating income and capitalization. Generally, development is a field for analytical people. Developers are risk bearers, income estimators, and, most of all, coordinators. They cannot abdicate responsibility in favor of decision making by committee.

Developers have great social responsibility because land has tremendous value and because society must ultimately endure the results for many years. The bottom line is whether the development functions satisfactorily for the residents and for society as a whole.

Historically, land developers have acquired their expertise from direct experience on projects but were educated in some related field: economics, business, planning, or engineering, for example. Only since the late 1970s have university graduate degree programs become available in real estate development. In 1989, four American universities offered graduate degrees in real estate development: Massachusetts Institute of Technology, Columbia University, University of Southern California, and New York University. About another 60 universities offer graduate-level courses in development as a major or minor concentration in a related graduate curriculum—primarily planning and MBA programs.[3]

A survey of builders conducted in 1988 reveals that over 58 percent of all builders buy and develop the sites on which they build houses. Only 27 percent indicated that they buy their sites from other developers. While land developers are concerned primarily with the conversion of land from nonurban to urban uses, residential builders are concerned primarily with the actual construction of houses. Some land developers also function as builders. In high-growth markets where volume production is the norm, however, the trend has been for real estate firms to focus on one or the other.

Typically, land developers are responsible for acquiring development permits, rough grading of the site, and bringing major components of infrastructure (roads, water and sewer, utilities) to the site. Builders purchase the site from a land developer, build the houses, complete on-site infrastructure (local streets and utilities, for example), and are responsible for marketing the completed product. The program for a particular development is usually limited to about 100 houses or fewer, which means that the job can be accomplished in one to three years, depending on the strength of the market. Land developers, on the other hand, might be involved in a project like a master-planned community, which could take 20 years or more to complete.

Attorneys

Good attorneys who are familiar with land development can save developers many times their own fees. Attorneys can be responsible for preparing and reviewing the documents for the project's legal structure and the corresponding documents for project financing, consultants' services, land purchase, leases, and rezoning. The extent of the attorney's role in zoning and processing permits tends to vary by

1-8   WHERE DO RESIDENTIAL BUILDERS
OBTAIN THEIR SITES?

When asked where they get the sites on which they build, residential builders responded as follows:

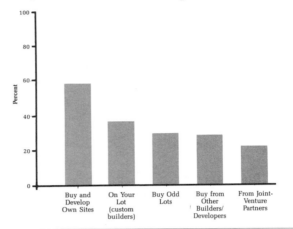

Note: Totals more than 100 percent because of multiple responses.
Source: "Consumer Builders Survey," *Professional Builder & Remodeler,* September 1988, p. 144.

region. For example, in the East, attorneys often play a major role in permitting and are directly involved in negotiations between developers and local governments. In most western states, however, attorneys have a less visible role in permitting and developers or professional consultants (the planner, for example) take the lead. Attorneys have two other important tasks: 1) to draft lease and sales contracts, especially those with subdevelopers and builders, and 2) to draft the declaration of covenants, conditions, and restrictions and other legal documents necessary to establish a community association.

If developers operate within their own local market, attorneys are probably already a member of the team. Attorneys become identified with a developer, and if the developer's track record is clean, negotiating with local public officials and lending institutions becomes increasingly easier. "Foreign" developers, those working outside their own markets, however, must create a sympathetic climate for their actions. They therefore must acquire a local image, and well-respected local attorneys can be key avenues of communication.

[3] For a directory of university programs related to real estate, see ULI–the Urban Land Institute, *Directory of Real Estate Development and Related Education Programs* (Washington, D.C.: Author, 1989). Updated periodically.

Planners

Like attorneys, professional land planners should have done the same type of work before. They should be familiar with local zoning policies and municipal regulations. If they are good, planners create not only better places for people to live but also value for the developer. Planners typically are generalists with a specialty; for example, most professional planning firms offer physical design with a subspecialty like architecture, engineering, or landscape architecture.

Land planning involves site evaluation, determination, allocation, and location for specific uses of land. It includes topography, access and circulation, vehicular and pedestrian traffic, open spaces, and areas for residential, commercial, and industrial uses—all coordinated to produce a unified development that can be built economically, operated efficiently, and maintained with normal expense. Land planning is really product planning—matching the right product to the land so as to produce profit. Land planners also have the primary role of relating the proposed project to the overall comprehensive plan for the area.

Land planners should be allowed to work freely at first, within certain market parameters. Only after they have made some preliminary plans should an engineer be consulted; that is, an engineering plan should not put a land planner in a straitjacket. Engineers should be used to verify and refine the planner's concept—not to drive the concept.

While planners have traditionally been associated with physical design, they often also play a key role in policy. In fact, services of professional planners not related to design have become very important in recent years with increases in regulations, environmental concerns, and permitting requirements. Many professional planning firms now retain "policy" planners who are experts in such areas as writing development regulations, processing plans through the permitting maze, and negotiating with public agencies and citizens. Such planners work closely with physical designers to ensure that the physical plan responds to the municipality's comprehensive plan and other relevant public and private planning programs.

Professional planners have also taken on much of the responsibility for processing projects through local, state, and federal agencies and obtaining development permits. Professional planners often coordinate preparation of the environmental impact assessment and are therefore key players in developing mitigation programs to lessen impacts, many of which are eventually built into the physical land plan as open space or other adjustments to the conceptual plan.

Overall, planners must be generalists capable of working with a variety of technical specialists. They must be able to communicate public concerns to the developer and must understand and convey the economic realities of development to government officials and citizens. In short, planners often serve as the developer's lead coordinator, in effect often serving as the middle man for opposing concerns.

Market Researcher

Market researchers collect data and analyze them to determine several issues: the market audience and its demographic profile, the size of the potential market and what percentage of it can be attracted to a project (based in part on an evaluation of the competition), the optimum sale price or rent and rate of absorption, the type and size of units the developer should build, and what amenities should be included in the project to attract the intended target market. Through objective analyses of available data, market researchers help developers perform the market and financial feasibility studies that will lead to the initial decision about whether to proceed with a proposed project site and concept of development. The research findings help the developer to fine-tune the proposal in terms of product type, product mix, and phasing.

Engineers

Engineers test the soil, establish the precise location of streets and lot and building lines, and furnish topographic maps, detailed data, and working drawings needed to establish grades, earthwork, street improvements, stormwater drainage systems, sanitary sewers, water supply mains, and other public utilities and the types of materials that can be used. Engineers can be a resource for preparing cost estimates. They are also responsible for preparing final subdivision maps and sometimes tentative maps. Council member David Jensen notes, "To ensure implementation of critical design concepts, planners are often asked to prepare tentative maps with the technical support of the engineers."

Some projects require specialists in various fields of engineering. A project located in an area where earthquakes are likely, for example, might require a seismic geologist to determine the precise location of faults on the site and recommend appropriate setbacks or construction standards. Other times specialists in soils, ecology, hydrology, or flood protection should be brought into the process. Not every civil engineering company has all of these technical specialists on its in-house staff, so it might be necessary to subcontract with a local expert. Normally, lead engineers can recommend qualified subcontractors.

Environmental Specialists

Most residential development projects now require some level of environmental assessment. Some states mandate this environmental review, while in other states, it is a municipal practice. Generally, the larger the project, the greater the degree of environmental analysis required. Specialists in various environmental sciences will likely be required if a full environmental impact report is necessary.

Various environmental specialists might become part of the developer's team of experts: historians, archaeologists, paleontologists, biologists, botanists, air quality experts, acoustical engineers, transportation engineers.[4] Project sites known to contain endangered species or habitats for endangered species could require several biologists. In recent years, projects containing wetlands have come under substantial scrutiny from federal agencies, and, as a result, new specialists in developing wetland mitigation programs and obtaining permits have emerged. Residential developers need to understand which environmental issues are relevant (and potentially controversial) to the site and be prepared to bring in the appropriate experts.

Architects

Architecture involves planning, designing, and constructing buildings, and most developers find architects to be essential members of the team. In residential development, builders must offer purchasers more than just a well-built structure on a good lot. They must produce an architecturally pleasing house, well adapted to the topographic features of the lot and with a good relationship to other houses, and a good, livable floor plan. But developers are finding that talented architects also provide them with aids other than a floor plan and an elevation: site planning; selection of building materials; exterior color, styling, and coordination; interior design; professional supervision; and suggestions on merchandising the finished product. These extra services can pay for themselves by helping to produce superior houses that sell faster. Council member Richard Michaux notes that architects can play another important role: "Architects are especially important to neighborhood groups and municipal officials who are concerned about the quality and appearance of a project. Their ability to convey design concepts to these groups can be instrumental in obtaining approvals."

1-9   Traditional-looking houses drawing upon regional architectural characteristics remain popular with housing consumers.

Although architects should not usually be leaders of the development team, they should be involved in the process early because of the decisions that must be based on architectural and planning concepts. Decisions about programming and budgeting made during concept planning without architects' participation can strip them of effective control over design. Excluding an architect at this early stage may lock the design into a preconceived solution, severely limiting the architect's future options. This concern is especially important when the development program calls for a higher-density residential product, such as detached units on small lots, where the size, shape, and grade of development parcels can substantially determine which products will work and which will not.

---

[4] Many residential developers make a transportation engineer part of the development team regardless of the need to prepare environmental documents. Transportation engineers can be independent consultants or associated with a diversified civil engineering or planning firm.

Landscape Architects

Landscape architecture deals with the treatment and arrangement of ground forms: studying the detailed relationships among buildings, circulation routes, and the site's physical features; creating open spaces around buildings; designing recreational spaces and other areas; and ultimately determining where and what type of plants should be installed. Thus, landscape architects do more than determine where trees and shrubs should be planted. Landscape architects are valuable because they think of the outdoors in three dimensions. For example, berms and similar topographic relief features can add much to a project's appearance and value. Landscape architects should be brought in early, before roads and buildings are built, for their trained eyes may perceive possibilities that planners, architects, and civil engineers miss.

Landscape architects play a large role in determining the image a residential project will convey to prospective buyers or future residents. Landscape architects design the project's entrances, and they are largely responsible for creating the streetscape—the features that often form one's first impression of a residential neighborhood. The landscape architect's contributions can add both perceived and real value to a residential project, which ultimately translates into quicker sales and increased prices.

Financiers

Almost all good real estate developments rely to a large degree on the proper supply of equity and borrowed funds for the risks of development. Financing is one element in the process that is subject to a great amount of fluctuation, yet adequate financing can in large measure determine whether a project ultimately is profitable. Developers must tap into this supply of funds at just the right time to secure the amount needed under the right terms.

Developers should shop thoroughly and be prepared to wait until better terms can be secured if possible. A knowledge of sources of money is indispensable to developers. In all cases, the source of money, whether an investor or a financial institution, must be convinced of the project's feasibility. That real estate developers must understand the techniques of financing cannot be overstressed, but if developers do not understand the techniques of financing, they should surround themselves with those who do.

Contractors

Usually much of a development's quality rests with the actual builder of houses, the products eventually marketed to consumers. Contractors, licensed professionals who construct a project in accordance with plans and specifications, perform the task of building. Typically, *general* contractors assume the lead role in residential construction, and they may retain the services of numerous *sub*contractors for specialized aspects of construction: roofing, drywall, windows, masonry, cabinetry, and so forth. General contractors are often referred to as "builders," but they may be just a contractor to the real builder as defined earlier. Most residential builders retain the full-time services of a general contractor within their organization, however.

Residential developers also require the services of contractors for a variety of construction projects that occur before houses are built—grading, installing utilities, paving streets. Most residential developers do not retain such contractors in-house, but larger organizations frequently employ an experienced individual to manage contractors.

Contractors are skilled in assembling and organizing materials and labor, supervising construction in the field, and hiring and managing subcontractors. They are responsible for quality control, managing construction schedules, and controlling construction costs. Their input to a development plan during preconstruction helps developers generate reasonable estimates of construction costs and schedules.[5]

Sales Managers

Once the houses are built, developers need assistance to market them, selling or renting the units. Most moderately sized and larger development companies maintain an in-house sales or rental staff who are responsible for developing and implementing the marketing strategy. Smaller developers and developers of small projects often contract with a local real estate broker to market units. A contract agent or in-house sales manager is a vital member of the team, because the project's success ultimately is judged by how fast the units are sold or rented. Sales managers or agents should be brought into the project early to be most effective—before the units are designed. Experienced sales personnel are usually familiar with the local market and can suggest ways to improve the pace of sales or rentals.

---

[5] For additional discussion of the contracting profession, see Mert Millman, *General Contracting: Winning Techniques for Starting and Operating a Successful Business* (New York: McGraw-Hill, 1990).

2.
Project Feasibility

The first step in residential development is to determine a project's feasibility. "Feasibility analysis is a generic term [that] groups a variety of predevelopment studies by generalists and specialists in a systematic philosophy of inquiry to determine facts that are reliable, assumptions about the future that are consistent with past experiences, and tactics [that] will minimize the variance between objectives and variations."[1]

Estimating a project's feasibility comprises several steps: assessing the physical characteristics and capabilities of the site, establishing the initial development concept, preparing a profile of the market and determining what it can afford to pay, delineating the market area in terms of location, and determining the effect of regulatory practices on the desired development program. The process also requires an estimate of development costs, an analysis of the financial package considering such elements as costs and terms of borrowing, equity position, and mortgage loan ratios, and an estimate of economic feasibility based on computations of income, expenses, and rate of return.

For simplification, feasibility analysis can be broken down into four primary components: 1) market analysis, 2) site considerations, 3) regulations, and 4) financing. This chapter addresses the first three. Because of the increased complexity of financing residential projects—brought about in part by tax reform in 1986 and the demise of much of the nation's savings and loan industry—financing is discussed separately in Chapter 3.

Market Analysis

Any well-conceived new housing project *must* begin with a thorough understanding of the marketplace where the property will be constructed. Market feasibility is fundamental to a development's financial feasibility and success. No matter how resourceful the financial structure, the numbers will not work without an appropriate market for the product.

Residential developers often marvel at the marketing instincts of well-publicized colleagues, but for every successful hunch player there might be many others who played one hunch too many, disrupting not only their own businesses but the marketplace as well. Developers use market analyses not only to validate their market instincts but also to identify new market opportunities. Today's most savvy and well-respected developers seldom make a move without thoroughly researching the market pertaining to the contemplated development.

Understanding the market involves classic factors of demand and supply. Analysis of demand covers

---

[1] James A. Graaskamp, *Fundamentals of Real Estate Development* (Washington, D.C.: ULI–the Urban Land Institute, 1982), p. 13.

2-1   Before selecting the product type and mix, the developer of California Meadows prepared a market analysis to determine general market trends and a specific target market for each housing type. The market study indicated a strong demand for affordable single-family houses, which was accommodated with an interlocking (or zipper) lot design that achieved 8.7 units per acre. Specific products were then designed for single parents with children, childless couples buying their first house, young move-up families, and empty nesters.

demographic and economic characteristics of the households within the marketplace. Analysis of supply looks at activity and trends in the marketplace and—most important—the potentially competitive properties that are likely to be marketed during the same period. The developer collects and analyzes data to help answer several basic questions:

1. What are the opportunities or gaps where a need exists within the marketplace?
2. What is the appropriate target market and market orientation for this project?
3. What is the size of the future market and what percent of that market can be attracted to the subject site?
4. What is the price range in the market?
5. What type of unit is justified by demand?
6. How large should the units be?
7. What amenities should be provided?
8. What are the indirect economic constraints? Or, what are constraints to development not related to supply and demand—regulatory issues, the physical site, community opposition? (This last question is dealt with more thoroughly later in this chapter.)[2]

Along with these classic questions about the market, another, more qualitative purpose for the market analysis is gaining importance among leading developers: a thorough research report with rigorous methodology becomes an invaluable aid for gaining financing. Analytical lenders and equity sources scrutinize the data about the market in a good report. Those who

move on instinct see the report as adding to the defensibility of their decision. Well-documented market analysis can help to obtain the necessary municipal approvals; innovative projects in particular might need the political support that can be fostered by clearly presented market rationale. And market studies provide invaluable guidance to planners, architects, and engineers in their designs.

A market analysis can address a broad spectrum of concerns. Developers use general market studies to survey local or regional markets when contemplating geographic expansion, gathering information about available land, determining where development is feasible from the standpoint of construction costs and regulatory constraints, and, most important, determining where the dynamics of supply and demand match the characteristics of the proposed housing development. This chapter concentrates on how market analysis is used to determine the nature and level of demand for residential development on a specific site.

Context

Market analysts begin by looking at the regional setting within which the proposed development will occur, including major shifts in regional population, recent or anticipated changes in the regional economic base, and patterns of employment. Then the focus narrows to the county, where more specific information is available about population, employment, housing needs, activity, the relative desirability of locations within the county, transportation patterns, and regulatory or development policy issues. From there, the focus narrows further to the subject property and the market areas that will more specifically affect its appropriate development program and ultimately its success in the market.

The Market Area

To conduct a proper market analysis, analysts must define the physical extent of the markets for the proposed products—the demand market from which potential buyers will be drawn and the supply market of planned or existing developments that will compete for buyers.

Housing markets are largely local and generally do not have fixed geographic borders except those dic-

[2] G. Vincent Barrett and John P. Blair, *How to Conduct and Analyze Real Estate Market Feasibility Studies* (New York: Van Nostrand Reinhold Co., 1982), pp. 28–30; and Margaret Waite, Robert Charles Lesser & Co., Los Angeles, California.

tated by physical barriers, manmade features, or political considerations. Market analysis should be targeted to identifiable regions where the infrastructure creates sectors (individual housing markets) of geographic, demographic, and socioeconomic interdependence. While no set guidelines define a marketplace, it is generally smaller than the entire metropolitan area but larger than a single community. The market area and its future performance depend upon the health of the metropolitan area's overall economy, however. ULI council member William E. Becker suggests, "County boundaries are often good areas to use as control points for determining market areas and for the collection of statistical data."

Consumers in the market for housing usually prefer certain geographic locales but not precise locations within those broad areas, reflecting the fact that within any given area a range of housing is usually available. Consumers select a geographic area—based on such factors as areawide prices, social amenities, quality of neighborhoods, reputation of schools, and ease of commuting—and shop among a number of competitive offerings within that area. Within the selected geographic area, the decision to purchase or rent, however, is likely based upon the perceived present and future value of the dwelling unit and the consumer's ability to pay rather than upon precise location.

The market analysis for a proposed housing development involves two kinds of market areas: the *demand side* (the target market area) and the *supply side* (the competitive market area). In most cases, a strong geographic correlation exists between supply and demand, but not always. In fact, in some instances, the two can be regions apart. For the second-home market in destination resorts, for example, the target market areas could extend to cities 500 or more miles away from the site-oriented competitive market area. Most market areas for primary shelter (first homes) are within a one-hour commute of employment centers or other key destinations, however.

Target Market Area (Demand Based)

Target market areas define the location where most logical demand for a contemplated housing project exists. Various factors are considered in delineating the target market area for a proposed development:

1. *Travel time from major population and employment centers.* With worsening traffic congestion in most metropolitan areas, decisions about the location of housing are increasingly based upon proximity to employment. By locating major employment centers (downtowns or emerging suburban activity centers) and making assumptions regarding "acceptable" commuting time, market analysts can approximate housing target market areas. Sites easily accessible to employment centers draw from wider target market areas.

2. *Mass transportation facilities and highway links.* Commuting patterns and times are based largely on ease of access; thus, the target market area is based on the availability of mass transit, the location of transportation corridors, and the speed at which they operate during peak travel hours. Sites offering efficient mass transportation draw from wider target market areas.

3. *Existing and anticipated patterns of development.* Most urban settings exhibit areas of strong and weak growth. Growth areas might be distinguished by certain housing characteristics (large luxury houses, entry-level houses, apartments, for example), which in turn influence the boundaries of target market areas. Growth is likely to continue to be strong in pockets of hot markets, which have larger target market areas. Likewise, developments offering products geared toward underserved markets within a region draw from larger target market areas.

4. *Socioeconomic composition of the population.* Income, age, household characteristics, and other socioeconomic characteristics of a given area influence the choice of housing and location and thus target market areas. Locations with a higher perceived status draw from wider areas.

5. *Physical barriers and time/distance zones.* Natural features like rivers, bluffs, and parkland and manmade features like jurisdictional boundaries or intensive development can sometimes form a wall through which boundaries of the target market area do not penetrate.

6. *Political subdivisions.* Municipal boundaries can be especially important when adjoining jurisdictions differ markedly in political climate, tax policies, or snob appeal or when different attitudes about growth exist. Further, boundaries of school districts are important to market segments with school-age children.

With these and potentially more localized considerations in mind, analysts should define target market areas with the objective of gathering meaningful indicators of the strengths and weaknesses of the market and the existence of a core of consumers able to purchase or rent the proposed housing products. That core is generally comprised not only of households already existing in the market but also of those that will relocate to the area. The existing location of this core group of consumers varies with the type and location of the proposed property; for example, a retirement community for active adults in a resort area draws from an area much beyond mere local influences, while a market-rate rental property inside the perimeter highway of a major city could draw most of its residents from within a mile or two of the site. To better understand the potential market for a particular housing project, target market areas can be categorized in a hierarchy based on the different strength of demand anticipated in these locations:

- The *primary target market area* is where the strongest potential demand is anticipated. Typically, 50 to 75 percent of the buyers or renters for a given project come from the primary target market area. Usually this area extends up to five miles from the subject property in urbanized areas and up to 10 miles in suburban areas farther away. Analysis of demand factors within the primary market area influences the design and pricing of the specific product.
- The *intermediate target market area* has a secondary influence on the primary area's population and economic expansion. Most of the remaining 25 to 50 percent of the prospects for the proposed property come from the intermediate target market area. It usually extends five to 10 miles from the site but in larger metropolitan areas can extend 10 to 20 miles from the site.
- The *regional target market area* is often the combination of the primary and intermediate market areas; in very dynamic or populous locations, however, the regional target market area could draw from significantly beyond those defined boundaries. A property located in a specific urban neighborhood, for example, might have thousands of households within a primary target market area that encompasses only a section of the city, while the intermediate target market area would be the city itself. The regional target market area, however, would include the affluent suburbs in the recognition that a market would exist for mature families and empty nesters moving back into the urban core. Typically, the regional target market area extends 20 to 40 miles from the site.

Identifying the demand-based target market area brings the analyst only half way to fully understanding market potential. For many market studies, the more significant definition of market area is the one on the supply side of the equation—the competitive market area.

Competitive Market Area (Supply Based)

Demand for new housing exists to some extent in most locations. What is important in market analysis, however, is *residual demand*—the demand for new housing that is not met within the marketplace. It can be determined only after the housing competition affecting the proposed property is thoroughly understood.

Residual demand is determined by a deceptively simple equation: *Total Demand* minus *Total Absorption by Competitive Products* equals *Residual Demand*. This equation is simple in concept, but defining its components is often an uncertain exercise. Furthermore, data about the supply side can prove elusive, erroneous, and contradictory.

The competitive market area encompasses the housing potential buyers or renters consider comparable to the proposed property. Competitive products include new and resale units existing in the area and units planned to enter the market during the marketing period of the proposed property. If the proposed marketing period is lengthy, the competitive analysis should also consider vacant and redevelopable properties zoned for residential use that may become active during the marketing period. Delineating the competitive market area provides a boundary within which the analyst can measure the competition and ultimately estimate absorption and capture rates.

Delineating Target and Competitive Market Areas

Target and competitive market areas can be defined in many ways. To a certain extent, every site is special, as are its areas of influence for supply and demand; certain standard and acceptable methods or guidelines for delineating market areas can be used in most instances, however. The primary target area is established by the location of and accessibility afforded by transportation routes, by what has been learned about the location of prospective consumers from surveys of competitive products, by the locations of current and future employment centers, by the general housing trends in the region, and by the spillover demand from unmet housing needs in surrounding jurisdictions. The location of competitive projects and physical barriers, such as rivers or large areas of open space, are less important determining factors. The boundaries of the primary target area are likely irregular and differ markedly for different types of projects and for different locations.

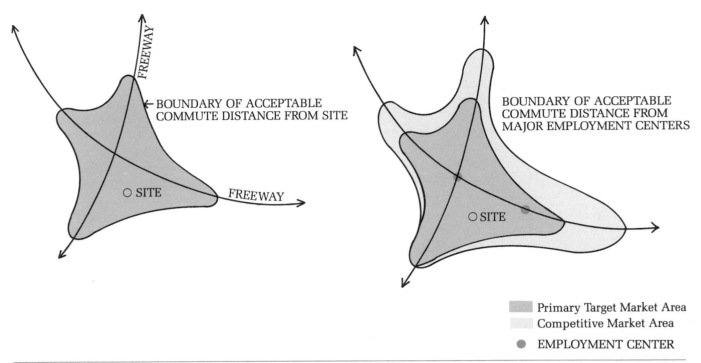

Note: The *primary target market area* is determined largely by the amount of time it takes to travel from the site to places of employment. As shown, the area is expanded through its access to transportation corridors. Other considerations affecting the size and shape of the primary target market area include urban growth patterns and infrastructure, socioeconomic conditions, physical barriers, and political boundaries (regulations). The *competitive market area* encompasses additional areas that are within acceptable commuting distance from major employment centers—areas that would be expected to compete with a given site. What constitutes an acceptable commuting distance varies between regions from under one-half hour to, in some cities, over one hour.

Computer-modeled planning data services can carve demographic information out of data from census tracts in virtually any shape. The most accurate data, however, conform to municipal boundaries or census tracts. No matter how sophisticated the computer model, the margin for error increases when artificial boundaries are used. Caution should be used with computer-modeled census data more than three or four years old, for computers are not aware of new housing developments, new highways, or recently imposed moratoriums.

Most development occurs in areas with significant growth dynamics. It is therefore often more useful to look at *corridors* of growth or patterns of migration and development that follow those corridors. An analysis of corridors studies the direction of growth and the areas from which a general location draws new households. The Internal Revenue Service can provide information about relocation for all taxpaying households, which shows the direction of movement, often from closer-in locations to the suburban fringe (or, where substantial highway construction is occurring, to rural areas).

Assuming similarities in target markets, the primary target market area could complement municipalities surrounding the site that contain similar housing and market dynamics. In this case, the intermediate target market area would include those counties from which the proposed property's county has historically drawn new households. The regional target market area for primary housing, then, would be the combination of the two. The competitive market area would likely coincide with the primary target market area, with some additional area accounting for transportation links and emerging employment centers.

On the other hand, the target markets for the proposed site may be different from those in municipalities surrounding the site. For example, the proposed property might offer a product not being provided elsewhere in the region, such as affordable housing. In that case, a specific portion of housing demand will be almost forced to the proposed property even though surrounding jurisdictions may be growing. Delineation of the target market area thus must also consider the specific nature of supply and demand within the larger region.

19

Factors Affecting Demand

Once the target market area is determined, analysts can study in detail demand factors that take into account a variety of socioeconomic and household characteristics. Because most market analyses are accomplished within limits of time and budget, however, it is not always possible to consider every factor that might influence demand. At a minimum, four factors are of primary importance: population, households, income, and employment. Appendix A provides a list of sources for much of these data, and Appendix B provides a list of housing-related associations and other organizations that may collect data useful to market researchers.

Population

Forecasting population and households as part of a market analysis is primarily to assess the number and nature of current and future households and thereby forecast the demand for new housing. An analysis of in-migration and out-migration also offers insight into present and future demand for housing in the market area.

Increases in population are typically based on two factors: more births than deaths within the market area and more in-migrants than out-migrants within the market area. Any analysis of trends in population should cover the period from the last decennial census. It may be necessary to study a shorter period if some other factor has significantly affected population in the target market area—the relocation of major industry in or out of a specific market, for example.

Because housing markets are local, developers would be wise not to rely on national population trends. In-migration, for example, varies widely between regions as well as between communities within the same metropolitan area. It is therefore essential to examine historical population trends for the target market area and to forecast future changes in light of local influences.

A thorough study of population includes an examination of trends and projections in the age of heads of households, information that gives an important indication of the nature of demand for housing in an area. Comparison of population age pyramids for the target market area and the nation directs the market analyst toward existing and future market opportunities; deviations from the national norm are the first avenues of investigation. For example, a proportionately high percentage of individuals aged 20 to 30 indicates a need for housing for first-time or first move-up buyers. Adults in their 40s, on the other hand, are usually approaching the peak of their earning power, and a preponderance indicates a need for

2-3   POPULATION PYRAMID OF THE UNITED STATES: JULY 1, 1989

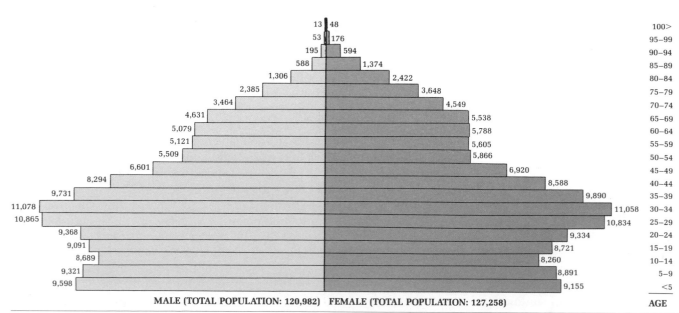

MALE (TOTAL POPULATION: 120,982)   FEMALE (TOTAL POPULATION: 127,258)   **AGE**

Source: U.S. Bureau of the Census, *Current Population Reports*, Series P-25, No. 1057, "U.S. Population Estimates, by Age, Sex, Race, and Hispanic Origin: 1989" (Washington, D.C.: U.S. Government Printing Office, 1990), p. 12.

2-4 Bishops Park, a condominium community of three-story stacked flats in Raleigh, North Carolina, was marketed to young professionals. As expected, this market group was not concerned about walking up stairs to the upper units and appreciated the proximity to the downtown that the infill site offered.

more expensive housing. Households comprised of ages above 60 suggest markets for move-down housing or specialized housing developments like active adult communities or assisted living arrangements.

Households

Of perhaps even greater significance in determining housing demand and market potential is an analysis of the number of households that make up a given population. Increases in population signal a corresponding increase in the number of households, but not in direct proportion. In many areas, increases in the number of households have been more a function of declining household size than of increases in population. Most demographic planners estimate household growth by correlating population data with trends in household size.

Another important factor influencing the demand for housing is the average size of households. Nationally, the decrease in average household size can be attributed to changing lifestyles—the declining birth rate, delayed marriages, a greater number of divorces, and an increase in the number of single-person households. Studying the specific trends in household size for a region can determine the demand for product

type (multifamily or single family), bedroom mix, and overall floor plan.

The broad category "household" includes several nontraditional family formations—single parents, persons of the opposite sex sharing living quarters, and persons of the same sex sharing living quarters. Each formation has specific housing needs. A thorough market analysis examines the trends and projections for such nontraditional families to determine which group or groups might constitute a significant market for the proposed development.

Income

An analysis of median household income within the target market area indicates the economic welfare of the region and provides valuable insight into the scope and magnitude of the available purchasing power for housing (not counting equity and appreciation). This part of the analysis involves tracking historic changes and projections in median and average household income for the primary, intermediate, and regional target market areas, including the rate at which incomes rise and the number of households in each income bracket (under $15,000, $15,000 to $24,999, etc.). Such information is invaluable in de-

Primary Segments:
Segment/Household Size

Young Singles/1–2

Under 30; gregarious; unmarried; active; mobile; many interests; entertain informally. *Design implications:* Glitz; color; excitement; variety; experimentation; interior privacy for sleep and bath.

Adult Singles/1–2

Over 30; presently unmarried (single, widowed, separated, divorced); serious social relationships; require privacy; more mature but still experimenting; early possession buildup; appreciate quality and dependable brands. *Design implications:* Glitz; design animation in ceiling, floor, room shapes; minimal daily maintenance; appreciate design features like fireplace, bathrooms, built-ins, workspaces.

Young Married Couples without Children/2

Discretionary/dual income; physically active; entertain often both formally and informally; independent; do-it-yourselfers; planning for future (financial, career, family planning); ambitious; travel often. *Design implications:* The look of success (emphasize entry, indoor/outdoor relationships); good wardrobe/storage spaces; combined living/dining room; master bedroom suite; dramatic spaces with good decorating potential.

Young Married Couples with Child/3

Under 35; child under five years; both spouses working; entertain informally; amateur gardeners; focus on child; planning on more children. *Design implications:* Emphasize kitchen; informal dining area; master bedroom; similar secondary bedrooms; family room with fireplace; yard areas (need roaming space for pets and children); interior "mess" or play area.

Move-up Family/3–4

The "monthly payment" group; focus on casual and informal family activities; numerous interests; mostly child-oriented. Amateur gardeners; transitional. *Design implications:* Emphasize kitchen; informal dining area; master bedroom; smaller secondary bedrooms; fireplace in family room; usable yard areas.

Established Family/3–5+

Making monthly payments comfortably; some discretionary income, approaching their economic and social peak; some formal entertaining; older children/teenagers; diverse interests; three-car family; prefer limited maintenance. *Design implications:* Separate formal living and dining areas; provide den and formal living room; private master bedroom suite; large secondary bedrooms, formal yard.

Luxury Family/2–4

Considerable discretionary income; entertain infrequently but formally; teenagers (maybe a small child too); less physically active; dine out often; desire minimal maintenance; privacy mandatory; will not compromise on space, quality, or prestige of address. *Design implications:* Formal entry; separate living and dining rooms; provide den; secluded master bedroom with "retreat" area; guest or maid's room; emphasize privacy and security; large walk-in wardrobes; gourmet kitchen; wine area; classic wet bar; formal entertainment room; library;

termining a range of prices that a significant portion of the population can afford.

The market analysis can be further refined by examining household income by age group. For example, the group of 35- to 44-year-olds, which tends to contain the largest proportion of professionals and managers, is often the key category to study for high-end, single-family detached houses. These numbers provide a base on which the analyst can calculate with reasonable accuracy the demand for and absorption rate of a proposed community of that type.

In residential development, income of consumers is a most important factor in demand. As incomes rise, people generally demand and can pay for larger, customized houses in neighborhoods with more amenities. Thus, demand for new housing can exist although the level of population has not risen correspondingly. Recently, however, housing prices have risen faster than incomes in many areas, and in some markets, many people now owning houses could not afford to buy them at today's prices. Countering this phenomenon is that many households today are will-

paneling; fine woods in kitchen, bath, and staircase; wide exterior facade with strong window and roof treatments.

Move-down Family 2–3

40–50 years of age; leaving large family house; prefer limited maintenance; entertain both formally and informally; travel often; occasional visits from family or guests; both active and passive recreational pursuits. *Design implications:* Quality over quantity; luxury features; focus on living room and master bedroom area; adequately sized secondary areas (bedrooms, den, dining room); provide breakfast nook or informal eating area, small private patio; have accumulated possessions so storage is important; provide features such as fireplace, bar, reading nook, and skylights; value nearby recreation and status neighborhood over interior space.

Divorcee/1+

Reestablishing social lifestyle; experimenting; exploring new relationships; want freedom to travel and pursue leisure interests; may be career oriented with social life focused on workplace. *Design implications:* Home may be a "launching pad" for social experimentation; smaller but full kitchen; master suite desirable; low-maintenance materials.

Single Female with Child/2+

Child oriented; must find a suitable place to live with child; child is focus of lifestyle. *Design implications:* Privacy from child yet ability to monitor (no matter what age); interior play area; space for television is important; bright, informal, easily maintained eating area with kitchen; no dining room necessary but perhaps an area for infrequent formal meals; quality (but not luxurious) appointments and materials; separate full bath for child.

Empty Nester–Never Nested/2

Mature, self-sufficient couple; no debts; occasional overnight guests; active in leisure activities; entertain often; want privacy; minimal maintenance and investment in house costs; mobile in attitude but permanent in residence. *Design implications:* Formal living and dining areas; den; guest suite; large master bedroom with retreat; informal eating nook in kitchen; low-maintenance yard.

Young Retiree (Active)/2

Active in community; enjoy passive recreation; semiformal entertaining at home; privacy important; may work part time; enjoy some sports; people oriented. *Design implications:* Quality rather than quantity; secondary bedrooms usable for hobbies; option of separate master bedrooms; storage space; room configuration should be functional, formal, and traditional; one-car garage.

Passive Retiree/2

Not physically able to engage in active sports; prefer walking, family and group activities, playing cards, and reading. *Design implications:* Avoid stairs and heights; conservative design; one-story and end units are preferred; grab bars and other safety features should be subtle in design; garden or patio area; nicely lighted, full but compact kitchen; lower appliance shelves, pantries, and switches.

Widow–Widower/1

Budget conscious and will listen to advice; privacy, security, and comfort are important. *Design implications:* Interior privacy; no fanciness unless affluent; wants a full kitchen and has time for maintenance; wants a "homey" feeling; fireplace; tends to use formal areas rarely so living and dining rooms can be smaller; has possessions that are vital links

▶

ing to pay a greater percentage of their discretionary income for housing than ever before, and this trend is likely to continue.

Employment

Information about employment growth for the target market area supplements trends and projections of population, households, and income. At a minimum, analysts compare total employment and unemployment figures for the region with national figures to determine the general economic health of the area, but they also study the occupational composition of the labor force, beginning with the broad categories of white collar and blue collar jobs and continuing with more specific types of employment (professional, technical, clerical, wholesale, retail, service, and health care). Projecting these data indicates not only the number but also the type of expected new jobs formed. Ideally, the quantitative study of employment figures should be supported by a specific survey of major employers in the ares. The expansion or con-

2-5 (continued)

to past so needs wall space and storage; security features appreciated; may want hobby or work area; extra sleeping area for visiting children or guests; neighborhood very important.

Special Segments:

Second Homebuyers–National Origin/2+

Affluent empty nesters who travel; preretirees; active retirees; self-employed; corporate chiefs. *Design implications:* Spacious luxury; detached house; many amenities with view of golf course or other premium features.

Second Homebuyers–Regional Origin/2+

Often same as above, but in lower income bracket. *Design implications:* Compact luxury; usually attached units; turnkey delivery as an option (with furnishings).

Investors

Local and out of state. Many may eventually live in community where investment home is located.

Aesthetics/1–2+

Often single, with a profession as a writer, artist, musician, architect, decorator, or similar occupation; borderline or actual elitist; freedom and the avant-garde are important. *Design implications:* Thematic or bold architecture; wood or masonry construction; dramatic roof lines and animated exteriors; interior features such as fireplace, interior garden, circular staircase, lofts, beams, skylights, and natural design elements; provide a work area; use thematic decoration (such as Oriental); likes to be in peer group neighborhood.

Glitz/1–2+

Seek that which is new and trendy; gregarious; spend much of their income. *Design implications:* Heavy design and merchandising orientation; market features with "sizzle," such as mirrors, chrome, large entertainment areas, interior balconies or decks, music room, wet bar, and European kitchen with every gimmick.

Snowbirds and Desert Rats

Fall into two groups: fun-loving escapists and self-gratifying achievers. Fun-lovers of all ages have a vacation mentality; want to live out their fantasies; travel often to exotic locations. *Design implications:* Both unusual and traditional interior and exterior designs; feature "drama," such as large party rooms, bold masonry fireplaces (with woodbox), and lofts that convert to sleeping areas; use natural wood. Small spaces are fine but must be "fun"; location is all important; timeshare may be appropriate.

Self-gratifiers of all ages want to live their fantasies now; transfer work ethic into wish fulfillment; often singles and divorcees; ambitious; heavy investors in brand-name material goods for prestige and comfort. *Design implications:* Showcase entertainment areas, bar, gourmet kitchen, and worksaving appliances; feature fireplaces, wood beams and paneling, and ceiling heights; they spend beyond their means, so will accept rental unit that satisfies their lifestyle and location needs.

Source: Sanford R. Goodkin, Peat Marwick Main & Company/Goodkin Real Estate Consulting Group.

---

traction of existing employers and the entry of new businesses into a region significantly affect demand for housing.

Most general demographic and economic information is available from government agencies. The Census Bureau provides totals from the most recent census and estimates of the current year's population and income. Similarly, a state department of labor can supply employment figures for a region. State and county offices of economic development often project future employment, but private demographic firms can also supply these data. Some firms provide information about households based not only on age and income but also on such intangible qualities as career goals, social aspirations, and self-perception.

Factors Affecting Supply

The current and projected housing supply within the competitive market area is determined to enable analysts to translate data about population, households, income, and employment into estimates of potential demand for a specific new development. A thorough analysis of the housing stock within the competitive market area includes a description of prices for new and resale housing *and* a compilation of private authorized residential building permits. The *current* housing market is determined through an extensive study of selected, existing residential communities in the competitive market area, but the *future* housing market can be assessed only by an analysis of housing developments proposed for construction within the competitive market area.

Inventory of Existing Housing

The characteristics of the existing housing inventory are determined by the types of housing prevalent in the competitive market area, the number of houses on the market, and the ratio of owned housing units to rental units. Perhaps the most crucial figures are the average sale price and the average absorption rate—an indicator of how quickly competitive products are selling. These statistics for the previous three to five years reveal the relative strength of the area's market.

To be useful, however, the numbers must be put into a larger context. Analysts must determine plausible reasons for abrupt rises (or falls) in the statistics as well as their long-term impact. For example, any changes in the infrastructure (e.g., the completion of a major transportation route) or land uses (e.g., the opening of a new employment center) can affect average prices and the pace of sales. Real estate brokers are the best sources for this statistical information. Multiple Listing Services provide information about total sales, average prices, and average days on the market for different types of housing in an area. Brokers can share their general insights and experiences in the market.

Trends in Building Permits

Recent historical trends in residential construction can also be tracked by compiling information about the number of private authorized building permits, available from the U.S. Department of Commerce. Some municipalities may be late in reporting their building permits, however, so the figures for the most recent year may not be complete.

The analysis should concentrate on the number of permits issued in the previous five years. Like average sale prices, a significant increase or decrease in permits issued from year to year must be explained in terms of general activity. Analysts should also study the number of permits issued by each municipality within the competitive market area to pinpoint the

most active jurisdictions. This information can be particularly valuable to a developer who has no specific site already identified.

This analysis should also consider the breakdown between permits for single-family houses and those for multifamily units, although these figures are not always accurate, because townhouses and certain other types of attached, for-sale houses are often counted as single-family housing. Thus, a significant portion—perhaps as much as 25 percent—of single-family units might actually be attached units. Analysts may need to adjust the data to provide a more accurate breakdown of single-family detached and single-family attached units. The number of building permits should be compared to actual sales of projects in the market area to refine the breakdown of unit types.

Analysis of building permits is important, because it indicates the level of historic activity and therefore the level of future building. These figures give the developer an initial indication of the size of the market and how it has changed over time—short-term or cyclical changes as well as long-term trends.

Analysis of the Competition

The study of the competitive housing market must begin with an analysis of single-family and multifamily communities where houses are currently being sold within the competitive market area. Though a representative sample of these projects may be a useful beginning, the only way to obtain the most accurate knowledge of the area is to account for each development through a visit by a member of the development or research firm—a "professional shopper."

Several facts about each community must be compared—floor plans, types and sizes of units (in square feet), current prices or rents, standard features and options, amenities offered in the community. The opening sales date and the total number of units sold or reserved contribute the key measure of the project's success. The number of sales in the previous three months or so enables the analyst to gauge the recent market, and information about original prices indicates how much prices have increased and over what span of time. The shopper should also note the values for various premiums like views, lot size or configuration, and frontage on a golf course that can result in major differences in price for the same product and determine a profile of buyers—their age and household members, place of employment, and location of previous residence. Any characteristics of buyers' lifestyle will be invaluable. Details about the physical

2-6 Empty nesters and active older families with children nearing adulthood were determined to be the market for Spinnaker Ridge in Gig Harbor, Washington. The market analysis also suggested design features that would help the developer market the houses to this group: single-level floor plans, spacious rooms to accommodate large pieces of furniture, views from primary rooms, and security.

characteristics of each community (views, amenities, and so on) contribute to the analysis. The reputation of the local school district should be factored in for projects designed to appeal to families. The advantages and disadvantages of the development's exact location, within the region and within the jurisdiction, must be noted. Availability of special financing and/or terms must be considered and the overall plan of the project and the design appraised.

Once data have been gathered about all communities, the information should be arranged in a form that permits easy comparison of the projects, best accomplished with a series of tables or charts in which differences in prices, sizes, and sales are readily apparent. Several factors must be considered when analyzing these properties, particularly jurisdiction and type of housing. Sales of certain types (garden condominiums, for example) may be strong in some municipalities, but not in others. On the other hand, some communities are perceived as more desirable places to live—so much so that most new housing will sell well, regardless of type.

This part of the analysis has two purposes: to identify voids or gluts in price or rent ranges and to offer reasonable explanations for the notable success or failure of existing communities (and ways in which those explanations can benefit the proposed property). The first goal is relatively easy to accomplish once the prices or rents of all units selling in the

competitive market area are arranged in increasing order. The second is more difficult, as it involves weighing a variety of other factors, notably type of units, size of units, price or rent per square foot, and certain qualitative considerations.

Comparison by unit type is the first logical step. Experience shows that most buyers, confronted with two houses of similar price or rent, choose the product that most resembles a single-family house. Thus, a townhouse is generally preferred to a garden condominium, and a duplex is preferred to a townhouse. The success of the "less desirable" housing types therefore depends on their being offered for more affordable prices or rents.

After comparing the different types of units, the next step is to gauge the success of different communities offering the same type of unit. Such an examination should concentrate on the range of prices and rents in relation to unit sizes. The simplest way to allow for variances in price and size is by computing the average price or rent per square foot for all units, even though consumers may not think in such terms. Logically, communities with the lowest prices or rents per square foot should report the highest monthly absorption and vice versa, *assuming similar location, features, amenities, and units of the same size.* If the analyst finds that consumers are not responding consistently to value—price per square foot—for similar products, other factors (financing,

26

design, amenities, specific locational advantages, for example) must be identified that cause consumers to prefer one development over another of similar market value.

Proposed Developments

The final component in analyzing residential activity in the competitive market area is an overview of proposed developments that have received municipal approval but have not yet received building permits. The number and type of units, the names of the project and the developer, and the street address of the project should be included. These data, which yield important information about the scope of future competition, can be obtained from the municipal planning or zoning department.

Analysts should also ascertain the length of time before a proposed project begins sales, which can be estimated from the time the project was approved. Units having final approval usually are on the market within six months. Units with preliminary approval are often six to 12 months from market entry, while those having conceptual approval are probably at least one year or more from entering the market. Any developments in litigation and properties zoned for residential use should at least be acknowledged in a market analysis.

Analysts should also determine the status of any vacant or redevelopable land within the delineated competitive market area that is zoned or could be rezoned for residential development. If these properties might be developed and marketed within the anticipated absorption period of the proposed project, they must also be factored into the analysis.

Information about these future communities, combined with knowledge of existing housing projects, can reveal gaps and potential opportunities in the competitive market area. An absence of proposed garden condominium developments in an area where existing condominium projects are selling well, for example, constitutes a significant void in the market. Similarly, a careful analysis might reveal an abundance of single-family houses, both existing and proposed, signaling that this product may have a future problem with absorption.

The total number of units planned by each jurisdiction within the competitive market area helps to put the proposed development into perspective, revealing which municipalities might experience the greatest near-term future growth. It can be particularly helpful when a builder searches for land for a prospective site.

Site Analysis

Once the competition has been evaluated, market analysts must cast a similar critical eye on the property for which the market analysis is being conducted. Specifically, the site's location, environmental characteristics, and amenities must be examined to establish its competitive position and relationship to the overall competitive market area.

The location must be evaluated in terms of gradually shrinking frames of reference: first the region within the state, then the municipality, and finally the neighborhood within the municipality. At each stage, analysts must consider the practical factors of transportation corridors and infrastructure and such intangible qualities as the area's desirability and reputation. Major highways and public transportation lines are obvious concerns, but a thorough analysis also accounts for airports, particularly if the developer is considering an upscale, professional market. Accessibility to major employment and shopping centers is vital to the success of any development, and the time required to drive to each major focus should be determined. The locations, reputation, and facilities of local schools should be considered when projects are targeted to a family-oriented market. Other factors, such as status, security, special features, and neighboring uses may be important to potential buyers.

The area around the site should offer amenities suited to the particular lifestyle of the target market that would make a prospect want to move to the community. Easy accessibility to particular restaurants, theaters, and other entertainment centers would probably appeal to young professionals, while empty nesters would favor nearby golf courses.

Analysts must also consider the immediate and long-term aesthetic appeal of the site itself. If views are a major source of appeal, for example, the developer should ascertain that future developments will minimally affect those views. Ideally, the analyst should walk through the property, assessing views and topography.

Calculating Demand, Absorption, and Capture

Perhaps the most valuable function of market analysis is the determination of future demand for a particular product and the estimation of absorption rates at a community offering that product. The concept of prospective housing demand is based on the premise that a given population will require a reasonable and ascertainable number of housing units. That number, as well as the type and mix of units, can be projected by employing data related to increases in population, households, and employment and to known and anticipated trends in the social and economic framework of the marketplace.

Housing demand must be distinguished from housing need. Housing need is based on two factors: households entering the marketplace and newly formed households. This information indicates the minimum number of housing units that will be required during a specific time. Housing demand includes the same two factors but also accounts for households moving within the market, or "internal mobility." Housing demand also takes into consideration unsatisfied or pent-up demand, households seeking larger houses because of a growing family or increased ability to buy (the move-up market), and older households whose children have created new, independent households and so no longer need their existing large houses (the move-down market). Nationally, close to 20 percent of households move in any given year.

The total demand for housing is directed toward newly constructed housing units, resale housing units, and rental apartments. Analysts must estimate shares of this total demand that major housing types will attract—detached single family versus attached single family versus multifamily or for-sale units (including townhouses and garden condominiums) versus rental apartments. This allocation should be based on historic trends in the marketplace and projected based on economic and demographic changes.

The next step is to determine the housing demand that each major housing type channels into new for-sale housing units. In areas with normal market dynamics, this figure can be estimated from previous trends in the ratio of new houses sold to resale houses sold, which can be derived from the Multiple Listing Services or from statistics kept by area real estate brokers. Housing demand should be further refined by adjusting figures for income and age; knowledge of consumers' income is fundamental for any market-rate housing, while knowledge about age becomes particularly important when special market segments—for example, empty nesters or retirees—are to be targeted. Estimates and projections of these data are available from demographic services.

Once these data are refined, analysts can then identify all the components of the basic equation for demand (*Total Demand* minus *Total Absorption by Competitive Products* equals *Residual Demand*). Total Demand is comprised of the refined data. Total Absorption by Competitive Products must be projected based on the sales performance of existing communities as well as projections of the influence of proposed communities that will be competitive during the marketing period of the proposed property. Calculation of the Residual Demand yields the number of prospective households for which the quantity and type of housing are insufficient or unavailable in the competitive market area—or the number of units of a particular product type within a particular range of prices and rents that can be absorbed (sold or rented) within a particular period of time (usually expressed in units per year).

Once the residual demand is known, analysts must still determine what share of that demand the project at hand is likely to capture. Determining this "capture rate" is highly judgmental and must take into account all of the advantages and disadvantages of the project being proposed.[3] For example, a project being proposed in a relatively poor location with few amenities should expect a low capture rate, while a project with many amenities located near employment centers and transportation corridors is likely to capture a much higher percentage of the market. In their enthusiasm for a project, developers and market analysts often lose their objectivity and overestimate the capture rate for the project. This mistake can lead to a seemingly deadly sales pace that ultimately can affect a developer's credibility with lenders.

A number of sophisticated mathematical models have been developed to calculate short- and long-term capture rates.[4] Any such model is only a tool for estimating capture, however, and should not be the sole source of projections. The instincts of experienced developers and market analysts must also be taken into consideration.

No new development can be expected to capture a majority of the residual demand. In all but highly specialized market positions, a new project can at best capture only up to 30 percent of the residual demand in its first year of sales, and that percentage is likely to decrease over the following years.

Qualitative Research

A thorough analysis concludes with an identification and description of the various categories of potential buyers, or "target markets," for the proposed development. Development programs—particularly house design, interior features, exterior amenities, and land plan—must be created based on profiles of potential buyers. Target market groups are comprised of people

---

[3] John McMahan, *Property Development*, 2d ed. (New York: McGraw-Hill, 1989), p. 143.
[4] See, e.g., John M. Clapp, *Handbook for Real Estate Market Analysis* (Englewood Cliffs, N.J.: Prentice-Hall, 1987).

Real estate professionals use market research to tap the pulse of consumers and professionals and learn their opinions about products, services, issues, and concepts. When people think of market research, they typically remember the telephone call they received at dinnertime or as they were ready to step into the tub that asked their opinion about a proposed new development in the neighborhood. Such surveys or polls are quantitative research. Quantitative research measures the volume of response to specific questions, for example, what proportion of people prefer fourplexes to townhouses. This type of research is valuable because it can produce numerical data on preferences and product appeal based on a large number of responses. But while the quantitative research can tell us how many senior citizens prefer to buy rather than rent a retirement home, it cannot explain why or under what circumstances widows might prefer to pay an entrance stipend rather than monthly fixed costs.

Qualitative research can provide that explanation. Considered by some to be "soft" because results cannot be tabulated, measured, or projected, the qualitative method explores the nature and nuances of underlying attitudes, opinions, beliefs, and values. This knowledge can provide direction or generate ideas in:

- Creating new products, services, designs, or plans;
- Changing existing products, services, designs, and plans;
- Identifying and exploring attitudes about national, regional, or local issues;
- Testing specific marketing and advertising strategies, concepts, materials, and packaging; and
- Understanding reasons for consumers' unexpected behavior.

A qualitative study can be undertaken *before* a quantitative study to identify key issues to be measured and ensure that the survey's terminology will be properly understood. It can be used *after* a quantitative study to explore and better understand the findings of a survey. Qualitative research takes the form of in-depth one-on-one interviews and focus groups.

A focus group is a directed discussion among a small group of participants, usually eight to 12, who were selected to participate because they have common characteristics of interest to the focus group's sponsor. For example, the developer of a retirement community might wish to hear the opinions of a group of single females over the age of 65 with incomes over $25,000 per year who reside in a specific geographic area. A professional moderator focuses the discussion on the desired topics and encourages respondents' participation and interaction. For a given project, the sponsor typically commissions a number of focus groups involving different categories of respondents. At the conclusion of the series of focus groups, the sponsor is given a written report analyzing the findings of the study.

Typical objectives for a focus group might include:

- Identifying and ordering what is appealing or unappealing about a particular community;
- Understanding what would motivate homeowners to move from their present residences to a nearby new community;
- Exploring respondents' attitudes toward specific aspects of the product or different designs;
- Understanding the image a development company projects;
- Understanding competitors' images;
- Ascertaining the components of "curb appeal";
- Asking respondents to comment upon specific floor plans, community designs, elevations, or amenities;
- Testing respondents' reaction to certain key marketing terms or materials;
- Understanding the lifestyle, attitudes, and preferences of a specific target market. ▶

who share not only demographic and economic characteristics but also lifestyle.

Qualitative research is essential to determine the features and qualities that will enable a product to meet the preferences for lifestyle of its intended target market. For example, two dual-income families with the same income, in the same age group, and with children the same age may have entirely different aspirations and lifestyles in different market areas. A finely tuned understanding of the market can be used to create a highly successful project if the appropriate product can be built in the proper location.

Focus groups are an expedient and cost-effective tool of qualitative research. In addition to helping the sponsor understand the target market's values and attitudes, focus groups often uncover unexpected issues. For example, the developer of a retirement community might not have considered including transportation services until a focus group of senior citizens identifies it as an important need. Another benefit of focus groups is that the turnaround time is convenient for the client: usually a study can be completed within six to eight weeks, from recruiting respondents to the final report.

Focus groups capitalize on the synergy of group dynamics and the willingness of individuals to share their opinions. Because the discussions can be monitored while they are happening, the *way* respondents communicate their opinions and attitudes provides an additional understanding of their attitudes. Nonverbal behavior (i.e., vocal emphasis and tone, body language) is as important as verbal responses—sometimes more so.

Respondents

Potential participants of a focus group might be selected according to demographic categories (age, sex, occupation, income), psychosociographics (mental, social, emotional, or attitude profiles and predispositions), and geographic location (individuals residing in different places may have different needs or outlooks). The desired mix of respondents' characteristics is determined by the objectives of the study. Members of related professions are often excellent sources of qualitative research. For example, to explore marketing issues, a developer might want to hear the views of potential consumers in one set of groups and of real estate salespeople in another.

Potential participants, especially those who have never taken part in a focus group, are often not easily recruited because people tend to be skeptical about what they might perceive as a marketing scheme. To offset their reluctance and to establish the study's credibility, respondents should always be assured that their participation in the research will not initiate future attempts at marketing—and, indeed, that promise should be honored. As an incentive, and to impress upon them that their opinions and time are valued, respondents are compensated with a monetary stipend or a donation to their favorite charity.

Respondents are grouped homogeneously to promote a comfortable atmosphere where they can discuss freely personal and professional insights—and sometimes emotional reactions. For that reason, it would not be a good idea to mix certain groups. For example, tenants and apartment managers should not be in the same group, even when the discussion deals with relationships between tenants and management. To obtain certain types of information or in circumstances where one sex might be inclined to defer to the other—for example, when discussing child-care facilities or alternatives for financing—men and women should be in separate groups. Ideally, to ensure anonymity and to encourage candid discussion, respondents should not know one another. While it is not always possible, at minimum, respondents should not live in the same household.

Procedures

Focus groups typically are commissioned through a professional focus group moderator/market analyst, who generally assumes responsibility for making all the necessary arrangements, conducting the groups, and analyzing the results at the conclusion of the study.

Focus groups conducted in a specialized setting or research facility produce optimum results. Re-

Qualitative research should be undertaken after it has been established that demand exists for various housing products. The most common methods of qualitative research are surveys and focus groups. Surveys can be done by telephone or, preferably, by direct mail. Focus groups, or structured group discussions with selected potential consumers, are considered more valuable, for the trained researcher can obtain more detailed information about lifestyle than a simple questionnaire (see the accompanying feature box for a more detailed discussion of focus groups).

Besides helping to fine-tune the product, qualitative research also serves as a valuable first step in marketing the community. The research establishes name recognition for the developer and the proposed development in the area. The consumers who are surveyed can also form the beginning of a mailing list for the sales or leasing program.

spondents sit around a table in a conference room or on comfortable chairs in a living-room setting. The moderator maintains a balance of control and freedom and introduces the session, exploring topics, asking key questions, keeping the discussion on track, yet permitting the group enough freedom to uncover feelings honestly.

A one-way mirror, located behind the moderator, permits interested clients to view the session from an adjoining room, out of view from participants. For obvious ethical reasons, respondents are informed that others are watching, but the mirror allows respondents to forget they are being observed and is less obtrusive than having observers in the discussion room.

When a research facility is unavailable, a two-room suite, such as a hotel conference area, can be used. With the proper technical set-up, observers may still watch the groups from another room through a closed-circuit television monitor. The group's discussions are audiotaped as a permanent record of the proceedings and so that the moderator can review the discussion later when writing the report. Although more costly, videotapes of the discussion provide a more accurate record and enable others who cannot attend the session to later see as well as hear the respondents' reactions.

The value of respondents' reactions in a qualitative study lies in their perceptions and behaviors and the intensity of their feelings. Individuals often are not aware of the motivations for their feelings or behaviors, and the moderator must extrapolate them in the analysis. The best respondents are those who are honest and frank about their own attitudes, opinions, and behaviors.

Final Report

The moderator of the focus group prepares a follow-up report for the sponsor, analyzing key findings based on all the focus groups that were held for the same purpose. In addition to a description and analysis of the overall findings, the report should include direct quotations from respondents to give the report specificity and emphasis.

The report serves not only as a record of what transpired in the groups but also, and more importantly, as a springboard on which to base marketing decisions. Further, it forces the moderator/market analyst to review all the groups objectively and put in perspective those attention-getting moments that occur in groups that can distract the observer from the whole picture. Reviewing the tapes enables the analyst to notice certain recurring themes that might not have been apparent during the session or to discern an issue that might have gone unobserved in the heat of discussion. Because these less obvious outcomes could be significant to the results, a professional moderator might be reluctant to discuss findings immediately after the focus groups are completed.

Clarifications and Limitations

Respondents' erroneous observations or faulty judgments revealed in the findings are still valid—and especially valuable. Such responses provide insights about inappropriate perceptions and may identify a need for clarification or consumers' education. Because of the nature of the qualitative research and its small sample size, findings from the qualitative study are not meant to be generalized or projected. By exploring attitudes, insights, and opinions, however, focus groups can provide real estate professionals a greater understanding of potential consumers' needs and behavior.

Source: Barbara G. Rosenthal, president, Qualitative Research Service, Potomac, Maryland.

Results of the Market Analysis

At the completion of the market analysis, residential developers should be able to answer the questions presented at the beginning of this chapter—whether a demand exists for new housing and if so what type, size, and price; what percentage of the market can be captured at a given site; and what particular amenities and features need to be provided in the project. The market analysis will also provide a basic level of information about indirect economic constraints like the physical site and regulatory constraints but, in most cases, not enough upon which to base a decision whether or not to proceed with the project. A final determination of a project's feasibility will require more detailed consideration of these issues. The remainder of this chapter discusses these indirect economic constraints in more detail.

Site Selection

While practices and standards for assessing a site's physical and environmental constraints have improved in recent years, the difficulty of locating buildable sites has increased markedly. Because of rapidly increasing land costs, sites that previously were considered unbuildable have become candidates for development; careful analysis is necessary, however, to determine accurately their current developability.

The precise nature of the property selected depends upon a number of factors, including type of development, the anticipated size of the development, its cost and location, and the market. In general, the worst reason for developing a parcel is "because I already own it." Only in rare instances should developers design a project around a piece of property they already own and wish to find a use for. Ideally, developers have a concept they wish to carry out (based on the findings of a thorough market analysis) and then locate a site with the necessary characteristics. An exception is when developers purchase a parcel based on a specific objective for development, only to have the objective change as a result of outside forces. In these circumstances, developers may be forced to shop for an objective, much as they normally would for a plot of land. (Appendix C provides a sample site analysis checklist.)

Location

Developers are fond of saying that site selection revolves around three factors: location, location, and location. Certainly the success of a residential development has a great deal to do with its location within the urban area, the position of major thoroughfares, the development's access to them, and the character of existing and prospective growth. The saying may be less of an axiom than it once was, however, because some entrepreneurial builders have in essence created demand in areas traditionally thought of as poor locations. Although location is very important in site selection, what appear to be balancing factors are the cost of the land and its suitability for development.

A "good address" for medium- to high-priced projects is especially important, and it is generally best to construct such projects in well-known, high-profile, established residential areas. Fighting tradition or creating demand in traditionally nonresidential areas or low-income areas may prove to be risky; however, because of the dynamic nature of cities and their economies, what is perceived to be a good address constantly changes. For example, the term "gentrification" has been used to describe the phenome-

2-8   Patterns and directions of urban growth are important considerations when evaluating a site's locational suitability for residential development.

non of young professionals' moving into traditionally low-income and nonresidential neighborhoods. If enough young professionals move in, the image, and in turn the housing, can increase in value. Although the trend toward gentrification of neighborhoods is a somewhat isolated phenomenon, it offers the entrepreneurial builder a chance for increased rewards from increased risk.

In projects geared toward low-income households, land cost and convenience to work, schools, and shopping are important considerations. Availability of public transportation becomes especially important to a low-income project. Because the economics of developing low-income housing have not been particularly attractive to developers in recent years, many such projects have been subsidized by public monies, community redevelopment programs, and public/private ventures.

Several locational factors should be considered in the selection of any site:

- Past trends of city growth should be carefully studied to determine the direction in which high-, medium-, and low-cost development has moved. Higher-priced residential areas usually show the same general direction of movement outward from the urban center over the years. If expensive residential development began northwest from the center, for example, successive outward extensions of higher-cost houses usually continue in the same direction. This trend holds true even when development takes place in suburban areas outside corporate city boundaries. It is usually unwise to ignore established trends in land development, especially when the project is a conventional subdivision. It is much easier to satisfy demand than to create it.

- If access to the site is available only on congested routes or through rundown commercial, industrial, or residential areas, it is probably wise not to consider the property for development. In some instances, however, it may be possible to acquire additional land or obtain rights-of-way that will permit a new or improved approach, thereby avoiding the negative image of existing land uses.

- The most desirable sites for new residential development are those near established or emerging employment centers. Studies have shown that most workers prefer to live within a 30- to 45-minute one-way commute to work.[5] Sites near major employment centers, however, tend to be the most expensive, and affordable housing often generates demand at urban fringes with commutes over one hour.

- Sites near commercial, recreational, and cultural services will be easier to market than those located in areas where such services do not exist. Developers will benefit by asking themselves the same questions a prospective buyer would: "How far must I travel to shop, play, and be entertained?"

- The location and quality of public schools are increasingly important considerations for young families seeking their first house or a move-up house. In fact, the quality of the school district where a site is located can prove an effective marketing tool. Developers should consider the access to and quality of the local public school district if the intended market consists largely of families with school-age children.

- Every prospective residential site is located within the regulatory jurisdiction of a county or municipality, which will be responsible for considering the eventual development proposal. Developers must therefore consider the agency's position on issues such as growth and development. Not all municipalities share the same attitudes about new development, and developers would be wise to understand fully their future dealings with the public agency before committing themselves to a site.

- The availability of utilities and public services must be evaluated carefully. In many parts of the country, permission to develop a site depends upon the availability of water and sewer lines, with municipalities deciding the location and timing of the installation of utility systems. In other areas, lack of capacity has resulted in moratoriums on residential construction until additional capacity can or will be provided. When a residential development has several phases, the *future* availability of utilities must be carefully assessed even though *current* hook-ups are available.

These locational considerations are not an exhaustive list but point to some of the most frequent issues that developers should consider before purchasing a site. Each site, locale, and intended housing product requires its own set of considerations. Prudent developers know what is important to their intended market and examine the site with respect to its advantages and disadvantages of location.

Accessibility

Transportation to places of employment, the central business district, shopping centers, schools, churches, and recreation places is a primary consideration in site selection and development. During the 1980s, the population of many urban areas grew substantially without a corresponding commitment to and funding of highway improvements. Vehicular trips generated have even exceeded "real" population growth as a result of such factors as two-worker families, more nontraditional households, and more young drivers (the children of baby boomers). The result has been severely congested freeways, arterial highways, and local streets and an overall increase in commuting times. With transportation problems foremost on the minds of today's homebuyers, developers must examine a potential development site in terms of both its regional and local accessibility.

[5] Yacov Zahavi, *The "UMOT" Project* (prepared for the U.S. Department of Transportation, Washington, D.C., and the Ministry of Transport, Bonn, Federal Republic of Germany, August 1979), p. 125.

Hamilton Proper is a 1,300-acre, irregularly shaped parcel located in Hamilton County, Indiana, under development by Mansur Development Corporation. Location, accessibility, surrounding developments, the potential for recreation, and proximity to employment, shopping, and schools were all important criteria that influenced Mansur's decision to develop the property. In addition, Mansur wanted a site suitable for a golf course residential community; thus, special consideration was given to selection of a site with the appropriate physical characteristics. Detailed site analysis before acquisition and planning was essential to ensure that Mansur's objectives for development could be realized.

2-10   SLOPES AND ELEVATIONS

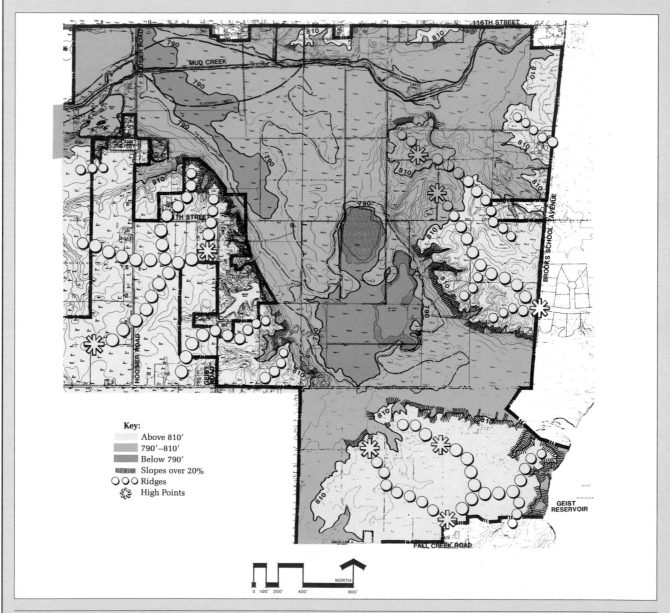

Key:
- Above 810'
- 790'–810'
- Below 790'
- Slopes over 20%
- Ridges
- High Points

Map shows only the eastern half of the site.

Locational Considerations

The property is located approximately 20 miles northeast of downtown Indianapolis. The primary factor supporting development of this site is its location with respect to Indianapolis and the relatively strong population and household growth projected for the metropolitan area. Because much of the metropolitan area's growth is projected to occur in Hamilton County, the property is well positioned for future residential development. Hamilton County's schools are among the best in the area. A comprehensive market analysis profiling historical and projected growth in the area was incorporated in the planning.

Access to the property is excellent and commuting times for residents relatively short. The site is bordered by primary collector streets on the north and south and secondary collectors on the east and west. Geist Reservoir, located just east of the site, is one of two reservoirs near Indianapolis offering a full range of water-related activities. The surround-

2-11 SOILS

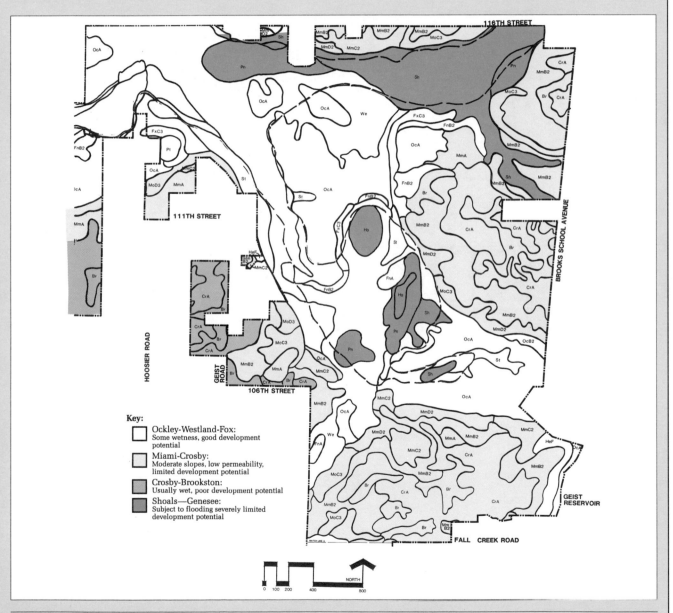

Key:

Ockley-Westland-Fox:
Some wetness, good development potential

Miami-Crosby:
Moderate slopes, low permeability, limited development potential

Crosby-Brookston:
Usually wet, poor development potential

Shoals—Genesee:
Subject to flooding severely limited development potential

Map shows only the eastern half of the site.

▶

2-9 (continued)

ing area is recognized for its exclusive, luxury single-family houses. In addition, the city of Carmel, approximately 10 miles away, offers retail and commercial space.

Physical Characteristics

David Jensen Associates, land planners from Denver, Colorado, conducted the site analysis, con-

cept planning, and master planning for the property. The objective was to complete an extensive analysis of all physical and socioeconomic factors that would influence development of the site. During the initial planning stages, maps of existing conditions, elevations and drainages, slopes and drainages, soils, opportunities and constraints, and ownership and subdivision patterns for surrounding properties were prepared.

2-12   DRAINAGE AND VEGETATION

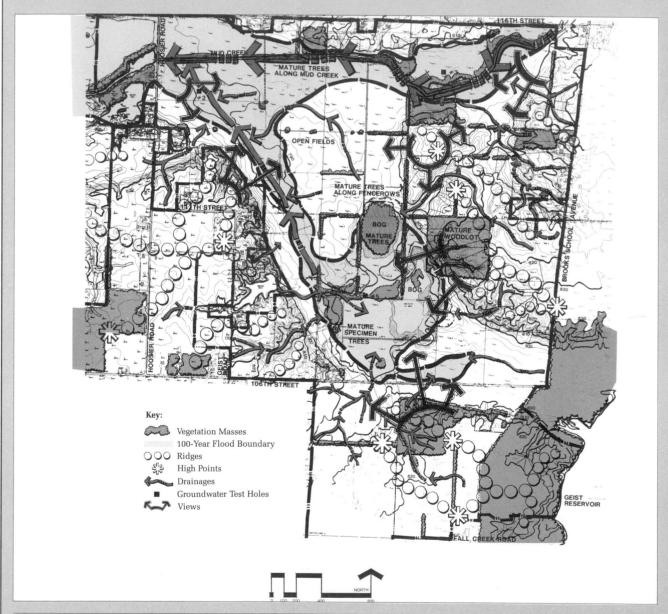

Key:

- Vegetation Masses
- 100-Year Flood Boundary
- Ridges
- High Points
- Drainages
- Groundwater Test Holes
- Views

Map shows only the eastern half of the site.

Past and present land uses for the site and surrounding area are for the most part agricultural. The site consists of gently rolling terraces and upland and agricultural land. Open fields provide potential parcels for development separated by hedgerows, wooded areas, and drainage pathways. The site has a distinctive irregular shape but can be developed relatively easily, based on the information found in the analysis.

The analysis of slopes and drainages shows topography that is flat to rolling in the valleys with abrupt slopes rising to uplands overlooking the valley. Mud Creek runs the length of the site from east to west, and wetland bogs occur in the east central portion. Floodplains and wetlands constitute a significant portion of the area and foster habitat for a variety of waterfowl. Although somewhat of a constraint for residential development, these features

2-13

OPPORTUNITIES AND CONSTRAINTS

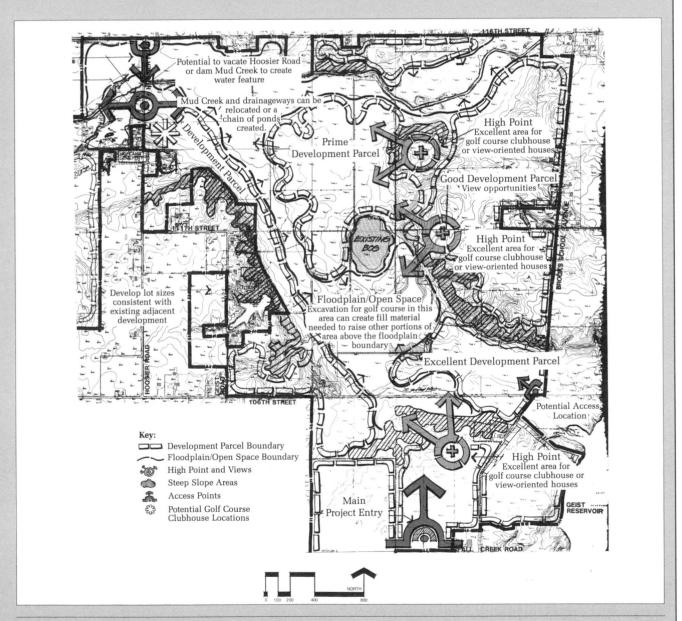

Map shows only the eastern half of the site.

offer an excellent opportunity for development of a golf course oriented toward conservation.

The analysis of elevations was critical for identifying a potential site for the clubhouse and the overall routing of the golf course. The upper areas of the site were found to be ideal for residential development, as they are on higher ground emphasizing views to the course and other features.

The map of opportunities and constraints represented a composite analysis of all other mapping analyses. It is an overlay, with the data reflecting the overall development parameters of the site and serving as the framework for concept planning.

Easements and Utilities

Because the site of Hamilton Proper was comprised of agricultural parcels, it is generally free of easements crossing the site. A sewer interceptor trunk line is planned along Mud Creek, which will supply the development with sanitary sewerage. Other utilities are provided in the adjacent streets bordering

the site. Requirements for storm sewers were fulfilled by the constructed and natural open drainages and wetland areas, making the construction of detention areas and extensive improvements to storm sewers unnecessary in Hamilton Proper.

Other Considerations

Although park and recreation facilities were not identified for the site in the county's comprehensive plan, a major portion of Hamilton Proper was set aside for open space and recreational amenities, incorporating and enhancing the property's natural characteristics. In addition to 27 holes of golf in the development, neighborhood parks, to be connected by an open space/trail system, are planned throughout. The wetlands and drainages provide valuable untouched natural areas for water and open space and will serve as a unifying element for all open spaces.

Source: Information for this feature box was submitted by David Jensen Associates, Denver, Colorado.

Accessibility takes several forms: regional, local site, pedestrian, and transit. In its broadest context, a site should be evaluated for its accessibility to major employment and commercial centers within the metropolitan area, which in the past usually meant a site's proximity and access to downtown. But increased distances and travel times to work have led to the restructuring of cities in many areas of the country. Today's cities and metropolitan areas are becoming groups of interdependent "activity centers" constituting business, retail, housing, and entertainment focal points amid a low-density cityscape. Each activity center acts as a new kind of downtown where the buildings are the tallest, the daytime population the largest, and traffic congestion the most severe. Each activity has its own outlying districts, which may stretch as far as 10 miles from the core.[6]

Los Angeles is perhaps the most evolved example of the "suburban activity center." Although downtown Los Angeles experienced an unprecedented boom during the 1970s and 1980s, the metropolitan area simultaneously gave rise to 16 smaller activity centers, among them Century City, Costa Mesa/Irvine/Newport Beach, Encino, Glendale, Los Angeles International Airport/Century Boulevard, Warner Center, Ontario, Pasadena, Universal City/Burbank, and Westwood. This pattern is replicating itself in

both cities of the Sunbelt and more archetypal cities along the eastern seaboard.

The emergence of new suburban activity centers is an important and relatively new consideration in residential site selection. A site with easy access to an existing downtown or an existing or emerging suburban activity center is easier to market than a site that is difficult to reach from regional employment and commercial centers. Developers should evaluate the growth dynamics of the metropolitan area and then determine whether a proposed site offers good regional accessibility.

Locally, property being considered for residential use must be accessible to streets and arterial highways. The actual nature of the streets connecting the project with the larger community depends on the type of residential development planned. Single-family detached houses, for example, generate more trips per unit than any other type of housing. "They are the largest units in size and have more residents and more vehicles per unit than any other residential land use; they are generally located farther away from

---

[6] Christopher B. Leinberger and Charles Lockwood, "How Business Is Reshaping America," *Atlantic Monthly,* October 1986, pp. 43–52.

shopping centers, employment areas, and other trip attractors than are other residential land uses; and they have fewer alternate modes of transportation available because they are not as concentrated as other types of units."[7] Per acre, however, single-family detached houses generate the fewest number of trips simply because each acre has fewer dwelling units.

If the project is to contain single-family detached houses at relatively low densities, a subcollector or collector street with pavement 26 to 36 feet wide usually provides sufficient access.[8] Ideally, low-density subdivisions should be designed with a minimum number of points of access to major thoroughfares. With higher-density development, expanded access may be required. Because projects containing garden apartments (15 units per acre) and denser development generate significant amounts of traffic and require greater access to support services, locations adjacent to collector streets and highways are common.

If a development site has poor or no access, developers must be prepared to invest in roadway improvements. Any evaluation of a site must include an analysis of the costs and feasibility of providing access and a determination of who will pay. If the points of access and proposed project conform with the city's future land use plan, the city might aid the developer in funding improvements. Alternatively, an improvement district could be created to fund improvements, in which all properties within the "benefit area" are assessed their fair share of costs, with the city's picking up the public's share.

Because of growing concerns about traffic congestion, almost every residential project benefits by good access to the local public transit system. Although reliance upon the private automobile for all transportation has become the norm for suburban areas since the 1950s, worsening traffic and rising costs of automobile ownership are contributing to increased use of transit, especially for commuting to work. Today, transit stops for rail lines and buses generally indicate a good opportunity for residential development.

Good public transit facilities become increasingly important to those who live in lower-priced housing, because such people are less likely to own a car. If development for low-income households is planned, a site within walking distance of employment centers is ideal. If the site lacks public transit and is over a mile from employment and commercial services, it is poorly located for low-income housing.

Another major consideration is a site's convenience for pedestrians. The concept of the planned unit development (PUD), which almost always provides an integrated pedestrian system, has become

2-14 SUMMARY OF RESIDENTIAL TRIPS
      BY TYPE OF HOUSING UNIT

	TWO-WAY VEHICLE TRIPS PER DWELLING UNIT	
	WEEK DAY	PEAK HOUR
Single-Family Detached	10.1	1.1
Apartments		
Average (all types)	6.1	0.7
Low Rise	6.6	0.7
High Rise	4.2	0.4
Townhouses/Condominiums	5.9	0.6
Low-Rise Condominiums	NA	2.2

NA = Not available.
Source: Institute of Transportation Engineers, *Trip Generation,* 4th ed. (Washington, D.C.: Author, 1987). Data synthesized by ULI.

tremendously popular among builders, municipalities, and residents. The creation of pedestrian links between residential and commercial, recreational, and public uses is one of the most noteworthy trends in residential development. Park areas, abandoned rights-of-way, public streets, private trails, and easements across private property should all be considered as opportunities to accommodate pedestrians.

Land Use

Existing, proposed, and historical patterns of land use on and adjacent to a potential development site should be studied carefully to determine whether a potential conflict exists. Well-documented land use studies can reduce a developer's liability against potential lawsuits filed by future residents of the project. A complete land use analysis is comprised of several subjects: 1) historical uses, 2) current use, 3) surrounding uses, and 4) possible conflicting uses.

Historical Uses

During the 1980s, it became increasingly important for developers to scrutinize the historical uses of the property under consideration. If past uses on the site resulted in contamination by hazardous chemicals, the landowner or the developer could incur potential liabilities. The Comprehensive Emergency Response, Compensation, and Liability Act (CERCLA), com-

---

[7] Institute of Transportation Engineers, *Trip Generation,* 4th ed. (Washington, D.C.: Author, 1987), p. 256.
[8] Donna Hanousek, *Project Infrastructure Development Handbook* (Washington, D.C.: ULI–the Urban Land Institute, 1989), p. 45.

monly referred to as "Superfund," includes provisions for joint and severed liability of both past and present property owners, even if those owners had no knowledge of or responsibility for the contamination.[9] Developers could be subject to civil or criminal liabilities, particularly if they were fully aware of the on-site contamination but did not disclose the information to buyers.

A case in point arose during the late 1980s, when the Environmental Protection Agency (EPA) investigated a residential neighborhood in Westminster, California, to determine whether the site qualified for inclusion on the Superfund list.[10] The neighborhood had been built in the 1950s on an abandoned underground waste pit that had been used for the disposal of oil field wastes from the 1930s to the 1950s. In the late 1980s, sludge from the pits began to seep into residents' yards, and residents complained of health effects they attributed to the odorous sludge. Both the developer and the city potentially were liable because they knew about the wastes before the site was developed. Even if liabilities are eventually waived in such cases, the frequently lengthy and costly legal battle can bankrupt a small builder and destroy the image of an otherwise reputable company.

Developers can protect themselves from such liability by thoroughly investigating a site and the surrounding area before purchasing property. Usually the municipal or county administrative building is the best place to begin researching historical uses of a property. Most planning departments maintain land use maps that reveal uses of a site over the last several decades. Tax records and historical societies can provide clues about historical land uses. If these avenues prove fruitless, long-time residents of the community may provide information.

To help reduce a landowner's risk of liability, Congress may eventually amend Section 101(35) of CERCLA to help define "due diligence" on the landowner's part. Legislation proposed in 1989 would qualify a landowner for a defense of "innocent landowner" under CERCLA if an environmental audit were conducted, to include the following documentation:

- The chain of title documents recorded for the property for a period of 50 years;
- Aerial photographs that may reflect prior uses of the property;
- County records to determine whether environmental cleanup liens exist against the property;

---

[9] David Salvesen, "Liability for Hazardous Cleanups: Caveat Emptor," *Urban Land,* April 1988, p. 36. For additional discussion of toxic wastes, see "Hazardous Wastes" later in this chapter.

[10] California Department of Health Services, Westminster Tract 2633, *Expenditure Plan for the Clean-Up Bond Act of 1984,* January 1989.

2-15 Developers can be held liable for health effects caused by locating houses on contaminated sites. A thorough survey of a site's historical use should be conducted during the feasibility analysis—especially for infill sites with a history of industrial use.

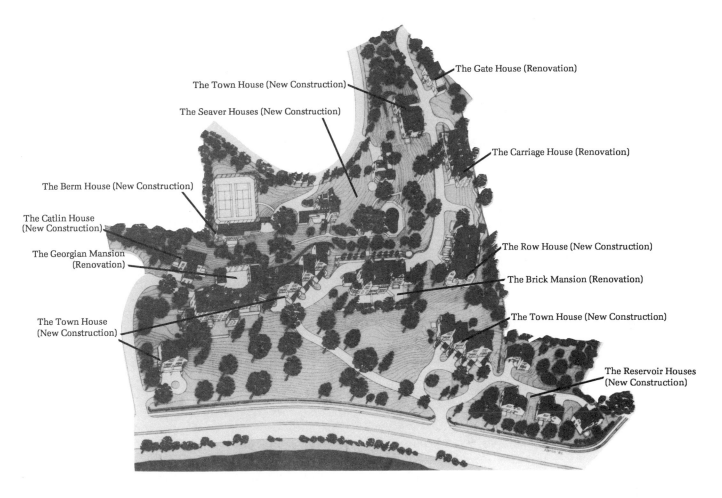

The Gate House (Renovation)

The Town House (New Construction)

The Seaver Houses (New Construction)

The Carriage House (Renovation)

The Berm House (New Construction)

The Catlin House (New Construction)

The Row House (New Construction)

The Georgian Mansion (Renovation)

The Brick Mansion (Renovation)

The Town House (New Construction)

The Town House (New Construction)

The Reservoir Houses (New Construction)

2-16 Fisher Hill Estates in Brookline, Massachusetts, was developed on a 13.2-acre infill site previously occupied by two historic mansions. The mansions, a carriage house, and a gate house were renovated and converted to 12 condominium units. An additional 26 detached and townhouse condominiums were constructed on grounds that were landscaped in the late 19th century by Frederick Law Olmsted. Preservation of the site's historical features factored heavily into establishing the project's distinctive character.

- Federal, state, and local government records of sites or facilities that have released hazardous substances likely to cause or contribute to contamination of the property;
- A visual inspection of the site and adjacent properties.[11]

The amount of time and effort spent on historical use surveys must be in proportion to the level of risk. A site that has been used only for agriculture may require only cursory examination, while a site with a history of industrial activities may require both research and field tests to determine the likelihood of contamination. Prudent developers undertake the appropriate level of analysis and then document their findings as protection against future legal action.

Residential developers should also be aware that not all historical activities occurring on a site are necessarily negative for development. In many instances, developers have capitalized on historical structures (houses, barns, public buildings) by incorporating them into the development's design. Properly treated, such structures can become a focal point of interest and help to set the development apart from its competition. Incorporating historical features into a new development implies additional costs, and developers need to weigh these costs against probable benefits.

[11] Warren, Gorham & Lamont, Inc., *Real Estate Financing Update,* vol. 6, no. 3, November 1989, p. 1.

Current Use

Developers also need to be aware of a site's current use. Nonconflicting uses that generate income, such as farming or grazing, can help carry the land economically during development. Other current uses—those requiring relocation or those that generate waste or damage the site's aesthetic quality—can be less advantageous. The concept and purpose of a proposed project influence a developer's willingness to accept the difficulty of site assembly, removal of existing structures and physical constraints, and other limitations.

In valuable inner-city locations, it is often economically justifiable to assemble several parcels with existing structures, clear the site, and provide a different, more intensive use, such as high-density housing. This economic reality has led to the loss of housing for low- and moderate-income families in many inner cities. As a result, many municipalities have offered incentives for developers to include affordable housing in new developments—in some cases have required them to do so. The economics of constructing single-family detached housing most often mandates an unimproved rural or suburban site with land assembly and clearance held to a minimum, for the costs normally incurred in purchasing and improving a site derive from the following factors:

- *Carrying costs.* When an existing use is removed to make way for something new, money is lost during the time it takes to clear the site and erect and occupy the new building. During that time, the developer incurs substantial costs without any return.
- *Demolition.* Improvements in techniques of demolition—heavy equipment to bulldoze small frame buildings and dynamite to remove high-rise masonry buildings—have greatly reduced the expense of site clearance; often the expense is further reduced by the sale of salvaged material.
- *Assembly.* Site assembly is most complex in highly urban locations where real estate has been continually used for many years and property has often been subdivided and redivided. Government renewal and housing assistance programs in most cities assist in the complex task of land assembly by acquiring blighted properties, clearing them, and making them available for use at less than cost.

Surrounding Uses

The nature of adjacent areas in large measure determines the use for which an undeveloped parcel

should be developed. If adjoining areas are compatible, they can enhance the desirability of a proposed residential project. When they are deleterious or conflicting, developers should proceed very cautiously.

Most desirable from the standpoint of residential developers are sites adjacent to open space and community facilities like parks, recreation areas, museums, and libraries. Such areas and facilities provide an attractive setting and frequently impart an aura of prestige. Because most sites are not blessed with these features nearby, on-site recreational facilities have become a standard in many, if not most, new housing developments. These amenities can include improved open space, tennis courts, pools, trails, and greenbelts. In large developments, major recreational amenities like manmade water features and golf courses are often incorporated into the project's design to create added prestige and value.

Existing residential areas are a desirable setting for new residential development, whether the development will occupy an undeveloped tract in the path of suburban expansion or a bypassed parcel in the midst of a built-up residential neighborhood. If a shift to higher density is being proposed for an infill site, however, problems may be encountered not only with regard to location, access, and other physical factors but also the attitude of nearby residents and their perception of what the change in density will mean to their neighborhood. Completely rural areas are generally viewed positively as long as incompatible uses are not approved for subsequent development adjacent to the site.

A concept usually applied to commercial or mixed-use projects but also applicable to residential site selection is "synergy"—the whole is greater than the sum of its parts. A good site for residential development is one with positive synergy with surrounding land uses. For example, a residential site near an established or emerging suburban activity center offers future residents the convenience of employment and commercial services within easy commuting distance. When selecting sites for residential uses, developers should always seek out sites with positive synergy with surrounding uses and avoid those where uses are likely to be incompatible.

Conflicting Uses

When the predominant image of an area has been created by uses incompatible with residential development, the probability of establishing a successful new development is reduced. Primary among the uses that may pose problems for new residential development are railroad tracks, rundown commercial devel-

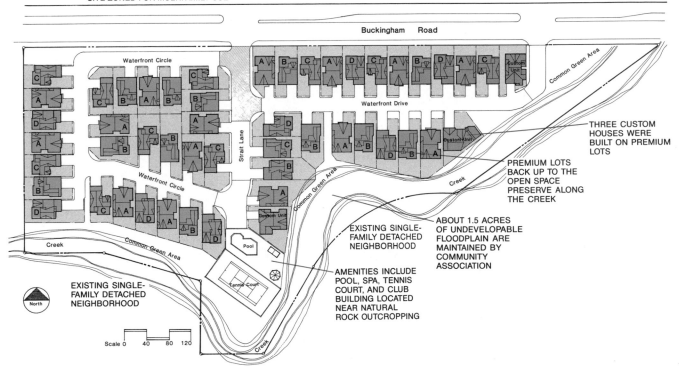

Buckingham Road

Waterfront Circle

Common Green Area

Waterfront Drive

Custom Unit

THREE CUSTOM HOUSES WERE BUILT ON PREMIUM LOTS

Strait Lane

Custom Unit

PREMIUM LOTS BACK UP TO THE OPEN SPACE PRESERVE ALONG THE CREEK

Waterfront Circle

Common Green Area

Creek

Custom Unit

EXISTING SINGLE-FAMILY DETACHED NEIGHBORHOOD

ABOUT 1.5 ACRES OF UNDEVELOPABLE FLOODPLAIN ARE MAINTAINED BY COMMUNITY ASSOCIATION

Creek

Common Green Area

Pool

AMENITIES INCLUDE POOL, SPA, TENNIS COURT, AND CLUB BUILDING LOCATED NEAR NATURAL ROCK OUTCROPPING

North

EXISTING SINGLE-FAMILY DETACHED NEIGHBORHOOD

Tennis Court

Creek

Scale 0   40   80   120

2-17 Surrounding residential development strongly influenced the product choice for Arbor Creek's 8.4-acre site in Garland, Texas. To the south was a single-family subdivision, whose residents had organized previously to block a proposed townhouse development; the property across Buckingham Road to the north was zoned for multifamily housing. The design strategy that emerged for Arbor Creek provides for the necessary density with a zero-lot-line development of detached houses, thus satisfying the developer's financial requirements and the concerns of the neighboring community.

opment, noxious industrial uses, shoddy, poorly subdivided residential development, and airports, heavily traveled highways, or other uses that generate noise.

In considering the issue of compatibility, developers should be aware of the potential liabilities that could be incurred as a result of building houses too close to conflicting uses. Proximity to large storage tanks of gas, oil, and other flammable materials should be avoided. Similarly, fire protection must be considered in heavily wooded or fire-prone areas and flood damage in flood-prone areas. Generally, protecting the public from such hazards is the responsibility of the municipality through its police powers (zoning), but developers also need to protect themselves against possible liabilities by studying the potential conflicting uses near a given site.

Freedom from the adverse effects of through traffic is important, as heavily trafficked streets exert an adverse influence; whenever possible, neighborhoods split by existing or potential major thorough-

fares should be avoided. If it is impossible to plan around a proposed highway, developers should work with the local planning and highway departments to have proposed road alignments relocated along the periphery of neighborhoods. Any additional land developers might be required to dedicate to the highway department can pay big dividends in terms of increased marketability for the project. To avoid interference with sleep and outdoor living, noise attenuation measures (walls, berms, building setbacks, increased insulation) might be required on lots abutting heavily traveled thoroughfares.

Airports present a special case as a result of the rapid expansion of air transport facilities in recent years. The possible adverse effects on a residential neighborhood caused by noise make it imperative for developers to investigate fully a site near an airport. Because airports generate business and have become employment centers, residential development around airports has been spurred despite the nuisance; however, if residential development is under

43

consideration for a site near an airport, noise attenuation measures must be factored into the project's design.

A common practice has been to place higher-density residential areas closest to commercial and industrial districts so the residential areas can benefit from proximity to the higher-capacity street system and the more extensive commercial and employment areas required for heavier population densities. In turn, cluster and attached housing is often located as a buffer between multifamily and lower-density, higher-priced, single-family development. In recent years, however, these planning practices have come into question. Local governments increasingly are willing to view development proposals in terms of integrating rather than separating different uses, a point partly illustrated by the increasing flexibility of land use controls through the widespread acceptance of PUDs and other concepts of mixed land uses. These devices to control land uses permit the mixed development of uses previously separated into exclusive districts, provided that they are properly designed. The result is often increased livability, efficiency, and attractiveness. The municipality's comprehensive plan and zoning regulations provide an excellent perspective of the public's position on appropriate uses for any property under consideration.

A wide gradation exists between potentially incompatible uses. While some can be accommodated with a minimum of difficulty, others (such as heavy industry) are virtually impossible to mitigate. In general, compatibility can be measured by the degree to which adjacent uses generate traffic, noise, pollution, and visual disharmony that would detract from residential environments.

Site Configuration

The optimum size of a development site depends on the type of development to be undertaken and the size of the market. In rapidly growing areas where large tracts of land still exist under few ownerships, developments can exceed 1,000 acres. Typically, such large-scale developments tie up the land with long-term options, and individual projects are constructed in phases. In some cases, forecast demand may warrant acquiring all the land at the outset. More typically, residential development sites tend to be much smaller, ranging from divisions of property along local roads to subdivisions of a few hundred lots.

The physical configuration and dimensions of a site influence the type of product, the layout of houses, and supporting uses. Options for design increase rapidly as a site increases in size. The larger the site, the greater the amount of unusable land that might be incorporated into the development. For small parcels under 10 acres, alternative designs tend to be somewhat limited, although this statement is less true when developers build townhouses, patio houses, zero-lot-line houses, and other cluster designs than it is for traditional single-family housing. When selecting sites for smaller projects, developers should avoid those with a high percentage of unusable land and carefully consider the tract's dwelling unit yield before purchasing acreage.

Because of taxes and carrying costs, it is not practical to carry too much acreage at any one time; many developers have gone broke trying to do just that. Whenever feasible, developers should make future expansion possible through long-term options on adjoining areas.

Sites come in a variety of shapes, although certain trends can be noted. In the Midwest, West, and much of the South, where land was developed on a grid pattern with roads usually at one-mile intervals, development sites frequently are square or rectangular. In eastern states, which were laid out by metes and bounds, a square or rectangular rural parcel is rare. Regardless of dimension and despite unusual shapes, however, a site's potential can be maximized by good site planning.

Skillful land planners can quickly prepare conceptual land plans showing alternative layouts for the desired product, which has emerged as a result of careful market analysis, on various proposed sites. Today's successful developers always take a market-based approach to land planning and selection of products. Potential environmental and regulatory constraints also play a major role in land planning. Zoning, land use designations, and other environmental considerations often determine the maximum densities of a project; however, this maximum density may not be realistically attainable. Only after deducting acreage for such items as streets, parks, school sites, and unbuildable areas can a planner determine a site's true dwelling unit yield.

"Outparcels"—parcels of land within a site that a developer is unable to acquire for one reason or another—can create an especially frustrating and complicated problem in site configuration. If these areas are large enough or badly located, they can compromise the integrity of the entire project. In such cases it might be necessary to modify the development plan or drop the project completely.

Another concern is whether outparcels will be developed to a standard or use incompatible with what the developer plans. When the outparcel is small, it might be no more than a small problem if

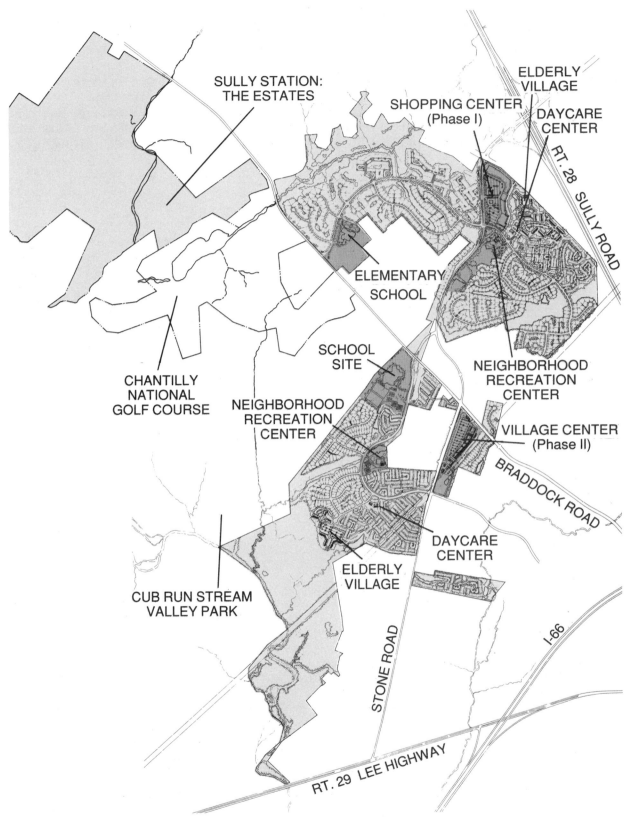

SULLY STATION:
THE ESTATES

SHOPPING CENTER
(Phase I)

ELDERLY
VILLAGE

DAYCARE
CENTER

RT. 28 SULLY ROAD

ELEMENTARY
SCHOOL

CHANTILLY
NATIONAL
GOLF COURSE

SCHOOL
SITE

NEIGHBORHOOD
RECREATION
CENTER

NEIGHBORHOOD
RECREATION
CENTER

VILLAGE CENTER
(Phase II)

BRADDOCK ROAD

DAYCARE
CENTER

ELDERLY
VILLAGE

CUB RUN STREAM
VALLEY PARK

STONE ROAD

I-66

RT. 29 LEE HIGHWAY

2-18 Sully Station—a 1,200-acre PUD in Centreville, Virginia—is indicative of the complex site configurations found in many eastern states. Because of existing development patterns and ownership of parcels by multiple owners, the site's boundaries are irregular and sometimes discontinuous. Maintaining a sense of community and cohesive design is an increased challenge when outparcels and development islands exist.

In recent years, land planning has become increasingly more sophisticated with the evolution of new computer applications. While computers have been used in financial analysis and construction management for some time, new applications have become

available that can improve the traditional methods of site analysis and land planning.

The initial phase of establishing a computerized data base may take as much time as traditional methods of land planning. When the data base is in

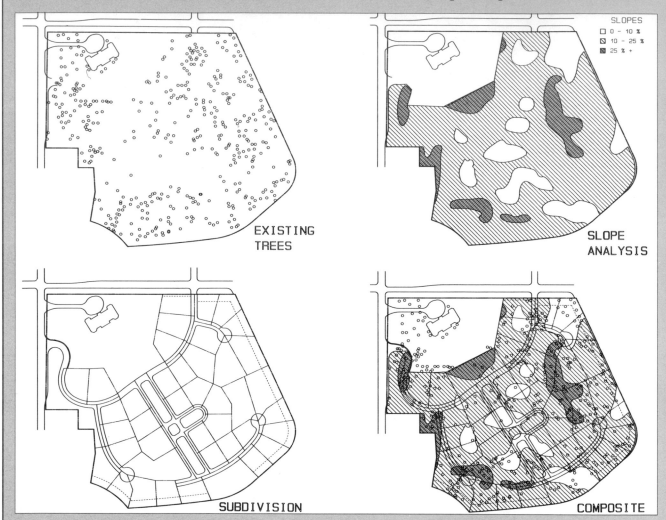

2-20 Site analysis and subdivision data can be stored in separate layers, which can then be combined into a single drawing that allows viewers to envisage a site more clearly.

municipal regulations are sufficiently strong to ensure compliance with the larger development or if the property owner is willing to coordinate the development of his property with that of the developer. Council member David K. Sunderland offers this advice on outparcels: "If you think you need it, you should be willing to bite the bullet and pay whenever economically feasible. It's always worth more to you than you think it is."

Physical Characteristics

Probably no other factors influence the actual selection of a site for development as much as a site's physical characteristics. In fact, residential land values are largely a function of a parcel's suitability for development in terms of slope, soil, geology, hydrology, and other physical limitations to development. Understanding a site and its environs requires some

place, however, alternatives can be studied much more rapidly and effectively than traditional methods allow. Alternative street alignments, building locations, and grading concepts can be developed in a matter of minutes on the computer, where hours or days would be required for drafting and calculations by traditional methods. This flexibility in adjusting design is a tremendous advantage over traditional methods.

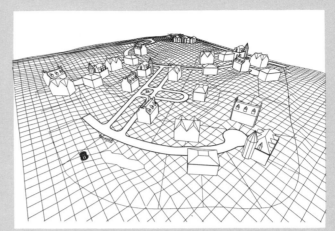

2-22 One of the computer's best uses is to produce multiple perspective views of a project.

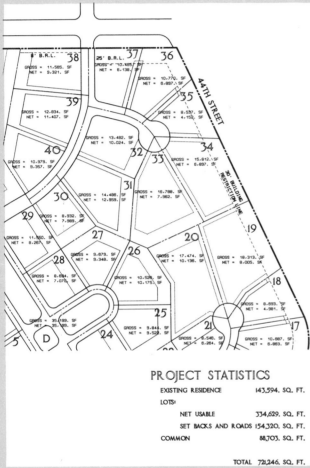

PROJECT STATISTICS

EXISTING RESIDENCE   143,594. SQ. FT.

LOTS:

    NET USABLE   334,629. SQ. FT.

    SET BACKS AND ROADS 154,320. SQ. FT.

    COMMON   88,703. SQ. FT.

                  TOTAL 721,246. SQ. FT.

2-21 The computer automatically recalculates development statistics as alternatives are tested.

Another advantage in the use of computers in land planning is the ability to overlay layers of environmental data, creating a matrix or model for identifying a site's potential for and constraints on development. A final advantage is in communication. Traditional land plans are typically presented as two-dimensional site plans, two or three perspective views (at most), and occasionally a scale model. The computer, on the other hand, offers an unlimited number of perspectives, virtually at the touch of a button.

Occasionally, savings of time resulting from computer applications have proven more illusory than real, but not for computer applications in land planning. Speed and accuracy have indeed been improved, and flexible designs are possible through public review and approval.

Source: Stephen P. Armington, "Computer Applications to Land Planning," *Urban Land*, September 1986, pp. 10–13.

time and effort on the developer's part. "Every site, natural or manmade, is to some degree unique, a web of things and activities."[12] This web must be understood because it imposes limitations and offers possibilities for a developer.

A number of analysts have attempted to formulate widely applicable techniques for investigation of the physical site. Ian McHarg suggests the following sequence of a topical analysis in his now classic *Design*

with Nature: climate, geology, physiology, hydrology, soil, vegetation, wildlife, and land use,[13] reasoning that each category of data follows logically from the preceding one, suggesting causality. With this se-

[12] Kevin Lynch, *Site Planning,* 2d ed. (Cambridge, Mass.: MIT Press, 1971), p. 5.

[13] Ian McHarg, *Design with Nature* (New York: Doubleday/ Natural History Press, 1969), p. 105.

quential procedure, McHarg believes that analysts can point out the inherent degree of tolerance a particular site has for development. The elements are all affected by one another and in turn are affected by man's activities. The procedure of evaluating a site's suitability by this technique has been made simpler and more accurate by the use of computers, which can code environmental data, overlay them in a matrix, and mathematically evaluate suitability based on the environmental data input.

Climate

Although easily overlooked as a factor in site analysis, climate nevertheless has a marked effect on the physical nature of the site. Climate determines to a great degree the type of soil and vegetation in a given area and the slope and nature of its terrain. In arid climates, for example, landforms tend to be more rugged, with less significant soil development over the rock base. Thus, if developers understand the specific factors of climate and what they mean, they will have a better idea of what to expect as analysis proceeds.

Each site has a general climate, which it shares with the surrounding region, and a number of microclimates, which may be peculiar to a very small area. General climate is determined by such factors as temperature, humidity, precipitation, wind direction and force, sun angle, number of days per year of sunlight, and frequency of major storms. Information on general climatic factors can be obtained through the EPA, the U.S. Weather Bureau, or the meteorological department of a local university.

Within a generalized climate exist a number of microclimatic variations caused by differences in ground cover and topography. "The form of the topography, the surface materials, the plant cover, the location of structures, the presence or absence of water all have a striking impact on the microclimate, on the quality of light, and on the propagation of noise."[14] Developers can discover these variations in a number of ways: by direct observation, by conversations with local people, by the way existing structures have weathered, and by the type and condition of existing plants. Natural vegetation is an especially good indicator, for it is a clue not only to the general climate but also to the soil and water conditions and to a locality's entire history.

A site best suited for residential development is one with good microclimatic characteristics: sun exposure and natural shielding from fog or wind. An understanding of the climatic conditions endemic to a site helps developers to understand the site's suit-

ability for development and allows planners to site houses for maximum benefit to future residents.

Geology

From a geologic standpoint, the earth is still young, but man can accelerate the aging process through his mistakes. In recent years, tremendous progress has incorporated scientific knowledge about geologic processes into development policy and environmental regulation. Even with this progress, however, planners, developers, and builders are still largely uninformed about geologic processes. Underlying bedrock is less frequently studied than soil, yet these rock strata are important as a source of raw materials, reservoirs for water, possible sites for waste disposal, and the support necessary to accommodate heavy structures.

The earth is a dynamic body, responding to factors and forces from within and without. Of importance to developers are those natural processes that act irrespective of man's activities as well as those that are set in motion, stopped, or altered as a result of man's intervention. While the settling of the earth's surface occurs naturally, for example, it can also be the result of man's removing rock or fluids from under the surface.

Movement of the land surface can be categorized under two headings: those caused by internal crustal movement (earthquakes) and those caused by surface mass movements (landslides). Perhaps the most well known of these phenomena are earthquakes, also known as tectonic movements. Earthquakes are caused by stresses that tend to disfigure the earth's crust and change its structure.

The earth is laced with faults or fracture zones, some of which have not shown any movement for thousands of years. Others, termed *active* faults, show evidence of more recent activity. If the land surface is believed to be very unstable, preservation of the land as open space or any other unoccupied use may be indicated. Checking with local, city, and county departments of building and safety and public works, and with the building inspector's or engineer's office will possibly turn up areas of active faulting. Also useful are the geology departments of local colleges and universities, state and geologic survey offices, or the U.S. Geological Survey (USGS).

A significant number of U.S. residents, especially on the West Coast, live in tectonically unstable regions, a fact that has caused planners and public

---

[14] Lynch, *Site Planning*, p. 17.

Energy conservation has become less prominent with the oil crises of the 1970s behind us. But ignoring opportunities to conserve energy is short-sighted. The long-term prognosis requires planners, designers, developers, and builders to provide energy-efficient subdivisions and houses.

The design of solar subdivisions, according to recent studies done for the Bonneville Power Administration (the regional power agency for Oregon, Washington, and Idaho), can save 10 to 20 percent per house of the costs for heating and air conditioning, compared to those for conventional subdivisions. Solar design, moreover, is achievable at little or no increase in cost to developers and with minimal change in a development's "character"—the conclusion reached after an exercise to redesign a number of existing subdivision plats in the Pacific Northwest to achieve the maximum number of solar lots (lots on which 90 percent of the winter solar radiation is available) while retaining the subdivision's other amenities and avoiding additional costs.

Conservation Management Services redesigned the plats. In each one, the developer established the basic characteristics of the site and parameters of design, while the city planning staff defined conditions and development issues. The parameters of design, which assured developers that redesign would not entail added development costs, generally included several goals:

- To maximize the number of solar-oriented lots;
- To maintain or increase the number of lots;
- To maintain or increase the average size of lots;
- To maintain or decrease the linear footage of roadways;
- To retain all access roads to and through the site;
- To maintain or enhance the character of the development;
- To maintain or reduce the slope of roadways and lots; and
- To maintain or decrease total costs for on-site infrastructure.

The primary change in design for each subdivision was the location and orientation of internal streets. Orienting streets within 30 degrees of

2-24 BEFORE AND AFTER SOLAR-ORIENTED REDESIGN

In eight existing subdivisions redesigned in accordance with solar design principles, the number of solar lots was significantly increased without reducing the total number of lots or the average lot size. In five of these subdivisions, the linear footage of roadway remained unchanged, while it was reduced by 300 feet in Sylvan Manor and by 215 feet in Centennial Park, and increased by 30 feet in Dawncrest.

SUBDIVISION	TOTAL NUMBER OF LOTS		NUMBER OF SOLAR LOTS		PERCENT OF SOLAR LOTS	
	BEFORE	AFTER	BEFORE	AFTER	BEFORE	AFTER
Waterhouse, Beaverton, Oregon	81	81	32	65	40%	80%
Dawncrest, Gresham, Oregon	112	112	32	92	29	82
Bridgeport, Portland, Oregon	39	39	29	31	74	80
Meadowlark Vista, Nampa, Idaho	149	149	54	122	36	82
Sylvan Manor, Caldwell, Idaho	100	101	39	83	39	82
Pierpoint #2, Boise, Idaho	36	36	11	26	30	72
Centennial Park, Tacoma, Washington	241	243	116	195	48	80
Lake Forest #2, Lacey, Washington	94	94	25	75	27	80

officials in California and in many other parts of the western United States to become increasingly concerned about the possible future effects of earthquakes and how to minimize damage from them. In 1971, California adopted an amendment to its state planning law that includes seismic safety as a mandatory element of any general plan along with other elements like land use, housing, and transportation. "A seismic element provides an analysis of the risk for any part of the planning area to enable the educated planner to make rapid preliminary evaluations of land use alternatives and the associated seismic

2-23 (continued)

east/west significantly increases the number of solar lots.

Does it cost more to integrate provisions for solar energy into the design of subdivisions? The Portland/Vancouver Metro Area Solar Access Project, a cooperative effort of 22 local governments and the private development community, estimates that it will cost an average of $20 per lot to implement these design standards for most subdivisions.

Source: Conservation Management Services, a division of The Benkendorf Associates, Portland, Oregon. Reprinted from *Urban Land,* August 1988, pp. 28–29.

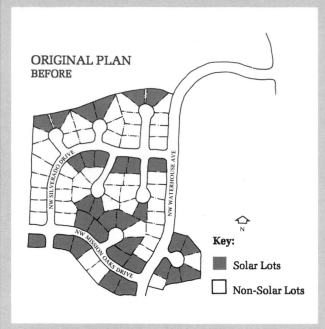 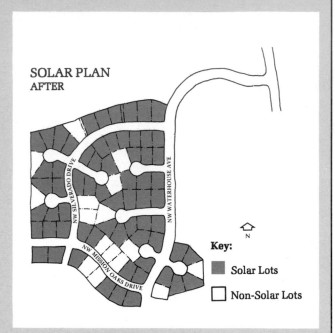

2-25 The Waterhouse site is on a north-facing slope with a grade variation from 2 to 14 percent. Clusters of mature upland vegetation lie at the center and along the north property line, across which lies designated open space. Besides adding solar lots, the solar plan reduces the size of lots along Mission Oaks Drive, increases the number of access points onto Waterhouse Avenue, and eliminates double-fronted lots. Costs for utility infrastructure rise by approximately $9 per lot.

2-26

ANALYSIS

	TOTAL LOTS	SOLAR-ORIENTED LOTS	PERCENT OF TOTAL	LINEAR FOOTAGE OF ROADWAY	AVERAGE LOT SIZE (SQUARE FEET)	SMALLEST LOT (SQUARE FEET)	LARGEST LOT (SQUARE FEET)
Original Plan	81	32	40%	4,400	9,500	6,400	12,000
Solar Plan	81	65	80%	4,400	9,500	6,000	13,200

hazards."[15] The risk analysis does not take the place of individual site investigation; it only provides a basis from which more rational and acceptable decisions can be made.

Another method used to protect against damage from earthquakes is a fault hazard easement, which requires a setback from active fault traces. The amount of setback varies with the type of faulting and

[15] William J. Petak, *Guidelines for Developing a Seismic Safety Element for the General Plan,* PAS Memo No. 12 (Chicago: American Society of Planning Officials, 1973), p. 1.

the degree of groundshaking and land deformation expected. Even more restrictive is the adoption of fault hazard zoning or broader geologic hazard zoning, which might include landslides and floodplains as well as faulting. This zoning—often called "overlay zoning"—overrides other local zoning ordinances, prohibits human occupation, and limits uses to those that would be compatible with the hazard.

Earthquakes cannot be prevented by any means we now know, nor have we yet developed techniques for accurately predicting quakes or their timing, severity, or location. Nevertheless, damage and loss of life resulting from earthquakes can be reduced by informed developers, planners, and engineers backed up by sound land ordinances, building codes, and site-specific geologic studies.

The other category of land surface movements, mass movements, do not occur deep underground but are movements of the earth's surface resulting from processes along the surface. Included in this category are landslides, rockfalls, mudflows, as well as gentle but persistent soil creep. All respond to gravity, and most are generally brought about by man's ignorance of natural forces at work.

Any mass movement of the earth's surface requires some topographic variation and a lack of friction between a moving mass and the stable plane beneath it. Geologists or soil scientists would be able to point out where these movements might occur—at weaknesses in the rock, such as joints or fractures (slip planes), or at unconsolidated or weakly consolidated surface soils.

Although not as sudden or dramatic as earthquakes and landslides, soil creep can also be highly destructive of property. Tilted telephone poles, fence posts, and road markings are general indicators of this phenomenon. Changes in volume in the earth's surface, such as wetting, drying, freezing, and thawing, all

2-27   SEISMIC RISK MAP OF THE UNITED STATES

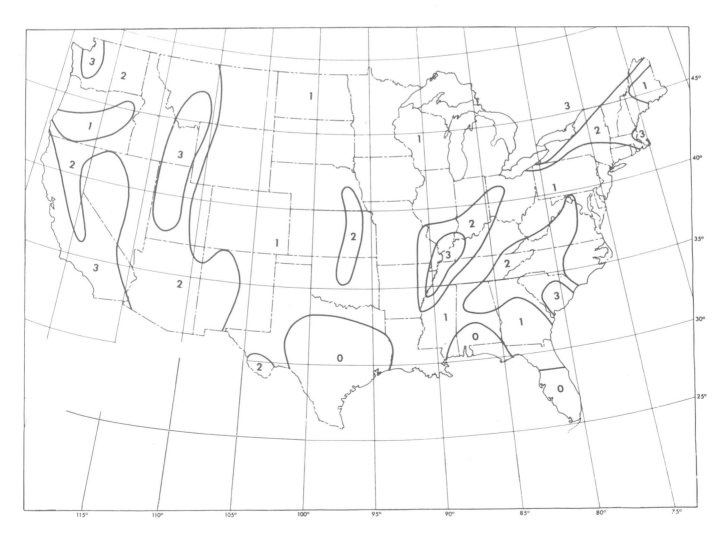

cause creep. Where soft unconsolidated sediments and water combine, however, conditions exist for a mudflow.

A collapse of the earth's surface generally occurs when subsurface material is withdrawn, either through natural or human forces. For example, if man has withdrawn large amounts of fluids from weakly consolidated soils, the soil can collapse. Moreover, it can collapse naturally where groundwater has dissolved or leached away subsurface elements.

A site exhibiting any of these geologic conditions can be rendered unsuitable for development or may require costly mitigation techniques to make it safe for residential use. Developers seeking sites for new housing projects must be assured through published materials and field tests that geologic hazards do not exist.

During the 1980s, a new geology-related hazard emerged as a major concern of both residential developers and homebuyers—radon. Radon is a naturally occurring colorless, odorless radioactive gas produced from the decay of underground uranium. Exposure to radon substantially increases the risk of lung cancer. Experts from EPA estimate that contamination by radon may be responsible for 20,000 deaths from lung cancer per year, although estimates range widely among researchers.[16]

While the natural decay of radon presents no health risks outdoors, where it dissipates to safe levels, it presents serious health risks in any environment where air is trapped. Radon can seep into houses through dirt floors, porous blocks, cracks in floors and foundation walls, floor drains, sumps, or joints.[17] The problem is compounded by poor ventilation.

Residential developers must be aware of the potential liability that exists for building houses that can ultimately become polluted with radon gas. Modified construction techniques can be implemented at little additional cost to the developer to reduce the potential for serious radon hazards and thus liability. (The accompanying feature box has additional information.)

Topography

Topography is a major determinant of a site plan because "topography influences the type and cost of development, controls the direction and rate of water runoff, adds variety to the landscape, influences the weather and climate, and affects the types of vegetation and wildlife."[18]

Topographic information can be obtained from many sources. The USGS provides general-purpose topographic maps at varying scales for all of the United States. Other federal agencies, including the Bureau of Mines, Bureau of Reclamation, Corps of Engineers, and Soil Conservation Service, have developed some system of land use inventory. Information can also be obtained from the state geology department, which might be known as the bureau or division of geology, natural resources, or conservation. This level of information is excellent for conceptual site studies, but it is often outdated or too general for detailed land plans.

To prepare adequate land plans and preliminary grading and drainage studies, up-to-date topography at an appropriate scale is necessary. With the new technology available through computers and aerial photogrammetry, computer-generated topographical maps can be obtained from the aerial photos quickly and cost effectively, at any standard scale. It is the recommended approach for developers, if recent, accurate topographical information cannot be obtained from other sources.

As a rule, moderately sloping sites are preferable to either steep or flat land. Costs of improvement rise sharply on slopes over 10 percent; without adequate engineering measures, heavy site grading creates problems with settlement, erosion, and slope stabilization. Although the initial cost per acre of raw, hillside land may be less, final costs of improved lots may be higher than if more expensive (and more level) land had been purchased. Because of high costs for grading and site improvements, hillside sites are often best suited to clustered, attached housing.

In many areas of the country where residential hillside developments are common, municipalities have enacted stringent regulations against hillside development. In some cities, this regulation is known as a slope-density ordinance. In concept, such ordinances establish a formula that reduces allowable density as slopes increase. Often development is prohibited or permitted only at very low densities on slopes with a grade over 25 percent. With this planning technique, allowable densities are based more directly on natural features than on traditional zoning methods. As a result of these ordinances, however, land that has traditionally been developable may prove off limits or uneconomical at the allowed density.

[16] "Indoor Radon Deaths Could Hit 13,000, Research Council Says in New Report," *Energy and Housing Report,* January 1988, p. 6.

[17] Mary Rose Kornreich, "The Invisible Trap of Radon Liability," *The Practical Real Estate Lawyer,* September 1987, p. 18.

[18] Michael Meshenberg, *Environmental Planning,* PAS Report No. 263 (Chicago: American Society of Planning Officials, 1970), p. 12.

Increasing public awareness of radon is indicated by a 1988 survey taken by the National Association of Home Builders (NAHB). One in three builders responding indicated that buyers ask about radon levels when buying a new house. Three in 10 builders indicated that they were taking steps to reduce levels of radon in houses under construction.

Unsafe levels of radon have been discovered in large numbers of houses, spurring concern among builders, government officials, and the general public. EPA has indicated that the only established safe level for radon in a house is zero,[1] although the recommended level for houses is below four picocuries per liter.[2] EPA surveyed 17 states in 1987, checking over 22,000 houses for radon.[3] The results indicate radon levels over four picocuries in one out of three, or 8 million to 10 million houses. The EPA tests have stimulated controversy over their accuracy, because short-term tests were used in areas where radon levels are highest, such as basements, which means that tests were designed to get the highest possible readings.[4] In recognition of the potential seriousness of contamination by radon, however, Congress and private industry have responded with national and state research and legislation.

It is difficult to get accurate readings on levels of radon, because they vary significantly from room to room and season to season, and according to how many windows are open or whether the building is air conditioned. To promote accurate measurement, EPA has devised a "radon measurement proficiency program" for companies. While this program falls short of certifying a company to measure levels of radon, it does permit companies to run a sample test, submit it, and be listed as a company that uses appropriate techniques to achieve accurate measurements.

Many states are developing their own certification programs, with Pennsylvania and New Jersey the first. Some states are also working to certify testing equipment.[5] Because liability could also arise from erroneous measurements resulting from unreliable testing techniques, developers should check to see whether companies are on the EPA list before they retain them to measure radon levels in new houses. The cost of measurement is minimal.

While the risk of cancer through exposure to high levels of radon is great, the cost to correct the problem is minimal. To modify an *existing* house contaminated by radon in the worst case would cost approximately $1,500, according to Bill Ethier, counsel with the National Association of Home Builders. To fit a *new* house with the basic equipment to reduce radon, meaning that it could later be upgraded if a problem with radon arises, would cost substantially less (generally between $100 and $500). ULI council member Sarah Peck notes that her residential development company is "equipping all new houses with devices that will allow for the easy removal of radon if problems are detected once construction is complete and the units sealed. The cost is only about $135 per house, and we are able to take advantage of this feature in our marketing program." After considering the risk of health problems and the risk of lawsuits for developers and those who sell houses with unsafe levels of radon, many developers are finding that the additional expense is a small price to pay.

EPA publishes reports for residential developers describing methods of abating levels of radon. Recommended methods include natural and forced-air ventilation, heat-recovery ventilation, sealing walls and floors through a variety of methods, sealing points where radon might enter, drain-tile soil ventilation, ventilating the subslab, block-wall ventilation, and preventing depressurization of the house. Subslab ventilation techniques can reduce radon levels by 90 to 95 percent, according to Mark Nowack of the NAHB Research Center.

For new construction, NAHB recommends putting a base course of aggregate under the slab, providing an interior drain tile loop in the slab, or providing a short section of pipe running from the stone underslab that is either capped in the basement or run through the side of the house to the attic, creating a circuit in the attic to install a fan later if needed.[6] (See Appendix E for more detail.)

Thus far, no court decisions have assigned a developer liability for the death from cancer of someone residing in a radon-contaminated house.[7] Given recent legal trends, however, the possibility increases that buyers will be able to sue developers for radon-related damages on legal theories of negligence (because a developer failed to take reasonable precautions in site selection and construction) and breach of implied warranty of habitability (as contamination from radon affects the habitability of

▶

a house). Developers could also be sued for misrepresentation or fraud if they are aware of unsafe radon levels and fail to inform a buyer.[8]

More and more purchase agreements for new and used houses contain warranties and representations by the seller regarding the levels of radon in a house. Contracts can require testing for radon or allocate the costs of remediation, if it becomes necessary. A cap can also be placed on how much the seller will be required to spend on remediation, if unsafe levels are discovered in initial tests.[9]

A growing number of real estate agents want a radon clause in sales contracts. In New Jersey, clauses in all standard contracts either provide contingencies for testing or provisions for escrow. EPA and NAHB plan a publication on radon and real estate transactions to guide homebuyers and sellers.

To avoid liability, residential developers should consider installing a roughed-in ventilation system that can be activated later if necessary by installing a fan. Doing so can be viewed as inexpensive insurance. Further, developers should put a provision in contracts warning consumers of risks associated with exposure to radon. Developers should also avoid any express warranties that would cover radon and should disclaim any warranties, express or implied, that are not specifically enumerated in a contract, which should be done in combination with adequate notice to the buyer of risks from radon. If developers also use reasonable techniques to prevent the entry of radon during construction of new houses, it should go a long way in reducing liability.[10]

In the Indoor Radon Abatement Act of 1988, Congress mandated EPA to create a model code by 1990 on abatement of radon and applicable standards, to provide technical assistance and guidance, and to establish regional radon training centers. A draft code was released for review in 1989.

EPA has a Radon Division in Washington, D.C., with a mandate to research and disseminate information on radon contamination and its abatement. It is a resource for those interested in radon abatement. As mentioned, some states have adopted their own radon programs and have passed legislation addressing radon standards, monitoring, or testing certification. EPA's regional offices can provide information on federal radon abatement laws and can provide referrals to appropriate state radon offices.

For additional information:

U.S. Environmental Protection Agency
Radon Division
Office of Radiation Programs
Washington, D.C. 20460
202-475-9605

EPA has published a number of reports, generally available at no cost:

"A Citizen's Guide to Radon" (OPA-86-004)
"Radon Reduction in New Construction" (OPA-87-009)
"Radon Reduction Methods: A Homeowner's Guide" (OPA-87-010)
"Radon Reduction Techniques for Detached Houses: Technical Guidance" (EPA/625/5-86-019)
"Removal of Radon from Household Water" (OPA-87-011)
"Summary of State Radon Programs" (EPA/520/1-87-19-1)

---

[1]Environmental Protection Agency, Office of Research and Development, "Radon Reduction Techniques for Detached Houses," June 1986, p. 2.

[2]A curie is a measure of radioactivity; a picocurie is one-trillionth of a curie.

[3]Environmental Protection Agency, "States of Emergency," Insurance Review, December 1987, p. 36. The states tested were Alabama, Arizona, Colorado, Connecticut, Indiana, Kansas, Kentucky, Massachusetts, Michigan, Minnesota, Missouri, North Dakota, Pennsylvania, Rhode Island, Tennessee, Wisconsin, and Wyoming.

[4]Telephone interview with Mark Nowack, NAHB Research Center, July 1989.

[5]"What to Do about Radon," U.S. News and World Report, September 26, 1988, p. 63.

[6]Telephone interview with Mark Nowack, NAHB Research Center, July 1989.

[7]Telephone interview with Bill Ethier, litigation counsel, NAHB, July 1989.

[8]Mary Rose Kornreich, "The Invisible Trap of Radon Liability," The Practical Real Estate Lawyer, September 1987, pp. 24–25.

[9]Kornreich, p. 23.

[10]Memorandum to Members and Executive Officers from William H. Ethier, litigation counsel, NAHB, August 8, 1988.

For higher-priced properties being developed at low densities, hillside sites can work very well. But for more conventional projects where the costs of improving lots are trying to be held to a minimum, gently rolling, well-drained land is most desirable. Very flat sites present problems of sewer and storm drainage that can raise costs of improvement. Flat sites must be sculptured into contours and elevations that create variety in the siting of the houses as well as a functioning infrastructure system.

Hydrology

Water is one of the most important variables in the selection of a site. It can be classified as surface water, which flows exposed in lakes or streams, or subsurface water, which occupies cracks and rifts in the soil, bedrock, or overburden (material lying over a useful geologic deposit). Subsurface water trapped within the soil is generally termed soil water, while that flowing within bedrock openings is termed groundwater. Both surface and subsurface water can significantly affect a development's feasibility.

Surface Water. Surface water can be both a resource and a nuisance. People enjoy living where they have an extended view of water and willingly pay a premium for the privilege of direct access to it. Residents near a body of water have the added advantage of being close to facilities for outdoor recreation—boating, fishing, swimming, water skiing. Because water is so much in demand for recreation, it adds value to surrounding land. But design, engineering, planning, land acquisition, and financing costs, among other aspects of development, are often complicated by working with water.[19]

Surface water can also be a good indicator of what is wrong with a site. If surface water is marshy and swampy, then the water table probably lies on the surface and contamination of the groundwater is possible if precautions are not taken. Pools of water left standing after a hard rain indicate poor soil conditions, hence structural and drainage problems. Such problems are often caused by a high clay content in

2-30 The Harford County, Maryland, zoning ordinance allows developers to increase residential density to the next highest zoning classification if more than 30 percent of a site is designated as a wetland. After an initial proposal to build 430 single-family houses was denied, the developer of The Villages at Thomas Run was given approval to build 530 townhouses. By clustering the townhouses, the developer was able to preserve nearly half the site, including over 20 acres of wetlands. *For additional information, see* David Salvesen, *Wetlands: Mitigating and Regulating Development Impacts* (Washington, D.C.: ULI–the Urban Land Institute, 1990), pp. 72–73.

2-29 Natural water features like this creek can appear to be a valuable site amenity but, if subject to periodic flooding, can constrain development by necessitating development setbacks or costly flood control improvements.

the soil, which is then subject to shrinking and swelling, which in turn causes problems with foundations.

Inland and coastal wetlands play a strong role in water management by storing water during periods of high flow and releasing it during periods of low flow. In addition, wetlands are vital for producing certain crops, as a haven for wildlife, and as a spawning ground for fish and shellfish. Because of these important functions, development of wetlands is being sharply curtailed.

Filling and/or dredging wetlands to accommodate development is becoming an increasingly difficult, if not impossible, process. The U.S. Army Corps of Engineers (the Corps) and the EPA jointly administer

---

[19] See Joachim Tourbier and Richard Westmacott, *Lakes and Ponds,* Technical Bulletin No. 72 (Washington, D.C.: ULI–the Urban Land Institute, 1976).

a permitting process that falls under Section 404 of the Clean Water Act of 1977 as amended. The program has been broadly defined to include virtually all surface waters and wetlands adjacent to those waters in the United States. In the guidelines developed by the EPA, the key criterion for determining whether a discharge will violate the objectives of the act is whether the potential discharge will have an "unacceptable adverse impact" on the environment. If a discharge will have such an impact, the permit will be denied. Although this test is subjective and leaves developers applying for a permit several options, the process of issuing a permit is at best stringent and time consuming and at worst can stop a project. *Project sites containing or near wetlands must be examined very carefully when evaluating the suitability of the potential site.*[20]

Subsurface Water. For residential development, a site should have good natural surface drainage. Clay loam, sand, gravel, or other porous material contributes to good soil drainage and economical construction. A sandy soil can absorb a hard rain and not lose significant capacity for infiltration. A clayish soil repels much of the rain into overland flow after saturation, leading to erosion and flooding. On potentially problematic sites, developers should make test borings in various parts of the property to identify soil-related drainage problems and areas where building might not be possible.

Water drawn down by gravity through the soil to rock strata below is commonly known as groundwater. This underground water flows horizontally though water-bearing (porous) rock, or aquifer. The movement is rather slow. Its depth below the surface can vary markedly, and it can fluctuate seasonally or over longer periods.

Supplies of pure groundwater are replenished at recharge areas where the aquifer comes close to the surface of the land. Protection of these areas is vital for keeping the quality of the groundwater intact. An aquifer recharge area is particularly vulnerable to damage from development because its capacity for absorption is reduced by covering the ground with buildings, roads, parking lots, and other forms of impermeable materials. Aquifers can become polluted from sewer lines (which commonly leak) and septic tanks, which can place contaminants directly into the groundwater supply. A polluted watercourse may also contaminate the aquifer; increased sediments and urban pollutants (oil, grease, heavy metals, pesticides, fertilizers) are contained in storm runoff and are carried to surface watercourses, where they can work their way into groundwater supplies or other sensitive water resources. Thus, if development

is permitted near or on an aquifer recharge area, adequate controls must be exercised, including restrictions on the use of septic tanks, protection against the discharge of untreated waste into the aquifer, and mitigation techniques to control urban contaminants in storm runoff.

Flood Control. Nature creates floodplains to accommodate the overflow of rivers and streams after a heavy rainfall or snowfall. In the desire to locate cities on waterways, man has undertaken large-scale public works projects, such as levees, reservoirs, and channels to curb the effects of natural flooding. Nevertheless, flood damage to urban areas continues to be a major problem.

Federal and state policy on flood control has gradually shifted from an emphasis on structural controls alone to a balance between structural and regulatory controls. Regulatory controls like floodplain zoning codes, building and sanitary codes, and open space programs prohibit certain types of structures from those areas most susceptible to inundation.

The Federal Insurance Administration (FIA) within the Federal Emergency Management Agency (FEMA) has mapped and delineated floodplains and their potential flood elevations for many communities nationwide. Cities and counties are using the flood insurance rate maps that resulted from this effort to guide future land use practices. To develop a national standard, FIA selected the "100-year flood" as the basis for managing floodplains. A 100-year flood is defined as the maximum probable flood that would occur within 100 years. Although the maps are a very good source of information, they might not delineate all potential flood hazard areas, particularly in the southwestern United States, where flash floods and intermittent streams are common. Because flood hazard areas are not always obvious even to the trained eye, developers should carefully research flood hazards and drainage patterns before committing themselves to a site. Additional information on the potential for flooding can often be obtained from the local flood control district, the municipal public works or engineer's office, or a consulting civil engineer.

If the site is large enough and is not entirely within a flood hazard area, recreational amenities and common open space can be provided within the flood hazard areas and a residential project incorporated in

---

[20] See also David Salvesen, *Wetlands: Mitigating and Regulating Development Impacts* (Washington, D.C.: ULI–the Urban Land Institute, 1990). Development issues regarding wetlands are discussed later in this chapter.

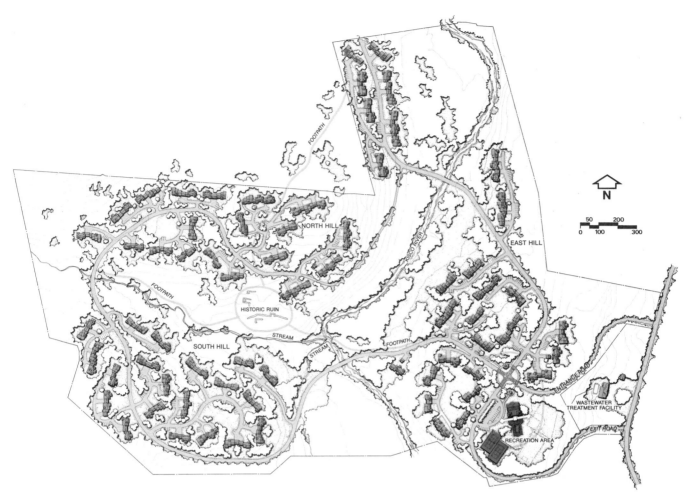

2-31 The 122-acre site for Riverwoods in Westchester County, New York, was skipped over during the first wave of suburban development because of constraints associated with rock outcroppings, historical sites, wetlands, and periodic flooding from the Kisco River and its tributary streams. Now, the site accommodates 148 luxury condominiums that are grouped in clusters located on knolls above the floodplain.

the design above the flood hazard elevation. Many communities, for example, include golf courses or similar open spaces located in the potential flood hazard areas.

Soil

An understanding of the principles of soil science is indispensable to developers. Soil acts as an engineering variable not only in construction but also in waste disposal systems and maintenance of the water supply. An analysis of the soil's properties follows logically from a study of the site's climate and geology, because more than any other factor, climate acts on the underlying rock to form soil. Other agents that form soil are biological activity (from trees, shrubs, and bacteria), time, and the configuration of the land surface.

A good soil for residential development is more than five feet deep, moderately pervious to water, free from the hazards of periodic flooding or a high water table, and level to gently sloping. Soil maps and information on properties of soil are readily available from the local office of the U.S. Soil Conservation Service. The local planning department often maintains maps of local soils.

Especially problematic for residential development are soils containing a high amount of clay. When clays get wet, they swell; when they dry and give up their water, they shrink. As a result, foundations that do not penetrate the zone where these volume changes occur are subject to stress, strain, and eventual cracking. In northern regions, this change in volume usually occurs during the periodic winter freezing of the ground surface. Roadways, sidewalks, and foundations constructed on unconsolidated or

2-32 The potential for soil erosion and sedimentation is intensified during construction. Temporary erosion control measures must be implemented during construction to prevent problems such as this one.

water-saturated sediments also tend to heave during freezing and settle after thawing.

Other soil conditions can affect a site's feasibility for development:

- Soils on hillsides tend to be shallow as a result of movement downward, either through gravity or water erosion. Removing vegetation through grading or other means exacerbates the problem of erosion.
- Water generally accumulates in low, depressed areas, and soils there are usually wet and spongy for long periods of time and therefore difficult to develop. Further, the density of these soils makes them largely impervious.
- Soil that has been forming as a result of upland water erosion and downstream deposits at the mouth of a waterway is alluvial. Without an adequate water disposal system, these areas are subject to periodic flash flooding after a heavy rainfall.
- Shallow soil over rock is easy to spot by checking where roads have been built and looking for

outcroppings. Costs of excavation for shallow soil over rock are 10 to 20 times greater than for deep soil and often involve blasting the rock before grading. Vegetation grows poorly on such soil because little room is available for roots and to store water and plant nutrients.

As a rule, deep, well-drained soils found on tops of ridges, gently sloping hillsides, and valley floors are the best for development. Surface and subsurface water management, problems with load bearing, and costs of site improvement can be held to a minimum.

Vegetation

Existing vegetation on any site is desirable. It is possible to build economically on wooded land by selective clearing, but too many times handsomely wooded acreage has been deliberately bulldozed before construction. Efforts should be made to preserve tree stands despite the temporary disadvantages of having to take some care with locations of trenches, workers' traffic between buildings, and storage of materials during construction. Mature trees provide a natural setting for any residential community and lend a new community an "established" air. The cost of locating and marking trees on a topographical map is minor,

2-33 The Woodlands in Darien, Illinois, is a 40-acre PUD based on a twofold theme—combining rustic architecture and materials with preservation of the site, an abandoned Christmas tree farm. The dense conifer forest located between clusters of houses gives the project a distinctive image and provides a marketing edge.

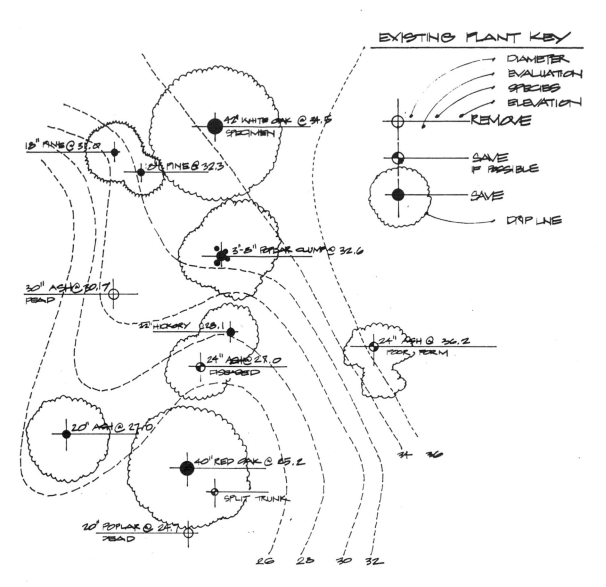

EXISTING PLANT KEY

DIAMETER
EVALUATION
SPECIES
ELEVATION
REMOVE

SAVE
IF POSSIBLE

SAVE

DRIP LINE

42" WHITE OAK @ 34.5
SPECIMEN

18" PINE @ 35.0

10" PINE @ 32.3

3"-8" POPLAR CLUMP @ 32.6

30" ASH @ 30.17
DEAD

22" HICKORY @ 28.1

24" ASH @ 28.0
DISEASED

24" ASH @ 36.2
POOR FORM

34   36

20" ASH @ 27.0

40" RED OAK @ 25.2

SPLIT TRUNK

20" POPLAR @ 24.7
DEAD

26   28   30   32

2-34 During the feasibility analysis, an accurate inventory and evaluation locating all trees and masses of vegetation by size, species, and quality should be completed. The inventory requires a thorough physical examination of the site so that selected trees can be preserved. *Source:* Robert Engstrom and Marc Putman, *Planning and Design of Townhouses and Condominiums* (Washington, D.C.: ULI– the Urban Land Institute, 1979).

and large, healthy trees can often be saved for little more than the cost of a small sapling.

Only in recent years has an actual monetary value begun to be placed on trees. A poll conducted for the Weyerhaeuser Corporation found that homebuyers estimate that trees contribute between 7 and 27 percent to the appraised value of residential property. According to a formula devised by the International Society of Aboriculture, a tree's worth is calculated to be $27 per square inch, based on its diameter at 4.5 feet above the ground. Thus, a red oak tree 25 inches in diameter would be worth about $12,000.[21] Assigning monetary value to existing trees has arisen, in part, as a result of homebuyers' suing developers for the death of a tree after a house was purchased but as a direct result of construction activity. Although a tree's worth is largely subjective, it is important to

[21] "Saving Trees Is Good Business," *Builder,* May 1989, p. 134.

note that homebuyers do place considerable value on existing trees and that developers can sometimes capitalize on that value through premiums for lots.

Some cities and counties have enacted programs to protect particular threatened or endangered species of trees. Such programs usually require a report by a biological expert that identifies size, type, and general health and conditions of the species. If some trees are permitted to be removed to accommodate a project, developers may be required to replace them (either on or off site) at a ratio of at least 2:1 or 3:1, depending on the species.

Although trees may be the most visible form of vegetation, they may not be the only form of vegetation related to a development's feasibility. During the 1970s and 1980s, many types of flora (grasslands, wildflowers, and so on) were added to federal and state lists of "endangered" or "threatened" species. The presence of one of these species on site generally requires a detailed biological survey and the preparation of a mitigation plan that could affect the density or design of a proposed residential project. Developers can often ascertain the likelihood of an endangered species's being located on a particular site by talking with the local planning department, botanical society, or college or university. The cost of this initial research is minor and will pay for itself may times over if it keeps the developer from having to implement a costly habitat preservation or mitigation plan.

Wildlife

Development sensitive to a site's natural condition also takes into account native fauna. Too often, developments are humanized to the point that mature native vegetation and groundcover—the habitat and food supply of small wildlife—are replaced with lawns and shrubs. The preservation of existing fauna, like vegetation, can do much to enhance a site's attractiveness and value.

Environmental awareness, water shortages, and the rising costs of maintenance have all led to a reevaluation of the advantages of retaining the natural landscape. These factors reinforce the importance of retaining natural flora, thereby protecting the habitats of native fauna. Merely providing open space will not attract or sustain wildlife; it can be accomplished by providing a diversity of open space habitats—grasslands, woodlands, or watercourses—where wildlife can live.

Like other environmental considerations, protection of endangered species of fauna has become an important issue affecting residential development.

2-35 An ongoing controversy in Riverside County, California, over the habitat of a little-known night creature—the Stevens Kangaroo Rat—could, if ever settled, set a precedent in negotiating disputes between environmental and growth interests. Should a compromise be reached that meets the needs both of the environment and of the landowners/developers, the tone might be set for handling such issues in the future.

Sites serving as habitats for endangered or threatened species (pursuant to the Endangered Species Act of 1973) are likely to face strong opposition to development and arduous project review and approval. If a project is permitted to proceed at all, it will likely be conditioned with costly mitigation measures.

According to the U.S. Fish and Wildlife Service, over 1,000 species of animals are nearing extinction—and about half of those species are native to the United States.[22] Destruction of habitat is a major cause of the problem. The Fish and Wildlife Service—supported by amendments to the 1973 act, court decisions, and environmental groups at all levels—has successfully blocked many development projects that would have removed critical habitat. For example, the Stevens kangaroo rat, native to arid grasslands of Southern California's Riverside County, was declared an endangered species in 1989. Faced with the potential for fines and imprisonment, county officials halted development on thousands of acres (affecting about 100,000 potential home sites) until a habitat conservation plan could be developed to create a 30-square-mile system of preserves.[23] Other endangered species have similarly complicated residential development in other regions of the country. Even if not on a federal list, some species may be considered rare to the locale, and their presence can raise controversy about development.

[22] Kirstin Downey, "Rare Rat Gains Ground in Turf War," *Urban Land*, May 1989, p. 30. Reprinted with permission from *The Washington Post*, February 23, 1989.
[23] Ibid., p. 29.

Easements and Covenants

An easement is generally defined as a "limited- or special-purpose right or interest acquired by one party in the land of another."[24] Where an easement exists, the owner of the property retains title but grants an individual or organization the right to use a specified portion of the property for his or its benefit.

Easements are of two types. *Easement appurtenants* are created by the owner of a parcel. The most common instance is their use when a property owner needs to cross an adjoining property to reach his own parcel. This type of easement is common in contemporary zero-sideyard houses where property owners must cross their neighbors' lots to perform routine maintenance on the wall that sits on the property line. The second kind of easement is an *easement in gross,* an agreement between individuals. An easement in gross is most commonly used for utilities like pipelines or telephone lines crossing private property.

Easements and the purposes to which they can be put are limited by legal agreement. Therefore, a pipeline company might acquire the right to build and operate a pipeline across private property but be prohibited from using the right-of-way for anything else. Equally important are the rights of use retained by the owner. For example, a utility easement might or might not permit the surface use of the easement as recreational open space, a parking lot, or a site for structures.

Beyond the more conventional application of the concept of easements, several newer applications are gaining widespread currency—scenic easements, conservation easements, solar easements, and air rights easements. All are designed for specific purposes.

Scenic easements have been developed as a mechanism to preserve underdeveloped rural areas with outstanding scenic or aesthetic value. Such easements are often used to protect important views in the natural landscape. Conservation easements are very similar but are usually used to preserve areas of ecologic or scientific significance. Solar easements are meant to maintain accessibility to the sun and are located generally at the southern exposure of a lot or building for passive and/or active solar use. Air rights, on the other hand, grant permission to develop in the airspace over property, as, for example, when a railroad allows construction of office buildings over a downtown railroad station. Air rights typically come into play if the income generated by a property can be significantly expanded without removing the original

---

[24] William Atteberry, Karl G. Peason, and Michael P. Litka, *Real Estate Law* (Columbus, Ohio: Grid, Inc., 1974), p. 73.

2-36 An existing high-pressure gas line easement was accommodated through the center of this golf course.

Drainage easements occur most typically in two locations: 1) between lots for the purpose of allowing runoff from the street to exit a cluster and 2) on each lot to allow runoff from adjacent roofs and private yards to exit the yard. In conventional projects where both houses are set back from the side property line, the easement is normally centered on the property line. In zero-lot-line projects, the easement is located adjacent to one side of the property line. Drainage easements between lots can be five to 15 feet wide and can occupy the same area as a pedestrian walkway. Easements on lots are normally smaller, often two to 10 feet in width.

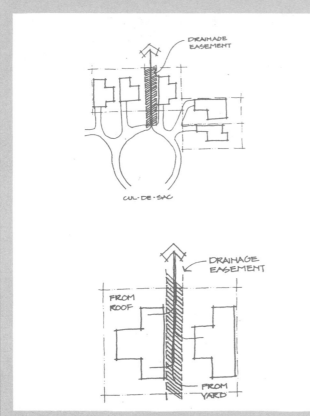

2-38 Typical drainage easements.

Maintenance/access/use easements are usually required in zero-lot-line developments to allow a homeowner access for use or to enter adjacent property to service the side of the house that is located on the lot line. Widths of these easements can be two to 10 feet, depending on codes or project requirements. The easements often are combined with covenants limiting any use that could physically prevent access to the wall located on the property line. An alternative to an easement on the adjacent lot is to set back the dwelling unit two to five feet from the lot line to allow access on the lot and then give the adjacent lot use of this area through an easement. Use easements may also be granted to owners of condominium units to allow limited private use of areas like patios and decks that are located on commonly owned property.

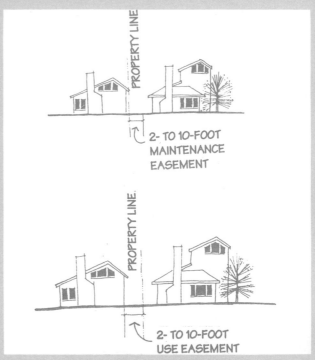

2-39 Typical maintenance/access/use easements.

Utility easements usually occur in one of three places: 1) in the public street right-of-way, 2) at the rear of the lot, or 3) in side yards. When a project abuts common area at the rear of the lot, this area can be used to accommodate utilities. Conventional rear easements are five to 10 feet. When lots do not touch on common area, utility easements typically occur in the public street right-of-way. Utility companies also usually require an easement across the lot to provide service connections to the house. These service easements sometimes are located on the side property line and are shared by adjacent property owners.

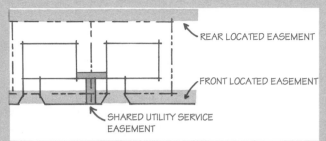

2-40 Typical utility easement.

Landscaping easements are not common in standard subdivisions but can be very useful in higher-density projects to enhance the streetscape's continuity and the project's identity. Landscape easements provide that certain areas, such as front yards or front setback areas, will be set aside and maintained in landscaping. The easement might prohibit the construction of fences or specify the number and type of plants that must be installed. Sometimes these easements may be landscaped by the developer and maintained by the community association, which can be especially useful as a marketing tool in higher-density projects. In other cases, the covenants may specify time limits within which the resident must install the landscaping and standards that must be maintained.

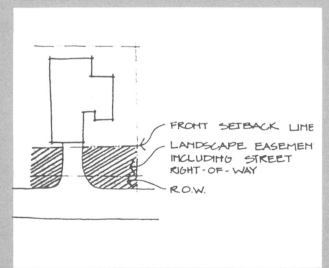

2-41 Typical landscaping easement.

Solar easements are intended to ensure that a property owner's access to the sun's rays will not be diminished by the actions of an adjacent property owner. Consideration of such easements is most relevant to those structures that are supplied in part or whole by a solar heating system. Basically, limitations on building orientation, building heights, roof planes, and plant material sizing and locations are involved in relationship to heights and seasonal sun angles. Because of the number of variables that exist in terms of regional location and use objectives, the precise locations and conditions of use for solar easements must be determined on a case-by-case basis.

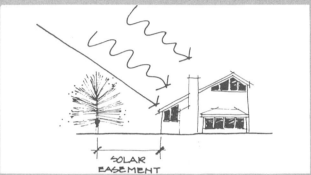

2-42 Typical solar easement.

View preservation easements can be implemented based on the total project, on project phases, or on selected lots. Such easements are most common to hillside developments or when a project abuts a scenic resource, such as a body of water. These easements can occur in horizontal planes (relating to structure placement) or in vertical planes (relating to structure or landscaping height). A very strong and thorough design review process is helpful in managing such a program.

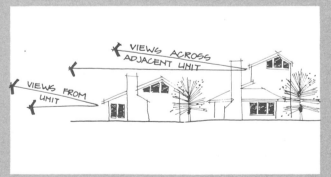

2-43 Typical view preservation easement.

Source: Adapted from David R. Jensen/HOH Associates, *Zero Lot Line Housing* (Washington, D.C.: ULI–the Urban Land Institute, 1981), pp. 17–20.

use. These forms of easements came into being as a way to regulate private property for the overall benefit of surrounding property owners or the general public.[25]

The size of easements depends upon the use for which they are created. Physical dimensions for most easements are well established, ranging from the narrowest single railroad line to those for electric power lines. The dimensions required for air rights or open space tend to be larger and more varied.

Easements have a number of implications for developers, because they influence the design of residential development. Existing easements are generally a constraint around which the design must be conceived. Providing for access to an adjacent parcel can usually be accomplished simply by adjusting the street layout. Pipeline, utility, and other easements in gross are best handled as common open space, because residential structures are almost always prohibited. Site planners can normally accommodate them in golf courses, greenbelts, pedestrian pathways, and other elements of open space in conjunction with easements.

Before acquiring a site or initiating a concept plan, developers must determine the extent to which easements may be used. It is not uncommon for utility easements written by the utility company to be so restrictive that, for all intents, they prohibit any placement of structures, surface improvements, or large landscape material. Such easements may also allow the utility company to enter the property with minimum notice to repair or maintain the utility with no liability or obligation to restore any damage done to owners' improvements.

In terms of development, therefore, the property itself should be thoroughly examined for any evidence of utilities crossing the property—either above or below grade. Outlet roads or travel ways over the property serving other properties that might result in adverse possession or have a deleterious effect on proposed development should also be checked. Particular attention should be given to any roadways used by other people, as the legal clearance of these travel ways can take a great deal of time and expense.

Because a visual examination of the property could show only those rights-of-way and easements that are in use, a qualified attorney or title company should make a title search for further determination of easements or encroachments. A title report also typically specifies the terms of the easement and all retained rights and obligations. In many cases, developers do not want to bother with a complete survey and title search during site study, but they should be aware that rights-of-way and easements are important considerations that can affect a site's feasibility for development.

Unlike mapped easements, protective covenants (sometimes called deed restrictions) exist between sellers and purchases of property. Typically, they extend beyond regulations enforceable by public authority, but they do not take the place of public regulations like zoning and both types of regulation can exist without necessarily overlapping. If they are not clearly spelled out in the deed or purchase agreement, a developer can find out whether any private covenants run with the land under question for purchase by retaining a qualified attorney.[26]

Some private covenants are drawn up with a definite termination date, while others "run with the land" (that is, they are passed on to successive property owners without a specified date for termination). While developers frequently want to establish covenants to ensure long-term protection of the quality of development, preexisting covenants (particularly those limiting the use of land) can constrain development considerably.

Utilities and Public Services

During the 1980s, many municipalities grew rapidly and were unable to maintain historical levels of services like transportation, sewage treatment, solid waste disposal, and emergency response. And maintaining basic services was aggravated further by increased environmental regulations and decreased federal funding to support improvements in local infrastructure.[27]

The availability of utilities and services and the financing policies of public and private surveyors can be significant enough to make or break a project. The days when developers could provide a house on a graded pad and the municipality would provide all necessary facilities appear to be over. Developers must now participate in either the funding or construction of public services, and many municipalities have adopted ordinances for collecting assessments,

[25] For additional information about the type and application of special-purpose easements, see Thomas S. Barrett and Putnam Livermore, *The Conservation Easement in California* (Covelo, Cal.: Island Press, 1983); and Janet Diehl and Thomas S. Barrett, *The Conservation Easement Handbook: Managing Land Conservation and Historic Preservation Easement Programs* (San Francisco: Trust for Public Land, and Alexandria, Va.: Land Trust Exchange, 1988).

[26] Covenants are discussed in greater detail in Chapter 7.

[27] For a more detailed discussion of development issues related to infrastructure, see Hanousek, *Project Infrastructure Development Handbook* .

fees, and exactions. These costs can be substantial, depending on the location of the site and the municipality's practices, and developers must understand the extent of this financial requirement before purchasing a site.

Although developers' participation in providing utilities and public services has increased, the way these improvements are financed can be a significant factor in judging a site's suitability. Some cities and counties, as well as private utility companies, are much more willing than others to help developers finance or construct necessary improvements to infrastructure. Public agencies can assist developers by issuing tax-exempt municipal bonds, establishing special assessment districts, coordinating special agreements between adjoining (or all benefiting) property owners, and a plethora of other financing techniques. In special circumstances, a municipality might even condemn property through eminent domain to assist developers in gaining access to the site or utility easements. The level of cooperation that can be anticipated from a municipality should be determined at the onset.

The following paragraphs discuss those utilities and services that are most frequently a subject of concern to residential developers: water, sewage, stormwater, solid waste, electricity and natural gas, emergency services, communication systems, schools, and parks and recreation.

Water

An existing, suitably sized public water supply main on or near the site is the least expensive and most desirable source of water. Thus, developers should determine whether it is possible to connect their projects with an existing public water supply system and where, as the answer may affect the planning and staging of development. If such connection is possible, then they should investigate with the proper public authorities the available capacity of the water and what capacity is already being captured by existing users.

Whether an existing water main will be adequate to serve a proposed project depends on the size and nature of the proposed development and the size and water pressure of the main. Logically, the greater the number of houses being proposed, the greater the demand for water. But other factors also come into play, including irrigation requirements and water pressure standards necessary to fight fires. Most fire departments mandate minimum water pressure standards, and if a proposed project will cause the pres-

sure in an existing main to drop below that minimum, then the developer may be required to assist in upgrading the water distribution system.

Beyond just examining the existing water system, developers need to consider whether the water supply is adequate to serve the proposed project. Many public supplies are already operating at full capacity and cannot meet the additional demand created by new residential development. The lack of water resources has reached critical proportions in recent years in some arid western states. The development boom in Southern California during the early and middle decades of this century was possible largely because water was imported from Northern California and the Colorado River. During the 1980s, however, Southern California's imported water supply was limited by a statewide population that is reluctant to fund expanded systems to import water from the north and by federal court rulings that have granted Arizona an increased share of water from the Colorado River, leaving Southern California with continuing growth and no immediate additional water resources.

Scarce water resources in Colorado have also threatened to curtail new development in metropolitan areas like Denver. According to council member Christopher Lee, "Water hookup fees in Denver were as high as $8,000 to $10,000 per unit in 1988. The lack of available water in the Denver metropolitan area is a major constraint to the future economic growth of the region, and no long-term solution is in sight."

Municipalities have responded to shrinking water supplies by imposing high water hookup fees on residential building permits, imposing strict water conservation practices that can include flow-restricting devices on plumbing fixtures, requiring installation of drought-tolerant landscaping, and in extreme circumstances limiting or prohibiting any new development until new supplies are made available. Residential developers would be wise to investigate the availability of water to a given site and, if it appears that supplies are limited, understand fully what will be required before hookup to the public system is permitted.

If they must develop their own water supply, developers could be faced with engineering, incorporation, and financing problems and the choice of providing either a central water supply for the project or individual water supplies (wells) for each dwelling unit. Small community water companies formed by developers in some areas are usually regulated by the state utility commission or health department. Though superior to individual wells, they add to the problems of development and are less desirable than a public water supply. Many states and municipalities are actively pursuing an antiproliferation policy that involves the creation of large looped systems and the abandonment of small private systems.

Sewage

A public sanitary sewer system to serve the site is the best alternative for sewage disposal. Only two other solutions are possible—a private community plant or septic tanks on site. If connection to a municipal system is not immediately available, then developers should check with authorities about scheduling extensions of the sewer main. Some local governments maintain a policy against such expansions, using limitations on infrastructure as a means of controlling growth or preventing leapfrog development. Other local governments are anxious to see urban growth and may assist developers in financing and negotiating complex reimbursement agreements with other benefiting property owners.

The determination of whether facilities are adequate to handle the sewage generated by a project focuses on two elements: the sewage transport system (sewer mains) and sewage treatment and disposal facilities. The first element is fairly easy to analyze: if existing mains are not large enough to accommodate the increased flow from a project, then they will need to be enlarged. Developers or consulting civil engineers should be able to quickly estimate the need for such upgrading and determine the likely cost of the needed improvements.

If adequately sized public sewers exist adjacent to the site, the site planner or engineer should carefully check invert elevations with all parts of the site to determine whether or not the entire site can be served. Sites lower than the adjacent sewage system involve a pumping station (not always permitted), entailing long-term costs for maintenance and energy.

The second element is often more difficult, as it relates to the existing capacity of the sewage treatment plant and whether the increased amount of sewage can be treated and disposed of. Many treatment plants in high-growth communities already operate at or above capacity, and municipalities have curtailed new development until funding is found to expand or construct new plants.[28] Developers cannot solve a municipality's or region's problems with treatment and disposal by themselves and in such cases are often left without recourse.

If hookup to the public sewage system is not possible, developers should investigate building a private community system. Small-scale wastewater treatment systems may become a more attractive alternative to capital-intensive, centralized plants. A variety of small-scale systems are available, usually combining small-diameter collection systems with common on-site disposal systems, package plants, or alternative treatment systems, such as lagoons.

For conventional subdivisions and PUDs of up to eight units per acre, such systems can be ideal if a public system is not accessible. Small-scale plants have not been used widely in the past, partly because they are perceived as land-intensive, environmentally unsound alternatives or only temporary. In some areas, the regulatory hurdles have been formidable as states try to reduce the number of discharge points for surface water. New difficulties in financing conventional technologies, however, may lead to fewer regulatory constraints on small plants.

Only as a last resort should developers consider individual septic tanks or cesspools. In some areas, individual septic systems have proven to be environmentally unsound, and regulations governing their installation have become increasingly stringent. In the future, only those areas with ideal soil conditions for septic systems and zoned for large lots (typically fewer than one unit per gross acre) will allow on-site disposal. Further, some homebuyers resist the use of septic tanks, because they require maintenance.

Stormwater

In the past, stormwater runoff has been handled through maximum convenience and rapid disposal of surface water through closed manmade systems. Stormwater runoff has often been mismanaged, however, and residential development built under the old philosophy has aggravated or caused problems downstream, including flooding. The aggravated conditions downstream often go beyond political jurisdictions, spawning lawsuits in which cities downstream sue cities upstream for approving projects that increase runoff, flooding, and erosion downstream. Developers would be wise to investigate the current method of managing stormwater runoff in the community where they seek to develop.

The preparation of a functional and aesthetic stormwater runoff plan requires cooperation among project engineers, planners, and landscape architects. For example, certain types of landscape plantings can effectively reduce the velocity of stormwater flow. Unless mass grading is proposed, how planners lay

---

[28] Patrick Phillips, "Wastewater Treatment: Impacts of the Shrinking Federal Role," *Urban Land*, June 1985, pp. 36–37.

out individual lots may be determined by natural drainage patterns. It is especially important that individual lots be drained; further, problems can arise with drainage easements located between lots unless provisions are made for periodic maintenance. Homeowners need to understand that altering the grade between houses can result in localized flooding or seepage into basements.

2-44, 2-45, 2-46, 2-47 Various techniques have been used to slow the rate of stormwater runoff from a site: A) stormwater outlet drains into an open channel lined with rocks; B) small detention area serves as a miniwetland; C) detention pond adds a valued site amenity; D) water flows over rolling grassy area before emptying into a catch basin.

Solid Waste

Each year, Americans generate about 150 million tons of municipal trash—about 3.5 pounds per person per day. Historically, picking up and disposing of this trash have been taken for granted. But during the 1980s, many municipalities were faced with landfills that had reached capacity or posed environmental risks to the community. And reduced federal funds made constructing new landfills difficult at best. Federal funding under the solid waste Subtitle D program was eliminated in 1986 (from $13 million in 1981), leaving local governments and states no option but to find new sources of funding.[29] Building new landfills or high-tech waste incinerators is a political, environmental, regulatory, and financial challenge that is likely to plague municipalities for the foreseeable future. Unless solutions are found to these challenges (which could include innovations in incineration technology), it is possible that new development could be limited in severely impacted jurisdictions.

Developers should determine the magnitude of a potential problem with solid waste disposal to ensure that building permits will not be delayed. They should also determine which agency or private company is responsible for picking up solid waste. Generally, trash pickup will not impose a constraint on development but will entail a tax or assessment that would be passed on to future residents, either individually or through a homeowners' association.

Electricity and Natural Gas

Electricity and natural gas services to the site are normally supplied by private utility companies at their own expense. The location and capacity of distribution lines in the vicinity should be indicated on existing utility maps. At the beginning of residential development, it is common practice for private utility companies to charge developers for the cost of constructing extended mains and then to issue refunds as customers are added.

Developers should check with the local electric power company for its policy on installing underground wiring. Underground power distribution produces a more attractive neighborhood, greater public safety, less maintenance, and more dependable service than overhead electric power lines. Most electrical companies now provide underground lines.

The 1970s focused on energy conservation, brought about by foreign oil embargoes, protests about nuclear energy, and dwindling domestic oil reserves. During that period, considerable attention was given to conserving energy through building and siting. The 1980s, however, saw generally low oil prices, which diverted attention from conservation. Still, some states and localities continue to require that developers incorporate energy-conserving building materials and techniques into new houses. In California, for example, Title 24 (established by the California Energy Commission) requires new residential developments to include energy-efficient insulation, caulking, double-glazed windows, and weather stripping.

Site design oriented toward energy conservation has also shown promise in isolated areas, but it is not used widely. Innovative solar ordinances in some isolated cities, such as Davis, California, require the longest side of a subdivision lot to be oriented toward the south, which receives sun for the longest period during the day. This ordinance also dictates that when structures are sited and built on such lots, they also be oriented toward the south.

Active solar energy systems were popular in the arid Southwest for a time, but they seem to have lost some popularity, primarily because of the loss of tax incentives. For the foreseeable future, it appears that residential builders need not be concerned with extraordinary construction practices to reduce energy use. Fossil fuels are a nonrenewable resource and nuclear waste remains an unsolved problem, however. Over the long term, energy conservation is likely to resurface as an important issue that could affect how houses are built and sited.

Emergency Services

Emergency services include primarily police and fire protection, which the local municipality almost always provides. In small or new suburban communities, these services might be contracted to a county government. In either case, responsibility for maintaining adequate levels of service to residents is a public function.

Many municipalities have found it difficult to maintain emergency services in light of cutbacks in funding and rapid growth. Developers may find themselves vying with police and fire departments for equipment, funds for increased personnel, and land for new substations. When evaluating a site's suitability, developers should consider the potential for these "unexpected" costs.

When examining fire protection services, developers should consider the site's distance from the nearest fire station and the expected response time in case of an emergency. Most fire departments maintain

---

[29] Fund for Renewable Energy and the Environment, *The State of the States* (Washington, D.C.: Author, 1987), p. 14.

objectives for response time and can estimate for developers the expected response time to a potential development site. If the response time is far greater than the department's objective, development of the site could be delayed.

Response times from police stations are less critical because police are usually dispatched from roving cars. Of greater importance is the department's level of staffing and equipment. Large residential projects in municipalities with overburdened police departments may be required to pay fees for expanded police equipment and staff.

In larger residential projects like planned communities, developers may also be required to reserve a site for a new fire or police substation. Some municipalities may require developers to dedicate such sites, without compensation. In other cases, the city reimburses developers for the cost of the land when it is needed. Developers of large tracts or communities should contact fire and police departments to determine whether site reservation is likely to be required and how much of the cost will be reimbursed from public funds.

Communication Systems

All new residential developments must be served by telephone lines, and in most metropolitan areas, new residents expect cable television (CATV) service as well. Private companies usually provide telephone and CATV, and their provision does not impose a constraint on development. Developers need to be aware, however, of the distance from a potential site to the nearest point of hookup and to obtain commitments for service from the purveyors before proceeding too far with a project.

Residential developers must closely coordinate the installation of communication lines with telephone and CATV companies. Some companies may require developers to share in their costs or to advance funds for installation that will later be reimbursed. Although such capital costs generally are minor, developers should be aware of each company's policies regarding financing of new service.

Residential developers and designers also need to consider the wiring of individual houses for communication systems. With rapid advances in communication technology, homebuyers are increasingly aware of the number and location of telephone jacks, CATV outlets, and other more advanced electronics, such as master computer and music systems. The advent of fiber-optic technology has opened vast new opportunities for linking homes and businesses and providing state-of-the-art voice, data, and video trans-

mittals. Before the end of the century, it is likely that all new residential projects will be built with fiber-optic cables as a matter of course.

The degree of high-technology wiring that needs to be included in a house depends on the intended market: higher-income households demand more state-of-the-art communications and electronics. So-called "smart houses" capable of performing maintenance through computer programs are becoming more common and require an extra degree of planning.

Schools

If the market analysis indicates a project's residents will be families with school-age children, the developer needs to be especially concerned with the location, quality, and capacity of nearby schools. Residential developers should not underestimate a homebuyer's willingness to investigate the quality and capacity of the local school district before deciding to buy a house.

Ideally, a residential site should be within walking distance of an existing elementary school with adequate capacity to absorb additional children generated by the proposed project. These circumstances are not always the case in rapidly growing suburban areas, however. During the 1980s, residential growth in many suburban areas outpaced school districts' ability to fund and construct new schools. Many states also reduced funding to school districts for the development of new facilities, resulting in overcrowded classrooms, the use of temporary buildings for classroom space, or busing children from crowded schools to other, less crowded ones. Many families will find any one of these results objectionable.

To mitigate the effects of rapid residential growth on schools, some districts, in cooperation with the municipality, have turned to residential developers for financial assistance. Developers may be required to contribute fees (typically established per dwelling unit), contribute temporary classrooms, dedicate land for siting new schools, or provide other contributions that the district has determined will help alleviate the problem.

Developers are likely to need to at least reserve sites for schools in large residential tracts or planned communities. These sites might eventually be dedicated to the school district, or the district might reimburse the developer for the value of the land when the school site is actually needed. Developers should contact the school district before committing themselves to a site to understand the extent of contributions likely to be required, especially when large projects are being proposed. Further, they need to factor in the school district's criteria for location and size of the site.

Wise residential developers understand the value of nearby, high-quality schools to the project's success: failing to ensure available classroom space can lead to a deadly pace of sales. Council member Richard Reese shares his experience:

> When we opened the first phase of the Rancho Santa Margarita planned community with 1,000 new houses, we knew we had to have an elementary school sitting there and ready to go. Our targeted buyers, young families, would not locate there, knowing that their children would be bused several miles away to already overcrowded schools. Because state money was not available immediately to build a school, we advanced money for the buildings and the playground equipment—right down to the last desk. We either advanced the money—some of which we will get back—or we did not have a competitive project.

When a residential development is an infill project in an already mature area, the availability of schools may pose an altogether different problem. Declining enrollments are causing school closings in some areas, resulting in changes to boundaries of service areas. After it is decided to close a school or change a service boundary, a site once considered well served by schools might prove to be poorly served. Changes to school service areas are reasonably predictable, usually occurring only after detailed study and debate by local school officials. Residential developers should investigate this possibility before committing themselves to a site.

Parks and Recreation

With rising incomes, shorter work days, and longer vacations, Americans have more leisure time than ever before. As a result, facilities and open space for recreation take on great importance in site selection. The amount and type of recreation needed vary with the lifestyle of future residents. Young families require playgrounds and ballfields, empty nesters prefer more passive forms of recreation, such as natural open space, and retirees want golf courses. The better developers know their intended markets, the better they will be able to ensure that their recreational needs are met.

The extent of recreational facilities developers need to provide depends primarily on three factors: 1) the size and number of units proposed in the project, 2) the availability of existing parks and recreation near the proposed site, and 3) regulatory requirements of the municipality. Clearly, the developer's obligation to provide parks and recreation increases with the size of the project. A subdivision of a few houses may require nothing of the developer, while a larger tract or entire community often requires the preparation of a comprehensive parks, recreation, and open space plan.

For smaller projects that will rely on off-site parks and facilities to satisfy future residents' recreational needs, developers must survey existing facilities and determine whether they will be adequate for the proposed project. Sites adjacent to or very near existing parks are usually preferred. If a site is far removed from existing or proposed recreational facilities, the developer may need to build these features into the project to attract the targeted market, thereby incurring expenses for both land and capital improvements.

If developers provide open space and recreational facilities within a site's boundaries, then they must carefully consider the types of facilities the market will want most and determine whether they can be provided economically. It is very difficult and costly, for example, to provide ballfields on a hillside or topographically diverse site.

Most municipalities maintain standards for the provision of parks with which new projects must comply. These standards are typically codified in a local ordinance and require that a certain number of acres of parks be provided per 1,000 residents or some specified number of houses. If developers cannot satisfy the provisions of the local code on site, the ordinance usually allows them to contribute a fee in lieu of land or improvements. Requirements for parks vary between municipalities and thus so too will a developer's contributions for land or improvements. Requirements for parks and recreational facilities can be substantial, and developers should understand them before committing themselves to a site.

Recreational facilities, including parks, built by developers can be dedicated to the municipality or handed over to a homeowners' association for long-term maintenance. In large projects, homeowners' associations as the vehicle for ownership and maintenance are becoming more popular, as municipalities become more reluctant to increase their responsibilities for maintenance and liability.

A growing trend is the use of school sites to meet at least part of a community's need for parkland. Because parks are used most intensively during evenings and weekends, school playgrounds can often serve both purposes. Locating schools and parks adjacent to one another is a practice that can work to the benefit of both. Members of ULI's Residential Council strongly encourage this practice because of its efficiency.

Regulations

Municipal, state, and federal bodies impose increasingly stringent regulations on residential projects. This trend developed gradually over much of this century but came to the forefront during the 1980s, in part, as a result of unprecedented urban and suburban growth. The net effect of these increased regulations has been to enlarge governmental control at all levels over the development process. Further, private developers are being required to contribute more fees, land, and improvements to help fill the gap in public funding. A result of these increased regulations and exactions from developers has been an increased premium placed on developable land. Each candidate site must be carefully studied in light of municipal, state, and federal regulations that in large measure will affect whether the contemplated project is feasible.

Municipal

Evaluation of a project's feasibility with regard to land use regulations should begin at the local (municipal) level. Although an array of regional, state, federal, and special interest issues may affect a site's potential for development, local regulations and perceptions about development are usually the most volatile. Because regulations vary between jurisdictions, they tend to be very important to site selection. A jurisdiction with stringent controls or a negative attitude about growth will likely require developers to expend more money, time, and effort to complete a residential project.

The arm of local government most involved with the regulatory and development approval process is the planning department, which in some municipalities may be known by another name, such as community development department. This division of municipal or county government is typically divided into smaller subdepartments by functional area: advance planning, current planning, land use control, and administration.[30]

Advance planning involves the preparation of comprehensive (or general) plans and the ongoing research necessary to keep them current. Planning policies typically originate in this unit. The current planning division is responsible for implementing plans—either by reviewing proposals that affect the plan or by initiating proposals to carry out the plan. This unit's work tends to be geared to short-term (often crisis-oriented) projects.

The land use controls division is involved in the application of the two principal regulatory tools in planning: zoning and subdivision controls. Residential developers find themselves dealing primarily with this division, which is most responsible for processing day-to-day applications for development: exceptions and variances, zoning interpretations and amendments, subdivision plats, and site plan reviews.

The administrative division takes care of the operations of the other three divisions, including personnel administration, library activities, budgeting, and support services. Other divisions within the planning department might include research, housing, economic development, environmental assessment, transportation, or a number of other special needs. Some municipalities may combine two or more of the divisions—for example, land use control and current planning—as a single entity. Each municipality structures itself somewhat differently, and residential developers need to know the organization of the planning department for each municipality where they propose a project to advance that project most effectively through the system.

Effective planning and development processing rest also with the political decision-making body. Decisions about zoning and land use often rest with the city council (or board of supervisors for a county government), the planning commission, or the zoning board of appeals (or the zoning administrator). Residential developers need to know what municipal approvals will be required for a proposed project and which individual or body will make the final decision on the application for a permit. This information can be obtained by meeting with representatives of the planning department or by retaining a qualified consultant or land use attorney.

The techniques by which a local government can regulate land use have grown considerably. Although zoning and subdivision controls are still the primary local regulatory devices, municipalities now can impose a host of other requirements on developers that can increase the cost of a project and in turn determine whether or not a project remains economically viable. These local regulatory techniques are discussed later in this chapter.

Regional

With the increasing urbanization of America, the need for regional planning structures has become more apparent. As suburbs have proliferated around urban cores and municipal boundaries have grown together,

---

[30] Frank S. So and Judith Getzels, eds., *The Practice of Local Government Planning*, 2d ed. (Washington, D.C.: International City Management Association, 1988), pp. 417–21.

cooperation and coordinated development policies and activities have become more important for neighboring jurisdictions. For example, transportation problems have been exacerbated by large volumes of commuters moving between municipalities, and provision of power and water for new development has become more of a regional issue because it is often regional supplies that are tapped. Many environmental problems are being addressed through state-coordinated agencies and programs, often managed regionally.

Regional conflicts in development have also arisen because one city may decide to limit growth, thereby placing a greater burden on neighboring jurisdictions. To prevent this shift of responsibility, several states have passed laws requiring cities and counties to assume their fair share of metropolitan or regional development needs, including affordable housing, air pollution control, water quality control, and waste disposal.[31] After the famous *Mt. Laurel* decision, for example, New Jersey passed legislation requiring that low-cost housing be allocated proportionately to jurisdictions so that each supplies its fair share of local housing.

Regional councils of government (or COGs) have also been created to address general development issues that cross city and county lines within a metropolitan region. A regional council often assists in coordinating unplanned development in unincorporated areas, provides technical assistance with development processes to smaller cities within metropolitan regions, and addresses important regional land use, transportation, and environmental issues. Special districts cutting across municipal boundaries address specific issues (such as environmental preservation) or provide specialized services (such as wastewater treatment and disposal).

Special Districts

In addition to familiarizing themselves with other regional agencies, developers should investigate the existence of limited-purpose government units (as opposed to general-purpose units) called "special districts." Special districts are commonly used to provide public services for local governments more cost-effectively. Typically, each district provides only one or two services.

The number of special districts has increased over time because of their usefulness in coordinating the provision of necessary infrastructure and other services. In 1988, more than 25,000 special districts (not including school districts) in the United States provided a wide range of services. Approximately 1,000

special districts provide metropolitan areas with water, energy, storm drainage, sewerage, and public transportation. Rural special districts provide flood control, soil conservation, irrigation, health services, and grazing management, among other services.[32] Special districts can have the power to tax, issue revenue bonds, and impose special fees to be collected by local governments.

In areas with low precipitation, several municipalities often form special districts to arrange and finance the importation of water. Such a large regional single-function special district is the Metropolitan Water District of Southern California (MWD).[33] Established in 1928, the MWD is a regional public agency that provides water for the Los Angeles area, including 5,000 square miles of area extending along the coast for 200 miles and inland for 75 miles. The area contains 13 million people in six counties and 135 cities. The MWD supplies 5 percent of Los Angeles's water normally and as much as 15 percent in dry years, but nearly all or all of the water supply for most other cities in the district.

The MWD became necessary because separate government units would not have been able to raise the large amounts of capital necessary to build facilities needed to provide water to the region. The MWD has over $1.5 billion in facilities, which include 242 miles of aqueduct, water treatment plants, power plants, and aqueduct pipelines. The MWD has the authority to levy taxes on property within its boundaries, establish water rates, sell bonds for construction projects, acquire property through eminent domain, and sell water. A corporate organization includes a board of directors, seven standing committees, and 135 representatives from the cities in the district. The MWD conducts long-range planning and forecasts. It derives its income from tax levies based on assessments of real property and manages cash flow after operational expenses, amortization, and interest expenses are deducted.

Smaller special districts in many municipal areas can also levy taxes to generate revenue to provide public services, such as sewer facilities. These districts are important to developers because they often act independently of local government in making decisions on where to place infrastructure, when it will be developed, and how it will be financed. The

[31] Melville C. Branch, *Regional Planning: Introduction and Explanation* (New York: Praeger Books, 1988), p. 104.
[32] Branch, *Regional Planning*, p. 107.
[33] Information on the Metropolitan Water District comes from Branch, *Regional Planning*, pp. 154–55.

levies of special districts also represent an expense for developers, in addition to taxes by local governments, in the development process.

During site selection, residential developers need to determine which, if any, special districts will affect site development. For those districts providing services like water or wastewater treatment, a meeting with the district staff should be considered to identify any constraints on service. If constraints exist, the district's staff can often help identify solutions and costs. Those costs can be substantial and must be factored into the feasibility analysis. If special districts do not exist, developers should investigate whether it is possible to establish one under state law to provide a needed service to the development site.

Regional Councils

The need to provide a forum for solving regional, multijurisdictional problems stimulated the creation of regional councils of governments. In 1989, approximately 550 regional councils were operating in the United States. Regional councils (also referred to as councils of government, planning and development districts, regional planning agencies, and regional development agencies) are generally made up of local governments as voluntary members. In all but seven states, regional councils are voluntary. Those seven states have some form of mandatory membership, although sometimes only for a program area.[34]

The form that regional councils take varies widely from state to state (and sometimes within states), depending on enabling legislation, the nature of the communities, and the political forces involved. Many regional councils have been put in place over the last 20 to 25 years, often to undertake major multijurisdictional programs that are too costly for individual local governments. The role of regional councils has grown in the last 20 years to be a significant factor in regional development and land use.

Virtually all regional councils have some voice in land use, economic development, and growth management. They are also generally involved in other programs that directly affect development or are affected by development. For example, management of regional transportation systems is a major responsibility of almost every regional council. Other activities of regional councils include assistance for small businesses, facilities planning, public/private ventures, commercial revitalization, and historic preservation.

Generally, regional councils cannot collect taxes, although in some exceptions, some councils are given a limited power to tax for a particular program. A few regional councils have bonding capacity. They typically have no governmental authority but operate on the cooperation of members to plan and coordinate regional operations.

Regional councils also serve as centers for analysis and dissemination of regional information, a forum for discussion of regional issues, and vehicles for the pooling of local resources.[35] They typically are the best single source of area demographic and marketing data, because they collect and analyze data regionally, the level at which markets actually operate. Regional councils work with the Census Bureau to collect and analyze data and sometimes market their services to the private sector.[36]

Historically, a major purpose of regional councils was to serve as a link between the local and federal governments, acting as clearinghouses to review and coordinate requests for federal assistance under the A-95 review system.[37] With decreased federal funds during the 1980s, however, the function of regional councils in A-95 review has lost importance. While intergovernmental communications improved with the establishment of a regional bureaucracy, the A-95 process is strictly advisory, and in some instances applications are merely rubber stamped.

Environmental issues are an area of growing concern for regional councils. In Florida, for example, regional councils are involved in the DRI (development of regional impact) review process. Water, air, solid waste, and land conservation all play prominently in many regional councils' activities—50 percent of all regional councils in solid waste programs, 45 percent in water quality, 25 percent in disposal of hazardous wastes, and 25 percent in land conservation. Of the major metropolitan area councils of governments, 72 percent are involved in water quality.

---

[34] Telephone interview with Carole Anne Nelson, Membership Services Division, National Association of Regional Councils, July 17, 1989.

[35] Branch, *Regional Planning*, p. 107.

[36] Contact the National Association of Regional Councils, 1700 K Street, N.W., Washington, D.C. 20006 for further information about and referrals to regional councils. NARC acts as the national coordinator for various councils of governments, lobbies Congress, conducts research, disseminates information to its members through various publications, provides technical assistance, and holds national meetings.

[37] The growth of modern councils of governments can be linked to three major pieces of legislation: the Demonstration Cities and Metropolitan Development Act of 1966, the Intergovernmental Cooperation Act of 1968, and the Housing Act of 1954. The first two acts were consolidated by the Office of Management and Budget's Circular A-95, which sought to establish a network of clearinghouses to review and coordinate applications for federal assistance.

State

Within the purview of state government rests all those powers not specifically mandated by the Constitution to the federal government—including the right to regulate and acquire land. Except for a flurry of activity in the 1930s and 1940s under the National Resources Planning Board, however, states have generally been more concerned with economic and industrial development than with land use planning. States have traditionally delegated almost all of their power over land use control to local governments (towns, cities, counties) and to special-purpose governments, placing them in a passive role in urban growth and development.

Patterns of population settlement established decades ago are now causing serious problems—traffic congestion, overloaded infrastructure, air pollution, surface and groundwater pollution. Many local communities have responded to these problems by limiting growth within their jurisdictional boundaries, but these piecemeal measures do not provide comprehensive solutions. As a result, some states have begun to intervene in the development process. State initiatives to control land use can be distilled into five major categories:[38]

- *State regulation of areas of critical concern.* A number of states have adopted single-purpose agencies designed to regulate and preserve a particular area of the state deemed valuable—an area of critical state concern (ACSC). In 1971, for example, Michigan passed the Shorelands Protection and Management Act to preserve and protect fish and wildlife and to prevent shoreline erosion. Similarly, with the passage of Proposition 20, voters designated the California coastline an ACSC. Florida's Environmental Land and Water Management Act of 1972 combined local participation and strong state authority, authorizing the state's land planning agency to designate ACSCs and empowering the state to approve local land use regulations within any of those designated areas. The Florida Supreme Court declared the state planning agency's power to designate ACSCs unconstitutional, however, and "excessive and unregulated delegation of legislative power."[39] The ruling did not question the state legislature's power to designate ACSCs—only the legislature's ability to delegate that authority.
- *Developments of regional impact.* States use DRIs to regulate land uses of potential regional impact. For example, Maine's Site Location of

Development Act requires a state permit for private projects over 20 acres or for single structures over 60,000 square feet. But, again, Florida uses regional impact review more comprehensively than any other state. Chapter 380, Section 6 of the state's planning law requires the regional agency to review large projects (including large housing developments) and prepare a report for the local government, including recommendations on the regional impact of the proposed development. The regional agency considers the project in light of several factors that "go beyond any narrow focus on environmental concerns. They constitute a broad mandate that regional agencies consider environmental, social, and economic factors and specifically that they consider the problem of adequate housing."[40]

- *Delegation of regulatory power to regional entities.* In some states, the power to regulate development has been delegated to regional bodies that function much like local planning agencies. In Vermont, for example, district commissions must issue permits even for relatively small development projects: residential projects of 10 or more units and subdivisions of 10 or more lots. Permits are often approved subject to numerous conditions—as would be the case with a local agency.
- *State review of local land use plans.* Oregon's Land Conservation Development Commission (LCDC), for example, reviews local agencies' comprehensive plans, land use maps, and policy statements to ensure their conformance with the LCDC's statewide planning goals. Local proposals conflicting with the state's land use planning goals must be changed, thereby usurping much local discretion in the planning process.
- *Direct regulation of land use.* Hawaii exercises the most direct control over land use. Since 1961, development has been regulated by county planning commissions pursuant to state controls—in effect, zoning by the state. Although no other state exerts such direct control over land use, some have started to move in this direction.

---

[38] An excellent source of information on what states have enacted in the way of land use controls is John M. DeGrove, *Land, Growth, and Politics* (Washington, D.C./Chicago: Planners Press/American Planning Association, 1984). See also Douglas R. Porter, "The States Are Coming...," *Urban Land,* September 1989, pp. 16–20; and Alexandra D. Dawson, *Land-Use Planning and the Law* (New York and London: Garland STPM Press, 1982).

[39] Dawson, *Land-Use Planning and the Law,* p. 90. See also *Askew v. Cross Keys Waterway,* 372 So.2d 913 (Fla. 1978).

[40] DeGrove, *Land, Growth, and Politics,* p. 119.

In the early 1970s, at roughly the same time that Petaluma, California, Ramapo, New York, Boca Raton, Florida, and other communities were pioneering the concept of growth management, a number of states also moved to impose more comprehensive controls over development. Vermont's Act 250 in 1970 was quickly followed by California's coastal program, Florida's land and water management and comprehensive planning acts, Oregon's local comprehensive planning requirements, Colorado's land use act, North Carolina's coastal program, and Hawaii's state planning act. Born of the environmental movement, these state forays into the nascent field of growth management were enthusiastically greeted by urban planners as signaling a new era in land use controls. Developers and builders thought differently, expecting their projects to be saddled with more restrictions and additional layers of approvals. Local government officials fell into two camps: those who detested the state's meddling in local land use affairs and those who welcomed a higher authority to blame for whatever went wrong with the regulatory process. As it turned out, no significant attempts at state-level planning materialized, and most state programs devolved into little more than project review exercises. Far from becoming the demonic scourge of development, state growth management appeared to have been a one-time effort.

But 1985 began what John DeGrove, an eminent expert in state growth management, calls "the second wave" of state regulation of urban growth. Florida passed a sweeping new state growth management act that year, followed by New Jersey's initiation in 1987 of a new state planning effort. These acts were succeeded by state legislation in Vermont, Maine, and Rhode Island in 1988 and Georgia early in 1989.

Whether or not states seize the authority to make day-to-day decisions on development—an improbable outcome—these recent acts have firmly established states' legitimate interests in coordinating the plans of local governments, curbing their regulatory excesses, and remedying their regulatory deficiencies. The new state legislation also recognizes that the domain of growth management extends beyond local jurisdictional concerns to affect the economic future and quality of life in large sections of states, if not entire states. For that reason alone, the push for state governments' role in managing urban growth is likely to continue.

The Second Wave

Momentum had been building for a new wave of state actions to corral growth. The new actions have gone well beyond environmental concerns to broader concerns about quality of life, including traffic congestion, uglification of the built environment, economic development, affordable housing, and funding and implementation programs to meet objectives for land use.

Florida led the way in 1985 with legislation to strengthen previous requirements for comprehensive planning and to engage in state-level planning. A study committee in 1982 had concluded that local plans were ineffective in the absence of regional and state planning, in particular because local plans contained no requirements for consistency with state goals, for a level of quality, or for implementation programs. The legislation framed to answer those criticisms required the creation of a state plan

▶

New Jersey—the most densely populated state—adopted the State Planning Act in 1986 to "provide a coordinated, integrated, and comprehensive plan for the growth, development, renewal, and conservation of the State and its regions, . . . which shall identify areas for growth, agriculture, open space conservation. . . ." The act placed a great deal of power in the hands of a state planning commission, which was given the task of formulating a state development and redevelopment plan.[41]

Early drafts of the plan sparked intense controversy by proposing that the state direct most growth toward existing urbanized areas and discourage development in agricultural and environmentally sensitive lands. The final draft plan retreated somewhat from those goals, offering instead a large array of potential growth areas to suit a variety of purposes. An elaborate procedure called "cross-acceptance" was devised to secure consistency between local and state plans. According to this procedure, each of New Jersey's 21 counties compares state proposals with existing municipal plans and negotiates to reconcile conflicts,

---

[41] See Barbara L. Lawrence, "New Jersey's Controversial Growth Plan," *Urban Land,* January 1988, pp. 18–21.

with goals and policies, state agency functional plans consistent with those goals and policies, regional and local plans consistent with state goals and policies, and local regulations consistent with those plans.

The 1985 law also required that development permits be issued only if infrastructure were available to serve it—the "concurrency" provision—and contained strictures encouraging compact urban growth and discouraging development in coastal areas. Today, Florida is beginning to approve local plans submitted for consistency review and is hotly debating the application of the concurrency requirement that infrastructure capacity be available for all new development (see Robert M. Rhodes, "Controversial 'Concurrency' in Florida," *Urban Land,* December 1988).

Hard on the heels of the Florida law came New Jersey's move to formulate a state plan, prompted in part by the *Mount Laurel II* court decisions that required the state to designate developing and developed communities to allocate lower-cost housing. In 1986, the legislature enacted a state planning act that created a state planning commission, which was given the task of formulating a state development and redevelopment plan (see Barbara L. Lawrence, "New Jersey's Controversial Growth Plan," *Urban Land,* January 1988). Early drafts of the plan sparked intense controversy by proposing that the state direct most growth toward existing urbanized areas and that development in agricultural and environmentally sensitive lands be discouraged. The final draft plan retreated somewhat from those goals, offering instead a large array of potential growth areas to suit a variety of purposes.

An elaborate procedure called "cross acceptance" was devised to secure consistency between local and state plans. According to this procedure, each of New Jersey's 21 counties compares state proposals with existing municipal plans and negotiates the reconciliation of conflicts, which could result in some modifications to the state's draft plan. That process is continuing. Once adopted, the state plan is supposed to guide future state actions, such as capital funding of facilities.

Maine, Vermont, and Rhode Island all enacted new legislation in 1988 requiring local governments to adopt plans consistent with state planning goals. Maine and Vermont also give regional councils responsibilities for reviewing and commenting on local plans. Maine's Comprehensive Planning and Land Use Regulation Act, citing the despoliation of the state's natural resources by unplanned growth and land speculation, requires each municipality to submit a comprehensive growth management program for state review. State agencies, regional councils, and contiguous municipalities are given opportunities to comment on such programs. The municipality may also request certification of its plans, which makes it eligible for state technical and financial assistance for planning and regulation.

Vermont's Act 200, over 100 pages long, responded to perceptions that Act 250 allowed too many small developments to escape review and fostered large-lot subdivisions. The act requires all local and regional plans to be consistent with 32 goals stated in the act. Although municipalities are not required to adopt plans, those without a confirmed planning process may not adopt impact fees or obtain planning assistance funds and are subject to regional plans. Authority is granted contiguous municipalities to form regional planning commissions, which are given a major role in approving

which could result in some modifications to the state's draft plan.

New Jersey's state planning process raised considerable controversy, and as of 1990, some uncertainty exists as to whether (or in what form) it will ultimately survive. Council member Robert L. Karnell offers this caution to other states that might use New Jersey's state plan as a prototype for their own legislation:

Adoption of an unbalanced plan in New Jersey would have adverse long-term consequence—for us and for others around the country. It could take years for New Jersey to recognize and correct imbalances in the plan and restore economic vitality to the state. In the short term, however, before the negative economic impacts are realized, the plan may serve as a model for other states, and they may embark upon the same path and commit the same errors.

The extent of states' involvement in planning and land use is likely to be in considerable flux for some time. States are trying to develop regulatory systems that will separate major decisions from minor ones. The danger, however, is the potential for regulation

municipal plans, assisting adjoining municipalities in coordinating their planning, identifying areas of special significance, such as agricultural and forest resources, and adopting regional plans as guides to municipal plans. The act also calls for the formation of a council of regional commissions to review and approve regional plans and act as an appeals board for regional actions on municipal plans. Finally, Vermont's act instructs state agencies to adopt plans consistent with the state's goals.

Rhode Island's Comprehensive Planning and Land Use Regulation Act expands on earlier provisions to require all municipalities to adopt comprehensive plans consistent with 10 state goals and containing nine specified elements. These plans must be approved by the state, after which state plans and actions must conform to the municipal plans. If, however, a state planning council finds that proposed state projects conform to state goals and vary "as little as possible" from municipal plans, the projects may be approved and affected municipal plans must then be revised to conform to the state action. If a municipality fails to submit and have approved a comprehensive plan, the state may prepare and adopt a plan for it. Because Rhode Island is a small state, no regional commissions are required, although joint municipal planning efforts are authorized.

In March 1989, following the report of the Governor's Growth Strategies Commission, Georgia's legislature enacted a law creating a three-tiered network of planning agencies. The law provides guidelines for regional and local planning and establishes a state development council to formulate a statewide development strategy. It mandates local plans, from which regional plans will be developed by revamped planning districts, now called Regional Development Centers (emphasizing the state's concerns about economic development). The regional centers will also mediate differences among local plans. Municipalities that fail to adopt plans will receive the lowest priority in allocations of state projects and funds.

The Reality Ahead

The development process in Vermont, Maine, Rhode Island, New Jersey, Florida, and Georgia will soon be affected by these new requirements for local comprehensive plans consistent with state goals, for active regional planning bodies, for more unified planning by state agencies, and ultimately for a more structured body of development regulations and implementation program. Statute drafters, of course, hope to create a cohesive set of development policies and a more predictable regulatory process among the various jurisdictions.

At the same time, however, the new laws raise issues and questions that are not easily answered. Will the enlarged maze of planning requirements simply clog the regulatory system, lengthening and complicating the development process? Are states serious enough about local and regional planning to provide adequate funding assistance to make it work? Will public officials and planners at all levels respond with truly effective plans attuned to the marketplace or simply go through the bureaucratic paces?

Clearly, the states have a long way to go to persuade either themselves or their critics that state growth management is a workable antidote to local regulatory anarchy. Meanwhile, planners, developers, elected officials, and just plain citizens will have to become adept at playing the land use game with state governments as well as with local ones.

Source: Adapted from Douglas R. Porter, "The States Are Coming, the States Are Coming," *Urban Land,* September 1989, pp. 16–20.

---

for its own sake. Any system of regulation imposes costs that are borne directly by taxpayers (staff salaries) and developers (carrying costs and processing costs) and are eventually passed on to consumers.

Like local regulations, the best way for developers to succeed with state-imposed regulations is to do their homework before confrontation. Developers should bear in mind that not all state regulations are negative to development or increase processing time. In some cases, state regulations have effectively corrected or improved local regulatory or processing practices. As they should with local governments, residential developers should be active in monitoring and improving state legislation that affects their interests.

Building Codes

Building codes are concerned mainly with structural requirements, performance of materials, and the arrangement of buildings for health and safety. But a building code may also influence site design and lotting as they relate to such items as attached garages, building heights, required exits, and setbacks, especially for multifamily buildings.

Statewide standards for building design and construction are increasing, largely because of the difficulty of applying numerous and varied local codes to actual development projects. Comprehensive statewide building codes take three major forms: codes applicable only to buildings constructed with public funds, mandatory statewide codes, and codes available on an optional basis for adoption by municipalities. Nearly half the states (24 as of 1989) still do not have any code at all, but all the rest have enacted some form of statewide code. Most state codes are based on one of three national model building codes. Other states have adopted their own codes, and still others have amended model codes until they are generally unrecognizable.

The most widely used model building code is the Uniform Building Code (UBC), which is used throughout the West and Midwest. In the Northeast, the predominant model is the National (or Basic) Building Code (NBC), while in the South, the Standard Building Code (SBC) predominates. The organizations responsible for overseeing the model codes are also members of an umbrella organization, the Council of American Building Officials (CABO). CABO was formed in part to improve communications among the model code organizations and to develop national standards for projects receiving federal funds. CABO also publishes a model code for one- and two-family dwellings, which is incorporated either directly or indirectly into the UBC, the NBC, and the SBC.[42]

The efforts of such organizations have helped greatly to reduce the variance between codes, but they are still widely diverse and it is a source of frustration for both developers and design professionals. For example, mandatory state codes have been somewhat of a problem in metropolitan areas that border more than one state: within the same market area, developers might be confronted with two or more codes, each with substantially different requirements. Further, many states have adopted minimum codes and then allow municipalities to amend them to meet local needs. Because of the complexity of most building codes, it is not easy to determine precisely what is required in a particular state or municipality.[43] While a national code would make it easier to know which building standards will be applied, it could also tend to limit flexibility (which is necessary between regions) and innovations that often arise on the job.

Subdivision Regulations

State statutes regulating the platting of land have long existed, and subdivision regulations have evolved over time. Modern subdivision regulations are largely patterned after three model acts: the Standard City Planning Enabling Act, the Municipal Planning Enabling Act, and the Municipal Subdivision Regulation Act. Subdivision of land became widespread after World War II, and the states widely adopted statutes based on these model and standard acts. Although enabled by state legislation, subdivisions are approved by municipalities. (See also "Local Regulatory Techniques" later in this chapter.)

Federal

Federal legislation affecting land use proliferated during the 1970s and 1980s, and the programs directly enacted from this legislation involve many agencies and departments in the federal government.[44] These programs and regulations have various effects on the use of land—direct impacts like regulatory controls over development and indirect impacts like restricting conditions of federal loans and grants. For the average residential developer, the degree of impact is not always easy to determine, and qualified consultants should be brought in at an early stage.

The increase in federal legislation and involvement has been generated from the actual or perceived notion that subnational and substate units of government were not performing satisfactorily on issues related to land use and the environment. It is federal policy to step in and act when local and state governments fail to do so. This function is generally reserved

---

[42] Steve Carlson, "Model Code Primer," *Journal of Light Construction,* January 1989, pp. 41–43.

[43] The National Conference of States on Building Codes and Standards, Inc. (NCSBCS), publishes a directory of residential building codes for states and for the 50 largest cities in the United States. The *Code Primer* is also available, which explains these codes in lay terms. For more information, contact NCSBCS, 481 Carlisle Drive, Herndon, Virginia 22070, 703-437-0100.

[44] For example, land use can be influenced by the U.S. Departments of Housing and Urban Development, Transportation, Interior, Defense, and Agriculture, the Federal Aviation Administration, the Forest, Park, and Soil Conservation Services, the Federal Energy Commission, the Bureau of Reclamation, the Army Corps of Engineers, the General Services Administration, the Environmental Protection Agency, the Federal Emergency Management Agency, the Water Resources Council, and numerous regional development commissions. For additional information on federal and state regulations affecting residential development, see Nicholas A. Robinson, *Environmental Regulation of Real Property* (New York: Law Journal Seminars–Press, 1987). Updated periodically.

STATUS OF RESIDENTIAL BUILDING CODES, BY STATE*

STATE	CODE
ALABAMA	No Code
ALASKA	No Code
ARIZONA	No Code
ARKANSAS	1982 SBC and 1982 Standard Fire Prevention Code
CALIFORNIA	1988 UBC
COLORADO	No Code
CONNECTICUT	1986 CABO
DELAWARE	No Code
FLORIDA	1986 CABO, 1988 SBC, or 1988 State of Florida Building Code
GEORGIA	No Code (CABO effective October 1991)
HAWAII	State Housing Code
IDAHO	1988 UBC
ILLINOIS	No Code
INDIANA	1987 CABO
IOWA	1988 UBC
KANSAS	No Code
KENTUCKY	1987 NBC, CABO (1988 Kentucky Building Code)
LOUISIANA	No Code
MAINE	No Code
MARYLAND	No Code
MASSACHUSETTS	Article 21 of Massachusetts Building Code (CABO with substantive amendments)
MICHIGAN	1987 NBC
MINNESOTA	1985 UBC (with 1987 administrative rules)
MISSISSIPPI	No Code
MISSOURI	No Code
MONTANA	1986 CABO
NEBRASKA	No Code
NEVADA	No Code
NEW HAMPSHIRE	No Code
NEW JERSEY	1987 NBC (with 1988 supplement) or 1986 CABO (with 1987 and 1988 supplements)
NEW MEXICO	1988 UBC
NEW YORK	New York Uniform Fire Prevention and Building Code (updated continually)
NORTH CAROLINA	1986 North Carolina Uniform Residential Building Code, Volume 1-B

STATE	CODE
NORTH DAKOTA	1985 UBC, Uniform Fire Code, Uniform Mechanical Code, 1987 National Electrical Code
OHIO	No Code
OKLAHOMA	No Code
OREGON	1989 CABO
PENNSYLVANIA	No Code
RHODE ISLAND	1986 CABO
SOUTH CAROLINA	No Code
SOUTH DAKOTA	1982 National Plumbing Code (with 1983 amendments)
TENNESSEE	No Code
TEXAS	No Code
UTAH	1988 UBC
VERMONT	No Code for single-family dwellings, 1981 NBC (with 1983 amendments) for two-family dwellings
VIRGINIA	1987 NBC or 1986 CABO (with 1987 supplement)
WASHINGTON	1988 UBC
WEST VIRGINIA	1986 CABO
WISCONSIN	1989 Wisconsin Uniform Dwelling Code
WYOMING	No Code
DISTRICT OF COLUMBIA	1984 NBC (with amendments)
PUERTO RICO	No Code
VIRGIN ISLANDS	Virgin Islands Building Code

LEGEND:

UBC:	**Uniform Building Code** International Conference of Building Code Officials
SBC:	**Standard Building Code** Southern Building Code Congress International
NBC:	**National Building Code (Basic Building Code)** Building Officials and Code Administrators International
CABO:	**One- and Two-Family Dwelling Code** Council of American Building Officials

*"No Code" indicates that there is no statewide code; however, local codes may apply.
Source: National Conference of States on Building Codes and Standards, *Directory of Building Codes and Regulations,* Volume II—State Residential Codes, July 1989. Reprinted with permission. See also Appendix F, which provides a more complete list of model building codes and organizations that administer those codes. For additional information, contact NCSBCS, 505 Huntmar Drive, Suite 210, Herndon, Virginia 22070, 703-437-0100).

for the legislature, but during the 1980s, the courts often acted as the final arbiter in many federal laws pertaining to management of resources and the environment.

The following federal regulations are particularly germane to residential development.

FHA Standards

The Department of Housing and Urban Development (HUD) has established property standards for those projects qualifying for federal mortgage insurance financing. These standards are similar to local housing and building codes and define the minimum level of quality acceptable to HUD under each specific condition. Like building codes, the requirements have been stated in terms of performance when practical. The requirements depend on nationally recognized standards of the building industry.

Although widespread use has not followed publication of these standards, they should be of interest to builders and developers as an indication of what HUD deems a minimum level of quality. But the use of the standards alone will not guarantee an acceptable or desirable project. Other factors, such as the physical site, must also be considered.

The package consists of three volumes of standards and a manual of acceptable practices, which presents current practices in residential design and construction technology.[45] It should be used for guidance and information only, as it contains no standards.

Flood Control

The National Flood Insurance Act of 1968 was enacted to provide property owners in flood-prone areas with previously unavailable flood insurance.[46] Before the act, flood-prone areas depended on the federal government for disaster relief following major floods—a costly and time-consuming process. Primary objectives of the act were to provide flood insurance at reasonable rates and to reduce flood damage through the imposition of local mechanisms for land use and control.[47]

The Federal Insurance Agency administers the National Flood Insurance Act. Under a presidential reorganization plan in 1978, FIA was transferred from HUD to the Federal Emergency Management Agency. FEMA has mapped and delineated floodplains and their potential flood elevation for flood-prone areas nationwide. The maps are available to guide local agencies in future decisions about land use.

FIA has adopted the 100-year flood as its standard, which represents "the flood level that, on the average,

will have a 1 percent chance of being equaled or exceeded in a given year."[48] Based on local flood elevation studies, FIA established flood elevations on flood hazard boundary maps and prepared subsequent flood insurance rate maps that take into account local risk factors.

Using these federal criteria, communities are using techniques to improve the long-range management of flood-prone areas, among them restrictions on the development of land exposed to flood damage and guidelines for shifting proposed development away from flood-prone areas. Most development is not allowed in a floodplain without mitigation, which might include constructing levees, deepening or widening channels, raising the elevation of the property, or diverting floodwaters.

Developers should check with the local planning agency or consulting engineer to determine whether a project is required to participate in the flood insurance program. Two sources of information are essential: a flood hazard boundary map, which is the official map of the community where floodplains and areas prone to mudslides are designated, and a flood insurance rate map, which is the official map of the community that delineates the area where flood insurance may be sold under the flood insurance program. Failure to check information on these maps could lead to costly delays.

National Environmental Policy Act

The National Environmental Policy Act of 1969 (NEPA)[49] was created to promote the restoration and maintenance of the environment. It consists of two elements: 1) development of a national policy for the environment under the direction of the Council on Environmental Quality, an executive-level, advisory council created by the act; and 2) preparation of regulations, the most notable of which include the requirement for an environmental assessment and possibly an environmental impact statement (EIS) before initiation of major federal actions, and creation

---

[45] U.S. Department of Housing and Urban Development, *Minimum Property Standards for One- and Two-Family Dwellings*, 4900.1; *Minimum Property Standards for Multifamily Housing*, 4910.1; *Minimum Property Standards: Care-Type Housing*, 4920.1; and *Minimum Property Standards: A Manual of Acceptable Practices*, 4930 (Washington, D.C.: U.S. GPO, updated periodically).

[46] 42 U.S.C. 4001–4128.

[47] Robinson, *Environmental Regulation of Real Property*, p. 10-12.

[48] Ibid., pp. 10-12–10-13.

[49] 42 U.S.C. 4321. See also Robinson, *Environmental Regulation of Real Property*, pp. 4-1–4-35.

of the Environmental Protection Agency as the regulatory agency charged with implementing the act.

The effect of the legislation on land development has been substantial. Following the passage of NEPA, similar legislation proliferated at the state level, extending EIS-like requirements to private real estate projects. The courts have also taken a central role in enforcing NEPA, often handing down tough interpretations of the law's intent and extending its guidelines.[50]

Two preliminary issues arise in complying with NEPA: is an impact statement necessary and, if so, what must it include? For an EIS to be required, a project "proposal" must first be prepared, which must require a federal "action." The action must be "major" and the potential environmental effects "significant."[51] If an EIS is required, it must include a detailed description of the proposed action, a statement of the significant effects, alternatives to the proposed action, and the impacts of the alternatives.

An environmental impact statement (or its state-mandated counterpart) basically reports on the potential effects of a proposed land use on the environment (although NEPA also requires an assessment of possible socioeconomic impacts). The content of an EIS is largely based on the enabling legislation (federal, state, and local), the administrative regulations, and the nature of the project. Regardless of scope, however, an EIS significantly increases the time necessary to obtain project approvals—generally from six to 12 months and longer for large or controversial projects.

A good part of what should be included in an EIS is a logical extension of the site evaluation and market and feasibility studies. Minimum effort expended toward meeting the requirements of an EIS will only subject the developer to challenges later (in many cases, court challenges) when project costs have escalated.

Residential council member Robert Engstrom discusses NEPA relative to residential development:

It is important not to confuse a requirement for an EIS for a federal dam with one for a routine residential development. Unfortunately, EIS in some cases has become a buzz word for delay. Likewise, the resultant delay often discourages creative development and absorbs scarce development funds that are used for bound volumes of paper instead of for features of livability, such as landscaping and recreational facilities. This is not to say that the impact of proposed development on natural terrain, traffic, schools, and other givens should not be considered in a residential development. More often than not, these factors are already part of a well-planned proposal. In many cases, the environmental assessment can serve as an abbreviated version of the environmental impact statement. The assessment also has a much shorter processing time.

Clean Air Act

The Clean Air Act of 1970[52] requires each state to develop state implementation plans (SIPs) to achieve federal standards for air quality. States are divided into Air Quality Control Regions (AQCRs) for the purpose of implementing the plans; the level of the problem with air quality varies considerably between AQCRs and thus so do control measures.

Because of persistent problems with air quality in many metropolitan areas, the Clean Air Act may play a larger role in land use regulation during the 1990s than it did during the previous two decades.[53] A major factor in air pollution is the automobile ("mobile" source pollution). Without major technological advances, regulatory efforts are likely to focus heavily on reducing automobile trips by curtailing growth or by rearranging land use patterns to shorten distances from home to work.

For residential developers, the Clean Air Act and its local implementing plans entail one more regulatory consideration. Projects proposed in outlying areas not served by public transit or near employment centers are likely to face the most resistance. "It is important to obtain a current copy of the SIP for the jurisdiction in which a land development or use is contemplated. Only by inspecting the SIP and relevant state regulations can it be determined which of these land use controls is in effect."[54]

Clean Water Act

The Federal Water Pollution Control Act Amendments of 1972 (later retitled the "Federal Clean Water Act"),[55] specifically Section 208, require the EPA to facilitate the planning and implementation of area-wide water pollution control programs. Typically implemented by regional agencies, the "208 planning process" often includes land use regulations designed to control nonpoint sources of water pollution. "Nonpoint-source pollution comprises all sorts of contamination that enters surface water by means other than ditches, drains, and pipes, such as street runoff, dumps and septic-system leachate, mining, forestry, and agricultural runoff, and construction erosion."[56]

[50] Daniel R. Mandelker, *NEPA Law and Litigation* (Wilmette, Ill.: Callaghan & Co., 1984), pp. 8–11.

[51] Definitions for these terms can be found in NEPA, Section 8:11.

[52] 42 U.S.C. 7401–7642.

[53] See David Salvesen, "The Clean Air Act's Impending Construction Ban," *Urban Land,* November 1987, pp. 36–37.

[54] Robinson, *Environmental Regulation of Real Property,* p. 16-9.

[55] 33 U.S.C. 1251 et seq.

[56] Dawson, *Land-Use Planning and the Law,* p. 119.

2-50 Tampering with wetlands usually results in rigorous and costly review. In this residential development, a small wet prairie became a multipurpose pond and now provides stormwater retention, a habitat for wildlife, and an attractive entrance.

Developers should check with the designated 208 planning agency as to how a particular site and design would be affected by the 208 process. Certain sites, for example, might be located in areas subject to a high amount of sediment or water pollution from construction activities and thus subject to extraordinary mitigation techniques during construction.

During the 1970s and 1980s, considerable legislative and judicial attention was focused on the regulation and preservation of coastal and inland wetlands. Section 404 of the Clean Water Act[57] requires permits for the discharge of dredged or fill material into the waters of the United States. The permit program, intended in part to prevent the loss of valuable wetland habitats, is administered jointly by the U.S. Army Corps of Engineers and the EPA. Because the two organizations do not always agree on policy, the bifurcated permit process has been a source of frustration for some permit applicants.

The Corps has been regulating discharge of refuse, including dredged and fill materials, into "navigable water" since the enactment of the Rivers and Harbor Act of 1899, which was intended to protect navigation and interstate commerce rather than the environment. Because of this experience, Congress in the Clean Water Act gave the Corps regulatory power over discharges into U.S. waters—but using EPA standards. The waters over which it has regulatory power were gradually expanded by court decisions,[58] environmental activists, Congress, the Corps itself, and EPA. The Corps's regulatory purview now includes not only traditionally navigable waters but also tributaries to navigable waters up to their headwaters, intrastate waters up to their headwaters that are used for interstate commerce, and wetlands adjacent to such waters.

[57] Enacted in 1972 as the Federal Water Pollution Control Act, 33 U.S.C. 1344 (renamed the "Federal Clean Water Act" in 1977).

[58] See *United States* v. *Riverside Bayview Homes*, ___ U.S. ___, 106 Sup. Ct. 455, 88 L.Ed.2d 419 (1985), *rev'g,* 729 F.2d 391 (6th Cir. 1984).

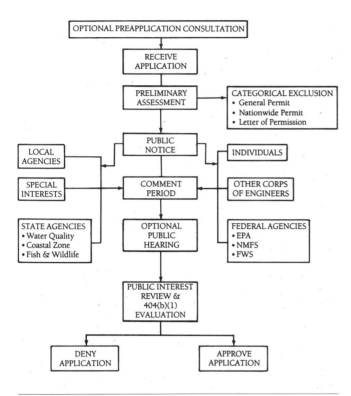

Source: The U.S. Army Corps of Engineers, in David Salvesen, *Wetlands: Mitigating and Regulating Development Impacts* (Washington, D.C.: ULI–the Urban Land Institute, 1990), p.29.

The Corps's regulations pursuant to Section 404 define wetlands as follows (EPA has adopted the same definition):

> The term "wetlands" means those areas that are inundated or saturated by surface or groundwater at a frequency and durations sufficient to support, and that under normal circumstances do support, a prevalence of vegetation typically adapted for life in saturated soil conditions. Wetlands generally include swamps, marshes, bogs, and similar areas.[59]

Because of this broad definition, many developers and landowners have been surprised to learn that their property is subject to the Corps's regulations. If even the slightest chance exists that a site might be designated a wetland, the developer should consult with the Corps or talk to a consultant before investing time and money into the site.

The process of actually obtaining a 404 permit requires a public review period, a "statement of findings" by the Corps (to provide the factual basis for a decision to be made), and a determination as to what other federal requirements must be satisfied. The Corps conducts a public interest review in which it

attempts to balance the public benefits for environmental protection with the property rights of landowners who want to realize the full development potential of their land. Although it sounds relatively straightforward, this permit process can become quite complicated.

The EPA has a strict policy against allowing discharges into wetlands and can invoke a veto power on a permit issued by the Corps. Although seldom used, this veto power is most often invoked when the EPA and the Corps disagree as to whether a particular discharge will have any "unacceptable adverse impact" on the environment. They can also often differ about what role mitigation should play in the analysis and what types of mitigation measures are acceptable. If such a disagreement arises between EPA and the Corps, the permit applicant can expect long delays.

Hazardous Wastes

A residential project may be complicated, either before or after development, by noncompliance with the Comprehensive Emergency Response Compensation and Liability Act of 1980, commonly referred to as "Superfund."[60] Amendments to Superfund and the Reauthorization Act of 1986 (SARA)[61] increased federal efforts to clean up toxic waste dumps; a budget of $8.5 billion was established to clean up over 200 of the worst sites in the United States.[62] For residential developers, the primary concern over toxic and hazardous wastes stems from potential liabilities.

The federal law provides that both past and present property owners of a site contaminated by hazardous chemicals or other toxic material may be liable for its cleanup. The liability pertains even if owners (past and present) had no knowledge of or were not responsible for the contamination. A case in point arose in 1985, when the Shore Realty Corporation was held responsible for cleaning up hazardous waste on newly purchased land, even though it did not dump the waste or even own the property when the contamination occurred (although it did know before purchase that the site was contaminated).[63] Shore Realty purchased the 3.2-acre site for $325,000 in 1983; in 1985, the estimated cost to clean up the site was $4 million.

[59] Robinson, *Environmental Regulation of Real Property*, p. 11-19.

[60] 42 U.S.C. 9601 et seq.

[61] 42 U.S.C. 6901.

[62] David Salvesen, "Liability for Hazardous Cleanups: Caveat Emptor," *Urban Land*, April 1988, p. 36.

[63] *New York* v. *Shore Realty Corporation*, 759 F.2d 1032.

Developers can reduce their liability by thoroughly investigating a site before purchasing it. SARA states that anyone who buys property, having made "all appropriate inquiry into the previous ownership and uses of the property consistent with good commercial or customary practice," will not be held liable merely because of such private ownership.[64] SARA directs the court to consider "any specialized knowledge or experience of the defendant, the relationship of the purchase price to the value of the property if uncontaminated, . . . the likely presence of contamination, . . . and the ability to detect such contamination by appropriate inspection."[65] Larger and more sophisticated developers will likely be held responsible for more research and documentation than smaller developers, but because case history on the law is limited, the smart approach is to investigate thoroughly previous uses and conditions of a property before closing a land deal.[66] Several states have also acted to reduce liability claims by prohibiting residential development within specified distances of known hazardous waste disposal sites.

Other Special-Purpose Federal Legislation

Federal protection reaches into many other areas that could affect the feasibility of residential development, depending on specific conditions of the site. Some of the federal laws that should be considered are described briefly in the following paragraphs.

Coastal Zone Management Act of 1972 (16 U.S.C. 1451 et seq.). Under this act, the 30 coastal and Great Lakes states are encouraged through the incentive of federal grants to regulate their coastal lands. The act was broadened with passage of the Coastal Zone Management Improvement Act of 1980 (16 U.S.C. 1452) to provide even greater protection for natural resources, such as coastal wetlands. The federal legislation is implemented differently by states, and, in some states, local land use authority can be superseded by other agencies. This latter point should be of special concern to developers building near coastlines; the developer may have to process plans through a statewide or regional entity before approval.

Endangered Species Conservation Act (16 U.S.C. 668). This act gives the Secretary of the Interior the power to designate plants or animals as endangered species and, once designated, to establish a program of conservation, including the purchase, donation, or other procurement of lands, waters, and interests.

Water Bank Program for Wetland Preservation (16 U.S.C. 1301). Applying only to inland freshwater wetlands, this act empowers the Secretary of Agricul-

ture to enter into 10-year agreements with landowners to preserve habitats for waterfowl and other wildlife to ensure that a landowner will not destroy an area's wetland character.

Marine Protection, Research, and Sanctuaries Act (16 U.S.C. 1401). This act enables the Secretary of Commerce to designate as marine sanctuaries any ocean waters, coastal waters, or the Great Lakes and connecting waters and to control any activities within them.

Fish and Wildlife Coordination Act (16 U.S.C. 661). This act provides that for any federal action that modifies a watercourse or any public or private action under a federal permit, one must first consult with the Department of the Interior's Fish and Wildlife Service and with the head of wildlife resources of the particular state. This provision could have a broad impact, considering the Corps of Engineers's regulations and activities in wetlands.

Qualified planners or real estate lawyers are aware of most of these federal regulations. Processing applications through many federal agencies takes time, but the job can be less frustrating if it is handled by qualified and experienced professionals. Often it is possible to combine requirements of two agencies, saving both time and money. To ignore these federal agencies and their requirements, or to postpone contacting them, can jeopardize an entire development.

Local Regulatory Techniques

Comprehensive Planning

The culmination of the local planning process is the development of the comprehensive plan, also called a general plan, a master plan, or a development plan. It is the product of a four-step process: 1) formulation of goals and policies, 2) research, 3) preparation of the plan's elements, and 4) identification of the procedures to implement it.

Usually the general plan contains a graphic presentation of what the community might look like in 10, 15, or 20 years. The bulk of the document, however, should contain the objectives, principles, and standards to guide the community toward its goals. Every plan includes three basic technical elements: land use, circulation, and community facilities. Elements

---

[64] Sec. 101(f)(35)(B).

[65] Salvesen, "Liability for Hazardous Cleanups," p. 37.

[66] See Bureau of National Affairs, *Environmental Due Diligence: The Complete Resource Guide for Real Estate Lenders, Buyers, Sellers, and Attorneys* (Washington, D.C.: Author, 1989).

addressing civic design, a result of aesthetic judgments, and public services/utilities, involving the relationship between water supply, drainage, sewage disposal, and other utility systems, are also usually included. Other elements related to a community's specific needs may also be included—preservation of a distinctive resource or protection against localized hazards, for example.

Although comprehensive, these plans are not permanent; rather, they are intended to be continually examined and revised to reflect new policies and goals based on changing conditions in the community. For this reason, comprehensive planning provides for local agencies' periodic amendments. The

procedures for amendment vary by state, but they are usually defined in the statute.[67]

In most areas, a general plan is an advisory document and does not bind a locality to a specific pattern of land development; rather, it provides guidelines to the local legislative body. The Standard City Planning Enabling Act, for example, states that "the plan shall be made with the general purpose of guiding . . . development."[68] Because the comprehensive plan is

---

[67] Douglas W. Kmiec, *Zoning and Planning Destop* (New York: Clark Boardman Co., 1987), p. 17-3.

[68] Standard City Planning Enabling Act, Section 7 (U.S. Department of Commerce, 1928).

2-52   TECHNIQUES USED MOST FREQUENTLY TO MANAGE GROWTH

- *Urban growth boundaries/urban service limits* are boundaries established around communities within which the local government plans for provision of public services and facilities and beyond which urban development is discouraged or prohibited. Boundaries are usually set to enclose growth over 10 to 20 years. Intended to provide more efficient services and protect rural land and natural resources, they are used extensively in Oregon, Florida, Colorado, Maryland, and California.

- *Designated development areas* are similar to urban growth boundaries in that certain areas within a community are designated as urbanized, urbanizing, future urban, and/or rural, and within those areas different policies for future development apply. They are used to encourage development in an urbanizing area or redevelopment in an urbanized area.

- *Adequate facilities ordinances* require that project approvals be contingent upon evidence that public facilities have adequate capacity for the proposed development. If facilities are found to be inadequate, development is postponed or developers may contribute to improve facilities.

- *Extraterritorial jurisdiction* is used in some states to give local governments power to plan and control urban development outside their boundaries until they can annex that land. It may also be effected through intergovernmental agreements—for example, between a city and a county.

- *Affordable housing allocations* are used in some states to require that local governments

plan to incorporate a fair share of housing types geared to regional housing needs. These targets can then be met through various programs to encourage or mandate lower-income housing.

- *Growth limits* establish an annual limit on the amount of development allowed. Usually applied to the number of building permits issued (most often for residential development), growth limits require some method for allocating permits, such as point systems (see below). They can be used as an interim or a permanent measure.

- *Growth moratoriums* temporarily prohibit development, based on an immediate need to forestall a problem involving public health, safety, or welfare, such as lack of sewage treatment capacity or major traffic congestion. Moratoriums may apply to one or more types of development and be communitywide or specific to an affected area. Moratoriums typically are in effect for one to three years to allow time for the problem to be solved but may last for many years.

- *Point systems* are a technique for rating the quality of proposed developments by awarding points according to the degree to which projects will meet stated standards and criteria. Various factors typically are weighted to reflect public policies. They are used most often in flexible zoning and techniques to limit growth.

Source: Mike Miles et al. *Real Estate Development Processes* (Washington, D.C.: ULI–the Urban Land Institute, forthcoming).

seen as advisory, it is not usually viewed as a controlling instrument. In fact, in many states, the advice of the plan can be ignored, while zoning or other land use controls contradicting the plan can be adopted. In a few states like California, however, zoning must be consistent with general plans, by state statute. In conflicts between a local zoning ordinance and a comprehensive plan, courts have usually held that the zoning ordinance is the controlling factor.[69]

A slow transition seems to be under way, however, as courts are beginning to give greater validity to plans in deciding the justification of zoning amendments. Municipalities must now justify land use changes more carefully, and the comprehensive plan serves as the essential criterion for evaluating any rezoning.[70]

Zoning

The authority for a municipality to enact a zoning ordinance comes from state enabling legislation, which in turn stems from the Standard State Zoning Enabling Act.[71] This enabling legislation lists specific purposes for zoning—the first being "promoting health, safety, morals, or the general welfare." In addition, the act specifies the purposes of a zoning ordinance as lessening congestion in the streets, securing safety from fire, panic, and other dangers, providing adequate light and air, preventing overcrowding of the land, avoiding undue concentration of population, and facilitating the adequate provision of transportation, water, sewerage, schools, parks, and other public requirements. The power to zone stems from the police power—that inherent power of government to protect its citizens—that the state delegates to municipalities.

Zoning is neither city planning nor comprehensive planning; it is but one of many legal and administrative devices by which comprehensive plans can be implemented. The reason the two have been confused is that many communities were "zoned" long before planning was initiated. (In fact, the Standard City Planning Enabling Act followed its zoning counterpart by two years.)

Zoning ordinances are usually comprised of a zoning map with accompanying text. The map delineates the boundaries of designated uses or "districts." The text of the ordinance outlines minimum standards to be met by uses in each district; they commonly define permitted use of land, building height, bulk, and placement from lot lines (setbacks), lot size, residential density (usually expressed in dwelling units per acre), parking, signage, and open space. The text also includes implementation of special exceptions, variances, and amendatory devices. Mechanisms for flexible zoning may also be included, such as floating zones, performance zones, planned unit developments, and transfer of development rights.

Zoning in its present form began to take shape during the early part of the 20th century, when the malaise affecting New York City was blamed on the unregulated mixture of conflicting land uses. At that time, the basis of zoning was the common law of nuisance, which, simply put, means that one may not use his property in ways that injure his neighbor's property. New York City's enactment of use districts soon spread, and districting became zoning. Upheld in numerous court cases, including the *Euclid* case decided by the U.S. Supreme Court, Euclidian (or conventional) zoning, as it became known, has evolved from preventing nuisances to a means for rationalizing controls over the use of space.

Zoning is prospective rather than retroactive—that is, it cannot be relied upon to correct existing conditions. It is generally effective in maintaining the character of existing built-up areas, however. As provided for in a typical ordinance, zoning does not encourage comprehensive land development. Further, zoning based on preservation of the status quo does not always meet the needs of a growing community or the needs of all its citizens.

During the 1970s and 1980s, zoning came under attack by housing organizations and civil activists for its sometimes "exclusionary" side effects. Whether or not intentional on the part of a community and its elected officials, zoning can be effective in prohibiting housing for low- and moderate-income groups by limiting development to low-density subdivisions or by imposing tough development standards that tend to raise the cost of construction. The legal backlash from these exclusionary zoning practices caused many municipalities to rethink their zoning ordinances and to provide for a greater range of housing.

Some communities have gone so far as to adopt "inclusionary" zoning provisions—a mandatory set-aside of a specified percentage of housing units for low- and moderate-income households within each new housing project. As an incentive to construct such affordable units, developers may be offered den-

---

[69] Kmiec, *Zoning and Planning Destop,* p. 17-3.

[70] Ibid., p. 17-7.

[71] Advisory Committee on Zoning, U.S. Department of Commerce, *A Standard State Zoning Enabling Act under Which Municipalities May Adopt Zoning Regulations,* rev. ed. (1926). This model act was first issued in 1924, but the 1926 revised edition serves as the model for most state statutes permitting zoning. An excellent overview of the zoning process is Herbert H. Smith, *The Citizen's Guide to Zoning* (Chicago: American Planning Association, 1983).

sity bonuses or relief from other standard exactions or development fees. Residential developers should become familiar with the zoning designation for each site under consideration to determine whether any inclusionary provisions exist and, if so, how they can best be met.

Another recent trend in zoning is the increased direct involvement of citizens in land use decisions. Residential developers have found it increasingly necessary and advantageous to begin working with neighborhood or citizens' groups early in the planning process to avoid controversial public hearings and potentially major changes to a proposed development plan. In most municipalities, citizens' groups exert tremendous influence over local decision makers and discretionary matters like development permits. Further, 21 states and the District of Columbia have constitutions that permit referenda and initiatives,[72] which permit citizens to vote on issues and effectively bypass the legislative process. Because zoning is a legislative action in most states, it is legally open to such direct decision making by citizens. The frequency of initiatives and referenda related to land use grew rapidly during the 1980s (especially in California), largely as a result of citizens' concerns about growth, traffic congestion, and loss of open space. "Letting the voters resolve land use issues seems like a good idea to concerned citizens, particularly in areas of high growth, where the complaint is that everyone talks about congestion but nobody does anything about it."[73]

An initiative is a proactive procedure allowing voters to propose and act on legislation. It is increasingly used at the municipal level to adopt amendments to the zoning code: for example, to prohibit certain uses, change zoning designations, revise development standards, or control levels of growth. A referendum is a reactive procedure that allows voters to reject or accept legislative actions—such as zoning amendments—made by local legislators. Both procedures are gaining use and have been used to block new residential (and other land use) development projects.

Whether an initiative or referendum can influence a particular development site and project depends on several factors. In general, these processes apply only to legislative actions, and zoning in most states is a legislative action, whereas other types of development permits are not. Although initiatives and referenda cannot be used to promote racial discrimination, such charges are often difficult to prove. And the opportunity for these processes to influence development varies widely among states. Courts in some states have ruled that these procedures do not apply to zoning because they preempt statutory procedures for notices and hearings.[74]

Despite these limitations, zoning by referendum or initiative is a growing regulatory problem for many residential developers. Developers should be aware of the opportunity for their occurrence and measure carefully the level of controversy a potential development project might entail. The direct involvement of citizens in making decisions can result in considerable costs, loss of time, and possibly the inability to gain entitlements to use.

Flexible Zoning

Critics increasingly attack traditional zoning as unnecessarily rigid, rooted in outmoded tradition, and lacking the framework for experimentation. "The fault, however, does not lie with zoning, which can be a very flexible instrument, but with the failure to take advantage of its flexibility. Attacks are generally against zoning of 30 years ago [that] still remains in effect, rather than against zoning as it could and should be."[75]

Because the single lot was the predominant pattern under which residential neighborhoods were developed in the past, specifications of the zoning ordinance were framed to fit the concept of development lot by lot. But many modifications were developed and refined during the 1970s and 1980s to recognize changing concepts of land use and land development. Most new residential communities are characterized by a mix of products and densities on relatively large parcels of land under single ownership, and these new communities do not fit the zoning for single lots. As a result, new or modified techniques are now being widely implemented to accommodate changing concepts of development.

Floating Zones. Floating zones allow a municipality to adopt a zoning district but not designate specific sites for that district on its zoning map. In theory, the zone "floats" over the municipality's jurisdictional area until a landowner petitions for a zone amendment and the municipality approves the request to establish a floating zone on that site. This flexible zoning technique recognizes that some land uses

[72] Iver Peterson, "Land Use Decisions via the Ballot Box: The Public Is Deciding Some Tough Questions on Zoning and Growth," *Urban Land*, August 1988, p. 33. Reprinted with permission from *The New York Times*.

[73] Ibid., p. 32.

[74] Daniel R. Mandelker, *Land Use Law*, 2d ed. (Charlottesville, Va.: The Michie Company, 1988), pp. 273–79.

[75] Fred H. Bair, Jr., and Ernest H. Bartley, *The Text of a Model Zoning Ordinance with Commentary*, 3d ed. (Chicago: American Society of Planning Officials, 1966), p. 2.

may be appropriate throughout the municipality and the impossibility of predetermining locations for certain uses.

Generally, floating zones are not applied to low-density residential uses; however, they are sometimes used for multifamily and special-purpose housing. In fact, the first major court decision upholding floating zones concerned a floating garden apartment district.[76] In that case, the court ruled in favor of both the apartment project in question and the use of a floating zone. Courts have been less favorable to the technique when municipalities use it as a way of exercising unreasonable discretionary power over zoning. Still, residential developers considering applying for a floating zone district should be aware of the considerable municipal discretion this technique implies. Applications for floating zones are often subject to long review periods, input from citizens, and/or resistance. Likewise, projects approved are often subject to a long list of conditions.

Performance Zones. First used to regulate industrial uses, performance zones offer a flexible alternative to conventional zoning ordinances. Rather than listing uses that are or are not permitted (as conventional zoning does), performance zoning relies on a set of standards to be met by new development, and whether or not a project complies with the standards determines whether it is or is not permitted.

In residential projects, performance zoning is most often based on the standard of density. The average density of the total site is held constant, but density over portions of the site may vary. Performance zoning often specifies limits on development or impact for various environmental resources. Some level of disturbance is allowed to less sensitive features, but more stringent restrictions are placed on rare resources, thereby protecting the environment. For example, if a sensitive habitat exists on a proposed development site, density can be limited in that area unless a way to lessen or eliminate impacts is proposed. Completely avoiding the area through cluster development may allow the developer the density needed to make the project economically feasible and still protect the resource.[77]

Planned Unit Developments. Planned unit developments came into wide use beginning in the 1960s and gained strength through the 1980s. This regulatory device entails many definitions and approaches, making it all the more desirable, as it can be molded to fit a variety of situations across the country. A PUD is a flexible way of developing land in a manner that might not strictly comply with traditional cookie-cutter zoning standards but usually results in a project of superior design and with superior amenities.

For example, a residential PUD can provide for a mix of many housing types and densities with more open space than would be possible under traditional zoning. A PUD allows more flexible design and is more adaptable to changes in the housing market.[78]

Transfer of Development Rights. Transfer of development rights (TDR) is another flexible zoning technique that was first suggested in the early 1960s by David Lloyd, a New York developer. Lloyd contended that if a community did not want development in a certain area, the community should allow landowners to sell their development rights to someone who owns land in the area where development is encouraged. The idea was largely ignored until the early 1970s, when John Costonis, a law professor, championed it as a way to preserve Chicago landmarks where no public funds were available.[79]

TDRs offer a person whose potential to develop land is limited the opportunity to sell development rights to a landowner in an area where the local government encourages development. They can be used to preserve open space, prime agricultural land, and sensitive ecological areas. TDRs can be cumbersome to administer, however, and they raise several constitutional issues.[80] When a site is subject to TDRs, it is best to contact a qualified land use attorney early in the process. In areas using TDRs, local attorneys, planning consultants, and public agency staffers have developed expertise in arranging such transfers and can provide residential developers with valuable guidance.

Subdivision Regulations

Subdivision regulations are a long-accepted method of municipal and county control over the development of land. Specifically, subdivision regulations allow a public authority to control the platting and conversion of raw land into building sites, and as such

---

[76] *Rodgers* v. *Village of Tarrytown,* 96 N.E.2d 731 (N.Y. 1957). See also Mandelker, *Land Use Law,* pp. 260–62.

[77] For additional information on performance zoning, see Douglas R. Porter, Patrick L. Phillips, and Terry J. Lasar, *Flexible Zoning: How It Works* (Washington, D.C.: ULI–the Urban Land Institute, 1988).

[78] For additional information on planned unit developments, see Colleen Grogan Moore, *PUDs in Practice* (Washington, D.C.: ULI–the Urban Land Institute, 1985).

[79] Frank S. So, Israel Stollman, Frank Beal, and David S. Arnold, eds., *The Practice of Local Government Planning* (Washington, D.C.: International City Management Association, 1979), p. 437.

[80] Mandelker, *Land Use Law,* pp. 443–45. For an overview of programs and practices related to TDRs, see Richard J. Roddewig and Cheryl A. Inghram, "Transferable Development Rights Programs: TDRs and the Real Estate Marketplace," Planning Advisory Service Report No. 401 (Chicago: American Planning Association, 1987).

These seven communities have all decided on performance standards as a central feature of their zoning ordinances. The jurisdictions represent a range of population from 1,250 to 90,000 and of geographic locations from Massachusetts to Florida to Colorado. All have had flexible zoning systems in place for at least five years.

Fort Collins, Colorado. The "Land Development Guidance System" formulated for this city of 82,000 in 1979 comes closest of all to the pure form of flexible zoning. Property owners may choose this approach as an alternative to standard zoning. The ordinance spells out absolute criteria (such as neighborhood compatibility) that must be met and relative criteria (such as location near a transit line) for which points are awarded. If all absolute criteria are satisfied and enough points are earned, the project is approved. Projects can be modified and/or amenities offered to increase point scores.

Breckenridge, Colorado. This town of 1,240 adopted a "development code" in 1978 to evaluate development applications. Its system is similar in some respects to Fort Collins's but with two important differences: the designation of 42 land use districts that specify preferable and acceptable uses and densities, and a much larger array of criteria, chiefly centered on design and environmental issues. Point scores are subject to negotiation with staff and public officials and can be influenced by project modifications and contributions from developers.

Largo, Florida. Largo's comprehensive development code was formulated in 1983 to compile numerous separate ordinances and to provide a less frenetic decision-making process than the then-typical extended negotiations. Complex in outline, the code rests on uses and densities defined in the land use plan, overlaying them with four "policy" districts (e.g., redevelopment). Within each district, 13 land use types (similar to those in the land use plan) are classified as permitted, permitted with mitigation, or prohibited. Thus, although use options are restricted, some flexibility is afforded. Most zoning decisions are made by zoning administrators.

Hardin County, Kentucky. This largely agricultural county had voted down conventional zoning several times before it adopted its "development

guidance system" in early 1984. The ordinance allows single-family houses and agricultural uses by right, but it decrees that all other uses will be evaluated 1) by a site assessment, which rates the developability of a site, and 2) by a "compatibility assessment," which is determined by discussion between a site's developers and its neighbors. The site assessment provides a performance-based evaluation, but the compatibility assessment is a highly discretionary approach to decision making.

Bath Township, Michigan. Replacing an overly elaborate and time-consuming county ordinance, Bath Township's new ordinance (1981) takes on some of the trappings of flexible zoning, especially in three of its five zoning districts, which permit a great variety of uses. Many "difficult" uses, such as junkyards, however, are placed in a special permit category that requires special review procedures and conditions. Performance provisions are highly simplified, and administrative procedures are much like those of other ordinances.

Buckingham Township, Pennsylvania. Lane Kendig's book on performance zoning [*Performance Zoning* (Chicago: American Planning Association, 1980)] came out of his experience with this early model, adopted in 1974, which focuses mainly on mixing dwelling types within the framework of a cluster subdivision. Permitted by right in some residential zoning districts, this design option provides performance standards for open space, control of nuisances, and environmental protection.

Duxbury, Massachusetts. This 350-year-old town of 13,000 residents enacted a bylaw in 1973 to provide for development of cluster-type subdivisions with varied housing types in an area otherwise dominated by large single-family, detached houses. After more than 10 years of well-designed subdivisions, which accounted for a majority of the town's new housing, both developers and public officials lost interest in the increasingly arduous negotiations and elaborate requirements the bylaw entailed. Since 1985, no one has activated its provisions.

Source: Douglas R. Porter, "Flexible Zoning: How It Works," *Urban Land*, April 1988, p. 8.

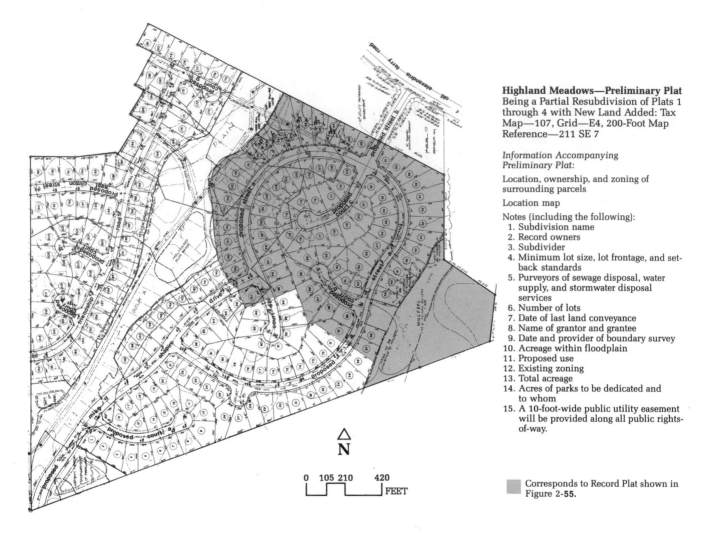

Highland Meadows—Preliminary Plat
Being a Partial Resubdivision of Plats 1
through 4 with New Land Added: Tax
Map—107, Grid—E4, 200-Foot Map
Reference—211 SE 7

*Information Accompanying
Preliminary Plat:*

Location, ownership, and zoning of
surrounding parcels

Location map

Notes (including the following):
1. Subdivision name
2. Record owners
3. Subdivider
4. Minimum lot size, lot frontage, and setback standards
5. Purveyors of sewage disposal, water
   supply, and stormwater disposal
   services
6. Number of lots
7. Date of last land conveyance
8. Name of grantor and grantee
9. Date and provider of boundary survey
10. Acreage within floodplain
11. Proposed use
12. Existing zoning
13. Total acreage
14. Acres of parks to be dedicated and
    to whom
15. A 10-foot-wide public utility easement
    will be provided along all public rights-
    of-way.

Corresponds to Record Plat shown in
Figure 2-**55.**

2-54   Preliminary plat of subdivision. *Source:* Greenhorne & O'Mara, Inc., Greenbelt, Maryland.

they have a much greater impact over a longer period
of time on all development than does zoning. Once a
residential development is created and sold to individual property owners, for example, it very difficult
to reassemble the land for another use.

Subdivision regulations are concerned mainly
with the layout and standards for lot-by-lot development, normally accomplished through plat approval,
whereby a developer is not permitted to make any
improvements on the land or divide and sell the land
until the planning commission (and/or city council)
has approved the map or plat of the proposed subdivision. Approval or denial is based on conformance
with the development standards set forth in the ordinance.

Planners' coordination of the unrelated plans of
individual developers is one obvious benefit of subdivision regulations; for example, subdivision regula-

tions ensure the alignment of streets and infrastructure between adjacent developments. For developers,
they are a safeguard against competitors who would
drive down the value of a well-planned subdivision with an adjacent substandard development. Subdivision regulations are most effective when their merits
can be judged communitywide against a comprehensive general plan. Like zoning, however, most cities
had subdivision regulations long before they had
comprehensive plans, and, in fact, much subdivision
regulation takes place without reference to the comprehensive plan.

[But] the practical need for conformity between planning
and subdivision control is greater than between planning
and zoning. While zoning regulates uses, bulk, and
height, it does so on developed and undeveloped land
and can be changed. Subdivision regulations affect undeveloped lands, and whatever is permitted initially—

Highland Meadows—Final Plat

Information Accompanying Final Plat:

Surveyor's certificate

Owners' dedications

Notes:
1. Approval of this plat is conditioned on the Washington Suburban Sanitary Commission's issuing the necessary water and sewer authorizations. Building permits may not be issued, however, until the planned water and sewer facilities are completed and determined to be adequate to serve the proposed development.
2. Subject to review and approval of conceptual grading plan by the Natural Resources Division before issuance of grading permits
3. This plat is subject to a Declaration of Covenants, Conditions, and Restrictions recorded in Liber-_____ and Folio-_____ and may be affected by a previous declaration recorded in Liber-_____ and Folio-_____.

Prince Georges County, Maryland, Health Department approval block

Maryland–National Capital Park and Planning Commission, Prince Georges County Planning Board approval block

Recordation date, plat book, and plat number

2-55   Final plat of subdivision. *Source:* Greenhorne & O'Mara, Inc., Greenbelt, Maryland.

street, sewer, and water main location, widths and standards for these improvements, park and school site locations, and lot size—will be present for a long time.[81]

Once streets and utilities are in, changing the subdivision layout is very difficult.

Generally, subdivision regulations require following a set of steps before an approved final plat is recorded. Many jurisdictions suggest that developers submit thumbnail sketches of proposed subdivisions showing locations and special features but do not actually require them to. Most planning agencies believe that a consultation before the application is submitted is helpful, because it gives them information that is useful later when they must review the formal plat. Likewise, developers can secure guidance from planners to smooth out the processing of the application before they incur great expense preparing detailed plans.

The first formal action required of developers is an application for approval of a preliminary plat. The local subdivision regulations specify in considerable detail what information is to be shown on the plat. Usually the plat must be submitted with multiple copies and in enough time for all affected agencies to review it and make recommendations. After interested agencies have considered the plat, the approval agency either approves (usually with conditions) or denies it. During review, considerable negotiations between the developer and the approval agency can be expected, often resulting in modifications to the proposed plat.

When a final plat is submitted, the approval agency has its last chance to do anything about a subdivision.

---

[81] Donald Hagman, *Urban Planning and Development Control Law* (St. Paul, Minn.: West Publishing Co., 1971), p. 249.

The purpose of approval of the final plat is to ensure that the recorded plat is in accordance with the approved plans and that construction will proceed according to those plans.

The final step before the development and sale of lots is recording the approved plat. When the required improvements have actually been completed, the public agency inspects them; a formal action is required to accept them for public dedication and maintenance. Many lending institutions require the filing of an approved plat before committing money to homebuyers in the subdivision.

Although subdivision regulations are clearly necessary, developers sometimes complain that municipalities have adopted unreasonable requirements as a prerequisite to subdivision approval. For example, requirements might include excessively wide street rights-of-way, unnecessary park or open space, and oversized utilities at the developer's expense to serve property (either developed or yet undeveloped) beyond the proposed development. Moreover, many conventional subdivision regulations have become obsolete in light of contemporary techniques of design and development. Many PUDs, for example, do not lend themselves well to traditional subdivision codes; such projects require greater flexibility if they are to respond to varying site conditions. A cul-de-sac serving 10 houses obviously does not require the same right-of-way as a residential street serving 100 houses. Likewise, applying rigid standards to a sloping site can result in excessive grading and removing too many trees.

Another frequently encountered constraint relates to minimum lot sizes. Usually, sizes of lots are regulated by zoning and subdivision codes that specify a minimum, for example, 10,000 square feet. Developers may find it very difficult to satisfy the requirement for minimum size when trying to preserve sensitive site features (e.g., a stand of trees, a stream course) or developing a sloping site. To provide greater flexibility, some jurisdictions call for an average (instead of minimum) standard, which allows developers to plat the lots more sensitively without compromising the jurisdiction's overall objectives for density. An average standard is also less cumbersome than requiring developers to file for a series of variances.

Residential developers should not take subdivision regulations as a given when standards are excessive for the development being proposed. Like zoning ordinances and most other local regulatory devices, periodic amendments to the subdivision code are necessary to keep pace with development practices. And the private sector must often initiate such amendments.

Exactions and Negotiations

The 1980s brought an explosion of costs related to the development of housing and most all other forms of land use. The decade was characterized by deep cuts in federal, state, and local funds for infrastructure, citizens' revolting against taxes at almost every level of government, and the strongest sustained housing market since the end of World War II. Faced with overloaded infrastructure and strong pressures for growth, municipalities turned to the private sector—especially developers—to provide an increased share of growth-related costs. Every indication is that the trend for private financing of infrastructure will continue. Residential developers—even those operating at a very small scale—must be aware of a municipality's requirements for fees and exactions to determine a project's feasibility.

Development Exactions

To recover what is perceived as the public costs of new development, local ordinances generally require developers to dedicate land, improvements, or fees as a condition of subdivision approval. In the past, these dedications were primarily for basic infrastructure necessary to serve the development site, such as on-site roads and utilities. Dedications or "exactions" now, however, are often required for off-site improvements above and beyond the immediate infrastructure needed for a development site. Today, exactions might be required for improvements to arterial streets, flood control facilities, sewage treatment plants, schools and parks, fire and police stations, open space—or almost any other public necessity.[82] Clearly, the trend has been in the direction of more exactions from developers.

For development exactions to be legal, they must be "reasonably related" to the need generated by the proposed development.[83] In land use law, such reasonableness is usually determined by the "rational nexus" test: the exaction and the need must be reasonably connected. For example, requiring a developer to improve a flood control channel from which the proposed development will receive no benefit is not permitted; however, if the subdivision will drain into the channel, an exaction can be imposed for the proportionate contribution to the needed improve-

---

[82] For an excellent discussion of exactions, see James E. Frank and Robert M. Rhodes, eds., *Development Exactions* (Washington, D.C./Chicago: Planners Press/American Planning Association, 1987).

[83] Mandelker, *Land Use Law,* p. 372.

ments. Exactions that benefit the community only (but not the development) are not legal, but developers do not always dispute this issue because court challenges are lengthy and costly and can jeopardize a developer's ultimate right to build.

On balance, the trend of the law seems to offer wide support for the use of development exactions for almost unlimited range of purposes as long as the purpose reflects a problem created to some degree by the particular development, the amount of the exaction bears some rough proportionality to the share of the problem caused by the development, and the exaction will be used to alleviate the particular problem created.[84]

Development exactions take a variety of forms: dedication of land, construction and dedication of public facilities, and, sometimes, cash payments. Some local governments have adopted standards by which to measure exactions, while others determine exactions case by case, thus complicating a developer's ability to judge the project's feasibility. When no standards exist, historical records of exactions imposed on similar developments can be a way to "price" exactions for a feasibility analysis and a basis for negotiating "equity."

Dedications of land usually take the form of a fixed percentage based on the total amount of land in the subdivision or a density formula in which a given amount of land is required per dwelling unit or lot. Some communities may give developers credit for private facilities within the subdivision that offset the need for public facilities. For example, a developer that provides for private recreation facilities on site may be required to dedicate less land (or pay a smaller in-lieu fee) for public parks.

Improvements to streets and utilities are specified on the final plat or map and, if the facilities are to be dedicated to the municipality, must meet public design standards. Improvements to be built by the subdivider that are to remain in private ownership are sometimes allowed to be constructed at standards less than the community would normally require. For example, private streets may sometimes be built narrower than would be required for public streets. Rarely do subdivision regulations require a developer to actually build a school or park. Such facilities are generally used by more than the residents of a single subdivision, so it would be unfair to impose the burden of such public improvements on a single developer.

In small developments, it is more likely that exactions will be made through fees instead of land and improvements. Requirements of land to be dedicated for parks, schools, and other public facilities would be too great a burden for a small site. Instead, fees are combined with those from other small developments to provide the necessary public improvements at some off-site location.

To ensure that developers complete the necessary improvements in accordance with the approved plat, some sort of security is usually required to be posted. Several options are available:

1) the subdivider may obtain a performance bond from a surety company; 2) the subdivider may obtain an irrevocable letter of credit from a lender (often the lender who is providing construction financing); 3) the subdivider may place cash in an escrow account held in trust by the local government or by a financial institution; 4) the subdivider may escrow personal property (stocks, bonds, equipment) or mortgage or give a deed of trust on real property; or 5) the subdivider, the subdivider's lender, and the local government can enter into a three-party subdivision improvement agreement. If one of these options is used, the bond may not be released, the letter of credit withdrawn, the account closed, or the contract completed until a representative of local government (often the engineer or public works director) has certified that the required improvements have been completed according to specifications.[85]

Developers clearly prefer an option that minimizes their outlay of cash or interest carrying charges; letters of credit, for example, are preferred to cash escrow accounts.

Development Fees

Development fees (also called impact fees, infrastructure fees, capital facility fees, and connection fees) are payments assessed on a development to recapture the proportional share of public capital costs required to accommodate that development with public necessities.[86] Development fees are similar to development exactions but are generally applied to improvements not related to a site. Many communities use development fees as an alternative to more traditional methods of funding large-scale capital improvements (e.g., taxes, bonds, and assessment districts).

We can define impact [development] fees as single payments required to be made by builders or developers at

[84] Fred P. Bosselman and Nancy Stroud, "Legal Aspects of Development Exactions," in Frank and Rhodes, eds., Development Exactions, p. 103.

[85] So and Getzels, eds., Practice of Local Government Planning, pp. 234–35.

[86] James C. Nicholas, Planning a Justifiable System (Gainesville, Fla.: Holland Law Center, 1987), p. 1. For detailed discussion of development fees, see Arthur C. Nelson, ed., Development Impact Fees: Policy, Rationale, Practice, Theory, and Issues (Washington, D.C./Chicago: Planners Press/American Planning Association, 1988); and Thomas P. Snyder and Michael A. Stegman, Paying for Growth: Using Development Fees to Finance Infrastructure (Washington, D.C.: ULI–the Urban Land Institute, 1986).

the time of development approval and calculated to be the proportionate share of the capital cost of providing major facilities (arterial roads, interceptor sewers, sewage treatment plants, regional parks, etc.) to that development.[87]

Development fees are a result of local government's efforts to manage the impacts of growth and development.

> In the late 1970s and early 1980s, rapid growth in many areas combined with increases in construction costs and interest rates and reduction in federal and state aid increased the cost to local governments of providing new infrastructure. Coupled with the fiscal decline of many cities, tax and expenditure limitations, and voter rejection of bond issues, the cost increases have forced many cities to reconsider the way they pay for new capital facilities. Hundreds of communities have already taken decisive actions to alter the distribution of the capital costs of growth between current and future populations by adopting development fees to finance at least some portion of new infrastructure.[88]

Some capital improvements for which impact fees have been charged to a development include police and fire protection, improving transportation, improving water and sewer systems, solid waste disposal, parks, drainage systems, public schools and libraries, and other public facilities. Fees vary widely between regions and municipalities but often exceed $10,000 or more per housing unit.[89] Fees that high contribute to the steady increase in housing costs as developers pass those charges on to consumers. Ultimately, much of the amount is figured into the homebuyer's mortgage and amortized over 30 years.

A form of development fee that gained much use in the 1980s is the "linkage fee." These fees require developers to contribute fees to help alleviate a particular problem or problems or fill a particular need created by a development. Linkage fees have been attached most widely on commercial projects in downtown business districts to provide needed uses (such as affordable housing) and services (such as daycare).

As with development exactions, facilities not benefiting new developments may not be assessed as fees to that development. In addition, capital improvements required for *existing* municipal needs legally may not be paid for by fees for new development, although in practice such distinctions are difficult to measure and surely occur.

Negotiations

Despite the plethora of ordinances regulating development actions, private developers still initiate most of the changes in the landscape and municipalities are the accommodators. At some point in the devel-

opment process, the public and private sectors must meet. It may be over a single variance from the zoning ordinance, or it may be over a complicated proposal for a planned unit development involving protracted negotiation and communication. Whatever the project's size, negotiation is important in building a rapport between the public and private sectors; it prevents the parties from becoming adversaries.

The development process is in the center of the political arena. Developers, builders, and other private real estate interests have large roles to play. The developer's role has diminished to a degree, however, because public involvement in land development decisions has increased tremendously. The arena is crowded with special-interest groups—citizens, local, state, and federal bureaucracies, and local planning agencies and commissions. Most recently, this trend has been manifested in initiatives or ballot measures that seek direct control over major land use decisions.

In short, communities are becoming more entrepreneurial and responsive to the needs of the entire community rather than strictly letting the marketplace dictate land use patterns as they have in the past. Council member Gary Ryan emphasizes, "As in any other partnership, there must be equity for both partners and a recognition of the objectives of each. Good development can be achieved only when the objectives of both are accepted by the other. Successful partnerships occur when each party provides unique resources to the deal. To the extent community plans reflect community needs and the ability to pay, such partnerships can succeed. When only one partner is expected to contribute, the deal suffers."

Municipal negotiations typically involve trade-offs and compromises, but not all those offered by a municipality will be useful to a developer. For example, a community might offer developers a density bonus because they have satisfied certain municipal requirements. But the density bonus will be useless to developers whose initial proposal for density represented the share of the market the project was capable of capturing; if they cannot succeed in capturing that bonus increment, it does them no good whatsoever. Developers need to be aware of what trade-offs and compromises are likely to be offered and then pursue those that will be of greatest benefit to the proposed project.

---

[87] James E. Frank and Paul B. Downing, "Patterns of Impact Fee Use," in Nelson, ed., *Development Impact Fees*, p. 3.

[88] Snyder and Stegman, *Paying for Growth*, p. 6.

[89] The *Los Angeles Times* reported on October 8, 1989, that impact fees in Southern California range from $3,000 to well over $20,000 per house.

2-56 The Wells-Robertson House in Gaithersburg, Maryland, offers transitional housing for 14 formerly homeless individuals. Renovation of the house in 1988 was the result of a coordinated effort between the city and the business community—including several local developers who donated over $100,000 worth of in-kind services, labor, and materials. The project provided an opportunity for developers to contribute to the community and promoted a cooperative spirit between the public and private sectors.

For developers, the best way to influence the development process is to begin long before it affects them personally and long before they need a particular type of zoning for a particular plot of land. Developers should actively support good local planning by pushing for a good planning staff and planning commission. They should also make sure that the community has up-to-date regulatory tools, such as zoning and subdivision ordinances, or even better, a combined development ordinance to complement its comprehensive plan. Developers should also participate in formulating and updating the municipal capital improvement plan, because it is important to the ultimate provision of infrastructure.

And developers can make it easy for themselves by improving their image with the public. It can be accomplished, as council member Ray Brock explains, "by being believable, by doing what you say you will do, and by doing it when you say you will. Build quality products (regardless of the price range) and establish a good track record. Do not overpromise when selling a project to the community. Provide a product that equals or is better than that represented during preliminary hearings." Performance is the critical measure of a developer's integrity.

Working from a basis of trust rather than hostility greatly aids developers when they seek approval for a project. Involving public officials early in the planning process gives them a certain sense of authorship in the proposal. Potential problems are more easily identified.

Almost always when dissension arises between planners and developers it is because each fails to appreciate the other's viewpoint. Council member Richard Reese says, "Public agencies must realize they are also developers with an entrepreneurial role to play in development." Council member Gary Ryan adds:

Disputes between public planners and private developers most often arise from planners' naivete concerning the social responsibility of the developer and concerning the willingness or ability of the consumer to pay for aesthetic or nonessential amenities. Conversely, developers may resist innovation when it deviates from the formula they had previously applied successfully, regardless of a changing market or physical conditions.

Before proceeding with a development plan, developers should analyze public interest; that is, developers should evaluate their proposals in light of the community's comprehensive plan and applicable ordinances. If developers find that their proposals do not fit in, then they should drop or modify them, for in the end it will save all parties a good deal of time and money. But if they find that the comprehensive plan and ordinances do not respect a community's present and future general welfare and must be amended to be responsive, then they should indicate the necessary changes and if necessary offer assistance in preparing the revised documents.

As mentioned earlier, it is advantageous for developers to establish contact with a public agency at a project's conceptual stages. A project's feasibility and acceptance can be discussed openly before substantial amounts of time and money are committed. Problems that might result from redesign can often be avoided through early and continuous contact. Before assuming financial commitments, developers can go informally to the planning agency when they need an indication of its receptiveness to the proposal. "Honesty is the best policy," explains council member William Rick. "Playing games with the planning staff can be the most expensive part of the process. It is often a great savings of time to request conceptual approval in broad terms before going into detailed planning."

A local community's political climate can change over time. A practice once accepted can become unacceptable, and developers caught in the middle may find that a project under way cannot be completed. Written agreements and statements of intent that address major issues can prove extremely beneficial to developers. They are the best and perhaps the only assurance that the community will follow through in good faith, but they are not always easy to get. Following California's lead in 1976, several states have provided enabling legislation authorizing local governments to enter into binding development agreements.[90] Although originally intended to better establish a developer's vested rights, development agreements have proven beneficial to both the public and private sectors by offering a forum for negotiating large-scale and long-term development projects.[91]

After meeting initially with local planners and after developing preliminary concepts, developers should plan meetings with local interest groups as a good way to get the community's advance reaction to a project. People seem to fear most what they do not understand, and they oppose most what they fear. It is essential not to overwhelm local citizens, however, in an effort to get them involved. Their concerns must be heard, and they must believe that the developer is hearing them. A developer's worst enemy is a rampant neighborhood rumor. Real estate councils, community groups, the local League of Women Voters, the school board, and various environmental groups all have sound opinions and good advice that developers should solicit and heed.[92]

All indications are that negotiation will become even more difficult in the future, because a greater number of agencies with many more requirements will be involved. Private and public awareness of the rights of consumers will make the process more lengthy. Successful residential developers will need to master the art of negotiation, but they will also need to establish a positive public image through actions, and not just words.[93]

Litigation

In residential development cases as in other land use cases, litigation generally results when a private property owner challenges the validity of a local or state government regulation because the owner's property rights have been infringed upon. Other types of litigation may occur during the course of development because of breaches of contractual relationships between the lender and the developer or between the developer and a contractor. (These types of litigation raise issues of contract law rather than land use law and are addressed only briefly in this section.)

Land use cases are usually litigated in state courts rather than federal courts. Conflicts over impact fees, zoning, moratoriums on growth, and other issues of growth control generally arise out of local or state laws rather than federal law and thus come under the jurisdiction of state courts. Cases involving a potential infringement of constitutional rights, however, such as violations of the takings, due process, and equal protection clauses of the Constitution or violations of the protections in the Civil Rights Act, raise federal issues that may be tried in federal court. Any conflicts arising over federal wetlands or other environmental laws may also be brought in federal court.

Most states have their own statutes and constitutions with provisions that parallel federal ones, and thus many claims can be brought in either federal or state courts. Often, when land use regulations are involved, developers must exhaust all administrative remedies

90 California Government Code, Sec. 65864 et seq.

91 For additional information, see Douglas R. Porter and Lindell L. Marsh, eds., *Development Agreements: Practices, Policy, and Prospects* (Washington, D.C.: ULI–the Urban Land Institute, 1989).

92 See Douglas R. Porter, Patrick L. Phillips, and Colleen Grogan Moore, *Working with the Community: A Developer's Guide* (Washington, D.C.: ULI–the Urban Land Institute, 1985).

93 For additional discussion of the project approval and negotiation process, see Albert Solnit, *Project Approval: A Developer's Guide to Successful Local Government Review* (Belmont, Cal.: Wadsworth Publishing Co., 1983).

before they can seek trial through the court system. Thus, only after they have attempted unsuccessfully to resolve the problem through local or state hearings and appeals can developers turn to the courts.

Traditionally, the courts have presumed that zoning and other land use regulations are valid as a constitutionally permitted exercise of the police power, unless they are shown to be clearly in violation of the constitutional rights of the landowners regulated. In recent years, however, the courts have been increasingly sympathetic to the perspectives of landowners, resulting in less latitude for municipalities to regulate land use as they desire. Basically, if the right to be protected falls under the category of "civil liberties," then any restriction of these activities by the government will be justified only by a strong demonstration of governmental purpose in upholding the regulation.[94] In fact, some would argue that all zoning decisions must further the public welfare rather than hinder it. The change in judicial attitudes toward land use restrictions, away from the absolute immunity and broad discretion previously accorded to local governments, has increased the risk of liability for governmental entities.

Increased Litigation

Recent years have seen an increase in litigious challenges to municipalities by developers as a result of the increasing popularity of growth management controls that prevent developers from the anticipated uses of their properties, decrease land values because of downzoning, or delay the development of sites because of phasing requirements imposed by a growth management plan, sometimes by means of moratoriums. The increased necessity to litigate, not only to prevent unconstitutional takings but also to challenge unfair development fees and regulatory practices, has caused a greater burden on developers in terms of costs. While large developers certainly feel the costs, they do not feel them as keenly as small developers. It can easily become so expensive to litigate to preserve development interests that smaller developers are seriously hampered. Litigation is a no-win situation for all developers: attorneys' fees are high, and the courts will award attorneys' fees to the winning party only if the case was based on a civil rights claim, a violation of due process, or an exercise of bad faith by the government.[95]

To avoid litigation, developers and city officials have begun to rely much more heavily on negotiations to prevent future conflicts, especially in the area of impact fees. Developers make concessions or dedications based on the requests made by elected officials

or citizens' groups. Negotiations are also possible at the state level, in the area of impact fees, proffers, and offers of contributions that go on behind the scenes. Although costly, negotiations have become a vehicle for both government and developers to avoid even more costly litigation.

Developers can also avoid litigation by working closely with citizens' or environmental groups, which are often the plaintiffs bringing suit against developers. If such groups are brought into the planning process early and back the proposed project, then developers are less likely to meet opposition from city officials and more likely to avoid litigation.

Fifth Amendment Taking

As mentioned, a major source of litigation for developers is the issue of a "taking," which is invoked under the Fifth Amendment's protection against the taking of private property without just compensation. The Fifth Amendment is applicable to the states under the Fourteenth Amendment, which, among other things, grants landowners "due process" protection. During the first several decades when zoning was put in place, local governments had wide discretion on how they chose to regulate the use of land. But more recently, the Supreme Court has imposed constitutional limits on how far a regulation can go before it becomes a taking. A "regulatory taking" is the excessive restriction of land use—often through the implementation of land use planning or zoning or building codes. A taking occurs when the government avoids bringing a condemnation action in court, as it would in a case involving eminent domain; the regulations can become a way for the government to avoid compensating people for the loss of the use of their property.

Cases involving a taking can be brought as a "facial" challenge (a direct challenge to the law) against the restrictive laws themselves or as an "as-applied" claim against the way the laws have been implemented to affect certain properties. The landowner may claim a remedy of either equity or damages. A remedy of equity means that the court orders the city to take some action to compensate the owner, like rezoning, rather than order that the landowner be paid damages for the loss of the use of the property. An equity action also may result in a city's being ordered

---

[94] Norman Williams, Jr., *American Planning Law: Land Use and the Police Power*, vol. 1 (Chicago: Callaghan & Co., 1974), p. 91.

[95] Telephone conversation with Bill Ethier, litigation counsel, National Association of Home Builders, Washington, D.C., June 13, 1989.

to permit the landowner to continue to use the land as originally permitted.

An action for damages, if successful, results in the government's paying the landowner whatever is determined to be the fair value of the rights to use the land that were lost as a result of a regulatory taking. Rights that have been determined to be compensable if they are restricted or lost include zoning rights, easements, access, lost profits, air rights, and other development rights.

In some cases, claims for inverse condemnation, or taking, are made in conjunction with claims of violation of Section 1983 of the Civil Rights Act. This provision gives relief for anyone who suffers the deprivation of "any rights, privileges, or immunities secured by the Constitution and laws. . . ."[96] Combining these claims has some advantages: the government can have no "good faith" or "qualified immunity" for claims under the Civil Rights Act, and the landowner can be awarded attorneys' fees if he wins.[97]

Two precedent-setting taking cases were handed down in the latter part of the 1980s that resulted in greater liability for local governments in regulatory taking cases. The first case, *First English Evangelical Lutheran Church of Glendale* v. *County of Los Angeles,*[98] established that landowners can receive monetary damages when land use regulations are determined to be a taking, even when the taking is temporary. The second, *Nollan* v. *California Coastal Commission,*[99] established that conditions attached to building permits must substantially advance a valid government purpose. *Nollan* weakens the presumption that the government can regulate land use with minimal justification. If a valid governmental purpose must "substantially" be advanced, then the government has a greater burden to justify its regulations to the courts, and landowners are more likely to win in challenges involving takings. In response to these cases, local governments have revised their procedures to show a close connection between the government's purpose and the conditions or procedures imposed.

Exclusionary Zoning

Another major source of litigation affecting residential developers involves claims of exclusionary zoning. In these cases, a developer challenges a municipal ordinance because it has excluded the potential for a specific type of development in that community—multifamily housing or mobile homes, for example—through refusing to zone land for that use. Typical exclusionary restrictions in suburban com-

munities include minimum requirements for size of houses and excessive street frontage.

If zoning totally excludes a type of development, the municipality must be able to demonstrate that the zoning serves the community's general welfare. Even some zoning regulations that serve the general welfare have been found to be exclusionary, however, because they are found to be mainly cost related, for example, to avoid the municipal expense of providing infrastructure for higher-density development. Controls on residential densities through large-lot zoning and restrictions on minimum house size are typical in many communities and may be found excessive, although the regulations serve a legitimate purpose in zoning.[100]

The courts have also invalidated zoning ordinances on a much broader basis, deciding that ordinances have excluded low- and moderate-income groups and racial minorities. Such cases, brought in federal courts, have concentrated on racially based exclusions that have been challenged as violations of the equal protection clause of the Constitution or the federal Fair Housing Act. In state courts, exclusionary zoning has been invalidated primarily because it excluded low- and moderate-income groups. The bases for these decisions have often been the violation of the due process and equal protection limitations of state constitutions and violations of provisions in state zoning acts.[101] Cases based on exclusionary zoning have been brought by developers as well as third parties, such as housing organizations and nonresidents of a community. Some courts have granted standing, or a right to sue, to these third parties, while others have not.

Environmental Issues

Environmental issues are a growing concern for developers, having become a major source of litigation because of federal, state, and local regulatory frameworks that restrict the use of land for development. The federal wetlands programs have become very controversial and have been subject to many congressional hearings. Increases in litigation probably will continue as a result of changes in these programs. Regulations covering hazardous wastes and the Superfund

---

[96] John W. Shonkwiler and Terry D. Morgan, *Land Use Litigation* (St. Paul, Minn.: West Publishing Co., 1986), p. 33.

[97] Telephone conversation with Bill Ethier, litigation counsel, National Association of Home Builders, Washington, D.C., June 13, 1989.

[98] 107 S.Ct. 2378 (1987).

[99] 107 S.Ct. 3141 (1987).

[100] See Mandelker, *Land Use Law,* Chapter 5.

[101] Ibid., Chapter 7.

The most famous of the exclusionary zoning cases is the 1975 case called *Southern Burlington County NAACP* v. *Township of Mt. Laurel.*[1] In this case, the New Jersey Supreme Court invalidated an entire zoning ordinance as excluding lower-income residents from the community by preventing the development of low-cost housing, which eventually spawned the development of a totally new statewide policy to monitor the zoning processes of all growing New Jersey communities. In *Mt. Laurel*, the court took a much more active role in evaluating the appropriateness of local zoning ordinances, determining that the zoning ordinance was invalid because it violated citizens' rights to equal protection under the law and violated their rights to due process. The most significant aspect of the decision was that the New Jersey Supreme Court concluded that municipalities must meet their "fair share of the present and prospective regional need" for low- and moderate-income housing. It held that a municipality could not refuse to provide sufficient zoning to meet its regional fair share simply because it did not want to shoulder the fiscal burden of providing necessary public services.

A second case was brought in 1983, after the township of Mt. Laurel had zoned only 20 acres out of 22.4 square miles for higher-density housing. In this case, called *Mt. Laurel II*, the New Jersey Supreme Court held that the obligation to provide the regional fair share applied to all municipalities designated in a 1980 state development guide plan as growth areas.[2] In *Mount Laurel II,* the court required affirmative governmental actions to meet the obligation of fair share. Municipalities could choose options that include the use of housing subsidies and tax abatements to meet their fair share.

More than 125 lawsuits were brought in response to *Mt. Laurel II.* Settlements reached in those cases required many municipalities to stimulate heavy growth because the courts required inclusionary development with, typically, 20 percent of all new units to be set aside for low- and moderate-income units. The state legislature also was pressured to step in; the Fair Housing Act was passed in 1985, the State Planning Act in 1986. The Fair Housing Act established the state Council on Affordable Housing (COAH) to determine housing regions and adopt criteria and guidelines for determinations of fair share, and provided municipalities with the opportunity to be certified by COAH that their housing elements responded to regional housing requirements, thus limiting their liability.[3] *Mt. Laurel* has significant influence throughout the United States, because it has exemplified the idea that the courts have the right to take an affirmative role in requiring that municipalities supply a sufficient amount of land for the development of low- and moderate-income housing to meet regional needs. Thus far, however, few other state courts have been so specific, and generally other states have not been quick to follow suit.

[1]336 A.2d 713 (N.J.), *appeal dismissed and cert. denied,* 423 U.S. 808 (1975).
[2]456 A.2d 390 (N.J. 1983).
[3]Daniel R. Mandelker, *Land Use Law,* 2d ed. (Charlottesville, Va.: The Michie Company, 1988), p. 296.

also stimulate litigation to determine who is liable for cleanup, as parallel liability for cleanup can exist under state law. If owners can prove they were innocent purchasers, then they may not be liable for cleanup, but that determination is made by the courts.

Because of the high costs associated with liability for hazardous waste, the large mortgage institutions have made a major effort to develop clear standards for "due diligence" or certain actions that developers can take to avoid liability. The language in the statutes covering Superfund is not clear, which means that the courts will resolve the ambiguities through litigation, creating different standards and confusion among developers on what actions they can take to avoid liability for cleanup.

Other Issues
Financing and contracts are also sources of litigation for residential developers, but they are generally related to individual differences rather than to nationwide trends. In development of subdivisions, litigation arises from a lender's liability, breaches of loan commitments by borrowers, conflicts between joint ventures and lenders, antitrust problems, and contractors' liability. Tax issues also produce specialized litigation that can be both costly and crucial to the success of a development. Developers can minimize the potential for major disputes over contracts or conflicts with lenders by using carefully drafted contracts and mortgages that are prepared by attorneys specializing in real estate contract work.

3.
Financing

This chapter was provided by Kenneth Leventhal & Company, Los Angeles, California.

More than $100 billion is invested each year in the development of single-family houses, townhouses, apartments, condominiums, and other residential housing in the United States. Private residential construction is one of the largest industries in the United States, accounting for about 5 percent of the Gross National Product. Unlike many of the nation's industries, which are dominated by a few giant companies, the U.S. residential development industry is fractionated and geographically localized. The 10 largest residential developers in the United States account for less than 5 percent of single-family and multifamily housing starts in the country. Most builders produce fewer than 100 dwelling units a year.

For small builders, arranging project financing can be a relatively simple exercise, a matter of investing their own capital, raising some equity from friends, relatives, or business associates, and obtaining construction financing from local lenders. Residential builders, however, increasingly are involved not just in building houses but in the full development cycle—acquiring raw land, planning and developing projects, obtaining entitlements to use, and arranging financing for buyers. They also are building larger and more complex projects to boost housing production and sales and to realize economies and efficiencies of scale. Along with their projects, their requirements for capital have grown, exceeding the resources of local investors and lenders. To raise the capital they

need, larger developers have financed their projects through large commercial banks and thrift institutions, credit company subsidiaries of diversified corporations, insurance companies, syndicators, pension funds, and other investors or lenders. With the help of their investment bankers, some developers have gone directly to the capital markets for funds, raising capital through the sale of mortgage-backed securities, for example.

Whatever the size of their projects and their capital needs, developers share common objectives for financing: to raise the maximum amount of funds at the lowest possible cost and to share as much of the risk as they can with their financial backers. For their part, investors and lenders seek the highest possible returns at the least risk.

In the past, thrift institutions have been the principal source of financing for residential development. Many thrifts, however, have curtailed or stopped financing development because of rules issued in 1989 by the Office of Thrift Supervision that impose more stringent capital standards and more restrictive investment regulations on thrift institutions. Some banks have trimmed or halted development financing to increase their capital reserves. As a result, residential developers are seeking new sources of financing for the long term.

The degree of risk that investors and lenders perceive in a project determines to a considerable extent whether the developer will obtain financing and the cost of that financing. Investors and lenders want a return commensurate with the risk—the greater the perceived risk, the greater the cost of financing.

The difficulty is in determining how much risk exists, for a developer's perceptions may differ from those of investors or lenders. But the failure of developer, investor, or lender to realistically assess the risk could have undesired consequences. An overly optimistic developer might persuade a lender to finance a project that never should have been built. An overly cautious investor or lender might refuse to finance—or demand an excessively high rate of return for—a project that should be built, thereby passing up an opportunity for profit and perhaps killing the project with high fixed costs that eliminate any potential profit.

One of the biggest risks is an external risk that an individual builder cannot control: an increase in interest rates. Because the residential development industry is so highly leveraged, rising interest rates can significantly increase the costs of building a project and holding it for sale or rental. And because homebuyers typically finance most of the cost of a house, rising interest rates significantly affect the affordability of housing and reduce the number of buyers in the market. Further, changes in interest rates could adversely affect sales or rentals of the completed houses or apartments, making them slower than expected.

Large, successful builders can usually command better loan terms, because lenders perceive that financing their projects involves less risk. Such builders have demonstrated the ability to control costs and to market effectively the for-sale or rental housing built; they also have the financial capability and commitment to carry the inventory until it can be sold or rented—even at a loss to the developer.

This chapter provides an overview of the residential financing process, examining the types of financing available for residential development projects, financing at each stage of development, from land acquisition to permanent financing, structures of ownership and how they affect financing, sources of financing, and analysis of financial feasibility. Its purpose is to help developers understand the process and use that knowledge in obtaining financing for their developments.

General Types of Financing

Land developers install roads and utilities and prepare land for construction, then sell the land to build-

3-1   Renaissance Park, a 170-unit stacked townhouse community in downtown Phoenix, was made possible through incentives provided by the city, including a writedown of the land cost from $600,000 to $100,000 and a zero-interest construction loan. The land writedown reduced costs by $15,000 to $20,000 per unit. The project was financed with $2 million in equity and a revolving, zero-interest credit line. *For more information,* see *Project Reference File:* "Renaissance Park," vol. 17, no. 8 (Washington, D.C.: ULI–the Urban Land Institute, April–June 1987).

ers who actually construct the housing. Frequently, however, developers organize and manage the entire development process: assembling the land, obtaining entitlements or approvals to build, developing the site, and building and marketing the final product. It is in this sense that the word "developer" is used in this chapter. While the developer might be an individual, a partnership, or a corporation, in this chapter, "developers" are considered individuals.

Equity Capital

To acquire land and build on it, developers require capital: equity capital or debt capital or both. Equity capital is money invested in a development for a share or all of the development's future profits that bears the first risk of any loss. The equity is represented by an ownership interest in all proceeds to be received from development greater than all mortgages and other claims against the property.

Debt Capital

Debt capital is money loaned to a developer to acquire or develop land and buildings. It is money on which specific interest is paid and that has a claim on the assets of the developer and the development superior to the claim of the equity capital. The developer's obligation to pay the debt is evidenced by a mortgage—an instrument that pledges real estate as security for an obligation. In some states, the mortgage instrument is called by other names (such as a trust deed), but its function is the same—to pledge real estate as security.

Debt financing can be recourse or nonrecourse. Recourse generally means the lender has the right to call on the developer to pay the loan out of personal assets; that is, the developer is personally liable for the loan. Nonrecourse means that in the event of the developer's default, the lender can find remedy only in foreclosing the mortgage and acquiring the property, collateralizing the loan. The developer is not personally liable.

Real estate development is a highly leveraged business. In general, developers believe that the more money they can borrow to finance a development, the greater their return on equity invested in a project. This statement is true, however, only if the project's cost of money (interest, points, and other considerations) is less than the return on the equity plus debt invested in the project. For example: Assume that a developer invests $500,000 of his own money and $500,000 of borrowed money in a one-year project. The annual interest charged on the borrowed capital is 10 percent, or $50,000. The project's return—the difference between its revenues and its costs and expenses—is $150,000, equal to a 15 percent return on the $1 million invested. After the 10 percent cost of the borrowed capital is deducted, the project's net return to the developer is $100,000. The developer's return on the $500,000 investment is thus 20 percent. The example in Figure 3-2 illustrates positive or upside leverage.

Leverage works both ways. Negative or downside leverage results when the cost of borrowed money exceeds the return on the equity and debt financing on the project. Assume that in the previous example the project's gross profit is $25,000 (see Figure 3-3). Interest on the borrowed capital is the same—10 percent, or $50,000. After the cost of the borrowed capital is deducted, the project's net loss is $25,000, the developer's loss $25,000.

Developers must carefully consider how much debt their projects can support. The greater the debt in relation to equity, the greater a developer's potential return on the investment—but also the risk that a project might not generate a return sufficient to cover the cost of the money.

Hybrid Financing

Joint venture arrangements involving the developer, the land seller, the lender, and the investors are com-

---

3-2 EXAMPLE OF POSITIVE LEVERAGE IN FINANCING A DEVELOPMENT PROJECT

Developer's Equity	$ 500,000	
Loan	500,000	(at 10% interest)
Total Investment	$1,000,000	
Gross Profit	$ 150,000	(15% return on $1 million investment)
Interest Expense	−50,000	
Net Profit	$ 100,000	(10% return on $1 million investment)
Developer's Return	$ 100,000	(20% return on $500,000 investment)
	$ 500,000	

3-3 EXAMPLE OF NEGATIVE LEVERAGE IN FINANCING A DEVELOPMENT PROJECT

Developer's Equity	$ 500,000	
Loan	500,000	
Total Investment	$1,000,000	
Gross Profit	$ 25,000	(2.5% return on $1 million investment)
Interest Expense	−50,000	
Net Loss	($ 25,000)	(−2.5% return on $1 million investment)
Developer's Loss	($ 25,000)	(−5% on $500,000 investment)
	$ 500,000	

mon in development projects. Occasionally, however, lenders prefer to structure these or similar arrangements as equity participation mortgages or convertible mortgages that have the characteristics of a combination of equity and debt. The equity participation mortgage is a debt instrument that provides the lender with a share of a development's gross profit, net profit, or cash flow in addition to a fixed-rate return. The benefit to the lender is that it receives a guaranteed minimum return plus a participation that provides a hedge against inflation and a yield potentially higher than normal if the project achieves or exceeds expectations. The benefit to the developer is the availability of financing at below-market fixed rates or a higher-than-normal amount of financing.

The convertible mortgage combines the elements of the conventional mortgage with equity ownership. Convertible mortgages are structured in various ways, but they essentially are long-term, fixed-rate mortgages with an equity "kicker" that gives the lender the option to convert the mortgage at some point during the life of the loan into a predetermined equity interest in the development project.

Bond Financing

Tax-exempt bonds issued by state or local governments and sold to investors have helped to finance housing development, directly or indirectly. Income from such bonds is free from federal income taxes; consequently, the bonds can be marketed at interest rates lower than those on conventional financing. Usually the issuer seeks a rating from one of the rating agencies to pay the lowest possible interest. To do so, the issuer may use some form of credit enhancement. For example, the bond issue could be secured by a letter of credit or by bond insurance. A letter of credit gives the bonds the same rating as the bank issuing the letter of credit.

The Tax Reform Act of 1986, however, restricts the range of private uses eligible for tax-exempt funding and reduces the annual volume of bonds that may be issued for the remaining permitted uses. Most bonds issued for private purposes, including bonds for ownership and rental housing, are subject to uniform state-by-state volume ceilings equal to the greater of $50 per resident or $150 million.

Entity Financing

The reduced amount of funds available from thrifts and banks to finance residential development has led to an increased use of "entity financing" (sometimes called "presale transactions"), in which a developer and investors enter into an agreement to form and capitalize an entity. The entity is a partnership or, less commonly, a Subchapter S corporation. The developer either sells or contributes projects to the partnership; the projects may be either under development or completed. In return, the developer receives a specified interest (usually a majority interest) in the partnership. The developer serves as the general or managing partner and, through a management company, manages the partnership's assets for a fee.

The investors are the primary sources of the partnership's capital; they may include pension funds, insurance companies, foreign investors, investment bankers, and other sources of long-term financing. The investors contribute equity or debt capital (or a combination of both) and have the option of making additional contributions under specified terms and conditions. The capital is used to finance the partnership's purchase of projects from the developer (in the case of a sale of the projects) and to help finance the partnership's future projects. How much capital the investors contribute and in what form and their return on the investment are negotiable.

The partnership typically has a life of seven to 10 years. It develops, holds, and manages projects for their long-term cash flow and appreciation, although some projects may be sold as soon as they are completed. At the end of the partnership's term, the partnership is terminated, its assets sold, and the proceeds distributed to the partners. In some cases, however, the developers and investors may extend the existing partnership agreement or enter into a new agreement.

Developers benefit from entity financing in several ways:

- *They have a ready source of capital for financing not one or a few projects, but a series of projects.* Developers usually must have the approval of their financial partners to develop each project in the series, but they do not have to go into the market for financing and to negotiate financing terms every time they develop a project.
- *Capital is available from a single source or a limited number of sources.* As developers grow and expand their activities, their need for capital sometimes exceeds the resources of a single lender. Further, thrift institutions are restricted in making loans to a single borrower, such as a developer. Thus, developers may have to seek financing from an increasing number of sources, and dealing with multiple lenders increases the complexities and difficulties of financing.

Through entity financing, however, developers usually can obtain capital from a single source or a limited number of sources with sufficient capital to finance a number of projects, including large-scale projects, and financing is simplified.

- *Developers are better positioned to take advantage of opportunities for development.* In rapidly growing markets, development regulations have severely limited the supply of land that can be developed. Developers backed by entity financing are best positioned to take advantage of opportunities to acquire land and to begin development when the opportunity occurs. They have a ready source of cash for acquiring land, which can give them a competitive edge over developers or investors that must arrange financing. They are also better positioned to obtain construction loans on more favorable terms. In short, they are able to develop more projects more quickly.
- *Developers have more flexibility in their use of capital.* Developers may be able to use capital raised from entity financing not only to develop residential projects but also to cover certain overhead expenses, to add to working capital, and to apply to other purposes.
- *Developers have access to "patient money."* Increasingly, many lenders are unwilling to take on the risks of financing projects that may take years to complete or that could be delayed because of regulatory problems or other roadblocks. With entity financing, residential developers have access to investors that are willing to finance long-term developments.

Financing at Each Stage of Development

Developers begin the development process with land that they want to acquire and a plan for developing it. The plan may be in the developer's head or on the back of the proverbial envelope. It may have gone as far as sketches of the completed development. But the plan, however crude or refined, will remain only a plan unless the developer can get capital to purchase and develop the land. For starters, capital is necessary to cover the costs of acquiring the land and developing the site. Obtaining capital to finance these front-end costs can be difficult because they are incurred before development is completed and the project is generating income to repay the borrowed capital.

Land Acquisition

A developer can finance the acquisition of land for development in various ways, the most common of which are discussed in the following paragraphs. Generally, lenders make such loans only to their strongest and best customers and only if developers have entitlements to develop the land and they can repay the loans from sources other than sale or development of the land.

Optioning the Land

It can be risky for developers to contract to buy land for development before obtaining the necessary government approvals (entitlements), securing long-term financing, and completing project feasibility studies. Instead, they can option the land, that is, have the right to buy it for a specified price within a specified time. Developers usually pay the landowner a small cash payment for the option and may pay taxes, mortgage interest payments, and other costs of carrying the property during the option period. They may agree to give the owner a share in the property's cash flow and appreciation should they acquire and develop the property. Owners can defer paying taxes on their proceeds from sale of the option until the option expires or the developer exercises it.

With an option, developers can control substantial tracts of land with relatively little cash. They can use the option as a hedge against not being able to assemble all of the land they want or obtaining the necessary government approvals. If they fall short of the goal, they can let the option expire. Developers can develop contiguous land parcels incrementally through the so-called rolling option, which covers a number of tracts. The developer buys and develops the initial tract and, if the development is successful, exercises the option to buy the next tract, and so on.

With an option, developers buy time. Before deciding whether or not to buy the land, they have time to effect any necessary rezoning, to determine whether the land has any environmental problems, and to secure a commitment from a lender or investor to finance development. At the end of the option period, they give up the option or negotiate its renewal. Or they exercise the option and buy the land, in which case some or all of the price paid for the option may be applied toward the purchase price (if the contract provides for it). The price paid for the land may be contingent on the density of development permitted. For example, the land may bring a higher price if the developer succeeds in persuading government authorities to approve rezoning of the land to permit an increase in the density from two houses per acre to four houses per acre.

Financing by the Seller

The seller could help to finance the developer's acquisition of land by taking a purchase money mortgage from the developer in lieu of cash. Typically, a mortgage covers a substantial part of the purchase price, with the developer and perhaps other equity investors in the property paying the balance in cash. How much cash the developer is required to put down depends on the seller's circumstances and sophistication, local customs, and demand for the land, but the amount of the downpayment usually ranges from 10 percent to 30 percent of the purchase price. Income tax and accounting rules sometimes govern the amount of downpayment the seller requires.

Historically, one incentive for the seller to agree to finance the sale was that the gain from the sale could be reported in installments. Generally, gain on a taxable disposition of property is reportable for income tax purposes in the year the real estate is sold. The tax can be burdensome to the seller, particularly if the seller has accepted a mortgage or other obligation from the purchaser and has not yet collected any cash. If the seller properly constructed the sale as an installment transaction, however, the gain could be reported over the period during which the installment note was collected, depending on the downpayment received, the amount of the liabilities assumed by the buyer, and the level of the seller's liabilities. The benefit of deferring the recognition of income was not allowed in the computation of alternative minimum tax, however.

Whether a seller agrees to finance a sale through a purchase money mortgage may be determined partly by the ability to structure the sale like an installment transaction under current tax law. As a result of the Revenue Act of 1987, the installment method is no longer available to *dealers* in real property, but *sellers* of real property who are not dealers can still use the installment method. If the seller has more than $5 million in installments receivable outstanding at the end of the year, however, interest must be paid on the tax that is deferred through use of the installment method. Consequently, the availability of financing by the seller may depend on whether the seller is a dealer in real property or, if not a dealer, on the magnitude of the outstanding installment receivables.

Leasing the Land

The annual rental in a land lease is generally based on a percentage of the land's market value. As the land is developed and individual houses, apartment buildings, or other dwellings are sold, the seller is generally paid for the land from the proceeds of sales. Alternatively, the buyers and the original land seller or developer enter into a substitute (or "sandwich") lease; the balance of the land remains under lease until successive tracts are released from it.

Land Acquisition Loan

Developers can obtain a land acquisition loan from an institutional lender, but many lenders will advance no more than two-thirds of the appraised value of the land—and often much less—because land loans are among the riskiest of all real estate loans, with their inherent uncertainty about whether or when the property will generate sufficient income to service the debt. Lenders that do make such loans—commercial banks, savings and loan associations or their service corporations, credit companies, a few real estate investment trusts and mortgage companies, and some life insurance companies if they have the right of first refusal to provide construction and permanent financing for the project—generally require strong financial guarantees and a substantial equity investment by the developer. Residential developers with superior track records, strong balance sheets, and long-standing relationships with potential lenders may be able to draw on a line of credit to finance land acquisitions.

In addition to borrowing money to acquire the land, developers may need to raise equity capital. Depending on the capital needed, they could raise the necessary equity from friends, relatives, or business associates, but if the need is substantial, they might have to go beyond their immediate circle. For example, developers could form a syndication, a device to raise capital from investors for a variety of real estate enterprises. Or they might obtain equity capital from large syndications that some leading brokerage houses and other sponsors have organized to invest in "predevelopment" land. In some cases, the equity raised might help to finance site development and construction as well as land acquisition.

Land Contract

If the landowner is unwilling to take back a purchase money mortgage and a land acquisition loan cannot be obtained from an institutional lender, the developer and owner may enter into a contract for the developer to acquire the land. A land contract is a written agreement to deliver the deed to the land to the buyer, provided certain conditions are fulfilled.

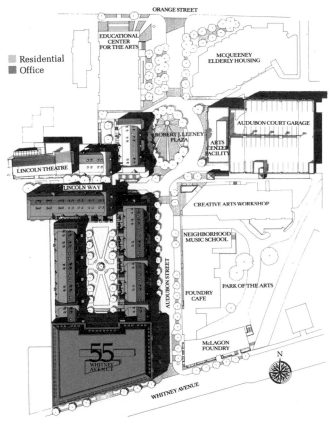

Residential
Office

3-4, 3-5 Audubon Court in New Haven, Connecticut, is a $30 million mixed-use project that includes 61 housing units. The nonprofit Arts Council of Greater New Haven acquired the site from the city redevelopment agency at writedown and leased it to a private developer—a partnership of Lawrence Investing Company, Inc., and the Guyott Company, an established local asphalt company. The Arts Council expects to earn more than $100,000 a year from land rentals plus the proceeds of a 1 percent interest in the project. *For more information, see Project Reference File:* "Audubon Court," vol. 19, no. 1 (Washington, D.C.: ULI–the Urban Land Institute, January–March 1989).

The advantage to developers is that they can control the land for a relatively small downpayment. The advantage to sellers is that they give the developer possession only, retaining title until most or all of the purchase price is paid. If the developer defaults on the installment payments, the seller may declare the contract forfeited and repossess the land. In the absence of state or other laws or regulations, the seller may keep all of the payments made by the developer before the default.

Joint Venture

The developer and the landowner might enter into a joint venture to develop the land. A joint venture is an association of two or more persons, partnerships, or corporations that combine their property, money, skill, and knowledge to carry on a single business enterprise for profit. The joint venture usually is organized as a partnership. The landowner might contribute the land in return for an equity interest equivalent to the agreed-upon value for the land, together with a profit interest in the development. The owner is paid for the land out of initial development proceeds. The developer contributes equity capital and arranges financing for the project.

Thrift institutions provide another potential source of development financing. The Financial Institutions Reform, Recovery, and Enforcement Act of 1989 (FIRREA) and the capital rules issued in 1989 by the federal Office of Thrift Supervision, however, prescribe more stringent capital requirements for thrifts. Many undercapitalized institutions are expected to sell assets and shrink in asset size to meet the new capital rules. In the process, they may sell or otherwise dispose of their investments in development projects and discontinue investing in further development. Consequently, developers could find it more difficult to secure development financing from thrifts.

Small developers might find it advantageous to enter into a joint venture with a large development company to develop a project. With its considerable financial resources, the large company could provide equity capital to acquire land and develop the site. It could provide equity financing in return for a share of the project's profits, and it also might help to arrange financing from an institutional lender. In some cases, small developers might be able to acquire land from a large development company that already has completed site development and obtained the required government approvals for development.

Foreign investors are potential joint venture partners in large-scale residential development projects.

The concept of joint ventures might take some explaining to foreign investors unfamiliar with the concept, however. Additional time will also be required to explain the project to investors and to give them time to consider the project. The time and effort could be well spent, however, for foreign investors could be important sources of investment capital for U.S. developers.

Various other combinations could be used as joint ventures to develop the project. For example, the landowner, the developer, and a financial institution might participate in a joint venture. In some cases, the landowners or financiers prefer to develop the project in their own names and to enter into a management contract with the developer by which the developer receives a fixed fee and a percentage of the profits.

Joint ventures are very flexible financing vehicles, but they can be complex and require careful planning and structuring. The authority and responsibility for controlling and managing the project, terms of equity contributions, distribution of profits and losses, and dissolution of the partnership should be carefully detailed in the partnership agreement.

Large Corporations

Some large corporations are developers of large, master-planned communities, providing ready-to-build parcels for sale to builders. In some instances, it is to the master developer's advantage to finance part of a homebuilder's purchase price of the parcel—for example, by taking a short-term note on a high percentage (70 to 80 percent) of the purchase price. The note usually pays market interest, is secured by an unsubordinated first lien on the parcel, and is repaid when the builder obtains construction financing. More commonly, the developer takes a subordinated note for a smaller percentage of the sale price, which is often the homebuilder's equity portion of the purchase. Such a note generally would have a stated interest rate, be repaid upon sale of the houses, and have additional interest calculated as a percentage of the houses' sale prices.

Land Banks

Some developers and other investors have formed joint ventures to invest in "land banks." The investors acquire raw land, obtain the necessary government entitlements to develop the property, and complete grading of the property and other site development. Then they hold the property until market conditions are right for development.

Land banks could be a source of land for developers planning residential projects, particularly in areas where stringent growth control regulations are in place and land that has the necessary entitlements for development is much in demand. In addition, investors in land banks could be potential partners with a developer in developing a project.

Title X

The U.S. Department of Housing and Urban Development through its Title X program provides insurance for the full amount of loans made by private lenders for the development of primary homes, including conventional subdivisions. Eligibility for such insurance is determined by local Federal Housing Administration (FHA) offices. Compared with conventional financing, Title X usually is less expensive, has a longer amortization period and lower debt service, and permits greater leverage with less personal risk to the developer. Developers have not used the Title X program widely, however. One reason may be that some developers simply do not want to spend the time and effort to qualify for the program and to administer the loan under complex government procedures. As of early 1990, funding for this program had been suspended by HUD, and its future is uncertain.

Land Development

To prepare land for housing construction, developers must grade the land, provide for flood control, arrange for sewer, water, and utility services, and install roads, pipes, and other infrastructure. If they are developing a new subdivision, they may have to put in roads and utilities not only inside the subdivision but also outside it to link it with existing streets and sewer lines. These initial site improvements are very costly—especially to developers of large projects—and often interest charges must be carried for many years. If a project is to be economically viable, developers must seek out the least costly source of money possible to fund up-front site improvements.

Residential developers should also keep in mind that as security for a development and/or construction loan, banks or other lenders require a "first mortgage" on the land being developed. Because the first mortgage is superior to any other mortgage, the seller of the land must subordinate any financing for the land-purchase mortgage to the first mortgage.

Bond Financing

In large-scale developments, municipal bond financing is increasingly used, not only for its tax and marketing advantages but also because such financing may be more accessible in some cases than large-scale financing from banks or other financial institutions. Another advantage of such financing is that developers do not have to increase the price of the finished lots or houses to cover the costs of infrastructure and other facilities. Rather, the costs are passed along to homeowners in higher property taxes or in annual assessment-bond payments. Either case is preferable from a marketing standpoint to increasing housing prices.

Counties, cities, or local government agencies issue municipal bonds for a variety of public purposes, including construction of highways, roads, bridges, sewer systems, parks, playgrounds, and other improvements and infrastructure. Various types of municipal bonds are available. One is the general obligation bond, for which the full faith and credit of the issuing municipality is pledged. Interest income on the bonds is not subject to federal income tax. The bonds are paid from a municipality's property taxes and other revenues.

In some municipalities, issuing general obligation bonds to finance improvements in development projects may be out of the question because of opposition from the local electorate or legal or budgetary constraints on general obligation financing. Increasingly, municipalities are issuing revenue bonds or special assessment bonds to finance such improvements. Such bonds are paid from specific revenues or property assessments and do not pledge the full faith and credit of the municipality. Special assessment bonds usually have a lien on all of the property that is included in an assessment district, and the property owners in the district make annual payments of principal and interest on the bond. The purpose is to have those who directly benefit from the improvements pay for them.

For developers, special assessment districts have several advantages:

- The district can include several property owners who all make payments to support bonds that finance common infrastructure serving all of the properties.
- When the developer sells a land parcel or a house, the new owner makes the annual bond payments, relieving the developer of that obligation.
- Development can be financed at a lower interest cost than with conventional financing because the bonds are tax exempt, so investors are willing to accept a lower return.

A disadvantage of such bonds, however, is that they add to the property taxes of homeowners in special assessment districts, which in turn could dampen housing sales in districts where property taxes and housing costs already are relatively high.

In California, where demand for housing has remained high, projects tend to be large, and the private sector is expected to contribute substantially to onsite and off-site improvements, the state legislature has adopted enabling legislation to permit special assessment bond programs for the development of community facilities. Local governments in California establish a community facilities district under the Mello-Roos Community Facilities Act of 1982. Because the community facilities district has bonding and taxing authority, it can issue bonds to finance public facilities or services. Compared with more traditional assessment districts, Mello-Roos financing can be used to finance a greater variety of public facilities and services. Mello-Roos bonds are repaid by a special tax levied by the community facilities district. The special tax must be approved by two-thirds of the eligible voters in the district. If fewer than 12 registered voters reside in the proposed community facilities district, however, the vote is by the landowners of the proposed district. Thus, developers who plan to develop single-family houses on land they own could vote to establish a community facilities district for such purposes as financing a new elementary school. The bonds to finance the school are repaid from a special tax levied on the owners of the new houses in the development.

Impact Fees

Voters increasingly reject increased property taxes and bond issues to finance public improvements. To compensate for the loss of revenue, municipalities increase development exactions and fees, further adding to private development costs and thus the price of housing.[1]

Local governments have long levied exactions to help finance the costs of public infrastructure and services in development projects. Exactions require a developer, as a condition of governmental approval of a development, to construct and dedicate streets, sidewalks, and other public infrastructure within a subdivision and to donate land for parks and other public uses. Developers also may be required to pay

---

[1] For a detailed discussion of impact fees, see Thomas P. Snyder and Michael A. Stegman with David M. Moreau, *Paying for Growth: Using Development Fees to Finance Infrastructure* (Washington, D.C.: ULI–the Urban Land Institute, 1986).

109

exactions and fees to help finance the costs of constructing new schools to serve a subdivision.

In contrast with exactions, impact fees are levied to help finance off-site improvements and infrastructure, such as a regional wastewater treatment plant or a street that may be miles from the development site. As impact fees spread, developers are trying to ensure that the costs of infrastructure are shared fairly by all those who benefit.

For example, developers say they sometimes must pay impact fees for off-site improvements that benefit not only themselves but also other developers and property owners, who are not required to pay. If they pass along the higher costs in housing prices or apartment rentals, they may find themselves at a competitive disadvantage in marketing houses or apartments. Developers also say that impact fees sometimes are used for general public purposes that, whatever their merits, should be borne by the entire community and not just by developers.

Responding to these problems, Texas in 1987 enacted what may be the first state law to set guidelines for the assessment of impact fees and to limit their use to facilities necessitated by new growth. It requires political subdivisions in Texas to show that the amounts of impact fees are reasonably related to the cost of providing services to a development and that the fees are spent on the projects for which they were raised.

California in 1979 became the first state to enact a law authorizing development agreements, by which developers seek to obligate contractually local governments to perpetuate the rules, regulations, and policies governing a development's land uses, density, design, improvements, and construction standards over the life of the agreement, which typically runs from 10 to 20 years. A few other states permit development agreements, but use of such agreements in those states has been limited.[2]

Construction Financing

Construction of houses, condominium units, or apartments on land that the developer has acquired and prepared for development is financed with a construction loan and the developer's equity. The loan also may cover some or all of the costs of site development.

Construction loans can provide lenders with substantial returns, but the risks can be considerable. One major risk is that the project will not be completed on schedule and within budget. For example, delays in construction could result from labor strikes, shortages of material, inclement weather, the discovery of toxic substances on the property, poor workmanship, or other problems. Another major risk is that the houses or apartments may not sell or rent as rapidly as projected as the result of a recession or poor market analysis by the developer. Meanwhile, interest charges, overhead, inflation in costs and real estate taxes mount, resulting in cost overruns that may require the developer to raise additional equity or go back to the lender to request an increase in the amount of the construction loan. Delays and cost overruns also could result from a developer's poor management or inexperience in developing the type of project being financed. To try to ensure that developers manage their projects efficiently, a lender may require them to give their personal guarantees on construction loans.

Principal sources of construction loans are commercial banks, S&Ls, and mortgage brokers. Lenders that provide permanent mortgage financing may in some instances also provide construction financing. Sources of equity capital for financing construction include the developer's own capital and capital raised from friends, business associates, other developers, and syndicators.

Some large development companies with strong balance sheets and credit ratings may use other forms of financing in addition to construction loans to finance some of the costs of developing projects. For example, a development company might issue "commercial paper"—short-term, unsecured promissory notes. Or a company might draw on a revolving line of credit, by which a lender allows a specified maximum line of credit to a borrower for a limited period of time and for a fee. Usually such forms of financing are less costly than a conventional construction loan, but because they may be unsecured or the value of the collateral may be less than the amount of the financing, the risks to creditors can be greater than for a construction loan secured by the development project.

Usually, the interest rate on a construction loan is 0.25 to 1.5 percentage points more than the prime rate (the interest rate at which commercial banks will lend money to their most creditworthy borrowers) and changes with the prime rate. Developers usually do not pay the interest from their own capital. Instead, the interest is accrued; that is, it is added to the loan balance.

---

[2] For a detailed discussion of development agreements, see Douglas R. Porter and Lindell L. Marsh, eds., *Development Agreements: Practice, Policy, and Prospects* (Washington, D.C.: ULI–the Urban Land Institute, 1989).

Developers sometimes pay a loan fee; if one is paid, it is typically 0.25 to 1 percent of the amount of the loan. Developers do not necessarily pay the fee out of their capital, however. Rather, the lender might deduct the fee from the loan funds advanced to the developer, or the fee might be added to the loan balance.

The construction loan is for a short term, from six months to two years. On an apartment project, it is repaid from the long-term (permanent) mortgage when construction is completed; on a for-sale project, it is repaid from the proceeds of sales. The construction loan is secured by a mortgage that gives the lender a first lien on the land and improvements. The lien is removed from each house when the house is sold and the loan is paid down by a specified amount. If the development/construction loan is used to finance the construction of single-family houses or condominium units, it normally contains a release clause that enables each housing unit to be sold free of the construction lien so that individual homebuyers can obtain permanent financing.

Hedging

A developer of a large project financed with a substantial construction loan may hedge against rising interest rates that could substantially increase his development costs by investing in financial futures contracts (which can be purchased from financial institutions) or other investments that yield a profit when interest rates rise. Any profits from the investment could then be used to offset any increases in the construction loan's interest rate.

Financial futures contracts also can be purchased for other interest rate hedges, including "swaps," "collars," and "corridors." A swap is a contract in which two parties trade individual financing advantages to produce more favorable borrowing terms for both parties. Typically, a party with a floating-rate debt agrees to make fixed interest payments to another party in return for that party's agreeing to make floating-rate payments tied to a specific index.

In a collar contract, developers set minimum and maximum interest rates that they will pay for financing, regardless of whether interest rates drop below the floor rate or exceed the ceiling rate during the term of the contract. For example, the floor rate could be 9 percent and the ceiling rate 12 percent.

A corridor contract is similar to a collar contract, except that developers set a floor rate and *two* ceiling rates. They pay the lower of the two ceiling rates when interest rates exceed the lower rate but do not exceed the higher rate during the term of the contract. If interest rates exceed the higher ceiling rate, however, developers are not protected. For example, the floor rate could be 9 percent and the ceiling rates 12 and 14 percent. If interest rates increase to 13 percent during the term of the contract, the developer pays only 12 percent. If interest rates exceed 14 percent, however, the developer pays the going market rate. Developers might use a corridor contract when they are willing to take the risk that interest rates will not exceed the higher ceiling rate, 14 percent in this example.

The costs of hedging can vary considerably, depending on the risk the developer is willing to assume, the duration of the hedge, current market rates, and the terms of the contract. The shorter the hedging period and the higher the ceiling or cap rate, the less the cost of the contract.

In determining which method of protecting interest rates is best for their situation, developers need to determine how much they can afford to contribute to a project, how long they plan to carry the project, and the effect that an unprofitable project would have on their overall financial picture. They should determine the course that they think interest rates will take over the life of the project and consider the effect of a possible increase in interest rates—including the effect on the project's costs and expenditures. Builders also should consider how much they can afford to pay initially for the cost of protecting the rate. Then they can determine what will fit their financial requirements, including the volume of financing they need to protect, when rate protection should be in place, and how long it should remain in place.

Disbursements

The construction loan is disbursed as construction proceeds; usually amounts are disbursed monthly, with the developer normally charged for interest just on the funds drawn. The lender may hold a percentage of the amount of each disbursement as a reserve against liens filed by subcontractors (who claim not to have been properly paid by the developer) or to ensure completion of improvements by each subcontractor. Typically, the range of the reserve is 5 to 10 percent of each disbursement. Generally, disbursements are made by one of three methods:

- *Vouchers.* The developer submits invoices from subcontractors to the lender for actual work completed to date. The lender then pays the subcontractors.
- *Monthly draw.* This method often is used in large projects requiring substantial loans. The developer requests a draw each month based on work

completed the previous month. If an architect employed by the lender verifies that the work has been completed, the lender disburses the funds to the developer, who pays the subcontractors. This method ensures that the economic value being created by the construction is in place and subject to the lender's lien as funds are disbursed.

- *Stages.* Funds are disbursed as stages of construction are completed. An initial disbursement might be made when the lender verifies the building is under roof, another when the building is plastered, and so on. Like monthly draws, stages verify that the security for the loan increases with the disbursement of funds.

Takeout Commitments

The construction lender may require the developer, as a condition of obtaining construction financing, to secure a written commitment from an acceptable long-term lender to provide permanent financing that "takes out" or pays off the construction loan once the project is constructed. This requirement depends on various factors, such as the type of project being built, prospects for selling or renting the finished housing units, and the developer's track record in building and marketing residential housing.

If, for example, an experienced residential developer builds single-family housing in a market where demand is strong and mortgage credit is readily available to homebuyers, the construction lender may not require a takeout commitment. But if the housing is being built for rental rather than for sale, the lender may well require a commitment for a takeout loan on the whole apartment project.

In another example, the lender might waive the takeout commitment if the developer gives a personal guarantee of repayment backed by his own collateral or that of friends or business associates, or if the developer has obtained a letter of credit from another lender or other third party guaranteeing that it will honor demands for payment by the construction lender. The waiver usually is made only for developers who have successful track records in building the type of project being financed and who have strong balance sheets and credit ratings. Sources of takeout commitments include S&Ls, insurance companies, pension funds, mortgage bankers, and mortgage brokers.

In some cases, construction lenders might provide financing without any assurance that permanent financing will be available when construction is completed, but again it usually is done only for top-rated developers. Or the construction lender itself may provide permanent short-term or long-term financing for the project.

The permanent lender usually charges a nonrefundable fee for making the takeout commitment. If developers fail to meet the completion date or other contingencies in the takeout commitment, they normally forfeit the commitment fee and the permanent lender is not obligated to make the loan. In addition, the permanent lender may retract the commitment for failure to satisfy contingencies, in which case the construction lender may have to finance the project until another permanent lender can be found.

In some cases, a permanent lender may try to renege on honoring the takeout commitment, even if the developer has satisfied all the contingencies to obtain permanent financing. This situation might occur if, for example, interest rates were rising and the lender had committed to financing a project at an interest rate that turns out to be below market at the time the loan is to be made. In seeking takeout commitments, therefore, developers would do well to assess realistically whether the commitment will be honored.

Commitment Fees

Lenders are not uniform in the pricing of commitment fees. The fee may be a function of the interest rate on the commitment or the time period of the commitment or both. For example, a lender may commit $5 million as follows: $2 million at 12 percent and one point, $1.5 million at 11.5 percent and one and one-half points, and $1.5 million at 11 percent and two points. Doing so gives developers some flexibility in marketing their products. For example, if developers build single-family houses at a time when demand is strong and home mortgage interest rates are around 12 percent, they might market some of the houses using the 12 percent money and reserve the 11 and 11.5 percent financing for buyers who could not qualify at the higher interest rate. Alternatively, the commitment might be at a 12 percent ceiling, with $2 million for eight months and one point, $1.5 million for 10 months and one and one-half points, and $1.5 million for 12 months and one point. Thus, developers have some flexibility in maintaining the commitment in case the construction schedule and pace of sales slip.

Interest Rate

The takeout commitment specifies the interest rate at which the permanent lender will provide long-term financing. The interest rate could be either fixed rate or floating rate. Developers could benefit from fixed-rate financing if the rate is less than the market rate for long-term mortgage financing at the time the permanent loan is funded. In the case of a single-family housing development, for example, the permanent lender might agree to provide mortgage loans to the homebuyers at a 10 percent interest rate. If mortgage interest rates are higher than 10 percent at the time the houses go on the market, homebuyers may use the commitment; if rates are lower, they may go to other lenders for financing.

The commitment may provide that the interest rate at which permanent financing is provided cannot exceed a certain level but can decline. In the example of the single-family housing development, the commitment might specify that the mortgage loans will be funded at the lower of 12 percent or the market rate at the time of funding. If the market rate is 13 percent, the loans are funded at 12 percent; if the market rate is less than 12 percent, the loans are funded at the market rate. The commitment would spell out how the market rate is to be determined; for example, the rate might be tied to an average yield of loans for single-family houses auctioned by the Federal Home Loan Mortgage Corporation. Alternatively, the commitment might specify that permanent financing will be provided at the rate that the permanent lender is charging at the time of closing, perhaps the rate it charges for loans for single-family houses to its most creditworthy borrowers.

Banks and S&Ls that provide permanent financing usually prefer that the loans be made at a floating rate of interest. The rate is a stated amount above a specific short-term market interest rate, such as the yield on six- or 12-month Treasury bills or a cost-of-funds index of the Federal Home Loan Bank or Federal Reserve Bank. For example, the floating rate might be 2.75 percent over the yield on six-month Treasury bills, so that at a time when the yield on six-month Treasury bills is 6 percent, the floating rate would be 8.75 percent. The lender adjusts the floating rate periodically, perhaps every six months, or the lender might fix the interest rate for a period of time, say one to two years, and then float the rate. The lender might also set a ceiling on the amount of the floating rate, for example, so that the maximum interest rate on the loan is 12 percent.

As an inducement to developers to take out a floating-rate loan, a lender usually sets the initial interest rate on the loan at 2 to 3 percent less than the prevailing interest rate on fixed-rate loans. For example, if the fixed rate were 10.75 percent, the initial rate on the floating-rate loan might be 8.75 percent. Devel-

opers face the risk, however, that sharply increasing short-term interest rates could result in interest costs of a floating-rate loan substantially greater than those of a fixed-rate loan. By contrast, a floating-rate loan reduces a lender's risk, because the interest rate on the loan normally exceeds the lender's cost of funds. The risk to a lender in making a fixed-rate loan is that its cost of funds will exceed its interest income from the loan at some point during the life of the loan.

Length of Commitment

The length of the takeout commitment can vary, but usually developers try to time the commitment to expire when the last house sells. If the commitment runs out before construction is finished, developers could miss an opportunity to lock in long-term financing at below-market rates unless they can negotiate an extension of the commitment, usually for an additional fee. But if the commitment continues beyond the date that the last house sells, developers could effectively pay more for the commitment than necessary.

Buy-and-Sell Agreements

In some cases, developers intentionally do not close a permanent loan, thereby forfeiting the commitment fee. To do so might be advantageous to the developer if interest rates have declined significantly during the construction period or if the developer can obtain long-term financing from another lender on more favorable terms. To protect against such an event, a permanent lender may require, as a condition of providing the commitment, that the developer, the construction lender, and the permanent lender sign what is known as a buy-and-sell agreement, which provides that the construction loan mortgage be delivered to the permanent lender on the date that construction is completed. In effect, the permanent lender buys the construction loan mortgage from the construction lender. As a result, the construction loan is repaid and the permanent loan closed simultaneously. A buy-and-sell agreement gives the permanent lender greater assurance that the permanent loan will close.

Standby Commitments

Like the takeout commitment, the standby commitment is a permanent lender's written promise to provide long-term financing once construction is completed. The difference is that neither developers nor lenders expect the standby commitment to be converted into a loan. Borrowers obtain the standby commitment with the expectation that during the construction period they will obtain permanent financing on more favorable terms from another lender. If they do not, they use the standby commitment to obtain permanent financing from the lender who made the commitment.

In some instances, lenders may choose not to honor the standby commitment; instead, they may seek to invalidate the commitment for technical violations, such as minor changes in the construction schedule that they did not approve. This situation could happen, for example, when the supply of money is tight and lenders have no readily available funds to meet the commitment. Because of the uncertainty, some banks may not provide construction financing to developers who have only a standby commitment.

Interim Financing

Interim financing—also known as "bridge" or "miniperm" financing or a "bullet loan"—is financing between the expiration of the construction loan and the funding of a permanent loan. It is more commonly used to finance rental apartment projects than single-family or condominium housing projects.

Developers who are unable or unwilling to obtain permanent financing at a given time use interim financing, repaying the construction loan with the interim financing and then making principal and/or interest payments on the interim loan until they secure permanent financing. Lenders that supply takeout commitments may provide interim financing, which generally is for two to five years.

Interim financing might be used when permanent financing is unavailable or too costly, or when a particular market is temporarily oversupplied with apartments and lenders are wary of extending permanent mortgage credit. Interim financing might also be used when apartment rentals and values are increasing and the developer (by waiting a few years) could obtain a larger loan based on the increased value of the apartment project.

Permanent Financing

Permanent financing is a long-term loan, usually seven to 10 or more years and up to 30 or even 40 years. Assuming that the developer has obtained a takeout commitment and the conditions of the commitment have been met, the permanent financing replaces the construction loan as an apartment project nears completion or as houses are sold.

The interest rates that lenders charge on permanent loans are a function of their cost of funds, their expectations as to future rates of interest and inflation, the returns offered on other investments, regulatory limits like state usury laws, and other factors. In the 1960s and 1970s, mortgage interest rates were relatively stable. As inflation worsened in the late 1970s, however, mortgage interest rates climbed, generally peaking in 1981—a year when home mortgage interest rates were more than 15 percent. Recent years have seen a return to lower and more stable interest rates, although real interest rates (after adjustment for inflation) remain high by historical standards.

The permanent financing instrument typically is a first mortgage (or first deed of trust). The mortgage is a pledge of the property under development as security for the loan. When the loan is paid in full, the lender marks the mortgage "satisfied" and returns it to the borrower. Usually the mortgage is secured by a priority lien on the property, which means that if the borrower's default results in foreclosure and sale of the property, proceeds go first to pay off the mortgage loan. Any remaining proceeds go to pay subsequent "inferior" or "junior" liens, such as a second mortgage.

Amortization

The permanent mortgage loan might provide for amortization of the loan. Sometimes the mortgage is fully amortizing, or self-liquidating, and provides for full repayment of the principal and for interest payments on the balance of the principal over the life of the loan, usually in periodic, level payments. In the early part of the loan period, most of each payment goes to meet the interest due; as the loan matures, an increasingly larger amount of each payment goes to reduce principal. Such mortgages commonly are used to finance purchases of houses. According to council member Richard Michaux, amortization of permanent loans for apartment projects is usually more complicated, with more interest loaded up front: "Typically, amortization is based on a 30-year schedule, but payments during the first two to three years are interest only, with a balloon payment due between years seven and 12." The balloon loan is a type of amortization that typically has a three- to 10-year term, regular monthly payments including some amortization of principal, and one large or balloon payment at maturity. The lender may or may not guarantee renewal of such a loan.

Amortization schedules can be tailored in a variety of ways to meet the needs of lenders and borrowers. For example, payments on the loan might be structured so that the amount of each payment is the same over the life of the loan and the payments are scheduled at uniform times, such as the first of every month.

Adjustable-Rate Mortgages

A principal need of lenders is to have alternatives to fixed-rate mortgage financing. During periods of rising interest rates and high inflation, the interest on a fixed-rate mortgage could be less than market rate, and the lender effectively has no interest income after discounting for inflation. As a result, lenders increasingly are reluctant to lend at fixed interest rates for long periods of time. To deal with this problem, the adjustable-rate mortgage (ARM) was created. The interest on an ARM is pegged to an index and moves up or down with the index. The loan term, debt service, principal balance, or a combination may change periodically with changes in the interest rate. Negative amortization is permitted; that is, the unpaid balance of the loan increases if loan payments are insufficient to cover the interest on the loan. The additional interest is added to the balance. Regulators generally set limits on the amount of negative amortization, and they generally require lenders to schedule "catch-up" payments periodically. Such payments are large enough that the regular debt service payment amortizes the current loan balance over the remainder of the loan term at the current interest rate.

During the 1980s, ARMs came into widespread use in the financing of home loans. A number of indexes have been approved for use; the most common are Treasury indexed and cost-of-funds indexed. To determine the interest rate of an ARM, the lender's "spread" (representing its overhead costs and profit margins) is added to the index. Spreads vary, but typically they are two to three percentage points. If the index is 8 percent, for example, and the spread is three percentage points, the interest rate for the ARM is 11 percent.

Regulators have set limits or "caps" on how much and how often the interest rate may increase over the term of the ARM. In doing so, they have tried to strike a balance between protecting borrowers from catastrophic rate increases that could increase defaults on home loans and providing sufficient incentive for lenders to make adjustable-rate loans.

Other Mortgages

Other mortgages are designed to give homebuyers a wide choice of financing options. According to the U.S. Savings and Loan League, from 40 to as many 100 alternative mortgage instruments (other than traditional fixed-rate mortgages) were available to homebuyers in 1988.

The graduated-payment mortgage, for example, provides for monthly payments to increase periodically during the early years of the loan. Its purpose is to assist buyers whose incomes are expected to increase. Graduated-payment mortgages usually are negative amortization loans. They are used during periods of high interest rates to qualify buyers who cannot qualify for fixed-rate loans.

In another variation, the growing equity mortgage, homeowners make higher principal payments than with a conventional mortgage, thereby building up equity and paying off the mortgage more quickly.

Home Mortgage Financing

If developers build single-family houses or condominiums for sale, they may have arranged financing for individual buyers through a takeout commitment from the permanent lender, usually an S&L, savings bank, or commercial bank. Some large development companies with mortgage financing subsidiaries may provide financing directly to buyers. Alternatively, buyers could arrange financing on their own, which they would do if they could obtain financing on more favorable terms than through the developer.

The amount of the mortgage loan is a function of the sale price of the house or condominium. Usually lenders finance 70 to 80 percent of the sale price, so that a 20 to 30 percent downpayment is required. For loans insured by the FHA or guaranteed by the Veterans Administration (VA), lenders finance most or all of the sale price. The VA and FHA set limits on the amount of each mortgage loan that they will insure, however.

During periods of high interest rates, developers may offer so-called "buydown" programs (or "teaser rates") as a means of qualifying borrowers for mortgage loans and selling houses. The developer pays a lender a fee to buy down the interest rate, that is, to charge a below-market interest rate in the initial years of a mortgage loan. The buyer's monthly interest payments are lower at first, step up over the initial three to five years of the loan, and then level off for the remainder of the loan term. For example, the rate might be 8 percent in the initial year of the loan, 9 percent in the second year, and 10 percent for the balance. The buydown enables the buyer to qualify for a larger loan and a higher-priced house than with conventional fixed-rate financing. Some or all of the developer's cost of buying down the loan may be added to the price of the house, or the cost may come out of the developer's profit.

Lenders themselves may structure lower initial payments as an inducement to homebuyers to take out mortgage loans. Interest rates on adjustable-rate mortgages usually are one and one-half to three percentage points less than on fixed-rate mortgages, which is a principal reason that, during periods of high interest rates, up to one-half the houses purchased in the United States are financed with ARMs.

Observers are concerned, however, that some owners of ARM-financed houses face the risk of "payment shock"; that is, they might have to assume substantially higher monthly payments after the initial discount period, especially if interest rates increase. Council member Dale Walker warns: "Liberal use of teaser rates could spell trouble for lending institutions in the future; if interest rates rise substantially, buyers may not be able to honor their mortgage payments over the long term."

Responding to this concern, private mortgage insurers that insure most ARMs have moved to limit the initial discounts on ARMs and to increase the income required to qualify for an ARM. And in 1988, the Federal Home Loan Mortgage Corporation (Freddie Mac) issued guidelines to protect marginally qualified homebuyers from the substantial payment increases during the second year that could result in foreclosure. The guidelines are likely to be followed by the many banks, thrift institutions, and mortgage companies that sell their home mortgage loans to Freddie Mac, because it will not buy loans that do not meet its standards. Lenders say that, under the guidelines, they will qualify buyers for ARMs at the maximum interest rate in the second year of loan payments if the buyers put down less than 20 percent of a house's purchase price. A borrower applying for an ARM with an initial 8.5 percent rate, for example, may have to qualify for the mortgage at 10.5 percent, because many ARMs carry a 2 percent annual interest rate ceiling.

Structures of Ownership

Direct Ownership

Direct ownership is the simplest form of equity participation in development. It usually is limited to small, relatively simple projects whose capital requirements are not great. The usual form of ownership is a tenancy in common, in which real property is owned by two or more entities or persons, such as a husband and wife. In most places, real estate is assumed to be owned tenancy in common unless otherwise specified. Each tenant has an undivided interest in the entire property to the extent of his or her ownership share. For example, four tenants in common with equal interests each own a one-fourth undivided share in the property.

Developers who are direct owners of a project are legally entitled to receive all of the profit and any tax benefits, but they are also personally and solely liable for all liabilities related to the project. In other words, direct ownership gives developers the chance to reap the most benefit from the project, but it also means they have no one with whom to share the risk. The developer alone directs and manages the project, depending on his own expertise and experience and those of employees.

Partnerships

A partnership is an aggregation of two or more persons or entities (such as corporations or other partnerships) to carry on a business for profit and to share profits and losses. Partnerships are a common form of unincorporated business organization, especially in the ownership and development of real estate.

A partnership is general or limited. In a general partnership, all the partners share in the profits and losses of the enterprise and in the management and operation of the partnership's affairs. Each partner is personally liable for all of the debts and obligations of the partnership. Thus, an individual partner's assets can be used to satisfy the partnership's obligations when the partnership's assets are insufficient to meet those obligations. Each partner by its conduct and actions can bind the partnership.

In a limited partnership, a general partner or partners manage the partnership's affairs and can bind the partnership. While the personal liability of the general partners for the partnership's debts and obligations is unlimited, limited partners in contrast are passive investors in the enterprise: they do not manage the partnership's affairs and they cannot bind the partnership. Their liability is limited to the amount of their investment in the enterprise.

Partnerships are free of many of the statutory regulations and taxes that bind corporations, which is why they are often used in real estate transactions. In contrast with a corporation, a partnership generally is exempt from federal income taxes, escaping the double taxation of a regular corporation. A partner is taxed on its share of a partnership's income and can use its share of any of the partnership's losses to offset other income (although the deductibility of such losses is restricted under the Tax Reform Act of 1986).

To qualify as a partnership for tax purposes, a partnership must demonstrate that it is not an associ-

3-6, 3-7 Located on a 26-acre site in Edina, Minnesota, Edinborough is a mixed-use project of 400 low-rise condominiums, 200 units of retirement housing in a high-rise structure, and a 115,000-square-foot office building. Each element of the project had a different developer and was financed separately to satisfy lenders' concerns about their precise financial responsibility. The developers, however, formed a partnership so that each owns portions of the other's projects. For example, the developer of the housing for seniors owns 15 percent of the office project and 24 percent of the low-rise condominium project (shown at right). This arrangement spreads the benefits and risks and ensures that each developer takes a lively interest in the well-being of the whole project. *For more information*, see *Project Reference File:* "Edinborough," vol. 17, no. 17 (Washington, D.C.: ULI–the Urban Land Institute, October–December 1987).

ation taxable as a corporation. Treasury regulations specify that an entity organized as a limited partnership under state law will not be classified as an association taxable as a corporation unless it has more corporate than noncorporate characteristics. Corporate characteristics include centralized management, free transferability of interests, continuity of life, and limited liability. Generally, continuity of life is deemed not to exist if the partnership is subject to a state statute corresponding to the Uniform Limited Partnership Act. According to Treasury regulations, an organization has the corporate characteristic of limited liability if under local law no one in the organization is personally liable for the debts or claims against the organization. The regulations say that a partnership has limited liability only if the general partner does not have substantial assets and serves simply as the limited partner's agent. If either element is absent, the partnership should not have the characteristic of limited liability.

A properly executed partnership agreement clearly spells out the rights and obligations of the partners. For example, the agreement includes provisions by which a partner can exit from a partnership or sell or transfer its interest in the partnership to another investor and defines how profits, losses, and cash flow are to be distributed among the partners.

Corporations

A corporation is a legal entity organized to carry on a profit-making enterprise or for other purposes. Corpo-

rations can be either publicly or privately held. The largest U.S. corporations are publicly held, but most U.S. corporations are privately owned—including most real estate development companies that operate as corporations. Publicly held corporations must register with the Securities and Exchange Commission and comply with federal and state reporting requirements of federal and state securities laws. Shares of publicly held corporations can be sold throughout the United States and may be traded on U.S. stock exchanges. Privately held corporations are exempt from government requirements for registration and reporting, but they are subject to restrictions that do not apply to publicly held corporations. Privately held corporations may not sell their shares across state lines, and the number of their shareholders is limited. The liability of shareholders of a corporation is limited to the amount of their investment in the corporation. Corporations, both publicly and privately held, are subject to federal and state taxation.

Corporations are very flexible financing vehicles. For example, a corporation could issue warrants that give holders the right to purchase a specified number of shares of the corporation within a specified period (which usually is long term, or even perpetual). Warrants can be traded separately, so investors who own warrants have a choice: they can exercise their right to buy the company's shares, or they can sell the warrants without ever exercising the right. Warrants can be issued not only by publicly traded corporations but also by private corporations, including real estate companies, that seek to raise substantial capital.

A drawback to the corporate form of business organization is that corporations are subject to double taxation. A corporation's income is taxable at corporate income tax rates, and income received by its shareholders as dividends is taxable at individual income tax rates. Corporate losses generally cannot be passed on to shareholders to offset their income from other sources.

S Corporations

A corporation may be exempt from federal and certain state income taxes if it and its shareholders elect to do business as an S corporation under Subchapter S of the Internal Revenue Code. The electing corporation is treated for legal purposes as a corporation and has all the advantages of operating as a regular (or C) corporation, including the advantage of limited liability for shareholders. But an S corporation generally is treated for tax purposes much like a partnership in that its income, losses, and credits flow through to its shareholders.

A corporation must meet numerous requirements to operate as an S corporation. An S corporation may have no more than 35 shareholders, none of whom can be nonresident aliens, and it can have only one class of stock. Moreover, the Tax Reform Act of 1986 contains new rules covering any C corporation that converts to an S corporation after December 31, 1986.

An important reason an S corporation could be selected over a partnership as a vehicle for doing business is that an S corporation is treated for legal purposes as a corporation. It therefore has all the advantages of operating as an ordinary corporation, including the all-important advantage of limited liability for shareholders, which is important to developers and real estate investors concerned about their exposure to liability. Concern has heightened in recent years as stricter standards of liability have been applied to real estate development and investment. For example, federal and state laws cast a wide net in assigning liability for hazardous wastes on a property. A property owner's liability for hazardous wastes deposited by former owners may exist even though the landowner may be without fault and may be the victim of previous owners' practices.

An S corporation, in contrast to a partnership, affords liability protection to its shareholders. To get around the problem of liability for general partners, a partnership could be structured as a limited partnership whose general partner is a corporation. If the corporation is a thinly capitalized shell, however, the Internal Revenue Service may tax the partnership the same as a corporation. The use of such a form of partnership organization could be impractical for some real estate developments and investments.

An S corporation, while not as flexible as a partnership, offers the benefit of limited liability while minimizing the tax disadvantages of operating through a corporation. Consequently, S corporations are the investment vehicle of choice for some developers and investors.

Sources of Financing

Thrift Institutions

Savings and loan associations and savings banks—also known as thrift institutions—are among the principal sources of mortgage financing for single-family houses and multifamily housing of up to four families. Only about a third of the states presently charter savings banks, and they are concentrated in the Northeast. All 50 states charter S&Ls.

Savings and loan associations are corporations chartered either by the state where they operate or by the Office of Thrift Supervision (OTS), which in 1989 became the regulatory successor to the Federal Home Loan Bank Board. Associations chartered by the OTS are known as federal associations and have the word "federal" in their corporate names. State institutions are supervised and examined by their respective state authorities and the OTS. Federal institutions are chartered under federal law and are regulated and examined by the OTS. Savings and loan associations and thrifts are required by law to have their savings accounts insured by the Savings Association Insurance Fund (SAIF), which is administered by the Federal Deposit Insurance Corporation (FDIC).

Many savings associations are mutually owned; that is, they are owned by their depositors, who, together with their borrowers, are entitled to vote at annual meetings. In recent years, however, the number of stock institutions owned by their stockholders has increased, resulting from some mutual institutions' converting to stock associations, mainly to raise equity capital.

Most states provide for the organization of mutual associations. In addition, some states and the OTS provide for capital stock associations that are authorized by state charter to issue and sell capital stock to investors.

Thrift institutions accept savings deposits from the public and invest the funds in various types of investments, mainly residential real estate mortgages. Mortgages held by thrift institutions account for more than half of all residential loans outstanding in the United

On August 9, 1989, President Bush signed into law a new bill, the Financial Institutions Reform, Recovery, and Enforcement Act of 1989 (FIRREA), mandating a massive restructuring of federal regulation and insurance of the savings and loan industry. As a result of the new legislation, new agencies have been created and old ones abolished. Now OTS and FHFB, plus SAIF and RTC—not to mention REFCORP—are doing the work that used to be performed by just one regulatory entity: the Federal Home Loan Bank System.

Even by Washington standards, all the new letters that make up the thrift regulatory alphabet soup can be a bit confusing. As the thrift industry enters this new era of regulation, it's helpful to have a road map of which agency, board, or office is responsible for certain activities.

Office of Thrift Supervision

One of several new agencies created by FIRREA, the Office of Thrift Supervision is the primary federal regulator of thrift institutions, including federally and state-chartered institutions that have federal deposit insurance and their holding companies. OTS is a bureau of the U.S. Department of the Treasury, as is the Office of the Comptroller of the Currency, which regulates national banks.

The OTS is the regulatory successor to the Federal Home Loan Bank Board (FHLBB), the Office of Regulatory Activities (ORA), the regulatory operations of the 12 federal home loan banks (also called district banks), and the Bank System Office of Education (BSOE). Headquartered in the former Washington, D.C., offices of FHLBB, the OTS staff includes the majority of the regulatory personnel of the predecessor agency in addition to approximately 3,200 employees located throughout the 12 districts.

Unlike the FHLBB, which was comprised of three members, the new agency is headed by a single director, who has the same authority as FHLBB had to promulgate regulations. Each OTS director will be appointed by the President and confirmed by the Senate to serve a five-year term.

OTS's Mission and Powers

Recognizing its role as primary federal regulator of the nation's savings institutions, OTS's working strategy is to prevent future thrift crises. Specifically, its mission is:

- To ensure the safety and soundness of the thrift industry;
- To foster public confidence in the thrift industry and its regulation;
- To ensure compliance with the full range of laws and regulations to which thrifts, their officials, and their shareholders are subject;
- To enhance the capacity within the thrift industry to adapt to changing economic environments and changing financial markets; and
- To ensure that the thrift industry can and does respond to its customer and community needs for housing finance and other financial services.

Although OTS's authority is more limited than that of the FHLBB, it takes from the former agency the responsibility:

- To charter federal savings and loan associations;
- To adopt regulations governing the operation of the thrift industry;

▶

States. Thrifts are required by federal regulations to have at least 60 percent of their assets in "housing-related" investments, including residential mortgages and loans for manufactured housing, equity investments in residential real estate, mortgage-backed securities, and state and local housing bonds.

Federal savings associations are permitted to establish and to invest a specified percentage of their assets in service corporation subsidiaries that can engage in activities prohibited to the parent associations. For example, a service corporation may originate, buy, sell, and service real estate loans and participations and may broker and warehouse loans. It can enter into joint ventures. And it can engage in the development of housing projects, for which purpose it may buy, hold, and rent unimproved property and perform any management and rental services. A number of savings associations have established service corporations.

In the early 1980s, Congress decided to deregulate thrifts, banks, and other savings institutions and to remove ceilings on interest rates on savings deposits. Thrifts were free to offer competitive interest rates, to

3-8 (continued)

- To conduct examinations of federally chartered and state-chartered savings institutions and their holding companies;
- To supervise institutions to effect their operating in a safe and sound manner and their compliance with federal laws and regulations and OTS directives; and
- To take measures as needed to enforce such compliance and rehabilitate troubled institutions.

OTS's Organization

The OTS is divided into six main areas, each contributing its share in fulfilling the agency's mission.

- *Supervision-operations*. Comprised of former FHLBB, ORA, and district bank employees, this division oversees the examination and supervision of savings institutions. Regulatory staff work in the Washington, D.C., headquarters as well as in the 12 federal home loan bank districts around the country. Each district has a principal supervisory agent, its highest ranking thrift regulator, whose responsibility is to ensure that all savings and loan associations in the district are in compliance with regulatory policy.
- *Supervision-policy*. This office develops regulations, directives, and other policies for the safe and sound operation of savings institutions and for their compliance with federal law and regulations. It is made up of former ORA and BSOE staff.
- *General counsel*. The staff of this division includes members of FHLBB's Office of General Counsel and Office of Enforcement. It is responsible for providing legal services to

OTS and for taking enforcement actions against savings institutions that violate laws or regulations.

- *Congressional relations and communications*. This office is responsible for communicating information about OTS and its actions and policies to the thrift industry, Congress, the public, and the news media. It makes agency documents, legal filings, and other written material available and handles consumer and Freedom of Information Act inquiries.
- *Management*. All of OTS's administrative functions are performed by this office. Its three main units oversee the agency's financial and administrative systems, information resources, and personnel.
- *Chief economist*. The chief economist's office is responsible for collection and analysis of data from the thrift industry. Its studies include comparisons of the thrift industry to other financial services, predictions of industry performance given certain economic conditions, and analyses of the industry in different areas of the country.

Other Agencies

As part of the reorganization called for by FIRREA, two principal areas that had been under the auspices of FHLBB—supervision of the 12 federal home loan banks and insurance of deposits—are now handled by two new entities.

The responsibility for supervising the federal home loan banks has been transferred to the Federal Housing Finance Board (FHFB), a new, independent agency. The FHFB is governed by a five-member board consisting of the Secretary of Housing and Urban Development and four other persons ap-

introduce their own money market funds, and to take other steps to attract more deposits and investments. They also were given more latitude to invest outside traditional housing loans, and some plunged into financing commercial real estate. The ability of deregulated thrifts to attract savings deposits, however, was hampered by the fact that their mortgage portfolios consisted primarily of long-term, fixed-rate, low-yield mortgages whose cash flows were insufficient to fund the higher yield that thrifts for competitive reasons paid on savings deposits.

The thrifts' problems were compounded in 1981 and 1982, when interest rates soared to historically high levels, followed by a slump in starts and sales of housing. Some thrifts added to their own problems by making construction loans to developers whose projects ran into construction delays, cost overruns, and a lack of buyers or tenants for their houses, apartments, or commercial buildings.

Losses and foreclosures among the thrifts persisted through the late 1980s, causing many thrifts to fail and the federal government to undertake a costly rescue

pointed by the President and confirmed by the Senate for seven-year terms. The President names one of the four appointees to serve as chairman. The federal home loan banks provide loans and other services to member savings institutions, which in turn own the district banks through the mandatory purchase of stock.

The FHLBB's role as provider of deposit insurance through the Federal Savings and Loan Insurance Corporation (FSLIC) has been transferred to the Federal Deposit Insurance Corporation. The FDIC now administers two deposit insurance funds—the Savings Association Insurance Fund, which replaced the abolished FSLIC, and the Bank Insurance Fund for commercial banks.

FIRREA also created the Resolution Trust Corporation Oversight Board, plus the Resolution Trust Corporation (RTC) itself. The Oversight Board has five members: the Secretary of the Treasury, who serves as chairman, the Chairman of the Board of Governors of the Federal Reserve System, the Secretary of Housing and Urban Development, and two independent members appointed by the President and confirmed by the Senate.

The Oversight Board, which has few employees, sets guidelines for and releases funds to RTC so that the latter may resolve failed thrift institutions by sale or liquidation. FDIC administers the day-to-day operations of RTC, maintaining separate FDIC and RTC staffs.

Since the reorganization, a thrift institution that fails is declared insolvent and placed in receivership by OTS, which appoints RTC or FDIC as receiver to handle the resolution of the institution.

By taking over FSLIC's responsibility for resolving failed thrift institutions through sale or liquidation, RTC fulfills the U.S. government's guarantee that savings institutions' depositors will not lose even one cent of their insured funds. Meanwhile, the FSLIC Resolution Fund, administered by FDIC, has taken over the task of liquidating failed thrift institution assets held by FSLIC before enactment of FIRREA. It is estimated that some 600 thrift institutions—including those already in conservatorship—eventually could be assigned to FDIC or RTC for resolution.

Footing the Bill

To pay for cleanup of the thrift industry, Congress authorized $50 billion—in addition to an estimated $40 billion already spent or committed by FSLIC before 1989—to make insured deposits available to customers of failed institutions and to dispose of those institutions by closing them or selling them to new owners. Of that amount, $20 billion was borrowed by the U.S. Treasury and turned over to RTC by September 30, 1989. Another $30 billion will be raised during the next three years for RTC from the sale of 30-year bonds by the Resolution Funding Corporation (REFCORP), another entity authorized by FIRREA.

The district banks are paying an amount required for the purchase of zero coupon Treasury bonds, which, when they mature, will repay the $50 billion in principal. Thus, the federal home loan banks—in effect, the thrift industry—will repay the principal as well as approximately $300 million a year toward the interest due on the $50 billion. The rest of the interest will be paid from proceeds of the sale of failed thrift institution assets and general tax funds. The total cost of the cleanup, including interest and amounts already spent, was estimated at $166 billion in 1989.

Source: Paul Lockwood, "OTS Stands for Healthy Thrifts," *Office of Thrift Supervision Journal*, special edition 1989, pp. 4–5.

---

effort. Fortunately, the problems afflicting the industry were concentrated in a relatively small percentage of thrifts. Most of the nation's thrifts remained relatively healthy and were able to restructure their loan portfolios to better match yields with interest rates paid their depositors. Central to this restructuring was the increased origination of adjustable-rate mortgages, reducing a thrift's risk of making a loan that over the long term falls below prevailing interest rates.

Because of the thrift industry's problems, thrift institutions are particularly sensitive to the risks in financing development projects. To hedge against such risks, thrifts want strong assurances that projects will turn a profit. They insist that applications for financing be supported by well-prepared feasibility studies and cash flow statements.

Commercial Banks

The principal function of commercial banks is to finance the commerce of the United States—the production, distribution, and sale of goods. The nation's commercial banking system is a dual system, with banks chartered either by the federal government or by individual states. National banks are chartered, supervised, and regulated by the Comptroller of the Currency under provisions of the Federal Reserve Act. State banks, whether or not they elect to join the federal reserve system, are regulated by the state that charters them. Deposits are insured by the Bank Insurance Fund (BIF), administered by the FDIC, and federally chartered commercial banks must belong to the FDIC. State-chartered banks may qualify for FDIC insurance, provided that they observe FDIC rules and regulations in addition to state regulations. Checking accounts represent about a third of commercial banks' total deposits; time deposits and various types of savings deposits account for the remainder.

A national bank may make loans secured by liens in real estate subject to conditions and limitations prescribed by the Comptroller of the Currency. Commercial banks are authorized to loan up to 75 percent of the appraised value on unimproved property or for new construction. Commercial banks can loan up to 90 percent of the appraised value of improved property secured by a conventional mortgage.

Commercial banks are the main source of construction loans for the real estate industry; they also are a significant source of loans for single-family houses. Of the approximately $2.3 trillion in one- to four-family home mortgage loans outstanding at the end of 1989, commercial banks held 12 percent, thrift institutions 28 percent. Banks are less active in financing multifamily housing. At the end of 1989, they held about 12 percent of the multifamily mortgage loans outstanding, while thrift institutions held 34 percent. Banks also issue letters of credit that are used to back equity investment commitments in development and to provide credit enhancement of bond issues. Banks also extend lines of credit—or bank lines—to their most creditworthy borrowers. Banks usually require that compensating balances be kept on deposit, typically 10 percent of the credit line.

Banks, including some of the nation's largest, in recent years have had their share of problem real estate loans. As a result, banks have taken steps to tighten their lending and underwriting practices for real estate ventures.

Life Insurance Companies

Life insurance companies, which are stock or mutual institutions, are subject to state regulation, including limits on the percentage of a company's assets that may be loaned to a particular borrower or on a partic-

ular property and limits on the amount of a loan in relation to a property's value. Life insurance companies generate a continuous flow of capital from premium payments. Because they can predict future cash flows with considerable accuracy, they can make substantial loans; indeed, given their size, they usually prefer to make large loans to reduce the cost per loan of originations. When mortgage yields are competitive with alternative investments, life insurance companies are active in the mortgage market. They are a principal source of financing for the development and ownership of income properties, including office buildings, shopping centers, industrial parks, and multifamily projects. Although they are less active in financing single-family houses, they can be an important source of financing for large-scale residential development projects. Often they demand "kickers," or additional payments over and above the stated interest on the loan, usually in the form of points or equity participation.

Credit Companies

Some large diversified industrial corporations have credit company subsidiaries that provide financing for real estate development. The financing includes land development and acquisition loans, construction loans (in some cases without a takeout commitment), and letters of credit for loans funded by third-party lenders.

Real Estate Investment Trusts

Real estate investment trusts (REITs) are trusts organized to pool capital for investment in income-producing properties and in mortgages. They raise capital by selling shares or debt instruments to the public and by borrowing from banks and other sources. Shares of most REITs are registered with the Securities and Exchange Commission and are publicly traded on stock exchanges or over the counter. Thus, they are a means by which individual investors can invest in real estate while benefiting from the liquidity of a ready market for REIT shares and the sharing of the investment risk among a REIT's shareholders.

REITs effectively are exempt from federal taxation to the extent that they distribute income to their shareholders. A REIT must distribute at least 95 percent of its taxable income to shareholders, who pay taxes at individual federal income tax rates on the income distributed to them. In addition, REITs must satisfy complex requirements for ownership, assets, and income, among others, of the Internal Revenue Code. In contrast with partnerships, REITs cannot pass through losses to their shareholders.

REITs generally can be classified as mortgage, equity, or hybrid REITs. The portfolios of mortgage REITs consist predominantly of mortgages on income-producing properties. Depending on the REIT's investment objectives, mortgages can range from relatively short-term construction or development loans to long-term mortgages on completed properties. Equity REITs take ownership positions in real estate through joint ventures, land leases, cash purchases, and other means. Hybrid REITs attempt to combine the advantage of mortgage lending, with its relatively stable cash flow, and equity investment, with its potential for higher returns in cash flow and appreciation in property values. Some REITs, for example, make short-term construction loans and invest in a diversified portfolio of income-producing properties.

Like life insurance companies, REITs generally have concentrated their investments in commercial properties. Some REITs, however, may be a source of capital for large-scale residential development.

Mortgage Bankers/Brokers

Mortgage bankers originate real estate loans from their own capital sources; they hold the loans in their portfolios or sell the loans to institutional lenders or other investors. Mortgage bankers may be independent companies or subsidiaries of other companies, such as industrial corporations or bank holding companies. Mortgage brokers also originate real estate loans in their capacity as an intermediary between developers and life insurance companies or other lenders that provide the capital.

Both mortgage bankers and mortgage brokers make their money through origination and servicing fees. They play useful roles as sources of financing and intermediaries for residential developers; they can also provide assistance to developers in packaging their products to attract investment capital.

Pension Funds

As of July 1989, pension funds had $2.7 trillion in assets, an 8 percent increase over the $2.5 trillion in assets a year earlier. Managers of pension funds have expressed a goal to invest 10 percent of their assets in real estate, which would make them a major force in real estate investment. By July 1989, pension funds had invested only 4.2 percent—$113 billion—of their assets in real estate, an improvement over the 3.8 percent invested a year earlier. Only 9 percent of pension funds' real estate investments had gone into multifamily developments (mostly rental properties), however, and only a small amount had gone into single-family developments. In addition, only 11 percent of the funds' investments in real estate had gone into new development, while 89 percent was directed to existing projects.

Many reasons are offered for the relatively slow growth of pension funds' investment in real estate. The most cogent is that pension fund managers are experienced in the fine points of evaluating stock or bond portfolios but are novices with real estate. As time passes, pension fund managers and their advisers will become more sophisticated in evaluating income real estate. This fact, coupled with a federal law requiring pension funds to diversify their investment portfolios, could in time result in increasing investment in real estate. Even with a substantial increase in investment, however, only a limited amount will probably be allocated to residential properties, with most of that amount going to existing multifamily developments.

Syndications

A syndication is an investment vehicle by which the syndicator or sponsor raises capital from investors for investment in a real estate enterprise. Syndications can be formed to acquire, develop, manage, operate, or market real estate. Syndicators, usually real estate professionals, receive fees for their services in organizing and managing a syndicate and may have an interest in the properties owned by the syndicate. Syndicates can give investors an opportunity to invest in a real estate enterprise that otherwise would be denied them. Investors benefit from being passive investors: they do not have to be concerned with managing the properties.

Developers could seek financing from an established syndication or might consider organizing syndications themselves. Syndications can be organized in a variety of forms, from simple joint ownership to a corporation. The most common form is the limited partnership, which, although having the advantage of limited liability for investors who are limited partners, also has a drawback in that it is an illiquid form of investment (that is, not readily convertible to cash). No central exchange exists for the trading of partnership interests. A secondary market is beginning to develop as some syndicators and other investors ac-

Amid the media-fueled jitters of October 1987 as stock values tumbled, calmer economic observers noted that the most important product of this episode in market volatility would probably not be another depression (as many dreaded), but rather some major structural shifts in the placement of capital.

By 1990, the real estate industry was just beginning to recognize the impact that one of those shifts could have. Pension funds, those cautious giants whose smallest steps can shake the earth, are moving assets out of the stock market into what they see as the profitable yet more placid realm of real estate.

"The total asset value of domestic pension funds is approximately $2 trillion," reports William J. Chadwick, chairman of the Pension Real Estate Association, a Hartford, Connecticut–based organization that provides information and a forum for discussion about pension-fund investment in real estate. "Of that, nearly 5 percent—about $100 billion—is currently invested in equity real estate. Reasonable projections estimate that, by 1995, pension funds will have shifted an additional 5 percent of assets into real estate. That's another $100 billion over the next five years."

That's a dazzling figure for the real estate industry to contemplate, especially at a time when a traditional source of capital—the thrift industry—is retrenching and more recent stars, such as retail syndication and private placement, are waning because of tax reform, high real interest rates, and more competitive yields from other investment opportunities.

The important question is how effectively developers will deal with this potential windfall and with those fund managers who direct it.

An Instinct to Build

History offers little guidance, as direct contact between developers and pension fund managers has, until recently, been minimal. It has been only about 20 years, in fact, since institutional investors of any type started to play a major role in commercial real estate development; in the late 1960s, insurance companies and banks were the first to seek diversification into real estate for their open-end funds.

The impetus for pension funds to invest in real estate began in 1974 with the passage of pension reform laws that required diversification among and within asset classes. "The response of the funds was to adopt the then-novel idea of asset allocation models," says Chadwick, former administrator of pension and welfare benefit programs for the U.S. Department of Labor.

"Modern portfolio theory provided a good structure for analyzing needs and goals and what investments could serve them," he says, "but there was no real documentation to back up the theory. Belief in the value of real estate was mostly intuitive: real estate is a hedge against inflation and has a negative correlation with stocks and bonds."

Allocation models increased in sophistication and began to recommend consistently that 10 to 15 percent of assets find a home in real estate. Still, pension funds took their time acting on this advice. "Don't forget that pension funds, in their own view, are immortal," reminds Chadwick. "Even when the stock market is volatile, they don't feel rushed. The larger funds are essentially indexed, anyway."

Yet, though even the crash of 1987 did not panic pension finds, it did acutely remind them of their accountability. They decided to pay better heed to the allocation targets—thus opening a period of "catch up" with real estate investment.

Just where will this money go? At a time when troubled thrifts are expected to disgorge a hefty lot of real estate, some of that first $100 billion could be quickly accounted for. But as Chadwick points out: "Pension funds are used only to quality. They will not buy trash." This could mean they will skim off the best available properties, leaving the bulk of potentially less profitable problem projects to others.

On the other end of the spectrum, pension funds, with their considerable financial muscle, could join the currently fashionable rush for "trophy" buildings. Yet the very competition that drives up the

quire partnership interests from the original investors, but the market is small and fragmented.

Publicly traded partnerships (PTPs) offer investors essentially the same benefits as a traditional limited partnership plus the benefit of liquidity. Interests in a PTP can be freely traded on stock exchanges or in over-the-counter markets. U.S. tax laws governing PTPs and PTPs' tax reporting and accounting require-

prices of these select landmarks is likely to cause consternation among pension funds, which are sensitive to both risk and return. They already realize that their substantial presence in any investment market will drive up values.

Rather, the basic instinct in pension funds is to build. Building creates value, creates jobs, and spurs the economy. Building makes intuitive sense, even to those funds that have never done it before. Pension funds looking for real estate opportunities will be open to new ideas, observes Chadwick. They will be willing to consider special opportunities and innovative strategies. "Because they recognize that they're new to the field, they have no strong bias toward product type, or even investment structure. Right now they need good developers who can take the initiative."

Need for Developers' Ideas

Chadwick, whose own job as president of Los Angeles–based Public Storage Institutional Realty is to develop and manage public storage facilities for institutional investment, believes that if developers expect to benefit from the influx of pension assets, they will have to change their approach.

"Very few developers have created successful relationships with pension fund managers in recent years," he observes. "I think the problem has been that too many developers have viewed pension funds as capital of the last resort. They have come to pension funds with marginal deals and inadequate business plans. Not surprisingly, the funds have not been interested."

Chadwick advises developers to emulate the approach of a manufacturer seeking to expand a product line: "Study the market, hire the experts you need, create a realistic business plan, and give it enough time to work." For example, he suggests getting familiar with the *Money Market Directory*, the so-called "green book," to be more selective about targets. "You'll find that there are more than 1,200 funds with assets around $100 million—but even they may not be ready to deal with you. Look instead at the 250 that are worth over $1 billion. They are more likely to have made policies toward

real estate deals and to have a dedicated real estate staff and the ability to do their own due diligence. You'll want that degree of sophistication."

He further recommends that developers look at their percentage of assets in real estate, types of projects, their location and individual value, tenant quality, lease duration—in other words, delve for the sort of information that allows a developer to present new ideas in a knowledgeable context.

"Most of all, be responsive to the needs of pension funds," says Chadwick. "They're interested in the most attractive investment—probably sophisticated and not plain vanilla. They probably want a seven- to 10-year holding term, with a real rate of return of more than 6 percent. Can you give them that or better? If you want to build a lasting relationship, you'll have to make the effort to speak their language."

Is it worth the developer's considerable effort to formulate a plan for pension fund partners? What about today's political talk of taxing pension fund income? Would that change the coming wave? "Not likely," says Chadwick. What about social and political pressure to use pension assets to address national problems, like relieving the housing shortage? Some public pension funds—such as those for state employees—operate under directives to invest at home, and some corporate funds have divested their South African holdings as an antiapartheid statement. But, as Chadwick points out, "The primary responsibility of pension fund managers is toward the beneficiaries, and there is nothing that would make them willing to sacrifice yields."

So, as America's pension funds move toward a basic allocation model of 10 percent for real estate, $100 billion will enter the real estate market between 1990 and 1995, with the likelihood that another 5 percent could follow. Developers are in an ideal position to shape much of the impact of this investment, if they take up the challenge.

As for those who still doubt the size of the opportunity ahead, consider one more projection: the total assets of domestic pension funds are expected to increase to $3 trillion by 1995. You do the math.

Source: Ed Mickens, "On the Horizon: A Bigger Development Role for Pension Funds," *Urban Land*, April 1990, pp. 28–29.

ments are complex. Changes in tax laws in 1986 and 1987 have had the effect of reducing the attractiveness of PTPs as investments. The Revenue Act of 1987 says a PTP is to be treated as a corporation for tax purposes unless 90 percent or more of its gross income is of a "passive-type character." PTPs that meet the 90 percent test are not taxed as corporations, but they are subject to special limitations under the passive loss rules of the 1986 tax act. Consequently, PTPs may not play as large a role in raising real estate investment capital in the 1990s.

Government Financing Programs

The 1980s were marked by a sharp reduction in the federal government's funding of housing programs. In 1970, starts of federally subsidized housing accounted for nearly 30 percent of starts in the country; in 1988, the figure was less than 10 percent. Federal appropriations for housing fell from $27.9 billion in 1980 to $9.7 billion in 1988.[3] The cutbacks were precipitated by the high cost of some programs, substantial federal budget deficits, and the Reagan administration's policy to shift more of the responsibility for housing programs to state and local governments. The decline in appropriations is also partly the result of a change in the emphasis of federal housing policy—from an emphasis on subsidies for production to subsidies for tenants, which some believe is less expensive. The change in emphasis has not added to the supply of low-cost housing, however.

Since the early 1980s, Congress has reduced the direct cost of housing assistance programs by raising the share of income that subsidized tenants must pay for rent. It also amended the U.S. Housing Act to target Section 8 and public housing programs more closely to the neediest households. (In the Section 8 Existing Housing Certificate program, for example, the federal government pays the difference between the established fair market rent for a housing unit and the amount that the tenant is required to pay.) Congress cut program costs further by repealing the components of the Section 8 program covering new construction and substantial rehabilitation, thereby limiting the program essentially to existing units.

Partly to offset the elimination of the Section 8 production program, Congress in 1983 created a new rental rehabilitation grant program and a housing development action grant program (HoDAG) targeted to areas with a shortage of low-income housing. The HoDAG program was short-lived; Congress in 1987 enacted a comprehensive housing bill that terminated the HoDAG program in 1989. The bill continued a housing voucher program, however, that permits qualifying households to receive rental subsidies for housing units costing more than the established fair market rents if the household can pay the difference between the subsidy and the actual rent.

Since enactment of the 1987 legislation, Congress has continued to reexamine the nation's housing policy. In 1988, the National Housing Task Force, comprised of respected individuals involved in housing

production, policy, and finance, made a number of recommendations to address the national shortage of low- and moderate-income housing. Essentially, the task force proposed that limited federal funds be leveraged to support the development and implementation of innovative, locally initiated housing production programs. As of early 1990, President Bush has proposed a series of initiatives based in part upon the task force's recommendations, including stimulating first-time purchases of houses, providing shelter and social services to the homeless, and encouraging economic revitalization of inner-city neighborhoods. Though new housing legislation is expected in 1990, no return to large-scale federal funding of low-income housing production programs is anticipated in the near future.

The one remaining federal effort to encourage production of low-income rental housing is the low-income housing tax credit (LIHTC), established by Congress in the Tax Reform Act of 1986. Administered by state housing agencies, the LIHTC provides a dollar-for-dollar credit against the federal tax on nonpassive income, based on the amount of money invested in qualifying units in mixed-income or low-income housing developments. The LIHTC is designed to return, over a 10-year period, either 70 percent or 30 percent of the costs of the investments in qualifying units, in terms of present value. The size of the credit is fixed at the time the property is placed in service and is based on an average of federal interest rates. For properties placed in service in 1987, for example, the percentages of the credit were fixed at 9 percent on a 70 percent return and 4 percent on a 30 percent return. Thus, a project using the 9 percent credit receives annually for 10 years a tax credit equal to 9 percent of the cost of developing the low-income units. The 9 percent credit can be used for costs of new construction or substantial rehabilitation not financed with federal funds (Community Development Block Grant funds excepted). The 4 percent credit can be used for federally subsidized new construction or substantial rehabilitation projects or for the acquisition of qualifying existing low-income housing.

The regulations governing the LIHTC are complex and discouraged early experimentation with its use. It has proved a strong incentive for corporate investment in low-income housing that otherwise would not have occurred, however. According to the National Council of State Housing Agencies, about

[3] Paul A. Leonard, Cushing N. Dolbeare, and Edward B. Lazere, "A Place to Call Home: The Crisis in Housing for the Poor" (Washington, D.C.: Center on Budget and Policy Priorities and the Low-Income Housing Information Service, April 1989), p. 32.

Crown Ridge Apartments is a $3.78 million multi-family rental housing development structured to take advantage of federal low- to moderate-income housing tax credits. Although limited in the amount of rent that can be charged, the project is comparable in design and cost to other apartment projects in the area. The design also allows for a possible future conversion to condominiums.

The 5.92-acre project is located in Dallas, Georgia, on the western edge of the Atlanta metropolitan area. It consists of 65 two-bedroom apartments plus a small building that contains an office and a laundry facility.

Housing Tax Credits

DeRand Housing Associates conceived the project to take advantage of housing tax credits available for the construction of low- to moderate-income multifamily rental housing. With the Tax Reform Act of 1986, Congress created a new tax incentive to replace previous incentives for the construction of low- to moderate-income housing. The housing tax credit program provides a 9 percent annual tax credit for projects built or rehabilitated without the use of any government guarantees or subsidies (except for Section 8 assistance). Alternatively, investors may receive a 4 percent annual tax credit for projects receiving assistance from some government program or using tax-exempt financing. Both tax credits last 10 years.

To qualify, either 40 percent of the units must be rented to tenants whose incomes do not exceed 60 percent of the area's median family income, or 20 percent of the units must be rented to tenants whose

3-11   Making use of federal low-income housing tax credits, Crown Ridge contains 65 apartments on a 5.92-acre site outside Atlanta.

income is 50 percent or less of the area's median family income. Furthermore, the tax credit is available only for that percentage of units conforming to the restrictions on income. Also, the rent for any unit may not exceed 30 percent of the tenant's qualifying adjusted income after deducting $75 per month as a utility allowance.

Unfortunately, the housing tax credit program has not worked as well as expected. The reason: in most rural areas, income levels are so low that to limit rent levels to 60 percent or less of the area's median income often makes a project economically infeasible. In urban areas, projects typically need rents higher than 60 percent of the median income level to recoup the high land, construction, and operating costs.

Thus, the only instances where housing tax credit projects generally have worked have been in

▶

120,000 rental units were developed, rehabilitated, or acquired for use through 1988—about 8 percent of all new housing units built during that period. In 1989, the LIHTC was refined and extended through December 1990 at 75 percent of its 1989 level. Based on expected full utilization rates for 1989, most observers believe that demand will outstrip supply. As of early 1990, efforts were under way to enact a permanent extension of the LIHTC.

In the absence of strong federal support for low-income housing, state and local governments have been creative in devising approaches to fill the gap.[4] State housing finance agencies have long been active in a variety of mortgage finance and housing produc-

tion programs. The Tax Reform Act of 1986 curtailed tax incentives for real estate investments and imposed restrictions on tax-exempt, private-purpose

[4] For detailed information on the nature and extent of state and local low-income housing activities and programs, see Michael Stegman and J. David Holden, *Nonfederal Housing Programs: How States and Localities Are Responding to Federal Cutbacks* (Washington, D.C.: ULI–the Urban Land Institute, 1987); Mary K. Nenno and George S. Colyer, *New Money and New Methods: A Catalog of State and Local Initiatives in Housing and Community Development*, 2d ed. (Washington, D.C.: National Association of Housing and Redevelopment Officials, 1988); John Sidor, *State Housing Initiatives: A Compendium* (Washington, D.C.: Council of State Community Affairs Agencies, 1986); and Diane R. Suchman with D. Scott Middleton and Susan L. Giles, *Public/Private Housing Partnerships* (Washington, D.C.: ULI–the Urban Land Institute, 1990).

conjunction with the Farmers Home Administration 515 low-interest loan program, where tax-exempt financing has been coupled with some state or local guarantee program, or in the outer fringes of large metropolitan areas with a relatively high median income but where land and other construction costs are fairly low. This latter scenario was the case with the Crown Ridge Apartments.

Another restriction of the housing tax credit program is a $7,000 limit on the tax credit that any one individual can use in a year. Also, unless using a public offering, one is limited to a private placement of 35 nonaccredited investors plus any accredited investors. But because of the tax credit limits, many accredited investors are not attracted to this type of investment. Consequently, the maximum total equity one can generally raise for an individual project of this type is about $1.3 million. Given the

amount of equity needed to make up the debt shortfall, the result is a limit to the size of projects using housing tax credits.

For Crown Ridge, DeRand chose to build 65 units. DeRand also decided not to use tax-exempt or Farmers Home Administration financing to qualify for the 9 percent, rather than the 4 percent, annual tax credit.

Financing

By doing a smaller project in a more rural area, DeRand was able to use a financing arrangement that might not have been possible for a larger project. DeRand negotiated with the turnkey builder, Dan Forsyth, to buy the land and secure permanent debt financing before DeRand's marketing of the equity syndication. As part of its turnkey purchase

---

3-12   FINANCIAL BENEFITS FROM HOUSING TAX CREDITS
FOR CROWN RIDGE APARTMENTS

Developer/Syndicator's Benefits:

Syndication Selling Commission: $126,000
Development Fee: $291,681 plus $69,939 in interest
Property Management Fee: 7% of gross rental receipts
Investor Services Fee: $3,000 per year
General Partnership Interest: a) 1% of all profits, losses, deductions, and credits resulting from operations and b) 50% of any net proceeds of a capital transaction, such as a sale or a refinancing.[1]

Investors' (Projected) Benefits:[2]

Return per Investment Unit:
Net Cash Flow: $33,908
Tax Deductions: $6,782
Tax Credits: $60,610
Residuals (proceeds from sale or refinancing):
a) return of capital contribution, b) 9% cumulative, preferred return, noncompounding, and c) 50% split with general partner thereafter.

[1] Only after investors have received a return of their capital contributions plus any unpaid portion of their preferred return.
[2] Based on a required equity contribution of $45,000 per investment unit. Assumes a 15-year holding period on the property.

---

bond financing that have posed new challenges for states seeking to finance production and rehabilitation of low-income housing.

Many state and local governments have developed innovative programs to increase the supply of affordable housing for middle- and lower-income families. The programs variously involve tax-exempt and taxable bond financing, allocation of remaining federal assistance, state incentives and subsidies, revolving loan funds, housing trust funds, funding through nonprofit corporations and lending consortia, and use of public/private partnership arrangements.

Private, for-profit developers can realize opportunities in low- and moderate-income housing indi-

rectly through programs to increase first-time buyers' access to low-cost mortgages and directly through use of LIHTCs and participation in state and local incentive programs in partnership with governments and/or nonprofit developers. For example, BRIDGE Housing Corporation, a nonprofit developer in the San Francisco Bay Area, operates in public/private partnerships and has entered joint ventures with private developers in several mixed-income developments, sharing risks, costs, and returns.[5]

---

[5] For detailed information on five program-based public/private housing partnerships, including BRIDGE, see Suchman, Middleton, and Giles, *Public/Private Housing Partnerships.*

of the project, DeRand assumed the mortgage loan previously secured by Dan Forsyth from First Federal Savings and Loan Association in Cedartown, Georgia. The $1,795,200 conventional mortgage, self-amortizing over 20 years with no prepayment penalty, has an interest rate of 10¼ percent that is adjusted annually to equal the Mortgage Contract Rate, with a maximum annual increase of 1 percent. The interest rate has a floor of 6¼ percent and a ceiling of 14¼ percent.

DeRand was also able to finance the payment of the turnkey builder's fee of $413,476 over 4½ years with interest. Although not secured by the property, this indebtedness is guaranteed by each equity investor on a prorated basis. Finally, a portion of the $1,575,000 in equity raised was set aside as a reserve fund to cover any operating deficits. If the project does not need all of these funds, any remainder will be used to pay down the mortgage.

Leasing and Marketing

According to the U.S. Department of Housing and Urban Development, the median family income for the Atlanta metropolitan statistical area in 1988 was $36,300. As a consequence, the project may rent units only to new tenants of four or more persons whose annual income does not exceed $21,780 (60 percent of the median). Income limits are proportionately lower for smaller tenant groupings. Because the median family income for Paulding County is only $22,000, a large pool of residents is eligible for this housing.

To determine whether tenants comply with the federally mandated restrictions on income, prospective tenants are asked to sign an income certi-

Sources of Funds:

Equity (from syndication)	$1,575,000
Mortgage Loan	1,795,200
Seller Financing	413,470
Total	$3,783,670

Uses of Funds:

Turnkey Construction	$2,081,676
Land	127,000
Syndication	196,000
Development Fee	291,681
Interest on Development Fee	69,939
Mortgage Debt Reduction	499,816
Repayment of Seller/Financing Note	413,476
Interest on Seller/Financing Note	86,643
Working Capital Reserve	10,000
Closing Costs	7,439
Total	$3,783,670

fication form and to identify an employer or other means of verifying income. Existing tenants must also sign an annual recertification form.

Because of the shortage of comparable rental housing in the area, marketing the project has not been difficult. In fact, the project has maintained over a 95 percent occupancy level since lease-up. Still, marketing strategies are careful not to portray the project as a low-income housing project; the income certification form is treated as a routine part of the tenant application process.

Source: Project Reference File: "Crown Ridge Apartments," vol. 18, no. 13 (Washington, D.C.: ULI–the Urban Land Institute, July–September 1988).

Secondary Mortgage Market

The rapid growth of secondary mortgages in recent years has done much to improve lenders' liquidity and indirectly increase sources of financing for residential developers. In the absence of the secondary market, the amount and number of mortgage loans lenders could originate would be limited by their ability to attract deposits. By selling their loans in the secondary market, lenders generate cash with which to make new loans.

In contrast with the primary mortgage market, in which lenders originate and retain mortgage loans, the secondary mortgage market is comprised of transactions between lenders who originate mortgage loans and investors who buy the loans to hold for income. The secondary market originally was created to correct geographic imbalances of mortgage funds: lenders in areas where the supply of mortgage money exceeded demand could buy mortgage loans from lenders in areas where the demand for mortgage money exceeded the supply. The federal agencies subsequently entered the mortgage market to serve a broader function, acquiring mortgages from lenders short of mortgage capital and selling mortgages to lenders with an overabundance of mortgage funds. As a result, the secondary mortgage market plays a critical role in providing substantial debt capital to the residential development industry.

Investors in the secondary market include individuals, thrift institutions, and the three organizations created specifically to service the market—the Federal National Mortgage Association (Fannie Mae), the Federal Home Loan Mortgage Corporation (Freddie Mac), and the Government National Mortgage Association (Ginnie Mae).

Fannie Mae is the largest purchaser of secondary mortgages in the United States. It buys conventional and government-guaranteed or -insured mortgages, financing the purchases mainly by issuing debt in its own name. It also services and sells mortgages. Fannie Mae is owned by private shareholders, although it has ties to the government.

Freddie Mac is under the direction of the Office of Thrift Supervision, which regulates the nation's thrift industry. It provides lenders with more funds by buying existing mortgages in their portfolios. Its programs cover conventional mortgage loans of various types, participations in conventional loans, and loans guaranteed or insured by the federal government.

Ginnie Mae is wholly owned by the U.S. government and operates within the Department of Housing and Urban Development. It was created in 1968 to assume certain functions previously assigned to Fannie Mae as well as to guarantee securities backed by government-guaranteed or -insured mortgages.

The Veterans Administration guarantees loans made by private lenders to eligible veterans of the U.S. armed forces. Because the VA guarantees part or all of the loan, lenders can require smaller downpayments than is usually the case with a conventional loan. The Federal Housing Administration, part of HUD, operates a variety of programs, including insurance of loans for single-family houses originated by private lenders.

Mortgage-Backed Securities

The mortgage-backed securities market has evolved into an important source of mortgage capital for financing home loans and residential development. Two basic types of residential mortgage-backed securities are available. One is the pass-through certificate, an investment in a pool of mortgages on residential properties in which prorated principal and interest payments from the mortgages are distributed or passed through directly to investors in the certificates. The other is a bond collateralized by a pool of mortgages. Usually interest payments are made semiannually, with full payment of principal when the bonds mature.

Some large builders have themselves issued bonds, based on a pool of permanent home mortgages that they originate on the houses they build. Groups of smaller builders have pooled the mortgages they originated on their houses and issued bonds backed by the pool.

The mortgage-backed securities market has attracted a broad range of investors, including life insurance companies and pension funds, which are, along with thrift institutions, the largest purchasers and holders of mortgage-backed securities. One reason is that credit enhancements have reduced the risk of investing in mortgage-backed securities, which are now routinely rated by the rating agencies. Another reason for the market's growth has been the introduction of innovative financing concepts, such as the collateralized mortgage obligation, a bond look-alike that combines the relative safety and high yield of mortgage-backed securities with the predictable cash flow of bonds. In addition, the 1986 tax act authorizes a new pass-through tax entity known as a real estate mortgage investment conduit. The tax act also provides specific rules that clarify several aspects of the treatment of mortgage-backed securities for federal income tax purposes. These developments should contribute to the growth of the mortgage-backed securities market and its importance as a source of capital for the residential development industry.

Financial Feasibility Analysis

Feasibility analysis is an analysis of a real estate project to determine whether the economic, legal, political, physical, and marketing environments are favorable for implementation of the project. Simply put, the feasibility analysis attempts to answer the question, "Will the project succeed financially?"

The question is easier asked than answered. Even the best-laid development plans can be upset by unexpected construction delays and cost overruns, delays in obtaining government approvals, slower-than-expected sales or rentals of the completed housing units, higher-than-expected interest rates, and a host of other problems. The more complex the project and the more time required to complete the project, the more uncertain its feasibility.

Given the element of unpredictability in any project, the feasibility analysis operates in the realm of probability. It can be used to make reasonable estimates of a project's financial feasibility. It cannot ensure the project's success, but it is an invaluable tool in helping developers to decide whether to pro-

3-14   PURPOSE OF FINANCIAL FEASIBILITY ANALYSIS

Type of Study	Purpose	Typical Conclusions
Market Study	• Determine the market for the proposed project or suitability of a site • Recommend product type, mix, pricing, and features • Analyze supply and demand and sales rate or absorption for the proposed products or uses	• Product type, size, features, and mix • Suitability of the site for the proposed use • Estimated absorption and pricing

Feasibility Study	• Determine whether project provides adequate profit or returns to make it worthwhile
	• Analyze project's sensitivity to:
	  a) product mix, pricing, uses, and absorption
	  b) costs
	  c) financing assumptions
		• Profit and/or project's internal rate of return
		• Recommendations for product or phasing
		• Analysis of financial alternatives

Appraisal	Determine market value of the completed project and/or land	Market value of the project and/or land at a certain date

Source: Kenneth Leventhal & Company, Los Angeles, California.

ceed with a project and in helping lenders or investors to decide whether to finance a project.

The nature and extent of the feasibility analysis depend on the size and complexity of the project, the budget for the project, and, most important, the developer's awareness of the value of feasibility analysis. Developers who fail to budget sufficient money or time for the analysis could base their decision to develop the project on inadequate or misinterpreted information—and doom their projects to failure.

If developers plan to build a few dozen for-sale housing units that can be completed in months, they can make do with a rudimentary analysis using in-house staff and information readily at hand. If they plan a large, complex project requiring substantial investment and a long construction period, they might require a sophisticated analysis, possibly using outside consultants skilled in large-scale data collection and interpretation.

This chapter focuses on the financial feasibility analysis, the principal analysis required by equity or debt investors who provide capital for the project. The purpose of financial feasibility analyses is to determine whether the project will generate enough net cash flow to pay in full the interest due on the loans that finance the project and to provide an adequate return on the equity capital invested in the project. The project is not financially feasible if it cannot generate the minimum required cash flow, and project developers will have difficulty obtaining the necessary debt and equity capital to finance the project.

Depending on the requirements of developers and lenders, financial feasibility analyses consist of one or more of the following elements: a market study, a feasibility study, and an appraisal. Some of the information contained in the three types of studies may be the same, but the studies differ considerably in their purposes and features.

Market Study

The purpose of a market study is to determine current and future demand for a particular use at a particular site.[6] It is usually done before the financial feasibility study. Not only does the market study help developers to decide whether a market exists for the proposed

---

[6] A more detailed discussion of market and site-related feasibility studies is provided in Chapter 2.

131

Market Study	Feasibility Study	Appraisal

• Project Description
  a) location
  b) access
  c) services available
  d) surrounding uses
  e) toxic contamination
	• Project Description
	
	• Assumptions: pricing, value ratios, absorption, unit sizes, etc. (usually based on market study), and projected project revenues
		• Project Description
		  a) location
		  b) access
		  c) services
		  d) legal description
		  e) surrounding uses

• Analysis of Key Economic Factors Affecting Uses
  a) population
  b) employment
  c) household growth
  d) income and age
  e) building permits
  f) development patterns
	• Projection of Project Costs
	  a) land
	  b) site development
	  c) unit direct construction
	  d) indirect construction and fees
	  e) overhead
	  f) property taxes
	  g) loan interest and fees
		• Analysis of Market Absorption and Pricing
		
		• Valuation Analysis (as appropriate)
		  a) discounted cash flow
		  b) market comparison
		  c) replacement cost
		  d) capitalized income

• Entitlements
  a) entitlements already approved for project
  b) additional entitlements needed and probability of obtaining them
  c) existing or potential ordinances limiting growth
	• Projection of Net Cash Flow
	
	• One or More Cash Flow Projections
	  a) before debt
	  b) after debt
	  c) after tax
		• Conclusions
		  a) market value when completed
		  b) land value before development

• Supply and Demand
  a) analyses of competitive projects, pricing, rents, sales, absorption, product type, mix, and features
  b) proposed additions to supply
  c) projection of aggregate housing demand or demand by housing product
  d) analysis of demand by price or rent range
  e) estimated market share of proposed project
	• Sensitivity Analysis
	  a) varying uses, mixes, pricing, absorption
	  b) analysis of financing alternatives	

• Conclusions
  a) determination of site's suitability for proposed uses or whether market exists for intended use
  b) recommended product sizes, mix, pricing, rents, and features
  c) projected sales or absorption rates for recommended products
	• Conclusions
	  a) total net cash flow (profit)
	  b) profit as a percent of sales revenue
	  c) discounted rate of return on equity
	  d) comparison of profit/return measures with profit/return requirements	

Source: Kenneth Leventhal & Company, Los Angeles, California.

project; it also helps them to decide the mix of products, size (square footage), and features.

The market study can be divided into macro and micro studies. The macro study measures demographic, economic, and political trends in the community or region where the project is to be built to determine that the environment is conducive to its development—or at least is not an impediment. The macro study examines growth in population, employment, household formations, personal income, and other trends.

The micro study examines whether the project can be marketed under conditions existing when the project is finished. It includes an analysis of zoning and land use controls that will affect the development, an analysis of competitive projects currently on the market or planned for development, an estimate of the rate at which the market will absorb the housing units to be built, the sale prices or rents that should be charged, and other data. It may include an environmental impact statement, not only to comply with environmental laws and regulations but also to enable developers and potential lenders to determine whether any environmental hazards (such as toxic wastes) exist on the development site and the cost of mitigating the hazards.

Feasibility Study

The purpose of the feasibility study is to determine the project's expected profitability or rate of return and whether the profitability (return) is adequate. Central to the study is the preparation of the project's pro forma cash flow statement, which contains an estimate of the project's revenues, costs, and net cash flow before and after debt service.

The cash flow statement measures cash flow over a period of time, usually the length of the project. For example, a statement may measure cash flow quarterly over the length of a three-year project. The statement can be structured to show pretax cash flow, cash flow after income taxes, and cash flow before and after debt service.

In determining the return from the project, developers might use discounted cash flow analysis to allow for the time value of money. This analysis applies an appropriate discount to cash to be received in the future, as future cash is worth less than present cash. How much less depends on the amount that present cash could earn in the interim. Various methods of discounted cash flow analysis are possible, including net present value analysis, reinvestment rate analysis, and internal rate of return (IRR) analysis.

As part of the feasibility study, a financial feasibility model may be prepared to test the economics of the project and to satisfy the financial objectives of the project's investors and lenders. For an apartment project, for example, the model could use estimates of the project's rental rates, size and number of housing units, development costs, operating expenses, net operating income, debt service, and other data to provide such information as the maximum equity investment required, return on equity, and the maximum loan that can be made on the project based on a criterion like the debt coverage ratio (the project's net operating income divided by the debt service).

Another important component of the feasibility study is an analysis of the project's financial sensitivity. Sensitivity analysis measures the impact of changes in assumptions about the project's financial and operating data on the project's profitability and return on equity.

Appraisal

The third part of the feasibility analysis is the appraisal. Its purpose is to provide prospective lenders with an estimate of the market value of the development project when completed and/or the value of the land on which the project is built. Market value generally is defined as the price that a willing and knowledgeable buyer would pay a willing and knowledgeable seller for a property. The estimate of market value commonly represents a synthesis of the traditional appraisal approaches to value, applied as appropriate for the project: the income approach (capitalization of the development's net operating income), the cost approach (the development's replacement or reproduction cost), the market approach (value of comparable properties based on recent sales), and the discounted cash flow approach (present value of the net cash flow generated by the project).

If the development project consists of for-sale housing, the market value of the completed project is estimated. If the project consists of rental housing, the estimate is based on the value of the project when it has reached stabilized occupancy. The estimate is included in an appraisal report prepared by a professional appraiser employed by the developer; it becomes part of the developer's application for a loan.

Pro Forma Financial Statements

The culmination of the feasibility analysis is the preparation of pro forma cash flow and profit and loss statements. These financial statements show whether the project is financially feasible, that is, whether the

CASH FLOW STATEMENT
(FOR A PROPOSED DEVELOPMENT OF 86 SINGLE-FAMILY DETACHED HOUSES)

INCOME AND EXPENSES	QTR 1	QTR 2	QTR 3	QTR 4	QTR 5	QTR 6
PROJECT REVENUES:						
Units Closed						42
Average Sale Price per Unit						150,000
Gross Sales Revenues						6,300,000
Less: Sales Commissions and Closing Costs (2%)						(126,000)
TOTAL NET REVENUES	0	0	0	0	0	6,174,000
PROJECT COSTS:						
Land Acquisition	(1,652,000)					
Planning, Engineering, Design	(186,943)	(170,485)	(122,572)	(94,736)	(82,009)	19,667
Site Improvements			(402,000)	(868,000)	(2,000)	(30,000)
Direct House Construction				(1,900,000)	(2,034,000)	(1,298,000)
Indirect House Construction and Fees		(97,000)	(94,000)	(72,000)	(72,000)	(72,000)
Marketing				(132,003)	(296,499)	(114,143)
General Overhead (3%)	(43,189)	(43,189)	(43,189)	(43,189)	(43,189)	(43,189)
Property Taxes	(6,500)		(6,500)		(6,500)	
TOTAL COSTS	(1,888,632)	(310,674)	(668,261)	(3,109,928)	(2,536,197)	(1,537,665)
NET CASH FLOW BEFORE FINANCING	(1,888,632)	(310,674)	(668,261)	(3,109,928)	(2,536,197)	4,636,335

FINANCING CASH FLOW

	QTR 1	QTR 2	QTR 3	QTR 4	QTR 5	QTR 6
LAND LOAN:						
Loan Disbursements	1,156,400					
Interest Due and Paid	(28,910)	(28,910)	(28,910)	(28,910)	(28,910)	(21,145)
Loan Repayments	0	0	0	0	0	(621,229)
Land Loan Net Cash Flow	1,127,490	(28,910)	(28,910)	(28,910)	(28,910)	(642,373)
CONSTRUCTION LOAN:						
Commitment Fee	(50,000)					
Loan Disbursements			1,215,567	3,109,928	2,536,197	1,537,665
Loan Repayments	0	0	0	0	0	(5,372,093)
Construction Loan Net Cash Flow	(50,000)	0	1,215,567	3,109,928	2,536,197	(3,834,428)
NET CASH FLOW TO THE DEVELOPER	(811,142)	(339,584)	518,396	(28,910)	(28,910)	159,534

LOAN INFORMATION

	QTR 1	QTR 2	QTR 3	QTR 4	QTR 5	QTR 6
LAND LOAN DETAIL:						
Loan Balance, Start	0	1,156,400	1,156,400	1,156,400	1,156,400	1,156,400
Add: Disbursements	1,156,400	0	0	0	0	0
Less: Repayments	0	0	0	0	0	(621,229)
Loan Balance, End	1,156,400	1,156,400	1,156,400	1,156,400	1,156,400	535,171
Interest Due	(28,910)	(28,910)	(28,910)	(28,910)	(28,910)	(21,145)
CONSTRUCTION LOAN DETAIL:						
Loan Balance, Start	0	0	0	1,389,720	4,586,802	7,281,133
Add: Disbursements	0	0	1,215,567	3,109,928	2,536,197	1,537,665
Add: Accrued Interest and Fees	0	0	174,154	87,154	158,134	119,287
Less: Repayments	0	0	0	0	0	(5,372,093)
Loan Balance, End	0	0	1,389,720	4,586,802	7,281,133	3,565,992

Source: Kenneth Leventhal & Company, Los Angeles, California.

INCOME AND EXPENSES	QTR 7	QTR 8	QTR 9	QTR 10	TOTAL
PROJECT REVENUES:					
Units Closed	18	18	8		86
Average Sale Price per Unit	155,000	160,000	165,000		154,535
Gross Sales Revenues	2,790,000	2,880,000	1,320,000		13,290,000
Less: Sales Commissions and					
Closing Costs (2%)	(55,800)	(57,600)	(26,400)		(265,800)
TOTAL NET REVENUES	2,734,200	2,822,400	1,293,600	0	13,024,200
PROJECT COSTS:					
Land Acquisition					(1,652,000)
Planning, Engineering, Design	8,221	19,947	21,621	16,816	(570,473)
Site Improvements	(3,000)	(2,000)	(1,000)	(45,000)	(1,353,000)
Direct House Construction	(150,000)	(60,000)	(60,000)	(8,000)	(5,510,000)
Indirect House Construction					
and Fees	(61,000)	(82,000)	(94,000)		(644,000)
Marketing	(74,925)	(59,740)	92,739		(584,571)
General Overhead (3%)	(43,189)	(43,189)	(43,189)	(10,000)	(398,700)
Property Taxes	(3,250)				(22,750)
TOTAL COSTS	(327,143)	(226,982)	(83,829)	(46,184)	(10,735,494)
NET CASH FLOW BEFORE					
FINANCING	2,407,057	2,595,418	1,209,771	(46,184)	2,288,706
FINANCING CASH FLOW					
LAND LOAN:					
Loan Disbursements					1,156,400
Interest Due and Paid	(10,051)	(3,395)	(34)	0	(179,175)
Loan Repayments	(266,241)	(266,241)	(2,689)	0	(1,156,400)
Land Loan Net Cash Flow	(276,292)	(269,636)	(2,723)	0	(179,175)
CONSTRUCTION LOAN:					
Commitment Fee					(50,000)
Loan Disbursements	327,143	226,982	0	0	8,953,481
Loan Repayments	(2,302,326)	(1,888,274)	0	0	(9,562,693)
Construction Loan Net Cash Flow	(1,975,183)	(1,661,292)	0	0	(659,211)
NET CASH FLOW TO THE					
DEVELOPER	155,582	664,490	1,207,048	(46,184)	1,450,320
LOAN INFORMATION					
LAND LOAN DETAIL:					
Loan Balance, Start	535,171	268,930	2,689	0	0
Add: Disbursements	0	0	0	0	1,156,400
Less: Repayments	(266,241)	(266,241)	(2,689)	0	(1,156,400)
Loan Balance, End	268,930	2,689	0	0	0
Interest Due	(10,051)	(3,395)	(34)	0	(179,175)
CONSTRUCTION LOAN DETAIL:					
Loan Balance, Start	3,565,991	1,647,600	0	0	0
Add: Disbursements	327,143	226,982	0	0	8,953,481
Add: Accrued Interest and Fees	56,792	13,692	0	0	609,211
Less: Repayments	(2,302,326)	(1,888,274)	0	0	(9,562,693)
Loan Balance, End	1,647,600	0	0	0	0

project's revenues will not only cover project costs, including financing, but also produce a profit or return on the equity that developers and other investors have invested in the project. Developers can then decide whether the projected return is acceptable, given the risks in developing the project. They can also decide whether the return on the proposed project is adequate compared to expected returns from other projects planned or under development. The pro forma financial statements are based on:

- Detailed market studies that document the demand for the residential units to be developed and the revenues that the units will generate.
- An estimate of the costs to develop and absorb the project.
- An estimate of the time required to develop and absorb the project.

The cash flow statement shows the project's cash flows period by period over the life of the development, from land acquisition to sales of the residential units or stabilized occupancy of an apartment project. It also shows the equity investment required to cover costs not financed by loans.

The profit and loss statement shows the project's total revenues, costs, and profits. It helps the developer to decide whether the project's potential profits are adequate.

The project shown in Figures 3-16 and 3-17 is to be built on 21.5 acres, with lots averaging 7,200 square feet. The houses range from 1,600 square feet to 2,000 square feet, and the average price over the life of the project is $154,535. The cash flow statement shows the project's cash flow over two and one-half years. It is presented by quarters, although a monthly format also is often used. The statement incorporates several major features and assumptions:

1. *Project Revenues*
   - Model homes are constructed in quarters 4 and 5.
   - Sales start in quarter 5.
   - Construction of production units starts in quarter 4.
   - Escrow accounts close and buyers take possession of houses beginning in quarter 6.
   - The starting average purchase price is $150,000 per unit, with quarterly increases of $5,000 per unit.
   - Sales commissions and closing costs are estimated at 2 percent of the sale price.

2. *Project Costs*
   - Land is acquired at the beginning of quarter 1 for $1.65 million with a 30 percent cash downpayment and the seller's financing 70 percent.
   - Planning, engineering, design, and subdivision approval require six months. The developer pays for these costs until being reimbursed from the construction loan, which is funded in quarter 3. During this period, the developer is required to make deposits for installation of utilities. Beginning in quarter 6 and continuing through quarter 10, the developer is reimbursed by the various utility companies as the houses are completed and occupied.
   - Site improvements are completed in quarters 3 and 4, with minor residual work after that.
   - Construction of housing units begins in quarter 4 and is completed in quarter 7, with minor residual and customer service work thereafter.
   - "Indirect house construction" includes building permits and fees, design fees, and other miscellaneous costs. It begins in quarter 2 and continues through quarter 9.
   - Marketing costs are heaviest in the early part of the period analyzed as a result of costs for decorating and furnishing models and landscaping. These costs start in quarter 4 and continue until quarter 9, when the models are sold. About 60 percent of the costs of decorating, furnishing, and landscaping are recaptured.
   - General overhead is estimated at 3 percent of total gross sales revenue; it includes project supervision and corporate allocation.
   - The developer pays property taxes on the land until the houses are sold.

3. *Land Loan*
   - "Loan disbursements" refers to the 70 percent note provided by the seller and is not part of actual cash flow. This note is subordinated to the construction loan.
   - Interest on the land loan is calculated at 10 percent per year, simple interest, and is paid quarterly by the developer. It is not funded by the construction loan.
   - Principal on the land loan is repaid as the houses are closed. The amount of the loan ($1,156,400) is divided by the total units built (86) and multiplied by 1.10 to determine the release payment made when each unit is closed ($14,791 per unit). This payment releases the unit from the lien of the land loan mortgage.

4. *Construction Loan*
   - The construction loan requires a 0.5 percent loan commitment fee paid in cash in quarter 1, when the land is acquired. Another 1.5 percent loan fee is incurred in quarter 3, when the loan is funded, and is included in the construction loan balance.
   - Disbursement of the construction loan begins in quarter 3; it covers all costs except land. The developer is reimbursed in quarter 3 for costs incurred in quarters 1 and 2.
   - Interest is calculated at 10 percent annually, compounded, and is accrued.
   - The total amount of the loan is $10 million, including all disbursements, loan fees, and accrued interest. It is the amount negotiated in quarter 1. Only $9,562,693 is actually used.
   - The loan is repaid according to a release payment schedule based on 110 percent of the total loan amount per unit ($127,907), which is paid when each unit is closed and releases the unit from the construction loan mortgage.

5. *Net Cash Flow to the Developer*
   This amount is the sum of "net cash flow before financing," "land loan net cash flow," and "construction loan net cash flow." Several different measures of a project's profitability and return can be calculated from the cash flow and profit and loss statements:

   - Profit per unit: $16,864 (from the profit and loss statement).
   - Profit as a percent of gross sales revenue: 10.9 percent (from the profit and loss statement).
   - Internal rate of return on the developer's initial equity invested: 49 percent (from the cash flow statement). The developer's initial equity investment is the total of the negative cash flows in the first two quarters.
   - Profit as a percent of initial equity invested: 126 percent (profit divided by the developer's initial equity investment).

Developers might use one or more of these measures in deciding whether or not the proposed project would provide a profit and return adequate to induce them to proceed. All of the measures of profit and return shown for the sample project are within ranges typically indicating that a project is financially feasible. All developers have their own standards of "adequate," however.

These measures of profit and return are only one factor—albeit an important one—to consider in deciding whether to develop a project. Entitlement,

3-17 PROFIT AND LOSS STATEMENT (FOR A PROPOSED DEVELOPMENT OF 86 SINGLE-FAMILY DETACHED HOUSES)

PROJECT REVENUES

Gross Sales Revenues	$ 13,290,000
Less: Sales Commissions	(265,800)
Net Revenues	$ 13,024,200

PROJECT COSTS

Land Acquisition	$ (1,652,000)
Planning, Engineering, Design	(570,473)
Site Improvements	(1,353,000)
Direct House Construction	(5,510,000)
Indirect House Construction	(644,000)
Marketing	(584,571)
General Overhead	(398,700)
Property Taxes	(22,750)
Total Costs	$(10,735,494)
Net Cash Flow before Financing	$ 2,288,706
Financing Costs:	
Land Loan Interest	(179,175)
Construction Loan Interest and Fees	(659,211)
Total Financing Costs	$ (838,386)
Net Income or Profit	$ 1,450,320

SCHEDULE OF RETURNS

Profit per Unit	$ 16,864
Profit as Percent of Gross Sales Revenue	10.91%
IRR	49.36%
Profit as Percent of Initial Equity Invested	126.04%

Source: Kenneth Leventhal & Company, Los Angeles, California.

construction, and market risks facing the project must also be evaluated.

Tax Considerations

The feasibility analysis would not be complete without consideration of the tax consequences of investing in the project to the developer and other equity investors. Tax planning for real estate investment and development has been profoundly affected by the Tax Reform Act of 1986 and the Revenue Act of 1987, and developers should be aware of some of the principal changes:

- The top corporate tax rate was reduced from 46 percent to 34 percent, the top individual rate from 50 percent to 28 percent.
- The top capital gains tax rate for corporations was increased from 28 percent to 34 percent, for individuals from 20 percent to 28 percent. Thus, capital gains are now taxed at the same rate as ordinary income.
- The life over which buildings can be depreciated was increased from 19 years (applicable to all types of buildings) to 27½ years for residential buildings and 31½ years for commercial buildings.
- The ability of individuals to shelter active income (income from services or material participation in a business activity) and portfolio income with losses from real estate and other tax shelters was drastically curtailed for individuals and somewhat reduced for corporations. Sheltering income with real estate losses (often attributable largely to deductions for depreciation) was a major factor behind many real estate developments.
- The benefits of reporting income by installments were greatly diluted. The installment method was eliminated for dealers in property and preserved for nondealers in property, but if a taxpayer has more than $5 million in installment receivables outstanding at the end of the year, interest must be paid on the tax that is deferred by the use of the installment method (to the extent that the receivables exceed $5 million).

The drop in tax rates, the lower deductions for depreciation, and the restricted ability to shelter active and portfolio income with real estate losses in large measure have achieved Congress's objective: to base business decisions on underlying economic factors rather than on tax considerations.

The Financing Process

Once the feasibility analysis is completed, developers are in a position to decide whether to proceed with the project. If the decision is affirmative, the developer seeks financing for the project, but how much financing and from whom depend on a number of considerations.

First is the size of the project. A small project may need a relatively modest amount of capital, and developers may be able to raise equity capital from their own resources and from friends, relatives, and business associates, and to obtain financing from local lenders.

Financing a large project that needs a large amount of capital is a more formal process. Developers might seek equity capital from a syndicator, a larger developer, or an S&L and construction financing from a large commercial bank, thrift institution, or mortgage banker/broker. They can reach prospective investors and lenders directly through their own business and personal contacts. Large developers experienced in building large-scale projects may have long-standing relationships with lenders ready and able to finance the latest venture. If not, they may have to go through mortgage bankers, mortgage brokers, or other intermediaries to reach potential lenders.

The Financing Package

Developers in some cases might be able to obtain construction financing without a takeout commitment—if, for example, plans are to develop single-family houses for sale to individual borrowers who will arrange their own financing. If the construction lender requires a takeout commitment, however, developers first have to get an insurance company or other permanent lender to commit to financing the project. To make that decision, the lender requires a financing package or loan submission package from the developer. (Construction lenders also generally require such a package.) The financing package is described more fully in Figure 3-18.

Negotiating the Permanent Loan

If, based on the information in the financing package, the lender is interested in funding the loan, the lender and developer open negotiations. Their objective is to produce a written contract containing mutually acceptable terms of the loan and the conditions under which the loan is legally binding.

Negotiations may begin over terms of the loan as proposed by the developer in the loan application. The lender may agree to the terms or counter with its proposed terms. For example, it may ask for some form of profit participation or equity interest in the project. If the developer prepared a financial feasibility model as part of the feasibility analysis, it can be used to determine the economic effects on the project of the financing alternatives proposed by the lender.

Once they agree on the basic terms of the loan, the lender and developer negotiate other issues. One of the most important is the issue of contingencies. Usually the commitment provides for contingencies, meaning the loan will be approved subject to satisfac-

Most lenders require the following items to be submitted before making a commitment to finance a residential project:

- *A description and characteristics of the property to be developed,* including a plot plan or survey, a topographical or contour map, aerial photographs, results of soils tests, drainage characteristics, and available utility connections and street access.
- *Legal documentation,* including a legal description of the property; a title opinion (for purposes of obtaining title insurance) that includes a description of any deed restrictions, easements, liens, and assessments; and a summary of land use controls and zoning and building code regulations that may affect the project. The documentation should also note any environmental hazards that could affect the project. One reason for the lender's requesting this extensive documentation is to protect its position as first lien holder in the event the loan is made. The lender wants to know whether any prospective liens could cloud its priority position and whether any restrictions could impede development and marketing of the project.
- *A description of entitlements,* including a description of government approvals already obtained, a plan for obtaining the remaining approvals necessary for the project to proceed, and the probability of obtaining such approvals.
- *Building and site plans,* including a rendering of the completed project, usually prepared by an architect.
- *Detailed development costs,* including estimates of financing costs and the time required to complete the project.
- *A pro forma financial statement* detailing the project's expenses, including land acquisition and construction costs, and the project's income and expected return.
- *A feasibility analysis,* including a market study showing expected demand for the completed product, a feasibility study showing the project's economic viability, and an appraisal.
- *The developer's financial statement,* including a list of assets and cash flow from other projects, which may provide additional collateral for the loan.
- *The developer's background and experience,* including its track record and current projects. Among other things, the lender wants to know that the developer has the financial and organizational resources to develop other projects in addition to the one for which financing is being sought.
- *The loan application,* including the requested amount of the loan, interest rate, terms of amortization, and method of repayment.
- *A description of any anticipated problems in developing the property,* including, for example, some form of proposed growth-control ordinance for the community where the project is located that has a potential effect on the proposed development.

tion of the specific conditions. If the contingencies are not met, the permanent commitment can expire without the lender's being obligated to make the loan.

Contingencies subject to negotiation include the time permitted for the developer to obtain construction financing or interim financing, the date for completion of construction, the expiration date for the loan commitment, and provisions for design changes and approval. For rental properties, developers might be required to rent a minimum number of units to obtain permanent financing or might have to guarantee rents if rents do not achieve a minimum level. The lender might advance only a portion of the agreed-upon loan funds until the required occupancy level is met, at which time it will advance the remainder of the funds. When the loan's terms include such a requirement, developers may have to obtain interim financing to cover the period from expiration of the construction loan until the required occupancy level is reached and permanent financing is available.

Negotiations usually cover a number of other issues—the developer's personal guarantee for the loan (or operating deficits in the case of income properties), terms and conditions of prepaying the loan, assignment of the mortgage securing the loan to a third party, the amount that the lender will be reimbursed for expenses of legal, appraisal, and feasibility studies, title examination, recordation and filing fees, and required insurance coverage for fire and other risks.

If the two parties agree on the loan's terms and conditions, the lender issues a commitment letter stating that the loan application has been approved and that the developer must accept the loan terms in writing within a specified time for the commitment to be effective. The commitment letter contains a legal description of the property securing the loan, the amount of the loan, annual interest rate, maturity date, terms of mortgage payments, required escrow deposits and finance fees, and other terms, conditions, and contingencies.

Negotiating the Construction Loan

With takeout commitment in hand, developers can seek construction financing for the project. Construction lenders often require a takeout or standby commitment as a condition of financing apartment projects; however, they often do not require such a commitment to finance construction of single-family housing or condominium projects. Obtaining a construction loan also requires filing a loan application and financing package with a construction lender and negotiating terms and conditions of the construction financing between lender and developer.

In considering the developer's application for a construction loan, the lender is concerned first of all with the developer's ability to complete the project in accordance with the requirements of the takeout commitment. For a variety of reasons—construction delays or cost overruns, for example—the permanent loan could not materialize because the project was not completed according to terms of the takeout commitment. Depending on the nature of the problems, the permanent lender may decide that they were of little consequence, or it may decide they were sufficiently large to reduce the amount of the loan or even cancel the loan agreement.

If the lender decides to provide construction financing, it issues a commitment letter stating the terms and conditions of the loan, including whether the developer or third parties provide a guarantee for the loan and the nature of the guarantee—for example, a full guarantee of the amount of principal, a guarantee of the top 10 percent of the principal, or a guarantee of payment of only the interest. Usually the permanent lender's loan requirements, as detailed in its commitment, are included in the construction loan commitment by reference. The commitment also includes the length of time that the commitment is effective, the lender's requirements as to its approval of the plans and specifications, its right to inspect the construction site, its requirements for title insurance policies, liability insurance during construction, and a performance bond, the lender's fee, and the lender's right to take over the project and finish construction if it does not proceed according to the terms of the loan agreement.

Before the commitment expires, the developer and construction lender enter into a loan agreement that contains the terms, conditions, and requirements of the commitment letter as well as other essential provisions, such as requirements for disbursement of construction funds and establishment of a reserve by which a percentage of the loan (usually 10 percent) is held by the lender until construction is completed satisfactorily.

When the developer and lender are ready to close the loan, a meeting attended by representatives of each party is scheduled. The loan documents are reviewed, including the note in which the lender states the amount and terms of the loan, the mortgage, which is the security for the loan, the title documents, and other necessary legal documents. Depending on the size and complexity of the project and how well prepared the parties are, closing can be completed in an hour—or take many hours.

4.
Product Programming

While developers and the public sector share responsibility for improving the urban environment, developers have a distinctive involvement, affecting both policy and projects. In 1971, an Urban Land Institute task force on environmental quality recognized the importance of a developer's role in shaping the quality of the urban environment:

> The developer's role should not only be that of a participant in improving environmental quality, but by virtue of his profession, that of a catalyst. The developer has significant impact on the face of our land and often carries the awesome responsibility of structuring the habitat of many people over a long period of time with great investments in capital.[1]

Council member Gordon E. Tippell believes that the real estate development industry is living up to this responsibility today: "The development industry is getting better organized every year to find solutions to the major problems facing the industry—shortages of infrastructure, traffic congestion, and environmental concerns. Developers will need to continue this kind of problem solving in the years ahead: local governments simply cannot do it alone."

Development is a long-term business—economically and physically. Unsound principles and practices applied to the land have long-term effects that cannot easily be reversed. And developers must consider these long-term effects with every decision. In short, they must address and foster concern for the urban environment where most people will continue to live.

For specific projects, developers have tremendous influence over quality of design through site selection, planning and engineering, construction, and maintenance and operation. While all development puts stress on the land, the degree to which the land is actually disrupted varies from project to project. Developers' first questions should ask how a particular parcel of land can be developed at a reasonable profit with the least detriment to its natural characteristics. Or, if the natural condition of the site is of questionable quality, they should ask what development practices, if any, will enhance the environment.

Good residential design begins with an understanding of how future residents might perceive their houses and the community where they are located. What do these future users consider valuable? And in choosing their housing, what is the extent of the geographic area that future residents will evaluate? The neighborhood remains the basic measurement urban planners use to evaluate elements linked with people and areas in the formulation of a comprehensive community plan. The concept of neighborhood

---

[1] Task Force on Environmental Quality and ULI–the Urban Land Institute, *Environment and the Land Developer* (Washington, D.C.: ULI–the Urban Land Institute, 1971), p. 6.

is equally valid for guiding the development of new suburban residential land and for redeveloping central cities.

A neighborhood is the geographic area within which residents conveniently share the common services and facilities needed in the vicinity of their dwellings. Neighborhoods are often set by physical boundaries: 1) natural features, such as topography or watercourses; 2) streets or highways; 3) manmade features, such as power lines, railroads, or other obstructions to development; and 4) planning elements, such as parks, open space corridors, and community facilities. But neighborhoods can also be set by social boundaries within which most residents share a common lifestyle or ethnic or socioeconomic characteristic, such as the neighborhoods that characterized much of New York City during the early part of the 20th century.

For contemporary planners, neighborhood boundaries are often defined as the service area of an ele-

4-1   PRINCIPLE OF NEIGHBORHOOD UNITS

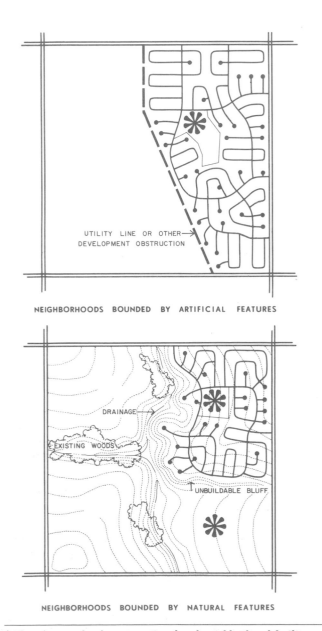

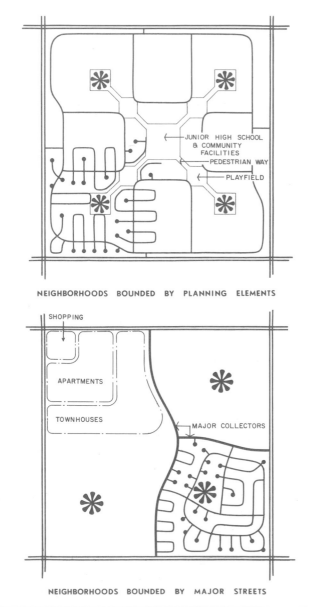

* Elementary school or recreational and neighborhood facility.

mentary school and convenience, "neighborhood-level" shopping center.[2] To promote the concept of neighborhood, major roadways should be designed around the periphery of the neighborhood, and only local streets serving the needs of residents should be built within the neighborhood.

New neighborhoods in planned unit developments or master-planned communities often contain various types of dwellings (or residential "products") at different densities. The trend has been to provide for a variety of housing, lifestyles, and ranges in prices or rents within what might be considered the same neighborhood. This concept permits developers to expand the market considerably by offering products that will appeal to a larger and more diverse segment of the population. Some localities, however, discourage such diversity by regulatory controls that prohibit higher-density housing. Existing residents within a neighborhood may also resist the introduction of substantially different types of housing or densities in an effort to preserve the status quo.

The concept of neighborhood is not limited to the development of raw land. Planning commissions use the concept as a basis in studies of new growth areas in cities or in replanning older sections. The size, type, boundaries, and community facilities of a neighborhood are often determined on the basis of existing physical barriers and an exhaustive land use survey, modified in accordance with plans for major thoroughfares, transportation, parks and playgrounds, and other physical, social, and economic factors.

Although the concept of neighborhood is valid for developers as an overall planning tool, perhaps more important is the creation of subneighborhoods that, more than anything else, lend a sense of place to the residents of a development. Residents perceive their immediate environment more vividly than any larger context called a "neighborhood." According to council member David K. Sunderland, "The neighborhood has lost any social meaning of consistent value beyond three blocks in any direction." Thus, it is wise for developers to build a sense of place and value into subneighborhoods to enhance a project's vitality.

This chapter addresses a key decision that developers must make with every residential development—the development "program" to be planned and implemented on the site. The selection and definition of this program is based on the results of the project feasibility analysis. After compiling all of the information learned about the market and the site, developers must begin to define a land use program for the land planners and other members of the development team to lay out on the site.

The development program is comprised of several distinct portions. The most basic decision about programming relates to how the land will be divided for development of residential uses, another major one to the type of residential dwellings to be developed. The choices range from single-family houses on large lots to high-rise, multifamily buildings. Developers also must establish the type and extent of amenities needed to support the number and type of houses proposed. Finally, developers must make hard decisions about how development of the housing, amenities, and supporting uses will be phased.

Alternative Forms of Land Development

The most basic decision about design that residential developers face is how the land will be divided and used to provide for new residential development. Many factors influence this decision: the physical conditions of the site, market forces, surrounding patterns of development, and regulatory limitations. The size of the site also often influences options for development; large parcels of several hundred acres can offer many opportunities for creative and diverse land plans, while small sites usually offer a more limited array of possibilities.

Conventional Subdivisions

Since the suburban explosion of the 1950s, the subdivision has been the most common mode of conversion and reconversion of land for residential uses. Subdivision is the division of a parcel of land into two or more lots, and it can take the form of a simple split or the creation of hundreds of residential lots from raw land. The practice of subdividing land is regulated by state laws enforced primarily by local (municipal or county) governments. Within the framework of a subdivision, residential developers can choose from numerous possibilities. The most common examples of a subdivision are those that grew in suburbs around central cities during the postwar era. Seemingly overnight, large tracts of land were subdivided for single-family houses, roads, schools, shopping centers, and other uses that support residents. Residential developers constructed tract houses on the lots created;

---

[2] A neighborhood shopping center provides for the sale of daily living needs like food, drugs, hardware, and personal services. Its principal tenant is a supermarket or superstore. See ULI–the Urban Land Institute, *Dollars & Cents of Shopping Centers* (Washington, D.C.: Author, 1990).

typically, three to five floor plans were used per subdivision with minor variations made to exteriors to suggest individuality. In many instances, a single trench was cut for footers, foundations, and basements to serve an entire block of houses.

During the 1960s and continuing through the 1970s and 1980s, subdivisions became more varied in terms of patterns and sizes of lots, street alignments, open space networks, and mix of residential products. A set "formula" for subdividing land for residential use no longer exists. Today, developers must create a land pattern that works within its physical and social context, one that responds to the aspirations of future users—homebuyers or renters.

Increasingly, it is almost impossible to separate the subdivision of residential land from the specific housing product to be built. Council member Jack Bloodgood says, "I started out designing houses.... Now I design houses and land together."[3] It is no longer economically feasible in many markets to subdivide land into one-quarter acre (or larger) lots capable of accommodating any type of single-family housing. Instead, the lot and choice of housing must be closely matched to maximize privacy, access, the streetscape, and relationships between indoors and outdoors. This need to design lots hand in hand with floor plans is most evident in small-lot, single-family houses that gained tremendous popularity during the 1980s.

When laying out the subdivision, developers must consider not only the pattern of residential development that will result (housing types, density, and mix, for example) but also all of the accessory uses of land that combine to make a residential neighborhood: streets, parks, open spaces, and community facilities. The subdivision's design must acknowledge both market forces and the site's natural quality.

Cluster Development

Cluster development is one form of subdivision in which houses are arranged in closely related groups. Rather than spreading houses uniformly over the entire site, developers of cluster projects build units at higher densities in certain areas and preserve natural features in others. Structures are usually placed on the most suitable terrain that minimizes site development costs associated with grading and installing infrastructure.

Clustering is most often based on the concept of "density transfer"; that is, overall density is within the limits established by the prevailing zoning code, but the individual density of the clusters is higher than the code permits. An excellent example of density clustering is Straw Hill in Manchester, New Hampshire (see the accompanying feature box). The 22-acre site was zoned for 12,500-square-foot lots, which would have yielded about 62 units once provisions were made for streets and a necessary retention pond for storm runoff. By creating nine clusters, the developer was able to build 65 units and to preserve almost 70 percent of the site as open space. Clustering not only improved unit yield but also resulted in substantially less cost for grading and site improvements.[4]

Within a cluster, all units typically are of the same type, although diverse housing types can avoid the sameness that becomes problematic as the scale of the cluster increases. Cluster planning requires attention to details of design to ensure that privacy is maintained. The approach can be adapted to any market in the country and has a proven track record as a viable alternative for land development. It is especially applicable for sites with physical constraints (such as wetlands, wooded areas, or steep terrain), because it offers an economic return on the land and still preserves important features of the site.

Planned Unit Development

A planned unit development embodies certain concepts of planning and design. A PUD is a land development project that 1) is planned as an entity, 2) groups dwelling units into clusters, 3) allows an appreciable amount of land for open space, 4) mixes housing types and land uses, and 5) preserves useful natural resources. A key factor in the popularity of PUDs among developers is the flexibility they offer in design in terms of such issues as lot sizes, densities, street layout, and product selection. Council member David Jensen adds, "The PUD's flexibility allows the developer to respond to changing market conditions by switching products as demand changes over time. Of course, these changes must be consistent with the PUD's original intent and ceiling on dwelling units, but the afforded flexibility gives the developer an edge over the developer of a conventional subdivision."

A simple PUD may contain a number of dwellings of the same type combined with common open space. A complex PUD may include a variety of housing

---

[3] Jerry Adler, "The House of the Future," *Newsweek,* Winter/Spring 1990 special edition, p. 73.

[4] *Project Reference File:* "Straw Hill," vol. 17, no. 18 (Washington, D.C.: ULI–the Urban Land Institute, October–December 1987). See also the related video.

CLUSTER PLANNING TO PRESERVE SITE FEATURES:
STRAW HILL—MANCHESTER, NEW HAMPSHIRE

Straw Hill is a community in Manchester, New Hampshire, of 65 single-family detached houses arranged in nine clusters of five to nine houses. In its land plan, landscape design, and architecture, the community strives to reflect the character of a small New England village. Located on a 22-acre hillside site, Straw Hill melds function, market demand, and concern for the environment.

Cluster planning provided for a series of small, social neighborhoods within a larger community. Each cluster can be reached from Straw Hill Road, a private street maintained by the homeowners' association. In addition to providing a livable scale for the project, the clusters permitted phasing in logical increments.

The community's design and success rely heavily on the blending of the units with the landscape. Clustering created blocks of open space—much like the open field of the site before development. To accommodate stormwater detention, seven ponds were designed into the landscape, serving as a visual amenity.

Perhaps the most immediately visible element of the landscaping is the use of wildflowers and native grasses on banks and around detention ponds—creating an amenity from a potentially negative feature of design. Requirements for grading around the ponds and on the steep, eastern portion of the site resulted in slopes of up to 2:1 gradients. To ensure

4-4   Aerial photograph showing houses situated around a cul-de-sac.

the slopes' stabilization and to minimize maintenance costs, a hydroseed mix of grasses and wildflowers was sown. The wildflowers bloom profusely during the spring and summer, providing enjoyment to residents, a habitat for wildlife, and a colorful symbol for the project.

Planning and Design

The design team first experimented with a plan based on the city's zoning, which permitted minimum lots of 12,500 square feet. Lots were arranged in a grid pattern similar to adjacent neighborhoods. Project engineers estimated that to meet the city's requirements for stormwater runoff, a detention pond about the size of the existing nine-unit cluster next to North River Road had to be located at the site's western edge. This plan yielded 62 units— within the developers' economic objectives—but was considered unsatisfactory from the perspective of design.

Instead of trying to replicate adjacent neighborhoods, the developers decided to create a community that would be compatible with them but distinctive in design. The concept that emerged was to provide a residential "village" reminiscent of a small New England town. And because the site had been a vacant field for years, the developers wanted to retain some of its qualities in the final plan.

Cluster planning was seen as a way to accomplish these objectives, but the 12,500-square-foot minimum prohibited optimal siting of units around clusters. The developers' criteria for solar orientation and privacy required greater flexibility in placing units and setbacks than typical lotting would

▶

4-3   The houses in Straw Hill are single-family condominiums; the condominium association performs all exterior maintenance. Cluster planning allowed houses to be sited around natural features like rock outcroppings, which were incorporated into the landscape design.

permit. To achieve flexibility, the developers structured the project as a condominium community of detached houses with private streets, which have less stringent design standards than public streets.

Although the city's zoning permitted them, detached condominiums had not previously been attempted in the area. When local residents learned that a condominium community was proposed for the site, they assumed the units would be attached and became concerned. To dispel controversy, the developers conducted door-to-door meetings with neighbors to explain the project. Ultimately, they achieved support with the proviso that access to Straw Hill be gained from North River Road instead of through the neighborhood on the south as originally planned.

Architecture

Given the primary design requirements for maximum southern exposure and privacy, the placement of all windows, blank walls, and outdoor openings had to be carefully considered. Each unit has a blank wall generally oriented to the north, which, along with the zero-lot-line concept, promotes privacy and provides energy efficiency. Additional privacy is gained by the placement of fences around the limited common areas (back yards) and by the strategic placement of trees or bushes on lines of sight between nearby units.

The southern exposure designed into virtually all units proved to be a major selling point in an area known for harsh winters. Orientation of units was so important to some prospective buyers that they brought compasses to better measure exposure to the sun. Inside, the houses feel bright and airy despite the blank wall and few multilevel volumes; heating and cooling costs are reduced considerably.

Grilled casement windows show a colonial influence, while wood siding, roof lines, and chimney treatments draw on rural New England design. To promote variety, shades of brown, green, blue, yel-

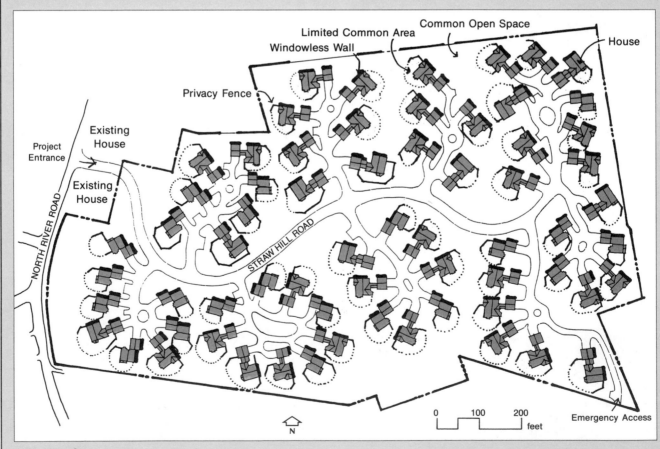

4-5   Site plan.

Land Use Information:

Site Area: 22 acres
Total Dwelling Units: 65
Gross Density: 3 units per acre
Parking: 2 garage spaces plus 2 driveway spaces per unit

Land Use Plan:

	Acres	Percent
Buildings	3.1	14.1%
Streets/Parking	3.0	13.6
Detention Ponds	0.8	3.6
Open Space	15.1	68.6

Unit Information:

Type[1]	Size (square feet)	Number[2]	Average Sale Price	Number of Bedrooms/ Bathrooms
A	1,820	22	$149,350	3/3
A+	2,780	4	$257,000	3/3
B	1,760	13	$151,760	2/2
B+	2,550	12	$184,000	3/3
C	1,820	5	$142,960	2/2
C+	2,820	1	$250,000	3/3

Economic Information:

Site Acquisition Cost: $396,000
Site Improvement Costs:[3] $1,587,500
Construction Costs:[3] $6,663,000
Total Hard Costs: $8,646,500
Total Soft Costs: $1,000,000

Notes:
[1]Unit types designated with "+" are designed for hillside clusters. The "C+" unit is a customized unit designed for a specific buyer.
[2]Fifty-seven of the planned 65 units have been constructed to date.
[3]Site improvement and construction costs are for the 57 units constructed to date.

low, and red are used. The architecture, clustering of units, and pastoral landscape work together to promote a sense of village.

Marketing

Because the developers had early reservations about the market's willingness to accept the concept of condominium ownership, Straw Hill was marketed as a single-family detached community rather than as a condominium community. Ultimately,

buyers were not concerned about the condominium form of ownership: most appreciated the convenience and lifestyle it offered. The first units were offered for sale in fall 1984, at $90,000 to $150,000. Prices have increased steadily and today range from $200,000 to $300,000; some resales command over $400,000. One cluster of eight houses remains to be built.

Fees for the homeowners' association are based on square footage and range from $90 to $150 per month. The fee includes maintenance of landscaping, unit exteriors, and all streets located within the community.

Experience Gained

- Creating several detention ponds instead of one large pond enabled the developers to better phase the project, to distribute costs over the phases, to use land more efficiently, and to create a series of amenities.
- Single-family condominiums require greater maintenance for landscaping than attached units. An underground irrigation system might effectively reduce maintenance costs.
- Security features are a primary concern to homebuyers. Original unit plans called for four doors opening to yard areas. Buyers felt that so many openings posed a security risk, so subsequent plans were modified to provide only two openings.
- Homeowners will respond favorably to the use of native wildflowers and grasses if landscaping is in place before occupancy. If they do not understand the concept, new residents will resist "natural" landscaping, fearing that it will look unkempt. It is important to keep the edges of wildflower patches mowed to demonstrate that they are intentional.

Developer

George Matarazzo and Mark Stebbins
P.O. Box 4430
Manchester, New Hampshire 03108

Architect/Planner/Landscape Architect

Matarazzo Design
9 Hills Avenue
Concord, New Hampshire 03301

Source: Adapted from *Project Reference File:* "Straw Hill," vol. 17, no. 18 (Washington, D.C.: ULI–the Urban Land Institute, October–December 1987).

types—detached single-family houses, townhouses, and multifamily units—along with open space and common areas containing recreational and community facilities. Residential PUDs can range from a few acres to well over 1,000 acres, but the number of units is often a better measurement of size than acres. The minimum number can be as few as five or six units, although principles of planning could better be applied with 50 units or more. Again, residential density averaged over the entire area being planned dictates the regulatory control, not specifications of minimum size and setback for individual lots.

Fundamental to the process of planning a PUD is negotiation among the principals involved—the developer, a public review authority (typically a professional planning staff and a lay planning commission), and the public at large. Because a PUD ordinance usually sets out parameters in very general terms, the local government has a good deal of discretionary control. Consequently, a PUD works best when all the parties understand the process and conduct their negotiations in a well-disciplined governmental framework.

Negotiation involves review of the site plan, although a wide range of alternative procedures exists. Review of the site plan is the major tool used to implement the PUD's objectives, and it offers a direct opportunity for tailoring development proposals to the community's objectives. Usually, general rules and standards are prescribed for the submission of site plans, which local officials then review and approve. In most jurisdictions that provide for PUDs, the process for approval consists of three stages: 1) the preapplication process, 2) submission of a preliminary development plan, and 3) submission of a final development plan. This procedure was first recommended by the American Society of Planning Officials in 1973 and has been incorporated and used by most jurisdictions since.[5]

During the preapplication conference (which in practice has not been mandatory), the planning agency helps to familiarize developers with the review process that lies ahead. It is also an opportunity for the agency's staff to convey to developers any parameters of design they hold for the land at issue. Developers in turn inform the staff of their ideas. Nothing during the preapplication stage is legally binding; it is an opportunity to share ideas and preconceptions about the project.

The second stage, submission of a preliminary development plan, is the most critical, because a major portion of project review takes place during it. The developer formally applies for a PUD to the local planning commission by submitting the required doc-

umentation—usually schematic drawings showing the site's visual character and how people will use it, a site plan, written design guidelines, and other supporting documents. The planning staff reviews the documentation and forwards its recommendation to the planning commission: approval, approval with conditions, or denial.

Following review and approval of the preliminary plan, developers have a set period of time before they are required to submit a final development plan. The final development plan is not a time to discuss matters previously agreed upon. Participants discuss any items that remain unsettled, especially how the developer has responded to any conditions of approval imposed at the time the preliminary plan was approved. Usually, the final development plan does not vary substantially from the approved preliminary plan. Following formal acceptance of the final plan, the planned unit development is recorded and the zoning approval phase is complete. Subsequent steps are typically administrative ones: a detailed site plan and architectural approvals for each phase of development, the issuance of grading and building permits, and construction inspections. In most cases, subdivision review and approvals are processed concurrently with the PUD; recording maps usually occurs in phases after review of the detailed site plan and before issuance of grading permits.

Contrary to most conventional zoning ordinances, which rely on a separation of uses, a PUD ordinance frequently allows (even encourages) mixed land uses. Nonresidential uses that are often included in a PUD include schools, churches, community centers, parks, neighborhood retail centers, and limited office and commercial space. The amount of nonresidential use included in a primarily residential PUD varies with the size of the parcel.

The flexible nature of the PUD provides an opportunity for creative land planning and residential design—and requires sophistication on the part of designers and developers. Approval authorities also must understand, evaluate, and endorse the concept.

Master-Planned Community

Government involvement in large-scale community development had its heyday during the 1930s under FDR's New Deal with the development of three

[5] Frank S. So et al., *Planned Unit Development Ordinances*, PAS Report No. 291 (Chicago: American Society of Planning Officials, 1973), pp. 14–24. See also Colleen Grogan Moore with Cheryl Siskin, *PUDs in Practice* (Washington, D.C.: ULI–the Urban Land Institute, 1985), pp. 21–25.

Widespread attention has focused on recent projects that promote walking at the expense of automobiles. This neotraditional movement in community planning has gained considerable recognition in the continuing public discussion about what constitutes a good place to live. Despite a growing interest in neotraditional communities by citizens' groups and planning agencies throughout the country, the verdict is still out on whether these communities can be economically feasible compared to the typical forms of suburban development they are meant to replace.

A key component of the new traditionalism is an emphasis on public places that accommodate pedestrian-oriented environments (such as unprogrammed open space or commons) and downplay the automobile as an element in the landscape. The "new traditionalism" encourages diverse housing types and architectural variety that increase a neighborhood's charm as well as small-scale neighborhood shopping that blends with nearby housing. Streets are designed as inviting promenades to encourage pedestrians' use, and parking lots are restructured to eliminate barriers between pedestrians and shopping.

The best-known example of the new design is Seaside, Florida, a resort community designed by the husband-and-wife team of Andres Duany and

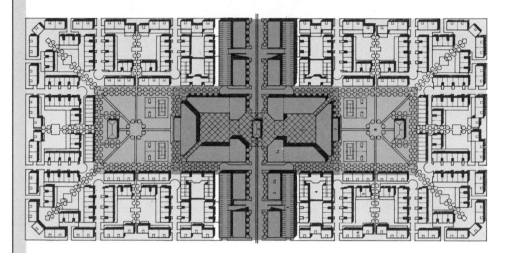

Key:
- ▬ Commercial Core: Office, Retail, Parking, Transit
- ▭ Residential
- ▬ Central Park/Open Space

4-8   A 60-acre pedestrian pocket, like the one shown generically above, is a balanced, mixed-use area within a quarter-mile or a five-minute walking radius of a transit station. The functions within this 50- to 100-acre zone include housing, offices, retail space, a daycare center, recreation, and parks. Up to 2,000 units of housing and 1 million square feet of office space can be located within three blocks of the transit station using typical residential densities and four-story office configurations. *Source:* Kelbaugh, p. 4. ▶

new towns: Greenbelt, Maryland, Greendale, Wisconsin, and Greenhills, Ohio.[6] A brief resurgence of the government's interest in the development of new towns occurred with Title VII of the Federal Housing Act of 1970, but since the demise of that program, it has been up to the private sector to plan and develop new communities. Although many private-sector developers may still use the term "new town" to describe a large development, these projects are generally never intended to function as freestanding, self-contained towns. Instead, they tend to relate closely with existing urban areas and become an extension of the suburban development pattern around an existing urban core. Although a number of terms have been used to describe this type of large-scale development, the one most universally applied today is "master-planned community." Such communities are often developed under PUD or similar regulatory procedures.

A master-planned community is a very specialized form of development because of its large size. Whereas a planned unit development can range from a few to a few hundred acres, master-planned communities

---

[6] See Lloyd W. Bookout, "Greenbelt, Maryland: A 'New' Town Turns 50," *Urban Land*, August 1987, pp. 7–11, for a summary of the federal "greenbelt" town movement.

Elizabeth Plater-Zyberk. Seaside is characterized by straight, not curvilinear, streets and uniform residential setbacks delineated by fences. Duany calls this orderly alignment a "...public room—a semi-enclosed outdoor area that feels properly delineated and seems to be a place in its own right, not just a void between buildings" (Langdon, p. 43).

Duany and Plater-Zyberk recently helped prepare a plan for a 352-acre project named Kentlands, near Gaithersburg, Maryland, 13 miles northwest of Washington, D.C. At buildout, the community will have 1,600 houses, 100 retail establishments, and 900,000 square feet of office space. The plan for the community, whose road network is configured on a

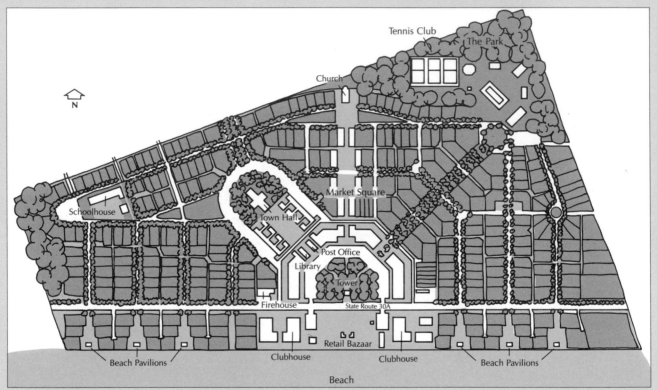

4-9   The plan for Seaside's 80-acre site provides for 750 dwelling units (including 200 hotel rooms) and a variety of "civic amenities": squares, gazebos, and arbors. The developer has reserved sites for a school, a firehouse, a post office, and other public buildings to reinforce the town's structure and identity.

typically range from one thousand to several thousand acres. In most instances, the site is acquired from a long-time owner of the property for a long-term, multiphase development program. Because of the project's size, developers can incorporate comprehensive design elements that might not otherwise be possible under multiple ownerships. According to council member David Jensen, master-planned communities are distinguished from more conventional subdivisions by an emphasis on neighborhood and community identities, a variety of housing types, a mixture of land uses (including centers of employment), coordination between land planning and architecture, and emphases on amenities and lifestyles.[7]

A master-planned community provides an opportunity for a large tract of land to be planned comprehensively from the outset and implemented (usually) by a single landowner or development company. Typically, a master developer assumes responsibility for constructing infrastructure and community services and makes building sites available to developers for the actual construction of houses. Sometimes the master developer also serves as homebuilder. In either case, as building sites become available, houses are

---

[7] See also "Planned Communities versus Traditional Subdivisions," *Land Development,* May 1988, pp. 23–27.

grid, resulted from an intensive series of workshops held with public officials and community groups. The plan's approval required the enactment of a new zoning category and amendments to a number of existing codes and other requirements.

Recognizing the need for alternative zoning regulations to encourage the development of other pedestrian-oriented communities, Duany and Plater-Zyberk wrote a "traditional neighborhood district" ordinance for general application. Key features of the ordinance are an emphasis on pedestrian orientation, mandatory dedication of land for neighborhood facilities like daycare centers, and encouragement of on-street parking. The maximum size of the district is 150 acres, so that all residents live within a 10-minute walk of a town center.

A variation on the neotraditional theme is evolving on an 800-acre site near Laguna Creek, 12 miles south of Sacramento, California. Laguna West, a 3,300-unit development, will be the first to demonstrate the "pedestrian pocket" concept of its planner, Peter Calthorpe. The project's town center will contain a mix of uses: shops, offices, and apartments laid out on a grid and linked to surrounding, lower-density residential and employment areas by a network of walking and bike trails. A principal goal of the plan is to provide sufficient density to support a light-rail line, which would connect the town center to other mixed-use, back-office, shopping-center, and park-and-ride "pedestrian pockets."

Even the proponents of these alternate patterns of suburban growth caution that they are not intended to displace urban renewal and acknowledge that they certainly will not eclipse suburban sprawl. Recognized obstacles to the implementation of the new traditionalism include rigid zoning and subdivision regulations and difficulties in marketing the

4-10 PROPOSED COMMUNITIES WITH NEOTRADITIONAL ELEMENTS

PROJECT	NUMBER OF ACRES	NUMBER OF UNITS
Belmont Forest Loudoun County, Virginia	275	800
Cascades Loudoun County, Virginia	2,804	5,995
Kentlands Gaithersburg, Maryland	352	1,600
Laguna West Sacramento, California	800	3,300
Montgomery Village Montgomery Township, New Jersey	200	490

new blended neighborhoods. Interest in the new urban concept is clearly growing, however, and its influence on residential development is likely to increase during the 1990s.

For additional information, see:

Doug Kelbaugh, ed., *The Pedestrian Pocket Book* (New York: Princeton Architectural Press, 1989).

Philip Langdon, "A Good Place to Live," *Atlantic Monthly,* March 1988, pp. 39–60.

"New Traditionalism in Suburban Design," *Zoning News,* June 1989, pp. 1–2.

Project Reference File: "Seaside," vol. 16, no. 16 (Washington, D.C.: ULI–the Urban Land Institute, October–December 1987).

"Reordering the Suburbs," *Progressive Architecture,* May 1989, pp. 78–91.

constructed in accordance with the original master plan's specifications for type and density.

The master developer is responsible for implementing the master plan, although the municipality normally reviews specific development plans along the way. Because most master-planned communities often require 20 years or more to complete, the original plan must often be modified; thus, the flexibility to make periodic changes must be provided in the original plan.

Large-scale master-planned communities are most prevalent in Sunbelt states like California, Arizona, Texas, and Florida, where large tracts of land near existing urban areas still exist under single owner-

ships. For the right parcels of land, master-planned communities can hold several advantages over more conventional (and fragmented) development. Because of the emphasis on coordinated planning and design, homebuyers have responded favorably to the concept. Council member David Jensen notes, "With their 'completeness,' highly visible image, and orientation, planned communities are better positioned in the marketplace than standard subdivisions." Council member Anthony Trella agrees: "When the housing market crashed in Houston during the 1980s, only projects within planned communities showed any signs of life; planned communities were also the first to stage a comeback."

In addition to potentially greater market acceptance, planned communities can be easier for municipalities to regulate than conventional development. Instead of dealing with perhaps hundreds of landowners or developers, each trying to maximize its development potential, planned communities usually reduce the municipality's negotiations to a single master developer, making negotiations and permitting easier to manage and making it easier to balance new residential growth with needed infrastructure and community services like roads, schools, and parks.[8]

Infill Development

Every city and its suburbs contain vacant parcels of land in otherwise built-up areas. These "infill" sites can result from a lack of or access to public services, physical or environmental limitations, or general unattractiveness to the market. Encouraging development of such parcels has become an objective for federal, state, and local governments faced with rising land costs, decreasing capability to expand infrastructure at the urban fringe, pressures to preserve environmentally sensitive or agricultural land, the need to strengthen older neighborhoods through preservation and rehabilitation, an interest in improving access to transportation, and a growing concern about the distance between jobs and housing.[9]

Developers are also becoming more interested in reconsidering the potential of previously skipped-over parcels as costs of land and development continue to rise in suburban fringes. Building on infill sites near existing infrastructure is often less costly than building on land at the urban fringe, where developers are now required to donate land or fees for such public services as schools, parks, roads, and utility extensions.

A fundamental concept underlies the design of infill development—sensitivity to context. No matter how obvious it may seem that infill development is distinguished from new development on raw land by the presence of the built environment, ignorance of or blindness to this environment often creates problems in design. The existing urban context must be fully understood in all its dimensions: physical, social, economic, and regulatory.[10] Designing an infill development to be consistent with its surroundings involves consideration of massing, scale, density, and architectural character. Infill projects hold a particular potential for controversy from existing residents of surrounding parcels, but developers can reduce the opportunity for controversy by designing a project that blends with the surrounding community. If the neighborhood is comprised of largely single-family houses, for example, a proposal for higher-density apartments is likely to face opposition. Developers must balance what is economically feasible for the site with what is perceived to be compatible with the existing urban fabric.

Opportunities for residential infill abound not only in inner cities but also in the suburbs. Many suburban sites were skipped over as a result of constraints on development that made them less attractive than other more readily developable parcels. With today's cost of land, however, these sites are proving to be economically viable. A case in point is Riverwoods— a 122-acre, 148-unit townhouse project in affluent

Michael Arden

4-11 The McClellan Apartments were built on a 1.2-acre infill site between single-family residences and high-rise office buildings in west Los Angeles. The design allows for three stories over a parking garage and a density of 54 units per acre.

[8] Reid Ewing, *New Community Development Guidelines* (Washington, D.C.: ULI–the Urban Land Institute, forthcoming).

[9] See Real Estate Research Corporation, *Infill Development Strategies* (Washington, D.C.: ULI–the Urban Land Institute and American Planning Association, 1982).

[10] Eric Smart, *Making Infill Projects Work* (Washington, D.C.: ULI–the Urban Land Institute, 1985), p. 15.

4-12 The Charleston Place rowhouses are located on eight infill sites in and around the historic district of Charleston, South Carolina. The "sidehouse" architectural style was used to blend the new houses into their historical surroundings. Each house actually contains two or three separate units.

Westchester County, New York. The site was passed over in the first wave of development because of problems associated with wetlands, outcroppings of rock, topography, and on-site historical buildings. Because of the site's history as open space, residents initially opposed any development. The developer was able to avoid the site's physical constraints, however, by clustering groups of townhouses on the least sensitive areas and thereby creating a plan that was acceptable to local residents. Planning and permitting required about three years of intense efforts, but the project paid off in the end.[11]

Types of Ownership

The design of a residential development must reflect the type of ownership contemplated. Newly constructed for-sale units—whether single-family, townhouse, or mid- or high-rise units—are created with a set of ground rules different from those for rental units. For example, for-sale products usually have different storage facilities (perhaps in the unit as opposed to common storage), different parking facilities, a different quality of construction and different life expectancy for the building, a different quality of interior finishes and building materials, and higher standards of sound attenuation. Thus, a for-sale unit may be completely different from a rental unit of similar size and floor plan. A project built for rent and eventually expected to become a for-sale unit must be planned for both types of ownership.

Housing ownership is of three primary types: fee simple, condominium, and cooperative. A fourth type, "interval ownership," describes a variety of options for ownership that allow the owner's use of real property on an occasional basis.

[11] Project Reference File: "Riverwoods," vol. 18, no. 17 (Washington, D.C.: ULI–the Urban Land Institute, October–December 1988).

Fee Simple

Most housing sold in this country is fee simple; that is, the owner is invested with the right to dispose of the property in any way he or she wishes. The owner can use the property so far as it will not interfere with the rights of others as typically controlled by zoning ordinances. The purchase of the property can be financed outright or, more commonly, through a mortgage arrangement.

Fee simple ownership is used for most single-family detached projects; the property owner owns the house in its entirety, the land the house sits on, and generally the property around the periphery of the house—the front and rear yards and two side yards. Most townhouse projects are also sold on a fee simple basis, with the homeowner owning the structure, the land under the house, and the front and rear yards.

The design of the lot and the house is largely a function of the sale price the developer hopes to receive as determined by the market analysis. As a rule, the larger the lot, the more expensive the house, although luxury, expensively finished attached houses geared to empty nesters are an exception. In this case, homeowners may actually prefer smaller lots to reduce maintenance chores.

Condominium

A condominium is not a design solution but a form of ownership. Each dwelling unit is owned outright by its occupant, not in common with other tenants like a cooperative. Each condominium may carry an individual mortgage, while a co-op has a common mortgage. A mortgage for a condominium might be reduced as the individual's financial position permits, while the owners of a co-op are bound by a set schedule of payments on the cooperative corporation's mortgage.

Condominiums may be structured so that a unit is defined as an airspace or as a portion of real property, such as walls and land. All parts of the condominium development not specifically owned by an individual (as described on the deed) are owned in common by all of the development's owners. Ownership of common elements is typically defined as a percentage proportionate to the square footage of each unit; the percentage interest in common elements is granted to owners by deed.

Owners of condominiums have a choice of owning their units free and clear of any mortgages or financing them through regular mortgage channels. Owners may sell, will, or give away the property. Each deed is recorded separately and taxes are levied individu-

ally. These advantages of actual ownership appeal to many—especially those who may not be able to afford a fee simple lot and those who may not want the responsibilities of maintenance associated with more conventional homeownership.

Because the condominium form of ownership is not tied to a particular design, it may appear in mid- or high-rise buildings, garden density units, attached townhouses, or even single-family detached houses.[12] It might also exist as a combination of two or more of these types of houses as part of a single condominium association. The condominium form of ownership is so versatile that it exists in commercial and industrial buildings as well as in residential housing; condominium associations can also include combinations of residential and commercial uses.

Management of a condominium is controlled by a condominium association.[13] The developer who has constructed the units within the condominium and established the condominium association usually assumes responsibility for managing the association initially before passing it on to the homeowners. Common responsibilities typically shared by the association may include maintenance of the building(s), landscaping, private streets and parking areas, recreational facilities like swimming pools and tennis courts, and any common interior elements like lobbies, elevators, heating and air-conditioning equipment, and hallways.

The association is also responsible for acquiring insurance coverage for the building; owners of individual units carry separate coverage for their personal belongings. Owners are charged a monthly fee to cover costs of maintenance, insurance, and a reserve account according to the value of their units. Often, fees are based on square footage so that those with larger units pay a proportionately greater share of the costs. Without agreement of the owners in accordance with the condominium's legal documents, neither the assessment nor the maintenance liability can change.

The condominium form of ownership first acquired legal status in the United States and its possessions in 1951 with the passage of a law in Puerto Rico. It was followed by another Puerto Rican law in 1958, the Horizontal Property Act, which governed the ownership of property categorized as condominiums. Congress amended the National Housing Act in 1961 to extend government insurance of mortgages to condominiums, and by 1968, all 50 states had enacted their own enabling legislation for condominiums.

---

[12] *Project Reference File:* "Straw Hill."
[13] Chapter 7 provides additional information about condominium associations and their management structures.

Typically, a condominium is financed in two phases: the developer finances the entire project through a blanket mortgage, and owners finance individual units through individual mortgages. Owners can obtain financing from many sources; such a mortgage is a conventional loan or a government-insured loan.

Cooperative

In the cooperative form of ownership, a single property is divided into units or use portions, with each user or "buyer" owning shares of stock in the corporation that owns the building. Typically, cooperative ownership is employed in a multiunit building—garden density, midrise, or high rise—where all the customary services are offered but where ownership and cost of operation are shared by the occupants in proportion to the value of the space they occupy. Co-op buyers are entitled to a proprietary lease of their space.

The predetermined rental rate for each unit is reached by prorating the costs of operation among tenants. The lease requires the co-op owner to make a monthly maintenance payment to the corporation to cover its operating expenses, mortgage interest, and real property taxes. Because interest and property taxes are obligations of the corporation, deductible only for calculating its taxable income, the proprietary tenant must be an individual, who is under strict requirements by the Internal Revenue Service to receive tax deductions.

To qualify as cooperative housing under IRS regulations, at least 80 percent of the corporation's gross income must come from tenant shareholders (defined as individuals entitled to occupy dwelling space in the building by virtue of ownership of stock in the corporation). Thus, not more than 20 percent of the corporation's income may come from tenants who are not individuals (i.e., income from commercial space, offices, garages, concessions, and restaurants).

The cooperative form of ownership has existed for some time, notably in major urban markets like New York City. The form of ownership appeals to confirmed city dwellers and those who seek the tax advantages of a corporation. But the cooperative has not caught on in this country as a popular form of ownership, although it is suitable for many suburban locations and offers advantages to the investor who might otherwise be merely a tenant. A primary disadvantage lies in the prorating of the building's operating costs among owners. Further, responsibility for mortgage payments is shared with other owners, each according to its own portion of ownership. Only that amount of the mortgage interest for which an individual owner is responsible can be deducted from his or her income tax.

Perhaps the most compelling reason that cooperative housing has not been more popular is that ownership rests with the corporation—not in the individual units. Thus, owners cannot pass their shares in the corporation through their estates or by any other means. The shares instead are sold back to the cooperative's board of trustees, which has ultimate authority over their disposition. Further, the co-op can incur liabilities, and stockholders may find themselves obligated for the liabilities of other stockholders.[14]

Interval Ownership

The most commonly known form of interval ownership is vacation timesharing. Most timeshare units are located in popular resort settings; owners of the units are guaranteed a period each year (usually a week) when they can use the unit. Ownership in vacation timeshare units is usually in fee simple title, with each owner holding a deed. Alternatively, owners may purchase a "right to use" the unit for some period (usually 30 years) without a deed. Most vacation timesharing developments are structured as condominiums, with all owners belonging to the condominium association and paying fees.

Another form of interval ownership is "fractional ownership." Rather than purchasing one week, owners purchase up to 13 weeks, or a quarter year. Thirteen-week purchases are often called "quarter-shares." Fractional ownership is most often purchased with a deed that gives the owners the right to use the unit in a solid block of time or in "floating" blocks that may be reserved in advance.

Vacation timeshare and fractional ownership programs have been most popular with active retirees, but as baby boomers age, they have found a new market.[15]

Residential Products

According to council member James W. Todd, "Given the economic choice, buyers still overwhelmingly prefer to purchase a single-family house—one with

---

[14] For additional information, contact the National Association of Housing Cooperatives, 2501 M Street, N.W., Suite 451, Washington, D.C. 20037 (202-887-0706).

[15] For additional information on interval ownership, contact the American Resort and Residential Development Association, 1220 L Street, N.W., 5th floor, Washington, D.C. 20005 (202-371-6700).

private green space all around it—even if it means a longer commute and a smaller lot. Most buyers are willing to squeeze themselves financially for a detached house. This long-term trend just does not seem to reverse itself." Several factors arose during the 1980s, however, that have made this American dream increasingly difficult to obtain. The most significant has been the lack of affordably priced houses in many major urban markets—New York, Los Angeles, Boston, San Francisco, and Washington, D.C., to name a few. Affordability has been affected by rising land costs, increased development fees, shortages of infrastructure, and generally higher financing costs. And the crunch came at a time of strong demand for first houses, as baby boomers moved into their homebuying years.

Despite the overall preference for detached houses, demand has also remained strong for attached housing. For some, a single-family attached house—a townhouse or condominium—is simply a matter of financial compromise. Others prefer attached housing because it is more convenient or secure or closer to employment or urban services than single-family detached development.

Whatever direction individual tastes run, the escalating cost of all types of housing and the desire to create a good living environment will continue to tax the imagination of designers and developers. The following paragraphs discuss the range of specific housing designs available in single-family housing—detached and attached—as well as in multifamily buildings.

Single-Family Detached

Single-family detached housing includes a wide range of densities and configurations. By definition, a single-family detached house is a freestanding structure that occupies its own lot. Conventional subdivisions rigidly prescribe setbacks for front yards, side yards, and rear yards.

In developing single-family detached housing, it is important to ensure that lotting and placement of houses respond to the site's natural features. Rigid adherence to preset specifications for lots can produce a uniform and monotonous pattern of development. A better neighborhood, net savings in site development costs, greater marketability of the product, and a greater benefit to purchasers will result from close attention to the relationships between houses and sites and to the provision of privacy and good orientation for each house.

Single-family detached units are generally arranged in a linear or curvilinear fashion, closely following the street pattern. A strong image and sense of place can be achieved in a neighborhood of detached housing if a consistent relationship between the houses themselves and between the houses and the site's features can be maintained in the site plan.

The identity of each single-family unit can be enhanced by providing some variety in building style and configuration. The front entrance to each house should be visible from the street, and garage doors should be placed or treated so as to minimize their street presence. On linear streets, blocks should be short to minimize long views of housefronts and driveways. Houses should be sited in groups with the same basic setback from and orientation to the street. Within the same neighborhood, these setbacks should reinforce the hierarchy of the street system—deeper on collector streets and shallower on minor residential streets like culs-de-sac. On corner lots, houses should usually be oriented to the lower-hierarchy street.

It might be appropriate to vary the size of lots within a project by as much as 25 percent to accommodate a site's natural features and to provide some variety in site planning and unit design. Price range, the intended character of the development, house design, and local custom are all important factors in determining the size of lots.

The strong demand for conventional single-family housing coupled with reduced affordability has brought major changes to the design of single-family houses. Overall, single-family lots have become smaller and more complicated in their configuration. And with smaller lots, designers need to consider issues related to privacy, usable yard area, entries, and streetscapes during the project's planning and execution. Developers must understand these issues and the potential pitfalls. The decision about which single-family concept to build will be determined after carefully considering the target market, the economics of the project, and the capacity of the land. Some of the single-family detached concepts that were popular in the 1980s are discussed in the following paragraphs.[16]

Conventional Lots

The typical residential lot in a conventional subdivision is square or slightly rectangular and may range from 10,000 to 12,000 square feet. A 12,000-square-

---

[16] A more detailed description of these and other single-family detached lots can be found in James W. Wentling and Lloyd W. Bookout, eds., *Density by Design* (Washington, D.C.: ULI–the Urban Land Institute, 1988). See also Debra Bassert, "What Shape Is Your Lot In?" *Land Development*, January 1988, pp. 22–23.

foot lot—100 feet wide by 120 feet deep, for example—would be common. In some markets in the Midwest and Northeast, minimum sizes can begin at one-half acre, especially when the site is heavily wooded. Lots of 10,000 square feet or more provide ample room for a house, a garage and driveway, and a yard around the entire house. Conventional plotting would place a single-family detached house somewhere near the center of its lot.

Sometimes it is impossible to maintain a uniform shape and size of lots, especially when it is necessary to accommodate sharp turns at the corners of the subdivision or when curvilinear streets and culs-de-sac are provided. Two of the most common variations of the conventional lot are pie-shaped lots and flag lots. Pie-shaped lots are common around culs-de-sac and sharp street turns; they are narrower at the street and wider at the rear of the lot. Flag lots are created to provide a building site and access to what would otherwise be a landlocked parcel; only the access drive of a flag lot actually fronts the street.

For conventional single-family subdivisions, zoning codes have been used to establish minimum lot

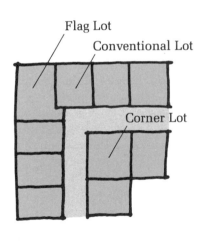

Flag Lot
Conventional Lot
Corner Lot

Pie Lot
Reverse Pie Lot

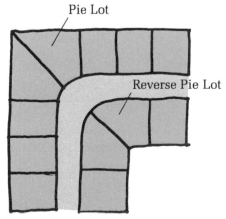

4-13 Typical lot types.

sizes and minimum setback distances from each of the four property lines. Most codes require the front of the house to be at least 25 feet from the street to allow space for cars to be parked in the driveway. Minimum setbacks from side property lines can range from five to 15 feet and from the rear property line, 25 to 30 feet or more.

To provide greater flexibility, some municipalities allow lot sizes to be averaged so that some lots can be smaller and others larger. In such cases, the zoning code typically specifies a permitted percentage of variation from the average size. For example, if the average lot size is set at 10,000 square feet but a 25 percent variation is permitted, lots may actually range from 7,500 to 12,500 square feet. Thus, developers have the flexibility to accommodate physical constraints, such as topography and environmental resources.

This conventional lotting pattern continues to be the most widely used for single-family detached houses. During the 1980s, however, rising land costs and an overall scarcity of developable land in many high-growth markets have reduced the size of the typical single-family lot. It is not uncommon in some markets to see conventional lots as small as 5,000 square feet—with in some instances houses as large as 3,000 square feet or more. Many municipalities have revised their zoning codes to permit smaller lots, higher lot coverage, and reduced setbacks to accommodate this trend.

Zero-Lot-Line Houses

Zero-lot-line houses were fairly common around the turn of the century. Council member David Jensen notes, "Most of these houses and their neighborhoods have strong value today because of their attention to architectural detail, mature landscaping, and location in close-in suburbs." During the 1960s, the concept of zero lot lines reappeared as the first expression of contemporary, higher-density attached houses. Since then, the concept has been used widely in almost every region of the country. Zero-lot-line houses are characterized by narrow but deep lots. Instead of providing two side yards that might each be only five feet wide, one side of the house is located on a side property line, thereby creating a more usable 10-foot-wide side yard on the other side of the house. The homeowner is granted an easement (usually five feet) across the neighbor's lot to provide for periodic maintenance of the exterior of the house and to provide for drainage off the roof.

Zero-lot-line houses are typically plotted on lots ranging from 3,000 to 5,000 square feet at densities of about five to seven units per acre. The lots typically range from 40 to 50 feet wide and 80 to 100 feet deep. Because lots are narrow, garages are usually located near the front of the lot facing the street, while the entrance is often located on the side of the house and not directly visible from the street. Another characteristic of zero-lot-line houses is the lack of windows and doors in the wall located on the property line. Original, turn-of-the-century zero-lot-line houses used rear alleys for service access and utilities; large windows were located on south-facing walls to maximize exposure to light, while north-facing walls contained only small windows.

Zero-lot-line houses offer advantages and disadvantages in design and lotting. The long, windowless wall located on the property line ensures privacy but

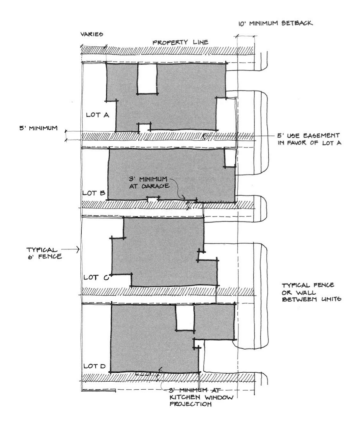

4-14 Zero-lot-line development involves locating the house next to a side yard property line. The most common variation is placement of the house three to five feet from the adjacent property line and the provision of a use easement along that side of the unit. Typical side yards total 10 feet wide except where windows or garages reduce that width to eight feet. *Source:* David R. Jensen/HOH Associates, *Zero Lot Line Housing* (Washington, D.C.: ULI–the Urban Land Institute, 1981), p. 11.

reduces the opportunity for light and air in the interior of the house. Usable yard space is efficiently concentrated in the rear and on one side of the house, where it is most needed. Garages pose particular challenges in design because of their typical placement near the street and because the garage door can occupy up to 50 percent of the total lot frontage. Without thoughtful design, streetscapes can be dominated by visually unappealing parallel garages. Further, with narrow lots, the amount of street parking available to each house is often limited to one car. Parking limitations become even more significant if garages are set so close to the street that parking in the driveway is precluded. Ordinances typically require that the garage be set back at least 18 feet from the sidewalk to ensure adequate space for a car to park or no more than five feet from the sidewalk to make parking on the short driveway apron infeasible. Placing the garage between five and 18 feet from the sidewalk only tempts residents to park on the apron, letting the car hang over the sidewalk or into the street. Despite the challenges of design, the concept of zero-lot-line housing has been successfully implemented for over 20 years.

"Z" Lots

The "Z" lot emerged in the mid-1980s as a way to overcome some of the design challenges inherent in zero-lot-line houses. The concept derives its name from the staggered side yard easements that allow each house to permanently borrow space from each adjoining lot. The front yard, house, and rear yard combine to suggest a "Z" configuration.[17]

A primary advantage of "Z" lots is that the long, windowless wall typical in zero-lot-line houses is broken by the staggered easements, allowing windows and doors to be placed on both sides of the house, providing more opportunity for light and air, and increasing the floor plan's flexibility. "Z" lots also create more usable yard space by locating the rear side yard on the side of the house opposite the entry. In most projects, this yard "borrows" space from the adjacent lot through an easement and thus becomes wider and more usable than for conventional zero-lot-line houses.

To maximize density, "Z" lots are almost always built on narrow lots, so streetscapes dominated by

[17] A more detailed discussion of "Z" lots and several other small-lot concepts can be found in Walter J. Richardson, "Designing High-Density Single-Family Housing: Variations on the Zero-Lot-Line Theme," *Urban Land,* February 1988, pp. 15–20. See also Wentling and Bookout, eds., *Density by Design.*

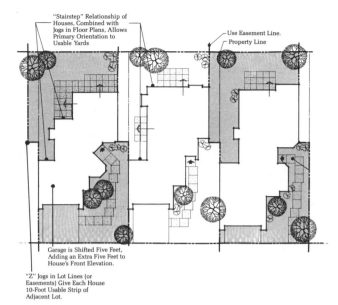

"Stairstep" Relationship of Houses, Combined with Jogs in Floor Plans, Allows Primary Orientation to Usable Yards

Use Easement Line.
Property Line

Garage is Shifted Five Feet, Adding an Extra Five Feet to House's Front Elevation.

"Z" Jogs in Lot Lines (or Easements) Give Each House 10-Foot Usable Strip of Adjacent Lot.

4-15 Typical "Z" lots and houses. *Source:* Richardson, "Designing High-Density Single-Family Housing," p. 19.

garage doors can be a problem. To reduce the expanse of garages, angled "Z" lots were introduced: the house and lot are rotated approximately 30 to 45 degrees from their traditional perpendicular relationship to the street. As a result, the front of the house and a portion of its side wall are both visible from the street, making the house seem larger and wider. Moreover, the garage door can be located on either the front or side of the house. By varying placement of garage doors, designers can avoid a monotonous repetition of driveways and doors.

Although "Z" lots lessen some of the problems typical to zero-lot-line houses, they also have some disadvantages. If used on very narrow lots (35 to 40 feet), the houses can give the impression of being attached, especially for angled "Z" lots, because the small side yards are not highly visible when seen from an angle (as a driver would view them from the street). Lotting patterns are more complicated than most buyers are accustomed to; sales brochures need to carefully describe the concept to alleviate buyers' concerns.

Wide-Shallow Lots

The concept of wide-shallow lots gained popularity in the late 1980s as an alternative to the various options for narrow lots. By keeping lots at a more traditional width (55 to 70 feet) but reducing the depth (to only about 55 to 70 feet), developers can achieve a density of about seven to eight units per acre. A wide-shallow lot offers the image from the street of a traditional single-family neighborhood by exposing more of the house's front and by orienting the front door directly on the street. The wider lots add proportionately to development costs for streets, utilities, and landscaping, but many buyers will pay for these additional costs for the more attractive and traditional streetscape.[18]

---

[18] The amount of additional site development costs varies between jurisdictions, but a rule of thumb is to add about $1,500 per lot over a development with narrow lots of comparable density.

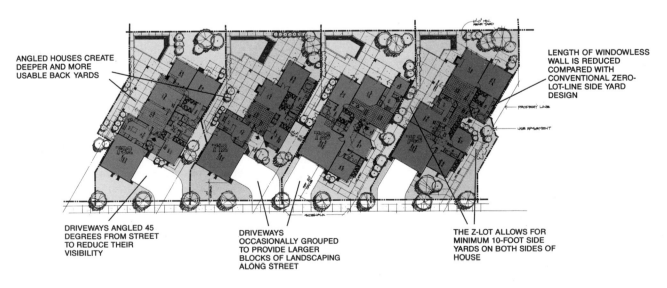

ANGLED HOUSES CREATE DEEPER AND MORE USABLE BACK YARDS

LENGTH OF WINDOWLESS WALL IS REDUCED COMPARED WITH CONVENTIONAL ZERO-LOT-LINE SIDE YARD DESIGN

PROPERTY LINE

USE EASEMENT

DRIVEWAYS ANGLED 45 DEGREES FROM STREET TO REDUCE THEIR VISIBILITY

DRIVEWAYS OCCASIONALLY GROUPED TO PROVIDE LARGER BLOCKS OF LANDSCAPING ALONG STREET

THE Z-LOT ALLOWS FOR MINIMUM 10-FOOT SIDE YARDS ON BOTH SIDES OF HOUSE

4-16 Typical angled "Z" lots and houses. *Source:* Richardson, "Designing High-Density Single-Family Housing," p. 17.

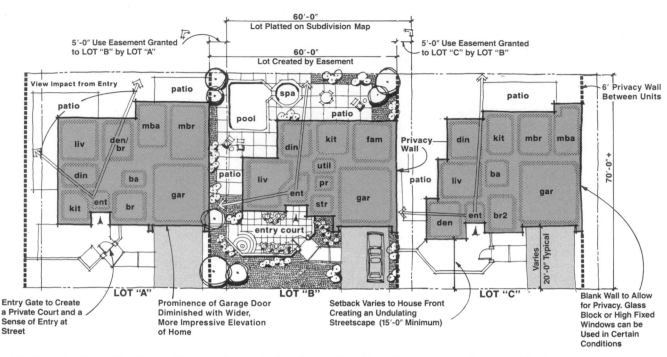

4-17 Typical wide-shallow lots and houses. *Source:* Arthur C. Danielian, Danielian Associates, Irvine, California.

Despite its improved curb appeal, however, wide-shallow lots also raise several design considerations. Floor plans tend to be less flexible because of the wide and shallow dimensions of the house. Standard requirements for front, side, and rear yards reduce the size of the house's footprint, which usually dictates a two-story design. If lots are very shallow, the distance between the backs of houses may be too narrow to afford privacy. According to council member Arthur C. Danielian, "The optimum size for a wide-shallow lot is 57 feet wide by about 80 feet deep, which allows a 20-foot driveway in the front for two cars to park and 25 to 30 feet for a rear yard."

Zipper Lots

Zipper lots are derived from the concept of wide-shallow lots and offer generally the same advantages and disadvantages. In this approach, the rear lot line jogs to vary the depth of the rear yard and to concentrate usable space on one side of the lot. The other side of the lot, left shallow, is located against the blank wall of an adjacent house.

Under ideal conditions that include straight streets and flat terrain, zipper lots can produce densities of up to 10 units per acre. The relatively wide lot—usually about 60 feet—allows the houses to look large from the street. But like wide-shallow lots, protecting privacy at the rear of the house becomes the primary challenge in design.

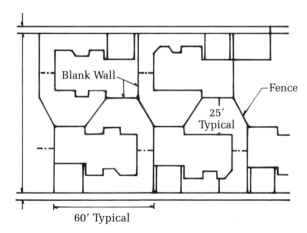

4-18 Typical zipper lots and houses. *Source: Project Reference File:* "California Meadows," vol. 17, no. 12 (Washington, D.C.: ULI–the Urban Land Institute, July–September 1987).

Alternate-Width Lots

Alternate-width lots (sometimes called "odd lots"), combine narrow and wide lots to offer a more varied streetscape. An almost countless number of combinations of unit plans and lot shapes and sizes can be created. Besides offering the advantage of a highly varied streetscape, the mixture of unit plans and lot sizes can help to diversify target markets. Generally, alternate-width projects do not achieve densities as high as those using one type of narrow lot, and match-

TEN IMPORTANT CONSIDERATIONS IN SUCCESSFULLY DEVELOPING
SMALL-LOT, HIGH-DENSITY HOUSING

1. The site must fit the concept. Narrow or "Z" lots do not work well on hillside sites with slopes of more than 3 or 4 percent. Conversely, the concept must fit the site; forced solutions are seldom successful.

2. Small lots are incompatible with scattered-lot or land sales involving multiple builders; the relationship between houses and adjacent lots must be carefully coordinated.

3. Land planning and plotting individual lots must be done concurrently and integrated with the design of unit floor plans. Floor plans must be specifically designed for the chosen lot configuration; seldom can existing single-family or townhouse plans be modified successfully for a zero-lot-line house.

4. Careful planning among architect/planner, civil engineer, and landscape architect is essential.

5. Sight lines into neighboring houses should be avoided. Orientation of second-floor windows should not compromise yard privacy.

6. Requirements for drainage must be carefully studied. Swales can inhibit the usability of narrow side yards.

7. Major rooms must be oriented toward outdoor patio areas to give each unit the appearance of spaciousness and to strengthen the relationship between indoors and outdoors.

8. The streetscape should be varied, with side and front entrances wherever possible. Any fences or walls visible from the street must be designed to enhance the streetscape. Front yards and streetscapes must be fully landscaped.

9. Any unusual approach may work only in selected target markets. Concepts involving use easements may appeal only to sophisticated buyers.

10. Complicated use easements needed for some lot configurations may not be legally feasible in many jurisdictions.

Source: Walter J. Richardson, "Designing High-Density Single-Family Housing: Variations on the Zero-Lot-Line Theme," *Urban Land,* February 1988, pp. 15–20.

School Access
Bridge by Developer

Existing Irrigation Canal

SOUTHFIELD COURT WALK

WISCONSIN

WEST

WEST MARYLAND PLACE

■ Typical Odd Lots

N
0 10 25 50 100

4-20 Typical odd lots and houses. *Source:* Site plan for Palomino Hill, Kephart Architects, Denver, Colorado.

ing specific floor plans to specific lots in particular must be considered. The alternate-width approach is versatile, however, and can be applied successfully in markets where other nontraditional lotting programs might fail.

Single-Family Attached

No question exists in the definition of single-family detached housing: a house that stands apart from others on its own lot with three or four yard areas that is intended for occupancy by a single family.[19] Other residential product types are less easily defined, however. Single-family attached housing and multifamily housing have been classified in various ways: by the number of dwelling units per building, by the scale of

[19] The definition of family varies among zoning ordinances, but typically the definition refers to one or more persons related by blood, marriage, or adoption, living and cooking together as a single housekeeping unit. In some instances, two unrelated persons performing the same functions may qualify as a family, but in cases of larger groups, the U.S. Supreme Court has determined that the designation of "family" should not be applied [see *Village of Belle Terre* v. *Boraas,* 416 U.S. 1, 94 S.Ct. 1536, 39 L.Ed. 2d 797 (1974)]. Since that decision, however, several state courts have ruled that certain group homes for mentally retarded persons do function as a family and should be considered a family for purposes of zoning.

the building (such as the number of stories), by some generic name (such as townhouse, garden apartment, or patio house), or by relating structures to one another (such as detached, attached, or row).

The use of generic names alone can cause confusion because terminology varies among regions. For example, a townhouse in some areas refers to a specific, identifiable design. In others, it is used to describe an individual dwelling unit within another entity, for example, a two-story unit within a midrise structure. In still other instances, it is used to distinguish for-sale housing from other units intended as rentals. This variation in terminology is perpetuated by marketing professionals, who often use such terms liberally to suggest more positive images about the product being marketed.

Generally, a single-family attached house is one where only one family is intended to reside within the building structure. Buildings (or individual houses) are attached to one or more other buildings (or houses), such as in the case of townhouses, which is still the most prevalent form of single-family attached housing.

Townhouses

Townhouses, once known as row houses, are single-family attached units with common (or "party") walls. Narrow lots are the rule in townhouse developments; widths generally range from 22 to 32 feet. Each unit has its own front door opening to the outdoors (usually to the street), and typically each house is a complete entity with its own utility connections. Although townhouses have no side yards, they can have front and rear yards. In most instances, the land on which the townhouse is built—and any front and rear yard—is owned in fee by the resident; however, townhouses can also be structured as condominiums. For decades, townhouses have proven to be popular housing options for urban dwellers.

More recently, townhouses have been adapted to suburban sites, because they usually are more affordable than detached houses. Townhouses have remained the most popular type of housing between single-family detached houses and various forms of multifamily dwellings. They may be offered for sale or rental, and how the unit is financed or owned (whether rental, straight sale, cooperative, or condominium) has nothing to do with its being called a "townhouse." Townhouses offer several advantages over single-family detached houses: lower costs for construction and land development, conservation of the land by using less land for a given number of houses and preserving open space, lower long-term

maintenance costs, energy efficiency, and increased security for both the house and the neighborhood.

Townhouses are characteristically built as individual units in a series of five to 10 houses laid out in a linear configuration. Only the end units have side yards. A unit may have one, two, three, or more stories, depending upon siting, room arrangement, internal stairways, whether a basement is included or slab construction is used, and whether a built-in garage is part of the unit. Like all housing forms, townhouses must be designed to fit a particular piece of land, its location, and the price range of the market. While rigid linear configurations work well in very urban settings, they can seem out of character for most suburban sites—especially sites with rolling topography. To reestablish the townhouse in a nongrid subdivision, the building form and site plan must be reconsidered.

Two of the most popular suburban adaptations of townhouses are the cluster and mews configurations. In a cluster, the units are arranged around a central courtyard that provides access to each townhouse. The clusters usually contain four to 10 units, which can then be sited to create minimal disturbance to natural landforms and sensitive site features. In a mews configuration, rows of townhouses are organized in pairs and are placed either facing each other or back to back. Front-to-front arrangements create a linear, landscaped courtyard that provides access to each unit's front door; back-to-back arrangements

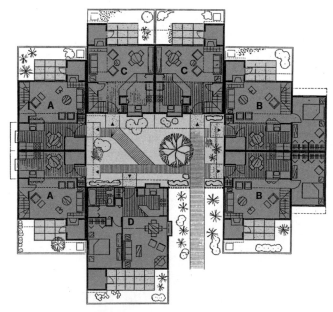

4-21 Whitman Pond in Weymouth, Massachusetts, includes 11 seven-unit clusters of townhouses like the one pictured above. Modular and prefabricated sections were used to maintain affordable prices, while the small clusters allowed the architect to work around rock outcroppings and mature trees.

allow for a shared driveway between the buildings to garages or carports.

Besides varying the layout of the units, designers and developers have begun to mix townhouses with other unit types in recent years. This mix of product types can effectively diversify the market range (by increasing unit sizes and price range) and provide for more varied architecture and design. For example, a row of townhouses can be anchored on each end by stacked flats; the flats help to increase the overall density and provide exposure to open space for four units at the ends of the building instead of the standard two units. Another widely used technique is to place a single-level flat either below or above a more conventional two-level townhouse or a two-level townhouse over another two-level townhouse. Stacking units in this fashion can be particularly effective on sloping sites where the natural grade permits both upper and lower units to have a walk-out patio at grade.

Privacy is a paramount consideration of design in all townhouse developments. Visual and auditory privacy can be enhanced through proper site design. Distances between buildings and the physical relation of one unit to another should be studied carefully.

The proper location of entrances, bedroom windows, patios, and decks is particularly important for visual privacy. Townhouse units can be staggered to solve the problem of second-floor views into adjoining ground-level patios. Privacy screens and heavy landscaping can also be used, but it is important for reasons of security that entrance doors be visible from other units and if possible from the street.

For acoustical privacy, party walls must be adequately soundproofed. In the construction of townhouses, the only completely soundproof party wall is made up of two separately constructed walls with at least two inches of air space between the walls, drywall on both sides of each wall, and insulation in each wall. This separation must begin at the footing at separate mud sills and continue all the way to the roof sheeting. No penetrations are allowed through the interior drywall barriers. Without such a separation, sound will be transmitted. The density, stiffness, and thickness of material used in party walls determine their efficiency. Nothing kills referral business faster than noisy townhouses.

The overall density that can be achieved with a suburban townhouse project varies with natural site conditions, with the size of the units and building clusters, and with the requirements for parking. Generally, eight to 12 units per acre is normal, but densities can be as high as 20 units per acre when building clusters are closely spaced, as in some townhouse mews projects. Providing attached garages for each

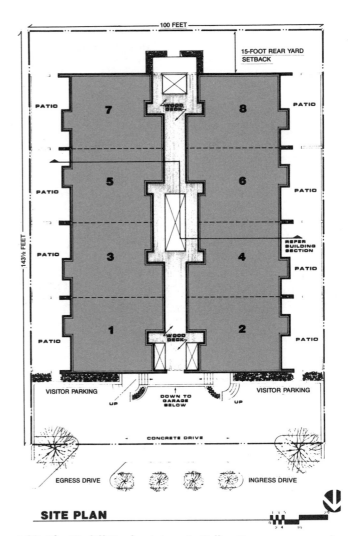

4-22 The Wycliff Condominiums in Dallas, Texas, are arranged in the typical mews design. Units front each other and onto the linear central courtyard. Each unit has direct access to the underground parking garage.

unit is a particular design challenge, especially when achieving a high density is a concurrent objective.

Patio Houses

The patio house is derived from the atrium house, which was tremendously popular in California during the 1950s. Atrium houses are characterized by an open court within the interior of the lot around which rooms are located and oriented. Although internally focused, atrium houses were most often placed on conventional lots with conventional side yards; thus, they were single-family detached designs.[20]

---

[20] For a historical overview of atrium houses, see Jack B.W. Ken, "From Bungalows to Atrium Homes," in Wentling and Bookout, eds., *Density by Design,* pp. 26–29.

4-23 The Patio Homes of New Seabury on Massachusetts's Cape Cod feature attached units with a strong relationship to the outdoors. Instead of being internally oriented to an interior atrium, these houses are oriented to the outside, with patios and decks to view the adjacent golf course and wooded open space.

A patio house usually retains a central atrium but uses the entire area of the lot by building up to at least two, and sometimes three, of the property lines. The customary side yards (and sometimes rear yard) are consolidated into one or more garden courts, either partially or completely bordered by rooms or walls. The outdoor and indoor areas become one secluded space for living, with no openings on two or more exterior side walls. This inward-directed house provides privacy yet allows increased density.

Patio lots are usually square and range from about 2,000 to 3,500 square feet, providing for a density of up to seven units per acre. Usually the houses are single level and are built without basements. Each patio house is attached to one or more other houses, yet privacy—from the street and from neighboring houses—is well protected.

The patio house has been used throughout the country but has been frequently modified to meet regional housing preferences. Today, the term "patio house" is often used to describe any housing type characterized by a strong orientation to the outdoors—even houses that are clearly detached.

Multifamily

The third primary type of housing design is generally known as "multifamily." Based purely on design, a multifamily unit is one contained within a single building that clearly houses several units. In most instances, units in a multifamily building are stacked atop each other and therefore are physically attached to three or more other units. Mid- and high-rise buildings are distinguished as multifamily buildings; garden apartments and other forms of mid-density housing (10 to 20 units per acre) also generally fall into the category "multifamily."

The term "multifamily" is particularly confusing, because to many residential developers it is used to refer generally to all forms of rental housing. While most rental units are in fact contained in multifamily buildings, the ownership of the units is not necessarily related to the size or design of the buildings. During the 1980s, a myriad of multifamily building types emerged specifically to house for-sale units. Again, residential developers should be aware of the dual meaning the term "multifamily" can imply.

Multifamily buildings can be categorized into three basic types based on the size and height of the buildings: garden density (sometimes called garden apartments), midrise, and high rise.

Garden Density

Garden density multifamily housing has come to encompass numerous housing types over the past two decades. The historical precedent for this form of housing was the garden apartment, which was built widely in suburban areas during the postwar housing boom. Still built today, typical garden apartment buildings are two or three stories, do not contain an elevator, and have 10 or more units within a single building. Buildings are placed around a site to allow generous areas for landscaping and surface parking lots, yet they still achieve densities of 10 to 20 units per acre.

Garden apartments are still a viable housing option for many developers. The design appeals to several markets—singles, young couples, empty nesters, and the elderly. Increasingly, they also appeal to families who may not be able to afford to purchase or rent a single-family house in an area with high housing costs. Council member David Lewis believes that rental communities for working families represent a major untapped market opportunity for the 1990s: "The number of middle- and upper-income renter families is large and growing—significantly outnumbering single renters at the same income level. These families have special needs, and rental communities designed to meet those needs are virtually nonexistent."

Garden apartments have evolved over the years to more closely resemble for-sale housing. Many projects have been built with carports instead of open parking spaces, for example, and some developers have begun to experiment with individual garages for tenants. Greater emphasis is being placed on amenities like swimming pools, exercise rooms, and spas. And more money is being spent initially to install lush landscaping and to provide higher-quality finishes. These changes have come about in part because of increased competition between apartment developers—but also because a growing number of apartment dwellers can afford to pay considerable rent but cannot afford to purchase a house. Such tenants want many of the same design features that historically have been associated primarily with for-sale housing.

Because of the increasing lack of affordable housing and the change in contemporary lifestyles, garden apartments have been adapted to numerous for-sale housing options, and, almost always, these units are sold as condominiums. While the density and overall site planning are similar to garden apartments, most condominium versions feature a higher level of amenities, finishes, and architectural character.

Mid- and High-Rise Buildings

A midrise multifamily building is generally from four to eight stories. In some markets with a tradition of living in high rises (New York City, for example), buildings up to 12 stories may still be considered midrise, although as a rule of thumb, any building over eight floors can be classified as a high rise. Mid- and high-rise buildings are now always equipped with elevators; the number of elevators is a function of the building's height, the level of sales or rent the developer has targeted, and local building codes. Luxury buildings are often equipped with more than the minimum number of elevators.

While garden density units are typically of wood frame or brick construction, taller buildings are required to meet higher building and fire protection standards. As a rule, buildings over six floors are constructed of steel frame or reinforced concrete, and buildings over three floors are typically required by state and local building codes to install a sprinkler system throughout the building. Because of the cost

4-24   The Barony on Peachtree in Atlanta's Buckhead district depicts two of the trends occurring in midrise residential development—an articulated roofline and parking located below a pedestrian platform.

of sprinkler systems, residential developers contemplating a mid- or high-rise project should investigate applicable building codes before proceeding.

Mid- and high-rise buildings vary in shape as well as height. Most common are the rectangular slab (which derives from the internal single- or double-loaded corridor), the tower (which consists of a centralized service and elevator core opening to a limited number of apartments), and the multiwing building (a combination of the rectangular slab and the tower or two or more adjoining slab buildings). Historically, midrise buildings have been characterized as rectangular blocks with unarticulated building forms. Double-loaded corridors with stairwells at the ends defined the building form as a linear slab of variable height. Parking was usually provided in a surface lot adjacent to the building. With the rising cost of land, contemporary midrise buildings often incorporate underground parking. Alternatively, parking could be provided at grade but below a platform that provides space for landscaping or recreational features like swimming pools or tennis courts.

Another trend in the design of midrise structures has been to more articulated building forms. Modern midrise buildings incorporate more typically residential elements like roof gables, varied roof slopes and heights, chimneys, and balconies to help reduce the perceived scale of the building and to make the buildings generally more appealing to middle-income markets.

High-rise buildings over eight floors are also shedding their box-like image in favor of greater articulation. While midrise buildings may cling to the ground plane for identity, high rises are more closely associated with the skyline. They are following the trend set by commercial office towers that seek to establish identities for their corporate owners by making a distinctive image on the skyline. Modern high-rise residential buildings are taking on more sculptural qualities stressing varied heights, changes of materials or texture, and other vertical and horizontal elements that can be used to dissolve the rectangular grid created by the units.

Products for Niches

A trend that developed during the 1980s and is expected to continue into the 1990s is the specialization of housing products designed for very specific markets (often referred to as "niche markets"). Such niches include houses for first-time buyers, "move-up" houses for second- or third-time buyers, housing for the elderly, housing for low- and moderate-income households, and second-home or resort-oriented

4-25 Fountainview is a 345-unit, self-contained rental community targeted to the special economic, psychological, social, and physical housing needs of elderly individuals who seek independent living in an active and secure environment. The residential product for this growing market niche extends beyond the design of the units and encompasses common facilities and services.

housing. Each market implies special considerations in product design.

During the 1980s, for example, demand soared for housing for first-time buyers, and residential developers responded by modifying typical single-family detached houses to make them appeal to that particular segment of the market. To make them affordable, many of these detached houses were built on small lots with inexpensive finishes to keep sale prices to a minimum.

In the years ahead, designing for particular market niches is likely to become much more complex. The aging of the population, for example, means strong demand for housing for the elderly. But the "elderly" will be a highly segmented group demanding different types of residential products and environments. Active retirees will likely seek detached or attached houses requiring low maintenance and offering access to amenities; those more advanced in age will need housing that offers convenient access to health care professionals and congregate-care housing. As markets become more highly specialized, successful developers will tailor products, amenities, and residential environments to these opportunities.

Factory-Built Housing

A trend is growing within the housing industry toward the use of prefabricated building parts in the construction of new houses. While the most obvious, long-standing prefabricated housing type is what was known until recently as the "mobile home," other types of factory-built housing like panelized and modular housing have grown in popularity because of their high quality, speed and ease of construction, and lower costs. For example, a 1,700-square-foot manufactured house that costs $45,000 to $60,000 (excluding land) can have drywall construction and solid wood cabinets and can be installed on site within a few days. Many past obstacles, such as difficulty in financing and design restrictions, have been overcome, further improving the popularity of factory-built houses.

Factory-built housing historically has suffered a negative image, but that image is changing. Projects like a 5,700-square-foot mansion in Mamaroneck, New York, made of nine modular boxes have demonstrated the increased flexibility in the design of houses using factory-built components. Now, hinged roofs and other design options can provide cathedral ceilings, and manufacturers can provide drywall finishes, high-quality siding, and other features that in the past would not be associated with a factory-built product.[21]

The majority of houses in the United States are now built with some prefabricated components. For example, nearly all windows and doors are completely preassembled and prehung in their frames, and many are prefinished. Manufacturers of factory-built housing carry this approach farther in prefabricating walls, roof trusses, and other major structural components and transporting them to the building site.

The broad category of factory-built housing accounts for nearly 60 percent of all single-family construction in the United States, with panelized houses making up 35 percent, manufactured houses 15 percent, and modular houses (those models made of preassembled sections) 6 percent.[22] Factory-built housing accounted for only 51 percent of the market in 1987; the growth demonstrates the steady increase of market share the industry enjoys.

All types of factory-built housing include several general advantages: lower cost, better control over cost of labor and materials, more assurance of quality control in the factory, less susceptibility to delays from weather, and shorter construction times and thus lower construction finance costs. With improved technology, a wider variety of design options has increased the popularity of factory-built housing. The single major advantage of factory-built housing, however, is its lower cost. The average price for a mobile home in 1988 was $75,000 (including land) and for a modular house was $71,300, contrasted with the overall average of $158,000 for a new house,[23] creating greater interest in factory-built houses by those concerned with affordable housing.

4-26 Steel-framed modules under construction in the factory.

Types of Factory-Built Housing

The nomenclature for types of factory-built housing has always been confusing. Initially, the most common type of manufactured housing was the mobile home, and factory-built components for other forms were not common. In 1980, however, the federal government, recognizing the growing diversity in design of "mobile" homes and their increasingly permanent nature, changed all references in federal statutes and regulations to "manufactured housing." (Analysts have estimated that less than 5 percent of manufactured houses [mobile homes] are ever moved from their original site.)[24]

This new name has created even greater confusion within the industry, as the term "manufactured housing" has often been broadly used to refer to any type of housing with factory-built components. While terminology still varies, this discussion employs the terminology adopted by the Manufactured Housing Institute.[25] The broad category of houses with factory-built structural components is called "factory-built housing." Six subcategories fall under this broad category: manufactured housing (previously mobile homes), modular housing, panelized housing, precut kit housing, log housing, and dome housing. The first

[21] Ira Wolfman, "Modular Construction Comes of Age," *Architectural Record,* December 1988, pp. 22–25.

[22] Telephone interview with Julie Bernstein, Building Systems Council, National Association of Home Builders, September 1989.

[23] Telephone interview with Bruce Butterfield, Manufactured Housing Institute, September 1989.

[24] California Manufactured Housing Institute, "Appreciation Rates for Mobile and Manufactured Homes in Four Urban California Counties" (Rancho Cucamonga, Cal.: Author, 1987), p. 2.

[25] Manufactured Housing Institute, 1745 Jefferson Davis Highway, Suite 511, Arlington, Virginia 22202.

three types are the most common. Generally, mortgage officers and building and zoning officials classify factory-built housing according to which body of law governs its construction. Manufactured houses must meet federal standards, while panelized and modular houses are built to local and state standards.

Manufactured Housing

A manufactured house is a three-dimensional, factory-built structure that is shipped from the factory to the site on a built-in chassis system (similar to those used in automobiles) that serves as a structural foundation. Such houses have been constructed to conform to the federal standards created in the National Manufactured Home Construction and Safety Standards Act of 1974 (24 CFR 3280). Manufactured houses contain plumbing, heating, air-conditioning, and electrical systems built into the units.

Approximately 40 percent of all manufactured housing is located in parks or land-lease communities. Generally, in such communities, the homeowner owns the manufactured house and rents the site. Thirty-six percent are located on private property and have a resident owner. Approximately 5 percent are located in subdivisions, 1 percent in condominiums or cooperative developments, and 18 percent on private property that belongs to someone other than the owner.[26] A 1987 study indicates that 66 percent of manufactured houses in California are located in land-lease communities.[27]

Manufactured housing is constructed in sections of 24 to 66 feet long by up to 14 feet wide to permit transport. In 1988, the average single-section house had 970 square feet and the average multisection house 1,435 square feet, with an overall average size of 1,175 square feet, compared with an average square footage for site-built houses of 1,995 square feet. In California, where the manufactured housing industry has grown increasingly sophisticated, triple- and quadruple-section houses are routinely sold.

The traditional interior design contains large open areas with few hallways. Typically, a master bedroom is located at one end and two bedrooms at the other. Houses with more than one section are generally built in two sections of 14 feet each, put together at the factory to ensure fit, and then unbolted, shipped, and rebolted on site.

The roof design of manufactured houses used to be limited by roof pitch, and no eaves were permitted. Now, however, manufacturers have devised a way to have steeper roof pitches by using hinged roof sections, and eaves can be included in some instances. High-end manufactured houses may have stucco siding, tile roofs, two-story foyers, hardwood floors, and virtually all the options available in a site-built house, with the only limitation that the basic section will always be rectangular.

Modular Housing

Modular houses are three-dimensional structures built in a factory and shipped to a building site.

---

[26] Telephone interview with Bruce Butterfield, Manufactured Housing Institute, September 1989.

[27] California Manufactured Housing Institute, "Appreciation Rates for Mobile and Manufactured Homes," p. 2.

Project architect, Steven Winter Associates

4-27, 4-28   Housing constructed of modular components is often difficult to distinguish from "stick-built" houses. Reywood Farms (left), luxury two-story townhouses under construction in Mamaroneck, New York. Lakeside Colony (right), affordable condominium flats in Mohegan Lake, New York.

Modular housing is generally 75 to 85 percent complete when it leaves the factory, with plumbing, heating, and electrical systems already installed. Modular houses are generally built in two or more sections.

The modular housing industry is one of the fastest growing within the homebuilding industry, accounting for 5 percent of the market in recent years.[28] Approximately 15 percent of sales of modular units go into multifamily buildings. Approximately 75 percent of modular houses are single story, 22 percent are two story, and 1 percent each are bilevel or split level. Modular houses have an average of 6.5 rooms; 22 percent have a full basement, 20 percent a partial basement, 65 percent a crawl space, and 12 percent a slab-on-grade foundation.[29]

Modular houses, because they are also three dimensional, have the same limitations on design as manufactured houses because they too have to be transported on public roads. Although modular houses are not held to federal standards, they must meet comparable state and local standards.

Panelized Housing

Panelized housing is built using major structural components manufactured in a factory and shipped to the building site to be assembled and finished. These structural components include wall panels, roof trusses, and floor trusses. Components are usually sold to a builder as part of a complete package of materials and equipment.[30] Two types of wall panels are possible—open and closed. Open panels, sometimes required by local codes, have only one wall finished in the factory to allow local building inspectors' easier inspection of electrical wiring and building standards. Closed panels have both the exterior and interior walls installed in the factory, with all the electrical and plumbing systems also built in before arriving at the site.

Typical construction involves assembly of panels and placement on site by crane, after which walls are finished. Floor and ceiling components also are produced at a factory, with gasketing or foam sealing making the finished product airtight.[31]

Some manufacturers provide their own crews to erect the shell of a panelized house to maintain quality control. Panelized pieces are used to construct a weather-tight shell, and then the builder does the finish work.[32] Often manufacturers offer builders an "integrated building system" rather than a specific product, and practically any architectural style and housing configuration can be built using an integrated panelized system. Panelized houses have basically no limitations on design that are not common to all

4-29 These three-story townhouses designed for moderate-income families are constructed of modules that were set onto their site in The Bronx, New York.

site-built houses, as panelized components are used in most site-built houses.

Financing

Financing varies considerably among types of factory-built housing. Modular and panelized houses are almost always conventionally financed, in the same way as any site-built house. Financing for manufactured housing varies considerably between jurisdictions, however, depending on how a unit is sited and sold.

A manufactured house can be financed in one of two ways: as real property, with land, or as personal property, without land. Most manufactured houses are financed as personal property through a retail installment contract arranged through a bank's consumer lending department, typically with terms that include a 10 percent downpayment, a 15-year term, and an interest rate two or three percentage points higher than conventional real estate mortgage loans. If a manufactured house is part of a land-lease community, it is usually financed with a personal property loan. Both the FHA and the VA have special financing programs for manufactured houses.[33]

[28] NAHB National Research Center, *Modular Housing Industry: Structure and Regulations* (Upper Marlboro, Md.: Author, 1987), p. 1.
[29] Ibid., p. 25.
[30] F.W. Dodge/McGraw-Hill, "U.S. Manufactured Housing Industry Remains Steady during 1987 Housing Decline," March 30, 1988.
[31] "Coming across the Finish Line," Builder, May 1987, p. 50.
[32] Telephone interview with Julie Bernstein, Building Systems Council, National Association of Home Builders, September 1989.
[33] Manufactured Housing Institute, "1989 Quick Facts," 1989.

The rationale for different treatments of financing has disappeared over the years, but the public perception has not. Experts now give manufactured houses an anticipated life of 36.5 years. The longevity of a typical site-built house is 40 years, so a reason no longer exists to assume that a manufactured house has a shorter lifespan and thus cannot justify a long-term mortgage.[34]

When a manufactured house is permanently affixed to a foundation and sold with land, it qualifies for conventional real estate mortgages available for site-built houses. Traditional mortgages are also available for them through FHA, Farmers Home Administration (FmHA), and VA programs.

Ginnie Mae has a secondary market program for personal property loans for manufactured houses, as long as those loans are guaranteed by the VA or insured under the FHA's Title I program. For manufactured houses that are permanently affixed and considered real estate under state law, Fannie Mae and Freddie Mac also have secondary market programs.[35]

If a manufactured house is permanently affixed to real estate, local property taxes apply, and it is treated as real property for purposes of federal income taxes. Deductions for interest are still allowed on loans for manufactured houses, despite the changes in the 1986 tax act. In some states, manufactured houses are still treated as motor vehicles and taxed accordingly. In land-lease communities, a manufactured house typically is taxed as personal property and the land as a business, with a standard property tax.

Regulation and Zoning

In many jurisdictions, manufactured houses are still treated differently from site-built houses for purposes of zoning, but modular and panelized houses are not. Many local zoning ordinances will not permit the installation of manufactured houses in standard, residentially zoned areas. To prevent this difference in treatment, 18 states now have laws that prohibit discrimination against manufactured houses. Because 54 percent of manufactured houses are constructed on individual lots similar to conventional single-family houses, no clear rationale exists for prohibiting them from residentially zoned areas. Eliminating discriminatory barriers is especially important in communities with a recognized need for affordable housing.[36]

Builders of all types of factory-built houses experience difficulties with building inspections and zoning. Standards for panelized and modular houses are still governed by local building codes, although most buildings must meet the standards set by the Conference of American Building Officials. Some local jurisdictions require that modular units or wall panels be partially disassembled to permit inspection of electrical wiring and plumbing, negating one of the advantages of factory-built components, because builders must disassemble and reassemble parts on site and costs increase as a result.

Various efforts have been made to create a uniform inspection law for factory-built houses, with some success. In 1976, the federal government began regulating the National Manufactured Home Construction and Safety Standards Act, called the "HUD Code." This code applies only to "manufactured housing," preempting all local building codes and setting performance standards for heating, plumbing, air conditioning, electrical systems, structural design, construction, energy efficiency, and other building characteristics. The HUD Code also requires specific procedures for monitoring and inspection during assembly at the factory, eliminating the need for inspections on site (except for building foundations, which are still governed by local building codes).[37]

Because local building codes are not uniform, it is very difficult for manufacturers of modular houses to sell their products in different markets. Often, builders are forced to build to the strictest code in their market to maintain a standardized product. To alleviate this problem, several states, including North Carolina and California, have initiated state-level preemptive standards for manufacturers of modular houses, which provide for uniform state inspections. In addition, the Council of State Governments and the National Conference of States on Building Codes and Standards created a model state "Manufactured Building Act," which was used as a base for industrial housing acts in 35 states. Thus, standards are somewhat uniform, making it easier for producers to sell in several states simultaneously. Approximately 80 percent of modular housing manufacturers sell their products in more than one state,[38] but regulatory barriers still plague the industry.

[34] Telephone interview with Bruce Butterfield, Manufactured Housing Institute, September 1989.

[35] Manufactured Housing Institute, "1989 Quick Facts."

[36] Telephone interview with Bruce Butterfield, Manufactured Housing Institute, September 1989.

[37] California Manufactured Housing Institute, 10390 Commerce Center Drive, Suite 130, Rancho Cucamonga, California 91730.

[38] NAHB National Research Center, *Modular Housing Industry*, p. 19.

Trends in Factory-Built Housing

Factory-built housing provides several advantages over site-built houses, with lower costs leading the list. The improved efficiencies of assembly-line production, with automated processes and production of large quantities of uniform products, create great savings. The existence of national standards for manufactured housing and the uniformity in some state codes governing other types of factory-built housing also improve efficiencies. Manufactured housing costs less than half as much per structural square foot as site-built housing, $20.61 versus $53.28.[39]

Factory-built housing also can be built much more quickly than site-built houses, reducing the cost of finance and labor and benefiting purchasers. A manufactured house or modular house can be ready for occupancy in a matter of days, compared to a typical construction schedule for site-built houses of several months. Some city housing authorities have opted to buy land and install factory-built housing for low-income residents, because construction is faster and cheaper and requires less skilled labor.

Because many of the electrical, plumbing, ventilation, and structural elements are installed in the factory, factory-built houses often provide an improvement in quality control over site-built construction, in which quality depends on the experience and quality of the contractor or subcontractor. This advantage is even greater in remote areas with a shortage of skilled labor. Factory-built houses are also being used for infill development because of these advantages.[40]

Factory-built houses have other advantages. Because materials are stored inside, vandalism and weather damage are nonexistent. Production can continue uninterrupted throughout the year, workers are permanent, minimizing expensive training, and materials can be purchased in higher quantities, making possible better-quality materials. Houses are delivered 75 to 85 percent complete from the factory, so that a minimum number of subcontractors is required, which also improves quality, as the work of subcontractors on site cannot be supervised as routinely as in the factory.

The historically recognized disadvantage of factory-built houses, lack of flexibility in design, has become less of a problem as the design of factory-built houses becomes increasingly sophisticated. Many factory-built houses sold today are indistinguishable in appearance from comparable site-built houses.

Most factory-built housing is custom built. The purchaser has the opportunity to select exactly the options desired for materials, location of windows, rooms, trim, fixtures, finishes, and so on. In addition,

Project architect, Steven Winter Associates

4-30 This colonial house manufactured by Key Loc Module Homes is part of a series designed to appeal to builders and homebuyers in the $200,000 to $600,000 range. This plan—constructed of six modules—features 3,200 square feet plus 1,600 square feet of attic space that can be converted to living area and an optional 1,600-square foot basement. Other features include cathedral and nine-foot-high ceilings, open floor plans, and a variety of luxury finishes. This colonial model received the 1989 Modular Design Award from *Better Homes and Gardens* magazine.

the purchaser can move into the house much more quickly. Closed-panel and modular housing take two days to one week to produce in the factory and about 30 to 45 days to finish readying the structure for occupancy. Open-panel houses can take as much as a week to install plus several more weeks to complete for occupancy.[41]

The public has historically viewed the fact that manufactured houses did not appreciate as rapidly as site-built houses as a disadvantage, partly because many mobile homes were taxed as motor vehicles and depreciated like automobiles. In reality, manufactured houses also appreciate substantially with time. A study in California indicates that manufactured houses appreciate at an average annual rate of 9.4 to 15.8 percent.[42]

[39] Manufactured Housing Institute, "Housing Affordability," 1988.

[40] "A New Look at Factory-Built Housing," unpublished paper, p. 6.

[41] Telephone interview with Julie Bernstein, National Association of Home Builders, September 1989.

[42] California Manufactured Housing Institute, "Appreciation Rates for Mobile and Manufactured Homes," p. 2.

Throughout the 1980s, the popularity of factory-built housing continued to increase in the United States, although it still has not touched the popularity of this product in countries like Sweden, where 89 percent of housing constructed in 1988 was factory built, primarily with closed-panel products.[43] Housing in Sweden is much less expensive to produce because production is vertically integrated, with manufacturers selling their own turnkey products without the involvement of a developer. Many regard the quality of Swedish-made factory-built housing as superior to its U.S. counterpart because of differences in manufacturing processes, volume of production, experience, and companies' vertical integration, which increases control over the final product. U.S. manufacturers may develop a greater interest in importing Swedish technology for that reason.[44] Some U.S. manufacturers of factory-built housing have begun to provide financing packages for their customers, although they still generally sell through independent builders.

Construction is faster in Europe than in the United States. A three-person crew can put up a weathertight panelized house in one day, and the same crew can ready the house for occupancy within seven to 10 days.[45] If current trends continue, what has occurred in the European market may foreshadow what will occur in the U.S. market. Regulatory barriers continue to be a major inhibiting force for U.S. manufacturers, and removing those barriers may serve to stimulate the factory-built housing market. It is also likely that cost advantages will favor factory-built construction as the U.S. industry matures. While the cost of factory-built housing is likely to drop with increased domestic production, the cost of site-built houses is likely to increase as the costs of labor and materials rise.[46] Congress has called on communities to identify ways to eliminate barriers to affordable housing and continues to explore options for federal legislation to increase the number of affordable houses built, specifically mentioning manufactured housing as a viable option for affordable housing.[47]

Recreational Amenities

How and where future residents will spend their leisure time are important considerations in planning and designing any residential development. The availability of recreational areas and facilities near the proposed development site, specific local requirements, market research about the interests and needs of future residents—and a certain amount of instinct—should guide developers in selecting a pack-

4-31   REFERENCES: DESIGN AND USE STANDARDS FOR RECREATIONAL AMENITIES

Joseph DeChiara and Lee E. Koppelman, *Time-Saver Standards for Site Planning* (New York: McGraw-Hill, 1984).
Charles W. Harris and Nicholas T. Dines, eds., *Time-Saver Standards for Landscape Architecture* (New York: McGraw-Hill, 1988).
National Recreation and Park Association, *Recreation, Parks, and Open Space Standards and Guidelines* (Alexandria, Va.: Author, 1983).

age of recreational amenities appropriate for a particular project.

> The notion of "amenity," as applied to real estate, is a rather broad concept that can encompass virtually any feature that is attractive to a given market and thus adds value to the land. Many amenities are inherent in a site or location: a splendid view, convenient access, or a mild climate. Amenities also include those features added to a particular development that, although nonessential to the project's main function, serve to attract a market.[48]

Standard recreational amenities for residential developments include trails and open space, play areas, recreation centers, swimming pools, and tennis courts. Some residential developments, by virtue of their sites and specialized markets, can be oriented around such amenities as golf courses, marinas, ski areas, and equestrian facilities.[49]

For any development to be accepted in the market, the selection of the correct type, quality, and number of amenities is important. Too often, amenities are not particularly useful to the future residents, who are the ones who must bear the burden of maintaining them. Changes in lifestyles are causing both renters and buyers to reconsider the value of amenities residential developers often provide. Council member Anthony J. Trella notes, "Many amenities, especially those built for large planned communities, are sitting un-

---

[43] Shep Robinson, "Manufactured Housing Trends," *Manufactured Home Dealer*, February 1988.
[44] Telephone interview with Paul Kando, Center for the House, September 1989.
[45] Ibid.
[46] "A New Look," p. 9.
[47] Telephone interview with Bruce Butterfield, Manufactured Housing Institute, September 1989.
[48] Patrick L. Phillips, *Developing with Recreational Amenities: Golf, Tennis, Skiing, and Marinas* (Washington, D.C.: ULI–the Urban Land Institute, 1986), p. 4.
[49] Ibid.

REQUIREMENTS FOR RECREATIONAL AMENITIES

	LAND REQUIREMENT	DEVELOPMENT COST	MAINTENANCE COST
Walking/Jogging Path	Variable	Moderate	Low
Open Space/Natural Areas	Variable	Low	Low
Sitting Areas	.1–.25 acre	Low	Low
Picnic Areas	.5–1 acre	Low	Low
Tennis Courts	.5 acre/2 courts	Moderate	Moderate
Paddle Tennis Courts	32'x60' for 2 courts	Moderate	Moderate
Racquetball Courts	60'x45' for 2 courts	High	Moderate
Swimming Pool	2 acres	High	High
Clubhouse	1 acre with parking	High	High
Weight Room	Part of clubhouse	Moderate (with clubhouse)	Moderate
Field Game Area	2–3 acres	Moderate	Moderate
Tot Lot	.1–.5 acre per lot	Moderate	Moderate
Golf Course	120 acres for 18 holes	High	High
Par 3 Course	60 acres for 18 holes	High	High
Putting Green	.25 acre	Moderate	Moderate
Basketball Court	60'x100' on parking lot	Moderate	Low
Horse Shoes	12'x40' for 1 run	Low	Low
Lawn Bowling (Boccie)	30'x80' for field	Low	Low
Shuffleboard	10'x64' for field	Moderate	Low
Pond/Lake	Variable	Depends on site	Low
Sailing	.25 acre for dock, etc.	High	High
Horse Facilities	2–5 acres for stable, etc.	High	Usually Leased

Source: Adapted from David R. Jensen/HOH Associates, *Zero Lot Line Housing* (Washington, D.C.: ULI–the Urban Land Institute, 1981), p. 46.

used, and residents are beginning to question whether it is worth paying for them. Residential developers must conduct market research before selecting the amenity package for a particular project; what is right for one community may not be right for another."

A developer's decision to include or exclude certain amenities is largely based on five factors: 1) what is being offered in similar local projects, 2) who the future residents are these amenities are planned for, 3) how much money is available to install and maintain the amenities, 4) what the climate will allow, and 5) what the marketing benefits will be.

A project's amenity package can provide an important edge over nearby resales that are competing directly with new houses. While a bad location for a development will hardly ever be overcome by a superior amenity package, a good amenity package might make the marketing difference in a marginal location. Opening memberships to nonresidents may make it possible to reduce the initial cost of the amenities and decrease their carrying costs to the developer or the community association.

The availability of existing amenities in the area is another important consideration. If public amenities are available nearby, fewer amenities may have to be provided on site; perhaps they can be omitted altogether.

Amenities should be phased in increments suitable to the phasing of housing construction. As a rule of thumb, the minimum number of amenities necessary to support sales and promotion of the first phase should be constructed. This approach keeps financing and maintenance costs to a minimum and avoids a situation where facilities are built and then perhaps not used for several years. It protects the community association from having to maintain amenities that could go largely unused in the event the developer is unable to complete the project.[50] Because of marketing objectives or municipal requirements, a developer might be required to build the entire package of amen-

---

[50] Chapter 7 discusses community associations in more detail.

ities during the first phase of construction. In most cases, residential developers should try to avoid this costly and often unnecessary expense, especially in large or potentially long-term projects. Residential developers should construct a phased schedule for delivery of amenities, if possible tying the delivery of certain amenities to a specific number of units sold. And developers should never promise amenities they are not sure of building.

The number of dollars per unit spent on amenities is determined by dividing the total number of units into the entire cost of the amenity package. Rules of thumb on how much to spend on amenities are difficult to apply because of regional differences, local competition, and varying expectations of local markets. Council member James M. DeFrancia offers this guidance, however:

> When preparing the preliminary estimate for a package of amenities, a good number to start with is $1,000 per unit, which then needs to be adjusted up or down in accordance with the size of the project, the competition, and the intended target market. If the emphasis of the development is on its affordability, then the budget for amenities could drop to just a few hundred dollars per unit. If the development is a larger community intended to offer a range of amenities, the budget could easily exceed $2,000 per unit.

Always included in the cost per unit is the cost of the developer's carrying a part of the maintenance and operating expenses until the succeeding phases are completed.

In all but exceptional markets, developers should stick with proven amenities rather than those that might prove to be fads. "For example," says council member Gary Ryan, "I would always put in standard tennis courts instead of platform tennis—even if it means fewer courts." Developers should consider untried amenities only for a project that is expected to sell out quickly. Amenities that may become less popular over time become part of the developer's risk.

As a general rule, residents should not decide the amenity package. They are usually inexperienced in such matters and will have trouble agreeing on the package. Moreover, if amenities are to be used as a marketing tool, it is very difficult to sell the concept of setting money aside for residents to decide their own amenities. Residents are likely to quibble over the extent and type of amenities and the costs associated with maintaining them. The development's design should be flexible enough, however, to permit residents to add to or change the package with their own funds. In many cases, this approach is excellent for additional recreation facilities after the basic facilities are installed. In Irvine, California, for example,

when residents felt strongly that additional soccer fields were needed to support the growing popularity of the sport and the number of children's leagues that were forming, space for the fields was taken from park lands that previously were set aside for more passive use.

An amenity package is often comprised of those amenities that are primarily sales tools plus those that residents of completed developments most often use. For example, people tend to get more excited about buying into developments with clubhouses, health facilities, and golf courses than they tend to use them, but swimming pools, tennis courts, picnic pavilions, and large play areas are used a great deal. Amenities used as sales tools often are heavily used early in the project's life, but then use declines. Developers should probably not plan to spend more than 25

4-33   BUDGETING RECREATIONAL FACILITIES FOR A MASTER-PLANNED COMMUNITY: SULLY STATION— CENTREVILLE, VIRGINIA

Sully Station is a 1,200-acre, 3,272-unit master-planned community located in Northern Virginia about 25 miles west of Washington, D.C. Designed and marketed as a traditional, small-town environment for its primary market of young families, the developer emphasized recreational facilities to serve a wide range of ages and tastes. The master developer, Kettler & Scott, completed all major site improvements and community facilities and made parcels available to individual builders. The cost for building recreational community facilities accounted for approximately 6 percent of the master developer's total costs, or about $1,200 per unit. The following costs are a breakdown of Sully Station's community facilities and the budgeted cost for each.

Community Center/Clubhouses (2)	$2,275,000
Pools (2, each 25 meters long)	450,000
Jogging Trails (12 miles)	495,000
Tennis Courts (6)	200,000
Multipurpose Courts (9)	175,000
Tot Lots (9)	160,000
Ballfields (4)	150,000
Total	$3,905,000

Source: Project Reference File: "Sully Station," vol. 19, no. 6 (Washington, D.C.: ULI–the Urban Land Institute, April–June 1989).

percent of the budget for amenities on amenities used as sales tools. Thus, developers should select amenities by weighting long-term use over sales appeal by at least a three-to-one ratio.

Certain amenities may require a daily management structure to be useful to residents. Such costs must be factored into the developer's budget for amenities as well as into the community association's long-term operational budget. For example, if the development is a tennis community, a full-time manager/tennis professional may be needed. The feasibility of daily management depends largely on the size of the community, the household income of residents, and the emphasis placed on amenities. Customer profiles can help determine the need for ongoing professional management and whether the cost will be considered acceptable.

Many homebuyers shy away from a developer's amenity package if it requires major, ongoing costs to them, or if they cannot strongly perceive their own regular use. Developers must carefully consider long-term operating and maintenance and possible replacement costs of an amenity—not just initial expenses of installation. Charges for maintenance and operations that escalate far above the developer's estimate damage his reputation. If the cost of a facility exceeds residents' willingness to pay, they can close it, but dissatisfaction will remain. Developers must make trade-offs so that operating costs are kept as low as possible. "Long-term operating success," says council member David Sunderland, "is an important design criterion in terms of what amenities will be used and the viability of operating costs for that use. Two factors affect long-term costs: 1) if amenities are wanted and used, residents will pay reasonable costs, unless 2) the operating costs do not correspond with the residents' income. Therefore, it is necessary to design what residents can afford, assuming of course that they like and can use the facilities."

Trails

When combined with the other elements of an on-site pedestrian network—sidewalks and paths—trails can be a relatively inexpensive and widely appreciated component of the total package of recreational amenities. Specialized and multiuse trails can be designed for bicycling, hiking, jogging, exercising, cross-country skiing, and horseback riding. Depending on the characteristics of the development where they are located, such trails can be located in public or privately owned open space and can be maintained by the community association, a public agency, or private groups.

4-34 This pedestrian path at Adams Woods in Bloomfield Hills, Michigan, leads to a wooded park.

The design of trails varies widely, depending on their intended use, the nature of the community, and the physical site. As a rule of thumb, trails should not exceed a maximum average grade of 5 percent, nor should any particular segment exceed a 15 percent grade. Approximately 40 hikers per day per mile can be expected to use rural trails, while about 90 hikers per day per mile will use urban trails.[51]

For jogging trails, the joggers' route should be carefully designed. It is helpful if paths are arranged in some variation of a figure eight to allow for shorter runs and a greater variety of routes.[52] Regularly spaced markers signifying distance traveled are highly appreciated. For jogging, paths should be of crushed stone or a similar resilient material smaller than one-half inch in diameter and angular enough to pack to a firm surface. Paths should also be well drained, at least four feet wide, and at least one mile long.

[51] National Recreation and Parks Association, *Recreation, Parks, and Open Space Standards and Guidelines*, Appendix A, Suggested Facility Development Guidelines (Alexandria, Va.: Author, 1983).

[52] Charles W. Harris and Nicholas T. Dines, eds., *Time-Saver Standards for Landscape Architecture* (New York: McGraw-Hill, 1988), pp. 520-16 & 520-17.

4-35 This par course exercise station in Rancho Santa Margarita, California, is located on a portion of a trail system that borders the community's manmade lake.

An exercise trail—sometimes called a par course—is a variation of the jogging trail, with exercise stations located periodically along the route. Depending on the total length of the track, exercise stations can be spaced as close together as 50 yards or as far apart as 400 yards, but 150 to 200 yards is the average. Patented tracks are available from several manufacturing firms and come complete with station equipment, signs, and guidelines for installation.[53]

Horseback riding is generally considered an exclusive sport without wide appeal to the general population, so few developers plan and construct equestrian trails. Tying a development of first homes to this single activity is risky. In large-lot equestrian communities where individual property owners are permitted to maintain private stables, however, equestrian trails can prove to be a valued community facility. Equestrian communities can also include communal barns, riding centers, storage areas for horse trailers, and riding trails.[54]

Play Areas

Play areas include tot lots, playgrounds, play fields, parks, and other open spaces used for a combination of active and passive recreation.[55] Clearly, play areas are needed to support most new residential developments, but often which facilities will be provided and maintained by a municipality and which will be privately constructed by the developer and maintained by a community association must be debated.

The type and size of play areas to be provided depend on the type of community being created. Condominium, rental, and other higher-density de-

velopments usually provide more space for children's active play than a single-family development where private yard space is available. Even single-family projects require play areas and tot lots for common use by neighborhood children, however. In for-sale developments, play areas are more often owned and maintained by the municipality, in condominium developments, they tend to be owned and maintained by the community association, and in rental projects, they are owned and maintained by the apartment owner.

As a general guideline, 5 percent of the gross area of a project is about the maximum amount of land a developer should expect to reserve for parks and recreational purposes. This guideline does not mean that 5 percent is all that is needed, as need is determined by the project's density and character. If the municipality desires more parkland than is necessary to serve the development project, the municipality should be prepared to purchase the difference. Under ideal conditions, play areas should be located within one-half mile of all dwelling units where children might live and be linked to residential enclaves with off-street pedestrian paths. Children's play areas should be visible from public areas and easily reached by emergency vehicles. A playground requires a level, well-drained site, but to maintain adequate drainage, the site should not fall below a 0.5 percent slope.

A full-service, neighborhood recreation area or playground usually need not be larger than one to five acres and should accommodate the following features:

- A section for preschool children.
- Apparatus for older children.
- Open space for informal play.
- A surfaced area for court games like handball, basketball, shuffle board, and volley ball.
- A field for softball and group games.
- An area for storytelling and quiet games.
- A shelter house with water and toilets.
- A corner for table games for older people.
- Landscaping.

Sturdy equipment is necessary, but it does not have to be expensive. Children prefer equipment that moves or that they can move on. When given the

[53] Ibid., p. 520-17.

[54] "Equestrian Centers and Residential Development," *Urban Land,* November 1986, p. 40.

[55] For a thorough discussion of the design and planning of playgrounds, see Peter Heseltine and John Holborn, *Playgrounds: The Planning, Design, and Construction of Play Environments* (New York: Nichols Publishing Co., 1987).

choice between designed play sculptures or conventional play equipment like swings or slides, studies show that children often prefer the latter. Council member David Jensen adds this advice: "Safety should be carefully considered in the selection of playground equipment for children. In hot climates, for example, reflective metal slides can burn a child." Accessories like trash cans, drinking fountains, and benches should be located appropriately on the playground.

If teenagers will live in the development, basketball courts should also be provided. Depending on the size of the development, several half courts for practice are probably better than one full court. Some goals can be less than standard height to ensure a court for younger children. If the area is to be lighted for use at night, it should be located away from houses to reduce noise and the effect of glare.

A good location for playgrounds is on or near an elementary school site, where the municipality or community association can ensure adequate supervision. Sharing space and facilities between schools and playgrounds is efficient for both parties.

Tot lots can be quite small—usually 2,400 to 5,000 square feet is sufficient—but they require special considerations in design.[56] They require a sheltered but sunny location, smaller play equipment, grassy areas for bike riding, and benches. As a general rule, tot lots should be designed for children four years old and younger and contain play equipment designed for this age group's preferences. The costs of building a tot lot vary with its size and facilities but should be budgeted for $10,000 to $20,000 each. In Sully Station, a 3,272-unit master-planned community in Northern Virginia, the developer planned nine tot lots, budgeting each at approximately $17,500.[57]

Market data usually indicate the expected population of children by various age groups. These data help planners to size and locate appropriate play areas throughout the development and help to determine the specific design and facilities for each. Generally speaking, materials that go into a play area or tot lot should complement those found in the rest of the project. Council member Robert Engstrom notes, "Tot lots and play areas should be integrated with natural landforms, making the architectural construction blend with the landscape rather than defying it."

A casual observation of children's play demonstrates that if an area does not present a certain degree of challenge, children will soon grow disinterested and seek more exciting territory. A balance must therefore be achieved between safety and challenge, much as the developer must also balance maintenance, budget, and aesthetics.

Recreation Centers

A large centralized clubhouse or recreation center offering a number of activities (swimming pool, tennis court, indoor game rooms, gathering hall, and so on) has been a common sales tool for residential developers since the 1960s. Maintenance and operating expenses for such facilities typically come out of homeowners' monthly dues to the community association, and the community association often uses the facilities as its headquarters. These facilities rarely pay for themselves, however, and residential developers must question the value of a large, central facility. Smaller clubhouses or recreation centers can often be built, maintained, and operated more inex-

[56] Harris and Dines, eds., *Time-Saver Standards for Landscape Architecture*, p. 520-21.

[57] *Project Reference File:* "Sully Station," vol. 19, no. 6 (Washington, D.C.: ULI–the Urban Land Institute, April–June 1989).

4-36, 4-37   Tot lots and play areas at Snow Creek near San Diego, California, were constructed of rustic materials that appeal to the imagination of children and blend with the architectural character of the community.

4-38 The developer of Sully Station in Northern Virginia used the community clubhouse as a primary marketing tool for the 3,272-unit, 1,200-acre residential development. The 4,200-square-foot clubhouse is sited on 7.5 acres and is surrounded by a 25-meter swimming pool, tennis courts, ballfields, and open park area. A second, comparably sized and fitted clubhouse will be built during a later phase of the project. The first clubhouse, which was built at a cost of over $1 million, serves as the community sales center and at completion of sales will be turned over to the homeowners' association. The raised porch at the rear of the clubhouse overlooks the pool, sundeck, and tennis courts. The lower floor, with a walkout entrance to the pool area, provides space for lockers, bathrooms, and equipment storage.

pensively and may prove to be of more use and value to residents.

The size of the residential development often determines the need for a recreation center. As a general rule, it is not feasible to support a recreation center with fewer than 150 houses. In fact, in most price categories, a minimum of 300 houses is needed to support the cost of maintenance and operation for a reasonable annual fee.

If a pool is planned for the development, it is sometimes easier to enlarge the pool building and turn it into a small recreation center than to build a separate clubhouse. Amenities that could be installed in this type of building include a sauna a spa, an exercise room, kitchen facilities, and meeting rooms.

Swimming Pools

"The well-designed swimming pool is a key feature of an association's recreation facilities and a mainstay of association vitality, to say nothing of the sales appeal generated during the development period."[58] A quarter-century after that statement was made, the sales appeal of swimming pools continues. Developers must evaluate their long-term usefulness to residents, however, before deciding to install one.

---

[58] ULI–the Urban Land Institute, *Homes Association Handbook* (Washington, D.C.: Author, 1964), p. 169.

Although most developers consider swimming pools low-cost recreational amenities, items like lighting for night use, heating, an enclosure, and pool furniture increase costs dramatically. The market's population should be carefully checked to determine whether a pool is needed in the development. The developer should investigate the number, location, and attendance figures for municipal and private open-membership pools in the area; if adequate facilities already exist in the immediate area, the capital and operating costs of constructing a community pool may not be warranted.

In townhouse, condominium, and multifamily communities, a swimming pool is often one of the most desired amenities. Even in areas with a short summer season, a swimming pool helps to establish an image for the community of a maintenance-free, leisure-oriented lifestyle and a certain prestige. It can also serve as a place to socialize with neighbors, a focus for open space, and a meeting ground for the entire community. After a project is completed and the community association takes authority, the swimming pool takes on another important function, becoming the key feature of the community association's recreation facilities and a mainstay of the association's vitality. All of these reasons are central to a developer's decision to install this rather costly amenity.

If research indicates that a pool would be a useful amenity, developers have a few options. They can provide the land, build the pool and its fixtures, and then operate the facility as a private commercial club or turn it over to the community association. Alternatively, they can donate the site and subsidize construction costs, helping residents to organize a community association and contract for the construction. The community swim club through its charter and bylaws would stipulate the assessment and dues to cover amortization, maintenance, and operation. In most cases, developers construct the pool and its accessory uses and turn it over to the community association along with other common open space and amenities.

The physical layout of a pool requires careful planning, because pools generate noise and activity. Adequate buffering between a pool and nearby dwelling units must be provided. Some families with children would prefer to live close to a pool, but others—particularly those without children—would prefer to be separated from this activity center.

Except for projects serving highly specialized markets (like retirees), developers should be prepared to serve the full range of the community's market, with shallow areas for young children, lanes for lap swimming, and areas for leisurely swimming. Some consideration should also be given to the construction of spas in addition to the community pool.

The pool and its paved apron must be completely fenced. In addition to the pool itself, the pool area should include some sort of appurtenant structure containing showers, toilets, a small office, and a storage room. This building may be part of a larger clubhouse, if one is needed for other purposes.

The size of the swimming pool varies with the number of residents it is intended to serve. The National Spa and Pool Institute recommends about 40 square feet of surface area for each swimmer. Thus, a basic 16-foot by 32-foot pool accommodates about 12 or 13 persons. Council member Robert Engstrom offers the following rough guidelines for sizing pools in a residential community:

Number of Houses	Pool Size in Square Feet
Under 50	800–1,000
50–100	1,000–1,300
100–150	1,200–1,500
150–200	1,400–1,800
Over 200	1,800+

4-39 Renaissance Park, near downtown Phoenix, Arizona, is a 170-unit townhouse community targeted mainly to singles and professional couples. The swimming pool and clubhouse are the featured amenities.

In large developments, a series of smaller pools relating to individual housing groups is an option instead of one centrally located, large pool. The depth of pools depends on the type of use intended: casual playing areas need be only three feet, while swimming areas should be about four feet deep to allow for turning.

The basic rectangular pool is the least expensive model to construct, but L-shaped or Z-shaped pools are more flexible because they separate different users. For example, one end of an L-shaped pool can be used as a play area for children while the other end serves adult swimmers. The design of oval and free-form pools is limiting, because they cannot accommodate lap swimming and competitive meets. Competition requires a pool approximately 82.5 feet (25 meters) long and approximately 42 feet wide for six lanes. Another important consideration is whether the pool will be designed for diving. Council member Judith Reagan offers this warning: "Residential developers should not consider designs for swimming pools that invite diving. The risks of injury and liability and the added insurance premiums for the community association are too great."

Concrete is the most widely used material for swimming pools, although fiberglass pools and vinyl-lined pools are less expensive options. Concrete in the form of "gunite" or "shotcrete" is air-sprayed onto pool sides and the bottom. Although prices vary regionally, a typical concrete-lined pool costs from $20 to $35 per square foot. Fiberglass and vinyl-lined pools the same size can range from $15 to $30 per square foot.[59] Typical decking, landscaping, lighting, fencing, furniture, and appurtenant structures can cost as much as, or more than, the basic pool.

If the projected market includes children and competitive swimming is popular in the area, a regulation 25-meter pool should be considered. On the other hand, if buyer profiles indicate few families with children, the wading pool can be omitted. In all cases, users' enjoyment will be enhanced if the deck or patio area is three to four times the pool area. Part of the patio area may be well-drained lawn. The main deck area should be located along the long axis of the pool.

The pool's filter-bathhouse structure, fencing, benches, and lighting provide the architect and landscape architect with an opportunity to complement the architecture of the community. Structures in the pool area can be constructed of similar materials and styles as houses in the community but in a more playful way. Typically, filtration pumps and heating equipment require approximately six feet by 12 feet, which is adequate for all but the largest pools. Each bath/dressing facility should have toilets and can

include showers, lavatories, mirrors, seating or benches, and several lockers. To save costs, a pool immediately adjacent to the houses it serves might not include toilets and showers. Local health ordinances often determine these requirements.

For safety, access to the swimming pool is usually limited by perimeter fencing. In most situations, a well-placed pool complex provides good general views of open space and screens out undesirable views. It is best to have two fence details or sections—one visually open with vertical, diagonal, or horizontal slats and another that blocks undesirable views, noise, and wind. In any case, the swimming pool complex should include a fence that is four to six feet tall, difficult to climb, and impossible to slip through. Again, local building and zoning codes dictate minimum requirements.

Maintenance and operating costs are important considerations that should not be overlooked. If the pool is to be maintained by a community association, the developer must factor those costs into the association's expenses. Developers must also determine whether the number of houses and the anticipated household income of residents will be sufficient to support the pool. Only in large communities is it likely that the community association will be able to hire a paid pool director. In most cases, it is advantageous to hire an outside maintenance contractor for periodic cleaning and repairs. Attendants and lifeguards also add to operating costs.

Tennis Courts

Tennis courts require little land (one acre is enough for four to six courts), are easy to maintain, and can be constructed rather quickly. Although the popularity of tennis reached a peak in the late 1970s and early 1980s, tennis will continue to be perceived as a necessity in a strong, balanced amenity package. Developers should be conservative, however, and consider providing tennis courts in a phased approach in response to actual demand.[60]

It is difficult to generalize about the number of outdoor tennis courts required in residential areas, because demand is related to such variables as the number of times per week people wish to play, climate and weather conditions, the availability of courts for night use, the availability of indoor courts,

---

[59] Based on 16-foot by 32-foot standard pool with pump, filters, steps, ladders, surface skimmer, and minimal decking. See National Spa and Pool Institute, *Pool Planning: Choosing Your Design* (Alexandria, Va.: Author, 1988).

[60] Phillips, *Developing with Recreational Amenities,* Chapter 4.

and whether they are operated using reservations or on a first come, first served basis. Two courts are generally adequate for a 300-unit residential development with a minimum recreation package. Space should be reserved for additional courts, however, should use dictate they are needed.

More courts should be built in some types of projects than in others. If the tennis facility is the primary amenity, it may be necessary to build more courts than if the tennis courts are ancillary amenities. A higher ratio of courts to units is often appropriate in second-home developments, where they could attract more tennis-playing buyers. Demand may also be higher in developments catering to empty nesters and upper-income families. In markets with a particularly high demand for tennis courts, developers might consider building a large facility and initially opening it to general membership. This concept, however, entails some risk and requires an expert operational staff as well as an operating budget.

The regulation size for a court is 60 by 120 feet, with a playable surface of 36 feet by 78 feet for doubles. Numerous playing surfaces are available.[61] Post- or pretension concrete courts are very durable, especially in areas with adverse soil conditions. The cost of construction should be evaluated in relation to costs of stabilizing and compacting soil. Such courts can also be depressed and serve very effectively for stormwater detention in higher-density projects.

Asphalt-mix courts (the mix varies around the country) are the most commonly installed courts in residential areas; they cost approximately $18,000 to $20,000 per court, excluding land, lighting, and fencing. An aesthetically pleasing, non-chain-link fence can add as much as $10,000 to the cost of each court, and lighting can cost from $5,000 to $10,000. Courts must be resurfaced every five years, at a cost of $2,500 to $3,500 per court.[62] Other equipment is needed: backstops, generally 10 to 12 feet high; windcurtains to deflect the sun, control the wind, and foster privacy (they should be easily removed); tennis nets and net posts; chairs or benches; drinking fountains; and backboards for practice. Depending on the expected caliber of the tennis players and whether tennis is a major or minor amenity, developers might also consider ball-throwing machines, a pro shop and racquet stringing service, locker rooms, toilets, and showers.

Glare is a possible problem with certain tennis surfaces, especially if the courts are lit. Developers should try to put courts as close as possible to units but not so close that they become a nuisance. Developers must also consider whether to cluster tennis courts or scatter them throughout the development.

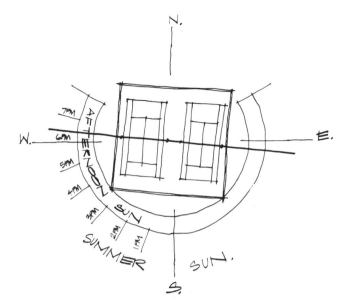

4-40 Orientation to the sun is one factor that influences the positioning of tennis courts. As a guide for orienting a tennis court, a line extending parallel to the nets should point in the approximate direction of the sun during the most popular hours of play. This plan shows a position for a court favoring late afternoon/early evening play.

While scattering may spread out the amenities, a tennis court is not the same as a tot lot. Courts should never be developed singly; they should be grouped at least in twos. If a tennis program is expected—requiring a reservation system and offering lessons or clinics—all the courts should be grouped so they can be managed. Scattered courts also create problems with maintenance and operation—clearing court surfaces, supervising dress regulations, and scheduling use.

Once a tennis court's general location has been chosen, it must be oriented properly relative to the sun's movement. Several factors should influence this decision:

1. Profiles of potential buyers should suggest the normal hours of play for the proposed tennis courts (generally, tennis courts for residential developments are used most frequently in the afternoon and evening).
2. Information about the sun's angle for the site's latitude should be researched.

---

[61] Much information on the physical characteristics of tennis courts—construction, maintenance, and equipment—can be obtained from *Tennis Courts* (published by the U.S. Tennis Association, 71 University Place, Princeton, New Jersey 08540). Published biannually.

[62] All costs are based on national averages as reported in *Tennis Courts,* 1990–91 edition. Costs vary regionally and according to local conditions.

3. The primary months of play and the anticipated normal hours of play should be considered.

4. The length of the court (the direction of play) should be oriented north/south to minimize the impact of the sun in players' eyes.

Themed Recreational Communities

Some recreational amenities are so large or costly that they cannot be provided in a typical residential development. Such amenities include, but are not limited to, golf courses, marinas, ski slopes, and equestrian facilities. The sense of identifying with a group offered by these kinds of specialized recreational developments, however, is increasingly important to many builders. According to council member Sanford R. Goodkin, "These developments make their marketing appeal not just in terms of pampering oneself but in terms of establishing a sense of community."

Golf Courses

Because of the popularity of golf, many developers are too quick to assume that their development should contain a golf course. This assumption is risky because golf courses require a large capital investment, consume a large amount of land, and once built are

difficult and costly to change. Moreover, aside from initial costs, developers must take into account the possibility that they will have to assume the expense of maintaining and operating the course for some years.

A golf course does add three basic benefits to a residential development. It provides generally 120 to 150 acres of maintained open space to a community and thus may be beneficial during negotiations with local officials. Second, it permits an additional activity to property owners in a sport that is in great demand and short supply. And, third, golf courses add substantial value to lots or houses fronting the course and some value to houses located in the community but without direct frontage.

Economic feasibility is the most important factor to consider in the decision about whether or not to build a golf course. Are the benefits to be derived offset by the cost, time, and responsibility involved in constructing and operating a golf course? In part, the benefits derived from a golf course are intangible. A golf course can be a great selling point for the developer, but whether it sells enough lots with higher premiums to justify the expense, especially in areas where play is restricted to six months or fewer, is debatable. Council member Gary Ryan observes, "If the developer has to operate the course and facilities, my experience is that premiums for golf course lots

---

4-41   THE VALUE OF RECREATIONAL AMENITIES

As a result of changing economics, a number of developers are holding on to their amenities and operating them as profit centers or structuring buyouts through which they can sell their amenities to the homeowners at agreed-upon prices. Companies disposing of their amenities are no longer practically giving them away. Developers are realizing substantial rewards from the sale of amenities, providing that they have structured the deal carefully in advance and have been careful to avoid over-promising memberships and other legal hazards in initially marketing their product. (For additional discussion of this process, see Patrick L. Phillips, "Thinking Ahead: Planning for Amenity Disposition," *Urban Land,* July 1986, pp. 10–15.)

Financial institutions increasingly recognize the value of recreational amenities as a basis for borrowing. Amenities, although they require nontraditional methods of appraisal, are being used to secure

financing for new residential and resort developments and to refinance existing developments.

A critical point is that the attention of management is an extremely important ingredient in realizing potential profits. The problem is that most managers of residential communities focus on the residential component of the development and have not expected to achieve profits from their amenities. It is a truism that if developers do not expect anything, nothing will be realized. Residential developers must assess their amenities to determine whether income or a better balance sheet can be generated by improving centralization, design, marketing, or management.

Adapted from J. Richard McElyea and Gene P. Krekorian, "The Changing Economics of Golf," *Urban Land,* January 1987, pp. 12–15.

4-42 The featured amenity is a golf course at Blackhawk Ranch, a community of luxury single-family detached and attached houses in Danville, California. Whenever possible, the golf course was located at the bottom of canyons so that hillside houses overlook the course.

will not justify the cost." Generally speaking, a golf course may be an amenity to consider if:

- Few golf courses are in the area, and public courses are overcrowded.
- The development contains luxury housing.
- Land costs are low.
- The golf course can be amortized over several years and several hundred dwelling units.
- The site is appropriate for use as a golf course, especially in terms of its terrain.

Developers should study the feasibility of a course: the number of courses in play in the area, increases in population, and per capita income. In addition, the study should look at existing clubs in the area, their size and classes of membership, existing initiation fees and annual dues, their waiting lists for membership, and the volume of players. The study should also look at causes for successes or failures in similar local projects.

Developers should remember that a quality course requires a substantial amount of time to construct and for the turf to mature: at least two full growing seasons in northern climates (18 to 24 months) and 12 to 15 months in southern climates before the course is playable.[63] Moreover, a minimum membership of 300 or more is typically required to break even for a golf course/country club. About 450 to 500 active players is the capacity of a regulation 18-hole course, so developers should be wary of overloading the course.

The development of a golf course is a large undertaking. The success of the course and the surrounding development are determined by many factors: economic feasibility, the site's suitability and location, selection of a capable golf course architect, detailed cost estimates for the course and for the clubhouse, financing, maintenance, and management. If a golf course is deemed feasible, developers should try to build an 18-hole regulation course with a par of 70 to 73. But developers should never insist that their developments contain only a championship course;

[63] Frederick D. Jarvis, "Golf: A Driving Force in Today's Real Estate Market," *Land Development,* Summer 1989, p. 15.

There's more at stake for the developer in the relationship between golf and housing than increased residential land values. Without careful planning, the relationship also has a down side: a significant risk of expensive lawsuits that can challenge the operation of the golf course itself. Careful land use planning, design of the golf course compatible with housing, and the use of sensitive construction procedures can do much to integrate golf and other land uses in a safe and aesthetically pleasing manner. The following guidelines suggest how developers can minimize the conflicts between golf and housing.

Uphill Housing

Generally, the best location for the real estate component of a golf course community is on the higher ground, with the fairways set in the valleys. At least three benefits accrue from this arrangement: first, uphill houses are less likely to be struck by golf balls; second, views down onto a golf course are generally better than views looking up; and third,

4-44 Without appropriate consideration of design, residential and golfing uses can conflict.

valley soils are usually deeper and retain moisture better.

Natural Buffers

Trees and tall shrubs provide a natural defense against poorly hit balls, but the effectiveness of the screen is directly related to the type of vegetation. Where climate, soils, and rainfall permit, tall, low-branching, dense evergreens provide the best year-round screen. Unfortunately, the more effective the vegetative screen, the less visible the golf course is to the residents who paid a premium to overlook it.

Farmland with a mix of open fields and woods is a typical location for golf course projects. In this case, it is advantageous to align fairways along the edge of the woodland. The part of the woods facing open fields gets more sunlight than the interior part and thus generally grows denser foliage and nurtures more low-branching trees. Additionally, the forest edge makes a handsome frame for fairways.

If appropriately placed vegetation is lacking, buffer plants should be made an integral part of constructing the golf course. It may make sense to transplant small trees from locations on the fairways to buffer zones. (For vulnerable homesites, nets or fencing are buffering devices of last resort.)

It is important to protect mature buffer trees while the course is being built. During planning, the development team should identify the locations of key trees and stands of trees, for example, trees along the edges of fairways between the tee and the fairway landing area. Retaining a forester to aid in this identification is often helpful. The trees to be saved should be shielded with snow fences or, better yet, with chain-link fences placed beyond

they should investigate other types of public and private courses as well.

If adequate property or money is not available for a regulation 18-hole golf course but including golf in the development seems to be warranted, then developers should consider the alternatives: a nine-hole regulation course, a nine-hole course with multiple tees, an executive golf course, or a par-three course. (In the other direction, an abundance of land may warrant either a 27-hole or 36-hole regulation course or a combination of a regulation course and an executive course. Developers should be aware of the main-

tenance costs involved, however, and whether or not the population will be large enough to warrant their creation. Many courses of 7,000 yards or so are too difficult to be enjoyed by the average golfer and too long to maintain.)

A nine-hole regulation course is a possibility, but they are not extremely popular with golfers because they must replay the course to get in 18 holes. A nine-hole course with multiple tees saves land area yet still offers golfers a variety of shots, choices of clubs, and visual excitement. But this type of course should be considered only if land and anticipated

their driplines to prevent earth-moving equipment from scarring their trunks or harming their root systems.

The seriousness of the effort to protect trees can be communicated by a system of fines for damaging trees during construction. The example of the McDonald's headquarters development in Oak Brook, Illinois, is instructive. A team of land planners and foresters tagged 1,500 choice trees on the heavily wooded site. A chain-link fence was placed around them and a two-part fine structure imposed: $20,000 for any identified specimen tree killed during construction and $100 per inch of trunk diameter for damage to other choice trees (with the fence to be rebuilt as well). Before starting construction, the crew was required to watch a video emphasizing the importance of staying away from protected trees. This approach may seem extreme, but when safety considerations make tree buffering extremely important, it can be a reasonable approach. Saving large trees is far cheaper than planting new ones.

Slanted View Corridors

Careful orientation of houses helps to solve the dilemma of views versus protection. If a house looks toward the green rather than straight onto the fairway, then trees should be cleared along an angled corridor facing away from the path of golf balls. Besides protecting windows from badly hit golf balls, view corridors lying in the direction of play are not very noticeable from the fairway—a plus for most golfers, who would prefer not to see houses as they play around the course.

Variable Setbacks

Starting with the late Ed Ault and others, golf course architects have long recognized the need for minimum setbacks from playing areas for reasons of

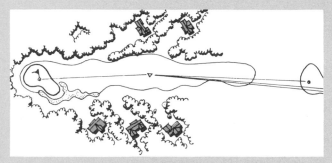

4-45 Oblique view corridors oriented away from the direction of play protect nearby homeowners while hiding surrounding houses from golfers.

both safety and aesthetics. In the early 1970s, golf course architects recommended a fairway "envelope" of 100 yards extending 50 yards on each side of the fairway centerline, within which no development could take place. Since then, golf course architects have recommended deeper setbacks of 200 to 210 feet from the center of the fairway to the facades of buildings. Near the tees, development is set back not so much to ensure safety from golf balls as to protect householders from the enthusiasm of early-rising golfers, and the distance to residences can be less. Some experts recommend only 100 feet. Around greens, architects favor setbacks of at least 200 feet from the hole.

These setbacks are, according to some course architects, minimum requirements. Conditions along fairways vary immensely, and each fairway has its own characteristics at the edge that should be considered in determining setbacks. A deep setback is needed for a fairway edge where the drive is downhill, where wind is prevalent, and where little buffering foliage exists. A shallower setback is needed along fairways framed by a dense pine forest. And, all other factors being equal, the setbacks

▶

play are limited. An 18-hole executive golf course is generally built on 45 to 60 acres and can be played in half the time of a regulation course. Its main function, however, is typically as a supplementary course. An 18-hole, par-three course uses only 35 to 45 acres.

Because of the premium prices paid for lots fronting on a golf course, a single fairway system may be used. In some cases, lots fronting on a golf course can command prices 50 percent higher than interior lots. Frontage also exposes owners to the sounds and hazards of badly played balls, however. If land is more limited, a double fairway system can be built, with

fewer lots fronting the course. Siting multifamily dwellings next to a golf course is a better option. Multifamily units overlooking a course often sell for as much as 10 to 20 percent more than their counterparts on interior lots.

As the design of golf courses has become more sophisticated, so has the planning of residential units around a course. Innovative planning can provide a consistent base price for units with direct frontage, increase premiums for off-course parcels and lots, and help to pick up the pace of sales. The 1950s and 1960s emphasized lining up lots along golf fairways,

185

(and buffers) along the first few holes, and especially along their slice side, will need to be deeper (and denser) than those farther along on the course, because golfers just starting their game are more apt to hit an errant ball. After golfers have warmed up, their accuracy improves.

Developers trying to maximize their lots with frontage on the fairway may, if zoning allows, include part of a privately owned lot within the setback, severely restricting active uses—structures, children's play apparatus, gardens, and so forth—within the privately owned portion. Thus, the golf course–owned property may extend 160 feet on both sides of the fairway centerline, and the property owner's (or homeowners' association's) restricted land another 50 feet.

Placement of Bunkers

In trying to avoid bunkers, many golfers drive far to their left or right and off the fairway. Therefore, to make the interface between golf course and housing safer, the placement of bunkers must be planned along with setbacks and buffering.

Orientation of Holes

Golf course architects generally agree that a north/south alignment of fairways is preferable to an east/west alignment that has early golfers playing into the morning sun and afternoon golfers playing into the setting sun. The glare is particularly hazardous on the first tee, where golfers starting out could lack the accuracy that comes from having played a few holes.

Legal Disclaimers

Developers must ensure that those considering buying golf course frontage are told of the possibility of personal injury or property damage from a stray ball. In fact, legal disclaimers shielding the developer and others involved in planning from liability should be made an integral part of the sales agreement and should be incorporated in any subsequent resales. Disclaimers reduce the chance that homeowners will litigate when bothered by golfers. Simple and to the point, they typically state that the property owner assumes the risks of the normal hazards of a golf course. Some developers have established easements for errant balls on their golf-front properties. Such an easement may extend 100 feet from the edge of the golf course property to include the house.

Developers should pool the talents of a land planner and a golf course architect to create the master plan for a golf community. With the planner looking out for the big picture and the architect making sure the course is well designed, the integration of golf with other kinds of development can be accomplished safely and aesthetically. Developers must be aware of the potential for personal injury and property damage stemming from poor planning and insufficient distances or buffering between golf and housing, roads, play areas, and other land uses. The temptation to locate housing as close to the golf course as possible must be balanced by the realization that closeness often leads to expensive lawsuits.

Source: William R. Firth, "Can Golf and Housing Get Along?" *Urban Land,* February 1990, pp. 16–19.

but today, designers maximize premiums by opening "windows" to the course that allow a greater number of residents to view it.

Residential developers should remember that all residential areas fronting a golf course are not valued alike, however. That is, premiums vary in accordance with interest, attractiveness, activity, and the creativeness of the landform at any given location. To boost the value of off-course parcels (parcels near the course but without direct frontage), the project's entry roads can be located at windows onto the course. Council member David Jensen advises, "It is always a good idea before laying out residential parcels for

residential developers to analyze sales premiums to set sales and marketing criteria with which street and lot layouts will have to conform."

Generally, it is better to construct the course before the houses on lots adjacent to it. Not only does doing so permit a visible selling feature, but it also is easier and more economical to establish the course before rather than after houses are built. In addition, maximum benefit from natural features—topography, drainage, vegetation, soil, and water—can be incorporated into the course.

Whenever possible, golf courses should be located in valleys or low flat areas. If a site can be used to a large degree as is, the cost of the course will be relatively low; if much contouring and grading are necessary, the expense will be greater. For a minimum amount of grading, developers should figure on 100,000 cubic yards to elevate tees and greens and perhaps another 150,000 cubic yards to create the fairways.

Totally flat sites make poor golf courses, because drainage must be improved by grading. Gently rolling terrain with some trees is preferable. It would be desirable to locate golf courses in those areas unsuitable for buildings, but construction on marshes and bogs may be prohibitively expensive as well as environmentally unsound. Developers who fail to recognize these locational considerations merely shunt expenses to the future.

Comfortably wide fairways (150 to 200 feet) are desirable, yet at the same time, existing vegetation should be preserved. Leaving trees gives the course a mature look and provides an adequate buffer between the lots and the course. Clearing a golf course in a wooded area increases the cost of the course, but it may offset the expense of landscaping a treeless course. Soils with a high degree of muck or peat should be avoided for the same reason that housing should not be built on them. Developers should also avoid soils with a high clay content. Sandy soils are often the best for golf courses; they percolate well, and good grass will grow on them if fed properly.

A water source capable of producing 1.5 million to 3.5 million gallons per week for irrigation should be available. This amount of course depends on the climate and the type of grass used. The source may be wells, streams, lakes, drainage canals, sewage effluent, or purchased water.

In contrast to the trends favoring increased revenues is a continuing upward spiral in the costs of new golf courses and their maintenance. Old rules of thumb that estimate construction costs at $100,000 per hole and annual maintenance at $20,000 per hole simply do not apply anymore. New high-quality courses costing from $4 million to $5 million ($225,000 to $275,000 per hole) are common, as are annual maintenance costs of $450,000 to $550,000 ($25,000 to $30,000 per hole).[64] Cost estimates for constructing a golf course in 1988 break down as follows:

- *Construction soft costs:* $75,000 to $150,000 (includes course design, engineering, planning, zoning, and approval)
- *Construction hard costs:* $1.9 million to $3 million (includes clearing land and earthwork, storm drainage, construction of features, irrigation,

grass and sod, car paths/roads, and bridging and headwalls)
- *Site and structures construction:* $1.25 million (includes parking, a 5,000-square-foot clubhouse, cart storage, a 5,500-square-foot maintenance building, shelters, and landscaping)
- *Equipment and furnishings:* $487,000.[65]

These figures do not include land acquisition or site preparation costs for mountainous, rocky, or forest-covered terrain. And the services of a capable golf course architect familiar with local conditions are indispensable if the decision is made to construct a course.

Marinas

The rising popularity of boating and the increase in boat owners have not seen a corresponding increase in the number of marinas and docks.[66] Much of the growth has occurred in smaller craft, which can be easily launched from a car trailer and therefore stored anywhere. At one time, a marina was merely a place for berthing recreational boats where the boater could obtain fuel, water, and sometimes other supplies. They have evolved into facilities offering more ser-

---

[64] J. Richard McElyea, "The Changing Economics of Golf," *Urban Land,* January 1987, pp. 12–15.
[65] "Golf Course Development," *Urban Land,* November 1988, p. 40.
[66] Phillips, *Developing with Recreational Amenities,* Chapter 6.

187

vices, however—restaurants, sleeping accommodations, repair facilities, and boating supplies. Like golf courses, houses located adjacent to marinas can command large premiums because of the views and access to a valued recreational activity they offer.

More complex commercial marinas are being built on inland waterways and oceanfronts. Marinas can be simple buildings with a parking area, docks, and rental boats, however. A complete marina furnishes docks with water and electricity piped to the berths, launching ramps, winter storage, marine railways, marine repair and supply shops, charter services, a sales agency, auto parking space, auto rental services, showers and dressing rooms, offices, a clubhouse, restaurants, a water travel bureau, complete shopping services, and a motel.

Because marinas are a service for boat owners, their designs vary according to the size and type of boats in the area. In areas with mostly outboard motorboats, services are specialized—smaller berths, large launching facilities, and parking areas for boat trailers. Services for sail boats, large-horsepower motors, and yachts vary accordingly.

Marinas are costly to build and operate and are not suitable for most residential developments. Before one is developed, a feasibility study is necessary. Construction techniques and methods of operation differ according to the climate, the clientele, and the body of water. Ultimately, a marina's success depends upon location, design, and management.

Ski Slopes

Although skiing continues to be an increasingly popular sport, the number of residential projects with downhill, or Alpine, skiing is largely limited to resort and second-home developments.[67] With the improvement in snow-making equipment, even lower elevations in southern states have developed ski facilities. But for developments containing primary residences, skiing will probably not be the primary amenity.

The cost of building ski facilities depends primarily on slope, tree cover, terrain, soil conditions, and

---

[67] Ibid., Chapter 5.

4-47 Prime homesites at Beaver Creek in Avon, Colorado, hug the shoulders of the valley and face the village core below. At completion, the 2,132-acre ski-oriented community will contain 3,223 dwelling units ranging in density from one to 26 units per acre.

market characteristics. Where the operation can be kept small and informal and mainly for local residents, surface lifts should be adequate and snowmaking equipment may not be necessary. If the market shows that snow skiing would be desirable but the cost of Alpine facilities is prohibitive, developers should not overlook the value of creating trails that can be used for bicycling or horseback riding in the warm months and cross-country, or Nordic, skiing in the winter. Equipment costs are lower for this type of skiing, and the sport can be learned with relatively little practice, thus broadening its appeal.

The demand for ski-oriented residential communities promises to be an especially competitive market during the 1990s and beyond.[68] The 1988–89 season had a total of 53.3 million skier-days, which was projected to grow by 1 percent for 1989–90, a considerable decline from the 3.5 percent growth between the 1985–86 and 1986–87 seasons. A number of factors are responsible for this slowdown: fewer and shorter visits by habitual skiers, a decline in leisure time, more competing choices for that leisure time, a slower growth in the population of new skiers, and the aging of the population. The last factor—an aging population—is of particular importance to residential developers.

The number of persons under 35 who ski is considerably higher than the number over 35. The average skier is typically between the ages of 18 and 35, with an annual income between $25,000 and $50,000. While most skiers are young, the majority of second-home buyers are over 35, and a typical empty nest or mature family is aged 40 to 55. This market is different from the second-home market of the 1970s and early 1980s. Buyers in the 1990s want to retain private use of their units both off- and on-season. They are typically less concerned with rental income and opportunities for investment and more concerned with family use. Empty nester, second-home owners frequently use their property as a means to bring together their extended families. Large (over 1,200-square-foot) houses (usually townhouses or condominiums) have performed best in recent years, consistent with the trend for the extended family's use.

Given these preferences of the market, perhaps the most important means of ensuring the long-term growth of mountain, ski-oriented residential developments is to extend their seasonality. By adding year-round attractions—golf courses, conference centers, theme-oriented commercial uses, and summer activities—ski resorts can expand their potential for growth in the residential market among skiers and nonskiers. The availability of all-season amenities puts ski-oriented projects in a better position to compete with alternative vacation locations and offers opportunities for growth.

Equestrian Communities

According to the American Horse Council, about 400,000 purebred horses were registered in the United States in 1986—a 477 percent increase since 1960. A Gallup Poll conducted in 1977 for the American Quarter Horse Association found that 13 percent of the population was interested in owning horses. In addition, one recreational community consultant estimates that at least 2 percent of homebuyers would find an equestrian lifestyle attractive, while the National Association of Home Builders suggests the annual demand for houses in equestrian communities may approach 35,000.[69] Despite this apparent interest in equestrian-related recreation and real estate, communities with an equestrian theme have been difficult to develop in most parts of the country, primarily because developers have been unable to obtain project financing. Lenders often perceive equestrian communities as risky ventures.

Equestrian communities have been most successful in areas where a "horse culture" already exists: Southern California (Fairbanks Ranch, San Diego; Saddle Back Estates, Simi Valley), Florida (Weston, near Fort Lauderdale; Palm Beach Downs), Kentucky, and Texas. In fact, this culture seems essential to the success of equestrian communities, although many lots in such communities are sold to households that simply like the atmosphere of the horse world. One study shows that only 23 percent of homebuyers in equestrian communities actually own and board horses.[70] Equestrian developments provide an economical way for horse lovers (and others) to preserve a certain way of life. Typically, they include communal barns and riding centers, storage areas for horse trailers, riding trails (many such projects are located adjacent to parks and forests), pastures, and other accessories. By putting facilities like barns and sta-

---

[68] See Gregg T. Logan and Ann E. Day, "Ski Resort Real Estate Development," *Urban Land,* December 1989, pp. 36–37.

[69] Much of the information for this section was taken from "Equestrian Centers and Residential Development," *Urban Land,* November 1986, p. 40. Additional information on this subject can be obtained from the American Horse Council, 1700 K Street, N.W., Washington, D.C. 20006, and the American Quarter Horse Association, 2701 I-40E, Amarillo, Texas 79168. In addition, *The Horse Digest: Journal of the U.S. Horse Industry* (published monthly by Equine Excellence Management Group, Inc., P.O. Box 3039, Berea, Kentucky 40403) contains occasional articles on equestrian-related real estate developments.

[70] See June Fletcher, "Equine Centers Rein in the Horsey Set," *Builder,* December 1987, p. 71.

A SUCCESSFUL EQUESTRIAN COMMUNITY:
HUNT CLUB FARMS—LAKE COUNTY, ILLINOIS

Nestled in the heart of the second largest concentration of horses in the United States, Hunt Club Farms in Wadsworth (Lake County), Illinois, stands as an all-too-infrequent success story for equestrian communities. Part of that success can be attributed to the site's location near the renowned Temple Lippizan Farm, the Arlington Park Raceway, and other popular equestrian facilities. But other lessons can be learned from Hunt Club Farms's success in terms of design, marketing, and financial structuring.

The 112 residential lots range in size from two to 13 acres and are grouped in clusters. Most have direct access to the 12-mile, white-fenced trail system. The trails are deeded to the lot owner with easements—they are not owned in common—and connect to the equestrian center, a preserved pasture area, and trails located outside the community. Boarding horses is permitted on some lots larger than four acres. Some lot clusters are prohibited

4-49   LAND USE DATA AND LOT/
                 HOUSE PRICES

Total Site Size: 621 acres
Field & Fences Equestrian Center: 28 acres
Preserved Pasture Area: 58 acres
Total Residential Lots: 112
Lot Sizes: 2 to 13 acres
Fenced Trails: 12 miles (on site)
Lot Prices: $90,000 to $170,000
House Prices (with lots): $450,000 to $900,000

from keeping horses on site for those buyers who like the idea of horses more than the reality.

Lots can be purchased separately or already complete with custom-designed houses—no two of the lavish houses are identical. To discourage speculation, deed restrictions require that the house be built within two years of sale of the lot. Owner-built houses must be at least 2,500 square feet and are subject to review and approval by an architectural review committee.

The equestrian center, called "Field & Fences," is a privately held, for-profit business owned by an arm of the development company developing Hunt Club Farms. As the first phase, the facility provides a barn with 29 stalls, one indoor riding ring, one outdoor riding ring, and a wide range of equestrian support facilities and services. Future plans for Field & Fences call for up to 200 stalls with three indoor and three outdoor riding rings. The developer chose to structure this facility as a private business (instead of eventually turning it over to a community association) so that control could be maintained over quality of both facilities and services.

According to the developer, only about 40 percent of the house and lot buyers actually own horses. The majority of the buyers just like the image that the community conveys. By and large, buyers are young families (in their 30s and 40s), but a few empty nesters have also been attracted to the community.

Source: The Fogelson Companies, Inc., Chicago, Illinois.

bles in a central location, expenses can be shared among homeowners and annoyances associated with odors and insects confined. In some instances, horse stables and care facilities can be operated by a community association, but this option is complicated by homeowners who do not own or board horses. Further, most community associations know little about managing or operating such a facility. Another option that should be explored is privatizing stables, operating them for profit for the benefit of community residents as well as others who may live outside the community but board their horses there.

Residential developers considering the development of a community with an equestrian theme need to carefully explore market potential and consider

various options for financial structuring of the community and the equestrian facilities. Further, targeting equestrian communities to other than high-income markets is risky. Even if market opportunities appear strong, the hardest part of the development process may prove to be obtaining financing.

Development Phasing

As residential projects grow in size from a few lots on a few acres to planned unit developments of several hundred acres or more with open space and recreational amenities, both developers and public officials need to become more aware of the timing and sequence of construction—the phasing of development. Developers desire flexibility, but it must be balanced against practical assurances that the pubic interest will be safeguarded.

If the principles of planned unit development are used, densities and general type of housing may vary from phase to phase, with the densities of all phases averaged to arrive at an overall density for the project. Problems can arise if, after an average overall density is established, some higher-density sections are built, after which the developer abandons the project before completing the lower-density sections. A community may be left with a project with a density higher than permitted. Some communities guard against this possibility by requiring simultaneous development of different elements of a project in proportion to one another. Others require individual stages of the project to stand on their own and meet the requirements of the entire development. But such solutions tend to dilute a developer's innovative design techniques. The dilemma for developers revolves around the fact that typically they get no assurance that financial and marketing calculations for the project will not be changed sometime in the future by zoning amendments, the composition of the planning and zoning commission, or the local climate for growth, even if they are proceeding on schedule and in good faith.

In contrast, development staging in conventional lot-by-lot projects generally refers to the developer's movement toward final plat approval of the project, which usually occurs after the preliminary plat is approved. In conventional development, then, approval of the final plat (usually within a specified period) is the assurance to the community that the final plat is in accordance with the preliminary plans approved earlier and that construction will take place according to those plans. The sale of houses cannot begin until this final plat has been recorded. Moreover, most local subdivision ordinances require that all public improvements be assured by the posting of an appropriate bond or money deposited in escrow. And in some cases the tax-assessed valuation of land is increased as soon as it is platted, not as soon as construction is completed.

With the outcome hinging on approval of the final plat, developers are discouraged—in many cases financially prevented—from seeking final platting of a whole project at once. Final platting all at once gives them more control over unforeseen hurdles, such as a locality's reluctance to grant further plat approval, but in the end developers normally plat only that portion of a project they are certain of completing and marketing in a short time. It is good business practice for developers to obtain final plat approval in stages.

A system that rests entirely on a single approval of development has some disadvantages. For example, a PUD cannot function within a framework that relates all commitments to a single filing, for the emphasis in a planned unit development is on continually upgrading site planning and architectural design. These innovative techniques do not come without a higher outlay of capital by the developer, but it may not be justified if the developer is uncertain about a municipality's changing the ground rules. The courts have recognized this fact yet have generally afforded developers protection only on that part of the project where they can demonstrate that they have already undertaken substantial construction.

Requirements for phasing vary from one community to another, based on existing ordinances and state enabling legislation. Regardless of legal requirements, however, developers of large, complex projects will find it necessary to phase development.

The size of the phases is based on several factors. Storm drainage and topography are obvious considerations. Confining phases to small drainage areas is a commonly used option because doing so minimizes siltation and erosion and provides a natural boundary within which to undertake construction. Developers must also consider the number of cut-and-fill operations needed and phase accordingly. Grading is an expensive part of development, and developers should strive to limit grading to only the area needed for each phase to reduce carrying costs on the land (interest on construction money borrowed to carry out grading and development) and to save the costs associated with protecting graded areas from erosion while awaiting construction.

Above all, the size of the first phase must be geared to what the market can absorb in a reasonable period of time. Absorption is based on anticipated demand and the existing supply of dwelling units. It is of prime importance to complete a section large enough in absolute numbers to offer a broad project mix and a sufficient number of unit types to get a good idea of the market's preferences.

Access to public services and utilities are also variables to consider when selecting the first phase. If the project is relatively inaccessible by existing roads, the first phase cannot be marketed unless roads are extended concurrently. It might be necessary to increase the costs of the lots and houses of the first phase to offset these initial costs; it is more typical, however, for developers to spread the costs of extending infrastructure over the entire project, which requires a carefully planned cash flow analysis. If long extensions of infrastructure and utilities are needed to service the first phase, it might be better to decide on a different phasing scheme. Council member Raymond Brock advises: "A development phase should be an absorbable entity geared to the market, with consideration given to minimizing front-end costs like excessive utility extensions."

Sometimes the location of the first phase is governed by marketing considerations, such as visibility or proximity to the primary amenity. The sequence of construction and the separation of construction traffic from potential and new residents' traffic are also factors. The order of importance varies, depending upon the particular type of product being marketed. Moreover, because many land contracts contain land purchase releases, developing a feasible phasing schedule to minimize carrying costs is vital. Council member David Sunderland says, "Make the most efficient choice. It is a balancing act to get the most market impact for your investment and still convey the product's message."

The planning agency's approval for staged or phased development should be geared to affording developers reasonable flexibility. It is best to get the public agency to approve a general overall plan with a firm overall density. The specifics of phase one should be set and approved, with parcels in the remaining phases zoned for an overall density by phase and an indication of general type of housing. Market conditions change over time, and, especially in long-term projects, it might become necessary to adjust the type of product offered in the original plan. Residential developers need to work with the municipality to devise a phasing program and procedure for amendments that allow for change without compromising the integrity of the original plan.

Perhaps the issue of greatest concern to municipalities when considering long-term developments is amenities. Consumers are not often willing to buy a developer's promises; they want to see the amenities proposed. But the carrying costs of some major amenities (clubhouses, tennis courts, lighted playing fields, for example) may well increase the prices of lots in subsequent development phases to the extent they are no longer competitive.

The balance between marketing, which may require all amenities in place before a project is completed, and the cash flow cycle, which would defer amenities until later, revolves around the product's salability. If developers cannot market the product for lack of amenities, cash flow will suffer. Again, developers must consider this tradeoff early and devise a phasing plan for amenities that will appeal to homebuyers without resulting in a dangerously low cash flow. Council member David Jensen advises, "As a general guide, it is best to locate the project's most prominent amenity in the first phase along with the highest-value product."

In large developments that extend over a period of years, amenities should be phased as units are constructed. Initial amenities should be representative of future amenities in terms of quality and type so that no question exists of misrepresentation by the developer. A general rule of thumb is to measure costs of amenities in terms of dollars spent per unit; each phase should include appropriate amenities to maintain a roughly equal expenditure per unit. Developers must include in the cost per unit of amenities the cost of carrying part of the maintenance and operating expenses pending completion of other phases.

With all types of development, a developer's credibility will bear on the type and amount of amenities and when they are included. If developers work outside their own territory, they might have to exert extra effort to justify their credibility to the municipality, to lenders, and to buyers. If so, a larger initial package of amenities may be called for. In one's own area, a developer with a proven track record may get by with less.

5.
Plan Preparation and Processing

Once a general program has been established for a development, it is necessary to prepare detailed plans. The preparation and processing of plans for residential development projects often seem unnecessarily complicated and time-consuming. As projects have grown in scale and complexity, however, so has the regulatory environment. Effective developers have adapted to increased public scrutiny with heightened sensitivity to the issues that must be addressed.

This chapter provides an overview of plan preparation and processing. The first section is a general, step-by-step description of site planning from concept planning to approval of the final development plan. The four subsequent sections review the implications of land use, circulation, utility, and landscape elements on site planning.

Planning and Approvals

Site planning is the process of designing a development project and obtaining the necessary governmental approvals to begin construction. It begins at the conceptual level with the study of alternative sites and becomes more formalized and specific when a site has been selected. When used as a tool in decision making, the site planning process minimizes the developer's risk and maximizes the project's long-term benefits.

Site planning proceeds through three general stages: concept planning, preliminary planning, and final planning. Each stage involves the collection and analysis of information about the site, the identification and evaluation of alternatives, and public review. The activities are highly interdependent and are normally undertaken in several cycles during each stage. Developers typically go through preliminary and final planning for each phase of a multiphase project.

Concept planning deals with site-specific issues at the broadest possible level and is often conducted before committing to a site to explore its opportunities for and constraints on development (see Chapter 2). During this stage, the developer evaluates alternative arrangements of generalized land uses (clusters of housing, sites for community facilities, corridors of open space, and so on) and alternative alignments for major roads. The product of concept planning is a diagram of the site where generalized land use areas and major road alignments are depicted schematically—the concept plan. During this stage, developers should attempt to obtain a clear understanding from local authorities of the amount of their contributions for roads, infrastructure, and other public services—information that is integral to evaluating a project's economics.

During preliminary planning, the concept plan is refined through the identification and evaluation of alternative locations for buildings, streets, parking areas, major elements of the pedestrian circulation network, and new landscape features. One of the most informative products that can be prepared during preliminary planning is an illustrative site plan that schematically depicts how the site might appear after development. (Illustrative plans are essentially an artist's interpretation of the plan, and developers should not let them drive future decisions.) By the end of preliminary planning, the local government and the developer often make commitments concerning such issues as the total number and type of housing units, the alignment and width of major roads, and the amount of land to be provided for other land uses, such as open space and community facilities.

During final planning, the preliminary plan is refined, detailed construction drawings are prepared, and final approvals are granted. After final approval is granted, minor changes can normally be made to the final plans through amendments.

Developers and the project planning team undertake site planning in consultation with representatives of public agencies and interested citizens.[1] Preparation of a realistic work program and schedule to guide site planning is essential. The work program and the schedule must reflect specific requirements for submitting materials and review periods that are necessary for the project's approval. Once the required approvals have been identified, a realistic schedule for completing the approval process can be prepared. As new requirements are identified during planning, the work program and schedule will need to be revised. The length of time required for a project to receive all of the approvals necessary for construction to begin varies widely between jurisdictions— from a few months to several years.

Concept Plan

A concept plan is a schematic diagram that identifies the organization of the major components of a proposed development. A well-prepared concept plan responds to the site's opportunities for and constraints on development, to the development program, and to applicable local, state, and federal requirements.

Preparation of the Base Map

To initiate site planning, a "base map" of the site is necessary showing site boundaries and features. In general, two base maps should be prepared for any residential development: a site map and a context map. A good base map is accurate, easy to read, and sized so that it is easy to handle and reproduce. Both base maps can initially be prepared from the U.S. Geological Survey's 7.5-minute quadrangle maps and updated as aerial photographs, site surveys, and other sources of information become available.

The site map should cover an area extending slightly beyond the boundaries of the site to provide a physical context and to allow for consideration of adjacent uses or physical features. Because the site map is to be used for recording site-specific information and for site planning, its scale and size should conform to any local requirements for submitting site plans. Most local requirements specify a scale of one inch equals 100 feet or one inch equals 200 feet. The boundaries of the site, topographic contour lines at regular intervals, and existing roads adjacent to the site should be included on the base map.

The context map should be prepared on a relatively small scale, for example, one inch equals 500 feet. The principal uses for this map are to orient the site in terms of location and configuration and to record relevant off-site information. The boundaries of the site, existing roads, and local boundaries and landmarks should be included on the context map.

Regulatory Analysis

The regulatory analysis involves identifying applicable local, state, and federal regulations and their particular requirements for submissions and reviews. These regulations directly affect the project's schedule and can often be an important consideration in evaluating alternatives.

Local requirements for approving similar projects can vary from jurisdiction to jurisdiction, and requirements for different types of projects can vary within the same jurisdiction. Local land use regulations for residential projects traditionally are contained in zoning and subdivision ordinances. Most states have some type of enabling legislation for local regulations, which often provides the best foundation for interpreting the intent and validity of a particular municipality's regulations. Depending on the nature of the project and applicable regulations, a proposed residential development can be processed under conventional, planned unit development, or flexible zoning standards. (Additional information on regulatory analyses can be found in Chapter 2.)

---

[1] See Douglas R. Porter, Patrick L. Phillips, and Coleen Grogan Moore, *Working with the Community: A Developer's Guide* (Washington, D.C.: ULI–the Urban Land Institute, 1985).

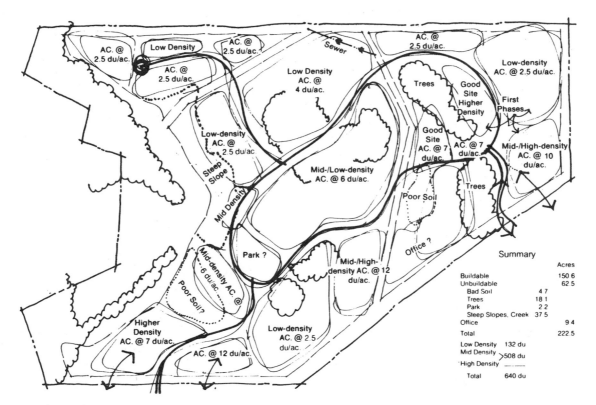

5-1 Concept plan studies provide information on buildable area, achievable density, and alternatives for land design. *Source:* Robert Engstrom and Marc Putnam, *Planning and Design of Townhouses and Condominiums* (Washington, D.C.: ULI–the Urban Land Institute, 1979), p. 31.

Site Analysis

Some useful data about the site may have already been collected during the feasibility study and site selection. This preliminary information is cursory because it was intended for use as a basis for comparing sites rather than for making detailed decisions about a specific site. The development team must therefore add to the preliminary data base, collecting information from both public and private sources.

The project team should always check to see what data are already available from local sources before looking elsewhere. Very often, information from local sources can be obtained free of charge or at a modest cost. A check with municipal agencies, public libraries, planning staffs, public works and building departments, utility companies, state highway departments, county offices, and local engineering firms will identify existing data, such as topographic maps, soil surveys, soil borings, percolation tests, and environmental assessments for other projects in the area. Tax assessment offices and recorded deeds are sources of information about existing easements, rights-of-way, and covenants that may be placed on the property. An initial inventory of locally available information de-

termines the amount and scope of material that still must be collected.

The National Cartographic Information Center (NCIC), part of the U.S. Geological Survey, is the primary governmental source of maps and other types of cartographic information. NCIC collects, sorts, and describes all types of cartographic information from federal, state, and local government agencies and, where possible, from private mapping companies. Aerial photos, topographic maps, satellite image maps, geologic maps, maps of floodprone areas, and information about maps in computer files are among the data that can be obtained from NCIC.[2]

As valuable as maps and data are, nothing can replace personal knowledge of a site. Developers thus should compile their own notes and photographs to gain a clear idea of important surface features for future reference, paying special attention to vegetation, slopes, rock outcroppings, vistas, wildlife, wet or potentially wet areas, easements, rights-of-way, and existing structures. Such a survey helps deter-

---

[2] For additional information, contact NCIC, 507 National Center, Reston, Virginia 22091.

mine whether or not construction equipment can move easily about the site.

Site analysis is most effective when information is collected systematically. Relevant information should be collected and mapped for all elements of the environment, including physiography (the lay of the land), geology, soils, groundwater, surface water, vegetation, wildlife, future land ownership, maintenance and use, the circulation network, and infrastructure. When all the information has been collected, the project planning team can analyze the information to establish a basis for the identification and evaluation of alternative sites.

One method for determining the suitability of specific locations for development on the site is to overlay maps to identify where various characteristics of the site coincide. After slopes, geologic features, floodplains, and other environmental considerations are located on the map, land parcels are classified according to suitability for various types and intensities of land use, graduating from those requiring protection and maintenance to those that can accommodate extensive modification and intensive development. The final map or maps that result from this synthesis provide an ecological description of the site and its natural processes that will enable the development team to understand and test the consequences of various alternatives for planning and design.

A second method for analyzing information about the site is to identify opportunities for and constraints on development. Opportunities are features that make the site attractive for development (views, well-drained soils, gently sloping terrain), whereas constraints are features that make the site unattractive for development (floodplains, steep terrain, biologically sensitive areas). Most sites contain both such areas, and creative design can often turn constraints into opportunities. The map showing opportunities and constraints also identifies potential design strategies for further consideration during subsequent and more specific site planning—planting buffer strips to screen unsightly areas, creating water features to contain stormwater runoff, orienting development around scenic natural features, creating pedestrian systems along watercourses prone to periodic flooding, and identifying the entity that will be responsible for maintaining these features.

Definition of the Program

Concept planning is the first opportunity to test a specific development program for the site under consideration. During concept planning, the develop-

ment team should articulate the optimum development program for the site based on the developer's understanding of the local market, regulatory constraints and requirements, the determination of the project's feasibility, and the site's character. In particular, the program should specify a minimum number of dwelling units by type. Information about the type and use of amenities, the character of the project, nonresidential land uses to be accommodated on the site, and functional relationships among the various land uses envisioned for the site should also be specified as part of the development program.

Study of Alternatives

The results of the regulatory analysis, site analysis, and definition of the program provide the basis for the study of alternative concept plans. From the regulatory analysis, it is possible to determine what type of development local authorities are willing to permit on the site. The site analysis indicates which portions of the site are developable and what opportunities and constraints exist for developable parcels. The development program identifies the developer's objectives and expectations.

Identification and evaluation of alternative concepts is an iterative process. Initially, alternatives can be based on any one or more of several variables: program mix (number of residential units by type, price range, acreage, or square footage of other land uses, for example), intensity of development, physical form (location of uses, patterns of access), development "themes," amenity packages, and responsibilities of the community association. Evaluation of the initial set of alternatives may suggest several new alternatives to evaluate. After several review cycles, the project planning team normally is able to identify an alternative that conforms to the municipality's regulatory guidelines, responds to the site, and fulfills the developer's objectives. Once the developer and the project team agree on a preferred alternative, it is useful to schedule a preapplication conference with the municipality. Following that meeting, the preferred alternative can be fine-tuned and documented.

Preapplication Conference

Even when not formally required, a preapplication conference with local officials during concept planning is generally a good idea. Failing to do so may result in the developer's finding that local officials are hostile to a particular development proposal after preliminary plans have been submitted, thus losing time and money for the developer. Rather than presenting a specific plan of action, developers may find it useful simply to review the range of development options for the site during the meeting to get a sense of the community's receptivity to various alternatives. In turn, the planning staff can inform the developer about requirements to be met and, in general, what factors should be considered during the planning process.

Officials of the planning department and representatives from related departments (engineering, public works, traffic, parks, police, and fire) normally attend the preapplication conference. The developer's submission of particular documents is generally not considered necessary or appropriate at this stage, and statements made during the course of the conference are not legally binding. The developer should bring key members of the project planning team to the meeting and the preliminary base maps, both site and context, as exhibits. Of special importance to local authorities is what portions of the site will be public and what portions will remain private. The more knowledgeable the project planning team is about applicable regulations, the site, and the potential range of alternatives, the more productive the meeting will be.

Preliminary Plan

In a word, what preliminary planning brings to a proposed development is scale. Council member Paul Reimer believes that this scale implies "a site plan scaled to the community or neighborhood that will surround it: access and circulation scaled properly to serve auto, bicycle, and pedestrian traffic; recreation and open space scaled to the needs of future inhabitants; and a sequential development plan scaled to the ability of the market to absorb the units produced."

Preliminary planning requires more detailed data than concept planning. Once the concept plan has been established, the project planning team will be in a position to identify additional information that must be collected and analyzed. At a minimum, topographic, boundary, and utility surveys of the site will need to be undertaken.

Topographic Survey

For any except the simplest of projects, a careful field topographic survey should be undertaken that, in addition to showing the precise contours of the property, should also indicate topographic features, rock outcroppings, springs, marshes, or wet areas, soil types, and the vegetative cover, including the location, size, and species of trees. Many municipalities,

townships, and counties have completed comprehensive topographic maps that are available to the public.

The topographic map for a typical site should clearly show:

- Contours at an interval of one foot for slopes averaging 3 percent or less, two feet for slopes between 3 and 10 percent, and five feet for slopes over 10 percent.
- All existing buildings and other structures, such as walls, fence lines, culverts, bridges, and roadways, with spot elevations indicated.
- The location and elevation of rock outcroppings, high points, watercourses, depressions, ponds, and marshes, with any previous flood elevations determined by survey.
- Boundaries of any floodplains or areas subject to periodic inundation.
- The size, variety, circumference, and accurate location of all specimen trees and an outline of all wooded areas.
- Boundary lines of the property.
- The location of any test pits or borings if required to determine conditions of the subsoil.

If existing topographic maps are not available, sufficient accuracy can usually be obtained at a savings in cost by using a plane table survey rather than a cross-section survey for these data. An aerial survey is another method to obtain topographic maps. It has the advantages of economy and speed, and the resultant topographic map will be current, accurate, and completely indicative of the site's physical features. Aerial topographic mapping (or "flown topo") is commonly used for large or remote sites and where a site's topographic features change frequently as the result of natural actions like landslides, rockslides, soil creep, and sedimentation.

Boundary Survey

A boundary map should be at a scale of one inch equals 100 feet for parcels 100 acres or smaller and at a scale of one inch equals 200 feet for larger parcels. The boundary survey should provide as much of the following information as pertinent:

- Bearings, distances, curves, and angles of all outside boundaries, and boundaries of all blocks and individual parcels.
- The location of any existing connecting streets along the boundary of the property and the intersection lines of any adjoining tracts.
- Any encroachments on outside boundaries as determined by survey.

- Existing easements of record.
- All streets within or contiguous to the property with reference to deeds or dedications; all existing and proposed street elevations.

- Names of owners of record or reference to recorded subdivision of adjoining property.
- Any cornerstones, pipes, or other physical boundary markers as determined by survey.

5-2   TEN WAYS TO EXPEDITE PROJECT REVIEW AND APPROVAL

1. *Know what approvals you will need.* Rules and procedures vary widely from one municipality to another and may change frequently. To avoid unpleasant surprises, get the most recent version of every regulation that applies, and be sure your team is completely familiar with the appropriate regulations. A further caution: Some permits may depend on others. A planning commission may not be willing to sign off on your project until the local traffic or utilities commission approves it. Plan your schedule and lead times accordingly.

2. *Know the agency's procedures.* How much notice is required for hearings and inspections? How much documentation is required? Some agencies will be satisfied with plans and specifications; others will require full details backing them up, including structural calculations, analyses of traffic capacity, survey notes, and logs of test borings.

3. *Inform yourself about local issues.* Elected officials and published regulations are only part of the story. Hidden agendas—concerns over land use development, traffic, aesthetics, water quality, requirements for open space, schools, or other issues—might affect how your project is perceived and evaluated.

4. *Make sure every application is as final and complete as possible before it is submitted.* If changes are necessary later, include detailed, specific information as early as possible, even if the changes seem negligible. Approval boards can quickly become highly suspicious when they learn of changes secondhand.

5. *Make your presentation as comprehensible as possible without compromising technical accuracy.* This requirement may be harder than it sounds. An accurate discussion of air quality, for example, may lead into a discussion of methods for predicting concentrations of pollutants and various models of emissions and dispersion. Your audience is probably unprepared to follow such a complex technical argument,

so revise and rehearse your presentation until you are sure your message is comprehensible.

6. *Whenever possible, use graphics to make your points.* You may have an inch-thick stack of tables and analyses to prove that your contingency traffic plans will protect local motorists during construction, but the review board may never read it. Presenting the same information on a large map with clear overlays can make it instantly and easily understandable.

7. *Disarm mistrust by cultivating a reputation for openness.* Be candid, and answer questions honestly—even if the answers are "bad news" for the approval board. Members will get the information anyway, and you will be better off in the long run if you are the one who provides it.

8. *Consider the regulator's point of view.* Members of review boards and regulatory agencies have their own orientation and mandate, which determine how they will regard your project and plan. By understanding the agency's position and rationale, you may be able to avoid unnecessary confrontations.

9. *Before making any formal submission, speak informally with those involved in the review.* Make a point of letting them know what you are doing, and learn everything you can about their concerns and what they expect to see. They will appreciate this courtesy, and they are much more apt to be reasonable about your project if they have had a chance to discuss it with you informally beforehand.

10. *Finally, get whatever expert help you need.* Seek out the professional experts—engineers, planners, construction managers, environmental specialists, and lawyers—who will understand what you are trying to do and put your project in the best possible light. Include experienced and credible local spokespersons on your project team who know the local influences and authorities.

Source: Peter Salwen, "Shepherding Large Projects through Reviews," *Urban Land,* July 1988, p. 13.

- All U.S., county, or other official benchmarks, monuments, or triangulation stations within or adjacent to the property, with precise position and description.
- Computed area of all parcels making up the property in square feet or acres (gross and net).
- True and magnetic meridian on the date of survey.

Permanent steel pipes or stone or concrete monuments should be set at each corner or angle on the outside boundary if not already established. "This is the first evidence of new development," says council member William Rick. "It takes tact. Sometimes we don't set them out because they tend to excite neighbors."

Utility Survey

If the amount of data would make combined maps confusing, it is desirable to provide a separate map of utilities at a scale of one inch equals 100 feet showing the following information, all of which the county surveyor should verify:

- All utility easements or rights-of-way.
- Location and size of existing water, gas, electric, and steam mains and underground conduits.
- Location, size, and invert elevations of existing sanitary sewers, storm drains or open drainage channels, catch basins, and manholes.
- Location of existing underground or overhead telephone and electric service and trunk lines, and street lighting with locations of poles.
- Location of any rail lines and rights-of-way.
- Location of police and fire alarm call boxes and similar appurtenances.

Site Evaluation

The site evaluation for preliminary planning is a refinement of the site analysis undertaken for concept planning. Detailed information about the environment is used to refine the analysis of opportunities and constraints and the analysis of the site's suitability for development. Where necessary, these analyses are supplemented by site-specific field investigations and studies.

The site evaluation provides a basis for assessing the potential environmental impacts of alternative plans considered during preliminary planning. The environmental impact assessment is useful in evaluating alternative plans and serves as the basis for the environmental impact assessment or report that may

be required as part of the submission for the preliminary plan.

Refining the Program

As new information about the site becomes available and as alternative preliminary plans are evaluated, the development program that was defined during concept planning also needs to be refined. By this stage, the project planning team should be able to identify prototypical building footprints for the various dwelling unit types being considered for the site. These building footprints may also need to be refined as the study of alternative preliminary plans proceeds.

Study of Alternatives

As in concept planning, the study of preliminary alternative plans is an iterative process. Typically, land planners prepare multiple alternative plans for the development team's review and critique. The team identifies advantages and disadvantages of each alternative and prepares a new set of revised, combined, or redefined alternatives for further evaluation. On the basis of this evaluation, the developer selects a preferred plan for refinement. The process of preparing and evaluating alternative plans can be shortened if a comprehensive, thorough analysis was prepared during concept planning and if the preapplication conference was fruitful in identifying public and private objectives of development.

Preparation of the Preliminary Plan

The developer normally initiates preparation of the preliminary plan by submitting a formal application. Requirements for submission vary, but they often include written documents as well as site plans and other graphic information. The list of required documents may include, but is not limited to, the following items:

- A legal description of the site, including ownership;
- A statement of planning objectives for the project;
- A construction schedule;
- Quantitative information, including the number of units proposed, the size of the lots, proposed lot coverage and densities, and total amount of nonresidential construction proposed (where allowable); and
- Any other market, feasibility, or other studies required by the review body.

INCREASED FLEXIBILITY OFTEN MEANS A COMPLEX APPROVALS PROCESS: PERRYWOOD—PRINCE GEORGE'S COUNTY, MARYLAND

Perrywood, in Prince Georges County, Maryland, is a multiproduct residential development comprised of 588 single-family detached dwelling units, 204 single-family attached dwelling units, 261 apartments for senior citizens, and 398 life-care units. An extensive 130-acre recreational network is woven into the community's design. Located on 516 acres, Perrywood is being developed under the guidelines for comprehensive design zones of the county's zoning ordinance.

Comprehensive design zones are a form of planned unit development distinctive in this jurisdiction. It allows for parcels to be planned comprehensively, from zoning through final site plan. A comprehensive design zone allows the applicant to propose regulations and guidelines that are tailored specifically to the project and development site at hand. This departure from the rigid development regulations associated with euclidean zones maximizes flexibility in design but entails an elaborate process for review and approvals.

The review process for comprehensive design zones comprises three stages: Phase I, the zoning or "basic plan"; Phase II, the "comprehensive design plan"; and Phase III, the "specific design plan." The comprehensive design zone provides for several

categories of residential use (based on density) and several categories for commercial and other uses that generate employment. For example, the ordinance provides for several subcategories and ranges of residential density: 1) *Residential–Suburban (R-S)*—1.6 to 2.6 dwelling units per acre and 2.7 to 3.5 dwelling units per acre; 2) *Residential–Medium (R-M)*—3.6 to 5.7 dwelling units per acre and 5.8 to 7.9 dwelling units per acre; and 3) *Residential–Urban (R-U)*—8 to 11.9 dwelling units per acre and 12 to 16.9 dwelling units per acre.

Phase I: The Basic Plan

Phase I is the zoning process that begins with filing an application to change existing euclidean zoning to one or more of the categories of comprehensive design zones. The Phase I zoning application for Perrywood requested R-S 1.6 to 2.6 dwelling units per acre for 446 areas of the property. The land uses proposed were single-family dwelling units and a life-care facility. The R-M 5.8 to 7.9 zone was selected for the apartment complex for senior citizens. The locations of these zones are depicted on a basic plan drawing for the property. The original application also requested an employment use zone for 35

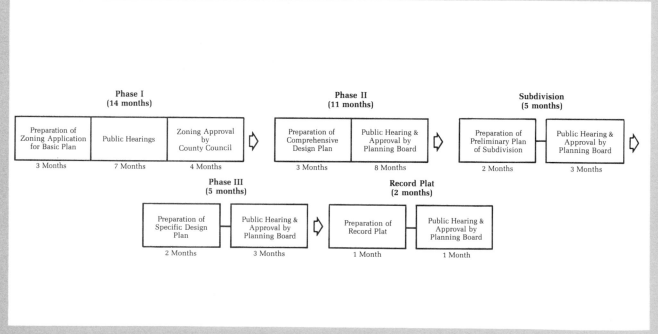

5-4   Comprehensive Design Zone Process—Prince Georges County, Maryland.

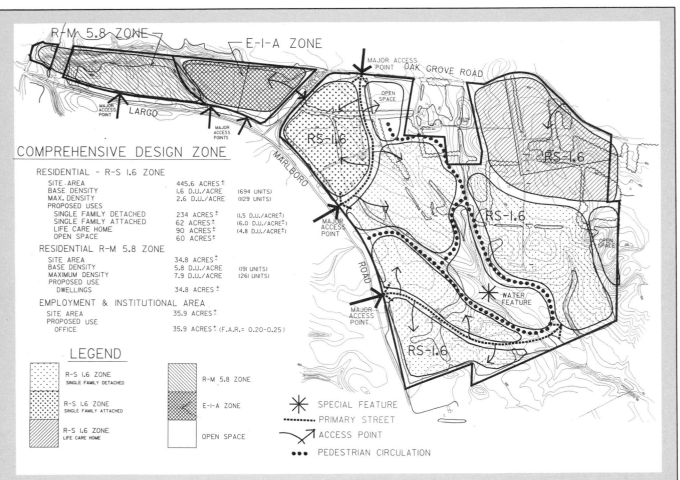

COMPREHENSIVE DESIGN ZONE

RESIDENTIAL - R-S 1.6 ZONE

SITE AREA	445.6 ACRES±	
BASE DENSITY	1.6 D.U./ACRE	(694 UNITS)
MAX. DENSITY	2.6 D.U./ACRE	(1129 UNITS)
PROPOSED USES		
SINGLE FAMILY DETACHED	234 ACRES±	(1.5 D.U./ACRE±)
SINGLE FAMILY ATTACHED	62 ACRES±	(6.0 D.U./ACRE±)
LIFE CARE HOME	90 ACRES±	(4.8 D.U./ACRE±)
OPEN SPACE	60 ACRES±	

RESIDENTIAL R-M 5.8 ZONE

SITE AREA	34.8 ACRES±	
BASE DENSITY	5.8 D.U./ACRE	(191 UNITS)
MAXIMUM DENSITY	7.9 D.U./ACRE	(261 UNITS)
PROPOSED USE		
DWELLINGS	34.8 ACRES±	

EMPLOYMENT & INSTITUTIONAL AREA

SITE AREA	35.9 ACRES±	
PROPOSED USE		
OFFICE	35.9 ACRES±	(F.A.R.= 0.20-0.25)

LEGEND

- R-S 1.6 ZONE SINGLE FAMILY DETACHED
- R-S 1.6 ZONE SINGLE FAMILY ATTACHED
- R-S 1.6 ZONE LIFE CARE HOME
- R-M 5.8 ZONE
- E-I-A ZONE
- OPEN SPACE
- ✳ SPECIAL FEATURE
- ┅┅┅ PRIMARY STREET
- ↗ ACCESS POINT
- ••• PEDESTRIAN CIRCULATION

5-5   Basic plan (Phase I).

acres of the property. While proceeding through review, however, the developer amended the application to a residential zone because of county officials' and citizens' opposition to nonresidential uses in a primarily residential area.

The basic plan is graphically expressed in bubble diagrams indicating the spatial relationships of development envelopes and the density or intensity of each. It also identifies vehicular and pedestrian circulation, access points, open space, and special features. The bubble diagrams evolved from planning, environmental, and engineering evaluations identifying and analyzing the physical features of the property. For example, streams, floodplains, wetlands, limitations of soils, steep slopes, unusual vegetation, existing structures, and historic sites all affect the design and thus are considered at this early stage of planning. The planning analysis also must take into consideration the county's comprehensive plans for recommended land uses and/or

locations for future public facilities, including potential sites for schools, public utilities, and public facilities. The results of these analyses provide the guidance for design of environmentally sensitive, aesthetically appealing areas that can be practically and realistically engineered.

The basic plan is accompanied by a text describing in great detail all the site's existing features, proposed development, and the adequacy of public facilities like water, sewerage, transportation, schools, and fire and police service. The text justifies the development with regard to the county's comprehensive plan and area master plan. Compliance with these documents is the main criterion the county uses to evaluate this initial request for rezoning.

The basic plan is submitted to the zoning division of the county's planning agency for review. That division in turn refers the submittal to various branches of the agency—natural resources, urban

▶

5-3 (continued)

design, transportation, comprehensive planning, fire, police, and hospitals, public schools and libraries, and economic development—for review and comment. The review requires approximately eight months. During that time, the development team organizes meetings with citizens' groups in the area to present the proposed project and discuss the various areas of concern they might have. Many times the application must be amended to reflect compromises. After the referral agencies have finished reviewing the application, the planning board and zoning hearing examiner hear the case. Both bodies present their recommendations to the county council, which has ultimate authority to approve or deny the application. This process takes approximately one year.

Phase II: The Comprehensive Design Plan

The phase of approval involving the comprehensive design plan involves preparation of a conceptual site plan and landscape plan to indicate how each development envelope indicated on the basic plan will be developed. This phase must maintain density ranges previously approved, and the layout must relate very closely to the basic plan's concepts for land uses, roads and access points, and amenities. The comprehensive design plan for Perrywood shows the lotting patterns and orientation of units associated with each development envelope depicted on the basic plan. It also shows recreational facilities to be included in the development, locations for stormwater management facilities, natural areas to remain undisturbed, areas where trees will be preserved, and types of new plants proposed.

The comprehensive design plan is also accompanied by a text that discusses how the proposed design will be served by water, sewer, and storm drainage facilities, methods for stormwater management and water quality control, and sediment control. The text also describes the development's projected impact on local facilities, such as schools,

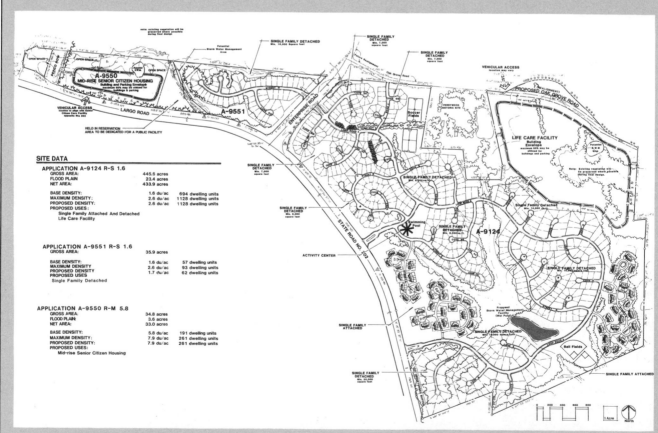

5-6   Comprehensive design plan (Phase II).

libraries, fire and rescue services, and transportation. During this phase, the applicant proposes design guidelines and specific regulations for the project. These design guidelines are meant to maintain flexibility but clearly define fundamental parameters of development. The text delineates these regulations and offers sketches of certain principles of design (buffering, landscaping, streetscapes, and recreational areas, for example) to more clearly convey the true intent of the proposed guideline. The text for Perrywood, for example, lists regulations covering size of lots (proposed to range from 7,000 to 40,000 square feet), setbacks, restrictions on building heights, number of attached units in a typical building cluster or multifamily building, undisturbed and landscaped open space, and parking.

The plan and text for Phase II are submitted to the planning commission's urban design division for review, and the project is again referred to other agencies for evaluation and feedback. The reviewer may suggest changes to the layout, design principles or guidelines, or proposed regulations as submitted. The applicant meets with the reviewer to work out compromises on those issues; the reviewer ultimately makes a recommendation to the planning board, which is the approval authority for the comprehensive design plan. This phase of the process usually takes about six months.

After the comprehensive design plan is approved, a subdivision plan is prepared and processed to refine the design and intent of the comprehensive design plan to a greater level of detail. Preliminary dimensions of lots, road alignments, grades, and other planning and engineering details are clearly established. The subdivision process again goes through all referral agencies for review and recommendation, and the planning board acts upon it within 70 to 140 days of submittal.

Phase III: The Specific Design Plan

After the comprehensive design plan and subdivision plan are approved, Phase III begins. The process involves the preparation of the actual detailed site plan and landscape plan so building permits

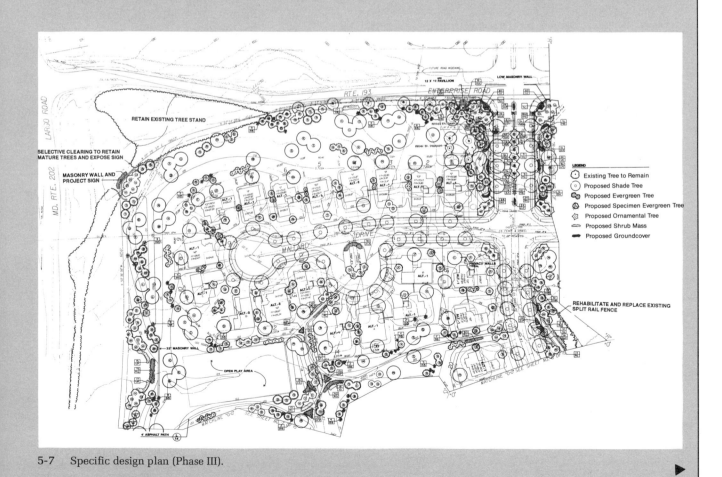

5-7 Specific design plan (Phase III).

203

5-3 (continued)

can be applied for. These plans must reflect in precise detail the layout, concepts, and design guidelines set forth in all previous approvals.

The applicant submits the specific design plan to the urban design division to review it for conformance with the comprehensive design plan and regulations. The plan is again referred to appropriate agencies for comment. The planning board again has authority to approve the specific design plan; this phase of the process usually takes four months.

Upon completion of this phase process, record plats for the property can be prepared and the lots recorded in the county's land records.

Summary

Although comprehensive design zones allow for increased density over existing euclidean zones and are programmed for maximum flexibility in design, they are subject to numerous reviews and revisions. The process may take up to three years to reach recorded plats for sale to builders and is quite costly. And the process is risky for developers, who must invest considerable time and money in a program that local decision makers ultimately might reject.

Source: Council member Bruce T. Yoder, AICP, Greenhorne & O'Mara, Inc., Greenbelt, Maryland.

Required graphic information may include, but is not limited to, the following items:

- Site plans showing existing site conditions;
- Proposed lot lines and plot designs;
- Maps showing the location and size of all existing and proposed structures and improvements;
- Maps showing the location and size of all areas to be reserved as common open space, developed as recreational facilities, or conveyed as public parks, school sites, or other uses;
- Existing and proposed utility systems;
- A general landscape plan, which may include the proposed treatment of the development's perimeter; and
- Any additional information regarding adjacent areas that might assist in the evaluation of the proposed project's impact.[3]

In addition, information about the design and construction of residential units and buildings, including typical floor plans and building elevations, may be required. In most instances, however, this specific building information is not required until final site plans or building permits are submitted. If possible, residential developers should avoid submitting detailed building information before it is required because doing so limits flexibility to change plans and features in response to changing market conditions.

Processing the Preliminary Plan

The planning staff normally reviews the preliminary plan submitted, often under a time limit imposed by the ordinance. During this period, staff members may confer with the developer to clarify information in-

cluded in the submission or to request additional material. The staff might also advise the developer to make minor changes that could contribute to a favorable review. Some planning departments also distribute copies of the plan to appropriate local agencies for review and comment. The planning staff then incorporates any comments received into its report of findings and recommendations, which is then transmitted to the planning commission.

The developer has an opportunity to make a formal presentation about the project at a hearing before the planning commission. As part of the hearing, the public is also given the opportunity to make comments about the project, both pro and con. The commission may pose some detailed questions about the proposal during the hearing and can render its decision either immediately after the hearing or within some specified period of time. The commission may approve, approve with conditions, or deny the application. More often than not, it grants conditional approval, requiring the applicant to change or modify some aspect or aspects of the proposal before approval is granted. All conditions should be put in writing, in language acceptable to both the commission and the applicant. If an application is denied, the applicant normally has the right to appeal the decision.

After the preliminary development plan is approved, the applicant has a set time period to submit a final development plan. If a final plan is not submitted within this period, preliminary approval is often

[3] Colleen Grogan Moore with Cheryl Siskin, *PUDs in Practice* (Washington, D.C.: ULI–the Urban Land Institute, 1985), pp. 21–22.

revoked. The purpose of such a provision is to discourage speculation.

If a development is to be phased, as most are, a preliminary development plan should be submitted for the first phase. The developer should work in increments that can be geared to actual sales. It is good policy, however, to submit the bare essentials of the remaining phases, even though the review authority will not approve them at this stage. Council member David Sunderland points out, "Many governments have a process for approving broad general plans for phase two and beyond 'in concept.' If the phases are interdependent, getting this approval in concept is a very important commitment for the developer." If within a specified time a developer has not moved toward completion of the final development plan for the phase under consideration, all of the prior approvals in some cases can be nullified and voided. In addition, if a zoning variance has been granted, it can be withdrawn, causing the zoning to revert to the original classification.

Final Plan

Most ordinances require the planning staff or commission to certify that the final plan substantially complies with the approved preliminary plan. Whether or not the municipality required certain changes to the plan during preliminary approval, the final plan typically varies slightly from the preliminary plan submitted. The appropriate regulations and the reviewing authority usually take into account the need for minor variations, perhaps specifying the parameters for such changes.

Preparation

The major difference between the submissions of preliminary and final plans is the level of detail required. Drawings that might have been presented in schematic form in the preliminary submission must be engineered for the final one. Site plans must be sufficiently detailed for legal recording, and any other graphic information, such as landscape plans, must also be submitted in final form. Where subdivision is involved, most ordinances require the submission of a tentative plat (or "map") for final approval. Legal documents required for establishing a community association or dedication of public land may also be required.

Processing

The final development plan is normally submitted to the planning staff, which may or may not issue another staff report documenting compliance with the preliminary plan and with any conditions of preliminary approval. The city council or other local legislative body often grants final approval because it entails some legislative action, such as accepting dedicated properties or accepting and recording site plans. If so, or if major changes have been made to the preliminary submission, a second public hearing may be required during review of the final development plan. Following approval of the final plan, other necessary administrative approvals can be obtained, building permits issued, and construction begun. Failure to begin construction within an allotted period normally results in revocation of the approval.

Developers should keep in mind that this process can take a long time (from a few months to several years), so it is necessary that the first phase be scaled to meet market need at the time construction can proceed. The longer the processing time, the more difficult it is to achieve this objective.

Amendment

Often, further changes in the final development plan become necessary. Minor changes will not affect the overall integrity of the development and are easily administered. Major changes, however, may force developers back through approval of the preliminary plan. Sometimes the limits of permitted deviations from the plan are specified; other times they are left to the discretion of public officials.

Changes to the final plan most often involve changing the product type or mix to better respond to the market. For example, after opening the first phase, a developer may find that one product sells much better than another. Changing building footprints is usually not a problem for the municipality, but more drastic changes in the product line (from single family to townhouse, for example) may send the developer back for new discretionary approvals. Residential developers need to be aware of the local agency's "limits" for allowing the final plan to be amended and, unless absolutely necessary, try to stay within those limits.

Land Use Elements

Local governments use many different standards of land use to regulate residential development. Most of these standards were initially created to regulate conventional lot-by-lot development and have been modified and adapted to apply to newer forms of development like clustering and planned unit development.

Conventional standards of land use for residential development seek to control the number, type, and placement of housing units that can be constructed on a given parcel of land by regulating such variables as size, coverage, frontage, width and depth of lots, building setbacks from lot lines, and building height. Codified in zoning and subdivision ordinances, these standards are responsible for the land use pattern and character of most residential areas developed in this country between the 1920s and the 1970s.

As clustering and planned unit development became possible, density replaced size of the lots as the most commonly used regulatory standard. Other variables normally regulated in conjunction with density include building coverage, floor/area ratio (FAR), open space ratio, building setbacks (from internal streets, the perimeter of the development parcel, and other buildings), building height, width, and depth, unit size, and the number of parking spaces per unit.

The current trend in regulating residential development seems to be away from traditional lists of permitted and prohibited uses and accompanying standards and toward the use of "a set of prestated criteria and standards that measure the performance of the proposed development."[4] The goal of offering more flexible treatment of building locations, sizes, and relationships is to make it easier to respond sensitively to specific conditions of the site and to create residential neighborhoods containing a mix of housing as well as workplaces and services. Performance standards are beginning to be incorporated into zoning and subdivision ordinances, and developers may encounter them more frequently during the next several years.

The challenge, of course, is to create livable neighborhoods and housing that is successful in the marketplace where people are concerned about such intangibles as image and identity, privacy, and security. The most well-intentioned and fine-tuned standards can never ensure that these expectations will be satisfied. In the final analysis, therefore, it is developers who must meet the challenge. Successful developers understand the market well enough to anticipate these concerns and respond to them throughout design and construction of the project.

The process of assigning land uses to a development site begins with "parcelization" of the site. The parcelization plan is based on the concept plan and establishes the framework for parcel-by-parcel site planning and subdivision. In residential development projects, a parcelization plan needs to account for rights-of-way for major arterials and collector streets, major areas to be reserved as open space, sites for commercial facilities, sites for public purposes (including common areas), sites for institutional use, environmentally and/or historically significant preservation areas, and land for residential development. The plan identifies the acreage of each parcel and its intended future use.

In larger residential developments that may have several phases, developers should strive to maintain as much flexibility as possible in assigning specific land uses to individual parcels. Market conditions can change rapidly, and it may become necessary to change the density or product type assigned to a parcel—or even to change the intended land use.

Streets

A community's comprehensive plan often contains a street plan that indicates future alignments and widths of right-of-way for major roads, such as arterials and collectors, whose function is to conduct traffic between communities and activity centers and connect to major state and interstate highways. If any of these planned roads intersect the development, parcelization will need to provide the necessary internal right-of-way.

Whether or not a street plan exists, developers often need to work with a transportation planner to identify requirements for major roads that will be necessary to serve the site. Decisions regarding internal street layout should result from evaluations of a variety of factors, including topography, soil and geologic conditions, drainage, and future land uses. General alignments for major roads identified on the parcelization plan are subject to further adjustment and definition during subdivision.[5]

Open Space

The inclusion of some types of open space in a residential development project increases the flexibility of site planning. Open space can be used to preserve natural features, vegetation, or ecosystems and to reduce the expense of grading and landscaping a site. It can also be used to increase the project's salability and property value.

Open space generally describes those portions of the development that are not included in the salable lots, houses, commercial properties, and so on. The open space may contain the stormwater management systems, lakes, creeks, ponds, landscape buffers, private roads and rights-of-way, natural topographical

---

[4] Douglas R. Porter, "Flexible Zoning: How It Works," *Urban Land,* April 1988, pp. 6–11. Techniques used to regulate residential development are discussed in more detail in Chapter 2.

[5] Streets are discussed in more detail in "Circulation Elements," later in this chapter.

features, entry (monument) areas, pedestrian pathways, parks, greenbelts, directional signage, walls or fences, and environmentally sensitive properties.

5-8   LOCATING OPEN SPACE

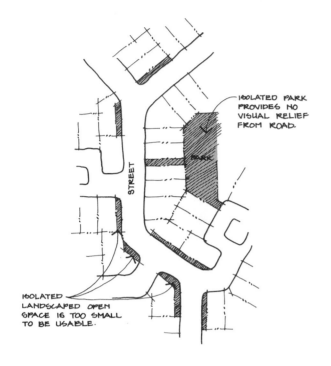

ISOLATED PARK PROVIDES NO VISUAL RELIEF FROM ROAD.

ISOLATED LANDSCAPED OPEN SPACE IS TOO SMALL TO BE USABLE.

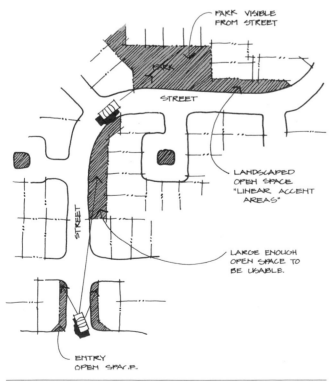

PARK VISIBLE FROM STREET

LANDSCAPED OPEN SPACE "LINEAR ACCENT AREAS"

LARGE ENOUGH OPEN SPACE TO BE USABLE.

ENTRY OPEN SPACE.

Source: David Jensen/HOH Associates, *Zero Lot Line Housing* (Washington, D.C.: ULI–the Urban Land Institute, 1981), p. 44.

Some developments include a golf course to satisfy requirements for open space.

Three types of open space are possible: private, public, and common. Private open space is usually land that is improved for use in a recreational capacity, for example, a golf course or tennis club. Its use, however, is reserved for members of the recreational facility. Public open space is land that has been purchased or dedicated for public use. Traditionally, roads, rights-of-way, and stormwater management systems are dedicated to the public for perpetual maintenance and ownership. Common open space is land that is deeded to a community property owners' (or homeowners') association that the developer creates and operates for the benefit of owners of property within the development. Common open space may contain a multitude of improved and unimproved property, including the entrance to the community, parks, pedestrian pathways, recreational facilities (pools, sports fields, bathhouses, and so on), landscaped buffers, the streetscape, walls, and signage.

Common open space is conveyed to an association that is responsible for its maintenance; the association is established by recording the declaration of covenants, conditions, and restrictions. All property owners, including the developer, pay prorated assessments for all of the costs relating to common open space, and payment of assessments is enforced through a lien against an owner's property. (This topic is discussed in more detail in Chapter 7.) Many governmental agencies require the formation of a property owners' association to maintain the common open space before it issues development permits.

Open space helps trigger sales, but it should not be such a large amount that it becomes a maintenance burden for the community association. Council member Ray Brock states, "To have value as an amenity, open space must either be usable or have such aesthetic appeal that it will enhance marketability. Some developments are such that economics will not permit much open space." In public requirements for open space in a PUD or in exchange for density bonuses, developers must recognize the value of the land as open space versus its value as developed land. In other words, developers can afford to give away a higher percentage of land at a smaller economic penalty when that land has a low cost and is unusable than if it is expensive and usable.

No universal ratio exists for how much open space developers should include in a development. Council member Gary Ryan explains, "The test is whether it will effectively perform some function, not how much is there." Requirements for provision and dedication of open space vary widely.

5-9 Open space at The Commons at Atkinson in Atkinson, New Hampshire, is located in a commonly owned green surrounded by houses.

The basis for defining open space is critical to understanding any percentage figures used in requirements for open space. In some cases, open space might be defined as any land not covered by buildings or paving. This standard might translate into ratios of 50, 60, and 70 percent open space to total site acreage. In other cases, open space might be defined as land not covered by buildings or paving but not including land that is private open space and land that is smaller than a certain area and not contiguous with other open space. A project that might have 60 percent open space under the first definition might have only 10 to 15 percent under the second. Another variable is water acreage, which may or may not be defined as open space. Comparison of percentages of open space is therefore meaningless unless common standards of measurement are used.

Some standards of quality must be maintained for open space. The physical characteristics, dimensions, location, slope, and physical improvements are all important factors in determining whether open space will be of value. Planning open space should be considered an integral part of overall site planning and design.

Paths and trails, recreational facilities, stormwater management, erosion and sedimentation control, and utility easements can be provided within a community's open space system. Open space can also be used as a buffer between separate neighborhoods or between the community and other surrounding land uses.

When planning open space, developers should be aware of short- and long-term maintenance costs. It is possible to set aside too much open space that requires maintenance, overburdening members of the community association or the responsible public agency if the open space is to be dedicated to the public. Council member David Jensen suggests that "the amount of open space should not be set in concrete but tailored to fit the specific project and market."

The type of open space provided should be tailored to meet the profile of prospective buyers or renters. For most markets, it is desirable to provide both maintained open space and natural open space. Some markets, such as empty nesters and retirees, may place a higher value on open space left in its natural state. The perceived amount of open space in a project is increased if adjacent areas like forests, hillsides, or lakes are maintained or managed as permanent open space by a municipal entity. According to council member Ronald Nahas, "This is the best kind of open space you can have because you don't have to pay for it or maintain it."

Commercial Space

Good planning often requires more than one type of land use within a development, which adds to functional convenience, character, and identity but may involve mixing residential uses with commercial or other nonresidential uses. Providing residential developments with convenient neighborhood-level commercial services is a common objective of planning.

Early concepts of planned unit development encouraged locating commercial centers near the center of residential communities so as to be accessible to all or most of the residents. These concepts also encouraged locating other institutional uses (schools and daycare centers) and commercial uses (professional offices, food service businesses) within the commercial "core."[6] Experience has proven, however, that commercial centers designed and located strictly for the use of one residential development are often not economical.

Commercial facilities should be located where merchants can draw from a large trade area. The best location for a neighborhood shopping center is generally at the intersection of an arterial street and a collector street. Still, the center should be accessible to pedestrians and bicyclists through a well-planned system of paths and sidewalks. The types of commercial development that should be provided include retail shops for convenience goods and the supply of basic services.

No accurate rules of thumb specify how much retail square footage to build within a given residential development. The determination depends largely on the availability of nearby (but off-site) retail services. The type of residential uses being proposed also influence commercial demand; for example, higher-income households generate higher demand for commercial services. ULI's *Shopping Center Development Handbook* suggests that neighborhood shopping centers (featuring a supermarket as the primary tenant) should range from 30,000 to 100,000 square feet, occupy a site of three to 10 acres, and require a minimum support population of 3,000 to 40,000 persons.[7] The trend has generally been toward larger neighborhood centers featuring a wider range of tenants, blurring the historical distinction between

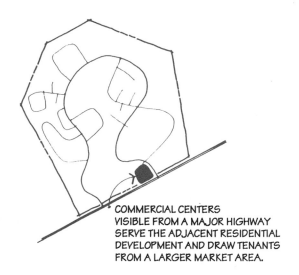

COMMERCIAL CENTERS VISIBLE FROM A MAJOR HIGHWAY SERVE THE ADJACENT RESIDENTIAL DEVELOPMENT AND DRAW TENANTS FROM A LARGER MARKET AREA.

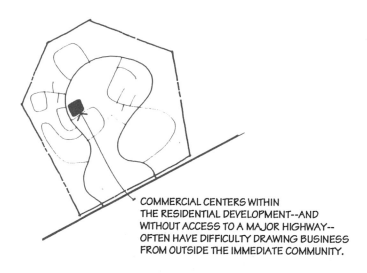

COMMERCIAL CENTERS WITHIN THE RESIDENTIAL DEVELOPMENT--AND WITHOUT ACCESS TO A MAJOR HIGHWAY-- OFTEN HAVE DIFFICULTY DRAWING BUSINESS FROM OUTSIDE THE IMMEDIATE COMMUNITY.

Source: Robert Engstrom and Marc Putnam, *Planning and Design of Townhouses and Condominiums* (Washington, D.C.: ULI–the Urban Land Institute, 1979), p. 41.

[6] For additional information on daycare centers, see Rob Seitz, "Day Care Centers: The Ultimate Amenity?" *Real Estate Forum,* February 1986, pp. 576–81; and "Day Care Centers: A New Building Amenity," *Professional Builder,* February 1986, pp. 158–61.

[7] John A. Casazza and Frank H. Spink, Jr., *Shopping Center Development Handbook,* 2d ed. (Washington, D.C.: ULI–the Urban Land Institute, 1985).

"neighborhood" and "community" shopping centers. Residential developers are advised to consult with a local market research firm to determine the potential demand for retail and other commercial uses.

Public Space

Public uses include schools, libraries, and facilities for public services like police protection, fire protection, and emergency rescue. The need to provide sites for these uses in a residential development depends on the existing availability of such services off site and existing plans for their provision in the future. Developers should therefore consult with appropriate public agencies and groups to determine whether it is necessary to reserve land for public uses. Appropriate locations for public uses within a residential development should be determined as part of overall site planning and design.

The availability of good elementary schools is an important consideration for residential developments where families with preschool and school-age children will form a substantial segment of the market. Frequently, the quality of the schools that serve an area significantly affects the potential price range of housing. The presence of nearby high-quality private or church-affiliated schools may also positively affect the market.

Like elementary schools, preschool or daycare centers may be an important consideration for family-oriented residential markets. Often such services are provided only institutionally or commercially. Commercial daycare centers may require less than one acre and need special exceptions to operate in certain zoning categories.

Providing schools has traditionally been a responsibility of the public sector, but the provision of land for schools is another matter. Subdivision ordinances

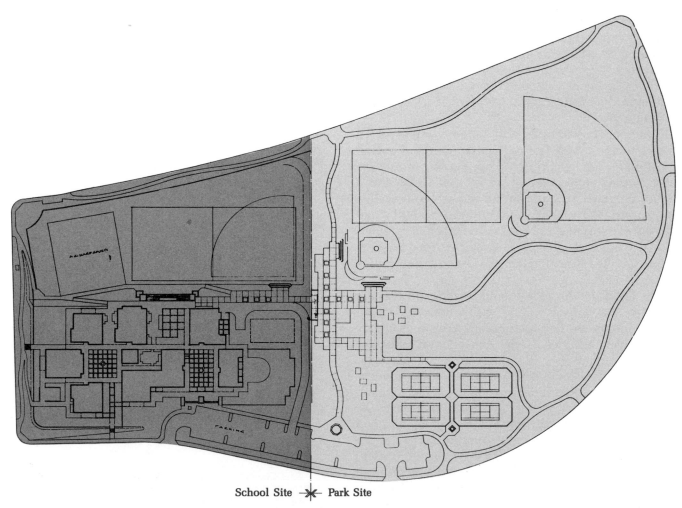

School Site ⸽ Park Site

5-11   The developer of Rancho Santa Margarita, California, increased efficient use of land by locating an elementary school adjacent to a local park. The two uses share parking and recreational facilities, such as ballfields and playground equipment.

requiring mandatory dedication of land or fees in lieu of buildings are a common method of providing land for schools. Courts have generally held this practice to be reasonable if the requirement placed on new subdivision is actually based on the need of the subdivision and if the subdivision benefits to the extent of the requirement.

From the standpoint of the developer and the community, an elementary school should be accessible to all sections of the project through a good pedestrian network. Sites for elementary schools should not front on a major thoroughfare, because doing so would expose children and the school to heavy traffic and noise. The preferred location is one that is easily accessible from a collector street and pedestrian circulation systems. Each school district has its own criteria for locating schools, and developers or land planners should meet with district officials before proceeding too far.

It is usually poor policy to place a school near the highest-priced housing planned for the development. Noise from outdoor activity can be a problem unless the playground is adequately buffered from adjoining housing. Further, the number of school-age children tends to decline as housing prices rise. The objective should therefore be to place the maximum number of units that will probably house the maximum number of school-age children closest to the school.

A site for a junior or senior high school should be on a major arterial thoroughfare for accessibility and to accommodate the school service area beyond the immediate neighborhood. That site should also be selected for access by pedestrians. Junior and senior high schools are sometimes combined on a single site to enable facilities like libraries, gymnasiums, indoor-outdoor swimming pools, auditoriums, and parking to be shared. School sites can also accommodate facilities for adult education, a community library, and other community cultural and social facilities. The obvious advantages are the elimination of duplicate services and the more efficient use of facilities.

Institutional Space

Developers should not overlook the value that institutional land uses, such as churches and synagogues, can bring to a development, particularly if the project is over 1,000 units or so. Such facilities require on-site parking, and freestanding sites must therefore be from three to five acres or more. Parking requirements relate to the size of the congregation and to the building's seating capacity. In a suburban area, parking requirements are approximately one space for each three to four seats, plus parking for staff members.

It is generally beneficial to provide institutional sites near commercial areas, schools, and other public facilities. Parking can often be shared and trips to these areas combined, perhaps reducing the amount of space required for parking. Institutional sites can provide a satisfactory buffer between neighborhood shopping centers and residential areas, provided that parking does not overflow onto residential streets.[8]

Residential Space

Density is the method of expressing the number of dwelling units in a particular area, normally per acre. For a residential development project, density is typically qualified as gross density or net density. Gross density is based on a site's gross land area, which includes streets, nonresidential uses, and open space. Net density represents the number of dwelling units per net acre of land devoted to residential buildings and accessory uses, excluding land for streets, public parking, playgrounds, nonresidential uses, and open space. In standard lot-by-lot residential developments, streets, parks, and recreation areas typically consume an average of 25 percent of the gross land area. Thus, a 300-unit development with a gross land area of 100 acres and a net area of 75 acres would have a gross density of three units per acre and a net density of four units per acre.

Density has always been a matter of interpretation. Historically, lower density was often interpreted as synonymous with higher quality, but today it is widely recognized that density in and of itself does not guarantee quality and that high-quality, livable neighborhoods can be developed at a wide range of densities.

Municipalities often establish permitted gross and net densities for residential projects. Other commonly used regulatory techniques for controlling density include the specification of minimum lot areas, sometimes based on the number of bedrooms, and the specification of maximum floor/area ratio, the ratio of permitted total floor area to available total land area. Maximum building height, building coverage, and front, rear, and side yard setbacks have also been used to control density. Another technique is to specify open space ratios that mandate requirements for usable open space. Most zoning and subdivision ordinances use some combination of these techniques.

---

[8] For more information, see Barton-Aschman Associates, Inc., *Shared Parking* (Washington, D.C.: ULI–the Urban Land Institute, 1983).

For developers, the development's productivity, or return on investment, is more important than density as a measure of acceptability. Productivity relates to a number of factors—the price of the houses, the number of houses, the pace of sales (and thus the length of time interest charges must be carried), and development costs. Clearly, density is one factor in determining productivity, because the fewer the number of units, the more each unit must share in the cost of land and improvements. While a low density may keep a project from being feasible, a high density will not guarantee its success. For the project to be viable, the market's expectations must also be met.

The trend in residential development today is toward higher densities.[9] This trend has been largely influenced by general acceptance of cluster subdivisions, which permit higher densities on some portions of the site to provide open space on others. When developing at higher densities, environmental impacts like increased runoff, increased traffic, and increased demand for services become important considerations during planning. Developing at higher densities also requires that more attention be devoted to the design of streetscapes and other public spaces. Sensitivity to these considerations can make the critical difference in the project's approval, market acceptance, and ultimately livability.

It is common practice in larger developments to segregate physically housing types, thus creating separate, uniformly dense enclaves of single-family detached, single-family attached, and multifamily housing. Although most local development controls encourage this practice, which has significant ramifications for construction and marketing, the practice can understandably be criticized for producing homogeneous and sterile residential landscapes. A more recent trend in residential development is to create more livable neighborhoods and communities through a blend of different housing types close to each other.

Phasing

As discussed in Chapter 4, a phasing plan for a residential development project identifies the proposed sequence and timing of development. It is based primarily on physical factors, such as the ability to extend roads and services, as well as on marketing factors, such as the anticipated rate of absorption. A well-thought-out phasing plan provides flexibility to respond to changing political and market conditions. The phasing plan is normally prepared as an overlay to the parcelization plan.

Circulation Elements

In residential developments, it is important to plan for easy and direct movement of both vehicles and pedestrians. Issues of convenience and safety must be considered and planned together. Ideally, vehicular and pedestrian circulation networks should be separated as much as practical and appropriate. The two systems should interface where people will get out of a vehicle and walk, such as where cars are parked and where buses pick up and discharge passengers. Wherever possible, the design of streets and pedestrian networks should facilitate residents' and visitors' use of mass transit. "People should be given more opportunities for traveling by some means other than the automobile, whether the means is rail transit, buses, van pools, or even bicycles or walking."[10]

Many municipalities have antiquated subdivision and design standards that result in higher-than-necessary costs for development and infrastructure. Development standards in the United States are contributing to the rising cost of housing, but big savings can be realized by changing design standards for streets. Past experience is no longer a good basis for determining future design and development standards, and high-quality development is possible by using innovative ideas for design and density and by implementing more cost-effective criteria for development. The Urban Land Institute, the American Society of Civil Engineers, and the National Association of Home Builders have cooperatively prepared a set of manuals for a program called Cost-Effective Residential Development Standards. One of the manuals targets cost-effective standards for residential streets and provides valuable information to residential developers about innovative ideas for street design.[11] Projects throughout the United States, for example, have reduced costs 12 to 30 percent by using innovative standards for street design.

Streets

Residential streets should be safe, efficient, convenient, and economical. They should also be designed and constructed for the particular function they serve.

[9] See James W. Wentling and Lloyd W. Bookout, eds., *Density by Design* (Washington, D.C.: ULI–the Urban Land Institute, 1988).

[10] Council on Development Choices for the '80s, *The Affordable Community: Adapting Today's Communities to Tomorrow's Needs* (Washington, D.C.: ULI–the Urban Land Institute, 1982), p. vii.

[11] National Association of Home Builders, ULI–the Urban Land Institute, and American Society of Civil Engineers, *Residential Streets,* 2d ed. (Washington, D.C.: Author, 1990).

Functions of residential streets differ according to purpose, traffic volume, and development density. Differences in function logically determine the rights-of-way and pavement widths to be provided.

Until recently, all types of residential streets were often lumped together as a single category behind major thoroughfares and highways. Standards for and advances in street design have historically been largely confined to highways and major thoroughfares, and standards for residential streets were either developed intuitively or adapted from highway design. Standards for most residential streets were set high in the event that a street might eventually be converted to a higher classification. These practices were insensitive to the characteristics of the users and resulted in needlessly expensive streets and standardized design.

> What seemed to have been overlooked was that residential streets are part and parcel of the neighborhood they serve. People live on them. It would seem desirable, therefore, not solely to move traffic safely and efficiently, but to see that the needs of people for a residential neighborhood that is quiet, safe, pleasant, convenient, and sociable are met as well. One must still provide for the necessary movement of the private automobile, for a place to park, and for access for service and emergency vehicles, but only because these too are part of the needs of the neighborhood. Streets should be designed to serve the neighborhood—not the neighborhood to serve the streets.[12]

The street plan of a new residential development should build upon the circulation element of a community's comprehensive plan, which normally identifies future alignments for major roads, such as collectors and arterials. New residential areas obviously need to be accessible from existing streets and highways, which might mean that a major road must be continued, extended, or planned to or through a development and be wider than necessary if it were serving the residential development alone. Residential streets, however, should be planned to discourage use by through traffic. The street plan should emphasize a minimum overall length of residential streets but still make dwellings accessible to service and emergency vehicles.

It is also important that the street plan relate to the natural contours of the site and that as many existing features of the landscape as possible be preserved. The street system should respond to the site's soil and geologic conditions, potential drainage and runoff, existing or abutting land uses, and the purpose, length, and intended character of the streets themselves. The street pattern can be curvilinear, linear, or a hybrid of the two, depending on existing site conditions and the intended character of the development.

Classification

In general, two types of residential streets are possible: collector streets and local streets. Collector streets convey traffic between local streets and arterial streets, such as highways and major thoroughfares. Local streets, which include both subcollectors and access streets, convey traffic between collector streets and dwelling units or off-street parking areas.

Collector streets are intended to carry a relatively high volume of traffic. Collectors typically carry an average daily traffic volume (ADT volume), the average number of vehicles using the road on a typical day, of over 1,000. Collector streets have one or more

---

[12] Bucks County Planning Commission, *Performance Streets: A Concept and Model Standards for Residential Streets* (Doylestown, Pa.: Author, 1980), p. i.

5-12 HIERARCHY OF RESIDENTIAL STREETS

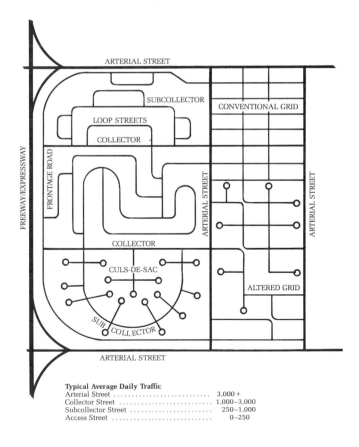

Typical Average Daily Traffic
Arterial Street .... 3,000+
Collector Street 1,000–3,000
Subcollector Street 250–1,000
Access Street 0–250

Source: ULI–the Urban Land Institute Real Estate Development School.

213

moving lanes in either direction, depending on the anticipated traffic load, and are intended to carry major public transportation, such as buses. On-street parking and direct access to individual dwelling units are not considered appropriate for collector streets.

Subcollector streets are intended to carry traffic between collectors and access streets. Subcollectors typically carry an ADT volume of 250 to 1,000. They can provide frontage and access to individual dwelling units and can accommodate on-street parking; they generally require one traffic lane in each direction.

Access streets, sometimes called places or lanes, are the lowest-order streets in the hierarchy and are not intended to carry through traffic. Examples of access streets include culs-de-sac, private drives, and short streets serving a few houses. Access streets typically carry an ADT volume of under 250. The primary purpose of this type of street is to conduct traffic between dwelling units and higher-order streets. They usually can accommodate on-street parking and can often require only one traffic lane.

In properly designed residential neighborhoods without through traffic, distances from residences to collector streets are short and actual traffic speeds are low. Lane capacity and design speed are not controlling design factors, and inconvenience or minor delays are inconsequential considerations. Brief delays or decreased speeds are expected for residential traffic. In residential areas, it is customary for individuals to drive protectively to avoid children and pets.

Alignment and Width

Residential streets need to be designed to discourage rather than encourage through traffic. The number of driving lanes provided, for example, can unconsciously encourage through traffic. Few if any access streets require two moving lanes to accommodate traffic generated in residential areas. Subcollectors rarely require more than two moving lanes.

Another method to discourage through traffic, a corollary of the number of driving lanes, is pavement width. Reducing pavement width does not indicate poor design, nor can wide streets be equated with better streets, which was often done in the past. Wide streets increase the potential hazard for pedestrians, and their maintenance is burdensome to taxpayers. "Selection of appropriate pavement widths must consider probable peak traffic volume, parking needs and controls, probable vehicle speeds, and limitations imposed by sight distances, climate, terrain, and maintenance needs."[13] To minimize street costs, the minimum width that satisfies these criteria should be selected.

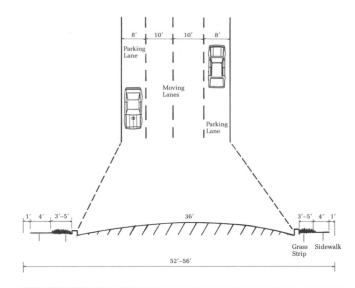

Source: National Association of Home Builders, ULI–the Urban Land Institute, and American Society of Civil Engineers, *Residential Streets,* 2d ed. (Washington, D.C.: Author, 1990).

Some municipalities request that superelevations (banked streets) be placed on all streets within a subdivision. This requirement can be waived on many streets if the developer requests it. Superelevations on subcollector streets can give a driver a false sense of security and result in excessive speeds. They can also cause ice and snow to accumulate on the roads where superelevations transition to the opposite drainage angle, such as on "S" curves. Superelevations should be evaluated carefully relative to need and not just arbitrarily applied because of a municipality's request.

For subcollector residential streets, pavement 26 to 28 feet wide is appropriate. This width allows for one active lane and two parking lanes, or one parking lane and two active lanes (one in each direction). For a short cul-de-sac, 22 or 24 feet is adequate. Widening this pavement a few more feet will not provide any significantly increased capacity but will tend to encourage faster driving. For collector streets, a pavement 36 feet wide is appropriate, providing two or four active traffic lanes. A 36-foot-wide pavement allows continuous movement at 25 to 30 miles per hour or more, depending on alignment and other

---

[13] Ibid., p. 32.

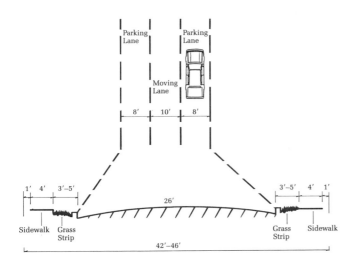

Source: National Association of Home Builders, ULI–the Urban Land Institute, and American Society of Civil Engineers, *Residential Streets,* 2d ed. (Washington, D.C.: Author, 1990).

Source: National Association of Home Builders, ULI–the Urban Land Institute, and American Society of Civil Engineers, *Residential Streets,* 2d ed. (Washington, D.C.: Author, 1990).

factors.[14] It is also sometimes appropriate to design collector streets without parking on either side of the street; in this case, the pavement could be reduced to 22 to 26 feet wide.

Horizontal alignment of residential streets should be based on terrain, sight distances, and probable roadway speeds. Vertical alignments should be sensitive to adverse weather conditions and limited visibility. Maximum permissible grades vary according to the severity of the weather. Automobiles can normally operate in high gear on maximum sustained grades of up to 7 percent. Local custom and such factors as energy conservation, aesthetics, and drainage will dictate vertical alignment. Short stretches of streets with grades of up to 20 percent may not be unreasonable.

Good drainage is of the utmost importance in street design, especially in areas subject to periodic freezing and thawing. With moisture below grade, expansion through frost heave can significantly damage the road surface. This problem can be especially severe on streets where water runoff from adjacent areas drains toward the road surface. The project engineer should recommend a street cross-section that ensures adequate drainage.

The thickness of the pavement should respond to environmental conditions, such as the bearing capacity of the soil and the traffic load. No other factor will have as great an effect on pavement thickness as the soil already there. If the subgrade material is well graded and compacted and if drainage is adequate, no additional base materials will be needed. The subgrade material actually supports the load, with the surfacing intended merely to prevent infiltration.[15] Developers also should not forget that the first traffic using the street will be heavy construction vehicles. To accommodate construction traffic, subgrade materials may need to be beefed up beyond what would be necessary for residential traffic.

Widths of street rights-of-way should be considered carefully, because every unnecessary foot of street right-of-way contributes to increased maintenance costs for the developer or the community. Unnecessary roads may also reduce final lot yields in jurisdictions where maximum allowable densities are calculated as a percentage of the net land area. Providing additional rights-of-way (for future widening of streets) should remain sensitive to the character of the community plan; usually, no reason should be available to allow the possibility of future widening through increased rights-of-way. For example, it would be inappropriate to allow additional right-of-way along an access street with individual lots fronting on it that

---

[14] See Donna Hanousek, et al., *Infrastructure Development Handbook* (Washington, D.C.: ULI–the Urban Land Institute, 1989), p. 45.

[15] For more information about pavement, see National Association of Home Builders et al., *Residential Streets,* 2d ed.

would later allow expansion of the street to collector status. The right-of-way must accommodate the required street pavement. Additional width, however, might accommodate sidewalks, utilities, drainage, snow storage, plant materials, and grading, but these features can also be located within easements on land owned in common by a community association or on other private property. By moving these features out of the street right-of-way, responsibilities for maintenance can be assigned more efficiently.

Intersections

The design of intersections is generally based on three characteristics: horizontal alignment, vertical alignment, and sight distances. It is best for all intersections to meet at approximately 90 degree angles. Acute angle intersections of less than 60 degrees should be avoided,[16] and little rationale exists for not offsetting pavements in these cases to improve the angle of intersection. Acute angle intersections often create excessive roadway paving, they are traffic hazards, and they create uneconomical block shapes.

The three-legged "T" intersection is the simplest and safest type. The more common four-legged intersection has 16 potential points of conflict where traffic lanes cross, and rights-of-way are often difficult to assign. The three-legged intersection has only three potential points of conflict, and assigning rights-of-way becomes more automatic.

The offset distance between two local streets intersecting a collector at opposite three-legged "T" intersections should be at least 125 feet to eliminate the possibility of corner cutting for crossing traffic and to provide adequate room for vehicles traveling in both directions on the collector to wait to make left turns without blocking one another. Intersections of two collector streets should be spaced at least 250 to 300 feet apart, intersections of collectors with local streets at least 200 feet apart.[17]

Where practical, the gradient within 100 feet of intersections of local streets should be no greater than 5 percent. In areas prone to heavy snow, this gradient should be reduced to 2 percent. The gradient for subcollectors and collectors should be as low as possible—generally not more than 2 percent, especially at intersections.

The minimum required sight distances at intersections vary with street classifications, design speed, and alignment. As a general rule of thumb, vehicles stopped on a local street intersecting with a 30-mile-per-hour collector should have an unobstructed view in both directions 300 feet from the centerline of the intersection; at an intersection with another 25-mile-per-hour local street, this minimum distance could be reduced to 250 feet. (These standards are not universal and must be tailored to specific conditions.) Ensuring adequate sight distances can be provided only by carefully siting buildings and avoiding high shrubbery or fences at street intersections.

Residential intersections should not be placed on a high point, a hilltop, or slightly below a hilltop. If it is impossible to avoid, however, an intersection on a hilltop is preferable to one slightly below.

[16] Ibid.
[17] Ibid.

5-16 TYPICAL CLEAR SIGHT DISTANCE

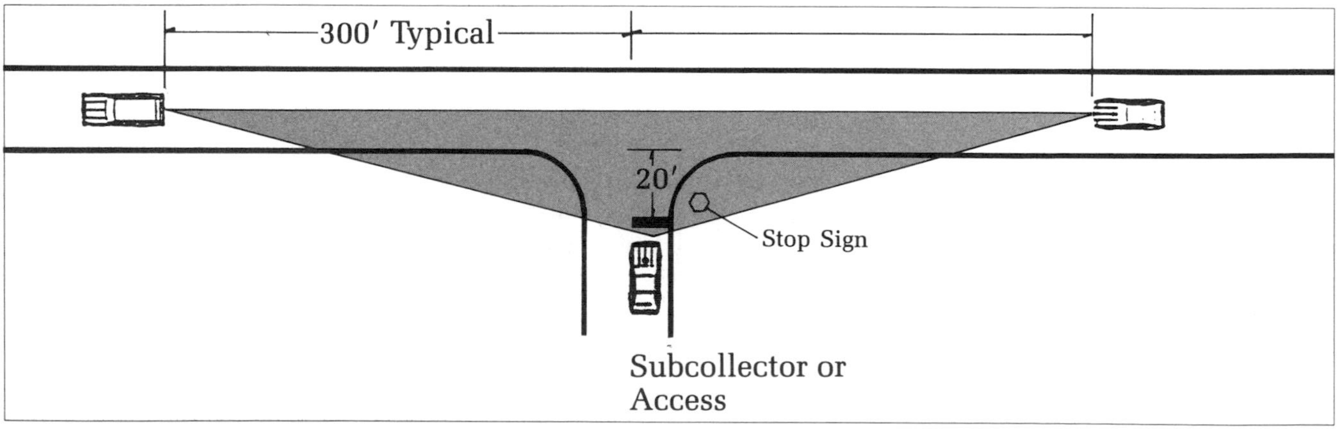
300′ Typical
20′
Stop Sign
Subcollector or
Access

Source: National Association of Home Builders, ULI–the Urban Land Institute, and American Society of Civil Engineers, *Residential Streets,* 2d ed. (Washington, D.C.: Author, 1990).

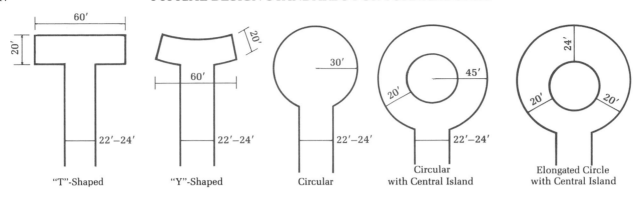

"T"-Shaped   "Y"-Shaped   Circular   Circular with Central Island   Elongated Circle with Central Island

Source: National Association of Home Builders, ULI–the Urban Land Institute, and American Society of Civil Engineers, *Residential Streets,* 2d ed. (Washington, D.C.: Author, 1990).

Culs-de-Sac

Culs-de-sac are dead-end streets with a turnaround at the end for cars. They are popular in single-family developments because of the privacy and freedom from traffic noise they offer.

Culs-de-sac up to 1,000 or 1,200 feet long are often satisfactory. In general, however, 500 feet is considered a reasonable maximum length for dead-end streets in urban areas, and a longer length should be considered only when:

- They are approved in writing by the local fire chief, the superintendent of streets, and the water superintendent or similar public authority;
- The street is divided by a median;
- An easement from the turnaround to another street provides a looped water system or the system is otherwise looped; and
- Hydrants are placed along the cul-de-sac and at the turnaround.[18]

Whatever its length, a cul-de-sac should serve no more than 20 or 25 dwelling units. This number of units can generate up to 200 vehicle trips per day, which is at the upper limit of what is considered acceptable for a local street.

The design of the turnaround at the end of a cul-de-sac should depend on the street's anticipated traffic volume and the type of vehicles that will use the street. Circular turnarounds are generally preferable to "T"- or "Y"-shaped turnarounds, whose use should be limited to short culs-de-sac serving very few dwelling units (usually fewer than 10). For slopes between 8 and 15 percent, they are excellent solutions because excessive grading for a turnaround can be avoided. Elimination of turnarounds is rarely justified on any cul-de-sac.

5-18   Located in Nottingham Estates outside Kansas City, Missouri, the central island in this turnaround is treated elaborately with special pavement materials, lighting fixtures, and architectural features.

---

[18] Carol J. Thomas, "Standards for Dead-End Streets," *PAS Memo* (Chicago: American Planning Association, 1985).

217

The recommended minimum radius for the paved area of a circular turnaround is 30 feet, the outside turning radius for large passenger cars. Larger vehicles will need to make one backing-up movement to negotiate the turnaround, but this minor inconvenience is considered acceptable in a residential area. In any case, a paved turnaround with a radius greater than 40 feet should be discouraged because it is more expensive to install and maintain, it results in increased stormwater runoff, and the large expanse of pavement is generally considered unattractive.

If a center island is used in a circular turnaround, it is desirable for the road around the island to be 20 feet wide and for low-maintenance landscaping materials to be used. The recommended right-of-way for circular turnarounds is a radius 10 feet greater than the paved area. Use of turnaround areas to store snow should not be a major consideration because such streets are low in priority in the overall street system for plowing snow and because snow can be stored in the right-of-way outside the pavement or on the edge of front lawns.

5-19 Rolled curbing is less expensive than vertical curbing and allows greater flexibility in locating driveways.

Driveways and Curbs

Driveways provide access to off-street parking or garages. The greater the number of driveways intersecting a street, the greater the number of points of conflict and the lower the street's capacity. The resulting decrease in traffic speed is desirable on local residential streets.

A minimum width of 10 feet is recommended for a single-lane driveway. Twelve feet wide allows a person to comfortably pass a car parked in the driveway. A minimum five-foot transition radius should be incorporated at the curb. For entrances to parking lots and other high-volume driveways, both a wider lane and a transition radius of 10 to 15 feet are recommended.

Street curbs may not be necessary on local streets in low-density residential neighborhoods unless they are required for stormwater management or road stabilization.[19] Curbs serve three basic purposes: to provide lateral support for the edge of the pavement, to prevent water's seeping under the pavement, and to contain pavement base materials and provide rigid channels for stormwater runoff. Aesthetically, curbing also provides a hard edge to the street that clearly defines the street area from the adjacent lot and open space. Curbing discourages off-street parking in unpaved areas, thereby lessening the potential for unsightly ruts.

The two basic types of curbing are vertical (or barrier) curbs and mountable (or rolled) curbs. Both types have advantages and disadvantages.

Neither type of curb acts as a safety barrier to protect those on sidewalks, as a car can generally mount both types when it is out of control. Curbs are much more a psychological than a physical barrier and are really only effective for preventing encroachment. Railings, posts, and shrubbery achieve the same effect.

Installation costs of both types of curb are similar. Vertical curbs' capacity to channel stormwater runoff is decidedly superior to that of mountable curbs. On steep grades of 8 percent or more, mountable curbs are impractical and are not recommended.

Mountable curbs are slightly less expensive than vertical curbs and make it possible to dispense with the installation of curb depressions. This feature increases design flexibility during construction in that the locations of driveways do not have to be determined before curbs are installed.

[19] Bucks County Planning Commission, *Performance Streets*, p. 17.

Alleys

Alleys are rarely used in residential development today. A rear property line easement is preferred to an alley when it is necessary to provide utility rights-of-way. Alleys can be beneficial, however, within certain densities and patterns of development. For example, alleys providing a second means of auto access to lots between 20 and 40 feet wide allow the number of curb cuts, driveways, and garage doors on the front street to be reduced, thereby improving the streetscape and increasing the safety and availability of on-street parking for guests.

Twelve to 16 feet is generally adequate for an alley, permitting use by service vehicles and normally providing just enough clearance for two cars to pass. The right-of-way should be coincident with width of the pavement. Garages and parking spaces should be set back from the alley three to five feet to provide adequate turning space for vehicles.[20]

Private Streets

The question of private streets versus streets dedicated to the municipality is in reality two questions—the first a question of design, the second a question of legal determination. Regardless of whether a street is public or private, however, streets should be designed to be responsive to needs. They should be designed for a specific traffic load with subgrade soil, drainage, groundwater, and climate conditions in mind.

Municipalities are sometimes concerned that private streets are designed with unusual configurations or to standards lower than those in force in the municipality. But making private streets respond to standards for public streets or flatly forbidding them is not always the best answer. Doing so may ensure consistent street design, but it is entirely possible that the municipality's street standards are arbitrarily high, lack innovation, and are generally unresponsive to new materials and new concepts of land planning. Strict standards can lock a developer into the costly cycle of providing overdesigned streets, which the city must then maintain.

If possible, developers should be afforded the opportunity for innovation. In keeping with the flexibility and discretion inherent in PUDs, private streets should be allowed to deviate from standards already in existence when a good reason exists for doing so. When the rationale is sound, innovative street design should be permitted.

Many developers propose that certain streets within a development be made private to escape public street standards. For example, some munici-palities do not allow medians, signs, lights, or certain types of landscaping in rights-of-way for public streets because of responsibilities for maintenance and the liabilities they incur. Most municipalities do not permit a guardhouse or security gate if streets are to be public. Developers must therefore consider how the streets will be used and how they can best be designed and maintained from the perspective of future residents before deciding whether streets should be public or private.

Developers are responsible for private streets until they transfer ownership to the community association. In protracted developments where phasing may take several years, developers participate in maintaining streets along with other property owners in the community.

One way to prevent misunderstandings about private streets is for the municipality to clearly set forth the terms under which it will accept dedication (for example, a surcharge for maintenance costs in excess of average costs to be charged directly to homeowners as a special district tax) and the physical modifications required for dedication (for example, the removal of entrance gates or the installation of curbing). Further, current requirements for full disclosure would presumably inform future residents of this special obligation, and the community association's financing structure should ensure adequate funds for ongoing maintenance and the gradual accumulation of an adequate reserve for repair and replacement.

Parking

The preparation of a parking plan for a residential development is highly affected by code requirements, costs, and demands of the topography. Parking is also a function of households' size, composition, and income, density, proximity to services like schools and shopping centers, and access to public transportation.

The parking plan should take into account new trends in the size of automobiles and their ownership. Small cars continue to capture a larger and larger share of the domestic market—just under 50 percent of the domestic market in 1978 but about 65 percent of sales by 1981.[21] At the same time, multicar families are becoming more and more common. According to the 1980 census, the national average of vehicles per

[20] National Association of Home Builders et al., *Residential Streets*, 2d ed.

[21] "Downsizing Cars and Parking Codes," *Zoning News,* January 1984, p. 1.

5-20 In higher-density housing developments like Arbor Creek, a zero-lot-line community in Garland, Texas, the location and design of garages can significantly affect the appearance of the street. Here, garages are set back to allow two cars to park on the apron. To further diminish the prominence of garages, garage doors are kept flush with house fronts, rooflines are varied to distract the eye, and overhangs are provided to cast shadows over the doors.

household in urbanized areas had increased to 1.5.[22] It is certain that changes in demographics and energy costs will continue to affect these trends.

Minimum parking requirements for residential developments differ from municipality to municipality. Regardless of what requirements are established by zoning ordinances, parking needs vary according to type of dwelling, locality, and composition of household. For example, more than a one-to-one ratio is likely to be needed for developments with households containing teenage children or apartments shared by unrelated adults. Less than a one-to-one ratio is more likely in housing for the elderly, especially in locations with good access to public transit.[23] Yet many ordinances stipulate the same parking ratio for the elderly that they require for family-oriented projects.

Off-street parking at a minimum of two spaces per dwelling unit must be provided for residents and guests in new single-family detached projects. Absolutes are difficult, however, and developers should check the market before deciding. Further, when two parking spaces per single-family dwelling unit are required under zoning or subdivision regulations, it must be made clear whether the requirement can be satisfied by a two-car garage or it means that space must be provided for two cars in the area between the street right-of-way and the front of the garage. If the garage or carport is to be counted as required off-street parking space, this allowance should be made clear in the covenants, conditions, and restrictions to prevent future conversion of the garage to living space.

Two parking spaces per unit should also generally be provided for residents and guests in new single-family attached projects. Traditionally, 1.5 parking spaces per unit have been provided for multifamily projects, regardless of the number of bedrooms, with additional space for guests' parking also advisable. Generally, 1.75 spaces per unit is a better measure. The recommended minimum requirements for off-street parking for multifamily housing projects are 1.25 spaces per unit for studio apartments, 1.5 spaces per unit for one-bedroom units, 1.75 spaces per unit for two-bedroom units, and two spaces per unit for units with three or more bedrooms.[24]

[22] Federal Highway Administration, *Transportation Planning Data for Urbanized Areas Based on the 1980 Census* (Washington, D.C.: Author, 1985), p. 35.

[23] See, for example, *Project Reference File:* "Fountainview Retirement Community," vol. 18, no. 19 (Washington, D.C.: ULI–the Urban Land Institute, October–December 1988).

[24] National Parking Association, "Recommended Zoning Ordinance Provisions for Parking" (Washington, D.C.: Author, September 1981).

Providing too much parking can be as problematic as not providing enough. Zoning ordinances that require an unreasonable proportion of parking in effect dictate the ultimate design of the project, and it is very difficult to relieve the wide expanses of pavement that typically result.

On-Street Parking

In general, on-street parking should be provided only for guests, and adequate off-street parking should be provided for residents. Two basic options are available for providing on-street parking: parallel parking lanes and diagonal or 90-degree parking bays. Compared to parking bays, parallel parking is generally considered safer and requires narrower streets, making it less expensive. Parallel parking lanes should be at least eight feet wide and can be provided on one or both sides of a local residential street.

In some situations, parking bays may be the best solution on local residential streets, such as in the center of turnarounds for culs-de-sac. Diagonal or 90-degree parking in recessed bays along access streets and interior service drives can be used successfully with single-family attached and multifamily housing. Based on actual experience, the best solution on internal streets that carry no through traffic is to make the street wide enough to allow diagonal or 90-degree parking on either side of two moving lanes, in effect forming an elongated parking lot. They might best be retained as private streets, because design standards for public streets usually do not permit 90-degree parking. This arrangement not only allows

5-21 In this community near Raleigh, North Carolina, guest parking is provided in parking bays located on private streets. Bricks are used instead of asphalt paving and railroad ties instead of concrete curbing to complement the community's wooded, rural character.

for a maximum amount of parking with a minimum installation of paving but also places cars in the most convenient location for residents and prevents the useless waste of open areas.

Off-Street Parking

All parking for residents should normally be provided off street. Locations for off-street parking include driveways, carports, garages, surface lots, and above-ground, below-ground, or integral parking structures. The choice depends on such variables as density, dwelling type, the market, and site conditions. In determining the area required for surface parking, a good rule of thumb is to reserve approximately 225 square feet for each automobile, including the parking space and a proportional share of moving lanes.

Awareness of cars parked in surface lots can never be completely eliminated, only made less noticeable. Large surface parking areas should be subdivided by landscaping. Surface parking should also be screened from adjacent structures and streets with hedges, dense vegetation, earth berms, changes in grade, or walls. The selection of plants should consider their size at maturity, differences in seasonal foliage, and maintenance, including feeding, pruning, spraying, watering, and eventually replacement.

Off-street parking facilities vary in price. A single uncovered surface parking space in a parking lot costs $1,000 to $2,500, depending on the total size of the lot and other variables. The average cost of a single space in an above-grade parking structure is over $7,000, and the average cost of a single space in a below-grade or integral parking structure is over $9,000, with integral parking slightly less expensive.[25] The use of structured parking can therefore be justified only if the market is willing to bear the higher cost.

The route from the car to the front door is a very important design consideration, perhaps more so than proximity to the unit itself. If parking is not possible immediately adjacent to a unit, it is best to designate parking for each resident as close as possible to his or her home. An indirect, inconvenient route that offers no protection from the elements is less than satisfactory.

Internal open space can be a project's best feature, so off-street parking should be located appropriately. Sometimes simple but well-designed carports in a

[25] Based on The Parking Market Research Company, *What's Going On Out There? A Statistical Analysis of Parking Construction in the U.S., 1986–1989* (Alexandria, Va.: Author, January 1987).

parking compound are a suitable solution to providing off-street parking. Garages under multifamily units save land on hilly sites, but they may raise construction costs because they must be fireproofed. Enclosed garages are seldom found in new multifamily construction except where land costs or the project's density dictate structured parking. In most parts of the country, apartment dwellers do not con-

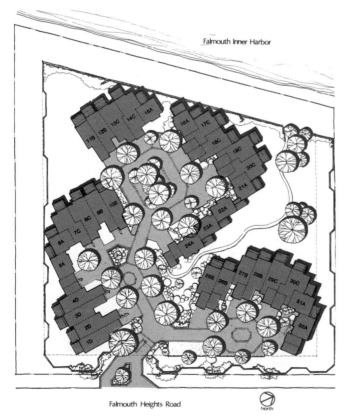

Falmouth Inner Harbor

Falmouth Heights Road

North

5-22, 5-23 The Boatyard in Falmouth, Massachusetts, uses a variation of the European motor court to provide access to garages and guest parking spaces. Parking space and access for automobiles become important elements of the project's design through landscaping and special pavement materials.

sider garages essential, and it is almost impossible to obtain sufficient rent to make them pay. Where winters are severe, however, some purchasers or tenants may insist on garages. In a townhouse development, enclosed garages may be the only large storage space available in the unit, particularly if basements are not provided.

Early marketing studies should establish the sales value of garages, the number required, and the importance of attaching them to individual houses. In almost all markets, a two-car garage is very important for single-family detached housing, but variations to this rule depend on sale prices and demands of the local market. Providing garages, however, means additional land coverage, greater setbacks, additional costs, and potentially negative impacts on the appearance of the streetscape. Especially in townhouse and small-lot detached developments, accommodating garages aesthetically is an increasingly important challenge in design.

In most cases where residents want a garage, they prefer a garage attached to the house, because a house is more functional if the walk from the car to the front door is short. Carrying in groceries during inclement weather can be a major accomplishment, and security is a growing influence on design. The convenience, privacy, and individuality afforded owners of a house with an attached garage are strong reasons for developers to consider their use.

If the walk to the house is pleasant, the market might accept separate garage clusters rather than attached garages. Clustered garages are seldom seen in single-family detached projects but can work quite well for townhouses, garden-density condominiums, and even multifamily rental apartments. For flexibility, a combination of both attached and detached garages as close as possible to individual houses is often possible and desirable.

Buildings housing garages should be a visual contrast to the houses rather than a uniform repetition of the same form. Using smaller garage clusters reduces the scale of the buildings, permits parking areas to be closer to the houses they serve, and adds another architectural form to accent and vary the development's visual image. Smaller-scale garage clusters bring architectural detailing closer to eye level and within human scale.

Strategies to deal with parked recreational vehicles, boats, and trailers are increasingly important. In general, oversized vehicles should not be permitted on residential streets, in front yards, or between dwellings because of their visual impact and potential fire hazard. The problem is particularly difficult in townhouse and multifamily developments. Special

222

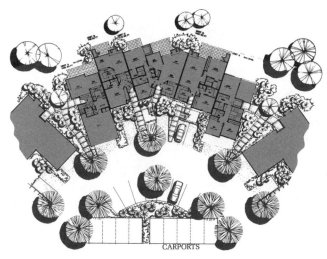

5-24 The eightplex buildings at Windrift in Laguna Niguel, California, are anchored at each end by two-story townhouses, each with a two-car garage. Stacked flats in the center have parking spaces located directly in front of each unit as well as carports in the center of each cluster. The use of clusters minimizes walking distances between carports and the units; the average walking distance is about 100 feet, and some units are as close as 40 to 50 feet from their assigned spaces.

garages and remote screened storage yards have been used with some success. The determination of how best to provide for or prohibit parking oversized vehicles must be based on market preferences.

Walkways

A well-planned system of paths and sidewalks is an important element in a residential area's livability. A number of design objectives have been identified in preparing a site plan in which pedestrians are recognized as a significant factor in shaping the arrangement of on-site facilities. Although the objectives seem simple, they make the difference between a

system that works and one that fails. One that works contains the following elements:

- A continuous pedestrian network connecting pedestrians' origins and destinations with direct and barrier-free pathways. Recreational pathways should be continuous but need not be direct.
- A minimum number of conflict points between pedestrians and motor vehicle traffic, with the site organized to reduce the number of places pedestrians must cross vehicular flows, particularly heavy flows.
- Clear delineation of pedestrian paths to ensure that effective walking routes can be selected. Visual cues should logically lead pedestrians to their desired destination, but signing may also be necessary, particularly on larger sites.
- Pedestrian facilities designed for easy maintenance. Failure to provide them has led to the demise of numerous well-intentioned and otherwise well-thought-out plans.
- Provision of amenities (greenery, shade trees, benches, and so on) to enhance walking.
- Consideration of pedestrians' special needs. Certain groups of pedestrians have special needs, which should be considered in the layout and design of facilities.
- Facilities designed to maximize pedestrians' security. Depending on the setting, a pathway that is not visible from parking lots or buildings can pose a threat to security, a problem of increasing concern.[26]

---

[26] S.A. Smith, K.S. Opiela, L.L. Impett, M.T. Pietrucha, R. Knoblauch, and C. Kubat, *Planning and Implementing Pedestrian Facilities in Suburban and Developing Rural Areas,* National Cooperative Highway Research Program Report No. 294A (Washington, D.C.: Transportation Research Board, June 1987), pp. 30–31.

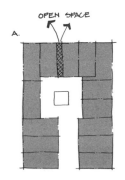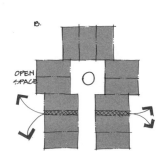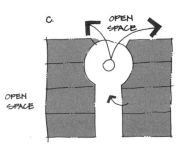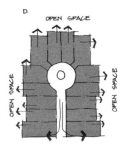

5-25 Access for pedestrians from each lot to open space can occur from the front, using sidewalks and easements, or from the rear of the lot. A and B use easements between lots, C uses a cul-de-sac opening up onto open space, and D uses access from rear lots and links to major open space. *Source:* David R. Jensen/HOH Associates, *Zero Lot Line Housing* (Washington, D.C.: ULI–the Urban Land Institute, 1981), p. 56.

5-26, 5-27, 5-28, 5-29   A) Mailboxes located along an interior trail system in The Woodlands, Texas. B) A perimeter trail system at Green Valley, Nevada, near Las Vegas. C) Fenced jogging and walking trail at Snow Creek, near San Diego, California. D) Path at Rancho Santa Margarita, California, providing pedestrians a shortcut to a community recreation facility and access for emergency vehicles.

Access for pedestrians from each house or cluster of houses to a variety of destinations—open space, recreational facilities, schools, daycare facilities, commercial centers—is an important consideration in planning. Such access can be from the front or the rear of a house. Traditionally, access from the front connects with a sidewalk that in turn links the house to the community's street-oriented pedestrian system. Access from the rear usually ties into an off-street pedestrian system built within open spaces, such as a greenbelt. The trend has been for increased use of off-street pedestrian paths where safety (especially for children) is most assured.

As a general rule, pedestrian and vehicular circulation should be separated. At-grade street crossings should be located only where sight distance along the road is good, and curb cuts should always be provided for users of wheelchairs, wagons, tricycles, bicycles, and baby strollers. At-grade street crossings on major streets require safety devices like appropriate signs, signals, and painted crosswalks. When paths or sidewalks intersect arterial streets, special signal controls, underpasses, or overpasses are necessary. Underpasses can be a security problem, however, unless they are designed for visual surveillance, and pedestrian overpasses are often expensive and not used unless they are readily accessible.

Sidewalks

Sidewalks provide a meeting area for neighbors and a play area for children as well as a circulation route. On streets with little traffic, the street itself can sometimes serve these purposes. Although many municipalities still require sidewalks on both sides of the roadway in all residential subdivisions, the need for either one or two sidewalks on any road can be determined based only on anticipated traffic volumes and the potential for conflicts between pedestrians and automobiles. For example, sidewalks are often not necessary in low-density developments with little street traffic, but they are generally needed on both sides of residential streets that serve as collectors from minor streets or that act as an approach to a school, bus stop, shopping center, or other focal point in the community.

Three questions must be asked in designing sidewalks: Are they necessary for the safety of children playing on the block? Are they necessary for children to walk to and from school and recreational facilities? And are they necessary for adults to walk to neighborhood centers?

If sidewalks are necessary and desirable, they should be located on a public right-of-way, on a public easement, or on a common open area. A sidewalk should normally be four feet wide, but six feet or more is often necessary along collector streets and near high-density pedestrian generators, such as schools and transit stops. Widths as narrow as three feet may be adequate for sidewalks on local streets. All utilities, such as utility poles and fire hydrants, should be kept out of the sidewalk area.

Integrated three-foot, six-inch sidewalks and curbs are possibly suitable for minor streets, although their use in northern climates complicates snow removal. In the snow belt, sidewalks should be at least three feet from the curb if no trees are present between the sidewalk and the curb. When trees are present, the distance from the curb may need to be increased, depending on the size of the trees.

As a general rule, a three- to five-foot border area or grass strip between the edge of the street and the sidewalk is desirable to provide a visual break between paved surfaces, enhance safety for pedestrians, and provide a storage area for plowed snow. In arid climates where water conservation is encouraged, the grass strip should be replaced with drought-tolerant groundcovers, gravel, or other low-maintenance, water-conserving treatment. While these border areas enhance pedestrians' safety, they can also become eyesores if they are not maintained properly; developers need to design for easy maintenance if grass is not feasible.

Driveway aprons that break the sidewalk level are an objectionable feature of combined sidewalks and vertical curbs, but this fault can be obviated by using rolled curbs. Local custom will help the developer choose.

Paths

Paths should supplement sidewalks in connecting all points of origin and destination within and adjacent to the residential development. For example, paths should be provided between residences and parking areas, commercial facilities, recreational areas, schools, clubhouses, and bus stops.

> [The] walk plan should be functional, built up of primary, secondary, and tertiary elements, each adjusted in location, width, and material to serve its purpose. Direct...access is essential; otherwise, most people seem inclined to shortcut, unless they are funneled into the intended paths by planting or barriers.... Walks must be laid out so that they follow the natural path of circulation. They should be functional rather than formal in design and layout.[27]

In addition to paths that directly connect points of origin and destination, recreational paths should be provided to take advantage of the site's natural amenities, following features like streambeds and shorelines. If a development includes wooded or conservation areas, paths can be developed within them for hiking and biking.

Pedestrian paths in well-drained soils may serve satisfactorily without any special surfacing. Where soils are soft or sticky when wet, pathway soils should be stabilized, surfaced, or paved as appropriate for the amount and character of their proposed use. An occasionally used footpath may serve adequately without improvement or with graveling. Heavy pedestrian usage or bicycle traffic usually requires a hard surface. Wood-chip or gravel paths are difficult to negotiate on a bicycle and are expensive to maintain.

---

[27] Joseph DeChiara, ed., *Time-Saver Standards for Residential Development* (New York: McGraw-Hill, 1984), p. 82.

Bikeways

A bikeway is "any road, path, or way [that] in some manner is specifically designated as being open to bicycle travel, regardless of whether such facilities are designed for the exclusive use of bicycles or are to be shared with other modes of transportation."[28] Three primary types of bikeways are possible: bicycle paths (Class I), bicycle lanes (Class II), and shared roadways (Class III). These three types can be connected to residential streets and pedestrian walks and paths to create a network for use by both recreational bicyclists and pragmatic bicyclists who use the bicycle for transportation to school, work, or shopping.

When they are provided, bicycle lanes and shared roadways are generally located on collector streets and arterials. A bicycle lane is a portion of a roadway that has been designated by striping, signing, and pavement markings for preferential or exclusive use by bicyclists. It should be four feet wide if located at the edge of the pavement and five feet wide if parallel to parked cars. A shared roadway is a right-of-way designated by signs or permanent markings as a bicycle route but also shared with pedestrians or motorists. For a shared path, an eight-foot paved area is desirable. Pavement striping helps separate different uses.

Bicycle paths are completely separated rights-of-way for the primary use of bicyclists. In general, the right-of-way should be at least 10 feet wide and the

5-30 Bicycle lanes can be accommodated on the street, separated from both vehicular and pedestrian traffic.

path itself at least five feet wide, permitting two-way traffic. Overhead obstructions should be no closer than 8.2 feet from the surface of the bikeway. The length of uphill grade that bicyclists normally tolerate drops sharply when the gradient reaches 5 percent. Uphill grades of 5 percent are tolerable for under 100 feet, but grades of 10 percent are tolerable for under 25 feet.[29]

Utility Elements

New residential development creates a demand for many types of facilities and services, both on and off site. This demand needs to be addressed during project planning to ensure that the required utilities and services will be provided efficiently and in a timely manner.

The entities responsible for providing these facilities and services range from the developer to private companies to public agencies at many different levels of government. In obtaining approval for the project, it is often the developer's role to identify the project's requirements and to seek the necessary commitments from the responsible entities.

Developers must plan ahead to ensure that installation of facilities required by the project goes smoothly. Often, municipalities' withholding utility connections, notably sewer hookups, has curtailed planned developments or severely delayed them at a time when the developer needs to proceed. Negotiation and continual communication are the hallmarks of coordination among the developer and the various utility companies. A preconstruction meeting on the site between the developer's construction manager and the utility company's installation supervisor is a good idea. Such a meeting can help each party keep the other advised from the outset, rather than having each try to solve problems alone after they occur. A coordinated installation schedule with specific commitments is also a good idea.

One inequality developers often face is a requirement for improvements and utilities in excess of those needed to serve a specific project. For example, a developer may be required to install a larger sanitary sewer main than the particular project needs to serve future development. The problem can be resolved in a number of ways. The municipality can pick up the

[28] American Association of State Highway and Transportation Officials, *Guide for the Development of New Bicycle Facilities* (Washington, D.C.: Author, 1981).

[29] Charles W. Harris and Nicholas T. Dines, eds., *Time-Saver Standards for Landscape Architecture* (New York: McGraw-Hill, 1988), p. 341-3.

costs for oversizing the improvement, or the developer can be reimbursed for costs of oversizing when new development is added. Developers should avoid installing more infrastructure than what is necessary to serve each phase of development. Advance installation greatly increases the carrying costs of land and reduces future flexibility in site planning.

This section discusses the primary utility services with which residential developers need to be concerned: water, wastewater, energy systems (electricity and natural gas), and communication systems.

Water

Water supply is typically the responsibility of a municipality or a special district. Particularly in the West, where long-term availability of water is a politically charged issue, it is often necessary for developers of new residential areas to assist the municipality or special water district in determining where the required quantity of water can be obtained. Only rarely are suitable sources of groundwater or surface water available on site. Once a source has been identified, developers might have to subsidize the construction of infrastructure required to tap the source and transport the water to the site. This infrastructure can include wells, reservoirs, storage tanks, aqueducts, and treatment facilities. If the availability of water is an issue, it will be in developers' best interests to incorporate water conservation measures into development plans, minimizing long-term water needs.

A central water supply is always preferable to individual wells, just as a central sewage disposal system is preferable to separate septic tanks. As areas are developed, the water supply and water quality of wells become undependable. Two or more wells placed near each other can interfere with one another, and saltwater intrusion of wells is a common problem in coastal areas.

Many different types of wells are available to meet different situations—drilled, jetted, bored, and dug—but the initial construction and subsequent maintenance costs of a central supply are often less and the results far more satisfactory. Small private water companies can render satisfactory service when larger municipal water services are not available.

When discussing extensions of water mains, developers must be aware of not only who pays the costs involved but also the legality of the extensions. In general terms, the obligation of a private water company to extend its lines within its franchised territory is undeniable. With nonfranchised companies or those operating outside their franchised territory, however, the obligation is based on the extent of their profession of service. Denial of application for extension can be appealed to the state public utilities commission and ultimately the courts.

With municipally owned water systems comes more discretion whether to extend service within municipal boundaries. Discretion can be abused, but in general the utility has a duty to supply water to all residents of a community. Extending its obligation beyond corporate limits is another question. A municipal utility must generally have made some profession of service in the area to service it, and in this regard it comes under the purview of the public utility commission.

The issue of financing extensions of water mains is clouded. In some cases developers bear the costs, either with or without reimbursement, in other cases the utility. Developers should check with the local utility or the state public utilities commission.

In an outlying area where the nearest public water supply may be several miles away, a last resort might be to create a private water company to serve the new development. Under most state laws, it will be necessary to obtain incorporation papers for the proposed utility company, a franchise from the local jurisdiction to lay mains in the projected streets, permission from a water control board to drill a test well after offering proof of need, and the submission of evidence of proper and safe construction and the safeguarding of other water supplies. The state board of health must approve plans for wells and the distribution system, and the public utility commission must approve rules, regulations, and rates. Public hearings are also required of the developer.

Once a source of water and the means of getting it to the site have been assured, the next step is to plan the on-site water distribution system. The primary purpose of this water distribution system is to convey potable water to dwelling units; secondarily, it is meant to provide water for fire protection. The on-site water distribution system often represents a high initial investment when compared to other utilities.

Water mains should be located in street rights-of-way or in utility easements. If curbs and sidewalks are contiguous, they could be placed behind sidewalks. Water mains vary in size, depending on demand from users; typically, residential mains are six or eight inches in diameter. Water mains are constructed in a loop system wherever possible to maintain water pressure. A civil engineer should be consulted to ensure adequately sized water mains.

Fire hydrants should be readily accessible without creating a hazard either to pedestrians or to automo-

5-31 Fire hydrants must be visible from the street and accessible to emergency personnel.

bile traffic. Like water mains, water lines for fire hydrants are often required to be constructed in a loop system. Traditionally, fire companies have needed large water mains to drown fires. With new types of fire-fighting equipment and chemicals like foam or fog, it may be possible to design water distribution systems that cost less.

Wastewater

Two basic alternatives are available for disposing of domestic waterborne wastes: piping the wastes off site to a municipal sewage treatment system or treating and disposing of the wastes on site. The use of on-site systems is expected to increase as areas beyond existing sewage collection systems are developed and as existing public treatment plants run out of capacity.[30]

Since the passage of the Clean Water Act in 1972, the federal government through the EPA has given construction grants to municipalities to help build sewage treatment facilities. Federal funding for this program is decreasing, however, and state and local governments are searching for alternative means of financing pollution control projects. Communities are likely to continue to insist that new development pay its own way through fees and exactions to finance

off-site improvements in public facilities. Furthermore, small-scale wastewater treatment systems are likely to continue to become a more attractive alternative to capital-intensive centralized plants. A variety of small-scale systems are available, often combining small-diameter collection systems with common on-site disposal systems, package plants, or alternative treatment systems, such as lagoons. For conventional subdivisions and PUDs of up to eight units per acre, these systems can be ideal if a conventional system is not accessible. Small-scale technologies have not been used widely in the past, partly because they are perceived as land-intensive, environmentally unsound, or only a temporary solution.[31]

From the developer's perspective, public sewer systems should be used whenever possible. The developer's next choice is an on-site, small-scale community system rather than individual on-lot disposal. Current pollution control regulations, however, are likely to prohibit community systems unless they are publicly maintained and operated.

In general, sanitary sewer lines should be located in utility easements or in street rights-of-way. When located in street rights-of-way, they should not be constructed under roadway paving unless laterals are extended to front property lines at the time of installation. If sewer lines are constructed only on one side of the street, laterals will be necessary and roadways cannot be completed until all laterals are installed. Requirements for laterals can be reduced by placing multiple units on each lateral.

The system should be coordinated with other utilities and located to avoid trees. The size of individual connections to sewers should be not less than six inches to avoid clogging. As a rule, lateral sewers should not be laid in the same trench with water supply lines. It is possible in some cases when permitted by local authorities, however, to combine the lines in a double-shelf trench that contains the sanitary sewer on the bottom and the water lines on the shelf. Preventing improper or illegal connections between surface water systems and sanitary sewer systems is extremely important.

Two types of sanitary sewer lines are available—gravity mains and forced mains. Gravity mains are used to connect individual dwelling units with treatment plants or pumping stations. Forced mains are used to connect pumping stations with treatment plants. The topography of the site, the arrangement of

[30] Ibid., p. 720-1.
[31] Patrick Phillips, "Wastewater Treatment: Impacts of the Shrinking Federal Role," *Urban Land,* June 1985, pp. 36–37.

units on the site, and the location of the treatment plant determine whether pumping stations and forced mains are required.

Municipal Systems

If developers plan carefully and overlook no short- or long-range opportunity to hook up with a public sewer system, they can probably save the cost and trouble of putting in high-risk septic tanks or tying up capital and time in community systems. In planning a sewer system, developers should investigate several questions:

- Is the existing system to which connections are to be made adequately sized? Is it a separate or combined sanitary and stormwater system? What is the present capacity? How many hookups are under contract but not installed? Normally more potential users are eligible than the system can handle.
- How does the municipality charge for installation of sewers? Is it charged entirely to the developer? Is total or partial recovery of the initial cost possible?
- Can a special sewer improvement district be set up to cover the area to be developed? How are costs allocated if mains and trunk lines must be constructed through the development to serve property beyond its borders? A municipality that charges fees for sewage disposal should also pay for the installation costs of sewage mains from the revenues produced by those user fees.
- Is a permit to discharge surface drainage into natural watercourses required by local or state government? And in what condition may it enter those waters? Developers should be sure to check this point as it will save trouble, litigation, and expense later.

Community Systems

Community systems include large septic tanks with subsurface leaching systems, large aerobic digesters (often called package plants) with surface infiltration beds, large aerobic digesters with evapotranspiration disposal of effluent, unaerated lagoons with overflow disposal to surface infiltration beds, and aerated lagoons with overflow disposal to surface infiltration beds.[32]

If an extension of public sewers is impossible, a small central community system should be used. The passage of the Federal Water Pollution Control Act Amendments of 1972 limits federal funding for the construction of small community systems dedicated to a municipality or designated as part of an areawide wastewater treatment program. In addition, a state permit for any discharge of sewage effluents into streams and rivers is required, and effluents must meet the standards set for the receiving body of water. In many cases, secondary treatment is required. Often a discharge permit can be denied if the community system does not comply with the local areawide wastewater treatment plan under Section 208 of the act.

Individual Systems

Individual on-site systems include septic tanks combined with any of a variety of subsurface leaching systems (leaching trenches, leaching beds, and leaching pits, for example), aerobic digesters combined with the same variety of subsurface leaching systems, aerobic digesters combined with surface infiltration beds, or aerobic digesters combined with evapotranspiration disposal systems.[33] Determination of effectiveness and feasibility of any of these disposal systems depends on site conditions, costs, and the local government's regulations and policies.

Sewage disposal by septic tanks and tile fields for each dwelling should be the last resort only when absolutely necessary, and then only after state and local departments of health have cleared their use. Individual on-lot disposal requires a parcel of land considerably larger than the normal suburban lot for an adequate disposal field. This consideration is not the only one, however. The disposal field must slope away from the house and be kept free of trees and shrubbery to ensure the action of sunlight. The type of soil and subsoil affects both the amount of area needed and the possibility of polluting nearby surface water or wells. Effluent from hillside disposal fields has been found coming to the surface a considerable distance from the field where it originated. The wide variation in the use of water by individual households (ranging from 30 to 150 gallons per person per day) causes the design of individual septic tanks to be very difficult. The addition of garbage disposal units to a septic tank system means doubling the capacity of the tank and more frequent attention to maintenance. These and other considerations often negate any benefits of septic tank systems.

It is impossible to adapt septic tanks to all of the various soils and uses found in a development. Even

---

[32] Harris and Dines, eds., *Time-Saver Standards for Landscape Architecture*, p. 720-3.
[33] Ibid.

229

if conditions are favorable in a residential community, the maintenance of individual septic tanks after a few years becomes a difficult problem. If individual septic tanks must be used, developers should first notify the state board of health and then be prepared to conduct percolation tests to determine the final required dimensions of the lots. They should also bear in mind that disposal fields might have to be abandoned after some years, as reconstruction of septic tank systems is very seldom practical or satisfactory. In any case, proper design and construction are absolutely essential.

Energy and Communications

Investor-owned utility companies typically provide infrastructure for telephone, natural gas, and electric service, and private companies typically provide infrastructure for cable television (CATV) service. Typically the companies finance this infrastructure, known as commercial or specialized infrastructure, and it is in the developer's interest to assist the companies with planning and installing any on-site facilities.

Underground lines for electric, telephone, and CATV service are now common. Advances in trenching equipment and protective coating for wiring and the elimination of tree maintenance costs associated with overhead lines have contributed to greater acceptance of underground utilities. New cost-reducing equipment is now available to power companies for quickly locating any interruptions in service, again lowering maintenance costs. Telephone companies find that underground wiring also eliminates paying

rent on power poles. Electric, telephone, and CATV companies routinely cooperate in common trenching, because it is more cost-effective and facilitates subsequent location of these utilities. Most gas companies, however, prefer to install gas lines in a separate trench, which may or may not be located in a common public utility easement.

Underground utilities are aesthetically superior to poles running along rear lot easements or within street rights-of-way. Some developers, however, have complained that electrical transformers mounted on pads are as ugly as overhead power lines. If surface appurtenances like pad-mounted transformers are used, developers should cooperate and compromise with utility companies to obtain a favorable location that will provide utility companies with adequate access yet not be prominently displayed. Transformers can also be screened with landscaping to minimize visibility from public spaces.

Current practice dictates the location of underground utility lines within the street rights-of-way or adjacent to them in separate utility easements. Moving utility easements to building lines has not been favored. The maintenance of underground utilities inevitably requires excavation for repair, and the political problems of disrupting private landscaping are more severe than cutting pavement.

Landscape Elements

Planning landscaping for residential development involves both natural and manmade features. Landscape architects work with such elements as terrain,

5-32, 5-33   Utility appurtenances should not be placed in full view of the street or pedestrian circulation areas (left). When matured, landscaping can effectively screen utility boxes from public view without blocking access for maintenance personnel (right).

water, plants, fences, walls, paving, street furniture, and lighting to create a landscape that not only is functional and attractive but also gives the site its character or sense of place.

Successful landscape planning and design require an understanding of a site's natural characteristics and the natural processes at work in the local environment. The landscape plan should attempt to preserve as much of the existing natural vegetation and landforms as possible while creating an environment that is pleasant and comfortable for future residents. New plant materials should be positioned in a manner that is compatible with native plants.

Grading

Grading is more than just an engineering tool to render a site usable for building, to create circulation routes and building pads, and to solve drainage problems. Grading is also an important design technique to enhance a site's distinctive and attractive qualities. Preparation of a grading plan is therefore an integral part of site planning and design.

In residential development, grading can be undertaken for a number of functional or aesthetic reasons:

- To create building sites for individual houses or groups of houses.
- To provide for proper drainage.
- To create berms as noise or wind barriers.
- To increase soil depth for planting or to increase the topsoil over unfavorable subgrade conditions, such as groundwater.
- To create acceptable sites for community facilities, such as playgrounds and playfields.
- To modify undesirable landforms.
- To create circulation routes, such as paths and roads.
- To create proper subgrade conditions.
- To emphasize the site's topography or to provide interest for a naturally flat site.
- To capture views or to hide undesirable views.
- To relate the site to the surrounding area and to relate structures to the site.
- To create illusions about the size or shape of spaces.
- To relate landforms to bodies of water.
- To emphasize or control circulation routes.[34]

Level terrain generally can be characterized as land with a slope less than 3 to 5 percent. With a little imagination, a relatively flat site can be transformed into one with subtle visual variety through the use of earth berms and other grading techniques. If foundations and basements must be excavated, fill can be deposited nearby to create berms, saving charges for trucking.

Berms can be integrated into the open space system, providing good sites for pathways between major open spaces and other community focal points. Berms can be used to provide a visual and physical screen between adjacent land uses without the need for elaborate walls and fencing. Berms can also be used to turn flat terrain into rolling, providing an opportunity to site houses in locations where they can obtain a better view of surrounding features.

Moderate terrain is characterized as land with slopes ranging up to about 10 percent. In developing areas of moderate terrain, economic considerations require that a balance be struck between the amount of grading and the resulting number of units that can be constructed on a given site. An advantage of planned unit development over conventional lot-by-lot development is that grading can be minimized by constructing houses on the more suitable portions of the site and reserving the remaining areas as permanent open space.

Steep terrain has average slopes exceeding 10 percent. Because of the potential hazards associated with the development of hillsides, such areas warrant special consideration by developers and planning departments. Imposing traditional subdivision regulations on hillside developments is rarely successful and often leads to improper or needlessly expensive development.

Engineering studies generally must be undertaken if development of a steep slope is contemplated. Such studies should focus on geological, soil, and drainage conditions and identify measures that will be required to ensure safe, stable, and functional building sites.

Flexible standards for lot size and shape, frontage, rights-of-way, street width, easements, and setbacks can permit sensitive and appropriate development of steep sites. In particular, steep topography frequently necessitates unusually deep or shallow lots to use the land efficiently without excessive grading. With regard to the design and placement of units, it is important to consider the view of the project from the surrounding area. Building profiles should be kept low, preferably below the skyline. The preservation of natural terrain, vegetative cover, rock outcrop-

---

[34] See John Sue, "Landscape Grading Design," in *Handbook of Landscape Architectural Construction,* edited by Jot D. Carpenter (McLean, Va.: Landscape Architecture Foundation, 1976), p. 35.

As prime development land becomes ever more scarce, so the prospect of building on difficult sites increasingly confronts planners, designers, developers, and builders. Ginsburg Development Corporation faced such a challenge when it chose to develop luxury townhouses on a steeply sloping, rocky ridge in Greenburgh, New York.

A former Salvation Army camp, the property that is now Boulder Ridge Condominiums spans 42 acres and includes rock outcroppings and stands of mature trees. The project includes 144 units in two- to six-unit clusters. An adjacent 11-acre parcel, a former country club that was annexed one year after construction began in 1986, provides a clubhouse, tennis courts, a swimming pool, and room for 18 estate houses.

In keeping with its philosophy of preserving the land, the developer wished to protect the site's

RECREATION LEVEL   FIRST FLOOR

SECOND FLOOR   SKY STUDIO

5-35   A townhouse cluster featuring the Dalton at both ends and the Bedford in the center. Both these models were designed for difficult uphill conditions, obviating recontouring the site. "The key to the attractiveness of Boulder Ridge," says its developer, Martin Ginsburg, "is the fact that we have designed models appropriate for the natural terrain rather than taking a house design and shaping the site to suit the plan."

5-36   The Dalton's side entrance, a pillared portico on the first floor, leads into an open foyer flanked by the living room and a raised dining area. Two pairs of French doors in the living room provide access to the unit's exterior deck, and another set of French doors in the dining room leads to a private rear yard. The Dalton model designed as an end unit is 3,946 square feet.

pings, and other special features should also be encouraged.

Massive cut-and-fill operations are obviously more expensive than minimal grading. The cost of grading for development of a given site is determined by several factors: 1) the composition of the material being moved, 2) geological and soil conditions (blasting rock might be required on some sites and compacted clays are difficult to move), 3) site location and access and distances required to haul dirt, 4) the

achievement of balanced cut and fill within the site, 5) the extent of stabilized slopes specified in the grading plan, and 6) weather conditions (for example, grading is prohibited in parts of California during the winter rainy season unless extensive measures to control erosion are implemented). To minimize requirements for cut and fill, roads in steeply sloping areas should generally be located on ridge lines or parallel to the contours of a slope. Roads in hillside and mountain areas should typically take on rural

Key:

E	Andover End
A	Andover
K	Kensington
C	Castle Hill
G	Greenwich
M	Melville
D	Dalton
B	Bedford
L	Lynwood

5-37   Site plan.

woodlands and other natural features. To avoid recontouring, an access road was built horizontal to the hillside, and building sites were clustered along both sides of the road.

Nine models of townhouses were designed for grades generally ranging from 20 to 30 percent. All models are essentially vertical (with small footprints) to diminish their impact on the site while still allowing large units. The houses are oriented to maximize privacy and are equipped with boulder and landscaped berms where streets, parkways, or nearby structures would intrude on privacy. All models contain four livable levels and measure from 3,490 to 5,020 square feet.

The most difficult models to design and execute were those on the road's uphill side, where front-facing garages and full-story basements below the entry and main living level made treatment of facades and entries critical. One model, for example, capitalizes on the possibilities of a cluster's end unit with a stepped ramp walk that curves around from the driveway and continues up several wide steps leading to an imposing side entrance portico. Uphill site conditions made interior units in another model prime candidates for a full-story front stoop. That design uses a series of gradual steps and landings combined with boulders, landscaping, and stone retaining walls to accommodate the uphill access gracefully.

Custom architectural and site planning for Boulder Ridge cost an estimated $2,500 extra per unit. In addition, approximately $20,000 per unit was necessary to provide stone retaining walls, berms, and mature plantings.

Source: Ginsburg Development Corporation, Hawthorne, New York. Reprinted from *Urban Land,* August 1989, pp. 28–29.

characteristics. Where feasible and appropriate, retention walls should be considered as an alternative to extensive grading.

Drainage

Land development alters the natural drainage patterns of landscapes, both on and off site. These modifications can sometimes adversely affect waters and land uses downstream. It is now generally accepted that development should have no more than a minimal impact on off-site drainage and that on-site drainage should respect or emulate natural drainage patterns whenever possible.

It is important that planning and design of a site drainage system be an integral part of project planning and design rather than a discrete aspect of site engineering. Major functions of site drainage systems include preventing flooding and erosion, minimizing soil swelling and frost heave, maintaining high water

233

quality, recharging the groundwater, protecting wildlife habitat, and creating an on-site amenity. Alternative strategies for site drainage must be evaluated in conjunction with the review of alternatives for other planning elements. The drainage plan should work in conjunction with other aspects of the overall site design.

Most site drainage problems can be solved in a variety of ways. Recently, minimizing use of engineering techniques and devices to control runoff has been widely accepted as a viable means of solving drainage problems. A major advantage of a "soft" approach to site drainage is a significant savings of both short- and long-term costs. When designed in conjunction with natural drainage techniques, conventional storm systems can be designed to carry smaller amounts of stormwater, thereby reducing costs of infrastructure.

Stormwater Management

In the past, stormwater management for residential development sites essentially was limited to the construction of underground storm sewers. The storm sewers collected runoff from the street system during and immediately following a rainfall and discharged the flow off site. This approach was very efficient for the rapid elimination of runoff from a site. Over time, however, it became increasingly clear that the cumulative effects of this approach often included increased flooding downstream and reduction of local groundwater reserves.

Current stormwater management practices recognize that every parcel of ground is part of a larger drainage area and that alterations such as regrading the land, increasing the impervious cover, or modifying natural drainage systems can lead to a series of environmental changes downstream. These changes can include flooding, erosion of stream profiles and undermining of stream banks, sedimentation, turbidity in waterbodies downstream, algae blooms and loss of water quality in waterbodies downstream, and loss or adverse alteration of the habitat of aquatic biota.

The following general concepts are offered as guidance for the design of environmentally responsible stormwater management systems.[35]

1. Ideally, water falling on a given site should be absorbed or retained on site to the extent that after development, the quantity and rate of water leaving the site would not be significantly different from the site's undeveloped state.
2. The design of any stormwater system should strike a balance among capital, operating, and maintenance costs, public convenience, risk of significant water-related damage, environmental protection and enhancement, and other community objectives.
3. Engineering techniques that capitalize on and are consistent with natural resources and processes should be implemented. Natural engineering techniques improve the effectiveness of natural systems and are frequently less expensive to construct and maintain than other alternatives.
4. Examples of sound stormwater management include use of on-site detention storage, increased use of on-site storage to balance peak flows, and use of land treatment systems for the handling and disposal of stormwater.[36]
5. Responsibilities and obligations for collection, storage, and treatment of stormwater are to be shared by individual property owners and the community as a whole.[37]
6. Stormwater is a component of an area's entire water resource system and should be used to replenish that resource.
7. Every site or situation is different, and design standards for optimal achievement of objectives for managing runoff must vary accordingly.

On-site stormwater storage facilities, including detention and retention basins, should be located in common open space whenever possible. Design of such facilities should consider safety, appearance, recreational use, and effective, economical maintenance.

Stormwater management systems, street layout, lotting patterns, and the horizontal and vertical locations of curbs, inlets, and site drainage and overflow swales should be designed concurrently. Streets play an important role in collecting and conveying stormwater runoff. Typically, runoff collected in the roadway is conveyed to the main drainage system through basins or inlets in the curb. The number and spacing of such inlets should be carefully regulated, and their design should consider the safety of pedestrians and bicyclists as well as efficiency in transporting water.

[35] ULI–the Urban Land Institute, National Association of Home Builders, and American Society of Civil Engineers, *Residential Storm Water Management: Objectives, Principles, & Design Considerations* (Washington, D.C.: Author, 1975), p. 11.

[36] See *Project Reference File:* "Straw Hill," vol. 17, no. 18 (Washington, D.C.: ULI–the Urban Land Institute, October–December 1988).

[37] Council member Judith Reagan notes, "In many contemporary large-scale communities, the community association is responsible for maintaining stormwater control systems, whereas in the past it was typically left to the local government."

- General-purpose governments should assess and develop plans for each drainage basin within their jurisdiction.
- All individual development proposals must contain drainage plans developed in accordance with a basinwide drainage plan or, lacking a regional plan, by estimating the impact of upstream development on the subdivision and the total discharge from the subdivision.
- The design of a stormwater runoff system must consider convenience and safety at the subdivision level, in addition to overall safety in the basin, as the area becomes fully developed.
- The design of permanent and temporary ponding storage should be an integral part of overall development planning.
- The design of permanent storage facilities should consider safety, visual appearance, and recreational use in addition to the primary storage function, and opportunities for temporary storage should be considered and planned for in the design of the system.
- The design of stormwater runoff systems should facilitate aquifer recharge when appropriate to compensate for groundwater removal.
- Some communities have a blanket per-acre storm sewer charge. When developers design on-site stormwater retention systems, they should receive a credit from the community against the stormwater assessment charge.
- The use of overland flows and open channels and swales should be the preferred choice in the design of a residential drainage system. They should blend into the natural features of the site, and they should be designed to minimize safety hazards.
- Alignment of an open drainage system must be coordinated with the design of lot and street

patterns, but the drainage system should not be arbitrarily located to avoid these features.
- Stormwater management systems, the layout of streets and pattern of lots, and the location of curbs and gutters should be planned simultaneously whenever possible.
- Depth of flow in the gutter and allowable spread of water across the pavement should consider the classification of the street according to its anticipated use and traffic load.
- The maximum flow in the deepest part of the gutter should not exceed 10 cubic feet per second.
- The number and spacing of stormwater inlets should be carefully regulated, and their design should consider safety and efficiency.
- Any enclosed portion of a system should be designed to manage stormwater, not just dispose of or disperse it.
- Energy dissipaters should be designed and installed for the outfall of enclosed systems when discharge is onto highly erodible soils.
- Pipe sizes in the enclosed system should be based on computed hydraulic data for the system.
- The use of enclosed components in a system should be minimized, consistent with the ability of the existing natural systems to accommodate storm runoff.
- Erosion from stormwater runoff should be minimized by the design of the system, and siltation ponds should be created at the start of construction.
- Maintenance costs as well as construction costs should be minimized.

Source: ULI–the Urban Land Institute, American Society of Civil Engineers, and National Association of Home Builders, *Residential Storm Water Management* (Washington, D.C.: Author, 1975).

Stormwater management systems should be designed to facilitate recharging the aquifer when it may be advantageous to compensate for groundwater withdrawn. In certain situations, perforated storm sewers can be used to distribute water to the subsoil. If perforated storm sewers are to be used in highly permeable soil, care must be taken to maintain them properly and to remove debris from the inlets period-

ically. Conversely, designs should avoid recharge where effects on the groundwater might be harmful. The design of all elements of the system must be coordinated and undertaken concurrently.

Natural overland flow and routing through open vegetated channels and swales are the preferred methods for carrying runoff from the street to storage basins. When large natural drainage swales exist,

5-39 The use of swales and culverts rather than curbs and gutters reinforces the low-density, rural character of Lochmere, near Cary, North Carolina.

to augment the flow of stormwater with an artificial recirculating water supply. A permanent water level should be maintained within a waterproof lower section of the basin, with the remainder taking up the necessary volume of storm retention.

Underground outfall pipes may be necessary to convey runoff when this surface method is not practical. Outfall pipes should be located in drainage easements that follow lot lines or preferably in the community's open space. Further, the amount of actual runoff can be decreased by reducing the amount of street surfacing through design and lessening driveway surface by reducing front yard setbacks.

Stormwater runoff from streets, parking lots, and roof drains is normally heavily laden with a variety of contaminants—phosphates, nitrates, putrescible organics—that often have severe adverse effects on surface waters downstream. The sources of contaminants are complex; they include airborne fallout from industrial air pollution, organic detritus, motor vehicle lubricants, detergents, and pesticides. Soil effectively adsorbs most contaminants, so the use of overland flow, vegetated open channels, and swales can be very effective in avoiding potential adverse impacts on surface waters downstream. Additional measures of control, if they are necessary, might include the use of sand filters or degreasers as part of the stormwater retention system.

overall site planning and engineering design should respect and even enhance them as landscape features. Constructed drainage swales should reflect their natural counterparts by looking less like artificially surveyed, trenched ditches. For practical construction, the minimum slope for a sodded or established turf drainage swale is 2 percent. Under exacting standards of construction, a 2 percent drainage swale permits flow, yet the slightest variation during or after construction results in ponding and possible damage from moisture to the lawn. These specifications for slope should be shown on preliminary and final grading plans.

Like drainage swales, stormwater retention ponds should be treated as elements of design and varied in shape, size, treatment of slopes, and plantings. Carefully designed stormwater flumes may be transformed into landscape features containing trickling water or noisy waterfalls. In some cases, it might be desirable

5-40 A series of retention ponds was created at Straw Hill in Manchester, New Hampshire, to ensure that the velocities of runoff after development did not exceed their predevelopment levels. The ponds—seeded with wildflowers—were made a featured amenity in the landscape plan.

Erosion and Sedimentation Control

Problems with erosion and sedimentation are primarily the result of improper grading, the wrong choice of plants, and poor plant maintenance. Erosion occurs when wind or water removes particles from the ground surface, and the rate depends on climatic factors, the soil's erodibility, length and gradient of the slope, and vegetative cover. Sedimentation most commonly occurs when particles suspended in water are deposited. The rate of sedimentation is influenced by the size and specific gravity of the particles, the temperature of the water in which they are suspended, and the motion of the water.[38] Sedimentation can also occur from windblown sources, especially in coastal or arid areas.

Careful site planning can reduce or prevent most erosion and sedimentation. Good planning responds to the site's conditions, avoiding development of portions of the site that are most highly erodible. Good planning also preserves natural site vegetation to the maximum extent possible and limits clearing and grading to the minimum necessary, reducing the percentage of the site exposed to erosion. A good site grading plan significantly reduces potential erosion and sedimentation by minimizing the total extent of disturbed areas and by phasing grading so that only a small area is disturbed at any given time. Measures to control erosion and sedimentation need to be employed as soon as it is determined that significant erosion and sedimentation could result from site development.

Measures to control erosion and sedimentation can be temporary or permanent, and often both types of measures need to be employed on a given development site. Although their functions are similar, temporary and permanent measures differ in design and construction materials. Temporary measures like putting sand bags around catch basins of storm drains or laying plastic sheeting over newly graded slopes typically are designed to last only for the duration of the construction period and generally cost less. The maintenance cost for temporary measures is directly related to weather conditions; maintenance costs are higher if frequent or intense storms occur during the construction period. Permanent measures, such as desilting basins or landscaping exposed soil, are typically designed to remain in place for many years beyond the end of construction and generally cost more to construct but require less frequent maintenance. To be most effective, permanent measures to control erosion and sedimentation should be integrated with stormwater management systems.

5-41 Measures to control erosion, such as plastic tarps and sandbags, are often necessary during construction.

The purpose of measures to control erosion is to reduce the loss of soil from a site by reducing the duration of the soil's exposure, protecting the soil by shielding it, and holding the soil in place. Measures to control water erosion include stabilizing the soil and controlling runoff.

Measures to stabilize the soil protect exposed soil from the impact of raindrops and subsequent erosion. Temporary measures protect soil during construction delays and until permanent vegetative covers are established. Useful temporary measures include mulches, nettings, and chemical binders. Mulches protect the soil from erosion and prevent seeds, fertilizer, and other soil additives from washing away. They also improve the soil's capacity for infiltrating rainfall, prevent wide variations in the soil's temperature, encourage retention of moisture by reducing surface evaporation, and shield delicate young plants. The most common mulch materials are hay, small-grain straw, wood chips, jute matting, glass fiber netting, plastic and asphalt emulsions, and various paper products. Most fibrous mulches must be anchored to prevent their dispersal. The choice of material should be based on economy, the future use of the area to be protected, and the degree of protection required.

Seeding can be used to stabilize the soil temporarily and permanently. When further grading will be

[38] This section is based on information contained in ULI–the Urban Land Institute, American Society of Civil Engineers, and National Association of Home Builders, *Residential Erosion and Sediment Control: Objectives, Principles, & Design Considerations* (Washington, D.C.: Author, 1978).

deferred, a temporary plant cover that can subsequently form the mulch for permanent vegetation is often appropriate. Hydroseeding, a common method for seeding relatively long, narrow, and steep areas, involves the application of seeds, fertilizers, and surface stabilizers in a spray mixture. Large areas with gentle slopes are more efficiently seeded by machine drilling in furrows. "Sprigging" is sometimes used to establish Bermuda grass and other easily propagated plants. Transplanting, which also includes plugging, is commonly used for propagation of grasses like Zoysia and to establish shrubs and trees. Sodding is used for the immediate establishment of a permanent ground cover and should be used on critical areas such as steep slopes, channels, and areas adjacent to paved land and buildings.

Permanent vegetative cover to stabilize the soil should be long-lived and require minimal care or maintenance. Grasses and legumes are generally superior to shrubs and ground covers because of their more complex root systems, which encourage formation of a water-stable soil structure. In addition, their leaves and stems protect the ground against erosion from wind and water. The selection of plants should be based upon what can be expected to grow at the site, the purpose of the planting, and foreseeable ensured maintenance.

Permanent nonvegetative measures of stabilization are used where conditions preclude the use of vegetation. Structural treatment may be required for excessively steep slopes, areas of groundwater seepage, soils that do not absorb or retain moisture well, or waterways subject to high flow velocities. Coarse crushed rock and gravel are commonly used for gentler slopes. Except in unusual circumstances, rock and gravel should not be used for temporary stabilization, as they will interfere with the establishment of permanent vegetative cover.

Structural measures for controlling runoff intercept surface runoff and convey it to a safe disposal area, keeping it away from erodible soil and preventing the erosion of gullies. Diversion structures, including soil or stone dikes, ditches or channels, and terraces or benches, collect water and direct it to an outfall, where it can be released without causing excessive erosion. Structural measures for controlling runoff can also include berms, waterways, downdrains, flumes, and level spreaders. To provide proper protection at all times at the most reasonable cost, temporary measures of controlling runoff must be relocated or removed as construction progresses. Maintenance is the primary need for continued effectiveness of permanent control measures. Regular preventive maintenance should be included in the con-

5-42 The sediment collected at the opening of this catch basin must be cleaned out periodically.

struction program, and ongoing requirements should be documented and assigned to the responsible entity for future reference.

Measures to control sediment generally act to slow the flow of surface runoff by filtering or trapping it, enabling sediments in the runoff to settle out. Measures of control based on filtering can be divided into two general categories: vegetative and structural. The choice depends primarily on economics and space available. Vegetative buffers are often economical and when properly used require little maintenance. Their disadvantage is that they require a relatively large land area. The more expensive structural filters, such as gravel inlet barriers, loose rock berms, and straw bale barriers, use less space by concentrating filtering in localized structures but require regular maintenance, particularly after storms.

Two basic methods are available for trapping sediment—sediment basins and sediment traps. Sediment basins are the more effective approach in terms of the percentage of sediment removed from runoff. Dry sediment basins are constructed on waterways that flow only during storms; wet basins are constructed on intermittent or perennial streams and may impound a permanent pond. Because trapped sediments must periodically be removed from permanent basins, a permanent disposal site for waste material must be provided. Sediment traps are small temporary detention structures used to intercept runoff and trap sediment. They are rarely practical for drainage areas larger than about five acres. Traps can be constructed with earth, pipe, or stone outlets, or they can be installed at storm drain inlets. Selection of outlets is based on construction costs.

Lake Management

In addition to their value as visual and recreational amenities, natural and manmade lakes and ponds can be used for controlling flooding, sedimentation, and pollution, storing water, managing wildlife, treating water, and recharging the aquifer. (Appendix D provides a summary of the intercompatibility of lake and pond functions.) Many issues must be considered when planning a residential development project that will include a lake or pond.[39] Creating a lake is a highly complex undertaking that requires a thorough knowledge of the natural processes at work on the site. A geohydrologist or lake ecologist should be consulted to determine whether a lake is feasible on a given site.

Creating a lake in a residential project involves upfront development costs. The cost of maintaining a lake in useful condition is an ongoing responsibility that affects the long-term value of the lake as an amenity. Another major concern is liability and insurance. It is therefore important to consider who will maintain the lake in the future. Local governments may be reluctant to accept responsibility for managing a lake, particularly if public access is restricted, and a community or homeowners' association may have difficulty funding the necessary maintenance unless it has been adequately financially planned and budgeted. As an alternative, maintenance could be entrusted to a separate management association specifically for the lake.

Lakes are major amenities for residential development projects. People enjoy living where they have an extended view of water, and if they have direct access to the water, they are even more willing to pay a premium for the privilege. An important consideration in planning is the structure of ownership and property rights along the shoreline. A cluster arrangement for lots away from the shoreline with access to the water through common property is one solution to providing limited public access while maximizing returns from the value created. Public access to the shoreline can reduce property values for landowners immediately adjacent, however, although the reduction is often compensated for by the views afforded to those houses.

The size of the lake or pond is affected by the nature of the source of water, the purpose of the water body, and characteristics of the site. Adequate depth is necessary to promote good water quality without a high degree of maintenance. A depth of at least 10 feet in some portion of the water body, possibly near the dam, has the benefit of allowing thermal stratification of the water and seasonal turnovers. Shoal waters, less than three to five feet deep, should be provided for near inflows to the water body. Rooted aquatic vegetation that becomes established in the shoal waters absorbs plant nutrients, partially denying the

---

[39] The North American Lake Management Society, P.O. Box 217, Merrifield, Virginia 22116 (202-466-8550) offers advice on constructing and managing lakes.

5-43, 5-44   The shorelines of lakes can be owned in common so that all residents of the development are provided access (left) or held under private ownership so that lots extend to the water line (right). Developers should consider these options carefully to maximize both the return on their investment in amenities and the residents' enjoyment of them.

nutrients to algae and preventing algae blooms.[40] In cold climates, 15 feet is desirable to prevent killing fish when the lake is covered with ice.[41]

An irregular shoreline adds visual interest to a lake or pond and can be used to great advantage in site planning. Wave action at the water's edge will eventually erode any embankment and form a wave-cut beach, the slope of which will depend on the texture of the soil involved. Shoreline treatments include riprap, stone armor, and various types of walls. The selection of an appropriate treatment should take into account the intended use of the shoreline and should provide for emergency access and egress. Shorelines of lakes or ponds that are expected to have fluctuating water levels may need to be planted with emergent vegetation to visually screen muddy edges or bottoms.[42]

For the lake or pond to hold water, the proposed lakesite should be generally impervious to water seepage. If it is well drained, it may be necessary to line the bottom with clay, concrete, asphalt, plastic, or other impervious material. When the amount of clay, such as bentonite, is sufficient, compaction can be an effective sealer.

The rate of siltation, or built-up sediment, is determined by the character of the watershed and the type and frequency of storms. The use of sediment basins upstream can minimize siltation of the lake or pond. The buildup of sediment is normally greatest near inlets. To minimize the need to dredge these areas frequently, waterfront recreation facilities like docks and marinas should be located elsewhere. Because dredging is inevitable, easements and other provisions for future access by dredging equipment and nearby disposal sites for dredged material should be provided whenever possible.

Standards for water quality for lakes and ponds vary, depending on how the body of water is to be used. The highest standards apply to water that will be used for swimming and other water contact sports, and a program to monitor water quality will be necessary to determine whether standards are being attained and to provide a reliable baseline of information to diagnose future problems. Restrictions on use of the lake by power boats may be necessary to protect water quality as well as to avoid increased wave action, which can aggravate erosion of the shoreline.

The shorter the period water is detained in a lake or pond, the more turbid and unattractive the water tends to be. A longer period of retention generally means the water is more transparent and attractive.[43] Water can also become visually unattractive if a large amount of suspended organic matter is present. In lakes and ponds where water is held a long time,

aerating fountains and other methods of recirculation act to increase levels of dissolved oxygen and prevent the occurrence of large amounts of suspended organic material.

Plant Materials

In residential developments, plants and hardscape features (walls, fences, paving, benches, trash receptacles, signs, mailboxes, light fixtures) are used to enhance the site and to increase residents' and visitors' physical comfort and convenience. Plants—trees, shrubs, and ground cover—have sculptural, textural, and color qualities that can provide visual coherence to manmade landscapes. Plants can articulate space, forming outdoor walls, canopies, and floors, and can conceal, reveal, modulate, direct, contain, and complete architectural features. Plants can also provide shade, modulate breezes, and, through transpiration, release water into the atmosphere and reduce evaporation from the soil. Hardscape features are important components of the landscape that, like plants, need to be considered during site planning and design. Landscape architects are trained to fulfill this role.

Existing vegetation should be preserved wherever possible in a landscape plan. Mature trees add value to a residential project, and the locations of roads and buildings can often be adjusted slightly to preserve mature trees. Root zones of these trees must be protected from compaction during site construction. In general, soil should be left undisturbed in a 10-foot radius around any tree to be preserved and fences or walls constructed to prevent encroachment. Dogwoods, beeches, and most conifers do not tolerate fill because they root near the surface. Other varieties may survive with two to three feet of fill, but a layer of coarse gravel or broken stone six to eight inches deep should be spread over the feeder roots before filling to ensure air circulation. A tree well built at least two feet from the tree trunk and extending to the old ground level should keep the trunk from rotting. Vertical tiles are sometimes set at intervals above the feeder roots down to the level of the gravel or broken stone to permit additional air circulation. If the site is graded, trees should not be left encased in small

[40] Harris and Dines, eds., *Time-Saver Standards for Landscape Architecture,* pp. 740-3 & 740-4.

[41] Joachim Tourbier and Richard Westmacott, *Lakes and Ponds,* Technical Bulletin No. 72 (Washington, D.C.: ULI–the Urban Land Institute, 1976), Chapter 2.

[42] Harris and Dines, eds., *Time-Saver Standards for Landscape Architecture,* p. 740-2.

[43] Ibid., p. 740-1.

5-45 A notice to workers helps to ensure that trees will be protected.

mounds; instead, mounds should slope gradually and be at least as wide as the tree's spread. A tree can be killed by changes in the soil's moisture conditions, increased exposure resulting from removal of its neighbors, or root damage during the installation of underground utilities.

New plants should be used to supplement rather than replace existing mature vegetation; they should be selected from native species whose growing characteristics are best suited to site conditions. Use of exotic species should be reserved for areas where a high degree of maintenance is warranted. The plants' size, shape, and density at maturity must also be considered.

Plant materials can have an important role in energy conservation. Tall deciduous trees planted on the south, west, or east side of buildings can block the sun's direct rays in the summer, but after leaves have fallen in the winter, the trees do not block the winter sun. As added protection, evergreens can be planted to the north of a building to break winter winds, which can cut down the sun's warming effect in winter. "If trees or shrubs are used as a wind barrier, it is important to plant vegetation that will provide a

dense growth and will grow to a height equal to or greater than the building. The maximum distance from the building to the windbreak should not be more than five times the building height, measured from the leeward wall."[44]

In the choice of plants to alleviate glare, deciduous plants can reduce unwanted summer sun but allow warming winter sun to shine through. When large water bodies reflect glare, reducing the glare may not be possible without disrupting the view. In such situations, it may be possible to funnel prevailing winds with foliage, producing ripples on the water to scatter the reflection.

Water conservation is a major concern in many parts of the country. During dry periods when conservation measures are imposed, the use of water for maintaining ornamental plants is often one of the first uses to be restricted. In areas where this possibility is likely, plant materials must be selected that have a high tolerance for drought.[45]

Lawns require a high level of maintenance and traditionally have been overused as a landscape treatment in residential areas. Lawns are best suited for use in fairly level outdoor living and play areas. The selection of a grass mixture should be based on site conditions and climate. Low-maintenance ground covers should be considered for use in other locations, particularly on steeper slopes where erosion control is necessary. Wherever possible, open areas should be retained in a natural condition to reduce maintenance costs and to minimize disturbance of the site.

The advantages of retaining natural areas that require little or no maintenance at a time when labor costs are rising and energy and water costs are increasing steadily are obvious.

> Further improvements can be accomplished by planting certain fruit-bearing trees and shrubs, such as sawtooth oak, Japanese crabapple, flowering dogwood, autumn olive, pyracantha, various hollies, and many other species. Wildlife food plots, consisting of a mixture of millets and sorghums, can also be planted in select areas at low cost to concentrate a wide variety of song birds. Increased cover for song birds can be provided by planting conifers, such as white pine and red cedar. They also make aesthetically appealing sight-and-sound barriers.[46]

[44] Chris Logan, "Air Motion and Ventilation," in *Low-Cost Energy-Efficient Shelter for the Owner and Builder,* edited by Eugene Eccli (Emmaus, Pa.: Rodale Press, 1976), p. 154.

[45] See Gary O. Robinette, *Water Conservation in Landscape Design and Management* (New York: Van Nostrand Reinhold Company, 1984).

[46] Stephen R. Seater, "Putting Wildlife in the Planning Process," *Environmental Comment,* August 1975, p. 3. The remainder of this issue touches on the subject of wildlife preservation and enhancing the natural landscape with planting.

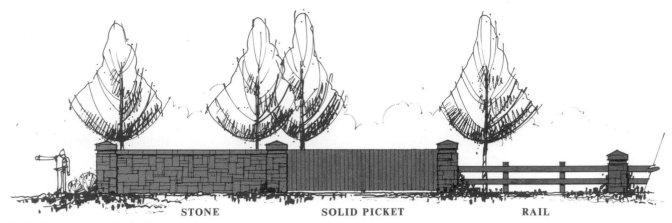

STONE   SOLID PICKET   RAIL

5-46 Typical materials for fences include stone or masonry at entrances or areas requiring special design treatment, wood pickets between lots and at perimeters of subdivisions, and wood railing when privacy or noise attenuation is not necessary or when views to feature areas should be accommodated. *Source:* David Jensen Associates, Inc., Denver, Colorado.

Walls and Fences

Walls and fences should be geared to overall lot sizes, housing types, and style of architecture, topography, and landscaping. On very large single-family lots, for example, privacy screening is often not necessary. In a higher-density area, fences and walls should be selectively placed to provide privacy and protection. Trees and shrubs can break up a monotonous row of fences or walls.

Fences

Fences can increase residents' use and enjoyment of the outdoors. Fences define property lines and create an outdoor "living room" by enclosing the private space. Beyond screening other houses and residents, fences (and walls) can mitigate many other undesirable elements—adjacent highways, roads, shopping centers, trash collection areas, and mechanical equipment. Noise from neighbors can be filtered. Wind can be lessened or redirected and snow accumulation in cold climates controlled. Off-site residential lighting and automobile headlights can be blocked from view. Fencing helps segregate private from public spaces and increases the security of neighborhoods.

As a landscape detail, fencing has a major impact on the visual environment:

- Fencing adds three-dimensional form, color, line, and texture to the landscape.
- Fencing can effectively divide a horizontal surface into two or more spaces, providing visual privacy within each space.

5-47, 5-48   Picket fencing is combined with a short rock retaining wall at The Commons at Atkinson in Atkinson, New Hampshire, to separate yard areas from streets (left). At The Ledges at Winchester in Winchester, Massachusetts, a four-foot wood and lattice fence complements the architecture and separates private from common spaces (right).

- Fencing can define separate spaces while retaining visual continuity.
- Fencing can establish an entire theme for a landscape; for example, a split-rail fence sets a rural character, while a white picket fence creates a nostalgic touch.
- Existing architectural concepts can be extended into the landscape or complemented by an appropriate fence. For example, a classic brick house or estate is complemented by a wrought iron fence, while a contemporary, wrought-cut cedar siding house may best be extended into the landscape with a low fence constructed out of similar material.

Fencing can often be prohibitively expensive, however, and should be used judiciously. Fencing that demands annual maintenance and repairs should not be used. On the other hand, not installing backyard fencing in a high-density development may make it impossible to achieve privacy.

5-49 This landscaped berm provides an attractive edge to a new residential subdivision and—through a combination of height and distance—acts as a buffer for traffic noise.

Perimeter Walls

The treatment required on the perimeter of a residential site depends on adjacent land uses and whether noise mitigation, security control, or visual screening is necessary. Image and identity are also important concerns where the perimeter of the site is perceived as a community or neighborhood boundary. Fences and walls should be used selectively only where they are needed to protect privacy and quality of the neighborhood. Fences or walls should not block views to open space or create a "fortress" around a neighborhood or subdivision.

Noise from traffic is a common problem when residential areas are adjacent to heavily traveled roads. Acoustical barriers can be used to reduce noise to acceptable levels. Noise is generally reduced more as the height of the barrier increases. Noise from around the ends of a barrier can compromise the effectiveness of the barrier, however. As a general rule, acoustical barriers must break the line of sight to the entire roadway corridor to be effective. Performance of a barrier is also affected by terrain, ground cover, and the heights of sources of noise.

The feasibility of noise attenuation and optimum height of barriers can be determined by acoustical engineers case by case. Various types of construction have been used for acoustical barriers, including precast concrete panels, reinforced concrete or earth walls, concrete blocks, bricks, plexiglass, and wood. All types of barriers can be effective if they are solid and sufficiently large, and selection of the proper type

should be based on acoustical effectiveness, economic feasibility, ease of maintenance, and aesthetics. Other methods of mitigating noise can be used during building construction, such as the use of double-glazed windows, and site planning, such as orienting buildings so that opening windows and doors face away from the primary source of noise.

Security control on the perimeter of a site can be provided by walls or fencing and sometimes lighting. Where walls or fences are installed, plants should be provided to soften the effect of large expanses of hard surfaces. Vines and evergreens are particularly effective in this regard.

If noise mitigation and security control are not necessary, vegetation can be used to provide an effective visual screen along the perimeter of a residential area. Plants requiring a minimum amount of maintenance should be selected.

Retaining Walls

Retaining walls provide many practical benefits beyond their primary function of retaining soil. Many sloped areas that are difficult to maintain can be developed and maintained more easily by the installation of retaining walls, making access to planting beds and sodded areas easier and the areas more manageable. The initial cost of retaining walls is high, but conditions corrected by the construction of the walls are often more cost-effective to maintain. Retaining walls usually become long-term solutions to a problem with a grade and if constructed properly

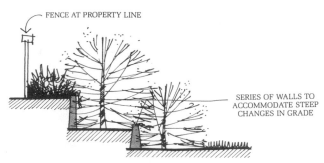

5-50 Landscaping beds can be made more manageable by a series of retaining walls.

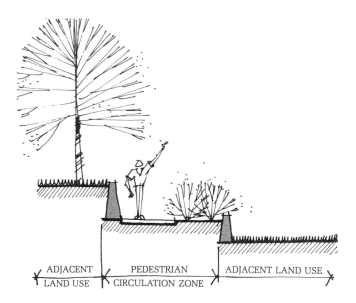

ADJACENT LAND USE | PEDESTRIAN CIRCULATION ZONE | ADJACENT LAND USE

5-51 Retaining walls promote separation of uses without the need for fencing. Changes in vertical grade are also an effective way to mitigate against noise by locating noise-sensitive uses (such as houses) on the higher elevation and noise-generating uses (such as roads) on the lower elevation. *Source:* David R. Jensen/ HOH Associates, *Zero Lot Line Housing* (Washington, D.C.: ULI– the Urban Land Institute, 1981), p. 100.

last for years. The methods used to construct retaining walls are critical, for the walls must accommodate natural water flow and drainage of the retained area. Reducing the slope minimizes soil erosion, but it also significantly reduces water runoff and eventual consumption of water in irrigated areas. It can, however, also reduce the cost of on- and off-site drainage.

The use of retaining walls on steep slopes can permit development that otherwise would not be feasible. Functional driveways, patios, and elements of the dwelling unit can be maintained on a relatively horizontal plane, closer together. Retaining walls can

generate more usable level space within a small lot. The higher installation cost of retaining walls, however, must be weighed against the project's economics.

Depending on their height, retaining walls can be used to define exterior spaces; they can easily be used to control access between levels. Retaining walls in combination with fencing provide privacy. Their use may provide one opportunity to segregate automobile and pedestrian circulation. They may eliminate the need to fence special areas, such as model home complexes, recreation clubs, and pocket parks, by physically and visually delineating such spaces.

The most commonly used materials for retaining walls are large rocks or boulders, wrapped rocks in bundles, wood timbers, railroad ties, brick, concrete blocks, and precast or poured-in-place concrete. The type of retaining wall can either complement the architecture or become an extension of it.

Entrance Gateways

Entrance gateways are very important for establishing the overall image and identity of the residential community or neighborhood. Gateways can also be important in providing security and privacy. Landscape

5-52 Retaining walls should be designed to complement a development's architectural character. They can be softened with landscaping.

5-53, 5-54, 5-55   Entrance gateways usually establish a first impression of a residential development. At Ocean Ranch in San Clemente, California, little expense was spared to create a positive image through the use of waterfalls, special paving, a guarded gatehouse, and extensive landscaping (top). At Eastern Point in Shrewsburg, Massachusetts, an unmanned gatehouse provides a sense of privacy and security (bottom left). Brick walls and landscaping provide a subtle entrance statement for this residential community in Forte, Michigan (bottom right).

materials requiring a high degree of maintenance may be appropriate for the entrance gateway, provided that the effect is compatible with the overall character of the project. Typically, maintenance of entrances is the responsibility of the homeowners' association.

For purposes of marketing, it is often desirable to have views of several major amenities from the approach to the entrance. A clear system of signage should begin at the gateway to direct visitors to those features, to the sales office, and to the model units. The signage system can be integrated with an overall signage system for the project that includes entry and identification signs, directional signs to provide orientation at major decision points, and street and regulatory signs. To be effective, signs should be uniform and compatible with the design of the project.

Streetscapes

The scale of residential streets should be consistent with the density and type of housing. As density increases and lot size decreases, a carefully planned strategy of design becomes more and more important. The character of a residential streetscape is influenced by the relationships between such factors as building height and setback, street width and length, plant location and height, street furniture, and signs. Where units are clustered around parking areas and courtyards, those areas need to be designed with the streetscape in mind.

It is standard practice to preserve mature trees or to plant new trees along residential streets, but street trees commonly are planted too close together. A distance of 50 to 60 feet is better than 25 to 30 feet, but it depends on the variety of tree and its growing habits. On narrow, short streets or those with one side higher than the other, the streetscape may be more attractive if street trees are planted informally, spaced varying distances from each other. If a local ordinance does not allow variations in planting, a variance may need to be obtained.

The selection of the type of trees to be planted along the street depends on climatic, aesthetic, and maintenance considerations. Trees whose wood breaks easily in storms should be avoided. Hardwood trees, such as oaks and Norway maples, are examples of trees that are generally well suited to planting along streets.

When choosing plants for yards and common areas, it is important to consider their height when mature and the function that they serve. Species that will maintain an acceptable appearance and height without constant trimming and pruning are preferred. Low-lying plants do well as ground covers and borders, and they are also effective at controlling foot traffic. Hedges can increase privacy and screen objectionable features, such as utility boxes. Shrubs should not be planted too close to buildings, and ample space should be allowed to prevent crowding when they are planted along walks. Only hardy varieties should be used. Protective covenants should require future owners to remove any vegetation at street corners that interferes with vision and creates a traffic hazard. For security reasons, shrubs should not be located where they will obscure the visibility of front entrances from neighboring units.

Where homeowners are to landscape yards, it is in the developer's best interest to provide guidance and assistance. In many development projects, the guidance and assistance are in the form of a set of design guidelines or controls. A series of typical landscape plans, a basic landscaping manual, or the services of a landscape designer can also be made available. Homeowners should also be made aware of any state or county requirements for landscaping along the street right-of-way. Many homeowners are not aware that a right-of-way exists on their property and landscape it, later having to remove the plants if they are inconsistent with local ordinances. Many local governments will allow landscaping in the right-of-way by permit only.

Lighting

Site lighting provides a residential development with character, security, and an aesthetic environment, and it extends outdoor use time. The selected light standard can emphasize a theme throughout the community. In some circumstances, the light fixture is a visual element; in others, it might be more appropriate to hide it from view. Decorative lighting at community or public facilities, for example, can accent public spaces. Lighting for vehicular or pedestrian circulation can be most effective in illuminating the ground plane while concealing the source of light. Five basic areas within most residential developments require lighting: 1) streets; 2) courtyards, mews, or clusters; 3) open space; 4) entrances to units; and 5) entry walks to units.

Outdoor lighting is expensive to install and can require a significant amount of energy. Unnecessary lighting should thus be avoided. If pedestrian traffic along local streets is expected to be minimal, lighting merely as a convenience may not be justified. In some cases, particularly single-family and townhouse developments, adequate lighting can be achieved by placing lamps on posts controlled from each house near the street. A check with the local utility company

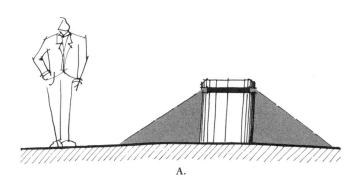

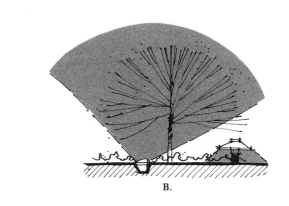

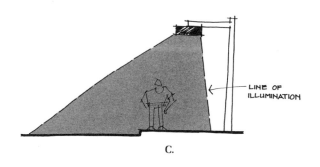

5-56 Lighting fixtures must be selected with regard to the intended use, scale, and avoidance of glare. A) For pedestrian areas, subdued lighting focusing on illuminating the ground is usually most appropriate. B) Lights to accent plants are often appropriate, especially at the entrance to a development. C) Glare and loss of privacy can be avoided by using street lighting fixtures with "cut-off" illumination features. *Source:* David R. Jensen/HOH Associates, *Zero Lot Line Housing* (Washington, D.C.: ULI–the Urban Land Institute, 1981), p. 93.

often helps developers and landscape architects select lighting that offers sufficient illumination but consumes low levels of energy.

Because of their higher traffic volume, collector streets must have adequate street lighting. Normally, the utility company installs standards for street lights. Developers should establish a close working relation-

ship with the utility company to ensure that light standards are placed on the right-of-way to best serve open space and to enhance safety and security while minimizing glare into houses. Where the municipality does not accept responsibility for street lighting, developers should have light standards installed early during the marketing program, thus avoiding the problem of residents who want lights but not in front of their houses. Platting should create the necessary easements to avoid later difficulties in locating lights.

When planning lighting along public streets that have private streets running off them, it may be possible to have light standards positioned at the intersections of the public and private streets to minimize the need for additional lights along the private streets. The selection of light standards and fixtures should be based on initial construction cost, long-term maintenance, and the ability to resist vandalism. Often, the intensity of light when traditional standards are used is too high. A lower intensity can be satisfactory while conserving energy and reducing costs.

Mercury vapor, metal halide, and high-pressure sodium lamps have generally replaced incandescent lamps for outdoor lighting. Such lamps should be mounted at an average height of 20 to 50 feet along residential streets and in parking areas and an average height of 10 to 15 feet along paths and walks. Several attractively designed and energy-efficient low standards are now available; although the costs of installing them may be higher, there is no question that more frequently placed, low lighting is more attractive.

Orientation within a residential development can be enhanced by providing a hierarchy of lighting that corresponds to the different zones and uses of the site. For example, major and minor roads can be subtly distinguished by varying the distribution and brightness of lights and by varying their height, spacing, and color of the lamps. Attaining high levels of illumination along circulation routes does not have to be a prime consideration in outdoor lighting. Low, uniform levels of illumination may be adequate if a clear, consistent system is provided.[47]

Residential developments should provide lighting for open spaces to gain the maximum benefit from them. Even marginal illumination of the pedestrian walkway system will improve the investment in amenities because of the added hours the areas can be used. Lighting should emphasize natural features or accent points of a pathway or open space. Unless very large areas must be illuminated, fixtures no higher

[47] Harris and Dines, eds., *Time-Saver Standards for Landscape Architecture,* pp. 540-3 & 540-9.

5-57, 5-58, 5-59   At Talcott Village in Farmington, Connecticut, lighting along the pedestrian path mimics the architectural style of the buildings (top). Path lighting at The Fairways in Valencia, California, is designed on a human scale (bottom left). Street light standards can be designed to blend with the character of the residential community (bottom right).

than 10 feet may be placed on center at intervals of up to 100 feet. Typically, budgets for amenities are inadequate for including lighting of even one footcandle uniformly along a pathway, but a spacing of typical landscape lights 40 feet to 75 feet on center makes pathways much more usable and secure. Greater security may require even more or brighter light fixtures.

Fixtures mounted at doorways are necessary for most types of housing; they are the least expensive on-site lighting fixtures. With proper architectural detail, low-cost incandescent fixtures can often lend a customized appearance. The decision about the type of fixture to use at entries should be based not only on appearance but also on maintenance costs (replacing deteriorated or vandalized bulbs and fixtures).

If the budget for lighting is limited, the next order of priority should be lighting the walkways that lead from houses to garages, parking bays, or lots. In some situations, walkways can be illuminated adequately and surprising visual impact gained by using ground-mounted spotlights, angled or directed up. They are particularly effective for uplighting trees or illuminating feature walls of buildings or garages.

With a plan that uses a rectangular design, it is typically good practice to locate open space/landscape lighting fixtures consistently on only one side of a given pathway. With an irregular or curvilinear site plan, alternating or irregularly placed fixtures are generally preferable, although the distance from the paving should be consistent.

Residents' privacy can be enhanced with the use of special fixtures with "cut-off" illumination patterns. Such fixtures avoid street glare into residential units and their private outdoor spaces. Areas requiring intense lighting, such as recreation centers, parks, tennis courts, or model home complexes, should also use cut-off fixtures when adjacent to residential units.

Design Details

Private Outdoor Spaces

Extending a house's interior to a private outdoor area is perhaps the most important use a developer makes of open space. Within this space, owners have the most freedom and spend much of their time. Private outdoor living areas buffer the house from nonprivate outdoor spaces. Acting as outside extensions of a house's interior, carefully placed windows, doors, and roof treatments adjacent to private outdoor space can visually expand inside rooms to the edges of patios and decks.

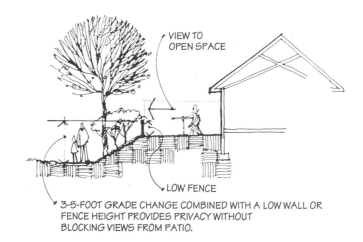

VIEW TO OPEN SPACE

LOW FENCE

3-5-FOOT GRADE CHANGE COMBINED WITH A LOW WALL OR FENCE HEIGHT PROVIDES PRIVACY WITHOUT BLOCKING VIEWS FROM PATIO.

Source: Robert Engstrom and Marc Putnam, *Planning and Design of Townhouses and Condominiums* (Washington, D.C.: ULI–the Urban Land Institute, 1979), p. 126.

Patios. On-grade, hard-surfaced patios are the most common type of private outdoor space. From the standpoint of marketing, having *no* patio would be better than building an inadequately sized, standard six-foot by eight-foot patio. Thus, homebuyers can themselves provide what they want in accordance with the community association's guidelines. If the developer offers a standard patio, an allowance should be made for people who want to build their own patios or add custom features to the standard design. In this latter case, it is helpful for the architect or landscape architect to prepare alternative designs that the developer approves.

The use of extensions to building walls, such as overhead arbors or trellises, enhances the indoor-outdoor relationship of inside room to patio. Privacy fences, earth berms, or plants should be used when the privacy of a person's patio would not otherwise be assured. A building offset, however, provides the greatest degree of privacy.

The interior dimensions of patio space depend upon the type of enclosure required. Many developments have erred by providing too much security, too much enclosure. For most sites, a six- to eight-foot-high fence blocking the view of well-landscaped open space may be a disadvantage in marketing. Some circumstances, however, may warrant a high, solid barrier. The final design—based on considerations of views and need to protect privacy—often is determined unit by unit.

The detailing of private open space enclosures may permit views through to adjacent open space. If security is a concern to residents, on-grade patios may require higher fences. In setting the final grades for a block of townhouses, developers should remember that a low fence permitting a seated person to look through it or over it, coupled with a three- to five-foot change in grade, achieves the same results. Because those elements that most frequently and directly affect residents should receive the greatest amount of design and budgetary consideration, the design of any open space adjacent to private patios and decks is very important.

Decks. Decks are a vital part of the design of many types of housing; they might represent the only outdoor space that extends interior functions. An on- or above-grade wooden deck is a popular solution, becoming an "outdoor room" that improves the archi-

5-61, 5-62, 5-63, 5-64   A) Each unit at the Patio Homes at New Seabury, on Cape Cod, has two patios—one off the living room and one off the bedroom. To protect privacy, the patios for each unit are located on opposite sides of the duplex buildings. B) Patios at Ocean Ranch in San Clemente, California, feature landscaping for privacy and a waterfall to mask noise. C) The small rear yards at The Gables in Newton, Massachusetts, are fenced for privacy and landscaped with raised wooden decks and a rock fountain. D) Some single-family condominiums at Straw Hill in Manchester, New Hampshire, have decks on the first level and balconies on the second.

tecture of the house. Different types of units and target markets require various sizes and locations for decks. In fact, it is good practice to be flexible in the positioning of decks. For instance, it might be desirable to locate a deck off a family room or a dining room, depending upon the preferences of the particular market.

The size and location of the deck affect not only the upper level but also the light admitted to the lower levels of the house. Angles of the sun should be considered before locating deep, second-level decks that overlap bedrooms or living areas below. In multi-level buildings where the depth of decks or balconies will affect views out of and sunlight admitted into lower-level balcony windows, shallower structures may be warranted. Decks may be cantilevered by beams or joists extending to the lower levels. If this latter method is chosen, care should be taken to avoid obscuring windows.

Screens and privacy are important aspects of a deck's design. Screens and fences should assure visual privacy and give a small degree of acoustical separation from adjacent decks, windows, and walkways.

Sitting Areas

Benches and sitting areas, while a relatively easy, uncomplicated addition to landscaping, are intangible elements that add to the way residents perceive a development. They can subtly indicate the lifestyle that residents can expect. Benches and sitting areas should be visible from the model home center and entrance to the development. Observation of residents' behavior indicates that benches located at the end of dead-end pathways tend to be used less than those situated along a continuous walkway.

While a bench may be all the sitting area necessary, certain areas within a development may warrant a more elaborately designed sitting area. Such an area could incorporate a special landscape feature, a spectacular view or vista, a rock outcropping, or a stand of mature trees with a combination of benches, planters, or a small water feature. In some climates, it may be appropriate to cover benches for protection from the sun or rain.

Fountains and Sculpture

Fountains can have a positive impact on marketing, particularly for higher-density developments in urban areas. Because of their high initial cost and

5-65 A neon and glass sculpture designed by local artist Paul Betouliere welcomes residents and guests to the Palm Square Apartments in West Hollywood, California. The sculpture helped satisfy the city's requirement of 1 percent of the total development cost for art.

requirements for maintenance, fountains should be centrally located and adjacent to as many houses as possible. Several functional and aesthetic rules should be incorporated into their design: 1) a fountain should be self-draining to avoid breakage in winter; 2) even if the development will have a full-time maintenance staff, an automatic water level valve and feeder line should be used; and 3) the fountain should serve as both a visible and audible feature, so it should be located where residents can hear it.

Whether the development is urban or suburban, another potential use for open space incorporates sculpture. The selection of an appropriate piece of sculpture should be guided by the architectural theme of the development and the profile of the intended

5-66 A fountain, lush landscaping, and tile pavers create a cool, tropical atmosphere within the courtyard of the 1550 Sunset Boulevard condominiums in Pacific Palisades, California.

near a street or parking lot so that postal carriers can reach them from their vehicles. Because centralized mailboxes often function as community gathering areas, residents appreciate their location in gazebos and other open shelters.

It is sometimes appropriate to provide a mail delivery or postal center at or near entrance gateways to larger developments. A delivery center is typically a freestanding shelter with 30 to 300 boxes for mail delivery clustered on a wall and facilities for outgoing mail. A postal center is similar to a delivery center except that customers can also purchase stamps and mail parcels. Generally, the number of boxes in a postal center should not exceed 300.

Trash Collection Facilities

Provisions for trash collection and storage vary, depending on density and housing type. At lower densities, curbside collection may be the most convenient and practical method. At higher densities, neighborhood trash storage areas can be a better solution if the areas are appropriately screened and are conveniently located. Such areas also provide an opportunity to store presorted, nonbiodegradable recyclable materials, which may need to be collected at different frequencies from other trash. During the 1980s, many localities adopted laws requiring recyclable glass, aluminum, metal, and paper products to be separated. Developers can assist homeowners to comply with these laws if they provide convenient containers for each house or building or for a neighborhood.

Signs, Names, and Graphics

Although the signage system normally does not make or break a project's success, signs constitute one of the many small details that produce character for a community and help to set the development apart from all others. Well-executed and -placed signs create an image of attention to detail. More important, they give a sense of order to what may be a rather complex site plan. One of the drawbacks of a curvilinear road system and some higher-density cluster developments is that it can be difficult to get one's bearings within the community. A well-designed signage system organizes the community visually, enabling residents and guests to know where they are. It can also enhance the identity of separate housing clusters or subneighborhoods. Lost drivers who are trying to read small, inadequate street signs or house numbers may pose a hazard to safety; thus, well-designed signs make the community a safer place.

market. For instance, a contemporary development targeted to young professionals would accept a more contemporary sculpture. Like fountains, sculpture should be located in a visually prominent area—along an entry road or in a courtyard, for example.

Mailboxes

If mail cannot be delivered to each unit, mailboxes should be centrally and conveniently located. A neighborhood delivery and collection box containing 14 to 18 locked boxes for mail delivery and receptacles for outgoing mail typically are mounted on a pedestal. For security reasons, neighborhood delivery and collection boxes should be visible from houses or apartments and lighted at night. They should also be

5-67, 5-68, 5-69, 5-70, 5-71   Mailboxes should be designed for easy delivery and collection of mail. They also can be important design details used to reinforce a community's architectural style.

During preliminary design, requirements for site graphics and signage should be analyzed and added to the list of amenities to be included in the budget. At this stage, it is not necessary to develop specific designs or standards, but collector and subcollector routes within the development must be named at this stage. Street names on the preliminary site development plan aid in communications among members of the design team, government agencies, utility companies, and others involved in the development. The creative or imaginative selection of a development's street names should not be overlooked for their value in enhancing image and identity. Living on "Smith Street" has a distinctly different psychological impact from living on "Berkshire Trail."

Graphics for the signage system should be located and identified on preliminary site plans—especially for townhouse and other attached housing developments. Doing so provides an accounting of units and indicates the comprehensiveness of the developer's planning. Most successful projects pay close attention to the design and placement of informational signs, including entry markers, groups of house numbers at the junctions of entry courts and loop roads, house or garage entry numbers, and notations for guest parking and open space.

Signs at the entry may provide the first impression of a new development. While the details of the design should not be selected until final contract documents are prepared, establishing locations early during site

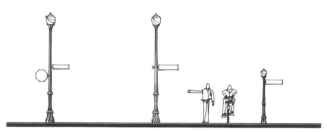

SIGNAGE COMBINED WITH LIGHT STANDARDS

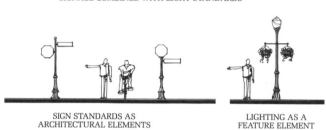

SIGN STANDARDS AS
ARCHITECTURAL ELEMENTS

LIGHTING AS A
FEATURE ELEMENT

Source: David R. Jensen Associates, Inc., Denver, Colorado.

planning is necessary. Discussions with local street departments or county and state highway agencies may be necessary to secure certain locations. Safe sight distances must also be considered in the placement of signs. A location close to the arterial roadway within the government's right-of-way may be approved only after review and only after agreeing with involved government officials that the sign will have a low enough profile and be far enough from the pavement not to interfere with lines of sight.

In a cluster community with a number of streets that terminate in turnarounds, it is important to provide visitors, delivery trucks, and particularly emergency vehicles with street name or number markers placed in the areas most visible from the prevalent direction of traffic flow. In cluster designs where parking bays are located away from the entries to houses, it is desirable to install arrows pointing toward groups of house numbers. Such signs help designate where visitors should park to minimize the walk to the house. In other cases, properly located individual house numbers attached to the house's entrance are sufficient.

In some developments with attached cluster housing, the view of entries may be obscured from the entry court or parking area (in designs where all front doors face a common courtyard, for example). From residents' standpoint, it may be a valuable feature because it increases privacy. From visitors' standpoint, however, it makes locating a specific house difficult. For this reason, individual residence numbers can be placed nearest the entry walk leading to the house. Sometimes it is desirable to also mount house numbers on garages visible from the street.

It is usually best to differentiate between informational and traffic control signs. Specifically, informational signs should not detract from or interfere with the visibility and prominence of traffic control signs. It is best to use the standard shapes for traffic control signs (octagonal for stop, triangular for yield, for example) or to frame them in a standardized framing system, as drivers can identify them more quickly than unusual traffic control signs. Informational signs need not be governed by the same rules, but they should be integrated using standardized materials and frames. Both types of signs should complement materials used in the architecture and other features of the site.

Standardized, die-stamped metal signs bolted to metal posts are the most familiar signage for most municipalities. They have several advantages: relatively low cost, resistance to vandalism, easy installation and replacement, and relatively low maintenance. Another standard municipal sign uses sheet metal with reflective material applied to the surface; it is also durable, moderate in cost, and comes in a variety of colors. Either type may be desirable for speed limits, pedestrian crossings, and parking control within the community. More distinctive designs can be used, however, if the developer and the design team want a fresh image.

On-site signage and other graphic materials prepared for the development (marketing brochures and letterhead, for example) must be consistent. American consumers are constantly presented with high-quality graphic materials in every medium, and developers hurt their image in a subtle way by failing to recognize the importance of quality graphics. Once a lettering style and logo have been prepared, they should be used consistently on printed materials and on signs and graphics.

6.
Marketing

Marketing a new housing community is a complex but vital component of the residential development process. Like most businesses and companies that employ marketing techniques to "move" merchandise, residential real estate developers also create markets for their products. Through the use of research and other investigations, they develop communities that will satisfy the demands of specific segments of the population. Successful developers examine the needs and wants of the local market, determine which demands they can realistically meet, and then develop a housing product and community infrastructure according to those findings. Successful projects are driven by the market, not by the developer's ego. Nevertheless, developers who are pioneering a new product or a new community concept must convince the market that the product or concept will meet its needs.

Developers often retain marketing specialists to identify psychographic profiles (e.g., family structure, lifestyle, personal tastes) of the members of the target market and then help design programs to attract them to the project. Marketing to reach those audiences involves presenting and merchandising the product, promoting the community, and training the sales team. Developers must constantly monitor sales, prospective buyers who visit the sales complex or view model homes, and buyer profiles to gauge consumers' acceptance of the product and the effectiveness of the marketing strategy.

The marketing program undertaken for a residential project might vary in response to such factors as the nature of the residential product and the size and characteristics of the target market. This chapter is concerned primarily with marketing conventional, for-sale housing products. Products designed to appeal to special niches or products new to a market may require a special marketing program. For example, housing designed specifically for elderly persons requires carefully tailored merchandising and promotion plans to reach this narrow but rapidly growing segment of the population.

This chapter also considers marketing programs for rental apartments and large-scale planned communities. While the tools used to market these types of residential developments may be the same as those used for for-sale housing, the techniques used are often different. Finally, this chapter considers the issue of construction warranties and how they can best be established to protect both residential developers and housing consumers. Clearly, successful marketing depends largely on developers' ability to convey a sense of quality and workmanship; their willingness to offer reasonable warranties against structural problems alleviates buyers' concerns and contributes to the marketing team's ability to sell houses.[1]

The Use of Market Research

The first step in marketing is compiling data through market research (see Chapter 2). Armed with this information, developers and marketing teams can then fine-tune final designs, floor plans, the site plan, product mix, and package of amenities for the proposed community. Fine-tuning is supplemented by tactics to create a marketing strategy that outlines the various advertising, merchandising, and sales programs necessary to achieve objectives for sales and profit.

The analysis of market research must be meaningfully applied to the subject property. Two applications in particular are crucial to a successful development. The first is determining the position of the subject property within the competitive market area, based on current and planned housing developments, to identify a concept or product that will satisfy unmet demand and give the product a competitive advantage.

Positioning has less to do with individual housing designs or pricing than with the overall range of products and prices and the property's location within a competitive market area. An analysis of the market may reveal an absence of housing products for a specific market group—move-up buyers, move-down buyers, or the luxury market, for example. The successful sales or leasing of particular communities might also serve as guides to pricing units in the proposed development.

This analysis also helps shape the community's overall concept. Based on what competing developments provide or fail to provide, for example, the marketing team or consultant can recommend a variety of features and amenities. The marketing team or consultant should also try to determine consumers' actual preferences (through focus groups, questionnaires, and interviews with buyers), but this information should be used cautiously because developers can be led to include expensive features that fail to influence the public.

The second important application of the research data is the realistic projection of absorption, based on analysis of the regions's demand for and supply of housing. The demand is the total number of age- and income-qualified households moving into the market area or created by births, deaths, marriages, and divorces. The supply is based on the number of unsold units in the existing community at the time the developer enters the market, allowing for the influence of the proposed project and those approved but not yet opened that will come on line during the marketing of the proposed project.

As explained in Chapter 2, absorption of the proposed property depends on residual demand, which is the total qualified demand in an area minus the units absorbed by the competition. Using residual demand, the marketing team or consultant can determine roughly how many households the proposed property can expect to capture per year. The accuracy of this figure can be checked by calculating monthly absorption and comparing it with the competition's sales. The market analysis should make this figure as realistic as possible; if anything, researchers should underestimate monthly absorption, for a project that is still feasible under the most conservative estimates will succeed in the real world.

The figure used to estimate absorption is crucial because it provides an approximate timetable for the project's selling out or being leased. This information in turn may cause the developer to modify the total number of units in the project or can help the developer determine the number of units to be built in each phase.

Developing a Market Strategy

With market research in place, developers and marketing teams can devise a comprehensive marketing plan for the proposed project. This marketing strategy should clarify the overall concept of the community, identify the appropriate target markets and the best ways to reach them, determine exact sizes, prices, and mix of units, provide for merchandising, advertising, and promotion, and determine the budget and timetable for implementation.

In clarifying the overall concept, developers and marketing teams must ensure that the project has a distinct identity. The proposed community should occupy a special position in the market, one that satisfies a demand that no other development in the competitive market area fills. The project's distinct identity is based on a combination of target markets, prices, housing types, and concept themes for creative marketing.

Perhaps the most misunderstood aspect of marketing is defining target markets. A profile of target

---

[1] For more detailed information on residential marketing techniques, see Dave Stone, *New Home Marketing* (Chicago: The Longman Group USA, 1989); and Charles R. Clark and David F. Parker, *Marketing New Homes* (Washington, D.C.: National Association of Home Builders, 1989).

markets, in addition to income and age, must provide qualitative information about the market, such as goals and aspirations, and current and future lifestyles. Demographic research companies are able to supply accurate numbers for each targeted market in the market area. Once the size and characteristics of target markets are defined, the market strategy can suggest ways to reach the prospects. The key to any such strategy is appealing to the market's self-image.

Based on the demographic data and information about the competitive properties in the area, experienced consultants can determine how best to position the product in the marketplace. Analysts can ascertain which segments of the population have needs that are not satisfied by the current supply of housing in terms of product type, features, and price or rent. The approximate size of units for the proposed development can also be determined by comparing the product to the competition, concentrating on providing a product that fills a demand unsatisfied by other housing in the market.

Most developers are likely to attract prospects from several different target audiences. For example, a project might contain small, two-bedroom units geared to young couples who are first-time buyers and four-bedroom units geared to growing families. As a result, consultants should estimate the number of units in each price range that each target market will absorb. Figures can be derived from the total number of households in each group in the target market and include estimates of the number of qualified households that will be attracted to the community. This exercise is particularly useful in planning the mix of unit types in the project.

The market strategy should also include the timing of development, allowing for a reasonable presale or preleasing period and the understanding that some percentage of preconstruction sales or leases eventually are canceled. The presales or preleasing period also provides an opportunity for the developer and sales staff to obtain feedback on the product and the market positioning strategy.

The phasing of the community is another important consideration. Council member Jim DeFrancia advises, "In most cases, the best locations in the development should not be the first ones released for sale. Developers might sometimes determine that they need to market a prime site initially to set the image and tone for the overall development, however." Because the final phase usually commands the highest prices, developers should avoid charging premium prices for less-than-prime sites, because it might make those units more difficult to sell. Instead, the project should be phased so that units in prime

David Zanzinger

6-1   To reinforce the "high country" theme of the Mountain Meadows single-family development in Moorpark, California, the entire cul-de-sac around which the model houses were located was landscaped with trees, flowers, turf, and a dry stream bed. The woodsy design blends into the landscaped front yards of the models.

locations are built and sold last—a process of building value incrementally. In the Straw Hill community in Manchester, New Hampshire, for example, the developer built the first phases on the low-lying, flat part of the site. The final phases were built on the hillside. The developer was able to realize high premiums on the last units sold because of the more dramatic lots on which the houses were built and the views they afforded and because of the community's overall positive image that had been established by the initial phases.[2]

Merchandising

Once the market strategy has been refined, developers should address ways to implement the plan. One of the first steps is the on-site merchandising of the community, which can be one of the most important elements in the marketing budget. Particular attention should be paid to graphics, the sales office, and the models. These features establish a tone or theme for the development and, when professionally executed, contribute to a prospect's good first impression.

Specific items to be considered in the budget include the costs of furnishing the model units (including accessories and their replacement), landscaping for the models, entry signs and lighting, other on-site

[2] *Project Reference File:* "Straw Hill," vol. 17, no. 18 (Washington, D.C.: ULI–the Urban Land Institute, September–December 1987).

signage, design and production of sales displays, and overhead for operating the models. While the gross budget can be considerable, the costs may be offset by eventual sale of the model units. The costs can also pay for themselves many times over if the merchandising program results in a quickened pace of sales or leasing.

The graphics should begin with a representative logo or distinguishing symbol that serves as the basic identification of the project. The logo must be used in all promotional materials that expose the project to the public, including signage, advertising, brochures, and letterheads, so it important that the design accommodate a variety of marketing applications. The total graphics package should be designed so as not to prejudice or preclude any group of buyers. Colors, style, and materials should be selected for maximum impact and appropriate emotional appeal to the primary target markets.

Often the entrance to the development is the potential buyer's or lessee's first exposure, so it is important to make a good first impression. The entrance should incorporate the logo and carry out themes consistent with the community's architecture and landscaping. All signage should be coordinated so that ancillary signs (such as those giving directions and information and identifying models) are constructed in the same style and with the same materials to the extent possible as the main entry sign. Telephone numbers and office hours are important pieces of information to be included on major signs. Colors should be selected for maximum appeal to the identified target market. Bright colors, for example, might not appeal to empty nesters but might be appropriate for young, first-time buyers.

The sales or rental office is the next step to consider. Presales or preleasing may actually start off site, depending on the local market, site conditions, project phasing, traffic patterns, and the use of brokers. In most cases, however, an attractively modified, landscaped, and furnished trailer, a freestanding temporary building, or an existing office can function as a sales office during the preconstruction period. Once the models have been completed and sales begun, a more permanent or finished sales office should be opened.

The location of the sales information center or leasing office should lend the best possible impression of the project and avoid conflicts with construction activities. In most cases, for the convenience of visitors, the office is placed immediately adjacent to the project's entrance. Council member Richard Michaux notes, "The location of the sales or leasing office is key. Ideally, it should be visible from the

6-2   The entrance to Villa D'Este in Longwood, Florida, conveys a strong sense of luxury and seclusion with mature landscaping, stamped concrete paving, a gatehouse, masonry walls, iron gates, and a fountain. The houses—priced up to $309,900—were targeted to second-home buyers but also appeal to young professionals and empty nesters.

entrance and, if possible, positioned to the driver's right side for more natural observation." In some cases, it is possible and desirable to create a temporary entrance from a perimeter roadway to the models, providing convenient access to visitors of the sales office and keeping sales traffic away from construction traffic and residents' traffic. In a large or multiphase community, the office may be placed well into the site, so that prospects drive past completed houses and landscaped areas. Signage, drawing on the theme of the entry sign, should clearly mark the direction to the office.

The most important consideration in selecting a site for the sales office should be presenting a sample of the environment *after* construction. In a townhouse development, doing so usually involves building a cluster of two or three blocks in addition to the model block to enclose a space that can be completely landscaped. In mid- or high-rise condominiums, the task may be more complex because of high initial costs and ongoing construction. For this type of development, visual displays may be necessary to illustrate the finished development. For a single-family detached development, the sales office (and model homes) are often located on a cul-de-sac or short street to achieve a finished look and accurate representation of the streetscape.

Developers should consider saving one or two lots adjacent to the sales office or model area to remain vacant (but nicely landscaped) to allow for the construction of a new model in case house plans change with changes in the market. Such lots can also serve as interim, off-street parking lots for visitors, which tends to concentrate their viewing during weekend periods. Traffic jams and conflicts with construction equipment around sales offices and model homes must be avoided; convenient, off-street lots provide the ideal design. Provisions for parking should be geared to peak flows, because buyers may turn into lost sales by having to wait to park.

Depending on the size of the development, the marketing budget, and the sophistication of the com-

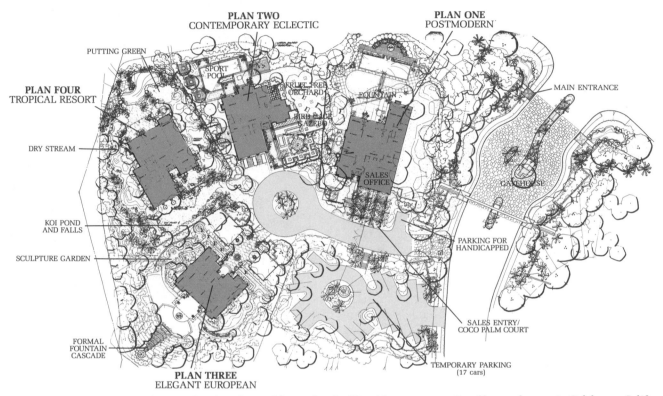

6-3   Little expense was spared to merchandize the model complex for Westridge, a community of luxury houses in Calabasas, California. The model home complex is located around a cul-de-sac to the immediate right of the entrance to the community. One lot was left vacant to accommodate 17 temporary off-street parking spaces. A temporary sales office was located in the garage of one model unit. Each of the four floor plans was elaborately landscaped and decorated to depict the ultimate lifestyle the house could offer.

Robb Miller

6-4, 6-5   The Plan Four model (left) was landscaped with enormous palm trees and enriched paving materials to convey a formal, European elegance. The rear yard of the Plan Four model (right) includes this curvilinear lap pool with cascading waterfall.

petition in the market area, the sales office can be one of four types:

- *A sales office within the model home* is the most economical, but often it is also the least functional. Invariably, the sales of that particular floor plan suffer as a result of confusion in the sales office. Nevertheless, for small developments, this arrangement minimizes expenses for merchandising.
- *A sales office within a partially completed model* may involve omitting some of the interior walls and postponing the installation of the kitchen until the model is sold. The model is usually a one-story plan permitting private offices for more than one sales person while still allowing for adequate display space.
- *A sales office in a double garage* is the most popular type of sales office around the country. It allows for a separate display area without impairing the salability of a particular floor plan. The major design decision is whether or not a private office is included within the limited available space. In some cases, a semiprivate informal sitting area substitutes for the private office; sales people then use another room in the model complex as necessary to have space separate from visitors for discussions with buyers. Two disadvantages of the garage sales office are its initial expense and the cost of subsequent remodeling.
- *A detached sales center* is sometimes used in larger projects with several phases. This type of sales office is often located in a building that is planned for the community association's later use. A large detached sales center has more display space, but it is also the most expensive option. It is most feasible when a community space is required as an amenity; however, it should not be used as a rationalization for building a clubhouse that is not needed. A detached sales office may be most applicable to the marketing of large-scale, multiproduct communities. If a detached sales center is determined to be necessary for marketing but a permanent structure is not needed for the development, the developer should consider using a temporary structure like a mobile home that can be removed upon completion of sales.

Like signage, the exterior of the sales office should be consistent with the project's architecture. The office should be merchandised as professionally as any of the models, and the furnishings and landscaping around the office should be selected with an eye to

6-6   The developer of Le Parc, a 300-unit community of low- to moderate-cost houses in Simi Valley, California, spent as much on this sales office as would have been typical for a much more expensive product. The contemporary interiors were designed to appeal to a primary market of first-time buyers.

the prospective market. Site plans, floor plans, renderings, photographs, video or audiovisual displays, and samples of finishes should all be considered for display in the sales office.

In large communities, it is often helpful to have a three-dimensional model of the development showing the street system, individual lots and houses, building clusters, amenities, and topographic features. A model gives prospects a quick understanding of the development's features and function; it generates excitement and interest. Houses or lots that have been sold can be identified on the model to indicate the success of sales.

Brochures describing the process for financing a unit are an effective way to increase buyers' interest after a tour of the models. Card systems can be used to show other services available for buyers—insurance, architectural and decorator services, appraisals, and landscaping. The office must incorporate space for signing and closing agreements for sale or lease. A round dining-style table is recommended, because it minimizes the adversarial potential of an "across-the-desk" arrangement.

The complex of models is the final step of merchandising. The number of models depends on the number of floor plans offered and the number of separate markets the developer plans to target. One model per floor plan may be desirable, but it is hardly an iron-clad rule, especially for projects with widely diverse unit types or a small number of total houses to sell. According to council member William E. Becker, "Many developers use a rule of thumb that allows for one model for every 25 to 40 production houses," and council member Fritz Grupe offers another guideline: "House plans can be furnished as models only if the builder expects to sell at least 20 of those units." To defray some of the costs of merchandising models, developers should consider a sale/leaseback arrangement with an investment-oriented buyer.

Models must be furnished with the appropriate target markets in mind, and the decorator must therefore have a sound understanding of the developer's intended market. For example, units for empty nesters should allow for the fact that prospects will bring treasured pieces of furniture with them; therefore, merchandising should focus on furnishings and standard accessories. Options like built-in bookcases and fancy finishes should not be emphasized unless they are relatively easy to provide and can bring substantial additional profit to the builder. Generally, models should be furnished and decorated a little more expensively than the income of the target audience, so that the house looks appealing but within reach of a prospective buyer.

Well-established local firms should be chosen to decorate the models to ensure continuity among units and to allow interested buyers to duplicate the decor after the sale. Decorating is of the utmost importance,

6-7   Interior merchandizing for the Signature Series townhouses at Princeton Landing in Princeton, New Jersey, appealed to their primary market, empty nesters.

and developers should always itemize what is and what is not to be included in a finished dwelling.

Council member Becker offers this guideline: "To do a quality merchandising job, budget 30 to 35 percent of the sale price of each model unit to cover the cost of draperies, furnishings, and accessories." Thus, on a $150,000 unit, the developer should plan to spend $45,000 to $50,000 for decorating. When the budget does not allow a fully decorated model, decorated "vignettes" showcasing certain features or areas of the house should be considered. For example, one or two key rooms might be furnished to help prospective purchasers visualize how the house will look after they move in.

Overdecorating should be avoided because it misleads buyers and fails to show off the housing unit. Displaying many nice but unnecessary options, for example, is a needless distraction that hinders the conveyance of accurate information on more important features. The model home also must not represent construction modifications that will be impossible for buyers to replicate. Council member Robert Engstrom warns, "The design of model homes and options should duplicate the approach the homeowner would use. For townhouses and condominiums especially, modifications to patios or, even worse, to common walls that are prohibited by the covenants, conditions, and restrictions should not be considered."

Developers should not overlook interior information signs in model units. Certain accessories, such as built-in bookshelves and upgraded appliances, and upgraded finishes like ceramic tile, hardwood floors, and crown molding can be clearly marked "optional" to indicate that they are not included as standard items. Professional, attractive plaques or cards can draw prospective buyers' attention to the important features that are included in the selling price. Restrictive signs prohibiting smoking and eating in model units, bringing pets inside the units, or using the bathroom must be handled wisely. The signs should be pleasant and inoffensive. Their style should also be related to other signs on site.

Background music at the sales center helps to create a mood. The use of aromas like fresh bread, cinnamon, popcorn, or potpourri stimulates the sense of smell and improves a prospect's memory of the house. Council member Sanford Goodkin suggests the use of television screens "all over the place, telling the same story"—who you are, the investment value of a house, the benefits of location and address.[3] These features,

[3] Sanford R. Goodkin, "How to Sell Houses to Couch Potatoes," *Professional Builder*, January 1990, p. 110.

coupled with a public address system that plays pre-recorded messages referring prospects to the unit's features, are effective techniques to enhance sales. If possible, models should be positioned on the lot to take advantage of afternoon sunlight, because most visitors arrive at that time.

The landscaping of front and back yards in model homes needs as much careful attention as the interior decoration of the units. Especially in townhouses, patio houses, and small-lot detached units, the yard area is seen as an extension of the interior living space and needs to demonstrate how the target market's lifestyle can be accommodated in small spaces. For example, yard spaces can depict how the homeowner can use the space for outdoor dining (decks and patios), outdoor cooking (a built-in barbecue), gardening (perhaps a rose or herb garden), and recreation (a pool or hot tub to add appeal).

Promotion

Choosing the promotional material and the public relations campaign constitutes the next phase of marketing. The entire promotional effort is intended to create an awareness of the development and a favorable public image. Unlike merchandising, most promotional efforts are conducted off site.

A good public relations image does not happen overnight. Developers who have been building in an area for some time can build good will with past performance. A house is a complex product and is purchased largely on faith in a developer; if the developer is well respected in the community, the task of selling houses is made easier. In some cases, the in-house marketing director may assume the role of public relations director; in other instances, it might be better to hire a public relations firm.

Outside firms typically establish their fees in one of three ways: a fixed monthly retainer, a fixed retainer with monthly billing for the staff's time, or a base fee, billed monthly. To better ensure performance by an outside public relations firm, developers might consider linking fees to the number of houses sold within a specified time or some other measure of performance. Bonus fees might be appropriate when sales exceed estimates.

For most developers working within a specific market, public relations and promotion are ongoing and include contributions to the community, working with civic groups, being active in the chamber of commerce, and serving on municipal committees. One can gain or retain the good will of public officials by having the best interests of the community at heart.

The most useful part of public relations is to develop and maintain a positive relationship with the press. Developers must concentrate their public relations efforts with local newspapers, more specifically with real estate, business, and city desk editors. Events affecting a local project should affect the community to be worthy of a story. Among the news items an editor might consider printing are plans for the project, the purchase of land, the unveiling of the development concept, breaking ground, a grand opening, or the first families' moving in.

The promotional budget also covers brochures, floor plans and site plans, price lists, and funds for photography, mailings, production, and follow-up mailings. The budget should allow for entertaining the media and a VIP party to be held before the official grand opening. A reserve fund for promotional materials is essential, as all promotional opportunities cannot be identified in the initial marketing strategy.

The promotional materials and literature represent one aspect of the promotion for a new development. But the first consideration should be the public relations campaign, which begins during presales or preleasing and continues through the project's grand opening and other special events. One effective form of preconstruction publicity is direct-mail promotion to qualified prospects. Mailing lists can be obtained from list brokers and from specialized publications, such as magazines that appeal to the individual target markets. Such lists can be further qualified by sending preliminary questionnaires that gauge the prospect's housing preferences in a friendly, nonthreatening way. These mailings promote the name of the development, and the responses can help modify and refine the housing program or marketing strategy. In addition, respondents form the basis of an invitation list to the VIP party.

The grand opening should be heavily promoted through advertising and also through stories in local newspapers and other media. The opening of the community to the public should be only one of several special events tied to the project. The groundbreaking ceremony is another opportunity for publicity. And the VIP party, either shortly before or shortly after the grand opening, would be open to respondents to the direct mailing, local civic leaders, the media, and other interested prospects.

Besides coordinating these events for the public, the developer and the public relations staff should also target the media. The promotional consultant must identify the local and regional newspapers, radio and TV stations, and business magazines that can carry word of the project to the widest number of qualified prospects. Regular news releases should be

ENHANCING THE IMAGE OF A NEW PRODUCT: NOTTINGHAM—FAIRFAX COUNTY, VIRGINIA

Nottingham introduces an entirely new concept, the diagonal Z-lot-line design, to the suburban Washington, D.C., housing market long dominated by two-story, red brick colonials. Miller and Smith Companies (M&S) risked rejection by the market and developed the high-density, detached units to compete specifically with nearby townhouses and condominiums.

Nottingham is located on a 20.7-acre site in Fairfax County, Virginia, 12 miles from downtown Washington, D.C. One of seven residential projects currently being built within Kingstowne—an emerging 1,200-acre, multiuse, planned community—it offers the only detached residential product in the development. Escalating land prices and scarce sites are forcing increased densities at close-in locations, where the demand for single-family houses is quite strong.

In response to these conditions, Spence Stouffer, a principal of M&S, wanted a high-density, innovative, detached design included with the apartments and townhouses planned for Kingstowne. He chose "Z" lots, a high-density pattern accepted in California, Arizona, and Florida but relatively untested in other parts of the country. M&S determined early during concept planning that success would depend on conveying a positive image about the lifestyle this new product would offer.

6-10 To demonstrate the livability of small lots, Nottingham's developer spent about three times more than typical on landscaping the model complex. The sales office was located in the garage of one of the units.

Planning and Design

Stouffer chose "Z" lots to attain maximum density. For assistance with concept development, he hired Walter Richardson of Richardson, Nagy, Martin—a California architect familiar with Fairfax County regulations and well known for his successful "Z" lot projects.

Typical "Z" lot projects permit seven to eight single-family houses per acre, but Fairfax County codes regulating street widths and parking result in

6-9   The exteriors of the model units were elaborately landscaped and included decking and hot tubs to demonstrate how the relatively small yard areas could be finished for maximum enjoyment and minimum maintenance.

▶

culs-de-sac, two-car garages, and wide driveways, reducing the density at Nottingham to 4.9 units per acre. Local codes and the site's configuration forced the developer to modify the concept of standard "Z" lots, resulting in a variety of lot sizes and shapes and adding complexity to the typically repetitive plan for "Z" lots: no two lots were the same, property lines had to conform to the actual sites of most houses, flexibility in interchanging unit plans and lots was limited, and privacy fencing between units had to be customized for each lot. Because of his success with high-density projects in other parts of the country, Richardson proved helpful in convincing local planners that detached small-lot housing was viable in Fairfax County.

Architecture

Nottingham provides three models: a one-floor, two-bedroom, two-bathroom unit, and two two-

6-11 This model interior demonstrates how to combine contemporary design elements like skylights and vaulted ceilings with traditional decor.

floor, 2½-bathroom units with a choice of two or three bedrooms. Every unit has a double garage, but only a few, those facing the floodplain, have basements. Because lots are small, grading and drainage are difficult, and basements are generally omitted from "Z" lot houses, again a departure from Fairfax County standards, where the market has traditionally demanded basements in single-family houses and townhouses.

The units average 2,400 square feet of usable outdoor space and 1,605 square feet of interior space, comparable to the size of most area townhouses with basements. To compensate for the smaller size, the houses have high ceilings to create volume, sliding glass doors to emphasize indoor/outdoor living, and a generous use of windows on all sides, placed strategically for privacy, a major concern for people living on small lots. The units are designed with ample light, outdoor views, and functional floor plans that include eat-in kitchens, fireplaces, and master bedroom suites. Most houses have wood siding exteriors, but one-third have brick fronts to conform with Kingstowne's architectural covenants that assume traditional Virginia-style designs.

Marketing

Marketing was important because Stouffer thought the project risky, with its small lots and units, lack of basements, and contemporary architecture. Research had identified the target market for Kingstowne as young professionals with a preference for single-family housing, and Stouffer felt Nottingham could best position itself with an innovative detached product oriented toward such a lifestyle to compete with the townhouses and multifamily units planned for Kingstowne. M&S increased its usual budget for the models by about 20 percent, presenting them as "city homes" accommodating an urban lifestyle. Interior decor was combined with extensive use of privacy fences and optional wooden patios, hot tubs, and lush landscaping to strengthen the relationship between indoors and outdoors and extend the livable space.

M&S's corporate director for marketing, Richard Tiller, explains more about the marketing program:

The marketing campaign was designed from the beginning to sell a concept of lifestyle rather than the specific product. The advertisements and marketing bro-

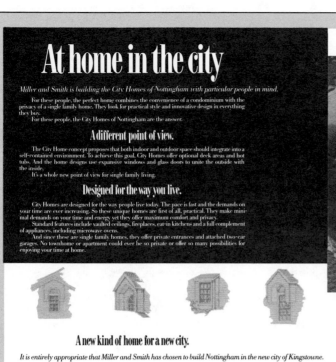

6-12   The sales brochure explains the concept of a home in the city as "a whole new point of view for single-family living."

chure, instead of showing pictures of the units, showed people relaxing in hammocks, blowing bubbles. We spent considerably more money on the brochure than we would have for a product that would be familiar to the market. We also spent more on merchandizing the units—in this case we spent $45,000 to landscape the model complex, where a more typical budget for this market would be about $15,000. The budget to decorate each unit was about $120,000, the budget for the sales office $25,000. In general, we enhanced the product through the decorating and landscaping to sell the indoor/outdoor elegance and comfort of the concept.

Nottingham was a market success. The 102 units sold out in 17 months, despite a substantial price increase raising the average cost per unit by about $40,000. The largest and most expensive model was the best seller. The demand for the detached product was great enough to overcome concerns about the unusual concept of lotting.

The Kingstowne Homeowners' Association assesses each unit $38 per month, which is used to maintain common areas and some streets and permits residents to use community recreational amenities. To reinforce the relaxed lifestyle of the community, M&S provided basic landscaping for each unit's front yard.

Summary

"Z" lots proved easier to sell than had been anticipated. A small yard and a small unit proved to be acceptable tradeoffs to gain an affordable, single-family, detached house in a relatively close-in area. But the risks were high, and the marketing program, targeted to the right segment of the market, proved essential to the success of the project. For example, selling the outdoor living space as an extension of indoor space by designing models with decks and hot tubs enhanced the appeal of the product.

According to Richard Tiller, "We learned that increased marketing expense for a new concept in a market can be rewarded many times over."

Source: Project Reference File: "Nottingham," vol. 19, no. 4 (Washington, D.C.: ULI–the Urban Land Institute, January–March 1989); see also the related *Project Reference File* video.

issued regarding plans and designs and progress of construction. The press should receive invitations to all special events, including the VIP party.

High-quality brochures or videotapes should be created from the outset, even during presales or pre-leasing. The literature or visual techniques should incorporate the graphic logo and designs employed throughout the community. Literature or brochures distributed should be a manageable size and should have a slit for inserting business cards of sales people or leasing agents.

The brochure also serves as a folder where related promotional materials can be placed—precise, legible floor plans, a list of features, a description of the project's amenities, a site plan, and a price list. The brochure should also include the developer's background and an explanation of the community's lifestyle. Other items that might be appropriate to mention in the brochure include information about local schools, a list of the area's conveniences, a description of public services, such as nearby recreational features, and a description of any responsibilities of the homeowners' association or common elements. Developers should be careful not to include too much information in a single brochure; inexpensive but attractively executed supplements can be handed out as a potential buyer's interest in the project increases. The brochure can be designed with a pocket to accommodate such supplements.

Developers pioneering a new concept in the market should consider appropriate explanations in the brochures. Many prospective buyers do not readily understand contemporary, higher-density single-family houses built on unusually configured lots ("Z" lots, zipper lots, and zero-lot-line designs). At the Casa del Cielo development in Scottsdale, Arizona, for example, the highly discretionary move-down buyers to whom the project was targeted were reluctant to commit to "Z" lots without understanding completely property lines, easements, and principles of planning. The project's developer devoted a full page in the sales brochure to explain "Z" lots as a new concept in patio houses. Using diagrams, the brochure compared the advantages of "Z" lots with more traditional zero-lot-line houses. The simplified explanation of the concept proved effective in reducing buyers' anxiety about purchasing an unusual product and quickened the pace of sales.[4]

Concurrent with design of the brochure, the developer should work with the advertising agency on additional materials—stationery (and a letterhead), envelopes, business cards, and press kits. Move-in kits for new residents and invitations to the VIP party are also recommended for the promotional budget.

Advertising

Even the best advertising does not sell houses; its function is only to deliver the highest number of qualified prospects to the development, and the rest is up to the sales staff. But because the public's perception of the development is reinforced by advertising, advertising plays a crucial role in the marketing strategy. The campaign should be focused on a central theme that is established early and carried throughout the various stages of development. The budget must allow for advertising during presales or preleasing, before the project's grand opening, and as an ongoing part of the development's operations.

The developer's in-house staff should have a general, working knowledge of the fundamentals of advertising, but it is best to hire an advertising agency to develop a fresh approach for each new project. An agency should be selected with care to ensure that the project is represented in the best possible way. Developers must make sure in advance that they and the agencies know the terms of compensation and what is expected from the agency. A system of commissions is still the traditional source of an advertising agency's income. It may be augmented by flat retainers paid monthly or yearly, a service fee, or markups on production charges.

An advertising agency typically develops a long-range strategy, plans individual programs, selects the best media for various presentations, prepares copy and designs layouts, and checks results of the campaign. The budget varies, depending on the project's size, the number of competitive builders, a developer's reputation in the market, and the introduction of new concepts to the market.

Items in the advertising budget should include the cost of advertisements in newspapers and other media, direct-mail marketing, the cost of producing advertisements, and the agency's fees. A reserve fund should be allocated, because an unexpected softening in the market may necessitate an increased advertising campaign. Advertising must be coordinated with merchandising and promotions to achieve a unified approach.

The initial advertisements, besides introducing the community and its location to the public, should work to establish the project's distinct position in the market. The text should include a description of the types of units available and the base price. The style and tone of the advertisements should be appropriate to the targeted markets, with text and graphics reflect-

---

[4] James W. Wentling and Lloyd W. Bookout, eds., *Density by Design* (Washington, D.C.: ULI–the Urban Land Institute, 1987), p. 64.

ing the current lifestyle, aspirations, and self-image of the various groups. Graphic elements appropriate for a community targeted to empty nesters will not help sell houses to first-time buyers or families. Ideally, advertisements should clearly delineate the main target markets without alienating any other qualified prospects.

The advertisements for a project's grand opening should sustain the market's awareness of the development; they should focus on introducing the model units and the community's lifestyle. Other points to emphasize are the specific advantages of the community's location and its package of amenities, particularly important for a pioneering community that is introducing a new type of housing or community environment to the market.

The advertising for subsequent phases must reinforce the community's image in the marketplace. Profiles of buyers or renters can be used in these advertisements after people have started to move in, with testimonials instituted for future advertising and promotional literature.

At each stage of the advertising campaign, developers and consultants should evaluate which media will be most effective in reaching targeted groups. Local and regional newspapers are a good way to reach a broad audience, while magazines, radio, and television can be more effective for specific target markets. Virtually every medium conducts its own surveys of the demographics of its audience, the results of which are made available to prospective advertisers.

Newspapers

Real estate advertising can achieve maximum exposure for its dollars in newspapers. A common place to start is the classified section, which is relatively low in cost. Although this section attracts readers who are looking for a particular product, the similarity of the advertising and, in some editions, the volume of such advertisements are obvious disadvantages. But in general, the overall advantages of the classified section outweigh the disadvantages.

Display advertising can be effective if it includes an attractive, high-quality layout and illustrations. The story should be told with pictures. Display advertising is especially good for weekend promotions like those found in a newspaper's weekly real estate section. On some occasions, developers of new projects can purchase a special section of the paper to explain a new concept. Teaser advertisements can be used

6-13, 6-14   The advertisements for the Signature Series at Princeton Landing attempt to convey a sense of Old World elegance and exclusivity.

effectively before big events like the grand opening to help create a mood.

Layout and copy should be simple and specific, not too clever and avoiding exaggerated claims. Advertisements must always include easy-to-follow directions to a project, and they should identify the developers.

Radio

Before setting up any radio advertising campaign, it is wise to check the profile of listeners, opting for stations whose general programming is similar to the tastes of the target market. The advertising agency for the project can be very helpful in selecting stations. Radio is an effective tool in attracting people's attention during the grand opening, but for developers who are not equipped to handle a large number of people on the site, radio advertising can do more harm than good. In addition to spot announcements, live remote broadcasts during times when many people are in their automobiles are effective. Typically an hour long, this type of broadcast features music and interviews with prospective buyers.

Television

Television is expensive per viewing minute and television advertisements expensive to produce, but the coverage afforded by the medium can offset its cost. If a project is located in a large metropolitan area, the television viewing population may be larger than the expected market; thus, other more localized forms of advertising may be more advantageous. Television can be effective in smaller markets for special events like grand openings and can be particularly effective for marketing large projects that feature several products within a community oriented toward a specific lifestyle.

Signs

Signs are an important aspect of the marketing program.

> The initial phase of extending [the] marketing message to reach customers begins with a thorough evaluation of signage needs and opportunities. Historically in the housing business, signs account for a very high percentage of closed sales. National averages range from 20 to 30 percent. In many markets, signs on major thoroughfares are far more important than ads in the newspaper.[5]

Billboards can be very effective in introducing a development's name to the public. Colors for billboards should be selected for maximum visibility; red, for example, catches the eye and is highly read-

6-15 A temporary sign in a developing planned community directs prospective residents to specific products. This sign is designed to be flexible so that product names can be changed as the community evolves without having to remove the entire sign.

able. Fluorescent colors are also striking; they have the advantage of increased visibility at night and are available now in a range of subtle hues. Nevertheless, the design of billboards and the colors selected should be compatible with the image of the development being conveyed in other elements of the marketing campaign.

Banners on buses and other forms of transit advertising (posters on benches at bus stops and commuter stations) also can be effective in making the public aware of a development. Developers should also consider placing off-site painted directional signs at key locations around the development—generally within a two- to five-mile radius—but should investigate the municipality's regulations concerning roadway signs to determine the extent to which this option is available. In areas where local ordinances restrict off-site signs, says council member C. Lewis Christensen, "the services of a company that places directional signs on Friday and removes them on Sunday might be appropriate. Doing so minimizes conflicts with local authorities yet allows signs to be in place for usually heavier weekend traffic." Developers should be aware of the aesthetic impact of off-site signs: offensive signs will do little to promote a project's positive image.

Other Media

Developers can reach a special market by advertising in special regional or city publications like *New York, Los Angeles, Washingtonian,* and *Southern Living* magazines or in the more specialized real estate jour-

[5] Stone, *New Home Marketing*, p. 422.

nals or smaller neighborhood newspapers. Advertising in local editions of national publications like *Wall Street Journal, National Geographic,* or *Time* is also an effective means of reaching target groups. In some markets, direct-mail advertising promotes a special project in a special way. Direct mail can also be used for exclusive showings or previews. Invitations to showings or previews hand delivered by sales people are effective variations of direct mail.

Wise developers will not overlook a time-tested method of advertising: referrals. Word-of-mouth advertising sells many units. Each time a developer opens a new project, an announcement can be sent to buyers at former projects, who might be ready to move up to a better house or could tell others. To understand whether an advertising campaign is working, developers should find out how each prospective buyer found out about the development and whether or not the advertising was pleasing. It might be advantageous also to survey those who bought a competitor's product. In the absence of an advertising agency or marketing consultant under contract, the marketing or business departments of local universities and colleges can usually perform this task at a reasonable cost.

Management of Sales and Leasing

Because the advertising and promotion campaigns are geared only to attract prospects to a community, a thorough market strategy plan should also cover the management and training of the sales or leasing team—the people who are actually responsible for closing deals. They are vital components of the marketing plan, but sales and management are sometimes treated as low-priority items in the budget.

A basic decision regarding sales personnel is whether to employ an on-site sales staff or to contract with a local realty firm. Council member Robert Engstrom notes, "In larger metropolitan markets, developers usually prefer to have their own staff, controlled by and accountable to the development organization. An exception might be a real estate company that specializes in a particular or special type of product." In smaller market areas and for smaller projects, developers should seriously consider using one or more real estate firms as the sales staff or as a means of generating referrals, making sure, however, that the outside firm has experience with selling new housing and preferably with the particular type of product being marketed.

With a projected sales forecast and program budget, it is necessary to decide how many people are needed (on staff or retainer) to market the develop-

ment. Usually a development needs a marketing director (sales manager), who is responsible for all phases of selling a project. Marketing directors should have a strong knowledge of sales techniques and of the product being sold. They must be able to motivate the sales force, convincing them that they are integral parts of the development program. Council member James Klingbeil offers some advice on the sales staff: "Let the sales people spend some time in the field so that they know the product inside out." Planning and design consultants for the project can offer valuable sales training by thoroughly explaining the rationale for the land plan and housing design. Using staff or consultants to train sales people is one of the best—but most neglected—ways of ensuring marketing success.

The sales or leasing organization should be carefully structured from the beginning of presales. All members of the team should be aware of how their efforts will be supervised and evaluated and how they will be compensated. From the onset, the mutual responsibilities of the developer and the sales or leasing staff should be clarified in a policy statement. The sales or leasing manager should also provide reporting forms to be completed by staff members—prospect cards, daily and weekly summaries of activities, and a monthly sales or leasing productivity report. By analyzing these reports, sales or leasing managers can accurately assess each staffer's productivity and know which ones might need more training or special assistance, using this information to determine whether staffers are following up on prospects. They can also determine the sales team's effectiveness by using a conversion ratio that indicates the number of contracts written as a percent of total traffic.

The policy for compensation should also be outlined in the statement. Compensation can take many forms besides direct financial remuneration, including recognition of personal achievement and indirect financial incentives. A sales person who decides to buy or lease a house in the development might receive a discount on the sale price or rent. A base compensation should be set, however, along with a minimum target of sales or leases for the year. Sales personnel who exceed the minimum should be rewarded with additional compensation or other bonuses.

Most developers believe that sales staff should receive salary plus commission, typically a minimum salary with an unlimited commission. This form of payment does not negate the incentive of commissions, and it helps sales personnel identify with the company's goals and policies. Prizes, bonuses, or other inducements have also proven to be good practice. Higher commission rates can be paid for speculative houses, and bonuses can be awarded if sales personnel exceed yearly or monthly quotas. Commissions can range from 0.75 to 1.5 percent, depending on the price range of a project, the rate of sales, and the project's location (some locations might be harder to market than others). Sales commissions can be based on a sliding percentage that increases with the volume sold and length of service in the organization.

According to council member Ronald Nahas:

> The structure of the sales department for rapid sales of low-priced housing is different from slower sales of high-priced housing. If sales are routine, the best method of compensation is a salary. For higher-priced housing, however, sales are seldom routine. Marketing for such houses may include special financing, many building modifications, and a good deal more salesmanship, because buyers with a substantial amount of money usually have a greater selection of places to live. Sales personnel in high-priced or difficult sales programs should be put on a commission at a rate they find attractive. Developers will get better sales people and more attention to the unusual items in each sale.

Salary or commission should be reviewed annually for all members of the sales staff. Changes in compensation should be avoided between reviews, except when a member of the staff assumes dramatically increased responsibilities between regular reviews. And each staff member should have the opportunity to discuss his or her present position and future work with the sales or leasing manager during the review.

The overall marketing strategy must allow for the training of sales or leasing staffs; a number of experts offer a variety of instructional manuals and tapes, courses, and motivational seminars. This training should be ongoing, with periodic education programs for all staff members. Developers should consider paying at least part, if not all, of the training fees for their employees.

Specific training should be undertaken for each new project so that the sales staff understands fully the target markets and the nature of the product being offered. A one-week, intensive training program at the beginning of a project is typical. Developers should continue with weekly meetings, preferably on Friday just before the active weekend selling period. Among the topics included in the initial training sessions and the weekly meetings are a description of the project, its benefits and conveniences, a tour of the neighborhood, the history of the development firm, and lectures and demonstrations on proper techniques of selling—the use of displays, how to conduct tours of projects, and understanding closing techniques. Council member Jim DeFrancia stresses, "It is essential that sales staff have a good knowledge of the neighborhood—the location of schools, parks, and shopping areas. A follow-up system should be established to answer prospects' questions to which the responses might not be immediately known, such as 'Where is the nearest soccer field?'" A sales person must learn how to answer questions, tackle objections, and handle customer service and follow-up. For rental developments, leasing trainees should gain a first-hand knowledge of the mechanics of leases. In for-sale developments, sessions on FHA, VA, and conventional financing should be offered to trainees.

Sales people also need to know how far they can go in adjusting the standard purchase contract when negotiating with a customer. Nonstandard upgrades, extended closing dates, contingency contracts, early dates for moving in, the form of payment of earnest money, and other such parameters can be established during the ongoing training program. Sales staff must know what adjustments, if any, can be made so that the initial contract written is acceptable.

Training sessions should also include instruction on the importance of following up with customers after the contract has been signed. Many sales are lost because sales people sometimes believe their work is done when the contract is signed. They should, however, maintain constant contact with customers to reinforce their decision to purchase housing, update them on the status of the loan application and of construction, and prevent the onset of second thoughts after such a large purchase.

The Marketing Budget

A key part of the market strategy is the budget for marketing. The budget begins with realistic projections of sales or leases, which are based on residual demand within the market, allowing for predictable seasonal fluctuations in activity. In most markets, sales peak during spring and summer and dip during winter. (For the sake of convenience, inflation should not be factored into the budget, so all figures are expressed in current dollars.)

Projections of sales or leases should be as detailed as possible. Ideally, the marketing staff or consultant should set up a chart that indicates how many units of each type will be closed in each quarter, along with the sale price of each unit. (For rental properties, the budget is based on the amount of rent that will be collected for each unit during the leasing period.) This chart allows the marketing manager or consultant to plot increases in prices or rents over the absorption period. They should be the base prices, not including options or premiums.

After income has been projected, the marketing budget pro forma should be estimated. Total expenses

MODEL/SALES OFFICE COSTS FOR START-UP (one-time expense for first year)

Three models furnished at $23/square foot	$164,000
Sales office set-up	50,000
Signage	10,000
Landscaping for two model areas	40,000
MODEL/SALES OFFICE TOTAL	$264,000

MARKETING COSTS

Brochures (8,000 at $3 each)	$24,000
Art and production for ads, logos	8,000
Advertising ($5,000/month)	60,000
Public relations ($800/month)	9,600
Model/sales office maintenance ($2,000/month for two single-family houses and $3,000/month for four townhouses), including all utilities and cleaning	60,000
Landscape maintenance ($500/month for eight months)	4,000
MARKETING TOTAL (2½ years)	$366,000
Marketing Costs for First Year	$165,600
Marketing Costs per Year Thereafter	$133,600

SELLING COSTS

In-house commissions for two sales people at 0.25 percent each	$128,210
Salaries (two sales people, one administrator)	75,000
Outside commissions (50 percent @ 3 percent)	384,630
SELLING TOTAL (2½ years)	$700,340
Selling Costs per Year	$280,136

TOTAL START-UP, MARKETING, AND SELLING COST	$ 1,330,340
TOTAL PROJECTED REVENUES	$25,642,000
MARKETING COST AS A PERCENT OF REVENUES	5.19%

Based on the Signature Series at Princeton Landing, comprised of 47 single-family houses (one decorated model) and 32 townhouses (two decorated models). *Source:* The William E. Becker Organization.

include costs of all promotion, public relations, advertising, merchandising, and management. The budget should estimate net and gross market costs as a percentage of total sales or leasing as well as the average cost per unit, or determine through "task allocation" what it will take to meet sales goals.

Typically, a marketing budget for for-sale housing can be based on 6 to 8 percent of gross sales. The marketing budget consists of three types of expenses: advertising, on-site merchandising, and sales. Advertising costs usually amount to 1 to 2 percent of sales, or $1,000 to $2,000 for every $100,000 of sales. This amount includes radio, television, and newspaper coverage, and off-site signage. In major metropolitan areas, however, developers should figure on 3 percent of sales as the minimum because media costs are higher. Brochures and other print material, displays, decorating for model homes, landscaping, and on-site signs usually run about 3 to 3.5 percent of gross sales, perhaps more. Sales commissions can run about 0.75 to 1.5 percent of sales, but the figure could be higher if overhead for the sales office is included here and sales people receive a salary plus commission.

The marketing budget pro forma should show the amount of money spent on each line item over the course of the absorption period. Like figures for sales or leasing, these expenses should be estimated for each quarter until all properties have been absorbed.

This method gives developers specific information on how funds should be allocated over time. Council member William E. Becker suggests spending most of the marketing budget up front: "If, for example, a development is expected to require one year to be sold or leased, it would be reasonable to spend 40 percent of the marketing budget during the first 90 days, another 40 percent over the next six months, and the remaining 20 percent to complete the project." Like other real estate pro formas, the marketing budget should be subject to periodic review and updated when new information warrants it.

Monitoring and Measuring Acceptance

The marketing effort does not end with the grand opening. Professional marketing consultants can analyze traffic through "exit polls" at the property to gauge consumers' acceptance of the project. They can also try to ascertain the effectiveness of each stage of marketing.

Because of the value of this information, all visitors to the community should be asked to fill out entry cards. At this point, they should register only their names, addresses, and phone numbers, together with additional qualifying information to ascertain the type of unit, price range, and occupancy date they prefer and their urgency to buy.

Potential buyers who visit the property should be surveyed on site after they have toured the models. Another option is to use the sales or leasing staff's follow-up call as an opportunity for a short survey. Prospects may also be selected at random for a more extensive telephone survey to assess their attitudes toward the community. The opinions of prospects who actually buy or lease units at the property must also be considered. These consumers might be asked to complete a short questionnaire when they sign a sales agreement or lease.

In addition to the units and the community itself, these surveys should probe the respondents' opinions on the

Welcome!

We'd like to get to know you better. Please take a moment to complete this form. (Please Print)

Name_____

Address:_____

City:_____ State:_____ Zip:_____

Home Phone:_____ Work Phone:_____

Age:
☐ Under 30 ☐ 41-50 ☐ 65 +
☐ 30-40 ☐ 51-64

Income:
☐ less than $50,000 ☐ $75 to $100,000 ☐ $125 to $150,000
☐ $50 to $75,000 ☐ $100 to $125,000 ☐ $150,000 +

Number of family members:
_____ Adults _____ Children at home _____ Children away

Occupation(s):
(1)_____
(2)_____

Date_____

Community_____

Current Residence:
☐ Rental apt. ☐ Single family home ☐ Three bedroom
☐ Condo ☐ One bedroom ☐ Four + bedroom
☐ Townhome ☐ Two bedroom ☐ Other_____

Principal reason for moving at this time:
☐ Relocating to the area ☐ Other_____
☐ Present residence unsuitable _____
☐ Change in family status _____

Planning to move:
☐ Immediately ☐ 1 year or more
☐ 3 to 6 months ☐ Must sell home
☐ 6 months to 1 year

How did you learn about our community?
☐ Signs ☐ Mail Magazines:_____
Newspapers:_____ Broker:_____
Referral:_____ _____

Thank you for your cooperation.

PRINCETON LANDING
A Value Group Community

6-17 The information gleaned from this entry card will assist the sales staff in determining which product(s) will best meet the potential buyer's lifestyle and budget. Such information should be collected as soon as the prospect enters the sales office. *Source:* The William E. Becker Organization.

HOW ARE WE DOING?
Part I

1. How do you rate your overall experience with our company?

☐ excellent ☐ good ☐ adequate ☐ poor ☐ unsatisfactory

2. Did our salesperson fully brief you on the benefits of the homes we build and about the special advantages of living in our community?

☐ excellent ☐ good ☐ adequate ☐ poor ☐ unsatisfactory

3. Did our salesperson answer all your questions about the purchase agreement before asking you to sign?

☐ excellent ☐ good ☐ adequate ☐ poor ☐ unsatisfactory

4. Did our salesperson keep you informed about the progress of your home during construction?

☐ excellent ☐ good ☐ adequate ☐ poor ☐ unsatisfactory

5. Were you satisfied with the condition of your home at closing?

☐ excellent ☐ good ☐ adequate ☐ poor ☐ unsatisfactory

6. Has our staff been responsive to your after-closing needs?

☐ excellent ☐ good ☐ adequate ☐ poor ☐ unsatisfactory

7. Are you satisfied with the quality of construction of your home?

☐ excellent ☐ good ☐ adequate ☐ poor ☐ unsatisfactory

8. Have our customer service representatives responded promptly to your complaints?

☐ excellent ☐ good ☐ adequate ☐ poor ☐ unsatisfactory

9. Have our customer service representatives fully corrected any defects?

☐ excellent ☐ good ☐ adequate ☐ poor ☐ unsatisfactory

10. Have our customer service representatives been courteous?

☐ excellent ☐ good ☐ adequate ☐ poor ☐ unsatisfactory

11. Do you feel our attitude toward you changed in any way *after* you bought your home?

☐ yes ☐ no   If yes, please explain.

_____

_____

Part II

1. If you could adjust the design of your home, what would you change?

_____

_____

_____

2. What do you like best about your new home?

_____

_____

_____

3. What do you like least about your new home?

_____

_____

_____

4. If we could improve our dealings with you, in what areas would that improvement occur?

_____

_____

_____

5. What has been the most positive aspect about dealing with our company?

_____

_____

_____

Thank you for completing this survey
and for letting us know how we are doing!
Please return in the enclosed self-addressed,
stamped envelope at your earliest convenience.

-Optional-

Name:_____

Address:_____

Phone:_____

6-18 A simple questionnaire like the one above will help a developer gauge consumers' level of satisfaction with the product and the service provided by the developer. *Source:* The William E. Becker Organization.

major aspects of the property's marketing. In this way, consultants and developers can ascertain the effectiveness of the advertising and merchandising programs. This information should be gathered from the beginning of preconstruction so that advertisements and other materials can be fine-tuned over the course of the project.

Monitoring the effectiveness of marketing and sales—by measuring traffic, absorption, and profiles of buyers against projections and corresponding bud-geted expenditures—ensures that the marketing plan is an appropriate strategy that maximizes market penetration. The essence of professional marketing is well-conceived strategy implemented through a carefully constructed plan.

Monitoring should not end with the completion of a sale. Residential developers should seek to learn from their successes and failures. They should obtain continuous feedback from a completed project so they can use the results to plan the next development. This final step is essential in residential development, one that is consistent with the principles and practices of good development.

Feedback is a dialogue between developers and community associations, if they exist, or between developers and individual residents. To be able to correct unwanted patterns of development that do not work (or work infrequently), developers should learn first-hand from residents what is wrong by soliciting their opinions.

The rate of sales tells whether buyers are pleased with the development initially. Even though a project sells well, however, other means are better indicators of residents' longer-term satisfaction with the development. "One of the best gauges," says council member Gary Ryan, "is the number of sales based on referrals. If developers are close to their projects, they'll get feedback from customers after the sales. Resales are another measuring stick."

Questionnaires or other survey techniques are sometimes helpful. Developers who use specific survey techniques usually employ their own marketing staff for this task. Others have used the services of a private public relations firm or the marketing department of a local university. Using one's own staff demonstrates a more personal commitment and exemplifies the desire to become involved; however, an independent consultant often can conduct a more skilled, professional assessment.

Marketing Rental Housing

Although the tools are largely the same, the techniques for marketing rental housing differ from those for conventional for-sale housing. While developers of for-sale housing can end the marketing campaign shortly after the last house has been sold, the rental developer/owner must constantly merchandise the product to maintain a profitable level of occupancy. Depending on the size of the project and the competitiveness in the market, the marketing program can be a big component of the operating budget.

The overall marketing program for a given community varies, depending on its location and the amount and type of competition. For example, a complex on a busy street that can generate most of its traffic through drive-bys needs a program quite different from a complex situated in a less visible planned unit development.

During the 1980s, competition within the rental market increased considerably, causing many developers to undertake ambitious market programs emphasizing amenities and services like laundry, housekeeping, and telephone answering. Elaborate recreational facilities are also common; swimming

6-19 The design of this combined clubhouse and leasing office was emphasized for the Hacienda Gardens apartments in Pleasanton, California, because it is instrumental in forming a potential tenant's first impression of the community.

The Chase at Wellesley is a 340-unit luxury garden apartment community in the far West End of Richmond, Virginia. Developed by Trammell Crow Residential, the property is situated within the confines of Wellesley, a 365-acre planned residential community, which will ultimately contain over 1,300 houses, 60,000 square feet of retail space, a 15-acre lake, and a tennis stadium. Wellesley is the first master-planned development in Richmond's West End, creating a distinctive market niche for the apartments and the community overall.

The location of Wellesley offers apartment dwellers an ideal residential setting, while still affording convenience to transportation and major employers. Interstate 64, connecting to downtown Richmond, is less than 1.5 miles away, and Innsbrook Corporate Center, an 800-acre multiuse office park, is within two miles. Other nearby employment centers are proliferating, as companies like Circuit City have chosen Richmond's West End to establish new headquarters.

Despite healthy trends in economic development, the feasibility analysis for The Chase at Wellesley was not without questions about the need for additional apartment units. In the early 1980s, Richmond, and particularly the West End, saw little new apartment construction. By the mid-1980s, at the height of tax-exempt bond financing, the volume of permits for apartment buildings rose dramatically. Many of the new communities were built by out-of-town developers, and because all of the apartments entered the market at about the same time and were clustered in a relatively small geographic area, rent increases were limited.

With minor fluctuations, the West End apartment market has remained quite competitive. Thus, the evaluation of The Chase at Wellesley focused on two specific concerns:

1. *The relative distance between Wellesley and existing, closer-in rental communities.* While Wellesley is close to highways, employment, shopping, and other conveniences important to renters, the site is about five miles farther west than most existing apartments, and the question was whether renters might consider Wellesley "too suburban."

2. *The lack of drive-by traffic.* The lifeblood of many apartment sites is their visibility to drive-by traffic. In a planned community,

6-21 An objective of the marketing program for this rental project was to build on the established reputation of the 365-acre Wellesley community where the project is located. The Chase at Wellesley Clubhouse (above) mimics the Victorian architecture of buildings found in Wellesley's town center.

these benefits are often foregone, generating additional marketing expenses for signage, advertising, and other related items. The benefits, however, of being in a planned community are the lifestyle and amenities that a freestanding apartment complex may not be able to provide.

The market strategy focused on understanding these issues as well as on housing supply and demand trends in Richmond's West End.

Market Strategy

The marketing strategy for The Chase at Wellesley comprised a product development component and an advertising and public relations component. Product development first involved identifying the potential market of renters. Good base data were available from Chase Gayton, Trammell Crow's 328-unit rental community developed in 1984 in Richmond. Analysts assumed that the renter profile at ▶

Wellesley would be similar to that at Chase Gayton—primarily young professionals, supplemented by 10 to 15 percent empty nesters or retirees.

Moreover, after analysts studied the unit mix of all existing apartments in the West End, they perceived a niche for a community geared more toward families. The number of three-bedroom apartments in the market was limited, and Wellesley's environment created the perfect setting for families. Further, the school district is one of the best in Richmond. The emphasis on families turned out to be well directed, as the implementation of the federal 1988 Fair Housing Amendments is expected to generate much higher demand from families than has historically been the case.

The profile of renters was expanded to include a small "corporate" element, capitalizing on Wellesley's proximity to major employers in the Innsbrook area. It was estimated that approximately 3 percent of Wellesley's renters might be on short-term business assignments, preferring a more home-like environment and the lower costs of a fully furnished apartment over the impersonal surroundings typical of an extended hotel stay.

With the profile established, the design team developed a product consistent with the perceived needs and desires of the target market. Over a three-month period, the buildings' architectural details were established and the floor plans refined to match expected lifestyles of the renters in each type of unit.

The marketing team worked with the architects and land planners to formulate the appropriate image for The Chase at Wellesley. The thrust of marketing was broadly based to appeal to the entire range of renters without necessarily overemphasizing one particular group. The marketing team helped develop interior designs for the clubhouse and furnished models and a package of media and other events that would draw traffic to Wellesley upon its opening. (The marketing program is described in further detail below.)

Establishing Community Identity

The theme established for The Chase at Wellesley was lakeside living, taking advantage of the 15-acre lake that forms the southern boundary of the property. Only one other community in the West End had a lake, but it was much smaller and therefore considered less of an amenity.

The theme of lakeside living was supplemented by an architectural theme. "Town Center" is the focal point of the overall Wellesley community. It contains all of the recreational amenities plus a clubhouse and administrative buildings. These buildings were designed as Victorian pavilions and served as the model for The Chase at Wellesley's clubhouse, which features barrel-vaulted metal roofs and Palladian windows. Abundant landscaping and seasonal color is used to enhance Wellesley's community identity.

Merchandising and Promotion

Merchandising and promotion for The Chase at Wellesley emphasized the benefits of planned community living and focused on drawing sufficient traffic to the site to meet monthly goals for leasing. With 18 planned neighborhoods and housing in varying price ranges, the master developers of Wellesley implemented a major marketing campaign. Parties, events for realtors, and frequent advertising were all part of the program. Wellesley was

6-22 The marketing brochure conveys the community's theme of "lakeside living." The brochure was designed to appeal to a broad market of young professionals, empty nesters, families, and corporate executives without excluding any particular market segment.

also the site of the 1988 "Homearama," Richmond's annual home show.

Wellesley's marketing program helped The Chase by creating name recognition. The challenge was to capitalize on the name and sell the "Wellesley lifestyle" while overcoming the perception that Wellesley might be too far away for potential renters. The program had to work within two constraints. The first was strict ordinances governing signage imposed by the local jurisdiction, Henrico County. The principal way of drawing traffic to a site that is not easily visible otherwise is to use ample directional signs along major roadways. Although billboards were allowed, other forms of off-site signage were restricted. Equally important, the marketing program had to work within the rules and regulations established by Wellesley homeowners.

Leasing takes place in The Chase at Wellesley's clubhouse. The clubhouse is integrated with the community's amenities so that when renters enter the club, they immediately see the pool, the jacuzzi, the tennis courts, and the lake. This approach helps sell the concept of community. Information about The Chase is displayed throughout the clubhouse, using a site plan, the builder's story, and color-boards. A well-trained and enthusiastic leasing team gives potential renters a brochure featuring the theme of lakeside living.

A comprehensive marketing plan (and budget) was compiled for The Chase at Wellesley, comprised of five key components:

1. *Advertising.* Newspaper advertising in the form of a daily line advertisement and a weekend display advertisement is an ongoing element of the marketing program. Most renters rely heavily on the *Richmond Times-Dispatch* to determine which communities they will visit. The local *Apartment Finder* has also been successful in generating traffic. Issued quarterly, it includes both a full-page color advertisement and a black-and-white property listing prominently displaying The Chase at Wellesley's features. Other advertising sources include *Richmond Surroundings,* a local magazine with wide circulation, *Inside Innsbrook,* distributed for area employees and residents, and *Style,* a weekly newspaper appealing to young professionals.
2. *Direct mail.* Shortly after Wellesley's opening, a direct-mail campaign targeted to renters in other apartments was implemented. The time for the mailing matched the time of year when most local renters move.
3. *Referrals.* Referrals from both residents and realtors are effective leasing tools. Satisfied residents are the best advertising a community can have, and if a property has a good reputation in the marketplace, local realtors active in corporate relocations will also be a fruitful source. Incentive payments reward residents and realtors for their referrals.
4. *Builders' co-op program.* Leasing consultants worked closely with Wellesley builders to provide rental housing in cases where a builder's delivery schedules were delayed or for prospective homebuyers contemplating a move to Wellesley.
5. *Employer/merchant outreach calls.* As an additional initiative, the marketing team visits local employers and merchants in and around Innsbrook weekly to generate interest in Wellesley. Calls to employers are effective for generating short-term corporate leases for furnished rental units.

Beyond these activities, the developer purchased a six-month billboard advertisement to announce the opening of the property. The billboards were located on major commuter routes and, using the bright colors of the brochure, were eye-catching to travelers. The leasing team also works closely with the sales and marketing staff within Wellesley, which has been an excellent source of referrals, especially from the high volume of weekend traffic that visits the Wellesley sales center.

Monitoring and Refinement

Unlike home sales, apartment leasing is ongoing, putting a greater emphasis on marketing to continually generate enough traffic to ensure stabilized leasing. The marketing program for The Chase at Wellesley will also be constantly adapted to meet changing market demands. The leasing team is responsible for monitoring the effectiveness of the marketing program as well as for noting residents' comments on the Wellesley community, floor plans, and other features. A good marketing program has to be thorough and implemented at the outset of leasing but monitored closely to determine its effectiveness.

Source: Information for this case study was provided by ULI council member Richard Michaux with contributions from Dennis Tomsey, Andy Isaacson, John Zwirecki, and Rita Bamberger, all with Trammell Crow Residential.

pools, spas, and weight equipment may be offered to appeal to young professionals. Regular social events, such as "meet your neighbor" parties, have proven to be effective for retaining residents.

Most rental projects over 150 units maintain a permanent, on-site rental office staffed by a full-time leasing agent who might also serve as the resident manager. Since the early 1980s, it is increasingly common for the permanent rental office to be located in a community clubhouse or recreation center building. This location allows prospective tenants to see the project's primary amenities when they visit the rental office. Often, a project's recreational and service features are as important to a resident's decision as the actual unit.

Apartment complexes over 200 units usually maintain at least one decorated model unit. For convenience, this unit should usually be located next to or near the rental office. In decorating the model unit, developers are advised to stick to standard features and furnishings. Tasteful furnishings professionally selected to appeal to the target market are a competitive necessity in most of today's larger apartment complexes. The unit should not include any built-in features or fancy wall and window treatments that would not be available to tenants.

The rental office should contain brochures describing the community's features. Floor plans for each unit type and a list of services and amenities available to tenants are important. The brochure may provide a space for a price list and possibly a site plan for the community.

Advertising is again an important part of a marketing program. Newspaper classifieds are typically the most effective and cost-efficient media, as they are where most prospective tenants start looking for apartments. Apartment guides produced in most local markets are also an effective source of generating traffic. For large projects, radio advertising may be successful in reaching a large number of prospects within a specific market segment; however, the effectiveness of radio is difficult to pinpoint. A radio advertising campaign should be considered most seriously during initial leasing to announce a grand opening or just to familiarize the public with the project's name and location.

During initial leasing, developers might need to consider special incentives to attract tenants—especially in highly competitive markets. Such incentives may involve concessions from the developer, such as offering new tenants free rent for the first month of the lease. Developers need to carefully evaluate the market, and if absorption is expected to be slow, it may be advantageous to make such concessions to shorten the leasing period.

Once the units have been leased initially, the next step is to maintain high occupancy levels. The key to meeting this objective is most often management and maintenance. If buildings, landscaping, and amenities are not maintained adequately and if repairs are not made promptly, vacancy levels are likely to increase. Supervision and funding of maintenance should be top priority, and most complaints should be handled within 24 hours. Resident managers should be skilled in supervising maintenance activities, for they are often the link between tenants and the maintenance staff.

Developers of rental housing should make special efforts to measure tenants' level of acceptance for a project and its management and maintenance. A high level of acceptance almost always translates into low turnover and stable occupancy levels. Further, measuring tenants' acceptance will help rental developers structure future projects for best positioning in the market. Council member Richard Michaux shares the following techniques used by Trammell Crow Company to get feedback and levels of acceptance from tenants:

- *Face-to-face contact.* Resident managers and leasing agents should keep notes of tenants' comments during casual contacts—when they drop off rent checks or at parties, for example.
- *Warm calls.* Generally 90 days before a lease is due to expire, the resident manager or another representative of the developer should knock on the tenant's door to check his or her level of satisfaction and to learn what the tenant likes or dislikes about the community.
- *Questionnaires.* Developers should consider sending questionnaires to tenants shortly after they move in and move out of a project.
- *Focus groups.* About 90 days after a project is completed, a focus group comprised of new tenants might be considered to learn how different demographic groups react to the project and why they chose the project over the competition. Information learned from the focus group can identify changes needed to both the physical plant and the management and is also helpful in planning new projects. (Trammell Crow's experience is that about one-third of those invited attend, and free gifts should be offered as an incentive to increase attendance.)
- *Open lines of communication.* A phone number where tenants can call to offer comments or ask questions may be displayed at some convenient location in the unit. If the developer's office is located outside the calling area, a toll-free number should be provided.

In large projects, tenant committees or associations can be formed to keep tenants informed of problems or changes in management policies. They should function as forums to address and solve minor problems before they become major ones. In both large and small projects, however, the key to successful marketing of rental housing lies in on-site management. In fact, on-site management is any apartment development's strongest amenity.

Marketing Large Communities

Not all residential developments involve small subdivisions that can be built and sold over one to two years. Increasingly, residential communities are comprised of multiple housing products—detached houses, townhouses, multifamily apartments, and condominiums—that may be built by several builders. In such cases, the master developer must assume responsibility for developing and implementing the communitywide marketing strategy, while individual builders implement separate (but compatible) strategies for selling specific products.

In some markets, particularly in the Sunbelt, it is not uncommon for planned communities to encompass 1,000 or more acres and require over 20 years to complete. Because long-term projects require substantial up-front costs and carry potentially large financial risks, a well-planned and aggressive marketing campaign is essential. A key element of this campaign is to establish a community identity or theme that appeals to the target market and then promote that theme through on-site merchandising and off-site advertising. Developers should also remember that today's buyers are not just interested in buying a house: with their decision to purchase a unit, they are investing in a community that represents their self-image and lifestyle. The marketing strategy must be able to convey the right messages about the community to the identified market.

Most large-scale communities are marketed from a permanent sales office constructed by the master developer, and the sales building (or "sales pavilion") is later turned over to the community association for a community clubhouse. The sales building must be designed to function well for both uses, and the developer must remember that the life of the building will extend many years after sales are completed.

The design of the sales building should convey the community's image and lifestyle; its architecture and proximity to amenities are typically important considerations. Functional qualities—parking and access from adjacent thoroughfares, for example—are also important. A highly visible location at the entrance to the community is usually preferred.

In most cases, the sales center's purpose is not to sell houses but to sell the community itself. Communitywide features—recreation, schools, pedestrian systems, the convenient location—are emphasized. The center should feature photographs, videos, models, maps, storyboards, and other techniques to convey positive information about the developer and the community. The sales staff should distribute promotional materials and help prospects identify particular housing developments that best meet their lifestyle and budget, helping them to narrow the range of choices and directing them to model complexes and the project's sales office for more information.

Marketing budgets for large-scale communities vary considerably between regions. As a guideline, a master developer should plan to spend about 6 percent of the total lot sales to builders on marketing. About half of this amount is generally considered the builder's contribution to cover the costs of media and promotional materials. The developer contributes the remaining half to cover the costs of the community sales office and on-site merchandising.

Because of the long-term nature of large projects, the community developer must continually monitor and refine the marketing strategy. It is common for the market at the beginning of the project to be substantially different from the market at the end of the project, and developers should document these changes through surveys of buyers, focus groups, telephone surveys, and other techniques to analyze the market. As new information about the market becomes available, the merchandising and advertising campaigns will likely need to be refined.

Construction Warranties

The construction of new houses has traditionally been backed first and foremost by the builder's or developer's reputation and willingness to make good on defects in materials or workmanship for a reasonable period of time after a unit has been sold. Until recently, the conventional practice was for a builder or developer simply to provide the purchaser of a new house with a gentleman's agreement to repair or replace any defects identified before the closing of the sale and to guarantee to repair for one year any structural defects in material and workmanship. Because this informal type of warranty was regularly supplemented by product manufacturers' warranties and guarantees, builders and developers frequently advertised the brand names of installed appliances and equipment when the product manufacturers' reputation for quality and performance could enhance the builder's or developer's warranty of the total unit.

To protect their reputation, responsible developers often corrected defects in materials and workmanship well beyond the conventional one-year limitation.[6] In contrast, developers with little stake in the community, a shaky financial structure, or limited financial reserves might have abrogated any responsibility to meet the warranty—or might already have gone out of business before the warranty expired—leaving the buyer to correct defects with little recourse for recovering the costs of repair or replacement. Units built under FHA or VA mortgage guarantee programs provided homebuyers with some additional protection, because the builder or developer had to conform with minimum property standards issued by the U.S. Department of Housing and Urban Development. Where applicable, local building inspections also provided homebuyers with some additional protection by certifying adherence to an acceptable quality of workmanship and conformance with requirements of the building code.

The residential development industry was badly hurt by the irresponsible actions of a few builders and developers, frustrating responsible ones. To remedy the situation, the National Association of Home Builders (NAHB) established the Home Owners Warranty (HOW) program in 1973 as the nation's first comprehensive protection plan for the construction of new houses. The program was modeled after the highly successful homebuyer protection plan of the British National House-Builders Registration Council (NHBRC), started in 1936. Over 99 percent of all builders and developers in Great Britain are registered with NHBRC and participate in the 10-year protection program for new houses by offering two-year warranty protection against major structural defects, backed by insurance coverage arranged by NHBRC. NAHB set up a subsidiary corporation, the Home Owners Warranty Corporation, to develop and administer a national warranty program in 1974, and in 1981 this corporation became an independent builder/member-owned company.[7]

Although the HOW program is today the most visible and widely recognized warranty program, several other private warranty programs and several government-sponsored warranty programs offer nearly identical coverage. The standard warranty program for new houses offers 10 years of coverage against structural defects (faults in load-bearing elements that support the weight of the house), two years of coverage on mechanical systems (plumbing, heat-

ing, electrical), and one year of coverage on materials and workmanship.[8] A developer's decision whether or not to participate in a warranty program should take into account local and regional market conditions, state and local warranty laws, and the increased potential for class action lawsuits when community associations are involved.[9]

A survey in 1986 found that over 90 percent of prospective homebuyers considered warranties important.[10] Prospective homebuyers have been advised to be more concerned about obtaining insured warranties in areas where soil conditions are likely to be unstable and in areas that lack tight regulation and enforcement of codes.[11] The age of consumerism has clearly arrived in real estate sales, and although responsible developers with a long-term stake in a community have always stood behind their developments and their products, organized warranty programs serve to protect responsible developers from complaints against irresponsible ones.

Private Warranty Plans

The Home Owners Warranty Corporation is currently the largest issuer of insured warranties for new houses. More than 2 million new houses throughout the country have been covered by HOW builders since the program was started in 1973, and the corporation currently has more than 13,000 builder/members. HOW operates like a mutual insurance company, screening members for technical competence, good customer relations, and financial stability.[12] It currently charges builders approximately 0.33 percent of the point-of-sale price when a single payment is made, which translates into a fee of approximately $375 for a $100,000 unit. Volume builders are eligible for significantly reduced charges.

Under the terms of the plan, builders retain responsibility for repairs to the house for the first two years.

---

[6] David D. Bohannon, past president of ULI and long-time builder/developer in California, cites an example of his firm's offering to buy back several houses it had built. Undetected soil conditions had resulted in settlement problems that could not be corrected. From the developer's viewpoint, his reputation required this rather drastic and costly extension of the warranty, even though it was well beyond his obligation under the terms of sale.

[7] The Home Owners Warranty Corporation's current address is 1110 North Glebe Road, Arlington, Virginia 22201.

[8] Peter M. Kendall, "Home Warranties," Sylvia Porter's Personal Finance, June 1987, p. 94.

[9] Joseph M. Cahn, "Developer v. Condo Association," Real Estate Today, April 1987, pp. 58–59.

[10] Kendall, "Home Warranties," p. 94.

[11] "Talking Warranties: When Is It Wise to Get One on a New Home?" New York Times, July 17, 1988.

[12] Kendall, "Home Warranties," p. 94.

During the first year, builders warrant the house to be free from all defects in materials and workmanship, in compliance with the program's approved standards. During the second year, builders continue to warrant against major structural defects and against defects in wiring, piping, and ductwork in the house's major systems. During this initial two-year period, builders carry insurance on the warranty. HOW administers the arbitration of disputes at no cost to the homeowner and provides that if builders fail to perform the work deemed to be their responsibility under the process for settling disputes within the time specified, HOW will take over and get the job done.[13] Complaints between builders and buyers are resolved first by negotiation between the parties, with unresolved issues decided by a neutral third party. Claims paid through the warranty company carry a $250 deductible. During the third through tenth years, HOW's insurance plan protects against the cost to repair major structural defects. The protection plan continues uninterrupted, regardless of subsequent resale of the house.

HOW's closest competitor is the Home Buyers Warranty Corporation (HBW). Like HOW, HBW requires that homeowners first take complaints to the builder before turning to arbitration. HBW also imposes a $200 deductible on nonstructural claims in cases where the warranty company, as opposed to the original builder, must pay on a claim. HBW imposes no deductible on structural claims.[14] The third major private warranty program is the Residential Warranty Corporation (RWC). In addition to these three plans, several regional or state-based private plans currently operate in Texas and Florida.[15]

Developers and builders participating in approved private warranty plans may be eligible to have certain requirements waived for inclusion in VA, FHA, and FmHA loan programs. The waived requirements can include relief from certain inspections, reducing paperwork, delays, and red tape. The agencies retain the right to require the inspections, either for individual developers or within specific geographic areas. Currently, all three major private warranty plans have relatively the same relationships with FHA, VA, and FmHA programs.

Warranty Laws

Many states have very general, implied warranty laws that are subject to interpretation, leaving it to the courts to determine what is implied to be warranted and thereby exposing homebuilders and developers to liability of uncertain scope and duration.[16] For example, California courts have ruled that builders

and developers of residential housing implicitly warrant that their products are constructed in a good, workmanlike manner and are of "merchantable quality"—that is, that they meet commonly accepted community standards for such properties. In states where this interpretation of the law has evolved the most, proof of negligence or guilt is not necessary for attaching responsibility to the developer or builder for common defects in construction, such as roof and basement leaks, soil subsidence, structural failures, and plumbing and electrical failures.[17]

In response to state builders' associations' seeking to clarify and limit their exposure to open-ended liability, both Indiana and New York have enacted legislation that allows implied warranties to be waived when a builder offers and the consumer accepts an expressed limited warranty.[18] In Indiana, this legislation requires builders to warrant more than would be warranted under standard private plan coverage, including HOW. In New York, the legislation allows the implied warranty to be waived if an approved insurance-backed warranty, such as HOW, is offered.

New Jersey is currently the only state that has a mandatory insured warranty law for construction of new houses.[19] New Jersey also enacted a 10-year warranty plan for new houses with its New Home Warranty and Builder's Registration Act of 1977. State regulations issued in 1979 require that individuals engaged in the construction of new houses be registered with the New Jersey Department of Community Affairs before obtaining a building permit for any new house. The regulations also require builders to participate in either an approved private warranty plan or the state's warranty plan before obtaining a certificate of occupancy for a new house. HOW is one of five private warranty plans currently licensed with the state of New Jersey. At the local level, a few counties and municipalities in states other than New Jersey, including New Castle County in Delaware and Montgomery County in Maryland, have enacted mandatory warranty requirements for the construction of new houses.

[13] Ibid.

[14] Ibid.

[15] Telephone conversation with Richard Biel, Home Owners Warranty Corporation, March 17, 1989.

[16] Ibid.

[17] Cahn, "Developer v. Condo Association," p. 58.

[18] Telephone conversation with Richard Biel, Home Owners Warranty Corporation, March 17, 1989.

[19] Ibid.

MARKETING MASTER-PLANNED COMMUNITIES:
SULLY STATION—FAIRFAX COUNTY, VIRGINIA

Sully Station, a 1,200-acre master-planned community of over 3,200 residences, exemplifies a successful marketing program undertaken for a large-scale planned community. The project includes single-family houses, townhouses, multifamily apartments, nearly 700 housing units for the elderly, and 70 customized estates located on five- to 10-acre lots. Community facilities include two schools, four child care facilities, one church, and about 400,000 square feet of commercial and retail space. Recreational amenities include two clubhouses, two swimming pools, tennis courts, jogging trails, tot lots, and 305 acres of open space and parks. Working with eleven homebuilders, the master developer, Kettler & Scott, Inc., opened the estimated seven-year project in 1986.

Located about 25 miles west of Washington, D.C., Sully Station is bordered by a regional park on the south, a golf course and country club on the west, and Westfields, a 20 million-square-foot corporate office campus, on the north. The community lies about seven miles south of Dulles International Airport in an area of strong commercial growth.

During the early 1980s, commercial development in the Dulles Airport area outpaced residential construction. Kettler & Scott's president, Robert C. Kettler, recognized an opportunity for development and began a major assembly of nearly 45 parcels that over the coming years could be rezoned for a new master-planned residential community. Several hurdles had to be overcome, however:

6-24, 6-25   The brickwork, intricate roofline, and welcoming arches of the community clubhouse and sales office (top) create a memorable building that serves as the visual symbol for Sully Station. The clubhouse inspired the project's logo used in all advertising and promotional materials (bottom).

- *No proven market.* At the time land was assembled, the market area was comprised of some existing small subdivisions built in the 1950s and 1960s interspersed with small non-working farms. Additionally, a few new subdivisions developed in the early 1980s failed as a result of high interest rates at the time and the location, which was considered to be on the edge of the metropolitan area. A strong marketing campaign would be essential to attract buyers to this fringe location, particularly during the early phases of the project.
- *No direct access.* Although well located next to major transportation corridors, Sully Station had no direct entrance from a major highway; in essence, the site had no obvious front door. Potential homebuyers would have to reach the community through the adjacent office park, Westfields.
- *Increasing competition.* Other developers also recognized the long-term market potential around Dulles airport and began assembling land; none would be as large and offer the same array of community facilities as Sully Station, however. The marketing plan needed to position Sully Station as the market area's premier planned community to first create the market and, second, to continue the lead over smaller communities scheduled to come on line within about a year of Sully Station's opening.

The marketing team's strategy confronted these primary issues.

The Marketing Strategy

The marketing strategy for Sully Station encompassed several tasks: 1) establishing an identity for the community that could be expressed in the project's design and reinforced through promotional materials and on-site merchandising; 2) developing an advertising campaign for carefully selected media; and 3) providing mechanisms for refining and monitoring the marketing strategy to keep pace with changing market conditions. The developer's in-house vice president for marketing oversaw the marketing strategy, which was drafted and implemented by consulting advertising agencies. An early market analysis projected that Sully Station's target market would be 25 to 45 with an annual income of $60,000 plus, largely young professional couples, many with young families. The marketing team knew it also had to attract a number of move-up and first-time buyers to meet objectives for sales.

Research conducted by Housing Research Reports, a local market research firm, qualified what the target market wanted: the beauty and friendly environment of an idealized neighborhood and "a good place to raise a family." Buyers wanted the comprehensive amenities and long-term security of a master-planned community (nearby Reston had helped establish this value in the market). An image of good neighbors, pretty streets, happy children, and a successful community had to be sent out to prospective buyers.

But the marketing strategy could not sell houses unless the community really offered the lifestyle it claimed. With information gleaned from the market analysis, project planners provided for a mix of product types and prices to appeal to a range of incomes. The project's amenities were selected and located, and the plan was tied together with a series of open spaces, parks, and jogging trails. In short, the master plan was designed to reflect the tastes and lifestyles characteristic of its primary market, young suburban professionals.

Establishing Community Identity

The first marketing task was to establish a theme for the community. The project is located near the Sully Civil War–era railroad stop and just off the present-day Route 28 transportation corridor, known locally as Sully Road. The theme that developed takes advantage of both historical and modern reference points. Research confirmed that in both England and America during the late 19th century, the village train station served as the visual front door to the community. Kettler & Scott decided to follow this nostalgic theme by designing the 4,200-square-foot community clubhouse and the nearby 200,000-square-foot shopping center with a train station motif and by locating them at the project's main entrance. In fact, the facade of the clubhouse became the project's logo, used in all advertising and print material. When prospective buyers see the clubhouse, they know they have arrived at Sully Station.

Merchandising and Promotion

With the target market, the master plan, and the community's identity in place, the next task was to merchandise the community and its various housing products. The perceived problem of having no direct access to the heavily traveled Route 28 corridor needed to be overcome. Kettler & Scott worked closely with neighboring Westfields's commercial developer to coordinate the treatment of entrances and streetscapes. The effort resulted in the appearance that both the office and residential communities were one, thereby creating the feel of a mixed-use development. Although Sully Station has no permanent signage on Route 28, temporary but attractive directional signs advise prospective buyers where to turn. The lack of permanent signage did not prove to be a problem.

In the early stages of development, Kettler & Scott made another important merchandising decision: community infrastructure and recreational facilities should be built in advance of actual need to give the community a more finished look when it opened and to alleviate any concerns of buyers about unfulfilled promises from the developer. This decision entailed increased financial risk, but the developer believed it would result ultimately in faster absorption and decreased carrying costs. Thus, roads were paved, landscaping along major roadways planted, key recreation facilities built, and the community clubhouse under construction when the first model homes opened. Model homes were deliberately sited to create the first completed houses on prominent streets. The merchandising strategy was to make Sully Station look successful and thriving from the day it opened.

Sully Station is merchandised through a sales center located in the main clubhouse. The clubhouse, surrounded by recreation facilities, includ-

▶

ing a pool and tennis courts, eventually will be turned over to the homeowners' association. In the sales center, prospective buyers learn about the amenities, facilities, and housing products available in the community. A brochure gives prospects basic information and an illustrative master plan

6-26, 6-27, 6-28, 6-29   Before the preview public opening, a unified system of signs, each featuring the community logo, was installed. The temporary signs included A) an off-site directional sign, B), C) on-site directional signs, and D) a builder/product identification sign.

6-30 The interior design of the community clubhouse follows the train station motif. The upper floor, entered at grade, is patterned after a 19th century manor hall and provides a spacious community sales and information center.

map they can take home. Trained sales staff are on hand to discuss the merits of the community and to answer questions.

Individual housing products are not marketed directly out of the sales center; each builder maintains a separate sales office in its complex of model homes. Kettler & Scott coordinates with each builder its individual marketing program to ensure that a consistent message is conveyed about Sully Station and the lifestyle it offers.

Advertising

Sully Station was introduced to the public through a teaser advertising campaign. A sequential three-week series of newspaper advertisements with "Get Ready," "Get Set," and "Go" headlines led up to a preview public opening. Before the preview opening, a handsome sales park of landscaped and facaded trailers was created for visitors and builders, the site's roads, grounds, and pathways were cleaned up, and a coordinated system of informative signage was put in place identifying amenities, homesites, and public areas.

Following the preview opening, an advertising campaign that told buyers "Your Timing Is Perfect" ran for 13 weeks and drew nearly 3,000 prospects. Homebuilders, operating without finished models and with the highest prices in the area, sold 79 units, which Kettler & Scott considered to be above the average in Fairfax County for comparable planned communities.

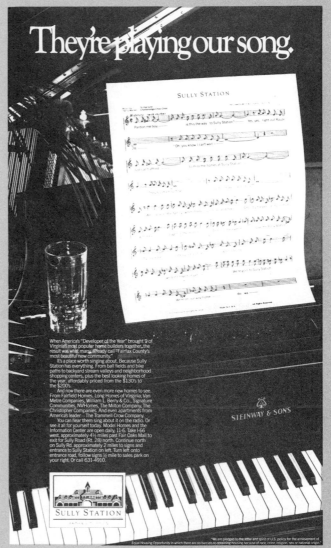

6-31 A print advertisement that accompanied the *Chattanooga Choo-Choo* radio jingle.

As expected, other residential communities opened nearby within the following year, competing heavily with Sully Station, many with "me too" messages. It was time to freshen the image, raise the public's awareness, and direct new attention to Sully Station. To do so, a jingle was created for radio, using the music of *Chattanooga Choo-Choo* and giving it new words about Sully Station. The entire message was sung; no announcer cut in to extol the community or give directions. The idea was to take a familiar, memorable song and make Sully Station the same. A companion newspaper campaign simply replayed the lyrics.

The next major advertising campaign took a different approach. Informal surveys conducted by the

▶

community sales staff revealed that prospective buyers walked through the door with three primary concerns about the project and its location: commuting, convenience, and opportunities for recreation and leisure. The concept was to address these concerns through children living in Sully Station; the advertisements portrayed the children as the most satisfied customers of all. The "kids as spokesmen" campaign effectively maintained traffic from prospects and the pace of sales and received a national advertising award.

Monitoring and Refinement

By the third year of sales, an entirely new advertising and promotion strategy was needed to reinforce the position of Sully Station as an upscale community. Surveys of buyers had shown that the market was becoming more affluent with the growth of high-paying jobs in the market area. Two additional phases had been opened, and the builders were ready to introduce new products.

Detailed data on every buyer had been maintained from the start of sales, and by this time the developer had recorded enough sales and data to accomplish highly accurate buyer profiles with which to fine-tune the marketing strategy. Using a research practice know as VALS, an empirically based system developed at Stanford Research Institute (Palo Alto, California) for segmenting people into groups based on their values and lifestyles, Kettler & Scott found that 80 percent of their market

SullyStation residents love to talk about their neighborhood:

"The bike paths are great. We can go everywhere!"

Sully Station has been Northern Virginia's favorite new community from the day it opened. A beautiful, established neighborhood covering 2 square miles, stretching from Sully Road south to Lee Highway, it is bordered by the golf course on the north, and vast public parklands

IT'S ALL RIGHT HERE IN THE NEIGHBORHOOD.

on the south and west.
"It's right here in the neighborhood" is a familiar comment for Sully Station residents, because they have their own shopping centers, schools, swim clubs, tennis courts, community centers and ballfields, more than 12 miles of biking and jogging paths, and nearly 300 acres of their own parks, playgrounds and open spaces.

In its first year, Sully Station was named "Community of the Year" by area homebuilders. Today, eleven of them are building their finest townhomes and single family homes here for this year's new residents.

31 DIFFERENT TOWNHOMES AND HOUSES FROM 11 GREAT BUILDERS FROM THE $150's TO THE $300's.

The new Visitor Center and model homes are open 12-6 daily. Take I-66 west past Fair Oaks Mall to exit for Sully Rd. (Rt. 28) north. Up Sully Rd. 2 miles to entrance on left. Follow into Sully Station to Visitor Center signs. Or call 631-4910.

"I like to fish in the park. Once I saw a deer."

"I can walk to my school and the playground by my house."

"Our daddy meets us at the swimming club when he gets home from work."

SULLY STATION

A Kettler & Scott Community.

A Sully Station resident talks about commuting:

Sully Station has been Northern Virginia's favorite new community from the day it opened. A beautiful, established neighborhood covering 2 square miles, stretching from Sully Road south to Lee Highway, it is bordered by the golf course on the north, and vast public

31 DIFFERENT TOWNHOMES AND HOUSES FROM 12 GREAT BUILDERS, FROM THE $140's, TO THE $220's.

parklands on the south and west.
"It's right here in the neighborhood" is a familiar comment for Sully Station residents, because they have their own shopping centers, schools, swim clubs, tennis courts, community centers and ballfields, more than 12 miles of biking and jogging paths, and nearly 300 acres of their own parks, playgrounds and open spaces.

In its first year, Sully Station was named "Community of the Year" by area homebuilders. Today, eleven of them are building their finest townhomes and single family homes here for this year's new residents.

The new Visitor Center and model homes are open 12-6 daily. Take I-66 west past Fair

IT'S ALL RIGHT HERE IN THE NEIGHBORHOOD.

Oaks Mall to exit for Sully Rd. (Rt. 28) north. Up Sully Rd. 2 miles to entrance on left. Follow into Sully Station to Visitor Center signs. Or call 631-4910.

*"Getting to school on my own is easy, 'cause there are bike paths all over our neighborhood. My mom also lets me ride to the store for her, since the shopping center is just up the street. And when I go to the pool or Bobby's house, I can even walk by myself.
My mom says she likes that everything is right here, so she doesn't have to drive me everywhere, and she can meet her friends at the tennis club. My dad even uses the jogging path by our house once in a while, but mainly he just rides the Metro to work.
I guess we're all glad we moved to Sully Station."*

SULLY STATION

A Kettler & Scott Community.

6-32, 6-33   Examples of the "kids as spokesmen" advertising campaign.

TIME STOPS AT SULLY STATION.

Underwhelmed by the overpromise of suburban living? Take heart. A better way of life waits at Sully Station.

As you enter the community, you're greeted by a lovely train station in an architectural style from the English countryside. This welcome taste of the 19th century is Sully Station's answer to the shopping center.

An award-winning community center follows the same, appealing motif. Neighborhood recreation centers are thoughtfully designed, situated harmoniously with parks, jogging trails, swim clubs and tennis courts. Beautiful new schools and day care facilities are on the way.

Little wonder that Sully Station has been chosen Community of the Year by Washington Area Homebuilders.

Townhomes and single-family homes are priced from $150,000 to $300,000, Sully Estates above $500,000. Call (703) 631-4910 for details. Models and the Visitor Center are open daily, noon to 6. To find them, take I-66 to Exit 28 North, proceed 2 miles, then turn left onto Westfield Blvd.

Take the time to stop at Sully Station. Time will stop for you.

SULLY STATION
BY KETTLER & SCOTT

6-34 This advertisement was designed to appeal to "achievers" by promising that Sully Station is different from other suburban communities.

fell within two groups: achievers and the socially conscious. The research helped to better target the advertising copy and graphics in new advertisements. For example, the "Sometimes It's Better to Live in the Past" advertisement appealed to the socially conscious, who were more directed toward tradition and harmony with nature. The "Time Stops at Sully Station" advertisement promised achievers that Sully Station has more to offer than suburban living and addressed the benefits of the award-winning community. The graphics for both advertisements were reproductions of famous paintings to convey a classic and upscale look.

The advertisements were run in the traditional media, such as the *Washington Post* and the area's *New Homes Guide,* which is targeted at residential homebuyers and brokers for immediate impact. The campaign also ran in upscale consumer magazines to generate awareness, build image, and extend reach; they included the D.C. edition of *Time* magazine, *National Geographic, Washingtonian,* and

the program for the Wolf Trap Center for the Performing Arts.

The advertising campaign provides for continual monitoring to understand the impact of the marketing program and to learn how Kettler & Scott is perceived compared to the competition. A survey of a random sample of the target market after about four years of sales revealed that 80 percent of the interviewees were aware of Sully station and that 56 percent had visited the community. As a result of the aggressive marketing and advertising program, the right people learned about Sully Station.

Source: Information for this case study was provided by Kettler & Scott, Vienna, Virginia. For additional information on Sully Station, see *Project Reference File:* "Sully Station," vol. 19, no. 6 (Washington, D.C.: ULI–the Urban Land Institute, April–June 1989).

7.
Community Governance

What happens after a development is completed? It is one of the most important questions residential developers must ask themselves before they initiate a development. Underlying the concept of good land use and development should be a concern for the proper long-term care and maintenance of the land and the development on that land.

Developers' responsibilities for stewardship should be constantly in mind during conception, implementation, and completion of a residential development. This concern shows itself in such matters as the developer's application of planning principles that respond to the distinct characteristics of the site. But just as important is the creation of a proper set of mechanisms providing for the community's governance and long-term maintenance of the development.

The stewardship of land takes many forms. The simplest is developers' general attitude and concern for maintaining the integrity of the design and the community's amenities. This form of stewardship is neither mandated by law nor ensured by creation of institutions but by the good will and concern of developers and their desire to build and maintain a reputation for excellence in the community. A more formal mechanism for the maintenance of the development is the creation of an organization that can assume responsibility for governance, maintenance, and provision of services necessary to the develop-

ment. Such organizations are generally grouped under the category of "community associations." The association's power is guaranteed by its legal documents, most often taking the form of a declaration of covenants, conditions, and restrictions (CC&Rs), which augment the municipal exercise of police power (zoning).

The association forms the base of governance that preserves the architectural integrity, maintains the common open space, and protects the development's property values. But an effective association does not emerge as a matter of course. Council member Ronald C. Nahas notes, "Homeowners' [community] associations are governments, born of the developer and nurtured by the developer. Once released of the developer's control and weaned of its subsidies, many associations have difficulty coping with the responsibilities thrust upon them. These difficulties may be the result of [the developer's] oversights or carelessness, but often they are the result of the inadequate management capabilities of board members due to a lack of experience."[1] The residential developer's role extends beyond good structuring of the association's legal documents; it encompasses education throughout the development's phasing to ensure that the

---

[1] Ronald C. Nahas, "Developer on the Defensive: Reflections on Developer/Association Conflicts," *Common Ground: The Journal of the Community Associations Institute,* May/June 1986, p. 17.

owners will be equipped to carry on the association's administrative duties.

Very often, the creation of a community association makes possible shared recreational and other facilities that might not otherwise be available or affordable to the owners. The industry has coined the term "common interest communities," which means owners share interests *in common* with other property owners in the community. But these interests often go beyond real property; they are often social, psychological, and political as well. According to council member Wayne S. Hyatt, "A common interest community is a community that is tied together with a strong common interest.... It is a community in which...interests [are shared with]...a cohesiveness that comes not only from a legal structure but also from sharing."[2]

A well-conceived program for community governance and maintenance can be a strong selling feature for a new residential community. Prospective property owners will be interested in preserving the quality of the neighborhood while they live there and in the potential appreciation of property values that can accrue to a well-planned and -maintained community. Thus, a single handbook for buyers that explains the community association and CC&Rs in simple terms can be an effective part of the development's promotional materials.

This chapter presents some of the most important issues that a residential developer must consider before starting a new development. It cannot be overstated that, because each development is different and because laws vary from state to state, the structure of the community association and the contents of CC&Rs must be tailored to the specific development. Set formulas or model documents that can be universally applied do not lend themselves well to this issue. Residential developers should surround themselves with the appropriate professionals—legal counsel, property manager, land planner, community association planner—before attempting to establish the association.

Community Associations: An Overview

When a developer creates a for-sale residential development project, maintenance of community-owned property becomes the shared responsibility of the community's property owners—including the developer. The community association, a generic term used to describe all forms of common interest associations, provides the process of governance required for main-

7-1 SERVICES FREQUENTLY OFFERED BY COMMUNITY ASSOCIATIONS

SERVICE	PERCENT OF ASSOCIATIONS PROVIDING
Landscape/Maintenance of Common Areas	94%
Painting and Exterior Building Maintenance	82
Offstreet Parking Area Maintenance	79
Waste/Trash Removal	74
Water and Sewer Facilities and Services	68
Private Street Maintenance and Replacement	62
Sidewalk Maintenance and Replacement	59
Exterior Street Lighting	56
Security Service/Protection (Passive)	39
Security Service/Protection (Active)	33

Source: CAI and the Advisory Commission on Intergovernmental Relations Survey, 1988. *Community Associations Factbook* (Alexandria, Va.: Community Associations Insitute, 1988), p. 10. Reprinted with permission.

taining community-owned property and enforcing CC&Rs. By definition, membership in a common interest community is automatic: the purchaser of a house or lot in a community association development automatically becomes a member of the community association. Thus, the community association is distinguished from a voluntary, civic, or club type of association by the provision for mandatory membership that is part of the owner's deed.[3]

Community associations under various names have existed since at least 1844, when an automatic homeowners' association was created for Louisburg Square in Boston.[4] This project—28 lots surrounding three sides of a commonly owned park square—was begun in 1826, but the recognized need for some mechanism to maintain the open space did not result in the establishment of the association until 1844.

While numerous other early examples exist, the major growth of community associations began to

---

[2] Wayne S. Hyatt, *Condominium and Homeowners' Associations: A Guide to the Development Process* (Colorado Springs: Shepard's/McGraw-Hill, 1985), p. 5.

[3] C. James Dowden, *Creating a Community Association: The Developer's Role in Condominium and Homeowners' Associations,* 2d rev. ed. (Washington, D.C./Alexandria, Va.: ULI–the Urban Land Institute and CAI–Community Associations Institute, 1986), p. 1.

[4] Ibid., pp. 2–3.

7-2　Maintenance of common area landscaping and recreational facilities like this pool area is the service most frequently provided by a community association.

occur in tandem with the growth of planned unit developments, where the inclusion of commonly owned facilities required creation of an organization for ownership, maintenance, and operation. This type of development began to appear frequently in the late 1950s and early 1960s in the form of subdivisions of single-family detached units with common open space. In the late 1960s and 1970s followed the surge of townhouse projects and new adaptations of the duplex, fourplex, and other attached housing on its own lot. At the same time, the condominium form of ownership became widely accepted, making possible the individual sale of dwelling units ranging in design from single-family detached units to units in high-rise towers.[5]

By the 1970s, it became clear that the continued acceptance of these concepts of land planning was in jeopardy because of widespread deficiencies in the effective application of the concept of community associations. Setting aside significant amounts of land as commonly owned open space and including

a wide variety of recreational amenities led to the creation of many new associations each year. Developers needed guidance in setting up community associations, and the community associations needed a continuing source of guidance and professional management after the developer was no longer involved in the project.

In response to these needs, the Community Associations Institute (CAI) was formed in 1973 with the support of the Urban Land Institute, the National Association of Home Builders, and the U.S. League of Savings Associations. CAI's purpose is to develop and distribute guidance on homeowners' associations and their shared facilities in condominiums, cluster hous-

[5] A good history of community associations and their application to a variety of residential developments can be found in Marc A. Weiss and John W. Watts, "Community Builders and Community Associations: The Role of Real Estate Developers in Private Residential Government," Working Paper No. 22 (Cambridge, Mass.: MIT Center for Real Estate Development, July 1989).

7-3, 7-4 Common areas can be in the form of natural open space, greenspace, or private parks, and may include entrance features, landscaped medians in roadways, drainage features, water features such as lakes or ponds, or recreation facilities.

ing, planned unit developments, and open space communities. CAI is an independent, nonprofit research and educational organization, and membership in CAI is open to associations and their members, builders/developers, managers, public agencies and officials, professionals, and other interested individuals and organizations. Because the field of management and operation of community associations is evolving constantly, this discussion of community associations is limited to a general understanding of the associations' role in residential development and some broad concerns that developers should consider. (For a more detailed understanding of this subject, residential developers are encouraged to contact CAI and investigate the many publications available though that association: CAI—Community Association Institute, 1423 Powhatan Street, Suite 7, Alexandria, Virginia 22314, (703) 548-8600.)

In addition to maintaining community-owned open space and recreational amenities, community associations frequently carry on many "public" functions and activities, including road maintenance, outdoor lighting, trash removal, and guard service. Although these activities reduce the burden placed on the public sector, property owners living within community associations often also pay local government property taxes that, in the absence of a community association, would pay for similar services.[6] In recent years, many local governments have begun to require the formation of community associations, in part to offset requirements for and costs of municipal services.

The need to create a community association largely depends on a project's design. The need is certain if recreational amenities are to be owned and operated as private clubs or if open space parcels cannot be deeded to a governmental entity or a private entity, such as a land trust. As council member Judith Reagan points out, however, "The amount of open space and amenities, the density, or the size of a project is not always a determining factor in whether a community association is necessary. The developer instead should consider how the community will operate over the long term. And community associations are essential whenever CC&Rs are placed on a development."[7]

To determine whether a community association is necessary, council member Wayne S. Hyatt offers this advice: "Three key words in determining whether or not a community association is needed in a particular project are maintenance, preservation, and sharing."[8] Residential developers should ask themselves the following questions:

- Does the community have common open space or amenities that must be preserved and maintained (e.g., a community recreation center)?
- Are services being offered to future residents beyond the scope of those typically offered by a municipality (e.g., yard maintenance)?
- Does the local government require private maintenance of portions of the development that

[6] CAI, *Community Associations FactBook* (Alexandria, Va.: Author, 1988), p. 15.

[7] Historically, subdivisions have been created with CC&Rs and without community associations. In this circumstance, CC&Rs function as deed restrictions and are enforceable only by individual property owners. CC&Rs without a community association have proven problematic, however, particularly with regard to enforcement, amendment, and interpretation. Residential developers are thus discouraged from establishing CC&Rs without a viable vehicle of enforcement (e.g., a community association).

[8] Hyatt, *Condominium and Homeowners' Associations*, p. 66.

would typically be maintained by a public body (e.g., environmentally sensitive land)?

- Will services, facilities, or amenities be shared among property owners?

If the answer to any of these questions is yes, then a community association should be formed at the onset of development.

Types of Associations

Membership in a community association is automatically obtained by purchasing real estate in the form of a dwelling unit or an improved lot within the community for which the association has been created. Builders who purchase land from a master developer generally become automatic members of the association until the houses are built and conveyed to the owners. The association may hold title to certain real property within the community and is responsible for its preservation, maintenance, and operation. The association may also be designed to maintain private property owned by some of the individual members. Members of the association have perpetual access to the common property established by the enabling declaration of the CC&Rs, the subdivision plat, and the articles and bylaws of the community association. Membership carries with it basic rights and obligations, including the payment of assessments to finance the association's responsibilities and conformance to the provisions of the covenants, specifically those for which the association has been given mutuality of interest.

Two basic types of community associations are possible: homeowners' associations and condominium associations. Housing cooperatives are not technically a community association because residents (shareholders) lease their units from the corporation rather than owning them in fee; still, housing cooperatives function much like community associations in that the cooperative maintains the buildings and grounds and pays the common mortgage.

Although all community associations combine individual homeownership with shared use or ownership of common property and operate according to similar principles of self-governance, each type of community association has distinct characteristics.[9] In most cases, all types of community associations are incorporated as nonprofit corporations. As council member Wayne S. Hyatt notes, however, "Some feel that incorporating condominium associations as nonprofit corporations is unnecessary, and it really turns on the applicable state law."

Homeowners' Associations

The homeowners' association is the prevalent form of community association in residential projects comprised primarily of single-family detached houses or in those townhouse or cluster developments where a house is conveyed in fee simple along with the land underlying the house. In a homeowners' association, the homeowner owns the lot, including the interior and exterior of the individual house, while the association owns and maintains the common property. Sometimes homeowners' associations also maintain the lot and the exterior of the units even though they are in private ownership. Maintenance easements can be established to grant the homeowners' association access to the private property for maintenance. A property owners' association, a lot owners' association, and a cluster association are simply types of homeowners' associations that reflect the real estate product sold.

Condominium Associations

The condominium association is the typical form of community association in multifamily residential projects with a condominium form of ownership. In a typical condominium association, an individual property owner owns the interior of each unit, and the common interior space (lobby, hallways, and so on) and exterior are owned "in common" with other owners. Less typically, condominiums are structured so that the units' exteriors are owned by individual property owners, particularly in townhouses and other forms of attached housing. The condominium association is responsible for maintaining the common property and delivering common services, but it does not *own* the common property; each unit owner actually owns an undivided interest in the common property in addition to his or her residence.

The purposes of a condominium association are similar to those of a homeowners' association, with the key difference being the conveyance of ownership. In a condominium development, the unit can be an "airspace" or it can be defined portions of the real property, including the land underneath the unit and some additional land. All parts of the development other than the units are *common elements* owned by all owners in common in accordance with their assigned percentage of interest. In other words, each owner has an individual percentage interest in the

---

[9] CAI, *Community Associations FactBook,* p. 3.

entire condominium project that is not specifically individually owned.

Owners are automatically members of the condominium association, sometimes called the council of co-owners, which typically administers the affairs of the condominium through a board of directors. To a large extent, the organization and structure of a condominium association are dictated by the enabling legislation, which varies from state to state.

Sometimes residential developers establish a condominium association to create product and lot configurations that are not yet recognized within the municipality's subdivision or zoning codes. For example, developers might find it impossible to build in conformance with requirements for setbacks or minimum street frontage if the objective is to cluster houses and preserve blocks of open space; they can avoid the limitations imposed by the creation of lot lines by structuring the project as a condominium.[10] This practice may prove to be the most expedient (and perhaps the only) alternative for developers who wish to vary from rigid development standards imposed by zoning or subdivision codes.

Forms of Community Associations

Associations for large residential communities can be structured in one of three ways: 1) as independent cluster associations, 2) as an umbrella association with independent cluster associations, and 3) as a single association with individual clusters structured as assessment districts. The latter two alternatives are types of "expandable" associations in which each individual phase (or residential "cluster") is added to the master association, which gradually grows larger as development progresses. This concept gives developers the flexibility to add properties to the association in the event that additional land is acquired for development. Expandable associations have the advantage of central management, continuity of leadership, and a unified body of owners concerned with the entire development.[11] To the extent that a single association maximizes efficiency and centralization, it is considered superior to umbrella associations.

If developments are to include nonresidential uses like a neighborhood shopping center, residential and nonresidential associations should in most circumstances be separate entities. Commercial and residential owners do not mix well and should not be forced into a marriage of convenience. Residential and nonresidential associations can be coupled with covenants to share appropriate maintenance costs. As council member Judith H. Reagan notes, however, "From a practical standpoint, creating separate entities is not always possible when the uses are highly integrated and share common areas."

A single community association is desirable even when a development contains a large number of units, multiple builders, a range of housing types, and a mix of land uses or will be phased over a number of years. Primary goals of forming an association are simplicity, certainty, and feasibility. The more associations in a project, the greater the administrative burden and cost. According to Wayne S. Hyatt, "The single association with neighborhoods or clusters gives the residential developer one entity to administer. It works very well in practice."

Independent Associations

In a series of independent associations, the overall development is divided into a series of housing groups or building projects, and a separate and independent community association is created for each group or project. Each association is totally responsible for common open spaces and facilities designed to serve the residents of that particular project.

This approach is the simplest for developers of large communities where improved parcels are to be sold to builders for construction of housing and where open space and amenities can be logically assigned to individual parcels. Usually, it also means that any open space for the overall development's benefit is not dedicated to and maintained by one entity but instead is divided up among the various independent associations. According to Reagan, "The down side to this approach is that each independent association operates as a little political subdivision that is not tied with other subdivisions to provide common services, maintenance, or unity of interest to the development." Over the long term, independent associations usually cost owners higher monthly assessments because of inefficiencies in scale.

---

[10] For an example, see *Project Reference File: "Straw Hill,"* vol. 17, no. 18 (Washington, D.C.: ULI–the Urban Land Institute, October–December 1987).

[11] Residential developers considering alternative structures of associations for large-scale developments should contact the Community Associations Institute. An excellent discussion of the advantages and disadvantages of alternative structures is contained in Hyatt, *Condominium and Homeowners' Associations,* Sections 5.07–5.21.

Umbrella Associations

In the past, large-scale, multiphased residential developments were often structured with an "umbrella" (or communitywide) association coupled with a series of smaller "cluster" associations for individual neighborhoods or housing products. For example, a single-family detached development built by developer "X" would have its own association, while a townhouse development built by developer "Y" would form another association. Both of these associations (and usually many more) would come under the umbrella of the communitywide corporation.

The umbrella association typically is responsible for managing and maintaining community-level open space and recreational facilities (for example, the community clubhouse). The separate cluster associations, on the other hand, provide services and maintenance for all matters pertaining *only* to that cluster (for example, trash removal). Usually, matters of enforcement and architectural control belong to the umbrella association.

The relationship between the umbrella and subassociations can take several forms. They can have interlocking boards or independent boards. In other words, the board of the umbrella association can be elected at large by all the members of the entire umbrella community association, or each subassociation can have a number of board seats that it fills from its own membership. The latter approach is less cumbersome. In the case of a very large development with dozens of subassociations, electoral districts may be established, or each association may elect members by proportional representation to an umbrella association assembly, which in turn elects a governing board. Subject to state law, the collection and financial management of the assessments could be independent within each association or combined into a two-part assessment collected by the umbrella association and distributed to itself and the subassociations. Service contracts could be administered centrally or independently by each association; again it is subject to state law in the case of condominiums.

Compared with the independent series of associations, the opportunity to have increased central management and unity of control is the principal advantage of the umbrella structure, provided that each subassociation is fairly represented. Because this

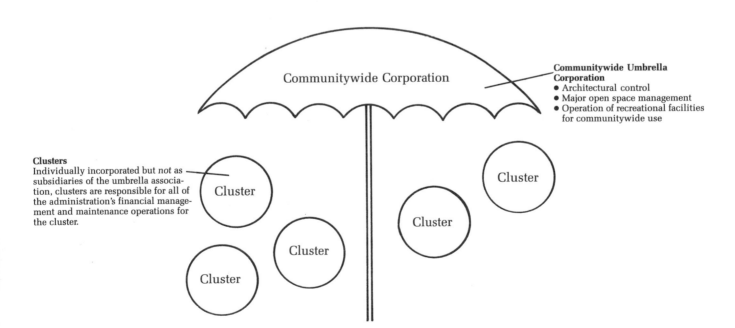

7-5   TYPICAL STRUCTURE OF AN
UMBRELLA COMMUNITY ASSOCIATION

Communitywide Corporation

Communitywide Umbrella Corporation
● Architectural control
● Major open space management
● Operation of recreational facilities for communitywide use

Clusters
Individually incorporated but *not* as subsidiaries of the umbrella association, clusters are responsible for all of the administration's financial management and maintenance operations for the cluster.

Cluster

Cluster

Cluster

Cluster

Cluster

*In comparison with the unified community association, the umbrella association structure lacks: the better controls of centralized administration and financial management; centralized communications; the economies of scale of centralized maintenance; uniform quality control of community appearances; and effective, centralized community code adoptions and enforcement.
Source: Wayne S. Hyatt, *Condominium and Homeowners' Associations: A Guide to the Development Process* (Colorado Springs: Shepard's/McGraw-Hill, 1985). Reprinted with permission. Further reproduction is strictly prohibited.

issue is complex and several examples exist of each type of arrangement, developers considering an umbrella structure should seek competent advice from a community association planner or professional management organization. If this structure is selected, the umbrella association must be established during the first phase of development, because its provisions must be established in the covenants recorded by the developer before any lots are conveyed.

Single Associations

In recent years, large residential communities have been structured under a single association capable of providing management and maintenance with maximum efficiency because of economies of scale. In single associations, individual clusters are established as special assessment districts instead of independent associations. Assessments are based on the cost of providing particular services to a cluster or district. For example, a townhouse cluster with extensive common landscaping and a neighborhood swimming pool would be assessed a higher monthly fee than would a single-family cluster without common landscaping and a pool. This structure offers the advantage of monthly assessments commensurate with the cost of services, while centralizing of administration and financial management.

STRUCTURE OF A SINGLE ASSOCIATION

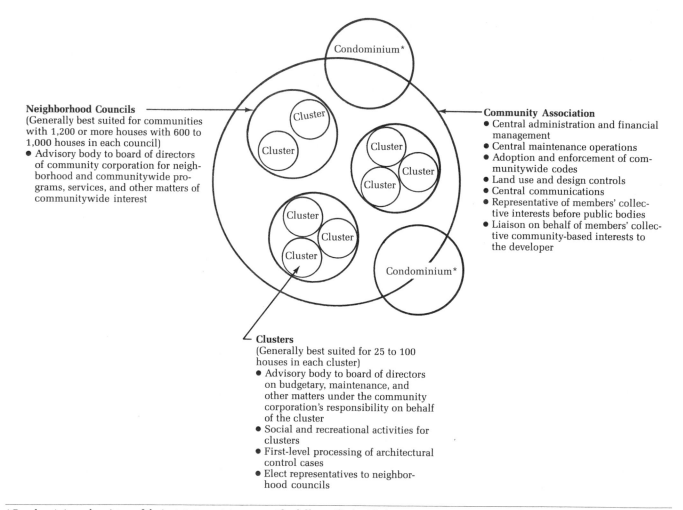

Neighborhood Councils
(Generally best suited for communities with 1,200 or more houses with 600 to 1,000 houses in each council)
● Advisory body to board of directors of community corporation for neighborhood and communitywide programs, services, and other matters of communitywide interest

Community Association
● Central administration and financial management
● Central maintenance operations
● Adoption and enforcement of communitywide codes
● Land use and design controls
● Central communications
● Representative of members' collective interests before public bodies
● Liaison on behalf of members' collective community-based interests to the developer

Clusters
(Generally best suited for 25 to 100 houses in each cluster)
● Advisory body to board of directors on budgetary, maintenance, and other matters under the community corporation's responsibility on behalf of the cluster
● Social and recreational activities for clusters
● First-level processing of architectural control cases
● Elect representatives to neighborhood councils

*Condominiums by virtue of their statutory status cannot be fully unified with the community corporation; however, they still come within the jurisdiction of the community corporation in matters of land use controls and code enforcement. Also, condominiums are within the community's network of social, recreational, and communications programs. Further, condominiums may contract with the community corporation for a variety of administrative and operational services, thereby benefiting from the greater economies of scale afforded by the central administration of the community corporation.

Source: Wayne S. Hyatt, *Condominium and Homeowners' Associations: A Guide to the Development Process* (Colorado Springs: Shepard's/McGraw-Hill, 1985). Reprinted with permission. Further reproduction is strictly prohibited.

Documentation

Residential developers rely on a team of support professionals to implement the residential development. The developer of a community association project needs to involve all team members—especially the attorney and community association manager or consultant—to create the necessary legal documents to deal with issues of ownership, to found the community association, to establish CC&Rs, to draw up design controls, and to establish the administrative structure to manage the association. The following discussion is intended to provide a brief overview of the issues that need to be considered in structuring this legal framework.

In general, five major elements make up the legal structure of a community association: 1) the declaration of condominium or CC&Rs, 2) the subdivision plat, 3) the articles of incorporation, 4) the bylaws, and 5) the individual deeds for each parcel. In a condominium, the document for transferring ownership of a unit may be called a deed or a certificate of title. Distinctions between the documents used in condominium associations and those in community associations are becoming blurred as states adopt uniform enabling statutes for community associations.[12] Again, the use of seasoned legal expertise is a must for developers wishing to prepare association documents.

Declaration of Condominium or Covenants, Conditions, and Restrictions

The declaration of condominium or CC&Rs states the developer's intent to charge purchasers with certain responsibilities and obligations, as set forth in the covenants.[13] In essence, the declaration creates the association. The enabling declaration is recorded with the subdivision plat or before the closing (escrow) of the first unit within the development. The association is created immediately upon recordation of the declaration.

CC&Rs have a long and successful history as a technique employed by the private sector to preserve the character, value, and amenities of residential communities. In combination with related public controls and a viable community association for enforcement, they ensure stability and additional protection against change.

For the purposes of the following discussion, no distinction is made between covenants, conditions, and restrictions. The words are used interchangeably, as are other frequently used terms, such as "protective covenants," "affirmative covenants," "restrictive covenants," and "private deed restrictions." The legal documents that contain covenants, conditions, and restrictions are often referred to simply as CC&Rs.

CC&Rs do not take the place of public regulations like zoning or other land use controls; CC&Rs and public regulations are mutually supportive and do not necessarily overlap. Zoning and other land use controls provide governmental exercise of the basic police power for the purpose of maintaining and promoting the public health, safety, and general welfare. CC&Rs can extend beyond regulations enforceable by public authority and be tailored specifically to the particular objectives of the developer establishing a community. In general, however, they must be applied uniformly throughout a project to be enforceable by any owner in the project or by the community association.[14] CC&Rs applying specifically to individual properties are enforceable by the contracting parties, their assigns, and heirs.

Many covenants are negative and restrict certain uses or activities, such as parking controls. These types of covenants typically are referred to as "use restrictions." Covenants can also be affirmative, however, by setting forth obligations of individual property owners, such as maintenance standards for landscaping. In a planned unit development where common space exists, an affirmative covenant calls for an affirmative act on the part of the community association—upkeep and maintenance of common areas owned by a community association.

CC&Rs provide a workable method for conserving the environmental characteristics and property values over time by addressing additions and modifications, landscaping, fencing, and architectural and design standards. In the past, design covenants dealing with such issues as architectural style, building materials, and landscaping were built into the declaration of CC&Rs, but experience has proven that design guidelines require greater flexibility than other types of covenants.

[12] Contact the National Conference of Commissioners on Uniform State Laws (676 North Clair Street, Suite 1700, Chicago, Illinois 60611 [312-915-0195]) for information about state adoption of the Uniform Common Interest Ownership Act (UCIOA), the Uniform Planned Community Act (UPCA), and the Uniform Condominium Act (UCA).

[13] "Covenants" are taken to mean covenants, both affirmative and restrictive, conditions, and restrictions, which as a group are often referred to as the CC&Rs. The declaration for a condominium is subject to state laws.

[14] See James D. Lawlor, "Subdivision Covenants in the Courts," *Urban Land,* September 1986, pp. 19–23.

7-7   The design controls for Seaside, a 750-unit resort community in Walton County, Florida, are intended to produce simple, durable structures that reflect regional materials and traditions. Although strict, the controls provide enough flexibility to ensure a diverse, though unified, collection of architectural forms.

For example, a design covenant might require that all roofs be constructed of wood shingles. Some years later, the municipality might revise its building codes to prohibit wood roofs to minimize risks from wildfire. Changing a covenant is often a difficult endeavor (especially in large developments) usually requiring approval of 50 to 90 percent of the owners. If even a small percentage of the owners vote against the change, the owners would find themselves in conflict with the municipality or the association. Developers of contemporary residential communities are structuring design guidelines so that the power to adopt and administer such guidelines is established in the declaration of CC&Rs but the specifics are contained in an exhibit to the declaration. The association's board of directors has the power to amend the exhibit as time passes and conditions change.[15]

Except for special situations, covenants should take the form of blanket provisions that apply to the whole development, and they should be specifically referenced in each deed. These CC&Rs together with the recorded plat (or condominium declaration and plat) legally establish a general scheme or plan for the development. In addition, if certain further special provisions are found to be necessary for groups of particular properties (usually called "clusters" or "neighborhoods") within a development, they should be added to the main CC&Rs with a supplemental declaration for that neighborhood. The general rights of enforcement for these owners in the neighborhood are then represented by the community association. An example is a project that includes common properties with individual properties abutting the common area or an arterial street that might require the application of specific covenants for screening or fencing that are different from those generally applied

---

[15] See "Design Guidelines" later in this chapter for further discussion.

throughout the community. The CC&Rs should expressly grant enforcement powers to the community association, in addition to individual owners.

CC&Rs should be drafted and checked for conformance with state statutes by thoroughly qualified legal counsel. An attorney who specializes in this field should be retained to prepare the legal documents. Certain limitations may be included in CC&Rs. For example, court decisions in the area of civil rights have clearly established that protective covenants seeking to exclude by race, religion, or ethnic background are unconstitutional. The Fair Housing Act of 1988 also makes it illegal to discriminate on the basis of family status and handicap.[16]

What covenants are needed and their application to individual sites should be worked out by the developer, the attorney, the land planner, and other members of the development team. A community association manager or planner should join the development team to provide a practical and operational perspective on the documents. Usually the final form of the documents should not be recorded until the developer has received preliminary approval of the subdivision from the local or state jurisdiction, as applicable. If any likelihood exists that the development will include FHA mortgage insurance or a VA loan guarantee for some of the dwelling units, the proposed CC&Rs should first agree with requirements of the FHA, the VA, and the Federal National Mortgage Association.

The CC&Rs recommended by the FHA (Form 1400) and the VA (Form 26-8200) have not been updated for many years and are therefore *not recommended* as a guide for residential developers. Even in projects that are being proposed for approval by FHA or VA, their model provisions should at best be considered only as a starting point. It should be recognized that if a residential development is to have a distinctive quality and character, it is highly likely that at least one or more special protective covenants will be needed to assist in the preservation and maintenance of its special characteristics.

If reasonably and diligently enforced, CC&Rs are in many ways stronger and more effective than zoning or other publicly enforced land use controls. The establishment of zoning and the resistance to rezoning are tied to the political climate in a community. As governments change, community objectives change. Thus, the specifics of zoning regulation may change over time, or rezoning can occur that might cause the loss of desirable controls. Likewise, the community climate for granting variances or modifying uses through special use permits can also jeopardize the character of a development. Even though some items of concern to the developer may be adequately covered by public regulation at the time of development, it may be wise to support those concerns in the CC&Rs whose life is ensured by their terms of establishment.

Effective Term/Amendments

While some covenants may be drawn up with a definite termination date, it is generally agreed that CC&Rs should be designed to renew themselves automatically and "run with the land" indefinitely. Amending CC&Rs should be permitted by approval of a stipulated percentage of the property owners. This percentage should not be less than a simple majority, but the percentage required for amendments or elimination of a particular covenant may vary so that major provisions may have a requirement for a percentage between 75 and 90 percent of property owners, while other less significant ones might require only a simple majority or perhaps simply a majority vote by the board of directors.

CC&Rs must be formulated so that amendments are possible. The absence of a workable provision for amendments can render the CC&Rs obsolete as developments mature and new planning concepts emerge. It is good practice for developers to encumber only that development phase in process—*not the entire development*. With this incremental approach, CC&Rs can be modified to meet changing conditions.

No one, including the developer, should have the right to remove any general covenant once it has been established; however, the beneficiaries of the covenants should be able to amend them at any time. The exigencies of the development process suggest that the developer should retain minor powers of amendment within fundamental limits, such as modifications in character of design from one phase to another of the project, so long as no one's rights are adversely affected. Alternatively, such modifications could be accomplished through supplementary declarations, thereby avoiding amendments. Frequent amendments should be used with great caution, because a developer's record of living up to its promises can be negatively affected.

---

[16] The Fair Housing Act virtually eliminated the possibility of covenants barring children from subdivisions and condominium complexes. Most retirement communities, except those that abide by rigorous federal guidelines on the age of the residents and the services provided, must now open their doors to families with children. Retirement communities can enforce age restrictions only if 100 percent of the residents are over 62 years of age or if 80 percent of the residents are over 55 years of age with extensive other requirements.

- Air conditioning/reflective material
- Clothes and drying facilities
- Commercial activities
- Design guidelines on units and landscaping
- Destruction of a dwelling
- Exterior antennas
- Fences
- Leasing
- Maintenance of private property
- Mining or drilling
- Nuisances
- Parking and types of vehicles
- Pets

- Signs
- Subdivision of lots
- Temporary structures
- Trash containers
- Timesharing
- Use of common areas
- Use of water bodies
- Wells and irrigation systems

This list is intended to provide only a sample of items subject to restrictions.
Source: Judith H. Reagan, Community Consultants, Inc., Deerfield Beach, Florida.

Enforcement

Unless adequate machinery is set up initially for proper enforcement, covenants may become ineffective through nonobservance and conscious violation. CC&Rs are typically enforced by the community association, although they can also be enforced by private individuals. Through CC&Rs, all parties seek to gain certain advantages: developers or subdividers to ensure that purchasers will use the land in conformance with the planned objectives for the community under development, the owners (or purchasers) to ensure that the subdivider or developer proceeds to use the land as planned and that other purchasers use and maintain the land as planned, and the public where a requirement for land use or maintenance may not be enforceable by a public body but may nevertheless serve a broad public purpose. Enforcement of suitable CC&Rs assures each owner that no other owner within the development can use property in a way that will destroy values, change the character of the neighborhood, or create a nuisance.[17] Strict enforcement of the CC&Rs, however, can best be assured by the creation of a viable community association.

If the association owns and maintains common properties, a solid management structure to handle day-to-day enforcement should be in place. An association with minimal enforcement responsibilities can easily be handled by one of the developer's employees (when the developer is in control), an employee of the association (after the owners are in control), or by the board of directors.

Use Restrictions

Covenants to control land use may simply restate the provisions of public zoning and limit the use of land to the residential use planned for the project (single-family dwellings, townhouses, and so on). They might, however, also eliminate one or more principal uses as permitted or conditional uses even though these uses are permitted by public ordinance—commercial activities, professional offices at home, keeping pets or livestock, agricultural activities, satellite dishes, and accessory uses, such as parking or storage of recreational vehicles or trailers. Developers should carefully examine all the suitable uses that might be possible under existing zoning and eliminate by covenant those that would be detrimental to the objectives of the development. Often activities not permitted also reflect municipal regulations: for example, no dumping of refuse, chemicals, or other pollutants into water bodies contained within the development or no drilling or mining activities.

Such use covenants should not be so restrictive that they prevent the reasonable use of land. Nor should they be onerous to the point that property owners may not perceive their merit and cause them to go into default by virtue of an unwillingness to enforce them diligently and consistently.

It is also possible with affirmative covenants to mandate specific use of land within the development for specific purposes. The most obvious example is the affirmative covenant to ensure that certain lands will remain as open space and that within that open space certain natural elements will be preserved. An example of this type of covenant is one that provides for preservation of a stand of trees or a stream in its

---

[17] See Dowden, *Creating a Community Association,* pp. 29–33, for more information.

natural state. Such covenants should allow for compatible future improvements (e.g., trails or nature study areas).

Covenants to ensure the continuance of open space may be in the form of open space easements. In some instances, these easements may be granted or irrevocably offered to a public agency (usually with use restrictions and maintenance requirements), because preserving this open space may be of great importance to the community at large as well as to the residents of the development. In fact, granting easements or comparable open space guarantees may be a basis for

The homeowners' manual for Briargate, a large residential community in Colorado Springs, Colorado, informs prospective owners in plain language about CC&Rs. Illustrated activities are prohibited.

Our goal at Briargate is to create a lastingly beautiful environment in which to live. Certain activities and objects can be detrimental to the overall impression of your neighborhood. These activities and objects are described in your Protective Covenants. The major ones are illustrated in these guidelines for clarity and easy reference.

Unscreened vehicles parked on your property or in front of your house: If a parked vehicle is not visually screened from the neighbors or adjacent streets, it is prohibited. This includes boats, trailers, motor homes, or vehicles being repaired.

Disturbing exterior sound systems: Sound systems that create noise that can be heard beyond property lines and annoy your neighbors are not allowed.

Annoying floodlights: Floodlights that light areas outside your yard, create glare, or annoy your neighbors are prohibited.

Disturbing odors: If odors emanate from your property and are disturbing to neighbors, they are not allowed.

Unscreened outdoor and garage storage: Trash, building materials, and/or maintenance equipment stored in your yard or garage without sufficient screening from neighbors' views or views from adjacent streets are prohibited. Please keep your garage door closed whenever possible.

Banners, streamers, and/or flags: Any objects designed to attract attention to help sell or rent property, other than one standard real estate sign, are not allowed.

Unscreened transmitters, antennas, or security alarms: Transmitters/receivers (e.g., satellite dishes), antennas, or security alarms must be screened from neighbors' views with architectural features, fences, or plants, or they will not be allowed. Rooftop antennas are specifically prohibited.

Livestock and poultry: Livestock, poultry, or any other animals that cause an unreasonable amount of noise or odor or are kept for commercial purposes are prohibited.

Unscreened clotheslines: If clotheslines are not adequately screened, they will not be allowed.

Excessive ornamentation: Driftwood, statues, animal skulls, wagon wheels, windmills, etc., in areas visible to your neighbors are not allowed.

Commercial activity: Any activity that is a business or commercial activity drawing customers or requiring business vehicles or employees (such as hair styling salons) will not be allowed.

Source: EDAW, Inc., Fort Collins, Colorado.

the approval of the development concept. According to council member Richard A. Reese:

> Integral to receiving our use entitlement for the 5,000-acre Rancho Santa Margarita planned community was our willingness to preserve about 2,000 of the acres for permanent open space accessible to the public. In this case, the county required that we make an irrevocable "offer of dedication" on the acreage. Until the county "accepts" the offer, it will be maintained by the community's master property owners' association. It is unlikely the county will ever "accept" every offer of dedication, because it would then also have to accept maintenance costs.

In addition to open space easements, it usually is desirable through CC&Rs to make reservations for future utility easements and possibly pedestrian systems that may not be constructed at the time of development but may be needed in the future.

A variety of other covenant provisions may need to be considered. With the advent of recreational equipment, including travel trailers, mobile recreational homes, campers, boats, vans, trucks, and an assortment of prefabricated storage structures, the location and storage of these vehicles and structures has become a problem that is often controlled by positive or negative covenants. For example, it may be a good idea to prohibit on-site parking or storage of various types of vehicles and recreational equipment if the development has a suitable common storage area. If a storage area is not possible, CC&Rs can prohibit the most objectionable vehicles from certain areas and require visual screening or specific locations, such as limiting the parking or storage of such vehicles to rear yards or garages. Council member David Jensen stresses, "It is very important to consider the preferences and needs of your market—the future residents—and design both project and covenants accordingly."

Other restrictions may also be made on cutting mature trees, maintaining or repairing automobiles, and parking inoperable vehicles. The list could go on indefinitely.

Subdivision Plat

The subdivision plat is the map setting forth the location and legal description of individual lots, common spaces, street easements, and other rights-of-way. The plat should be interrelated to the declaration by specific reference on the plat. It is desirable to include on the plat certain specifics of the declaration dealing with the title to the common property, the granting of easements of enjoyment, the indication that designated areas are not dedicated for use by the general public, and the conveyance or the intent to

convey these properties to an association. The reason for doing so is that all too frequently prospective purchasers view the plat or subdivision map without seeing the declaration and the documents therefore need to be referenced to each other. The specifics of the items that may be included on the recorded plat are governed by state and local legislation on subdivisions, and developers must be guided by these regulations.

Articles of Incorporation

Most community associations are incorporated, and the articles of incorporation establish the association as a corporation pursuant to applicable state law. The articles set forth the name of the association, the names and addresses of principal officers at the time of incorporation, and the purpose and powers of the association, tied to the subdivision plat and declaration. They also set forth terms of membership and voting rights; create the initial board of directors; and establish procedures for dissolution, the duration of the association in the absence of dissolution, the basis for amendments to the articles of incorporation, and the severability of provisions.

Bylaws

The association's bylaws are the procedures by which the association conducts its business. In the case of community associations, the developer's attorney prepares the original bylaws, but their adoption is also the first function of the first board of directors (which is controlled by the developer's appointees). The bylaws set forth the meetings of the association, the basis for a quorum, provisions for vote by proxy, and the notice of meetings. Bylaws also set forth the terms of office for the board of directors, the composition of the board, the method of nomination, the method of election, the handling of resignations, removals, vacancies, and compensation, and the conduct of board meetings. They set forth the power and duties of the board and describe the means of election, terms of office, and duties of officers. They define the committees required or the basis for their establishment, establish the fiscal year, spell out the indemnification of officers, describe the role and composition of special subboards, such as the design review board, and set forth the basis for amending the bylaws.

The community association, normally through the board, enacts rules under the authority of the declaration and other organizing documents. The developer usually drafts the initial set of rules in consultation with a community association planner or professional manager, and the rules are formally adopted at the first meeting of the developer-controlled board of directors. Rules should be enacted only if they are necessary, and they should regulate the fewest activities possible. Bylaws should be structured to permit these rules to be amended easily by a majority of the board following the basic concepts of fundamental fairness and reasonableness in their development and application.[18]

Individual Deeds

Each individual deed should contain a clause referring to the declaration and clarifying the title to common property adjacent to a lot (if any). At the time of conveyance, new owners should be apprised of the association and its function in relationship to their use of the property and the declaration with its associated covenants. Several states require sellers of property in a community association to include a disclosure of the existence of the association in the sales contract.

Information Brochure

While not one of the five major elements of documentation, an informational brochure about the association is required for FHA and VA processing. Further, a guide to the functions and operations of the community association has proven to be a viable marketing and enforcement vehicle for developers. An informational brochure will help to ensure that all purchasers are better informed of the association. It restates in clear text the relationship among the association, the purchaser, and the developer and covers major elements—identification of the common area, ownership and use, the structure of the association, assessments, selection and election of officers and directors, architectural controls, liens, annexation, dissolution, and so on. The brochure can take many forms; see Appendix G for an example of one such brochure, prepared for Cedar Creek in Olathe County, Kansas.

Design Guidelines

Often referred to as "architectural controls" or "design review," design guidelines set forth restrictions on building and site design, including exterior modifications and additions, accessory buildings, fences, walls, landscaping, architectural styles, building materials, colors, and other elements of site development. The association publishes design guidelines after the board of directors adopts them. Typically, they are adopted as an exhibit with the declaration of CC&Rs and may be amended from time to time by the board. "The purpose of design review or architectural

control is to keep the community attractive for the enjoyment of residents and for the protection of property values."[19]

Design guidelines and review procedures are typically necessary for new construction and for additions and modifications that occur after initial development. Because developers are compelled to maintain control over design review on all matters affecting new construction, they have historically structured the declaration of CC&Rs to give themselves full control of the design review committee until all development is completed. More recently, however, developers structure design review with two committees: one to review all new construction controlled by the developer and another to review all additions and modifications controlled by the owners but subject to oversight by the developer. This structure gives developers control over that aspect of design review about which they are most concerned and brings the owners into the process on matters about which they are most concerned.[20] Developments with custom lots often present a particular problem. In developments targeted toward buyers of primary housing, this form of residential activity is usually limited to upper-income housing (but may be open to a much broader market segment in the second-home market). Experience has clearly shown that affluence does not guarantee good taste in design and that incongruities in housing design may lead to an unattractive overall appearance, even though individual designs are attractive.[21] Developers can easily be accused of trying to exert their personal preferences for design if they try to enforce design guidelines without other owners' participation. In a development of custom houses, it may therefore be advantageous for developers to include homeowners on the design review committee as soon as possible to help remove themselves from the hot seat.

The design review committee is typically comprised of three to five individuals. During the period

---

[18] CAI, *Drafting Association Rules*, CAI-GAP Report No. 7 (Alexandria, Va.: Author, 1980).

[19] Byron R. Hanke and Thomas S. Kenny, *Architectural Control: Design Review*, GAP Report No. 2 (Alexandria, Va.: Community Associations Institute, 1986), p. 2. This report provides an excellent overview of design guidelines and design review procedures.

[20] The structure of design review committees is discussed further under "The Developer's Role."

[21] Probably the simplest and most effective method of establishing quality is to specify a minimum habitable floor area (excluding garages, basements, and other accessory structures) and to include minimum requirements for landscaping. Such restrictions can be directly interpreted and in combination with design review can be an excellent basis for maintaining standards of size, scale, character, and value.

of control by the developer, the developer appoints the members of the committee, often including representatives from the developer's organization and members of the development team (for example, the architect, planner, or landscape architect). These appointed members are gradually phased out as the committee is changed to control by owners. The design review committee preferably includes members with expertise in architectural and design matters if the body of owners includes such individuals. And it is generally not a good idea to have members who serve on the board of directors to also serve on the design review committee.

The range of design guidelines is almost limitless. The design guidelines for Piney Creek, a 700-acre development in Arapahoe County, Colorado, provide an example of some of the considerations that might be controlled and subject to review.[22] Other residential communities might require more or fewer design guidelines; residential developers must tailor guidelines to the development at hand.

1. *Building guidelines.* Roofing materials, colors, window treatments, window coverings, masonry finishes, solar panels, antennas (including microwave dishes), garages
2. *Fencing.* Permitted types (and materials), location
3. *Screening.* Garbage and refuse, vehicles, firewood, swimming pools and hot tubs, mechanical equipment/utilities, dog houses/runs
4. *Landscaping.* Plant materials, gravel, ornamentation, maintenance, water conservation
5. *Miscellaneous items.* Signage, mail boxes, exterior lighting, street lighting, basketball backboards, ancillary structures, driveways, retaining walls, site grading

To promote quality development, developers may set forth minimum and maximum setbacks for side, front, and rear yards, including dictating the location of or prohibiting accessory buildings. If a development is to be processed under an ordinance for a planned unit development, a special opportunity exists to modify yard requirements or other physical limitations on buildings lot by lot or unit by unit. In single-family detached housing, for example, it is possible through design guidelines to vary the setbacks on individual lots to create a more interesting streetscape. This tool can be used to respond to variations in topography and existing trees or other natural elements.

In terms of open space and its relationship to adjacent lots or other units of ownership, design guidelines can set forth limitations on fencing, landscaping, and other elements to control the physical

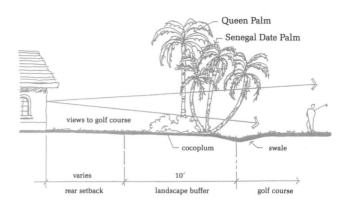

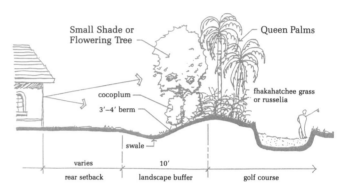

7-10 Design controls can be established lot by lot to promote compatibility between residences and the golf course and to minimize future disputes between landowners. Above, design controls specifying landscaping materials ensure the preservation of views between houses and the golf course in situations where the risk of poorly hit balls is low. Below, design controls protect the rear yards of lots from hazards. *Source:* Judith H. Reagan, Community Consultants, Inc., Deerfield Beach, Florida.

relationship of the boundaries between private ownership and common open space. For example, lots bordering a golf course may be restricted as to fencing and landscaping to ensure that views between the house and the course are preserved or to protect the lot from poorly hit golf balls.

The best methods to ensure good design are developers' constructing quality buildings, using talented design professionals in the development and as participants on the design review committee, and preparing and distributing detailed design and architectural criteria and guidelines. This last point is particularly important.

The manual of policy [design] guidelines serves two basic purposes: first, it assists the homeowner, both in

[22] *Piney Creek Guidelines,* prepared for Piney Creek Development Company, Denver, Colorado, by EDAW, Inc., Fort Collins, Colorado (n.d.). The list in this paragraph is intended to provide only a sample of some of the most common elements of design subject to design guidelines.

Design guidelines for Piney Creek in Arapahoe County, Colorado, explain the design review process to prospective homebuyers.

To obtain Architectural Control Committee ("Committee") review of proposed site or building exterior construction, the homeowner or his representative ("Applicant") initiates the review process by submitting an application to the Committee.

The Committee meets regularly on or near the first of the month and will render a decision on an application within 45 days from the date of submittal. For a typical application, two copies of the Required Information (see following paragraph) must be submitted. One copy will remain on file with the Committee and one copy, with comments, will be returned to the Applicant.

The applicant starts the formal review process by submitting the following *Required Information*:

A. Project Data

1. Name of Applicant (homeowner or builder, as applicable).
2. Address and phone number of Applicant.
3. Description of proposed construction.
4. Construction schedule (start and completion).
5. Names and phone numbers of all homeowners with properties within 500 feet of the subject property, when those homeowners are able to view the proposed improvements from their properties.

B. A site plan drawn accurately to scale, showing location and extent of:

1. Lot lines.
2. Location of house.
3. Layout of proposed construction, including dimensions, as appropriate.
4. Details describing the construction, including (as applicable) color, materials, sizes, etc.

C. Building elevations (as applicable).

D. A landscape plan showing proposed plantings, including sizes, species, numbers, mulch materials, landscape features, description of irrigation system, etc.

When the Applicant is a homebuilder, the following additional material shall be submitted:

1. Complete working drawings and specifications for all proposed construction.
2. A sample of the proposed house siding not less than two square feet in size with the proposed stain or paint color applied.
3. A sample of the proposed trim material, not less than 12 inches long with the proposed stain or paint color applied.
4. A sample of any proposed brick or other masonry to be used, including grout color.
5. A written statement of the type and color of roofing to be used.

▶

designing the proposed improvement and in determining how to apply for approval; second, it provides criteria for consistent decisions by the design review committee and between successive committees.[23]

Preparation of the procedures manual for design guidelines should be a joint effort of the developer, the design team (architect, landscape architect, engineer, and other design professionals), the attorney, and the community association's consultant or manager.

Inevitably, a question arises about excessive controls on the reasonable use of privately owned property. Like all regulations, reasonableness, fairness, and need should be the measures of four conditions: 1) whether or not a requirement for design guidelines or design review is desirable to preserve and protect owners' common interests; 2) whether or not it is likely to be enforced diligently and therefore not lose its effect through failure to enforce it; 3) whether or not the parties to the covenants can reasonably interpret it; and 4) whether or not it is so rigid that changing circumstances requiring modifications cannot be accommodated.

Management

The long-term success of a for-sale residential development hinges on the quality and effectiveness of its management, and the community association is the most prevalent tool used for this purpose. Small as-

---

[23] Hanke and Kenny, *Architectural Control,* p. 6.

EDAW, Inc.

6. A colored perspective rendering of the proposed residence.
7. A detailed site and grading plan showing finished contours, building elevations, spot elevations on pavements, retaining walls, drainage swales/structures, curb/gutter/sidewalk locations, etc.
8. A landscape plan for all model sites.

The Committee will meet to consider the application and will render a decision by voting. An affirmative vote of a majority of the Committee constitutes approval.

Within 15 days of completion of approved construction, the Applicant shall notify the Committee. The Committee then has up to 15 days to inspect the work. If the work is not done according to the approved application, the Committee has the authority to require the Applicant to remedy the defect within 45 days or be subject to action by the Committee to remove any unapproved construction.

Source: EDAW, Inc., Fort Collins, Colorado.

sociations can be managed and governed by volunteers. Those sufficiently large can retain professional management. The growth of associations has brought about corresponding growth in the number of qualified managers for community associations and management firms that specialize in providing management services to community associations.

Early in the development process, developers need to establish competent association managers within their own organizations or seek outside management services. Council member William E. Becker believes that "developers should undertake management only when they have solid experience, and they should not consider it a new profit entity. It is a service-oriented function that is quite different from the business of residential development." Management should not be left as a subordinate function. Further, early partici-

pation of the owners in the association and their training in the proper methods of management and operation will help make the transition from the developer's to the owners' control smooth.

Whether developer-controlled or homeowner-controlled, the community association board has four options for management: 1) self-management by volunteers, 2) self-management by employees on the association's payroll, 3) contract management by an outside management company, and 4) a management system combining these methods.[24] Developers must think through the kind of management most suitable for a particular project and must plan the management

[24] For additional discussion of the options, see Hyatt, *Condominium and Homeowners' Associations*, Sections 11.17–11.21.

program in conjunction with initial planning for the project. Ideally, independent professional management is the best course of action to follow. Most larger cities (250,000 or more) now have competent management companies that can perform the functions of professional management.

Self-management is most typical of small associations (50 units or fewer) and associations that are several years old where the developer is no longer involved. With a staff paid by the association, the association board identifies responsibilities and hires the necessary employees. Under management by a third party, a totally independent management firm provides all services, with minimal participation by the developer or the association. Some developers choose to contract for certain specific services, such as lawn maintenance, with a third-party contractor while the developer or the owners handle general governance, depending on the stage of the association.

The Developer's Role

Developers need to address several key areas of concern in creating an association relating to ensuring that the initial planning and design of the association are carefully tied to the planning and design of the development it will serve. Developers need to be concerned with planning the association's financial structure, including the establishment of initial assessments and the development of interim and final operating budgets. And developers must know the extent of their financial obligation to the association during their control. Appendix H provides an example of a developer's projected annual and cumulative association budget deficit for a highly amenitized 125-acre residential community containing limited hotel and retail uses. As shown, the developer's deficit during the 10-year sellout period (until the association is turned over to the owners) is estimated at about $11.7 million. Because operating deficits can be substantial, developers must factor this cost into the projects overall pro forma and financial feasibility analysis.

Developers must carefully consider the type and structure of management that should be designed for the association, including a consideration of self-governance versus the use of a professional management service, for these decisions will have important financial implications. The final area of developers' concern is control of the association's affairs through the period of development.

In general, the community association will evolve through five phases, each with its own special nature and needs:

- *Predesign.* Developers determine whether a need exists for a community association and whether it would be accepted in the market, form alternative types of associations, identify common open space and facilities, assemble the development team, and begin to draw up legal documents.
- *Design.* Developers design the community association by producing its legal documents, operating manuals, budgets, design and architectural criteria, and information for owners.
- *Start-up.* Developers incorporate the association, convey common properties to it, and begin to market the units. The association begins its operation as a separate entity. The developer controls a majority of the association's votes, and the association depends on the developer to provide most of its operating income and to administer its documents.
- *Transition.* Developers involve homeowners in the association's operations through membership on the board and committees. They gradually turn over control of the association's operations to the homeowners.
- *Governance.* Developers no longer control a majority of the association's votes. Independent of the developer's control, the association grows to full membership as the developer sells out the development. The association, with a full membership of homeowners, performs its ongoing functions of operating the common facilities, administering the covenants, and providing self-governance for the community.

Appendix I contains portions of an operational plan prepared for the Willoughby Golf Club, a 659-acre planned unit development in Stuart, Florida. This plan was prepared for the developer by a consultant specializing in community association operations and governance. It represents the types of issues that should be studied at the early stages of a project's planning and feasibility analysis. For example, the plan delineates matters such as: 1) the responsibilities of the developer and the owners, 2) the areas of private versus common maintenance, 3) the voting structure and the transition to owner control, and 4) the preliminary budget.

Predesign and Design

Perhaps the best way to describe a developer's concern in the initial planning of the association is to set forth the questions that need to be asked and answered:

ASSOCIATION PHASE:	Predesign			Design	
DEVELOPMENT PHASE:	**Choice and Evaluation of Site**	**Design Assessment**	**Market Approach**	**Financing the Project**	**Marketing the Project**
ASSOCIATION-RELATED DECISIONS OR ACTIVITIES	Assessment of natural features or barriers and of common property. Decisions about clustering and land conservation. Decisions about housing type.	Selection of common areas and open space. Determination of common facilities. Decisions about major capital items requiring long-term maintenance. Decisions about whether to develop all at once or in phases.	Acceptance of design and project by market. Exploration of alternative approaches to ownership of common property: •association •joint ownership •private club •dedication to local entity •funded trust Decide on condominium or homeowners' association. Acceptance of design and development by municipal officials. Assembly of team. Initiate preparation of association's legal documents.	Complete the preparation of the legal documents. Make sure the project conforms with requirements of FNMA, FHLMC, VA, FHA, and other lending-related institutions. Prepare initial association budget and management procedures. Submit preliminary association management and sales program to lender.	Explain the association concept as a sales tool. Inform the salesforce about the legal aspects of selling a house with an association. Prepare brochures for homebuyers and homeowners.

Source: C. James Dowden, *Creating a Community Association: The Developer's Role in Condominium and Homeowners' Associations*, 2d rev. ed. (Washington, D.C., Alexandria, Va.: ULI–the Urban Land Institute and CAI–Community Associations Institute, 1986), pp. 22–23.

- Is an association needed to support and sustain the concept for development?
- If an association is needed, what type and organization are most appropriate?
- What special features of the development require special treatment in the documents creating the development and the association?

- Do the types of common properties and amenities proposed require an initial or future assessment that may prove onerous to the association members and thus jeopardize the community's long-term viability?
- Are the covenants proposed necessary and enforceable? Are they complete in their purpose to preserve the community's character?

	Start-up	Transition		Governance	
Management	**First Phase of Construction (presale and sales) up to 25 Percent of Closings**	**Second Phase of Construction with 26 to 75 Percent of Closings**	**Final Phase of Construction with 76 to 90 Percent of Closings**	**Operational Project with Construction Completed and 91 to 100 Percent of Closings**	**Operational Project with Sales Completed**
Finalize management procedures and program. Designate the management approach. Refine the initial budget and set initial assessments. Arrange for maintenance. Prepare financial and administrative management programs. Record the legal documents. Appoint (elect) initial board, which will meet to adopt the budget, management approach, assessments, and rules. The board will let outside contracts for maintenance, etc., and contract for insurance.	Advise prospects of the nature and requirements of association living. Distribute homebuyer brochure with appropriate data and documents. Distribute homeowner information, including association legal documents, budget, and brochure. Solicit homeowners for involvement and participation in association. Identify potential association leaders. Initiate association committees. If a homeowners' association community, deed the common elements before the first closing.	Continue association-related sales activities. Management functions should be as follows: •owners on committees •annual membership meetings conducted •officers and board members elected •some, if not a majority, of owner seats on board •most administrative and financial functions assumed by owners.	Continue sales program. Owners control association and proceed with management, with increasing emphasis on: •an architectural review committee •establishing firm administrative procedures and systems •owner-controlled committees •owners' review of budget and assessments •finalization of transition process with common area inspections and transer of books, records, plans, and specifications. Developer continues minority position on board and key committees.	Continue sales program. Owners assume all management function. Owners control all financial, physical, and administrative functions.	Owners prepare annual budget and set assessments. All committees are owner-controlled and functioning. Owners control capital improvement programs.

- What design guidelines will be required, and what should be the mechanism within the developer's organization and ultimately within the association for their administration?
- Who will be responsible for managing the association? (The management staff or a community association planner familiar with operational issues should be on board at the development's onset.)

Typically, developers donate the commonly held land and facilities to the association, with their cost recovered from the overall income from sales of individual units or lots. For purposes of establishing their worth, it is important that their cost be isolated during development. All too often, for example, the paving of tennis courts is thrown into a contract for paving driveways or streets and cannot be isolated when the developer wants to establish the value of the capital assets that are part of the association. More important, the association's budget must include the cost of the assets for maintenance and repair.

By the same token, real estate taxation must be considered.[25] Open space that is permanently dedicated to a community association should not be assessed at the same rate as residential lots if appropriate language is inserted on the declaration and face of the subdivision plat and if the association cannot dissolve without offering the common properties to the public.[26] The value of such open space should already be reflected in the assessed valuation of individual houses. According to council member Fritz Grupe, "In California, for example, county tax assessors have generally taken the position that the taxation of common area recreation facilities should be minimal because the homeowner has paid for these facilities in the price of the house. Any other interpretation could be considered a form of double taxation."

Start-up

During the course of development and until the developer turns over the control of the facilities to the association for maintenance, the developer maintains the open space and facilities. Most frequently, the developer's own crews maintain the property, and unless developers properly account for funds expended, they cannot therefore properly budget and collect assessments for the cost of operating and maintaining the facilities.

Developers are responsible for setting up initial assessments. (See Appendix J for a sample chart of accounts.) Assessments must be realistic in terms of the expenses that will be incurred against this source of income for the association. Good recordkeeping by developers of their own costs will assist them in determining realistic assessments. Excess maintenance for marketing purposes should be counted separately—for example, planting flowers at the sales center or community entry. Because the size of the assessment must grow as the responsibilities for maintenance expand, a realistic determination of future assessments may be the best discipline for developers in controlling the amount of common area and the extent of facilities initially provided.

Developers must keep careful financial records from the date of the association's inception. Council member Judith Reagan notes that "developers can get into major difficulties with association members if the costs of the association's operations, including maintenance costs, are not isolated and accounted for from day one." Failure to account for the association's

expenses can also lead to inaccurate assessments; if all costs are not segregated, developers will be forced into "guesstimating" an appropriate assessment.

Transition

The rules and regulations about the number of directors on the association's board, the basis for eligibility, the method of initial selection, and the voting power of members and the developer are the basic methods for control set forth in the bylaws and in the articles of incorporation. However written, this framework typically allows developers to retain voting control of an association until some percentage of the units (usually 50 to 75 percent) are sold (in the case of a typical planned unit development) or a specific date, which is usually based on the estimated rate of sales. The control of a condominium project is handled similarly, with limitations set by state enabling statutes. The VA, FHA, and Fannie Mae also have requirements for relinquishing the developer's control.

Disregarding the developer's legal prerogatives, the need for owners' participation as the development proceeds is important. In the early years of community associations, many developers felt that benevolent paternalism was the most appropriate approach. Developers retained control to ensure the ability to achieve objectives for development with limited interference from purchasers. Some well-reported, if isolated, instances of developers' abuse of control, however, led those with expertise in association management to encourage the earliest possible involvement by association members to build competent and responsible leadership for the association. This approach prevents the creation of a dissident power structure within the association when the first problem occurs in the relationship between developers and purchasers. Early involvement is time-consuming for developers and residents, but it leads to a better community and better sales referrals.

Developers should be most concerned about their control of the association during the early and middle stages of development with respect to control over design, enforcement of rules, modifications of the plan to meet new market requirements, and the level

[25] For more information about this issue, see CAI, *Property Taxes and HOAs,* CAI-GAP Report No. 6 (Alexandria, Va.: Author, 1980).

[26] The following states, by law, have no assessment of common open space: Virginia, Illinois, Colorado, Connecticut, West Virginia, Alaska, Oregon, and North Carolina. By court decision, the following states require only a nominal assessment of common open space: New York, Maryland, and Florida.

of quality for maintenance of common areas and private houses and lots during marketing. If early control of the association by residents is valid, then developers' objectives need to be protected by alternative means. For example, developers might retain certain prerogatives longer than others, or they might have specific veto powers over the board's actions. An example might be the developer's right to appoint or approve appointments to the architectural or design review committee (or approve new design criteria) until the development is completed. Developers need to keep abreast of current experience in the use of these approaches, because successes and failures in actual application are the best measure of the potential for future application of evolving ideas.

Developers should be sure that they have the established legal right to use certain common facilities during a specified marketing period. For example, most developers establish the right to maintain marketing signs within the common areas, to use the parking lot for parking at model homes, and so on. Overall, developers must think through the development process and reserve all those rights that will be necessary to complete the project. Controversy with the emerging association can be avoided if developers have structured flexible covenants that protect their development interests.[27]

One of the most important issues during transition can be in the area of design guidelines. Because developers need to be certain about design guidelines, they often structure the association to give themselves control over the design review board until the development is completed. This control can conflict with owners' perceived need to be involved in decisions affecting their community. Owners are usually most concerned about decisions during postdevelopment, however, such as those involving modifications and additions, while developers are most concerned about decisions during development (new construction). Some developers have resolved this conflict by structuring two design boards: one concerned with additions and modifications controlled by owners and another concerned with new construction controlled by the developer until development is completed. In some instances, it might be prudent to include residents as members of the new construction committee so that they can participate in the development of design guidelines that will be effective after the owners take full control of the development. Because the committee's responsibilities vary from development to development, it is almost impossible to construct a model that is of any general value. A continuous process of education during development to build leadership is the optimum solution.

Perhaps the most traumatic point in the life of the association is when the common area is turned over to the association for maintenance.[28] The key to a successful transition is the development of an orderly process. Such a process is possible only if developers have kept complete, accurate, and understandable records in creating the properties and their maintenance during the period of their control. The transitional phase is most difficult when developers have commingled funds for the association with those of the development entity; ensuring that this difficulty does not arise begins during the project's conceptual stage.[29]

During transition, developers should also try to instill a positive attitude on the new board of directors. New association boards are often faced with many neighborhood-type problems, and they can begin to see themselves as just problem solvers. Developers should strongly attempt to get the new board aggressively interested in positive aspects of the community by forming committees, such as those for social events or community improvements.

A logical process for transition from developer to owner is shown in the accompanying figure. This model is based on a moderately sized hypothetical project (200 to 250 units) and must be adapted for larger or smaller projects.

Governance

As development progresses and the association takes control of its own affairs, developers theoretically are gradually relieved of all the responsibility for managing the association. Without regard to legal obligations, responsible developers should perceive a responsibility for the stewardship of the land. Further, developers carry a fiduciary responsibility for the interests of the association and its members. The association is a separate legal entity from the developer, and the legal duties of one in control of a corporation apply. Council member Wayne S. Hyatt notes, "Good business judgment is required through the process of forming an association. The developer must avoid self-interest and self-dealing. It is not

[27] See James J. Scavo, "Flexible Covenants Critical to Success of Large Communities," *Developments,* February 1986, pp. 18–25.

[28] See *Financial Management of Condominium and Homeowners' Associations* (Washington, D.C./Alexandria, Va.: ULI–the Urban Land Institute and Community Associations Institute, 1985), pp. 113–14, for additional discussion of the transition phase and the methodology for transferring private property.

[29] Ibid., pp. 114–15, discusses problems associated with commingling in greater detail.

TRANSITION PROCESS FOR A COMMUNITY ASSOCIATION

Point of Closings	Committee Activity	Committee Control	Association Governance
By 25 percent of closings	Newsletter Rules Enforcement	Developer controls, owners chair	Developer controls all seats on the board, and the owners may elect one owner. Quarterly board meetings open to owners.
	Management Budget Grounds Maintenance	Developer controls through board, owners may volunteer	
By 50 percent of closings	Maintenance Newsletter Architectural Controls* Rules Enforcement Insurance	Developer controls, owners elected	Transition board with developer controlling and electing additional owners to the board but developer still retaining a majority.
	Management Budget	Developer controls through board, owners elected	
By 75 percent of closings	Maintenance Newsletter Rules Enforcement Insurance	Owners control	Transition board, and depending on the existing legal statutes and the documents, the developer should shift to a minority position with a majority of board seats retained for owners. A membership meeting is held to elect board members and to effect the transfer of control. Complete control of board by owners but developer may be asked to maintain liaison.
	Architectural Controls* Management Budget	Owners control, with developer involved	
	Transition	Joint committee of developer and owners	
By completion of closings	Maintenance Newsletter Rules Enforcement Insurance Architectural Controls Management Budget	Owners control	Complete control of board by owners, but developer may be asked to maintain liaison.

*Developers may elect to maintain complete control of architectural/design review committee until the development is completed. Alternately, developers may structure an architectural review committee for postdevelopment matters (additions and modifications) and turn control of this committee over to owners by 25 to 50 percent of closings.
Source: Adapted from C. James Dowden, *Creating a Community Association: The Developer's Role in Condominium and Homeowners' Associations*, 2d rev. ed. (Washington, D.C./Alexandria, Va.: ULI–the Urban Land Institute and CAI–Community Associations Institute, 1986), p. 64.

always an easy task, but it can be done well if done thoughtfully."

If an association has been properly structured, has a good financial basis, and has strong, responsible leadership, developers have performed well and little follow-up support should be necessary. But continuing contact with the association and the offer of assistance with problems that arise will serve the developer's good reputation in the community and may be highly valuable toward maintaining the development's long-term value. An example might be assistance in estimating replacement and repair reserves or the negotiation of contracts for maintenance. Developers' expertise in this area may be invaluable to the association. Simply expressing a willingness to assist may be a major contribution to maintaining strong leadership in the association. It is most true when the association relies heavily on self-management.

The association's ongoing successful management is not the developer's responsibility, but providing the best possible management structure to meet the needs of the association and the tools to assist in developing good management is. This effort begins with the orientation of potential buyers and new residents.[30] The explanation of the association and its functions should be an integral part of the marketing program, and initiation to the association should be an integral part of the orientation for new residents.

---

[30] For additional information, see CAI, *The Homebuyer and the Community Association* and *The Homeowner and the Community Association* (Alexandria, Va.: Author, 1985).

8.
Rehabilitation and Adaptive Use

Rehabilitation and adaptive use projects have contributed significantly to total residential development in the United States for several years, and, for many who undertake them, they offer challenging and exciting opportunities. Like all development, risks and potential rewards are involved. Those who undertake a residential rehabilitation/adaptive use project—real estate developer, private citizen, or the public sector—do so for any number of reasons: return on investment, the desire for an architecturally well-done rehabilitation of a historic building, or an interest in community development. This chapter focuses primarily on rehabilitation and adaptive use in the context of opportunities for residential developers.

Rehabilitation and Adaptive Use Defined

Rehabilitation (or "rehab," as it is commonly called) is a distinctive element of residential development. Generally, the term describes a variety of repairs or alterations to an existing building that allow it to serve contemporary uses while preserving features of the past. It might include overall repairs for maintaining the property, bringing substandard units up to code, or totally gutting the interior, leaving the exterior structure, and installing modern systems and appliances. This latter form of rehabilitation is not merely a cosmetic cleaning or simple improvements. Often the building is stripped to its most important structural elements: foundations, walls, roof, and possibly floors. Extensive work then begins with modern mechanical systems and newly designed interiors inserted.

An adaptation of a building from a prior use (factory, railroad station, school, for example) to housing—that is, "adaptive use"—is a component of the rehabilitation industry. Improving facades, such as repainting or repointing, or realigning fenestration might occur as well. But rehabilitation (and adaptive use) are not necessarily "restorations" that accurately return a building to a particular period in its history by removing later additions or replacing materials with those appropriate to the architectural style and period.

Of the existing pool of residential and commercial buildings needing rehabilitation, many have a sound structure and large units by today's standards. Interior finishes are often of high-quality materials, such as solid wood interior doors, hardwood floors, and elaborate millwork, that are seldom affordable in new construction. Depending on the budget, developers can do as little or as much as they like to upgrade finishes. Necessary building components are already there, and it is a matter of deciding where the available budget money should be spent for the greatest return.

In many cases, a building can remain 80 to 90 percent occupied during the renovation, depending on the scope of work, type of building, and condition of mechanical systems. With some planning, existing utilities and mechanical systems can be kept operating and adapted for a smooth change to the permanent system as newly renovated units become ready for occupancy. Other benefits of rehabilitation over new construction include the absence of subsurface site risks, little or no delay in construction as a result of the weather, good community support, as renovators are usually perceived as ridding the neighborhood of a rundown building, and proximity to existing urban services and infrastructure.

Most housing rehabilitation is the product of individual homeowners, who undertake such projects with an interest in their singular investment purpose and who may wish to contribute to architectural preservation and revitalization of the neighborhood and community and in the process own a house, obtained for an affordable price. This chapter, however, focuses more on rehabilitation as an opportunity for developers and on larger public and private rehabilitations. Rehabilitation occurs in both the public and private sectors and is both subsidized and unsubsidized. Groups that contribute to rehabilitation include homeowners, planners, preservationists, contractors, lending institutions, real estate brokers, and developers/entrepreneurs.

Historic Overview

Historically, societal concerns for American housing can be traced to the social welfare reform movement of the late 19th and early 20th centuries. Many of these concerns grew out of substandard living conditions in urban centers as populations of new immigrants, migration from the South to the North during the post–Civil War era, and transitions from rural to urban locations overflowed the number of affordable housing units in the major cities as a result of the Industrial Revolution. Ethnic enclaves and urban ghettos of the poor were standard in cities. Advocates for more healthful housing conditions mobilized their forces, and social reformers of the day began an assessment of America's housing needs. From these efforts, standard codes for public health, safety, and welfare were written with powers of compliance backed by the weight of federal, state, and local governments.

The ideas and works of early 20th century architectural pioneers, the foundations of the "City Beautiful" movement, and the seeds of the emerging planning

8-1   The Sheffield Court Apartments in Arlington, Virginia, were built during World War II and served initially as housing for enlisted officers. After 43 years of heavy use, the garden apartment buildings showed signs of severe deterioration. Rehabilitation by The Artery Organization included refinishing each building's masonry surfaces to their original condition, installing new service and utility systems, and modernizing the interiors of each apartment.

profession took root. An interest in beautiful cities through architecture and urban design created an overwhelming interest in public spaces, building design, and building uses. Technological innovations provided further excitement concerning opportunities.

The suburbs, a phenomenon of the railroad, trolley, and private car, were well under way after World War I, although early examples had been developed shortly after the Civil War. The return of the GIs in 1945 and 1946 after World War II, linked with government financing initiatives for young families, allowed for the suburban explosion across the American landscape. Land, financing, and access to the downtown core were widely available throughout the country in new suburban housing developments.

Meanwhile, the established housing stock within cities was aging. As new families chose to locate in the suburbs, the cities began to suffer. The transitions from factories to modern office buildings, from downtown central business districts to new shopping centers in suburbia, and from rail transport and trolley to airline carriers and private cars left downtown buildings—houses, train stations, or businesses—looking tired, underused, and dirty. The "urban renewal" pioneers of the 1950s sought to rectify the situation with a wholesale elimination of blight in the form of mass demolition of structures, followed by new construction.

As the nation recovered from the social conflicts of the 1960s and the Vietnam era, the abandoned urban centers enjoyed a blossoming back-to-the-city movement after a 50-year hiatus since the "City Beautiful" movement. By the mid-1970s, a component of Americans labeled "urban pioneers" ostensibly had recaptured old houses in urban centers. An outgrowth of the movement toward historic preservation resulting from the National Historic Preservation Act of 1966, these pioneers concentrated on the preservation and restoration of historic landmarks and old houses now made affordable by the ravages of neglect.

In the mid-1970s, conflict grew between preservation efforts and urban redevelopment projects supported by Urban Development Action Grants (UDAGs) and other federal programs. Meanwhile, however, the tax laws were changing. Section 2124, "Tax Incentives to Encourage the Preservation of Historic Structures," part of the Federal Tax Reform Act of 1976, permitted owners of structures on the National Register or within a historic district listed on the National Register who invested in rehabilitation the opportunity to recoup their investments either through rapid amortization of expenses for rehabilitation over 60 months or, in certain cases, through accelerated depreciation of the value of the entire rehabilitated structure.

Further changes occurred in later tax laws. Effective January 1, 1982, the Economic Recovery Tax Act allowed an investment tax credit of 15 percent for structures at least 30 years old, 20 percent for rehabilitation of structures at least 40 years old, and 25 percent for certified historic structures of any age. The law covered residential structures used for commercial purposes if they were certified as being historic. Thus, the statute provided significant incentives for the use of historic buildings as rental housing. Projects certified under the act were to be for "substantial" rehabilitation, defined as exceeding $5,000 or the taxpayer's adjusted basis in the property, whichever was greater. The new law also allowed owners to recover the costs of all depreciable real estate in 15 years if they chose instead of the 40 to 60 years required by previous legislation. The write-off could be accomplished either by a straight-line or accelerated method.

While other changes have been made to tax laws since the 1981 act, none has had as significant (or negative) an effect on rehabilitation as the Tax Reform Act of 1986. Congress not only agreed to trim the investment tax credit to 20 percent from 25 percent but also curbed tax shelters in general by virtually eliminating the use of "passive losses" to offset income from salaries, dividends, and interest. A single 10 percent credit for nonhistoric commercial buildings built before 1936 was added, and real estate depreciation periods were increased from 19 years to 27.5 years for residential real estate and 31.5 years for commercial real estate (all straight line). The exclusion of 60 percent of a long-term capital gain was repealed, and capital gains were now taxed as ordinary income. Along with other provisions of the law, the changes eliminated the tax benefits that led many upper-income individuals to invest in rehabilitation of historic buildings.

The public sector has built a large chain of programs to spark investment in cities and neighborhoods. While many of these programs were initiated to encourage low- and moderate-income housing for the period 1976 through 1986, specific financial and tax incentives also encouraged private funding and public/private partnerships for the rehabilitation of historic buildings. In recent years, however, rehabilitation and adaptive use have been greatly affected by the Tax Reform Act of 1986 and by the systematic withdrawal of the federal government from supporting the production of low-income housing.

Despite the volume of rehabilitation and adaptive use in the nation's cities over the past 40 years, most Americans continue to favor suburbia over the city or the country. The U.S. Census Bureau reports that of more than 46 million people who moved between March 1986 and March 1987, 43 percent moved within, between, or to suburbia. The suburbs gained 4.8 million people during this period from the central cities of metropolitan areas and 1.6 million from nonmetropolitan areas. With all the moving about, the suburbs registered a net gain of 1.97 million people, while cities and nonmetropolitan areas registered net losses of 1.04 million and 930,000, respectively.

Private and Public Rehabilitation

Private developers who undertake rehabilitation projects often view themselves differently from those developers whose main interests are new construction. Advocates of rehabilitation must enjoy the challenge of rehabilitation, for they face additional risks and constraints from the beginning: they must investigate the feasibility of an existing building, their designs are limited by structure and square footage of the building shell, and they face uncertainties about what might be found within the building's structure— the "surprises" that may cost time and money and test current plans or designs. Even the regulatory approval process can be riskier for rehabilitation projects, especially when a structure with historic significance is involved. Many developers involved in rehabilitation have found themselves struggling through a historic

317

ULI council member Paul Z. (Pete) Rose is president of The Klingbeil Company, a San Francisco–based development company that has undertaken dozens of residential rehabilitation projects around the United States. Rose cautions all developers contemplating rehabilitation or adaptive use to "beware of what you cannot see—surprises have a way of arising in almost every project." A few of the company's experiences (below), demonstrate the range of issues that can go wrong—or right. "It is a little like trying to describe an earthquake," says Rose. "You have to live through one to understand the meaning of surprise."

- *840 Powell Street (San Francisco, California).* The seven-story apartment building was being converted to luxury condominiums. All of the bathrooms on the street frontage side of the building were connected to a drain pipe that ran down the outside of the building's front facade. To our surprise, the pipe was not connected to anything, so when people drained their bathtubs, soapy water ran down the building's front.
- *The Queen Anne Hotel (San Francisco, California).* Our project was to create a fashionable boutique hotel from a falling-down, Victorian ladies' home built in the late 1800s. Painfully slow removal—by hand—of 100 years' worth of white enamel paint revealed absolutely beautiful paneling throughout the building. This unexpected resource quickly became a factor in our marketing plan.

- *University Village (Columbus, Ohio).* The 848-unit apartment building had a basement, but the basement's floor-to-ceiling height appeared insufficient to accommodate additional units, so we based our financial analysis accordingly. In rehabilitating the building, we discovered false floors and ceilings in the basement that, when removed, made basement units possible. We found that we could add 128 units in the basement for an insignificant sum per unit—and our cash flow improved measurably.
- *Executive Clubs (Alexandria, Virginia).* The project is located in the city's historic district. The city wanted the unsafe and unsightly "widow's walks" left in their broken state, even after studies determined that they had been added to the building in the 1950s and were not part of the original architecture. City officials thought the disrepair looked authentic.
- *Waldorf (Pittsburgh, Pennsylvania).* This project is a good example of how thorough, early inspection of the building paid off. Our inspection revealed that a 10-story building in this cluster of apartment buildings we were converting to condominiums had twisted on its foundation and broken the concrete floor. Studies also showed that this particular building contained asbestos. We were able to negotiate a sufficient discount from the seller to be able to repair the foundation, remove the asbestos, and still have a financially feasible project.

certification process that has involved considerably more time and money than ever envisioned. And when it happens, developers and investors must have the resources to wait out the approval process and sometimes to undertake a more costly project than originally anticipated. But when a project is completed, rehabilitators often believe they have a product superior to new construction in quality and market appeal. When the rehabilitation is of a historic building, rehabilitation developers view the project as particularly exciting.

Housing rehabilitation undertaken by private developers uses a mix of financial packages that ultimately produces a financial return to the participants. The primary incentive toward rehabilitation is the potential return, yet developers firmly see themselves

as taking financial risks to produce a desired product in demand by consumers. Further, developers' efforts often precipitate a change in neighborhoods—in both financial and social terms—that sparks other opportunities for investment. Decayed neighborhoods find new life through better housing and associated retail and commercial uses, which support additional residential rehabilitation.

Rehabilitation that is directly subsidized by public monies (as opposed to rehabilitations indirectly subsidized by favorable tax treatment) has generally been associated with the goal of assisting the housing needs of low- and moderate-income families. Some governmental programs offer direct dollar aid to families, while others guarantee low-cost loans. Governments at all levels—federal, state, and local—offer a multi-

William F. Johnston

T.W. Prendiville

8-3, 8-4 Rehabilitation of Commonwealth—a 14.2-acre, 392-unit, low-income housing project located fewer than four miles from downtown Boston—involved gutting all the buildings to provide larger units, demolishing two midrise buildings to make room for a community center and a daycare center, and modifying the site plan to improve the relationship between parking and housing units, improve street circulation, increase landscaping, and better define public and private spaces. The project demonstrates the potential for reuse of aging public housing developments (left). Disrepair had fallen on Commonwealth before rehabilitation (right).

tude of programs for developers who undertake rehabilitation, again stressing the goal of assistance to low- or moderate-income families. While subsidy programs are offered as incentives to engage the private sector, developers should beware of the risks and costs associated with filtering through regulations and reviews among the many governmental agencies involved in the process. Gaining cooperation among local public officials, banks, developers, and citizens is one important aspect of public officials' role in sponsoring residential rehabilitation projects in community development.

The Rehabilitation Process

Residential rehabilitation for the most part comprises the private sector in unison with public officials. Although public officials play a role in initiating rehabilitation, it is most often the private sector that takes on the burden of processing the project from feasibility through implementation. Like any other development, rehabilitation involves acquiring property (land and buildings), obtaining required permits and approvals, seeking designs and ideas for use, and putting financing options into place.

Fundamentally, rehabilitation/adaptive use is a process not unlike the process described earlier in this handbook for new construction. Differences exist, to be sure, but many of the same basic factors and procedures involved in any successful real estate venture apply to rehabilitation and adaptive use. In essence, the process of successfully bringing new life to older structures has four basic steps: initiation, feasibility, planning and financing, and marketing. The links among these steps cannot be overstressed, for a project can fail at any step in the process.

Initiation

Many actors in the development field can initiate rehabilitation and adaptive use projects. The public sector initiates some projects. For example, a city might own a property and declare it surplus, or the property might be transferred from one agency to another (for example, from the school board to the department of community development), acquired by eminent domain as part of a larger revitalization effort, or acquired through abandonment. The city can then sell, lease, donate, or swap the property, develop it with the private sector's participation through a partnership agreement, or develop the property itself.

The development of the Lewinsville Center residences is one example of the public sector's initiative in rehabilitation and adaptive use. The Fairfax County (Virginia) Housing and Redevelopment Authority rehabilitated the Lewinsville Center residences as part of an effort to develop affordable housing for lower-income elderly people in the absence of federal subsidies. Using a $500,000 capital grant for renovation from the Fairfax County Board of Supervisors, the developer's concept was to adapt a surplus elementary school for housing by reducing the square footage in each apartment without sacrificing livability and to provide congregate living, dining, and kitchen facilities.

The reuse of the surplus elementary school provided for the collocation of a number of services, including two daycare centers for children (one privately operated, the other county operated), a comprehensive adult daycare center (operated by the Fairfax County Health Department), and a senior center (operated by the County Department of Recreation and Community Services), all located on the first floor of the building, with living units on the second floor. The Housing and Redevelopment Authority leases the second floor of the facility from the school board.

The public sector has undertaken other roles in initiating rehabilitation and adaptive use: advocate, regulator/facilitator/broker, and funder. In such instances, private real estate developers and nonprofit organizations acting as developers have used advice and assistance from the public sector to help bring projects to fruition. For example, using an $8.4 million loan from the District of Columbia Housing Finance Agency, federal historic tax credits, a syndication by private investors, and HUD Section 8 rent subsidies, a partnership between a local private developer and a neighboring church adapted a 1920-era commercial/bank building in Washington, D.C., listed on the National Register of Historic Places, for reuse as housing for the elderly. Based on a preliminary site assessment, the developer, Winn Development Company, determined that it would be more cost-effective to rehabilitate and adapt the upper floors of the building for housing while maintaining the street level for retail use (in fact, previous tenants have rented most retail space). For financial reasons, the developer decided to build two additional stories to increase the total number of residential units from 100 to 150. Because the building was listed on the National Register of Historic Places, the additional stories were set back so they would not be visible from the street, thus preserving the historic tax credits. The building opened in early 1986.

Nonprofit sponsors have undertaken rehabilitation and adaptive use for a variety of reasons. In some cases, the motive is to provide shelter for those potentially excluded from the housing mainstream—low-income individuals, the elderly, and the disabled. In other instances, sponsorship of such projects is simply good business. In Charlotte, North Carolina, a consortium of seven banks agreed to lend money to the city, which would relend the money to people interested in buying and renovating houses in the city's Fourth Ward. With no private developers willing to take a chance on the area, with private redevelopment moving slowly, and with a direct investment in the area in the form of a new headquarters building, North Carolina National Bank (NCNB), one of the original seven banks, established a wholly owned nonprofit subsidiary, NCNB Community Development Corporation, to become the development catalyst for the area. Any profits realized by the corporation are returned into operations and future development projects and according to its charter cannot be returned to NCNB's balance sheet.

In addition to the strong sense of corporate citizenship involved, NCNB also recognized that its initial below-market mortgage loan money had been lever-

8-5, 8-6 One of dozens of historic preservation projects undertaken by Philadelphia-based Historic Landmarks for Living, The Chocolate Works comprises five separate buildings transformed into 135 modern units designed to appeal to young professionals. Landscaping, decorative lighting, and a Victorian-style trellis give the former candy factory a residential feeling. Large industrial windows provide units with natural light.

aged into nearly $30 million of private investment in the Fourth Ward. NCNB got much of that spinoff investment but this time at market rates, contributing earning assets to the bank and returning the neighborhood to a net contributor in the community.

More recently, as rehabilitation and adaptive use have become more commonplace as a development activity, some private development firms have begun to concentrate solely on market-rate rehabilitation of housing. For example, Philadelphia-based Historic Landmarks for Living was started in 1978 as a full-service real estate development, management, and syndication organization specializing in the conversion of historically certified buildings into high-quality, multifamily housing. Until the 1986 changes in the tax law, Historic Landmarks for Living completed over 35 adaptive use projects, most in the Philadelphia area.[1]

Feasibility

The word "feasibility" is used to describe the preliminary analysis of a project, leading to a decision whether or not the project can proceed. The main areas to be examined are the project's marketability, the site, the structural integrity of the building, an architectural or historic evaluation, and financial feasibility. Developers often undertake a preliminary analysis of the property on their own and then seek outside help for more detailed analyses.

Analysis of Market and Demand

Analysis of market or demand verifies the overall idea of the project and identifies would-be consumers (buyers or renters). Developers seek to understand the demographic trends in the area—population characteristics by age and level of income, number of households and their general composition, the current stock of housing types available, housing costs, and vacancy rates. Interviews with public planners in housing and with real estate agents and an assessment of what is selling or renting in the market form a solid base for analyzing what the product type should be. Because most rehabilitation involves substantial changes to the building, developers through market analysis test their original idea for the product or formulate what products are most in demand in their geographic region. If, for example, the analysis finds that the absorption of new or rehabilitated space is slowing and that a significant inventory exists, then the probability of immediate acceptance is diminished. (See Appendix K for a checklist of items essential to a market analysis.)

An analysis of competitive projects in the market area and outside the market area where local examples are scarce (as might be the case with rehabilitation projects) uncovers such information about successful types of products, an inventory of competitive units, rental rates and/or selling prices, absorption, occupancy rates, waiting lists, operating histories, and physical characteristics, including unit mix and sizes. The analysis also addresses an area's development trends in terms of planned and proposed projects. A final task is to reach a series of conclusions addressing the potential pace of absorption and identifying general type, mix, and size of units and the range of sales and rents for the proposed project.

The extent of market analysis for a given project depends greatly on the nature of anticipated consumers. Rehabilitation or adaptive use undertaken at market rates with little or no public subsidy requires a rigorous market study commensurate with that undertaken for any new construction project. A project undertaken for more discrete market niches may require less analysis; for example, a project geared specifically to low- and moderate-income households would have little difficulty finding a market, and the developer's feasibility analysis would likely focus more on site and economic issues than on market issues.

Site Analysis

Site analysis includes an assessment of the location of the building in its immediate neighborhood and in a wider context, such as its regional access. Distance to downtown work centers, to major retail districts, and to major transportation routes forms part of the locational aspects of site analysis. Locational factors are often foremost in consumers' minds and should play a major role in the developer's analysis of the project's merit. Public investment and private initiatives in the immediate area should also be examined. The availability of public infrastructure, opportunities for leisure activities, the neighborhood's socioeconomic profile, and nearby comparable and competitive projects must be ascertained.

Most opportunities for rehabilitation are located in highly urbanized areas close to employment, transportation, and urban services. Such sites are often already served by electricity, gas, sewer, and water and do not require the developer to fund extensions

---

[1] For an example of an adaptive use project completed by Historic Landmarks for Living, see *Project Reference File:* "The Chocolate Works," vol. 17, no. 4 (Washington, D.C.: ULI–the Urban Land Institute, January–March 1987).

DISPLACEMENT AND RELOCATION:
A FACTOR IN DETERMINING A PROJECT'S FEASIBILITY

The displacement of tenants in residential buildings has been a concern since the 1960s, when sweeping federal urban renewal programs uprooted existing, often low-income, residents. Such displacement continues to occur as a result of some of today's publicly funded programs and of private market activities.

Many cities have experienced extensive revitalization by the private sector as a result of the existence of attractive, well-located, reclaimable housing stock in a market with constraints on supply and a growing demand for housing. Private activity involving the preservation or rehabilitation of housing or in some cities the conversion of apartment buildings to condominiums has often focused on older neighborhoods with low-income households. As a result, they are most affected by displacement yet are the least able to afford it.

Studies have found that displacement affects between 1 and 6 percent of all households in any given year and is the consequence of increased rent, the sale of the house, conversion to condominiums, eviction, or the renovation of the unit.

Displacement occurs when any household is forced to move from its residence by conditions [that] affect the dwelling or its immediate surroundings and...are beyond the household's reasonable ability to control or prevent; occur despite the household's having met all previously imposed conditions of occupancy; and make continued occupancy by that household impossible, hazardous, or unaffordable.[1]

Concern over affordable housing and increasing homelessness has made the issue of the displacement and relocation of existing tenants more visible. Some federal and local legislation is in place to protect the rights of existing tenants. In certain cases, the legislation specifies some financial obligation on the part of the developer whose actions have caused households to be displaced.

Displacement and relocation assistance from developers is required under federal law in projects involving federal monies. The basis for this requirement is the Uniform Relocation Assistance and Real Property Acquisition Policies Act of 1970, which mandated uniform relocation requirements for all federal and federally assisted programs. The act, which was revised in July 1989, can require that rental assistance be given to displaced and relocated tenants for up to 42 months for the difference between former and current rents in a comparable unit plus moving expenses. Further, HUD requirements for the Section 312 program stipulate that a developer using Section 312 funds to rehabilitate a project comply with the act.

---

of infrastructure. As a result, developers involved in rehabilitation can often be less concerned about physical site conditions than they might be for a new construction project and can concentrate more specifically on the quality of the neighborhood and the condition of the existing structure. While the characteristics inherent in most rehabilitation and adaptive use sites appeal to some market segments, they may not appeal to others (such as young families, who still generally prefer suburban, single-family settings). Residential developers need first to understand the intended market and determine that market's preferences for location and lifestyle before being able to judge a particular site's suitability for development.

Another specific characteristic that should not be overlooked is the availability of parking. Many older structures suitable for rehabilitation were built before the use of automobiles, and thus the site may not accommodate modern requirements for parking. Further, many rehabilitation projects result in an increased number of dwelling units, which further increases the demand for parking. When examining a site, developers should determine whether adequate spaces are available for residents to park and, if not, whether marketability will suffer if each unit does not have at least one off-street space.

Building Integrity

"Integrity" may refer to the solidity of the building's construction (a building lacking structural integrity will be rife with construction and engineering problems), or it may refer to a more elusive quality, such as architectural or historic integrity. A building of high architectural integrity generally means a building in solid structural condition whose original design or form has not been altered beyond recognition. Historic integrity refers to a building that has not lost its chain of documentation regarding its use or its significance.

Many municipalities rely on the Uniform Relocation Act as the basis for state or city regulations to protect tenants in projects redeveloped with public funds.

- *San Francisco* requires developers to assume the full financial obligation of providing the benefits and assistance available under the federal act to existing tenants who are temporarily or permanently displaced. In that high-rent city, the amounts can be so costly that developers may think twice about using city funds for a project that will require relocation.
- *Washington, D.C.,* allows existing tenants both protection from conversion and relocation assistance. After a contract is signed on a building, tenants are allowed a period of time to form a cooperative and purchase the building themselves. If the original contract goes through, tenants who have had a lease longer than one year can continue to rent indefinitely month to month. When substantial rehabilitation is undertaken for the purpose of conversion, tenants must be given 120 days notice to vacate the unit, and the developer must pay moving expenses for tenants to move to a comparable unit.
- *Portland, Oregon,* requires a 120-day notice similar to that in Washington, D.C., when a building is being converted. In addition, developers must pay moving expenses and the last month's rent for all low-income residents.
- *New York City* has extensive laws to protect tenants. Most conversions to cooperatives and condominiums in the city are completed under noneviction plans, which require 15 percent of existing tenants to agree to the conversion. The dissenting remainder are allowed to continue to rent with the same rent control or rent stabilization laws governing their tenancy.

Displacement and relocation thus become an issue for any developer who acquires a residential building with existing tenants, intending to undertake a program of rehabilitation that will affect the availability of those tenants' housing. Developers who plan to proceed using federal or private monies would be well advised to understand thoroughly the costs involved, for such costs can be substantial, involving either immediate expenditures to relocate tenants or future costs of a prolonged effort to increase rents.

[1] E. Grier and G. Grier, "Urban Displacement: A Reconnaissance," in S. Lasky and D. Spain, eds., *Back to the City: Issues in Neighborhood Renovation* (Elmsford, N.Y.: Pergamon Press, 1980), p. 256.
Source: Prepared by Cynthia Angell, senior research associate, ULI–the Urban Land Institute.

A building's physical and structural qualities must be thoroughly inspected at the outset to determine its suitability for the proposed residential use. For example, utility systems that were once considered state-of-the-art might require complete and expensive replacement. Particular problems can arise regarding fire codes and, in areas prone to earthquakes, seismic codes. More important, some buildings may have severe structural problems that will render them poor candidates for rehabilitation. While the quality of original materials and craftsmanship in older buildings may in some ways be superior to new construction, years of neglect can leave bricks, interior details, and structural and support systems in need of extensive work.

Concealed conditions constitute the greatest risk in the rehabilitation of older buildings. Design consultants can, with a cursory look throughout the building, detect major structural problems and the condition of existing equipment and the roof and can form an overall opinion about the building's condition. Problems most commonly found include dissimilar adjoining metals, failure of exterior walls, unserviceable plumbing mains, corroded electrical wiring, and hazardous materials.

Hazardous materials, particularly asbestos, constitute the greatest financial risk. Asbestos may be found in insulation, roof shingles, floor tiles, plaster compounds, and ceiling tiles. An example of such financial impact is provided by a construction company official in the Washington, D.C., area. The scope of work called for removing plaster from the kitchen walls to work on the plumbing and electrical systems; the plaster was found to contain traces of asbestos. If a regular demolition crew removed the plaster, the cost would be about $80 per apartment; if the plaster was removed as a hazardous waste, the cost would be about $650 per apartment. A careful check of maintenance records can uncover trends and problem areas, such as plumbing, leaks and stoppages, roof leaks, and so on. Technology today allows inspection of the plumbing system through tiny, closed-circuit television cameras.

When certain building components are retrofitted in a building without considering how the new components will mesh with the existing system, additional problems can occur. For example, replacing old windows and exterior doors in a building that had no insulation in the exterior walls could create a problem, because new, state-of-the-art windows and doors create an air-tight environment that does not allow moisture to escape from buildings, causing condensation on exterior walls. In this case, a well-designed heating and ventilating system is necessary.

Bringing an older building up to full compliance with present building codes is not always economically feasible, especially in buildings constructed before the 1960s, because many do not have adequate fire separation walls between units and common spaces. Electrical, mechanical, fire, and life safety codes are much more stringent today. The Building Officials and Code Administrators International (BOCA) code that is widely used does not address renovation and rehabilitation in terms of which non-complying building components can remain and which must be brought up to code. As a result, planning and budgeting for these items are difficult. Issues involving codes can usually be negotiated with local building officials, however. A developer might successfully negotiate with the electrical inspector to waive the code's requirement for one electrical outlet for every 12 feet of wall space in return for replacing the outlets in the bathroom and the kitchen with ground-fault interrupter plugs, for example. The bargaining chip in this case is that the developer is willing to correct a life-threatening situation in return for waiving a code requirement that exists solely for residents' convenience.

If compliance with the code is not possible, insurance for the project may be jeopardized. Many insurance companies hesitate to provide fire, building risk, and extended coverage insurance for a structure that does not fully meet code requirements. In certain cases, when only partial insurance is available, developers must be self-insured for the balance.

The cost of upgrading building materials and structural and support systems for compliance with codes must be carefully examined before the developer makes a financial commitment to rehabilitate a particular building. Such costs may be a major factor in determining the economic viability of rehabilitation. In most instances, developers retain the services of a qualified engineer to help ascertain structural integrity, but even a very thorough inspection does not always reveal all of the building's potential structural pitfalls. It is not uncommon in rehabilitation projects for structural difficulties to arise throughout the process as portions of the building are uncovered. Developers of rehabilitation projects should be aware of these risks and be ready to undertake unanticipated structural improvements.

The federal government plays a large role in ensuring that the historical integrity of significant buildings is not lost as a result of rehabilitation. Buildings that have been and will be rehabilitated to take advantage of investment tax credits for historic rehabilitation must undergo a process of historic certification administered by the National Park Service of the U.S. Department of the Interior. Tax incentives for federal historic preservation are available for any qualified project that the Secretary of the Interior designates as a certified rehabilitation of a certified historic structure. These incentives were established and modified by the Tax Reform Act of 1976 (P.L. 94–455), the Revenue Act of 1978 (P.L. 95–600), the Tax Treatment Extension Act of 1980 (P.L. 96–541), the Economic Recovery Tax Act of 1981 (P.L. 97–34), and the Tax Reform Act of 1986 (P.L. 99–514). To qualify for the tax incentives, property owners or developers must complete and send the appropriate parts of the three-step application for certification of historic preservation, either to the state historic preservation officer, who then forwards the application to the National Park Service, or directly to the park service's regional office.

Parts 1 and 2 should be submitted together.[2] Part 1 is used:

- To request certification that a depreciable building contributes to the significance of a registered historic district and therefore qualifies as a "certified historic structure" for the purpose of rehabilitation;
- To request certification that a depreciable or nondepreciable building contributes to the significance of the registered historic district where it is located for a charitable contribution for conservation purposes;
- To request certification that a building does not contribute to the significance of the registered historic district where it is located;
- To request a preliminary determination of whether an individual building not yet on the National Register meets the National Register's

---

[2] Owners of buildings already listed on the National Register of Historic Places need not complete Part 1.

Criteria for Evaluation and will likely be listed on the National Register when nominated;

- To request a preliminary determination that a building located within a potential historic district contributes to the significance of the district;
- To request a preliminary determination that a building outside the period or area of significance of a registered historic district contributes to the significance of the district.

Part 2 is a description of proposed, ongoing, or completed rehabilitation work. It is recommended, however, that Part 2 be submitted before beginning any rehabilitation. Completion of Part 2 seeks to have the rehabilitation work certified by the Secretary of the Interior as consistent with the historic character of the structure or the historic district where the structure is located. Each project is measured against the Secretary of the Interior's "Standards for Rehabilitation and Guidelines for Rehabilitating Historic Buildings." While the wording has been modified slightly since first published, the intent has not changed. Some developers have lost the ability to use the tax credits provided by the tax law because they have ignored or misinterpreted the intent of these standards.

A project does not become a "certified rehabilitation" eligible for tax incentives until it is completed and designated as such by the National Park Service. The last part of the application is a request for certification of the completed work, including photographs, to document that what was proposed in the submission of Part 2 was actually completed. Fees for

---

8-8   THE SECRETARY OF THE INTERIOR'S STANDARDS FOR REHABILITATION AND
GUIDELINES FOR REHABILITATING HISTORIC BUILDINGS

1. Every reasonable effort shall be made to provide a compatible use for a property that requires minimal alteration of the building, structure, or site and its environment, or to use a property for its originally intended purpose.
2. The distinguishing original qualities or character of a building, structure, or site and its environment shall not be destroyed. The removal or alteration of any historic material or distinctive architectural features should be avoided when possible.
3. All buildings, structures, and sites shall be recognized as products of their own time. Alterations that have no historical basis and that seek to create an earlier appearance shall be discouraged.
4. Changes that may have taken place in the course of time are evidence of the history and development of a building, structure, or site and its environment. These changes may have acquired significance in their own right, and this significance shall be recognized and respected.
5. Distinctive stylistic features or examples of skilled craftsmanship that characterize a building, structure, or site shall be treated with sensitivity.
6. Deteriorated architectural features shall be repaired rather than replaced wherever possible. In the event replacement is necessary, the new material should match the material being replaced in composition, design, color, texture, and other visual qualities. Repair or replacement of missing architectural features should be based on accurate duplications of features, substantiated by historic, physical, or pictorial evidence rather than on conjectural designs or the availability of different architectural elements from other buildings or structures.
7. The surface cleaning of structures shall be undertaken with the gentlest means possible. Sandblasting and other cleaning methods that will damage the historic building materials shall not be undertaken.
8. Every reasonable effort shall be made to protect and preserve archeological resources affected by, or adjacent to, any project.
9. Contemporary design for alterations and additions to existing properties shall not be discouraged when such alterations and additions do not destroy significant historical, architectural, or cultural material, and such design is compatible with the size, scale, color, material, and character of the property, neighborhood, or environment.
10. Wherever possible, new additions or alterations to structures shall be done in such a manner that if such additions or alterations were to be removed in the future, the essential form and integrity of the structure would be unimpaired.

Source: Historic Preservation Certification Application (Washington, D.C.: U.S. Government Printing Office, 1989-0-619-549).

this last step of the application are based on the dollar amount spent on rehabilitation and range from $500 to $2,500.

Planning and Financing

Planning the program for the building includes determining the number, size, and type of units, the overall design and size of common areas, placement of mechanical systems, landscaping, and amenities to be offered. In rehabilitation work, certain constraints bind designers and engineers to the volume of the building, its mass, and its material. Most rehabilitation work is completed around the shell of the building; that is, its foundation and structural elements remain in place, but new mechanical systems and interiors are designed.

8-9   Standing on a 26-acre site in a residential area of Dayton, Ohio, 10 Wilmington Place provides 223 congregate-care housing units in a structure previously occupied by the Dayton State Hospital. Local preservation groups and residents of the surrounding neighborhood rallied to save the building from demolition and succeeded in having the structure placed on the National Register of Historic Places. The main entrance provides elements of Italianate and Greek Revival architecture.

While individual homeowners probably have the convenience of time and can pace rehabilitation to suit a financial schedule (or other personal reasons), developers' interest in rehabilitation is to finish the unit to produce a salable or rentable product. Depending on the target market, decisions about construction (such as interior finishes) must be resolved as soon as possible. Developing a product for an upscale, amenity-conscious market implies different floor plans, materials, and finishes from those for a rehabilitation project designed for low- and moderate-income tenants or buyers. Parameters should be based on intended consumers' ability to pay.

Especially for a major rehabilitation project, a reputable construction company is crucial to the project's success—a job completed on time, within budget, and done well. As rehabilitation is completed on existing buildings with structural quirks or modifications of their own, however, surprises often are discovered. Anticipating them is next to impossible, and developers should plan contingency funds to weather such problems.

Many old buildings no longer have construction documents or blueprints available, and, for those that do, the paper plan and the built plan may not be consistent. At 10 Wilmington Place in Dayton, Ohio, for example, the program for the conversion of a state hospital for mental patients into congregate-care housing involved the conversion of the double-loaded hospital corridors to single-loaded corridors that could accommodate apartment units.[3] The building's thick bearing walls dictated the redesign, but determining the location of those walls was time-consuming, as no original structural plans for the building existed. Day by day, as previously unknown features were uncovered, decisions on structural design were changed.

Requirements for public approval or licensing are necessary at every step of planning and engineering to ensure basic standards for health, safety and welfare. Prior agreements between the developer and public entities come to the surface at this juncture of the project.

Economic Evaluation

The market analysis will have demonstrated comparable sales and rental costs per size of product. It will also have formed a barometer of what is selling in the area and at what rates. Based on such information, developers ascertain going rates in the area and price

[3] *Project Reference File:* "10 Wilmington Place," vol. 16, no. 10 (Washington, D.C.: ULI–the Urban Land Institute, April–June 1986).

the new product accordingly. Financing packages then must be put together, including permitting and license fees, architectural design fees, and contingency funds. Many developers provide (and some lenders require) a contingency fund of at least 10 to 15 percent of the total construction costs for unanticipated problems in construction. Private lenders, developers, and public officials often work closely to secure the financing package. The developer and the lender examine a pro forma statement detailing pretax income and after-tax income available to investors. (A sample pro forma for a typical rental rehabilitation project is provided in the accompanying figure.) If the return is sufficient to justify the

8-10   SAMPLE PRO FORMA

PROJECT INCOME

A. RESIDENTIAL UNITS

UNIT TYPE	NO. OF UNITS	RENT PER MONTH PER UNIT	RENT PER YEAR PER UNIT	GROSS INCOME
Efficiency		$	$	$
1 Bedroom, 1 Bathroom		$	$	$
2 Bedrooms, 1 Bathroom		$	$	$
2 Bedrooms, 1½ Bathrooms		$	$	$
Etc.				
TOTALS		$	$	$

B. RESIDENTIAL PLUS OTHER (Note: Assumes other income)

UNIT TYPE	INCOME	LAUNDRY	PARKING	OCCUPANCY RATE	EFFECTIVE ANNUAL INCOME
Efficiency	$	$	$	%	$
1 Bedroom, 1 Bathroom	$	$	$	%	$
2 Bedrooms, 1 Bathroom	$	$	$	%	$
2 Bedrooms, 1½ Bathrooms	$	$	$	%	$
Etc.					
TOTALS	$	$	$		$

PROJECT EXPENSES (Note: Cost basis for illustration)
A. Management Fee (@ 5% effective annual income . . . . $
B. Operating Costs ($250 per unit per year) . . . . $
C. Maintenance/Insurance ($200 per unit per year) . . . . $
D. Operating Reserve ($150 per unit per year) . . . . $
E. Property Taxes (@ 1.2% of value) . . . . $
                                                      TOTAL PROJECT EXPENSES $
                                                                NET INCOME $

MORTGAGE CALCULATION
A. Net Income . . . . $
B. Owner's Profit (@ 10%) . . . . $
C. Available for Debt Service . . . . $
D. Annual Cost of Existing Debt . . . . $
E. Net Available for Rehabilitation Loan . . . . $

FEASIBILITY CALCULATION
A. Projected Cost of Rehabilitation . . . . $
B. Amount of Public Subsidy . . . . $
C. Amount of Loan Application . . . . $

Source: U.S. Department of Housing and Urban Development, "How to Design a Rental Rehabilitation Program" (Washington, D.C.: Author, 1985).

financing, the project can proceed given no unforeseen dilemmas.

The 1986 Tax Reform Act

Perhaps the most critical aspect of planning a rehabilitation/adaptive use project is its financial feasibility. The bottom line for most developers and other project sponsors is whether the project will make a profit or break even, or whether a gap exists between income and expenses and if so how it can be remedied. During the heyday of rehabilitation projects sponsored by the tax act, many deals were predicated on tax losses initially, with a profit turned when the units could be converted to condominium ownership.

At present, residential rehabilitation is in a transitional state in the United States. Effects of the 1986 Tax Reform Act, which replaced earlier tax laws and limited allowances for tax shelters and passive losses for investors, have resulted in approximately a two-thirds drop in historic rehabilitation projects, according to the National Park Service. Major allocations of funding at HUD were discontinued after 1989. Both of these effects have severely constrained opportunities for private real estate developers to rehabilitate buildings. Such operating limitations swing with many tides within the industry, however, as a result of its dependence on private lenders and financial packages put together by public/private partnerships, and they are often affected by federal, state, and local politics as well as the mood of the private sector.

The effects of the 1986 Tax Reform Act on rehabilitation projects by the private sector cannot be overstated. Projects that before January 1987 were results of the historic investment tax credits dropped 43 percent between 1987 and 1988. In 1988, dollars invested dropped 20 percent, to less than $1 billion, compared to the peak years of 1983, 1984, and 1985, when investment was well over $2 billion per year. The Department of the Interior, which oversees the program, estimates that nearly 75 percent of projects before 1988 would not have been considered without the advantages of the tax incentives. In addition, Interior states that *half* of all projects undertaken under the tax act were housing projects. Total national statistics from the Department of Interior demonstrate that nearly 20,000 historic projects were undertaken and "certified" between 1976 and 1986 using the tax incentive program, with investment of nearly $13 billion.

The possibility always exists that newer legislation might neutralize or counteract the results of the 1986 Tax Reform Act. Any discussion must therefore recognize that an overwhelming constraint to residential

8-11

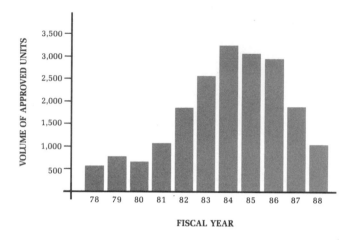

TRENDS ANALYSIS:
HISTORIC REHABILITATION PROJECTS
APPROVED BY THE U.S. DEPARTMENT
OF THE INTERIOR
1977–1988

*Figures are estimated maximum private investment, assuming all approved projects are completed.

Source: U.S. Department of the Interior, National Park Service, Technical Preservation Services, Preservation Assistance Division, "Tax Incentives for Rehabilitating Historic Buildings: Fiscal Year 1988 Analysis" (Washington, D.C.: Author, November 1988).

rehabilitation and adaptive use projects has been the flight of investors from historic projects because they desired the shelters provided by rules governing passive losses of the pre-1986 laws. Under the 1986 act, the tax credit for those investors with incomes of more than $200,000 has been reduced and for those with income of $250,000 or more has been eliminated. Developers now have sought to target investors earning $50,000 to $200,000. Many supporters, especially within historic preservation interests, are calling for a reinstatement of the rules governing passive losses for historic rehabilitation and low-income housing projects.

Federal Programs

The federal Department of Housing and Urban Development has long been a source of funding for residential rehabilitation programs. Building upon the very strong interests in community development and neighborhood revitalization of the recent past, most HUD programs, such as Community Development Block Grants (CDBGs) and UDAGs, have been useful as aids to cities and are currently listed as "active" (a term the agency uses to mark an ongoing project). Other successful programs that encourage residential rehabilitation (through grants, direct loans, or subsi-

WHAT'S LEFT AT HUD?
FEDERAL GOVERNMENT PROGRAMS TO
ASSIST LOW- AND MODERATE-INCOME HOUSING AS OF 1988

Program Name	Dollar Use (FY 1988) (Audience or Recipient)	General Criteria Intent of Program	Cumulative Activity to Date over Life of Program
Community Development Block Grant (entitlement)	$2,041 million obligated for 736 metropolitan cities and 121 urban counties	Grants for promotion of quality community development, economic development, neighborhood revitalization, and improved facilities/services; 60% or more of funds must benefit low-/moderate-income residents	1974–1988 obligations totaling nearly $33 billion
Community Development Block Grant (nonentitlement)	$850 million obligated for 51 states for 3,250 small communities (including Puerto Rico)	Similar to above but states have the option to administer to nonentitlement units of government, i.e., areas in nonmetropolitan regions with populations of 50,000 or fewer. All states have exercised the option to administer, except Hawaii and New York.	1974–1988 obligations totaling nearly $12 billion
Urban Development Action Grant	$275 million grant "Announcements" for 160 projects; obligations of $402 million for 202 projects	Grants to economically distressed cities and urban counties; 2.5 private dollars for every Action Grant dollar is required; 25% of each year's distribution may go to small cities of 50,000 or fewer. No new funds enacted for program in FY 1989.	1978–1988 announcements totaling $5.5 billion and obligations of $5.3 billion
Rental Rehabilitation	Obligations of $206 million	Grants to encourage rehabilitation of rental housing for lower-income tenants; after rehabilitation, 70 to 100% of units must be occupied by low-income tenants; for metropolitan areas with population of 50,000 plus.	1983–1988 obligations totaling $800 million
Section 312 Rehabilitation Loans	Loan obligations of $102 million	Direct loans, repayable over 20 years at 3% interest for low-income homeowners, used to finance rehabilitation, upgrading of single-family or multifamily residential, or mixed-use nonresidential housing in certified areas. Currently operating on repayment of loans with uncertain future for continued funding.	1964–1988 loans totaling $1.5 billion
Section 221(d)(2) Homeownership Assistance for Low- and Moderate-Income Families	5,426 units for $146.4 million	Mortgage insurance program to increase homeownership for low- and moderate-income families for purchase, construction, or rehabilitation of one- to four-family housing units	Through September 1988, 886,075 units insured for a value of $13.3 billion
Section 223(e) Housing in Declining Neighborhoods	1,406 home mortgages for $51.5 million; none for multifamily units	Mortgage insurance to purchase or rehabilitate housing in older, declining urban areas	Through September 1988, 174,522 home mortgages insured with a value of $2.9 billion; for multifamily units, 28,148 units insured with a value of $2.3 billion

▶

8-12 (continued)

Program Name	Dollar Use (FY 1988) (Audience or Recipient)	General Criteria Intent of Program	Cumulative Activity to Date over Life of Program
Section 207 Multifamily Rental Housing	None in 1988	Federal mortgage insurance to finance construction of rehabilitation of a broad cross section of rental housing	Through September 1988, 2,501 projects with 324,435 units insured with a value of $4.1 billion
Section 223(f) Existing Multifamily Rental Housing	8 projects with 1,950 units for $10.5 million	Federal mortgage insurance for purchase or refinancing of existing apartment projects	Through September 1988, 489 projects with 111,628 units insured with a value of $1.7 billion
Section 221(d)(3) and (4) Multifamily Rental Housing for Moderate-Income Families	9,919 units for $501 million	Mortgage insurance to finance rental or co-operative multifamily housing for moderate-income households	972,774 units for $24.3 billion
Section 106 Assistance to Non-profit Sponsors of Low-/Moderate-Income Housing and loans for Section 202 housing for elderly and handicapped	98 loans reserved; $903 thousand obligated	Technical assistance to nonprofit sponsors of low- and moderate-income housing. Also provides interest-free "seed money" loans to nonprofit sponsors of public housing agencies (currently limited to sponsors of Section 202 housing for elderly and handicapped)	Through September 1988, 1,078 loans reserved; $17.8 million obligated
Section 108 Loan Guarantees	Loan guarantee commitments of $144 million	Loan guarantee provision of CDBG program that provides assistance for community development. Provides front-end financing for large-scale community and economic development projects (including housing rehabilitation). Loans provided through private lending sources.	Total loan guarantee commitments of $1.1 billion
Section 8 (Total) Lower-Income Rental Assistance; includes voucher and certificate programs	$5.8 billion in new budget authority enacted in support of Section 8 program in FY 1988	Assists low- and very-low-income families in obtaining decent, safe, and sanitary housing in private accommodations. Permits families to rent units beyond the fair-market rents. Project sponsors may be private owners, profit or nonprofit organizations, public housing agencies, and state housing finance agencies.	Through September 1988, 2,332,462 units receiving subsidies
Section 231 Mortgage Insurance for Housing for the Elderly	290 units for $8.4 million	Federal mortgage insurance to finance the construction or rehabilitation of rental housing for the elderly or handicapped	Through September 1988, 67,047 units insured for $1.2 billion
Section 223(f) and Section 221(d) Multifamily Housing Coinsurance	340 projects with 68,958 units for $2.1 billion	Joint mortgage insurance by the federal government and state housing agencies and authorized private lenders to finance rental housing	1,140 projects with 270,670 units for $7.3 billion

Source: U.S. Department of Housing and Urban Development, *Programs of HUD 1988–1989*, HUD-214-PA-(16) (Washington, D.C.: May 1989). Table reviewed and updated by Albert J. Kliman, Director, Office of Budget, HUD Office of the Assistant Secretary for Administration.

8-13 Located on the banks of the Suncook River in Suncook, New Hampshire, this once-thriving industrial mill was adapted for use as 71 apartments with public financing that included a HUD Section 312 rehabilitation loan. About half of the units at the Emerson Mill Apartments benefit from the sights and sounds of the adjacent river, which is still flanked by the original rock walls.

dies) have been contained in various pieces of legislation since the 1934 National Housing Act.

Figure 8-13 profiles active programs for residential rehabilitation under HUD's authority, the dollar value of their contribution where available, and the general intent of each program. The enormity of HUD's investment in residential rehabilitation is evident. The CDBGs and UDAGs are monies awarded for a variety of public/private partnerships, of which only part may have been directed for investment in residential rehabilitation. The Rental Rehabilitation Program, begun in 1983 but authorized only through 1989, invested a total of $772 million by the end of fiscal year 1988.

Section 312, a direct loan program authorized in 1964, invested a total of $1.5 billion. Emerson Mill Apartments in Suncook, New Hampshire, was financed partially through a Section 312 rehabilitation loan and resulted in the adaptive use and rehabili-

tation of a turn-of-the-century textile mill into 71 market-rate apartments.[4] To qualify for the Section 312 loan, a project had to be located in an eligible area (a CDBG-, UDAG-, or Urban Homestead–designated area). The total cost of the rehabilitation had to include all work necessary to meet not only local rehabilitation standards but also HUD's standards for energy conservation and efficiency and historic preservation. In addition, multifamily properties seeking financing under Section 312 must meet certain criteria for income: the property must be located in a neighborhood where the median income of the residents does not exceed 80 percent of the median income for the area (adjusted for family size), or at least 51 percent of the property's initial residents after

[4] *Project Reference File:* "Emerson Mill Apartments," vol. 18, no. 10 (Washington, D.C.: ULI–the Urban Land Institute, April–June 1988).

rehabilitation must have family incomes not exceeding 80 percent of the median income for the area.

HUD, by virtue of its status as a federal agency, is affected by political tides, and many current housing programs face uncertain futures. A number of other non-HUD programs have been used to help finance rehabilitation and adaptive use projects, however, that private developers should explore. Two of the most widely used are preservation easements and programs administered by the National Trust for Historic Preservation.

An easement is a right or privilege in land or a building acquired from an owner that at the same time restricts the rights of use or privilege of that owner. Often, preservation or facade easements may be written between a building owner and a local historic preservation organization or government agency in return for certain tax advantages. Such easements may be treated as a charitable contribution, or the future assessed valuation of the property may be lowered. "Alone or in tandem with the rehabilitation tax credit, facade easements can contribute significantly to making restoration of historic buildings [more] financially attractive."[5] Developers should consult an attorney familiar with the issue of facade easements and historic tax credits, however, before granting such an easement. A recent ruling of the IRS (Ruling 89-90) held that, for tax purposes, a facade easement is treated just like any other easement and the conveyance of the easement is considered a partial disposition of the original property. This event would result in the recapture of the rehabilitation tax credit.[6] In one case, a taxpayer created and sold a facade easement to a local historical society. In another, a taxpayer created and donated a facade easement to a local historical society and then claimed a deduction for a charitable contribution.

The National Trust for Historic Preservation is a national private, nonprofit organization chartered by Congress with the responsibility for encouraging public participation in the preservation of sites, buildings, and objects significant in American history and culture. The Trust's National Preservation Loan Fund provides low-interest loans, loan guarantees, interest subsidies, and in special circumstances grants and technical assistance to help organizations create or expand preservation revolving funds and with preservation development projects for historic buildings, sites, and districts. The fund can be used for acquisition, rehabilitation, and related capital costs for projects involving historic properties.

The Trust's Inner-City Ventures Fund provides a vehicle for revitalizing inner-city historic areas without displacing people. It provides low-interest loans

and development expertise to neighborhood non-profit organizations incorporated under Section 501(c)(3) to rehabilitate buildings for housing, jobs, and services for current, low-income, primarily minority, residents. The fund's assistance can also be used for acquisition, rehabilitation, and related capital costs for historic properties.

Local and State Programs

As federal funds have been curtailed and the effects of the 1986 Tax Reform Act have made their mark on the rehabilitation industry, many local and state programs have been instituted to help fill the gap. Local efforts to address housing needs often revolve around increased local revenues to fund a variety of housing programs, including rent supplements, housing rehabilitation, and new construction. These activities, formerly funded largely with federal funds, are now frequently funded with a combination of state, local, and nonprofit revenues.

Communities that in the past depended on CDBGs to fund rehabilitation are now using local revenues to replace nonexistent federal funds. Many local governments are developing their own rent subsidy programs to meet the needs of residents formerly served by Section 8 subsidies. While their local programs frequently are unable to provide the extensive subsidies offered by federal programs, the somewhat more modest subsidies fill an important gap.

State housing finance agencies (quasi-public corporations with the authority to issue and sell tax-exempt bonds) have issued state bonds to finance housing projects. States also have provided other incentives to promote housing, such as state revenues, special taxes, reserve funds built up in some finance agencies through interest investments and fees, and trust funds (casino revenues in New Jersey, lottery funds in Pennsylvania, for example). These funds have been used for both new construction and rehabilitation.

Housing trust funds, created by ordinance or legislation and considered dedicated sources of revenue, use nonfederal financial sources and programs as local supplements to traditional federal monies. The trust funds are earmarked for providing or rehabilitating low- and moderate-income housing. The money in the funds comes from taxes on the sale of real estate, interest on real estate escrow accounts, and required

---

[5] Stephen L. Kass et al., *Rehabilitating Older and Historic Buildings: Law Taxation Strategies* (New York: John Wiley & Sons, 1985), p. 19.

[6] "When Rehabilitation Tax Credits Can Be Revoked," *Corridor Real Estate Journal,* August 11, 1989, p. A-6.

contributions by developers of office buildings. By the end of 1987, existing trust funds had collected an amount estimated at over $300 million, and through the use of the funds, over 8,000 units had been built or rehabilitated.[7]

The types and level of financial resources available from local sources vary tremendously from city to city and county to county because of a number of factors: local experience in dealing with housing rehabilitation, state and local statutes limiting the amount of capital that can be raised, the extent of the existing tax base, and the relationship of the city or county to quasi-public authorities like housing finance agencies, local housing authorities, and school districts.

Cities and counties have used three types of bonds to produce housing, both new construction and rehabilitation:

- *General obligation bonds* are secured by a pledge of the issuer's full faith and credit, including a pledge to levy taxes unlimited (or limited, in some instances) as to rate or amount.
- *Revenue bonds* are payable solely from a specific source of revenue, typically derived from the operation of a municipal enterprise, but excluding ad valorem taxes. Primary types and purposes are airport, bridge, college and university, electric (public power), hospital, housing, natural gas, parking, pollution control, port, recreation, stadium, student loan, telephone, tollway, water and/or sewer, and transit.
- *Industrial revenue bonds* are issued to finance the construction or purchase of industrial or commercial facilities and/or equipment for a private corporation; such bonds are payable solely from the revenue of the private corporation or an affiliate.

One of the largest preservation projects under way in the country using local and state programs, Tobacco Row, occupies 15 contiguous blocks near the Richmond, Virginia, central business district. It will provide 259 rehabilitated residential units in its first phase. Reconstruction of Tobacco Row originally was set to begin in June 1986 but got caught in the 1986 Tax Act. Tobacco Row's developers successfully lobbied Congress for a transition clause that allowed investors to maintain the 25 percent tax credit for certified historic rehabilitation. The developers also obtained construction and permanent loan financing through $100 million in tax-free bonds specifically authorized and allocated to the project. To help move the project, the city of Richmond agreed to suspend all ad valorem taxes for a period of 10 years following the completion of each building, and it will provide

$6.5 million from the city's capital improvements program for the reconstruction of public areas. Additional financing will come from equity investment from corporations and individuals through the sale of limited partnership units with entitlement to the rehabilitation tax credit.

Another example of the complexity of financing rehabilitation of housing, especially large-scale projects, is Quality Hill, a commercial, retail, office, and residential (366 housing units) project west of downtown Kansas City. A mixture of rehabilitation and new construction, Quality Hill involved the acquisition of 33 pieces of property. Forty businesses and 296 tenants had to be relocated at a cost of $850,000. It took two years to amass the $32 million in debt and equity financing through commitments from the federal government (a $6.5 million UDAG), the city, 16 local banks and corporations ($4 million), and more than 130 private investors ($11 million).

Other city resources to assist in the development of rehabilitation/adaptive use projects have been tax incentives and abatements or direct assistance to developers. Developers of Washington Court in Brooklyn, New York, were able to take advantage of New York City's J-51 Tax Abatement Program, which results in zero property taxes for a number of years, followed by gradual increases in taxes until the 20th year.

The District of Columbia's program offers direct assistance to developers through a sale/leaseback arrangement. The District acquires the land underlying a new or rehabilitated multifamily housing project and leases it back to the developer on a long-term basis at a modest annual rate. Enacted in 1985, the Land Acquisition for Housing Development Opportunities (LAHDO) program funded or generated 471 multifamily units from 1985 through July 1987. The program seeks to improve the economic feasibility of developing low- and moderate-income housing by eliminating the value of the land as a mortgageable cost of development. Land purchased by the District through the program may be leased back to the developer on a long-term basis with a predetermined provision for buying it back. Program funds may also be used to pay for certain costs of site improvement. Projects developed under LAHDO must set aside at least 20 percent of the units for lower-income residents.[8]

[7] David E. Anderson, "Trust Funds Rise to Fill Housing Aid Gap," *Richmond Times-Dispatch,* May 21, 1989.

[8] For additional information, contact the Program Development Officer, D.C. Department of Housing and Community Development, 1133 North Capitol Street, N.E., Room 204, Washington, D.C. 20002 (202-535-1415).

In conjunction with federal, state, and local programs, private developers also have used a variety of conventional financing sources to fund rehabilitation and adaptive use projects—commercial banks (short-term construction or interim financing), savings banks, savings and loan associations, real estate investment trusts, life insurance companies and pension funds, credit unions, individual investors, and syndications.[9]

Marketing

The marketing program undertaken for a rehabilitation/adaptive use project will vary greatly with the size of the project and the intended target market. A large project geared to an upscale market usually entails a marketing effort similar to that undertaken for a new construction project—the creation of an on-site sales or leasing office, model unit(s), media advertising, and the preparation of promotional materials. Many rehabilitation projects, however, are smaller scale and would not support the costs of an elaborate marketing program. Smaller projects (fewer than 20 units) generally are sold or leased through an independent real estate agent, thereby avoiding costs associated with a sales office. Advertising and promotion budgets must also be commensurate with the scale of the project. Rules of thumb are difficult to apply, and developers must determine a marketing budget in line with a project's particular needs.

Because existing structures are in most instances protected from the outside elements and potential floor layouts are visible, early marketing is possible, unlike new buildings, where marketing is more constrained by construction phasing. Thus, with rehabilitation projects, space requirements can be discussed with potential users earlier during the development process. Early marketing and thus potentially earlier occupancy can mean the difference between paying higher interest rates on a construction loan and reduced financing costs on a permanent mortgage commitment.

Marketing rehabilitated units to middle- and upper-income tenants often focuses on the charm of the structure and the convenience of the location. In the initial stage of a neighborhood's transition, it is necessary for incoming residents to feel that the housing purchased—the size and design of units, the materials, and amenities like fireplaces—exceeds that that could be purchased at a comparable price in other areas. Issues of safety, schools, and public services must also be addressed, but often they do not constitute the major reasons that young professional are likely to move into the central city.

Marketing programs geared to specific niches need to be tailored accordingly. Projects aimed at low- and moderate-income households are typically in such high demand that little or no marketing program is necessary. Other niches, such as projects for the elderly, often require extensive marketing programs. For example, 10 Wilmington Place in Dayton, Ohio, is a 223-unit congregate-care facility built within a former hospital. The aggressive marketing program included a leasing office, furnished models, models of common areas and facilities, a direct-mail and telephone campaign to reach the target market, and radio, newspaper, and television advertising. A large professional sales staff was employed full time to answer questions.

Case Studies

The remainder of this chapter is devoted to case studies intended to demonstrate the diversity of rehabilitation and adaptive use projects that have been developed around the country. The case studies illustrate issues of financing, design, and marketing that must be taken into consideration when undertaking a development of this nature.

- *Washington Court (Brooklyn, New York)* used federal historic preservation tax credits in conjunction with New York City's J-51 Tax Abatement Program to restore a turn-of-the-century apartment building. The building, which provides a mix of market-rate and low-income units, was an impetus for revitalization of the neighborhood.
- *The Queen Anne (Seattle, Washington)* provides market-rate apartment units primarily for young, urban professionals in a structure adapted from a high school. The project was made feasible with federal historic preservation tax credits and assistance from local public agencies.
- *The Paddock Kensington (Beatrice, Nebraska)* is one development that resulted from an investment syndication program using federal low-income and historic tax credits. The former hotel was transformed into an assisted-living facility for the elderly.

---

[9] U.S. Department of Housing and Urban Development, *Financial Leveraging in Community Development Rehabilitation: A Technical Assistance Guide* (Washington, D.C.: Author, July 1979).

WASHINGTON COURT
Brooklyn, New York

Washington Court consists of 114 units of market-rate and moderate-income multifamily rental housing in the Clinton Hill area of Brooklyn, New York. This restoration of three buildings, built at the turn of the century, combines the original architecture with a modern interior design. The quality of design and attention to detail have made the project—the first large certified historic rehabilitation project in its market area—a success.

Clinton Hill, now designated a historic district, was an established middle-class neighborhood in the 1930s and 1940s. Migration to the suburbs in the 1950s and 1960s resulted in the area's physical and economic deterioration. Many apartment buildings dating from the early 1900s and brownstones built from 1860 to 1880 had become vacant and uninhabitable. In the 1970s, new homeowners, attracted by the distinctive architecture, began to renovate brownstones in the Clinton Hill area and the adjacent historic district of Fort Greene.

In 1984, after several successful small-scale projects in the Clinton Hill/Fort Greene area, Stephen B. Jacobs, an architect specializing in historic preservation, decided to restore three vacant, partially burned-out buildings—which would become Washington Court. Jacobs's rationale for rehabilitation has been to choose dilapidated buildings that no one else would touch, leaving moderately deteriorated buildings for individual rehabilitators. He has found that eliminating a neighborhood's eyesores encourages more renovations, which leads to higher property values. With the completion of Washington Court in 1987, Jacobs's firm has rehabilitated 27 buildings and has been the major force for revitalization in the Clinton Hill/Fort Greene area.

Washington Court faced two major obstacles: historic restoration was difficult because of the buildings' severe deterioration, and no evidence indicated that the market would support the project and its projected rents ranging from $875 to $1,650—rents as high as those in areas already revitalized. But with a combination of tax incentives, an innovative organization structure and approach, and an exceptional concept and product, the developer overcame these obstacles.

The Site

Washington Court is located near downtown Brooklyn, within one block of two subway stations. Manhattan, where most of the tenants work, is a 10- to 20-minute commute. The surrounding areas are pri-

Stephen B. Jacobs and Associates, Architects/Todd Henkels

8-14 Originally known as St. James Court, the building located on Gates Avenue was designed by J.S. Fonner in 1907. The dark red brick laid in a Flemish bond with limestone trim relects the influence of English Edwardian architecture and is a departure from the brownstone buildings nearby.

marily residential, with scattered commercial and industrial structures. To the south, a major urban renewal project, Atlantic Terminal, is being developed. To the north and east of the project is the Bedford-Stuyvesant area, a low-income, deteriorated neighborhood with pockets of restoration. Directly west are the Fort Greene and the Brooklyn Academy of Music historic districts. Washington Court is also near Pratt Institute and Long Island University and is within one-quarter mile of Borough Hall, the commercial and governmental center of Brooklyn.

Planning, Financing, and Governmental Approvals

The development of Washington Court began with the acquisition of the buildings. One of the three buildings, a six-story American Georgian apartment building situated on Gates Avenue, was acquired from a private owner; it was phase one of the project. The other two buildings, both located on Washington Avenue—one a six-story beaux arts–style apartment building and the other a Georgian-style townhouse—were phase two. These buildings were acquired through the city of New York's "dollar" program, which offered buildings needing rehabilitation for the price of one dollar.

The city selected Jacobs's proposal because rather than offering only the required one dollar, he offered market value less the amounts necessary to replace a missing cornice on one of the buildings and to create an internal subsidy on some of the units. This subsidy enabled seven units to be rented at moderate rates: four efficiency units for elderly persons at $350 and three two-bedroom units at $550. Market rates for these units are $750 and $1,200 (1987 dollars), respectively.

To make the project financially feasible, the developer used New York City's J-51 Tax Abatement Program and the federal tax incentive for historic preservation. The city tax abatement is a 20-year program that results in no property taxes for a number of years, followed by gradual increases in taxes until the 20th year. The Historic Preservation Tax Credit permitted tax write-offs of about $8 million.

Using the tax credit resulted in a longer approval process. Although the New York City Department of Buildings approved the construction plans almost immediately, the project also was subject to review by the New York City Landmarks Preservation Commission, the New York State Office of Historic Preservation, and the National Park Service. The city's historical review was limited to the exterior of the structure, while the state and federal reviews encompassed both the interior and exterior of the buildings.

Engineering and Design

The Washington Avenue building was structurally unsound to the degree that a series of collapses occurred during construction. To save the exterior walls, replacing beams was necessary. A hybrid structural system of steel and wood was constructed by alternating demolition and replacement, using 85-foot steel columns threaded through the roof.

Original wood window frames and sashes were restored wherever possible; otherwise, they were custom made to match the original profiles. The windows were thermal glazed, and all brick exteriors were chemically cleaned and, where necessary, repointed. Deteriorated mortar was chipped out by hand and replaced.

Interior spaces were almost totally redesigned. The original apartments consisted of tiny rooms strung along narrow corridors. A wide range of designs for units was developed to make the best use of each area within the existing buildings. A unified circulation design leads residents through restored lobbies, then across bridges above garden courtyards, to provide secure access to the new elevators. Common areas include a lobby with 24-hour security, a street-level laundry room with a sitting area, a landscaped interior courtyard, and a private, vest-pocket park and playground.

The apartments range from a 450-square-foot efficiency unit to a 1,200-square-foot three-bedroom unit. Most of the ground- and top-floor units are duplexes; the top-floor duplexes are penthouses with private roofdeck gardens. In keeping with requirements for historic preservation, the penthouses were designed

Stephen B. Jacobs and Associates, Architects/Todd Henkels

8-15, 8-16 The cornice of the Washington Avenue building, intact only on the south end of the facade, required almost complete replacement. At right, the building after restoration, cleaning, and repairs to ornamental trim, doors, and windows.

Stephen B. Jacobs and Associates, Architects/Todd Henkels

Stephen B. Jacobs and Associates, Architects/Todd Henkels

8-17, 8-18 Washington Court's courtyard—before, filled with debris, and after, as the project's focal point with landscaping.

so they cannot be seen from the street. All units have oak floors and either poplar or restored hardwood trim and doors.

Marketing

The project is geared to professional households with annual incomes of $35,000 to $60,000. Although the first phase—consisting of 45 units—took one year to lease, it was partly attributable to the ongoing construction of the second phase in the neighboring building. The 67 units in the second phase (one unit was kept off the market as a construction office) were leased within 90 days of completion.

Experienced Gained

- The success of Washington Court is largely based upon the unified organizational structure of its development company. Architectural design, development, and construction management are contained within the firm. In addition, the development company includes a millwork shop, where most of the finishing work is done, and in-house staff do much of the carpentry, masonry, plaster repair, and painting, enabling the developer to ensure quality while controlling costs.

- The mill and a branch of the development office are located in the Fort Greene/Clinton Hill area, providing jobs for neighborhood residents.
- The success of Washington Court demonstrates that rehabilitating the worst buildings in an area can dramatically affect an area's overall revitalization. The price of building shells has increased tenfold over the past four years.
- The community's response may be mixed to a project that contributes to the gentrification of an area. It is important to assess the neighborhood's support to determine a project's potential impact before it is under way.

Developer/Architect/Planner
Stephen B. Jacobs and Associates
677 Fifth Avenue
New York, New York 10022
(212) 421-3712

Management
SBJ Management
88 South Portland Avenue
Brooklyn, New York 11217
(718) 643-4421

Source: Project Reference File: "Washington Court," vol. 17, no. 16 (Washington, D.C.: ULI–the Urban Land Institute, October–December 1987).

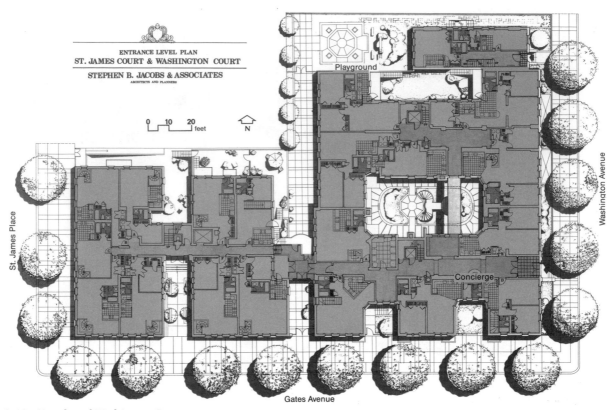

8-19 Site plan of Washington Court.

PROJECT DATA

Land Use Information

Site Area: 26,915 square feet
Gross Floor Area: 109,320 square feet
Number of Dwelling Units: 114
Density: 184 units per acre
Parking: None required

Economic Information

Site Acquisition Cost:

Privately Owned Building	$600,000
City-Owned Buildings (two)	125,000
Total	$725,000

Construction Costs:

Demolition	$ 300,000
Structural	684,000
Carpentry	1,710,000
Electrical	410,000
Plumbing	798,000
HVAC	350,000
Elevators (three)	240,000
General Conditions	790,000
Contingency	125,000
Other[1]	3,493,000
Total	$8,900,000

Total Hard Costs: $9,625,000
Total Soft Costs: $2,926,000

Annual Operating Expenses:

Insurance	$ 50,000
Taxes[2]	0
Sewers	8,500
Repairs/Maintenance	85,000
Utilities	16,800
Legal/Accounting	5,000
Marketing/Miscellaneous	126,700
Total	$292,000

Unit Information:

Unit Type and Number	Number of Units	Unit Size (Square Feet)	Monthly Rent
Studio	4	450	$350
1-Bedroom	36	650–750	$875–$950
2-Bedroom	64	800–1,000	$1,050–$1,350
3-Bedroom	10	1,100–1,200	$1,400–$1,650

Notes

[1] Includes exterior restoration, windows, skylights, flooring, tiles, stairways, cabinets and appliances, refuse chutes, landscaping, and finishes.
[2] J-51 Tax Abatement.

THE QUEEN ANNE
Seattle, Washington

Queen Anne High School has long been one of Seattle's most noteworthy architectural landmarks. Inspired by English late Renaissance palaces, the 1909 building is considered the finest work of architect James Stephen, who designed dozens of Seattle schools. A 1929 addition, while somewhat simplified, was true to the character of the 1909 building's load-bearing masonry facade. Two 1955 additions (for a cafeteria and industrial arts classes) with facades of simple, unornamented curtain walls, stand in contrast to the older buildings. The building complex illustrates a half-century progression in construction methods and attitudes toward educational facilities.

The school was closed in 1981 because of declining enrollments, but the neighborhood wanted to save the building. Neighbors were involved early in planning, and a feasible alternative—converting the school into a housing complex—received strong support from the community. In 1984, the school district, in cooperation with the Historic Seattle Preservation and Development Authority, chose Lorig Associates and The Bumgardner Architects in a design and development competition to convert the vacant buildings to residential use. As a first step, the development/design team succeeded in placing the school on the National Register of Historic Places, making it eligible for historic renovation tax credits totaling $1.6 million.

The Site

Queen Anne Hill, approximately two miles north of downtown Seattle, overlooks downtown and Puget Sound. The site is surrounded predominantly by residential uses, including single-family dwellings on the immediate south and multifamily units on the immediate east. On the west side is a gymnasium, and

8-20 Inspired by English late Renaissance palaces, the original Queen Anne High School was expanded through several additions. It now contains 139 rental units.

Jim Ball

8-21, 8-22 A 1929 auditorium addition blocked off the attractive rear facade of the building; the developer chose to demolish the addition to open the center of the site for a new main entrance at grade, with an entrance courtyard giving access to new parking and landscaping.

a new elementary school is being built to the north. Because of its location atop the hill, the school is visible from numerous points around the city.

Development and Financing

In selecting the developer, the school district acted through the quasi-public Historic Seattle Preservation and Development Authority. A request for proposals specified that proposals be submitted by a team, including a developer, an architect, and a contractor. Six teams originally bid for the project, and Lorig Associates was chosen in 1984. The deal that was then negotiated involved a 50-year ground lease of the site, with two 20-year options to extend the lease.

The developer was not required to pay ground rent until construction was completed; thereafter, the annual ground rent of $60,000 would accrue for three years, with 12 percent interest on the rent not paid. After three years, the developer was required to pay

$60,000 rent per year, or 8 percent of the net operating income, whichever was greater. Any rent exceeding $60,000 per year would be used to retire the accrued rent, which had to be paid off in 10 years. The structure of the deal allowed investors to be repaid early in the process.

The partnership that was established involved 55 units of $40,000 each, or $2.2 million in equity. The remaining funds necessary—about $7 million—were obtained through a construction loan from Crosslands Mortgage of Brooklyn. A permanent loan was later arranged with Northwestern Mutual Life. The project was set up to allow conversion to condominiums, but no plans have been made to do so in the foreseeable future.

Construction began in March 1986, and the project was completed in March 1987.

Planning and Design

The site consisted of the original 1909 building on the north side, a 1929 classroom and auditorium/gymnasium addition in the middle, and two separate 1955 additions separated by a court on the southern end. Turning a space the size of a large department store into housing—while dealing with existing windows, two-foot-thick masonry walls, and a jumble of deteriorated or poorly placed additions and breezeways—is a bit like working a big Rubik's cube, according to the architects.

In evaluating the existing site, the team first determined that the 1929 auditorium/gymnasium should be demolished to reveal the attractive south facade of the original building. Doing so would also provide a pleasant open area at the center of the site, which was

8-24 The project includes this four-story addition to the 1929 classroom building.

8-23 Original blackboards were retained in many units, and some residents have commissioned artists to create murals.

subsequently designed to include a grand porte cochere, a formal courtyard paved in cobblestones, parking, and a circular drive with a large fountain at its center.

The remaining buildings were redesigned according to their structure. The 1909 building, for instance, was converted into 90 apartments, including lofts in the high-ceilinged library. The developer constructed a small, four-story addition to the 1929 classroom building, which was too narrow for a double-loaded corridor, to create 21 apartments in the addition.

The 1955 industrial arts addition was converted into 16 apartments—eight of which are two-level, two-bedroom units with rooftop terraces—through the addition of a third floor. The ground floor was converted into 38 parking spaces. Finally, the 1955 cafeteria addition was converted into 53 secured parking spaces.

A high school, where rooms are interspersed with laboratories and study halls, presents a much bigger

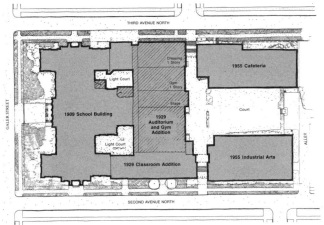

8-25 Site plan before conversion.

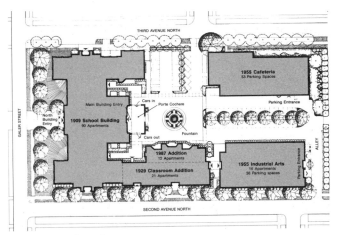

8-26 Site plan after conversion.

challenge in redesign than an elementary school, where the pattern of rooms is repetitive. The redesign of the Queen Anne involved exploration, photography, and a study of old drawings, and the designers had the contractors test the strength of the masonry walls and analyze the structure. Very little bolstering was required, as the already massive 1909 building was reinforced after a 1949 earthquake. Among the problems in restoration the developer faced were the replacement or restoration of 900 windows and the removal of asbestos used to insulate steam pipes.

A variety of unit configurations accommodate such diverse prospective renters as single parents, young professionals, families, and unrelated singles. Although virtually every unit has some distinctive feature, the 139 units come in 39 basic shapes. In contrast with standard apartments in Seattle, the Queen Anne offers high-volume rooms (12-foot ceilings are typical) with many details, including classroom chalkboards in many of the units.

Marketing

The developer did extensive market research before proceeding with the project. It involved checking every building in the neighborhood for size of units, rents, and so on to eliminate guessing about what the market would tolerate. Rents at the Queen Anne range from $523 per month for a studio to $1,050 for two-bedroom, two-level units (1988 dollars). The building now has 200 residents, half men and half women, with an average age of 32; 80 singles, with the remainder couples, including nontraditional couples, live there. Average annual income is $28,000, and 63 percent of the tenants moved from within the city limits.

The press covered the project closely—so closely that the leasing team did not have to spend nearly what had been planned on marketing; people kept pouring in the front door. Seattle's two major newspapers did full-page features the week before the grand opening, and Historic Seattle organized a tour weekend that turned out 8,500 people. As a result, 40 percent of the units were leased with barely any advertising before the Queen Anne formally opened. The remaining units were rented within three months.

Experience Gained

- Each of the team members—the developer, the architect, and the contractor—had prior experience with both rehabilitation and residential construction. As a result, construction entailed no major pitfalls or unforeseen problems. The project was actually completed two months ahead of schedule.
- Working with a negotiated contract with a pre-selected contractor avoided the sort of adversarial relationship typical of projects awarded to the contractor submitting the lowest bid. The team worked together from the start with an eye always on the budget, and the contractor was involved in the design process.
- Through previous experience, the developer recognized that the success of a residential rehabilitation project largely depends on the quality and character of the building and the neighborhood. A good building and a good location afford the opportunity to charge higher rents, making the difference between a profitable and an unprofitable venture.

Developer/Manager
Lorig Associates
2001 Western Avenue, Suite 300
Seattle, Washington 98121
(206) 728-7660

Architect
The Bumgardner Architects
101 Stewart Street, Suite 200
Seattle, Washington 98101
(206) 223-1361

Construction
J.M. Rafn Company
Seattle, Washington

Landscape Architect
Robert Shinbo Associates
Seattle, Washington 98101

Source: Project Reference File: "The Queen Anne," vol. 18, no. 6 (Washington, D.C.: ULI–the Urban Land Institute, April–June 1988).

PROJECT DATA

Land Use Information:

Site Area: 2.85 acres
Gross Density: 48.8 dwelling units per acre
Total Dwelling Units: 139
Current Vacancy: 2 percent

Parking

Total Spaces: 173
Parking Index: 1.25 spaces per unit
Visitor Spaces: 12
Handicapped Spaces: 7
Compact Car Spaces: 66

Economic Information:

Site Acquisition Cost: Option fee $7,500
Site Improvement Costs:

Excavation and Grading	$ 47,470
Sewer/Water	23,063
Paving	25,853
Curbs/Sidewalks	10,145
Landscaping	60,575
Demolition (if any)	405,970
Other	59,418
Total	$632,494

Construction Costs:

Structural	$134,227
Carpentry	648,177
Electrical	512,920
Plumbing	363,423
HVAC	62,290
Elevators (if any)	96,859
Other	3,904,610
Total	$5,722,506

Amenities Costs:

Fountain ($25,000 + $12,500 installation)	$37,500
Roof Deck	2,500
Tanning Room	5,000
Total	$45,000

Total Hard Costs: $6,400,000[1]
Total Soft Costs: $2,860,000

Unit Information:

Unit Type	Number Built	Monthly Rent	Number of Bedrooms/ Baths
Studio	6	$523	0/1
Loft Studio	25	$558	0/1
Studio Alcove	16	$591	0/1
1-Bedroom	31	$716	1/1
1-Bedroom Platform	27	$720	1/1
2-Bedroom Flats	15	$1,004	2/1–2
2-Bedroom Townhouses	8	$1,050	2/2
2-Bedroom Platforms	6	$942	2/2
1-Bedroom Townhouses	5	$775	1/1–1½

Total Projected Monthly Income: $97,500

Monthly Operating Expenses:

Taxes (historic building leased from public agency)	$ 0
Insurance	2,500
Sewer	1,500
Repairs/Maintenance	6,420
Utilities	2,700
Legal	100
Accounting/Management	3,500
Marketing	500
Miscellaneous Salaries	7,900
Total	$25,120

Note
[1] Includes site improvement, construction, and amenities.

THE PADDOCK KENSINGTON
Beatrice, Nebraska

The Paddock Kensington is one of several projects developed in small midwestern and southern communities by The Westin Financial Group as part of its Historic Housing for Seniors (HHS) program. This investment program seeks to provide investors with cash flow and a combination of historic rehabilitation and low-income housing tax credits. The approach taken by HHS is to acquire the most prominent or notable building in a community where a strong market exists for a residential care facility and then to develop that property as a full-service senior citizen facility. Westin organized the HHS program in 1987 to provide equity financing and has recently organized a preferred income fund to provide development financing. Bank financing for this type of project is difficult to obtain; small local banks typically have loan limits that are too low, and large city banks generally consider the risk too great.

Each HHS facility offers a package of services that includes lodging, food, and assisted care, each of which is managed as a separate profit center. The lodging component includes residence in a comfortable and well-appointed setting, social and recreational programs, a scheduled minibus service, and optional personal housekeeping and laundry services. The food component includes three meals a day in a restaurant-style dining room plus unlimited snacks and beverages. The assisted-care component includes a full range of personal home health care services available through an independent, licensed

8-27 The Renaissance Revival–style hotel was constructed in 1924 using concrete post-and-beam construction. The building's conversion to housing for the elderly was made possible in part by historic and low-income tax credits.

provider with offices and staff in the building. By offering safety, comfort, and dignity at affordable prices, the HHS facilities enable elderly people to avoid early and unnecessary institutionalization; they compare favorably with local nursing homes, which generally provide fewer social services in a medical-type environment at a much higher cost.

The Site

The Paddock Kensington is the centerpiece of Beatrice, a small town in southern Nebraska. The site was formerly occupied by a hotel built in 1887 by U.S. Senator Algernon S. Paddock. The original hotel was destroyed by fire in 1919 and was replaced by the existing structure in 1924. The Paddock Hotel was popular with traveling salespeople and served as the focus for the community's social life, hosting political rallies, conventions, graduation ceremonies, ballroom dances, and club meetings. Over the years, the hotel's business declined, and during the 1970s several new owners tried, with varying degrees of success, to manage the property as a residence for the elderly.

Development and Financing

The Westin Financial Group acquired the property in January 1988 for $549,000. The company has a full-time acquisitions staff that seeks out economically distressed hotels and motels, hospitals, and other residential buildings that contain a minimum of 50,000 square feet, are structurally sound, and are located in smaller downtowns that are still viable as business districts. Before the property was acquired, a detailed feasibility study was undertaken to identify the number of elderly persons in the community, the affordability index, the time it would take to fill the facility, the percentage of market penetration necessary for success, local competition, a five-year operating pro forma, and local demographic information. Under a turnkey fixed-price construction contract, renovation of The Paddock started in March 1988 and was completed by March 1989.

The project is one of five properties in Historic Housing for Seniors I (HHS-I), a public real estate limited partnership that raised over $10 million in equity. Conventional financing was obtained for the project at a loan-to-value ratio of approximately 60 percent. With a basis of $1.5 million in investors' equity, the project is eligible for $474,000 in rehabilitation tax credits and $1.7 million in low-income tax credits. To qualify for low-income tax credits, the property must be maintained as low-income housing for 15 years.

8-28 The lobby, which is open to the second-floor mezzanine, is furnished with period pieces and features a simple black and white mosaic tile floor and original ceiling details and columns.

Planning and Design

The objective of rehabilitation was to accommodate the new program while being sensitive to the original structure. Working closely with the state historic preservation office, the project architect identified building features that had been added or substantially modified in recent years. Partitions that had been added to create office space in the lobby area were removed to expose original ceiling details and columns. Ventilation equipment that had been installed in the open court on the back of the building was removed to permit the replacement of the central skylight in the former ballroom on the second floor. A central air-conditioning system was installed for the public areas, and the building's plumbing, wiring, and boiler steam-heating systems were replaced. Original bathroom fixtures and woodwork were preserved wherever possible.

The hotel's coffee shop and restaurant on the first floor were converted to a dining room and kitchen, the hotel ballroom on the second floor was converted to a lounge, and basement rooms were adapted to accommodate a home health care center, a chapel, a storage area for residents' use, and two clubrooms, including a fully equipped residents' kitchen and

private dining room available for family meals and gatherings. Other common areas include a game room on the first floor, an exercise room and a laundry room on the second floor, and an arts and crafts room and an outdoor deck on the third floor. Two street-level retail spaces—a beauty parlor/barber shop and a men's clothing store—provide an additional source of income.

The fifth floor was the first floor to be completed, and 16 residents of the former building who stayed during the renovation process were relocated there for the remainder of the construction period. The upper four floors contain a total of 65 units, ranging from standard studio units comprising one bedroom and one bathroom to deluxe suites containing two bedrooms, two bathrooms, and a living room. Units are unfurnished and, except for two units for live-in caretaker couples, do not contain kitchen facilities—a kitchen area with a refrigerator and a microwave oven is located on each floor.

A radio-transmitter emergency call system is installed throughout the building, with wall units in all bathrooms and bedrooms; this system is monitored by the live-in caretakers, and all members of staff are trained in cardiopulmonary resuscitation. The public areas and a number of the units are accessible to disabled individuals.

Marketing

The average age of tenants in all HHS facilities is 83. Within three months of completion, the Paddock had 20 residents (12 women and eight men) whose average age was in the 90s. Because it takes time for a new

8-29 The dining room serves three meals per day, seven days per week; the kitchen also provides catering and banquet services to the community.

facility to establish a local reputation and because the market is targeted to specific needs, lease-up is scheduled to take about three years. Referrals often come from existing residents as well as from physicians and clergy in the community.

Marketing for each HHS facility initially benefits from free publicity during renovation and the grand opening. When renovation is completed, each facility holds an open house that typically attracts 20 to 40 percent of the local population. The no-pressure mar-

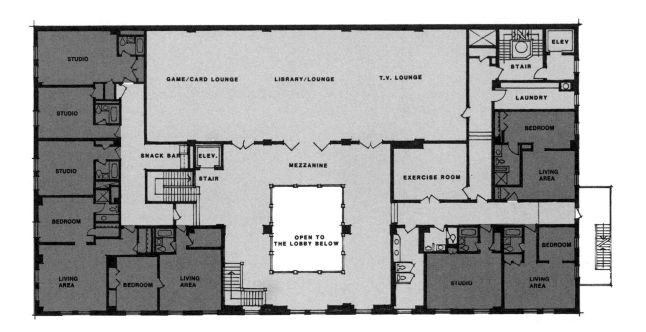

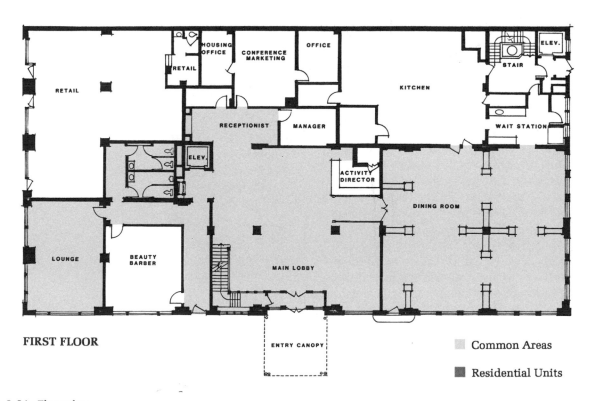

FIRST FLOOR

ENTRY CANOPY

Common Areas

Residential Units

8-30, 8-31 Floor plan.

keting program involves direct mail to age- and income-qualified households. Potential residents are encouraged to reserve the room of their choice with a nominal, fully refundable, high-interest-bearing deposit and are placed on a mailing list for newsletters, menus, and activity calendars. To relieve the pressure of decision making, prospective tenants are offered a 100 percent refund during the first 60 days at any HHS facility. The marketing staff also frequently works closely with the potential resident's family during decision making.

Management

Base rent at The Paddock includes 24-hour on-site security, transportation, monthly hair care, free laundry facilities, cable TV, all utilities (except telephones), maintenance, professional management, and membership in the Kensington Club (a private social club offering planned activities, classes, cultural events, group travel, and discounts from local merchants). Membership in the Kensington Club is also available to nonresident seniors for an annual fee. Additional services are offered at extra expense: $100 per month for meals, $25 per month for a linen and housekeeping service, and $25 per month for a personal laundry service. Complete packages range from as low as $550 per month to $850 per month, depending on the size and/or location of the apartment and the services requested. The Paddock charges no entry fee and tenancy is on a month-to-month basis.

The Paddock is operated by Evergreen Management, Inc., a subsidiary of Westin Financial. The on-site manager for each facility is encouraged to capitalize on the historic relationship that the building has had with the community. In addition to an on-site manager, the Paddock's staff includes a director of programs and a coordinator of resident services.

The activities program includes entertainment, games, and outings in a 16-passenger bus. Most activities are open to the public, and intergenerational mixing, including activities with local daycare programs, is encouraged wherever possible to prevent the elderly from becoming isolated.

Meals are served in a central dining room to promote interaction among residents. Through the sponsorship of the federal government's Older American Act, The Paddock also operates as a Senior Diner's Site, serving lunch for suggested donations to between 60 and 70 people seven days a week.

The presence of an on-site home health care facility regularly staffed five days per week is a strong selling point for potential residents. Space and furnishings are leased to a local home health care agency, which evaluates potential clients before leases are signed and offers screening clinics, nutrition and medication consultation, consultation and assessment of health problems, and maintenance of health profiles. The agency also contracts directly with facility residents for services ranging from personal care and assistance with medication to physical therapy, speech therapy, occupation therapy, and 24-hour skilled nursing care.

Experience Gained

- Historic buildings can be successfully adapted to senior housing by creative use of tax credits to lessen economic risks.
- Small, viable downtown areas offer an ideal location for assisted-living projects for the elderly. Senior citizens can maintain an independent lifestyle in a safe, pedestrian-oriented environment. At the same time, the downtown area is given an economic boost.
- Personal associations often play a large role in a prospective resident's decision whether or not to move to this type of facility. For this reason, the presence on its staff of members of well-respected local families may help a facility attract residents.

Developer
The Westin Financial Group
2614 Telegraph Avenue
Berkeley, California 94704
(415) 548-6600

Manager
Evergreen Management, Inc.
1111 West 39th Street
Kansas City, Missouri
(816) 753-2147

Architect
Galpin Ciaccio Klick Associates
5801 Cedar Lake Road
Minneapolis, Minnesota 55416
(612) 545-7674

Source: *Project Reference File*: "The Paddock Kensington," vol. 19, no. 15 (Washington, D.C.: ULI–the Urban Land Institute, July–September 1989).

PROJECT DATA

Land Use Information:

Site Area: 10,785 square feet
Total Units: 67
Gross Density: 268 units per acre
Gross Building Area: 47,940 square feet
Floor/Area Ratio: 4.45

Development Cost Information:

Site Acquisition Cost: $549,000
Site Improvement Costs:[1] **$100,000**
Construction Costs:

Structural	$ 200,000
Carpentry	300,000
Electrical	300,000
Plumbing	350,000
HVAC	200,000
Elevators	120,000
Other	130,000
Total	$1,600,000

Finishing Costs:

Lobby Furniture	$ 15,000
Common Area Furniture	35,000
Kitchen Equipment	100,000
Total	$150,000

Soft Costs: $400,000
Total Development Costs: $2,799,000

Notes
[1] Interior demolition.
[2] Initial lease-up.
[3] From residential units, based on full occupancy.
[4] Includes rental plus meals and personal care package.
[5] Per person.

Estimated Annual Operating Expenses:

General Administrative	$80,000
Dietary	90,500
Supplies	7,400
Maintenance	34,000
Services	9,500
Transportation	11,600
Utilities	55,000
Insurance	5,200
Real Estate Taxes	6,000
Marketing[2]	76,000
Sewer	3,300
Health Care Services	7,900
Total	$386,400

Projected Annual Rental Income:[3] **$578,400**

Unit Information:

Unit Type	Number Built	Average Size (Square Feet)	Average Monthly Rent[4]
Studio	22	208	$725
Studio	9	270	$800
One-bedroom	10	396	$850
Two-bedroom/ one-bathroom	4	166	$550[5]
Two-bedroom/ two-bathroom	18	275	$625[5]
Two-bedroom/ two-bathroom	4	535	$775[5]

9.
Trends

This final chapter discusses the possible future directions of residential development. For private developers, an awareness of new opportunities and constraints is essential. Because private residential development is foremost a business operation, any future direction that private development might take must be based on profitability—which is not to say that developers should not be innovative, for innovation is often the cornerstone of economic success. But innovation must be grounded in project feasibility and a sound understanding of the market. For the public sector, an understanding of the activities of the private sector and public/private partnerships is needed to help attain objectives for housing.

Forecasts of trends must be approached with caution. Often apparent trends disappear or change markedly as new, unexpected societal, economic, and political forces surface. The first edition of this handbook, published in 1978, noted examples of such changes:

- The prediction that single-family houses would shrink in response to smaller families did not come to pass. While the size of families dropped, the size of houses continued to climb throughout the 1980s, as buyers bullishly refused to compromise on quality or quantity despite sky-high prices.
- The predicted effects of the "energy crisis" on the residential development industry (construc-

tion standards, implications for location, and alternative forms of transportation) vanished with the return of inexpensive imported oil in the early 1980s. The decade proved that solar subdivisions and building designs were not, in fact, here to stay.

- The return of foreign oil in part triggered a chain of events that left much of the nation's Oil Patch states (Texas, Oklahoma, Colorado, and Louisiana) in economic shambles. Could anyone have predicted the magnitude of this nearly decade-long recession on the real estate and banking industries? The effects will surely be felt well into the 1990s.

Other predictions in the 1978 handbook were realized in the 1980s, however. As anticipated, the incredible strength of the housing market persisted through most of the decade as maturing baby boomers moved into their first (and many into their second and third) houses. The demand for child care in residential communities soared as working mothers solidified their place in the work force; however, this need was left largely unfilled and continues to be a pressing issue for the 1990s. And the cost of land for the average single-family house did in fact rise as a percentage of the total sale price—almost beyond what was conceivable in the 1970s.

Thomas L. Hodges, ULI council member and chair of the Housing and Community Development Research Subcommittee, offers this truth: "The residential development industry is highly cyclical, so solutions are a constantly moving target. Realistically, developers can see ahead only about 18 months with a reasonable level of confidence." Still, residential developers must strive for a longer vision, because residential development is a much longer process than it was even 10 years ago. Almost every element in the process will take longer to complete in the 1990s—land acquisition, planning, regulatory processing, and, probably, sales or leasing. Developers in many cases will need to begin a project three to five years before they can expect to complete it. Residential developers *must* have a sense for the future.

Demographics

A sound knowledge of demographics lies at the heart of determining housing demand, location, and type, and demographic factors important to residential developers include population size and growth rates, age, household characteristics and growth rates, income, employment, and immigration. These factors are highly interrelated, and developers should not rely on data for any single factor as the basis for determining demand for housing. Instead, these fac-

tors must be considered as a whole, with data weighted and logical conclusions drawn.

Population and Age[1]

People—their numbers and ages—represent the initial baseline for viewing future demand for housing. Because the primary housing consumers (over 21 years old) of 2010 are already alive, their future numbers and ages can be anticipated with reasonable certainty. Immigration, however, is much more difficult to predict and could prove to be a key variable in future demand for housing.

Within this expanding adult population, variations will be evident according to age. The dominant growth is associated with maturing baby boomers (see Figure 9-1). The cohort of 35- to 54-year-olds (the age group of peak housing consumption) will be the major demographic target for homebuilders during the 1990s. Conversely, the 1990s will be characterized by

---

[1] Information about population and age was drawn largely from James W. Hughes, "Demand Considerations: Future Housing Needs Based on Demographic and Economic Projections," prepared by the Department of Urban Planning and Policy Development, Rutgers University, June 1989, for the ULI Low- and Moderate-Income Housing Task Force.

9-1   PROJECTED INCREMENTS IN POPULATION GROWTH BY AGE: 1985 TO 2010
U.S. TOTAL (000)

	1985–1990	1990–1995	1995–2000	2000–2005	2005–2010
TOTAL	11,131	9,728	8,128	7,337	6,970
Under 5	404	(609)	(901)	(287)	288
5 to 13	2,283	1,471	(381)	(1,503)	(979)
14 to 17	(1,628)	1,273	822	159	(745)
18 to 24	(2,609)	(1,859)	950	1,687	237
25 to 34	1,687	(2,963)	(3,813)	(1,152)	1,575
35 to 44	6,058	4,439	1,575	(2,959)	(3,750)
45 to 54	2,890	5,810	5,926	4,395	1,589
55 to 64	(973)	(39)	2,833	5,605	5,667
65 to 74	1,363	557	(687)	167	2,629
75 and Over	1,656	1,648	1,804	1,225	459
Under 17	1,059	2,135	(460)	(1,631)	(1,436)
18 to 64	7,053	5,388	7,471	7,576	5,318
65 and Over	3,019	2,205	1,117	1,392	3,088

Note: As of July 1. Includes armed forces overseas. Projection data from middle series. Shaded section encompasses the baby boom generation (born 1946 to 1964).
Source: Gregory Spencer, U.S. Bureau of the Census, *Current Population Reports*, Series P-25, No. 1018, "Projections of the Population of the United States by Age, Sex, and Race: 1988 to 2080" (Washington, D.C.: U.S. Government Printing Office, 1989); and U.S. Bureau of the Census, *Current Population Reports*, Series P-25, No. 1022, "United States Population Estimates by Age, Sex, and Race: 1980 to 1987" (Washington, D.C.: U.S. Government Printing Office, 1988).

a considerable dip in the number of 20- to 34-year-olds, the years of first household formation and first homeownership.

Subsequently, 45- to 64-year-olds (the beginning and expansion of empty nesters) will represent the growth node of the first decade of the 21st century. Also coming into consideration during the latter part of this decade will be the baby boom "echo"—the children of the baby boomers born between 1976 and 1990. The first decade of the next century will see renewed growth in the number of Americans in their 20s after more than a decade-long interval; young housing consumers will again increase in aggregate numbers.

On the basis of age alone, it is apparent that a maturing baby boom will dominate housing demand in America for the balance of the 20th century and for some time beyond. The "youth generation," yielding to middle age, will be the potent market reality of the 1990s. These data alone suggest a continued strong demand for traditional, family-oriented housing through the 1990s, with a slackening of demand for entry-level housing. Demand for suburban housing and move-up products is likely to remain a factor.

Also likely to be in demand are second homes for the maturing and still economically mobile baby boom generation. Purchases of second homes—encouraged by current tax law, which permits a deduction for interest on the mortgage—could easily double in the 1990s. The strongest markets for second homes will be those within two hours driving time of major metropolitan areas.

After entering the next century, baby boomers will initiate a major shift in demand for housing, toward that geared to empty nesters. Preferred products are likely to be higher density, have numerous amenities and luxury appointments, and require low maintenance. Security and a convenient location will be key factors in marketing. Some predict that the preferences of this empty nester market may result in an imbalance in the housing stock, with an oversupply of large, single-family houses nationally.

But these conclusions are based simply on data about age. The population itself, despite its relative certainty, provides only the broadest of contexts for considering future housing markets. It is only when the population is partitioned into households that expectations can be refined.

Household Characteristics

The basic unit of currency for housing demand is the household. The long-term shrinkage in the size of the American household has generated housing demand

9-2   HOUSEHOLD SIZE: 1940 TO 1987

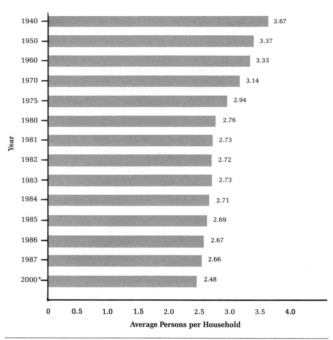

* Projection.
Source: U.S. Bureau of the Census, *Current Population Reports*, Series P-20, No. 417, "Households, Families, Marital Status, and Living Arrangements: March 1987" (Washington, D.C.: U.S. Government Printing Office), Table 2, p. 4.

far in excess of the magnitude dictated by population growth alone. Between 1960 and 1970, for example, the population of the United States grew by 24.3 million people, while households grew by 10.6 million. Between 1970 and 1980, however, the population increased only 22.7 million, while households grew by 17.4 million. The baby boom generation, en masse, came of age in the 1970s, redefining the nation's household profile and precipitating a virtual revolution. In those 10 years, the average household size fell by over 12 percent (from 3.14 to 2.76 persons) and households were formed at a frantic pace, sending demand for housing soaring at a time when population growth rates were declining. Further, this trend to smaller households is expected to continue into the foreseeable future. By the turn of the century, the average household size is projected to decline to 2.48 persons, which will continue to generate household growth in excess of population growth.

The demographic revolution associated with baby boomers' coming of age is reflected in the process of household diversification and segmentation. Households once considered atypical—single-parent families, persons living alone, and unmarried couples—surged in number, while traditional families headed

351

by a married couple grew slowly. Between 1980 and 1988, such households accounted for only 2.7 million out of the total growth of 10.3 million households, barely one in four. As late as 1970, married couples accounted for 71 percent of all households; in less than 20 years (by 1988), their share had declined to under 57 percent. Between 1980 and 1988, "nonfamily households" (either persons living alone or households comprised of two or more unrelated individuals) and "other families" (predominantly single-parent families) accounted for 7.6 million out of the total growth of 10.3 million households, or nearly three out of four. Thus, America's pool of households continued to diversify throughout the 1980s; whether it will continue to do so through the 1990s is a question of vital importance to homebuilders.

Figure 9-3 projects the number of new households by household type from 1985 to 2000. Every household type is projected to grow through the end of the century, but nonfamily households are expected to continue to eclipse traditional family households during the 1990s, with families headed by a married couple showing the slowest rate of growth. From 1990 to 1995, only 370,000 of the total projected 1.2 million new households each year will be married couples (a 3.5 percent increase), compared to 610,000 new nonfamily households annually (an 11.1 percent increase) and 164,000 households headed by a female

(a 7.3 percent increase). A similar profile is expected from 1995 to 2000. To the degree that the future brings more "atypical" households, affordable housing and smaller, more efficient housing will be in demand.

Household Growth

Annual household growth fell by more than 500,000 in the first half of the 1980s, to 1.2 million. One of the underlying causes was the massive economic downturn in 1981 and 1982—the worst recession since the Great Depression—when household formations plummeted and housing production fell to postwar lows. The Census Bureau projects a rebound to an average annual increase of almost 1.4 million households, a level still 300,000 below the peak of the 1970s. Projections for 1990 to 1995 show another decline, to 1.2 million households per year. For 1995 to 2000, projections show an even lower average annual growth, to 1.1 million households.

This pattern of growth should not be misconstrued. It does not mean that the demand for housing is about to disappear. The level of annual growth projected for the 1990s—from 1.2 million to 1.1 million households per year during the decade—is still far greater than for any period before 1970. It is eclipsed only by the special events of 1970 to 1980, when the number of baby boomers forming households exploded. The

9-3   PROJECTIONS OF HOUSEHOLDS BY HOUSEHOLD TYPE: 1985 TO 2000
U.S. TOTAL (000)

| | | FAMILY HOUSEHOLDS | | | | NONFAMILY HOUSEHOLDS | | |
| | | | OTHER | | | | | |
	TOTAL HOUSEHOLDS	TOTAL	MARRIED COUPLE	MALE HOUSEHOLDER	FEMALE HOUSEHOLDER	TOTAL	MALE HOUSEHOLDER	FEMALE HOUSEHOLDER
1985	86,789	62,706	50,350	2,228	10,129	24,082	10,114	13,968
1990	94,227	66,758	53,012	2,581	11,165	27,469	11,946	15,523
Change: 1985 to 1990								
Number	7,438	4,052	2,662	353	1,036	3,387	1,832	1,555
Percent	8.6	6.5	5.3	15.8	10.2	14.1	18.1	11.1
1990	94,227	66,758	53,012	2,581	11,165	27,469	11,946	15,523
1995	100,308	69,787	54,863	2,940	11,984	30,520	13,666	16,854
Change: 1990 to 1995								
Number	6,081	3,029	1,851	359	819	3,051	1,720	1,331
Percent	6.5	4.5	3.5	13.9	7.3	11.1	14.4	8.6
1995	100,308	69,787	54,863	2,940	11,984	30,520	13,666	16,854
2000	105,933	72,277	56,294	3,282	12,701	33,656	15,452	18,204
Change: 1995 to 2000								
Number	5,625	2,490	1,431	342	717	3,136	1,786	1,350
Percent	5.6	3.6	2.6	11.6	6.0	10.3	13.1	8.0

Note: Data as of July 1, except for 1985, which is as of March 1.
Source: U.S. Bureau of the Census, *Current Population Reports*, Series P-25, No. 986, "Projections of the Number of Households and Families: 1986 to 2000" (Washington, D.C.: U.S. Government Printing Office, 1986).

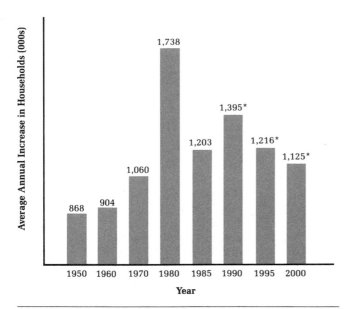

9-4   AVERAGE ANNUAL HOUSEHOLD
FORMATIONS: 1950 TO 2000

*From the middle series.
Source: U.S. Bureau of the Census, *Current Population Reports,*
Series P-25, No. 986 (Washington, D.C.: U.S. Government Printing
Office, 1986).

composition of demand in the 1990s and beyond will
continue to evolve, however.

Household Income

The maturing of Americans that will take place in the
1990s will mean a general increase in incomes. The
baby boom generation will swell the ranks of the
cohort aged 35 to 54 years, the classic peak-earning
and peak-income age group. Those baby boomers who
are also married couples (particularly couples comprised of two working professionals) will command
peak resources, with incomes approximately 50 to
100 percent greater than the overall household median. Those who settle into different configurations—
particularly households headed by a female and other
nonfamily households—while experiencing growing
incomes will have incomes still substantially below
the overall household median. The variations will
thus be an amplification of the 1980s.

Employment

The regional variation in America's economic landscape evolved considerably during the 1980s. After
booming in the 1970s, the Oil Patch states and their
major metropolitan areas struggled through most of
the 1980s, as cheap imported oil undercut domestic
energy-related industries. By contrast, the Northeast

experienced an enormous wave of new jobs and housing development fueled by renewed growth in financial, service, and defense-related jobs. During the
1980s, the "bicoastal economy," bolstered by international trade on the East and West Coasts, captured
most of the economic gain and real estate development.

But regional economies are dynamic and ever-
changing, and residential developers must be able to
anticipate the changes. One way to do so is to consider
emerging patterns of employment, which may be the
most decisive indicator of demand for housing.

The U.S. Bureau of Labor Statistics projects that
virtually all of the 21.4 million growth in jobs projected between 1986 and 2000 will occur in the service sector (see Figure 9-5). Thus, the total 133 million
jobs in the United States by the turn of the century
will, to a far greater degree than today, be concentrated in the service sector. This pattern of growth
means that highly skilled jobs requiring the most
education and training will grow the most rapidly but
that the overall labor force will grow more slowly and
will become increasingly older and dominated by
minorities and females. ULI council member Richard
Kately, president and CEO of Real Estate Research
Corporation in Chicago, predicts that as a result of this
change in the labor force, "the distribution of income
will result in more rich and more poor families.
Traditional middle-income families will experience a
decline in spending power, which will limit their
choice of housing."

Based on age, fewer people will enter the work
force during the 1990s. This fact, coupled with the
ever-increasing requirements for skills, sets the stage
for a sizable shortage of labor. Council member M.
Leanne Lachman notes, "The first businesses to experience the shrinking labor force are those that depend
on young, low-wage workers—the hospitality, tour-
ism, construction, and food service industries—but
others will feel it soon. This shortage of new workers
will not be felt uniformly across the nation because
of variances in local birth rates, migratory patterns,
and immigration. So far, it is most pronounced in the
Northeast." In part, this shortage will be filled by
elderly people who will take many of the lower-paying
jobs traditionally held by younger people. Further,
older workers can be expected to delay their retirement, as many will be financially unable to retire at
the traditional age. Employers will be more accommodating to workers (for example, by offering flexible
hours) to entice special groups like the elderly and
women into the workplace. Still, employers will compete heavily for workers—especially young, skilled
workers—and will need to entice them in creative
ways. Two principal factors in securing labor will be

EMPLOYMENT BY MAJOR SECTOR: 1972 TO 1986 ACTUAL AND 1986 TO 2000 PROJECTED
U.S. TOTAL (000)

	1972	1986	2000	CHANGE: 1986 TO 2000 NUMBER	PERCENT
TOTAL EMPLOYMENT	84,549	111,623	133,030	21,407	19.2
Nonfarm Wage and Salary	73,514	99,044	119,156	20,112	20.3
Goods Producing	23,668	24,681	24,678	(3)	0.0
Mining	628	783	724	(59)	−7.5
Construction	3,889	4,904	5,794	890	18.1
Manufacturing	19,151	18,994	18,160	(834)	−4.4
Service Producing	49,846	74,363	94,478	20,115	27.0
Transportation and Public Utilities	4,541	5,244	5,719	475	9.1
Wholesale Trade	4,113	5,735	7,266	1,531	26.7
Retail Trade	11,835	17,845	22,702	4,857	27.2
Finance/Insurance/Real Estate	3,907	6,297	7,917	1,620	25.7
Services	12,117	22,531	32,545	10,014	44.4
Government	13,333	16,711	18,329	1,618	9.7
Agriculture	3,523	3,252	2,917	(335)	−10.3
Private Households	1,693	1,241	1,215	(26)	−2.1
Nonfarm Self-Employed and Unpaid Family Workers	5,819	8,086	9,742	1,656	20.5

Source: Valerie A. Personick, "Industry Output and Employment through the End of the Century," *Monthly Labor Review*, September 1987, p. 32.

the availability of housing and the proximity of jobs and housing.

Figure 9-6 shows employment projections for states, regions, and regional divisions for 1990 to 2005 and the rank of each state based on its absolute growth in employment during the 15-year period. The Northeast and the Midwest trail the national pace of growth, while the South and the West exceed it. The top three states in terms of growth in employment—California, Texas, and Florida—are projected to capture 31.8 percent of the nation's total growth in employment through 2005. The same three states are projected to capture nearly 55 percent (17.5 million out of 32.2 million people) of the national population growth between 1990 and 2010. H. James Brown, ULI Fellow and director/professor at Harvard University/Joint Center for Housing agrees: "The historical trend of population movement to the South and West will continue during the 1990s. California and Texas will likely experience tremendous growth in population during this decade as a result of a combination of in-migration and low death rates." Thus, a stronger demand for housing in a number of Sunbelt states seems inevitable.

Another factor likely to affect regional dynamics between jobs and housing is the growing trend to major corporate relocations. In the late 1980s, several major corporations announced moves from New York City to Dallas, Houston, and Washington, D.C., among others. Such moves can affect thousands of employees with a single decision. While most major relocations during the 1980s affected New York, other high-cost cities, such as San Francisco and Los Angeles, are candidates for losing major employers in the 1990s.

One primary reason a large corporation chooses to move its operations is clearly the availability of a qualified labor pool. Increasingly, young professionals are unwilling—or unable—to live in a city where reasonably affordable housing is not available; neither are they willing to commute long distances each day from the distant suburbs, where housing is affordable. Council member Thomas L. Hodges notes that major corporate relocations to the Dallas area in the late 1980s were related directly to the low cost of housing and office space, and council member Dale R. Walker adds, "Affordable housing is becoming such a big issue in San Francisco that many major

EMPLOYMENT PROJECTIONS BY STATE, DIVISION, AND REGION: 1990 TO 2005
(000)

	1990	2000	2005	CHANGE: 1990 TO 2005		NUMERICAL GROWTH RANKING
				NUMBER	PERCENT	
UNITED STATES TOTAL	123,071	138,338	143,257	20,187	16.4	
NORTHEAST	26,124	28,776	29,456	3,332	12.8	
New England	7,429	8,484	8,818	1,389	18.7	
Maine	578	639	661	83	14.4	44
New Hampshire	584	702	748	165	28.2	34
Vermont	302	345	362	60	20.0	48
Massachusetts	3,523	4,006	4,144	621	17.6	7
Rhode Island	514	572	590	75	14.6	45
Connecticut	1,928	2,220	2,313	385	20.0	16
Middle Atlantic	18,695	20,293	20,638	1,943	10.4	
New York	9,085	9,881	10,044	958	10.5	4
New Jersey	4,006	4,508	4,664	658	16.4	5
Pennsylvania	5,603	5,904	5,931	327	5.8	20
MIDWEST	29,745	32,284	32,960	3,215	10.8	
East North Central	20,177	21,743	22,110	1,934	9.6	
Ohio	5,136	5,484	5,565	429	8.4	15
Indiana	2,721	2,928	2,991	271	10.0	25
Illinois	5,689	6,181	6,294	606	10.7	9
Michigan	4,122	4,380	4,411	289	7.0	22
Wisconsin	2,510	2,772	2,849	339	13.5	19
West North Central	9,568	10,540	10,850	1,281	13.4	
Minnesota	2,415	2,753	2,865	450	18.6	14
Iowa	1,495	1,597	1,624	129	8.6	38
Missouri	2,665	2,881	2,940	275	10.3	24
North Dakota	382	423	438	56	14.6	49
South Dakota	364	403	417	52	14.4	50
Nebraska	910	1,014	1,051	141	15.5	37
Kansas	1,338	1,470	1,516	177	13.3	33
SOUTH	41,546	46,968	48,925	7,379	17.8	
South Atlantic	21,053	23,868	24,887	3,834	18.2	
Delaware	333	366	379	45	13.6	51
Maryland	2,218	2,408	2,467	248	11.2	28
District of Columbia	711	761	772	61	8.5	47
Virginia	3,045	3,392	3,521	476	15.6	13
West Virginia	769	835	859	90	11.7	43
North Carolina	3,367	3,711	3,849	482	14.3	12
South Carolina	1,671	1,867	1,951	279	16.7	23
Georgia	3,182	3,584	3,755	573	18.0	10
Florida	5,756	6,944	7,335	1,579	27.4	3
East South Central	7,012	7,680	7,944	932	13.3	
Kentucky	1,674	1,811	1,859	185	11.0	32
Tennessee	2,393	2,644	2,755	362	15.1	17
Alabama	1,794	1,964	2,022	229	12.7	29
Mississippi	1,151	1,261	1,307	156	13.5	36

9-6 (continued)

| | 1990 | 2000 | 2005 | CHANGE: 1990 TO 2005 | | NUMERICAL GROWTH RANKING |
				NUMBER	PERCENT	
West South Central	13,481	15,421	16,095	2,614	19.4	
Arkansas	1,115	1,252	1,304	189	16.9	31
Louisiana	2,079	2,331	2,428	348	16.7	18
Oklahoma	1,640	1,837	1,901	261	15.9	26
Texas	8,646	10,001	10,462	1,816	21.0	2
WEST	25,656	30,310	31,917	6,261	24.4	
Mountain	6,870	8,434	9,038	2,169	31.6	
Montana	418	471	491	74	17.6	46
Idaho	490	566	594	104	21.3	41
Wyoming	305	368	397	92	30.1	42
Colorado	1,963	2,416	2,581	618	31.5	8
New Mexico	676	792	841	165	24.3	35
Arizona	1,653	2,123	2,299	646	39.1	6
Utah	791	970	1,043	251	31.7	27
Nevada	574	728	793	219	38.1	30
Pacific	18,787	21,876	22,879	4,092	21.8	
Washington	2,334	2,704	2,849	515	22.1	11
Oregon	1,378	1,606	1,690	313	22.7	21
California	14,139	16,459	17,161	3,022	21.4	1
Alaska	329	411	447	118	36.0	40
Hawaii	607	696	731	124	20.5	39

Source: U.S. Department of Commerce, Bureau of Economic Analysis, *BEA Regional Projections*, vol. 1, "State Projections to 2035" (Washington, D.C.: U.S. Government Printing Office, 1985).

employers—including financial institutions headquartered there—are considering moving to other locations." In sum, according to council member Nina J. Gruen, "The 1990s will be a decade of labor shortages during which companies will make their decisions about location based on where the labor is—and labor will not be in areas with very expensive housing. The communities most likely to benefit from this labor shortage are those that now have a large, low-wage labor pool."

Immigration

The final demographic issue that must be considered with respect to future housing demand is immigration. Between 1980 and 1987, legal immigration averaged 570,000 persons per year, 30 percent higher than the average for the 1970s.[2] This estimate does not include illegal immigration, which ranges from 100,000 to 1 million per year. Hispanic and Asian households especially are increasing rapidly and account for large, but different, housing opportunities.

Between 1980 and 1987, the Hispanic population grew by 28.6 percent, while total U.S. population grew by only 7.4 percent. In fact, Hispanics accounted for one out of every five new households formed during that period. This growth rate is particularly significant in California, Texas, New York, and Florida, where much of the Hispanic immigration has been concentrated. Also significant is that Hispanics tend to be less educated and less skilled than the total U.S. population. "Some 71.6 percent of all employed Hispanics currently work in low- and mid-level skilled jobs, as opposed to 5.9 percent of the total population."[3]

While the numbers and growth rate of Hispanic households suggest a strong demand for housing, homeownership by Hispanics has historically been

[2] National Association of Realtors, *Demographics in the U.S.: The Segmenting of Housing Demand* (Washington, D.C.: Author, 1989), p. 76.

[3] William B. Johnston and Arnold H. Packer, *Work and Workers for the 21st Century* (Indianapolis: Hudson Institute, 1987), Fig. 2, p. xxiii.

low because of comparatively low levels of education and wages—and these factors are expected to persist into the next century. Still, opportunities will exist for affordable single-family houses and for family-oriented multifamily rental housing. To appeal to this market, residential developers will need to pay attention to issues like size and structure of families (often extended families) and cultural values.

Asian households (including groups from the Middle East and Pacific Islands) present a less difficult opportunity for residential developers. Like Hispanics, Asians are a rapidly growing segment of the population—from 1.5 percent of the total population in 1980 to an estimated 4 percent in 2000 (10 million persons).[4] Asian households tend to be more educated and have higher incomes, however, than any other nonwhite group, with some nationalities outpacing white Americans. Asian families, therefore, are as able (or more so) to afford housing as the general population. Residential developers can best capitalize on this growing segment of the population by understanding cultural and family values and accommodating those values in the design of housing. Council member Arthur C. Danielian offers some practical experience: "It is important to pay close attention to details of design when designing housing targeted to certain Asian buyers. For example, some cultures will not consider a house where the staircase is oriented toward the front door, because superstition suggests this design to be bad luck. And semiprivate areas for members of the extended family are important considerations when designing the floor plan."

Patterns of Residential Development

The rapid increase in the cost of land and housing and the complexities of providing new infrastructure have contributed to a redefinition of the suburbs. But long-standing suburban growth trends will not be reversed overnight, and the suburbs will likely remain a focus for residential developers through the 1990s. ULI Fellow H. James Brown predicts that "decentralization of cities is likely to continue, with both population and job growth increasing more rapidly in fringe areas. Population will tend to migrate away from large cities to smaller cities and rural areas." Council member Nina Gruen adds: "The trend toward de-densification appears to be occurring worldwide."

But central city and close suburban locations should also show strength in the coming years. The anticipated growth in nontraditional households, singles living alone, and empty nesters will provide a strong market for locations near major urban services and employment centers. Such locations will also benefit from traffic congestion in the suburbs, which will almost certainly grow worse. Further, the costs and complexities of installing infrastructure and the growing sentiment against urban growth in fringe areas will increase the attractiveness of building new houses on underused infill sites.

A large percentage of the new housing in suburban locations can be expected to be constructed in large planned communities—many of which were initiated in the 1970s and 1980s when assembling such large sites (typically over 1,000 acres) was economically viable and use entitlements could be reasonably obtained. Such communities have the ability to fund the infrastructure and development fees necessary to obtain approvals from local governments. Council member Norman H. Dyer suggests, "Large-scale developments are becoming more important in meeting

9-7   IMMIGRATION BY REGION OF ORIGIN: 1965 TO 1988

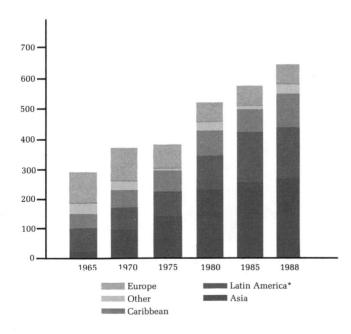

*Includes Mexico, Central America, and South America.
Source: National Association of Realtors, *Demographics in the U.S.: The Segmenting of Housing Demand* (Washington, D.C.: Author, 1989), p. 66.

[4] National Association of Realtors, *Demographics in the U.S.*, p. 48. See also Leon F. Bouvier and Anthony J. Agresta, "The Future Asian Population of the United States," in James T. Fawcett and Benjamin V. Carino, eds., *Pacific Bridges: The New Immigration from Asia and the Pacific Islands* (Staten Island, N.Y.: Center for Migration Studies of New York, 1987), p. 290.

Employment and housing growth can be traced from before World War II to demonstrate the suburbanization of both housing and employment. A) Before the war, employment existed primarily in the urban core with housing located nearby; small towns with limited employment existed on the outskirts of the urban core. B) The postwar period brought massive housing growth to the suburbs and a reduction of housing in the urban core; only limited employment opportunities existed in the suburbs. C) Beginning around the early 1970s, employment-dominated centers emerged in the suburbs, often consuming areas that were once small rural towns; these suburban centers accommodated new residential development in more distant locations. And baby boomers sparked a revived interest in housing near the historical downtown. D) The 1990s promise to bring increased suburbanization as a "second wave" of employment centers begins to emerge at the new urban fringe. The trend, however, will be for increased efficiency of land use and an emphasis on mixing employment uses with housing. Opportunities for residential development also will occur on infill and underused sites near existing employment centers (the historical urban core and the "first wave" of suburban employment centers).

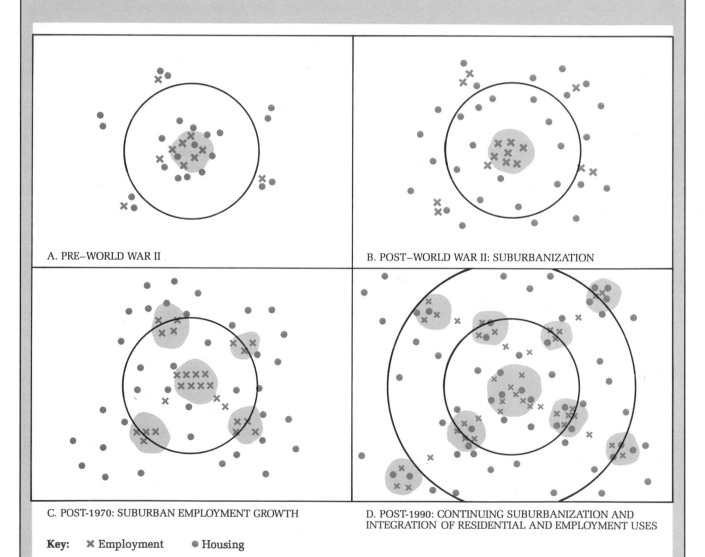

A. PRE–WORLD WAR II

B. POST–WORLD WAR II: SUBURBANIZATION

C. POST-1970: SUBURBAN EMPLOYMENT GROWTH

D. POST-1990: CONTINUING SUBURBANIZATION AND INTEGRATION OF RESIDENTIAL AND EMPLOYMENT USES

Key: ✖ Employment   ● Housing

9-9 Rancho Santa Margarita is an emerging 5,000-acre master-planned community in Orange County, California. At completion, the community will provide about 15,000 housing units of mixed type and density and a wide array of supporting employment and service uses.

market demand because they can provide builders with a ready source of available land."

Council member H. Pike Oliver believes that the popularity of planned communities will increase in the foreseeable future, not only with homebuyers but also with local governments.

- Large-scale planned communities make it much easier to isolate and assign costs of infrastructure; if a local government can be assured that a project is paying its own way, it will more likely grant entitlements.
- Large-scale projects make it possible to undertake more comprehensive master environmental planning and mitigation programs. Conscientious developers, inspired by the prospects of a long-term development program, can address environmental issues more comprehensively than local governments can piecemeal. Planned communities can therefore act as vehicles for "packaging" entitlements.
- Planned communities provide opportunities for "privatizing" growth management. The master developer can work continuously with local government to better maintain a balance between new development and public services and be better able to avoid emergency growth moratoriums.
- Through community associations and maintenance districts, large communities have proven effective in providing long-term maintenance that municipalities increasingly are unable to provide.

For these reasons, planned communities should remain a staple of suburban residential development, despite their high economic exposure and risks. Master developers will package such communities in terms of use entitlements, basic infrastructure, and overall planning and design, thereby acting as middle men between sellers of raw land and homebuilders. Master developers will minimize their financial risk by phasing large communities in villages that can be built incrementally.

Although forecasters believe that job growth will slow in the coming decades, the trend for jobs to decentralize to suburban sites can be expected to continue. The 1990s will likely see continued job strength in large suburban activity centers, where much of the employment occurred during the 1970s and 1980s. But during the 1990s, employers will be enticed to more distant suburban sites to be closer to lower-priced housing (and thus employees). Such moves will open up new opportunities for housing demand at even more distant locations, continuing the process of urban decentralization. This process, however, could be hindered by nonmarket forces like moratoriums on growth and the inability to provide new suburban sites with infrastructure and public services. The relationship between jobs and housing will become even more critical in the future as homebuyers become more concerned about affordable housing.

Financing

The availability of money—not the supply of and demand for housing—has always been the real determinant of building cycles. Until the 1980s, the limited availability of mortgage funds controlled development, but that check on construction disappeared with the introduction of new financing vehicles designed to promote a constant flow of funds into real estate.

Residential financing was the first to change. After deregulation of the S&Ls in 1982, borrowing rates rose to market levels. The continuous appetite of the secondary market allowed S&Ls to originate and sell new mortgages quickly, whether or not they had new cash to invest. Ready financing resulted in overbuilding in many real estate markets—most notably in offices. In comparison, residential developers adapted to deregulation quite well. They learned that ready access to end loans was not enough and that they had to monitor the demand for new houses while remaining attentive to prevailing mortgage terms.[5] Multifamily projects, however, were developed more like offices, with less regard given to demand and primary consideration given to the availability of financing and tax writeoffs. But all that changed with the Tax Reform Act of 1986.

While the 1980s were characterized by this ready flow of capital, the 1990s are more likely to experience a squeeze on financing. The failures of S&Ls of the mid- and late 1980s will be felt well into the 1990s. Tighter regulations and requirements for liquidity for lending institutions will severely limit money available for new residential development—regardless of demand. Council member H. James Brown states, "The S&Ls' problems of the 1980s will profoundly affect housing production for years to come, with the most immediate effects on acquisition, development, and construction." Residential developers attending ULI's spring 1990 meeting in Dallas confirmed that financing for residential projects was scarce in all markets and nonexistent in some and that the credit crunch had arrived.

To obtain financing for their projects, residential developers in the 1990s will need to put up more equity. Council member Susan L. Giles believes that foreign investors will play a role: "A trend for the 1990s will be to draw Asian financiers as equity partners (joint ventures) and as construction partners. The financing will still probably come from American banks, but the Asians will supply the 'paper money' or good credit." She sees four primary sources of Asian money for financing residential development: Hong Kong, Japan, Korea, and Taiwan. So far, such investors have shown interest primarily in acquiring completed multifamily projects, but that role may be expanded over the 1990s to include new construction.

Council member Lachman agrees that foreign investment in U.S. real estate will be a trend for the 1990s: "The globalization of financial markets that characterized the 1980s will incorporate real estate finance thoroughly in the 1990s—construction lending, direct investment in all types of properties, mortgage lending, resale of mortgages, and interest rate and currency. Overseas banks' financing of U.S. properties will be far more extensive, keeping competitive pressure on domestic lenders." Council member

Richard L. Michaux agrees that globalization will be a trend in the 1990s but adds, "Much of this capital—especially Asian capital—could be diverted to Eastern Europe because of the potential for higher returns and the opportunity to enter a new market. Increased competition for Asian capital would mean requirements for higher returns for U.S. projects and higher interest rates." But U.S. developers will also play a larger role in international real estate development, in part because of shrinking markets at home. Some American residential development companies have already found success abroad; an example is Los Angeles–based Kaufman and Broad, which builds production housing in suburban Paris.

Legislation curbing S&Ls' risk taking will reduce the role of that source of lending, requiring other sources of capital—commercial banks, pension funds, insurance companies, and foreign investors—to assume a larger role. Except for commercial banks, these sources have thus far been interested mostly in multifamily projects, and it may be some years before they become major players in financing for-sale residential development.

Residential financing in the 1990s will also be affected by federal legislation, which is almost impossible to predict. The Tax Reform Act of 1986, for example, dealt a serious blow to multifamily and rehabilitation projects by virtually eliminating the tax shelters that generated much of the capital for financing. Saved from the tax reform ax was the deduction for mortgage payments, which is still the major incentive for homeownership. But many experts believe that deduction's days may be numbered. Council member Ronald C. Nahas says, "The mortgage deduction for homeownership may not be as sacred as once thought." If the deduction is eliminated in the future, the effect would certainly be to encourage renters to remain renters. Existing homeowners might also be encouraged to sell their houses and invest their equity elsewhere.

Another concern for the 1990s relates to the overall stability of housing prices. Some real estate experts believe that prices will fall dramatically before the end of the century in response to decreased demand and the overinflated prices of the 1980s. If housing prices do start to tumble, the implications for homeowners and real estate developers will surely be profound:

At the very least, the retirement plans of many Americans might be blighted by further erosion in the value of their most valuable asset. Moreover, rising home prices

---

[5] M. Leanne Lachman, "A New Climate for Development in the 1990s," *Urban Land,* February 1989, p. 30.

The demographic trends that will affect rental housing in the 1990s are complicated, inconsistent, and sometimes contradictory, according to council member Richard Kately, executive vice president of Real Estate Research Corporation (RERC). Overall trends point to the need for more specific marketing of products. Structural changes in the economy will affect the size and composition of the labor force and distribution of income. RERC expects employment to grow by only 18 percent (21 million jobs, largely low-paying service jobs in wholesale and retail trade) by 2000. Nine out of 10 of these new jobs will be filled by minorities and women.

These changes in the nature of the labor force will affect the distribution of income. Middle-class America will shrink in comparison to the expanding ranks of the affluent and the poor. Historically high rates of homeownership will continue the decline begun in the 1980s as lower-paid workers are unable to afford to buy their own houses. As a result, the rental housing market should be strong.

According to Kately, several demographic segments will support multifamily rental development during the 1990s:

- *The elderly*. Seventy-five percent of persons aged 65 to 75—the young elderly—are homeowners, but because 47 percent of persons in this group live alone, they are good, though reluctant, targets for rental products.
- *Baby boomers*. Now aged 25 to 43, baby boomers fall into two distinct subgroups. Those born before 1955 are more educated, more affluent, and more likely to be homeowners. Those born after 1957, Kately believes, are

likely to remain less affluent and more prone to rent.
- *Single people*. By 2000, the population will contain 40 million singles, most with insufficient income to become homeowners. RERC estimates that only 20 percent of singles will earn more than $30,000 annually. Single persons will thus loom large as renters.
- *Hispanics*. This rapidly growing demographic segment has increased 30 percent since 1980 and is expected to account for 20 percent of the U.S. population by 2010. Hispanic households are typically larger and poorer than the average U.S. household. They are concentrated in primarily a few metropolitan areas (Los Angeles, New York, Miami, and San Antonio), where they constitute an especially important segment of the rental market, but they constitute sizable populations in many other metropolitan areas as well.

Rental housing demand, like total housing demand, will decline from the peak years of the 1980s. Products tailored to specialized market segments, however, will provide opportunities for development in many locations.

High-Rise Apartments

Council member Richard L. Michaux, a national partner of Trammell Crow Company, believes that opportunities for high-rise apartment development will exist in certain markets. In the suburbs of Washington, D.C., for example, professionals, executives, and semiemployed singles and couples con-▶

helped fuel the consumer spending boom of the eighties through the "wealth effect." [Dropping resale values] in the coming decade could correspondingly hobble economic growth. Finally, weakness in housing could seriously debilitate an already overextended American credit system. For residential real estate constitutes perhaps the most important stable class of collateral backing U.S. consumer, institutional, and government debt.[6]

Other experts believe that housing prices are more likely to increase modestly (in line with the rate of inflation) or, at worst, stabilize over the coming decade. Referring to one forecast, known as the "Harvard Study," which predicted a 30 percent drop in residential real estate prices during the 1990s, council member H. James Brown comments: "The study fo-

cused on the demand side of the equation and did not give adequate consideration to supply. Building houses entails increasing constraints (regulations, growth controls, construction costs), and it is not likely that the housing industry will be able to supply the estimated 1.1 million units that will be demanded each year during the 1990s. The combined effects of supply and demand will tend to keep housing prices from dropping substantially."

_____

[6] Jonathan R. Laing, "Crumbling Castles—The Recession in Real Estate Has Ominous Implications," *Barron's,* December 18, 1989, p. 8.

9-10 (continued)

stitute a market for high rises in or near commercial and business centers. The ideal product mix for this group is two-thirds one-bedroom and efficiency units and one-third two-bedroom or two-bedroom-plus-den units, averaging 750 square feet overall.

Leasing to this market is like selling; such renters are making a decision based on lifestyle and only 10 percent sign a lease during their first visit. This market demands a location that is convenient to employment centers and/or rapid transit and a high level of amenities and services, such as maid service, plant and animal care, concierge services, business services, and handyman help. To gain a competitive edge, projects should offer not only high-quality appliances, finishes, and recreational facilities but also convenience stores and high-tech amenities, such as antisurge outlets for computers.

Compared with garden apartments, high rises require greater front-end investment, are more difficult to phase, take longer to construct, are more complicated to operate and manage, and lease more slowly. In the right markets, however—those with appropriate locations and proven demand—they will be an important market niche in the 1990s.

Infill Apartments

Robert Wagner, president of Prometheus Development Company, has found good market opportunities for rental housing on infill sites in the San Francisco Bay Area, a market where developable land is scarce and expensive and 85 percent of the population now have incomes too low to purchase an average-priced house. Wagner looks for vacant or redevelopable properties like school sites or old R&D sites that are located close to employment

centers. Redeveloping such sites typically involves a change of use and requires working with neighborhood groups and navigating a lengthy approval process.

Tenants for infill projects tend to be older and affluent; they demand a good location, large units, extensive amenities, and an array of well-managed services. Light, airy apartments with vaulted ceilings are popular, and tenants want security systems, fireplaces, and walk-in closets. Pools and clubhouses with exercise rooms are desired amenities.

Infill projects work well at densities up to 50 units per acre. Higher densities are difficult unless the project is part of a mixed-use development. Mixed-use projects on infill sites appeal to many employers and create opportunities for shared amenities and parking. About 10 to 20 percent of the units can be leased as corporate apartments.

Garden Apartments

As for-sale housing becomes less affordable in many markets, garden apartments become more attractive. Council member William B. McGuire, Jr., partner of The McGuire Group, believes that garden apartments should be targeted to specific market segments. Even within a single project, buildings can be divided into areas where architecture, unit size and design, amenities, and services can be tailored to meet the needs of specific market segments.

Apartments for the Elderly

Thomas Bozzuto, formerly with Oxford Development Corporation, characterizes housing for the

If housing prices drop in the future or if interest rates rise substantially, many experts believe that the number of mortgage defaults will rise dramatically. Betting on continued price inflation, many households stretched their mortgage payments to new limits in the 1980s, often using ARMs and buydown mortgages to qualify for loans that would otherwise be beyond their reach. Other households borrowed heavily against the equity in their houses to take advantage of permitted interest deductions on home equity loans. Some lenders are now concerned that instability in the housing market or a major recession could lead to a rise in defaults, which would deal

another blow to an already crippled real estate finance industry. As of early 1990, the likelihood for any major upheavals in housing prices or defaults was still a matter of conjecture, but raising these flags suggests much more cautious lending practices are in order in the 1990s.

Regulations

According to council member Gordon Tippell, "If a developer is not already a politician, then he better become one." The regulatory climate for development

362

elderly as an imperfectly understood infant industry. Oxford's initial market studies indicated a growing market, especially for high-end rental products. According to these initial studies, large projects (up to 360 units) could achieve economies of scale, but leasing them would be slow. It would be important, but not critical, to locate projects near a nursing home.

After developing several projects, Oxford found it was experiencing a 25 percent turnover each year in its portfolio of rental housing for the elderly, making leasing long and difficult. The company achieved occupancies of 50 percent overall, but projects varied considerably. Oxford expected to attract young retirees but found the market to be driven by need. The average age of tenants entering its projects is 80. Based on this experience, Bozzuto believes that projects of about 150 to 170 units are the best risk. Assisted units lease more quickly and make money. Bozzuto believes a nursing home on site is essential. Overall, he cautions that developing projects for the elderly is extremely difficult, complex, and imprecise.

Family Apartments

Noting that twice as many families as singles rent, Bozzuto sees family apartments as an underserved, strong market. Bozzuto Associates follows several guidelines: provide large apartments (many three-bedroom units, no one-bedroom units), services, and daycare; locate projects in good school districts; and keep projects small (up to 200 units), because housing children entails potential management problems. The locations of projects do not have to be highly visible.

Financing

Council member Philip J. Ward, senior vice president of CIGNA Investments, Inc., believes that money will be available for feasible apartment projects, particularly as pension funds attempt to diversify their portfolios. Investors will look for distinctive projects in larger cities on sites that offer locational advantages.

Council member Richard B. Saltzman, managing director of Merrill Lynch's capital market, agrees that pension funds will invest in apartments, at first favoring existing projects to test the market at lowest risk. Sophisticated investors like CIGNA will be willing to look at new apartment developments. Foreign investors will generally be attracted only to high-profile investment opportunities downtown. Individuals will be reluctant to invest unless the tax law changes.

All in All

Council member J. Ronald Terwilliger, managing partner of Trammell Crow Company–Residential, sums up the prospects for rental housing in the 1990s: "The market surge begun in the 1970s by the coming of age of the baby boomers, sustained by high divorce rates and immigration, and intensified by problems of affordability will continue into the 1990s." An effective development response to the demand for rental units will be more carefully targeted to specific segments of the market and will emphasize the provision of services and good management.

Source: Diane R. Suchman, "Rental Housing in the 1990s," *Urban Land,* June 1989, pp. 32–33. Based on a program session, "Rental Apartment Product for the 1990s," at ULI's 1989 spring meeting in New Orleans.

will almost certainly be tougher in the foreseeable future. Environmental issues will continue to gain the attention of the public and elected officials. Hot issues promise to include groundwater pollution, solid waste disposal, preservation of wetlands, disposal and cleanup of toxic waste, and air quality. The federal government will continue to take the lead on most of these environmental concerns by adopting standards that state and local governments must meet.

But residential developers will probably be the most affected by local politics and the burgeoning antigrowth sentiment that has already swept through many of the nation's hottest real estate markets like California and Florida. Fueled by concerns over degradation of the environment, loss of open space, traffic gridlock, and insufficient public services, growth management regulations are extending beyond local politics and encompassing entire regions and even states. Several state planning acts adopted in the 1980s, such as those for Vermont and New Jersey, clearly have as a primary objective to control, direct, or limit growth. Council member Norman H. Dyer notes, "In Hawaii, which has had state planning since 1961, housing production is governed by the approvals process, with little relationship to demand."

Speaking before an audience of ULI Residential Council members, architect Barry Berkus of Santa Barbara, California, noted that "housing consumers essentially are holding land hostage. Wasteful development of land and infrastructure has led to a consumer backlash against new development." The NIMBY attitude will intensify as a major obstacle for residential developers during the 1990s, and residential developers will certainly need to invest more time and money to overcome inherent opposition to new development. They will also need to invest more in design, quality control, infrastructure, and direct community contributions to overcome such roadblocks. In short, there is every reason to believe that development costs and fees will increase during the 1990s, contributing to higher for-sale and rental housing prices.

Affordable Housing: Public and Private Roles

In the early part of this century, the production of housing at all levels was considered an activity of the private sector. The federal government's role was limited to expediting mortgage lending associated with homeownership. From the Great Depression through 1980, the history of the federal government's involvement in housing—through financial assistance to producers and occupants, direct production, tax incentives, insurance and credit programs, specialized thrift institutions, and neighborhood revitalization programs—was one of expanding responsibility. Especially during the 1970s, federal housing programs supported the massive production of low-income housing.

Housing policy shifted dramatically in the 1980s as the federal government withdrew its commitment to housing by eliminating or substantially reducing funding for a broad cross-section of programs. Federal authorizations for housing dropped 80 percent between 1980 and 1988.[7] By 1990, only about one-fourth of eligible low-income households received any kind of housing assistance.

Because of the size of the federal deficit, little money will likely be available for new or expanded federal housing programs during the 1990s. This factor is significant because of the federal government's special ability to redistribute resources effectively. As council member and Senior Fellow Anthony Downs observes, "If local jurisdictions tax the rich to serve the poor, the rich can—and often do—move elsewhere."

| 9-11 | RATES OF HOMEOWNERSHIP BY AGE OF HOUSEHOLD HEAD (PERCENT) |

Between 1973 and 1988, total homeownership declined by 0.5 percent to 63.9 percent. Declining homeownership was most evident, however, in the youngest age cohorts, dropping between 7 and 8 percentage points. Some experts believe that homeownership will stabilize or rise slightly during the 1990s as the baby boom generation moves into its 40s, an age associated with high rates of homeownership. But other factors may work to offset an increase: a growing percentage of nontraditional configurations among newly formed households and higher and higher costs of becoming an owner.

AGE	1973	1976	1980	1983	1988
Under 25	23.4	21.0	21.3	19.3	15.5
25–29	43.6	43.2	43.3	38.2	36.2
30–34	60.2	62.4	61.1	55.7	52.6
35–39	68.5	69.0	70.8	65.8	63.2
40–44	72.9	73.9	74.2	74.2	71.4
45–54	76.1	77.4	77.7	77.1	76.0
55–64	75.7	77.2	79.3	80.5	79.6
65–74	71.3	72.7	75.2	76.9	78.2
75+	67.1	67.2	67.8	71.6	70.4
Total	64.4	64.8	65.6	64.9	63.9

Source: Joint Center for Housing Studies, Harvard University, *The State of the Nation's Housing 1989*, 1989, p. 12. (Data from *American Housing Survey, 1973–1980*, Current Population Survey, 1983–1988.)

The decreasing federal role in housing programs has shifted the burden to state and local governments. State administration of federal programs has enabled some state agencies to develop a sound base of experience. In fact, many state housing programs are modeled after now unfunded federal initiatives. The types and levels of local housing programs vary tremendously from one jurisdiction to another for reasons including the extent of local experience in the production of low-income housing, state and local statutes that limit the amount of capital that governments can raise, the depth of the existing tax base, and the

---

[7] William Apgar and H. James Brown, *The State of the Nation's Housing* (Cambridge, Mass.: Joint Center for Housing Studies, MIT and Harvard Univ., 1988), p. 19.

BRIDGE Housing Corporation is a public-benefit, nonprofit 501(c)(3) corporation established in 1982 to provide new or rehabilitated housing in the nine-county San Francisco Bay Area. Its goals are 1) volume production, aiming at and now approaching 5 percent of total multifamily housing starts in the area per year; 2) high-quality housing to satisfy both subsidized and market-rate consumers and to make projects acceptable to neighboring communities; and 3) affordability, with approximately 40 percent of units produced overall within financial reach of the target client group—households earning $12,000 to $25,000 per year. For both political and economic reasons, most of its projects have been mixed-income, rental and for-sale developments.

BRIDGE accomplishes its goals through a variety of roles. It functions as a private developer, participates in joint ventures with for-profit or nonprofit developers, does turnkey projects for public agencies, and provides technical expertise and assistance to nonprofit developers. Its key resources include a development trust fund, a revolving loan fund that provides working capital for projects; a talented and experienced staff; and the credibility of an excellent track record.

The nine-county San Francisco Bay Area is considered one of the most difficult development environments in the nation. Several constraints limit the supply of new housing developed in the area: limitations on available land, political pressures to limit growth, environmental regulations, and restrictions on public spending that affect development. The most serious limitations on the supply of land (and therefore of housing) are the growth regulations enacted by area governments. As a result, housing in the Bay Area is scarce and expensive, and lower-income households have few housing choices.

BRIDGE takes advantage of the various subsidies and incentive programs offered by different levels of government, including a state law that gives BRIDGE, as a tax-exempt, nonprofit organization, the legal right to purchase surplus public property (land, abandoned school buildings, and so on) for its projects at fair market value before the property is offered for competitive public sale. To make its projects affordable, however, BRIDGE relies primarily on the negotiation of land development conces-

9-13　Picklewood is a 32-unit low-income rental project in high-priced Marin County.

sions, density bonuses, reduced parking requirements, and waivers of development fees. Increasing the number of units that can be built or lowering the development costs in these ways adds value to the project. By formal written agreement with the governing jurisdiction, the increase in value gained from regulatory concessions and added density is plowed back into the project to support the development and occupancy of the affordable units. BRIDGE can negotiate these concessions because it can clearly demonstrate the flow of value back to lower-income consumers.

All of BRIDGE's projects are supported by a combination of subsidies in addition to density bonuses and land use concessions, including grants, below-market loans, fee waivers, regulatory concessions, below-market land acquisition, and rent subsidies. Each project is structured and financed individually, and each is therefore time-consuming, difficult, and not usually replicable for future projects. BRIDGE's system of production includes the use of the development trust fund to initiate projects, the reliance on donated or low-cost land and negotiation of concessions to reduce the level of financial subsidization required, the continuing relationships with lenders that have come to trust BRIDGE's judgment and capabilities, and its ability to keep rents down over time and to manage completed projects.

BRIDGE has three sources of financing:

- *Predevelopment funds.* The development trust fund determines the number of units that ▶

BRIDGE can produce. The money is used to invest in projects, and the project's earnings form the basis for the subsidy. Money from the development trust fund is recaptured, returned to the fund, and reinvested in other projects. The fund provides venture capital for predevelopment activities and occasionally provides equity capital to fill the gap between total development costs and the amount raised through loans. Monies from the fund are sometimes used to bring rents down to eligibility levels for Section 8 Existing Certificates.

- *Debt financing.* BRIDGE typically obtains construction loans for debt financing from regular construction lenders. Permanent financing is often obtained through tax-exempt financing obtained by working with state, county, and/or city governments. BRIDGE has used mortgage revenue bonds of different types, some taxable. For its condominium projects, BRIDGE often buys mortgage funds for its consumers.
- *Equity financing.* Equity financing is accomplished through syndication of tax credits, although occasionally the development trust fund is used for equity money.

For individual projects, BRIDGE can use a wide variety of sources of funding and techniques. It specializes in putting together creative, highly leveraged financing packages, using a number of different resources from lenders. BRIDGE likes to have each project totally financed. To do so, the project's

appraisal is based on the land use that includes increased density rather than on the purchase price of the land as originally zoned. Thus, what to the lender is a 50 percent loan-to-value ratio might actually be a 100 percent loan-to-value ratio based on BRIDGE's actual costs.

BRIDGE's ability to generate additional subsidies for affordable housing is illustrated by a 167-unit project in Alameda County, Richards Manor. The project began when a landowner in the city of Livermore (about an hour's drive east of San Francisco) proposed to donate 10 acres of land for housing for senior citizens. The site was zoned for eight units per acre and valued at $10,000 per unit, or $800,000. The city referred the landowner to Eden Housing, which in turn brought BRIDGE into the picture. Working together, BRIDGE and Eden secured the required project approvals.

First, the project had to receive special consideration under Livermore's growth control ordinance, which limits the number of building permits that can be issued each year. The project was allowed to use permits that had been allocated—but not used—in previous years. Next, BRIDGE and Eden obtained a density bonus over 100 percent, according to the incentives for affordable housing and housing for senior citizens available under the law. These bonuses increased the planned project from 80 to 167 units and more than doubled the value of the site, to $1.67 million.

BRIDGE and Eden entered a joint venture with a for-profit partner, Calmark Development Corporation, a Southern California–based firm specializing in housing for the elderly that had shown interest in the Northern California market. Calmark built the project with financing from tax-exempt bonds issued by the Livermore Housing Authority.

Under federal law, bond-financed projects must set aside 20 percent of their units for low-income families. Because of the added land value, however, Richards Manor has twice that number of low-income apartments. Subsidies come from payments on a land lease made by Calmark to BRIDGE/Eden, which maintains long-term ownership of the land. By pumping all available revenues back into the project, the participants will be able to keep rents at approximately $400 per month.

9-14 Holloway Terrace consists of 42 condominium townhouses and a community center built on a former school site in San Francisco. Architectural style and materials were selected to be compatible with the surrounding neighborhood.

Source: Diane R. Suchman with D. Scott Middleton and Susan L. Giles, *Public/Private Housing Partnerships* (Washington, D.C.: ULI–the Urban Land Institute, 1990).

9-15 The Sara Frances Hotel is one of several projects to be privately constructed in downtown San Diego under an innovative city program that provides private developers with financial incentives and the flexibility to vary from rigid construction standards and zoning regulations. The project provides 160 single-occupancy hotel rooms targeted to elderly, disabled, and low-income individuals.

relationship of the city or county to quasi-public authorities like housing finance agencies, local housing authorities, and school districts. But many, including past ULI president Fritz Grupe, Jr., believe that state and local governments cannot adequately fill the void left by the federal government: "Because of initiatives like Proposition 13, communities and states do not have any money. Unless the problem of low-income housing is addressed at the federal level, it won't be addressed."

Given the lack of federal initiatives as well as state and local funds, the provision of affordable housing in the 1990s will likely depend more on public/private partnerships. Players from the private sector will include nonprofit and for-profit developers, banks and other lending institutions or organizations (such as trade unions, insurance companies, and pension funds), quasi-public intermediary organizations, and foundations or other philanthropic groups. Employers might also become more involved in helping their

employees locate, rent, or purchase housing through a variety of programs that could include employers' direct construction and ownership, assistance with downpayments and/or closing costs, and mortgage guarantees. Given the predicted shortage of labor, employers might use housing assistance programs as a means of enticing or retaining qualified workers.

Some housing experts believe that affordable housing will become such a pressing problem in the 1990s that both government and private developers will be compelled to increase their efforts. Council member Lachman is one who believes the federal role will eventually be expanded somewhat: "Tax credits are likely to come back as an incentive to increase the supply of rental housing. A federal housing trust fund might also be established." It is also likely that the federal defense budget will be reduced during the 1990s; while most of these cuts will go toward reducing the deficit, some might be diverted to social programs, such as housing. From the private sector's perspective, the market for low- and moderate-income housing might prove too big to ignore—especially in light of dwindling mainstream markets.

Design

Throughout most of the 1970s and 1980s, houses grew steadily larger, with the median square footage increasing almost 18 percent between 1975 and 1988. This trend can be attributed to a number of factors, including the proportionately high percentage of houses built during that period for young (and growing) families. The market demanded larger houses, despite concurrent escalations in price. Buyers seemed willing to stretch their mortgage payments but also wanted evidence that they were getting their money's worth with larger houses and fancier finishes.

It is unlikely, however, that houses will continue to grow larger throughout the 1990s, given demographic trends. By the early 1990s, most baby boomers who potentially could become homeowners had done so—and many had already advanced to their first or second move-up house. And the trend toward nontraditional households implies a demand for smaller housing units.

The soaring land prices of the 1980s that greatly affected the design of single-family houses in many high-growth markets (for example, California and Florida) promise to continue to be a force for the remainder of this century. Although land prices are linked to demand, which is forecast to slacken in the

367

Robb Miller

9-16, 9-17   The trend for regionalism in design is expected to continue throughout the 1990s, influencing architectural forms, materials, and land planning. Lakemont (left)—a development of duplex and triplex units in San Ramon, California—and Whitman Pond (right)—clustered townhouses in Weymouth, Massachusetts—are two examples.

1990s, other factors must be taken into consideration: the decreasing supply of available building sites caused by local growth-control initiatives, increased regulations on development, tougher environmental controls, and escalating development impact fees. The land squeeze felt through most of the 1980s will intensify in the 1990s.

Given continued high land costs and the inability of both government and the private sector to finance major improvements to infrastructure, the trend to higher residential densities can be expected to continue. Firmly established in some markets in the

Sunbelt (most notably Southern California), the small single-family lot (about 5,000 square feet) will become more commonplace in midwestern, northeastern, and mid-Atlantic suburbs. The days of the typical quarter- to half-acre lot appear to be over. Nevertheless, single-family houses are not likely to disappear from the U.S. housing market, given consumers' strong historical preference for them.

When asked by *Newsweek* magazine to design the "house of the future," council member Jack Bloodgood complied with a three-bedroom house on a 6,800-square-foot lot specifically for a traditional move-up family (see Figure 9-19). One notable feature of the house is the smaller lot on which it is built—about 3,000 square feet smaller than the typical lot in 1989. "I started out designing houses," says Bloodgood. "Now I design houses and land together."[8]

Bloodgood's house makes maximum use of both indoor and outdoor space. Gone are such traditional features as front and rear yards and long driveways for parking cars. Instead, this house of the future offers an active play area for children, a secluded garden and spa for adults, a lap pool, space for a vegetable garden, a storage area for recyclable materials, and a walled, landscaped entrance courtyard. The house and lot back up to a common path restricted to bicycles and pedestrians that leads to community facilities—schools, recreation areas, and shopping centers.

One of the house's notable interior features is a multipurpose area with private entrance; this flexible room could house an extended family member, provide an additional bedroom, or serve as an in-home

9-18   MEDIAN SQUARE FOOTAGE OF NEW HOUSES: 1975 TO 1988

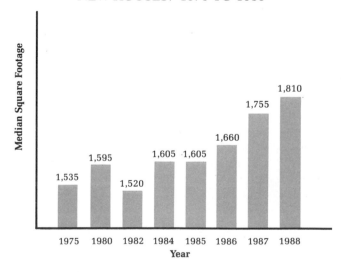

Source: U.S. Bureau of the Census, *Characteristics of New Homes*, Series C-25 (Washington, D.C.: U.S. Government Printing Office, 1989).

[8] Jerry Adler, "The House of the Future," *Newsweek,* Winter/Spring 1990 special edition, p. 73.

office. Overall, the floor plan is designed for flexibility; it separates adults' and children's sleeping areas and provides "common" spaces for them to come together. Formal, seldom-used rooms—a dining room, for example—are not present.

This house is designed for traditional family units with perhaps an extended family member also living in the unit. During the 1990s, however, the increase in the number of nontraditional households suggests a need for new product designs as well. For example, single-parent households and individuals living alone will require smaller and more affordable units geared to their lifestyles and incomes. Because affordability will probably continue to be a problem for most housing consumers, products, such as one designed for two single-parent households to share, may begin to emerge. Such a product is now being designed for a site in Columbia, Maryland, with assistance in financing provided by the Maryland Department of Housing and Community Development. As planned, the units will feature separate sleeping areas for each family and shared kitchen and living areas. The location and the design of the units will offer convenience to employment and schools and will open opportunities to share responsibilities for child care.[9]

Residential developers in the 1990s will need to build housing that responds to increasingly diverse households, ethnic backgrounds, and incomes, which suggests that developers must be ready to respond with products for specific niches. While single-family housing is expected to remain a strong preference, affordability and an aging population indicate that higher-density forms of attached housing will also be in demand.

A trend in planning and urban design that began in the 1980s—often referred to as neotraditionalism or village planning—will begin to leave a significant mark on new suburban developments in the 1990s. This approach draws upon historical prototypes as inspiration for the future. Notable features of design include small lots, higher densities, straight streets, abundant public spaces, and an emphasis on forms of travel other than automobiles. The concept embraces a mix of land uses, densities, incomes, and ages: an integral part of the concept is to allow residents the opportunity to walk, bicycle, or use convenient public transportation to get to work. By 1990, only a smattering of such projects had actually been completed, but dozens of other were on the drawing tables. One of the primary constraints to implementing this concept is getting past the roadblocks of zoning and subdivision codes, which usually do not accommodate the densities, mix of uses, and design

MAIN FLOOR

9-19 Bloodgood Architects & Planners, Inc., of Des Moines, Iowa, offers this design for 21st century living that would cater to a traditional family household. Built on a 6,800-square-foot lot, the house features plenty of flexible use areas to accommodate the growing diversity of household types and family activities. *Source:* Jerry Adler, "The House of the Future," *Newsweek*, Winter/Spring 1990 special edition, pp. 74–75.

[9] Presentation by Jacqueline Rogers, secretary, Maryland Department of Housing and Community Development, "Employer-Assisted Housing Workshop: Addressing the Region's Housing and Labor Needs," sponsored by the Metropolitan Washington Council of Governments, May 17, 1990.

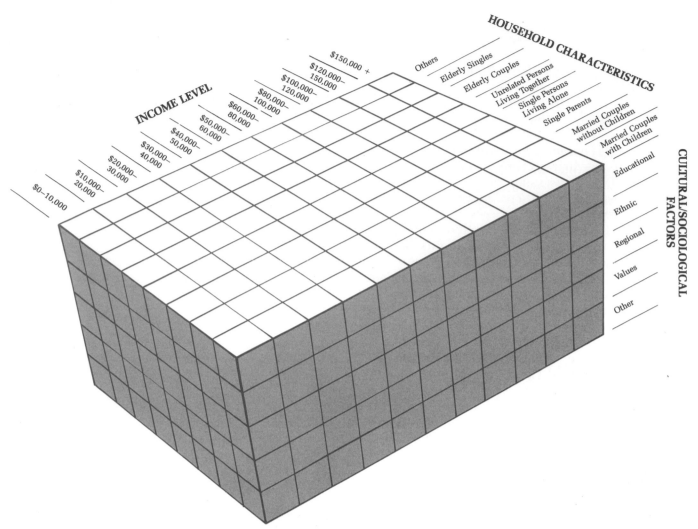

9-20 During the 1990s and beyond, residential markets will become increasingly segmented. In the past, developers targeted their products to market niches based on a two-dimensional matrix—one matrix consisting of income levels and the other consisting of household characteristics. In the future, however, consideration of a third matrix accounting for diverse sociological and cultural characteristics will also need to be considered. The number of "cells" or market niches is thus increased dramatically. Successful marketing will require careful targeting to specific cells within the matrix. These matrix categories are illustrative only; developers should determine their own matrices based on local and regional conditions.

standards (like narrower streets) inherent in the neotraditional approach. It may be too soon to determine whether this "back-to-the-future" approach to planning and design will be the answer to suburban woes, but the concept has gained much attention from the media and will certainly leave a mark on the "postsuburbia" of the 1990s.

The architectural trend that developed in the 1980s toward "regionalism" can be expected to continue into the next century. Consumers have responded favorably to house designs that draw upon historical and regional architectural prototypes, because such designs convey a sense of tradition and individuality. According to architect William Devereaux, "People want something a little different, but they do not want a house that looks like a spaceship landed on their lot."[10]

Rehabilitation

The Tax Reform Act of 1986 made it extremely difficult for developers involved in rehabilitation to put financial packages together. With opportunities for syndication harder to find, rehabilitation and adaptive use dropped significantly by the late 1980s from the peak of 1984 and 1985. The lost tax incentives had the secondary effect of reducing "patient money"— funds often required to wait out unpredictable approval and construction associated with rehabilitation projects. Other constraints to rehabilitation surfaced in the late 1980s, with overbuilding in some

---

[10] H. Jane Lehmen, "Future Shock: Society Redefining Home Buyer," *Washington Post*, May 12, 1990.

markets (not unlike the simultaneous occurrences in new construction). Increasingly, finding a match between a "good market" (consumers) and a "good project" (a salable project) was most likely only in certain niches.

In some markets, developers see abundant opportunities for rehabilitation, but they cannot make the numbers work without subsidies. In other markets, given the extensive rehabilitation of the 1980s, fewer opportunities may in fact be available because developers have already reused the best buildings for other, higher-income-producing uses and only buildings with a preponderance of negative factors remain. In short, a "creaming" process may have occurred in some markets.

But the outlook for residential rehabilitation and adaptive use is not totally negative. Resourceful developers are finding niches, building projects to house special segments of the population, and working in cooperation with local governments to find creative financing. Such developers generally believe that a city with a historic building stock and a solid employment base provides opportunities for rehabilitation and adaptive use. And some developers are convinced that the breathing space caused by the Tax Reform Act of 1986 may prove positive for rehabilitation, as both the private and public sectors reassess priorities and opportunities within an overbuilt real estate market.

Geographically, developers during the 1990s will seek out markets where it is known jobs will continue to grow. State capitals and university towns, for example, are likely to remain stable growth centers. Other opportunities for rehabilitation and adaptive use may result from no-growth/slow-growth ordinances affecting many of the country's fastest-growing metropolitan areas. As new suburban growth is limited (and land and housing prices as a result increase), the market for quality rehabilitated houses at closer-in locations may also increase. And as traffic worsens, existing older housing stock near downtowns may become an increasingly attractive alternative to housing located on the urban fringe. Council member Ronald C. Nahas believes that "rehabilitation and gentrification of inner-city neighborhoods are likely to continue as a result of reduced affordability and increased traffic congestion in the suburbs."

Rehabilitation might not be limited to older, inner-city areas and close-in suburbs. A large pool of aging single-family houses exists in more distant suburbs that will be prime for rehabilitation in the next 10 to 20 years. So far, rehabilitation of suburban single-family housing has been completed piecemeal by owners. But as this huge pool of housing ages and

development of new housing becomes increasingly more expensive, the opportunity for developers' involvement on a larger scale becomes more feasible. Developers might find it possible to purchase groups of houses—perhaps entire subdivisions—and modernize them while preserving the mature, suburban ambience. Rehabilitation might include dividing large single-family houses into two or more units to make them more affordable and to better accommodate smaller families. In effect, the process of rehabilitating and converting large dwellings into multiple units that has been occurring in inner cities since the 1970s might apply to the suburbs in the years ahead. The existing trend toward creating "granny flats" and accessory apartments on suburban single-family lots might be a harbinger of more comprehensive suburban rehabilitation.

During the 1990s, a particular opportunity for rehabilitation may exist in areas where localized housing issues are hot social and political concerns. Local officials, concerned about providing housing for special populations, indicate a willingness to provide incentives for private developers—although generally not with the same advantages earlier investors received with previous tax incentives. Some developers see group houses for the mentally ill and drug rehabilitation units as real opportunities for rehabilitated housing for the 1990s. Others see resort-quality housing projects for the still active elderly (55 to 75 years old) as the trend. Developers have assessed the rehabilitation industry of the post-1986 tax act era and developed new strategies for the 1990s:

- Restructuring and downsizing the scale of developers' operations;
- Capitalizing on state and local funding partnerships in cases where federal money previously was used;
- Searching for niches, such as housing for special populations; and
- Targeting projects in areas where housing demand is expected to remain strong (job growth centers) and/or where limitations may be placed on new construction (communities with growth controls).

Another form of rehabilitation—remodeling—offers other opportunities for residential developers in the 1990s. According to a survey in *Development Digest*, 32 percent of the 20,000 respondents indicated that they would remain in residential development in the 1990s even if their local housing market declined. Respondents indicated they would shift their focus to remodeling: "Many homeowners who can't afford a new home can get a home equity loan

9-21 The Tax Reform Act of 1986 eliminated most tax incentives for residential rehabilitation, making financing more difficult for developers of such projects. Clocktower Close in Norwalk, Connecticut, built before 1986, offers 132 rental units in a building constructed originally as a hat factory.

to remodel their existing home. These people are prime prospects for homebuilders who have already developed quality reputations locally."[11] The National Association of Home Builders reports that the percentage of members active in remodeling increased from 11 percent in 1969 to 40 percent in 1986. Although the remodeling business is vastly different from merchant building, it is likely to be a growth industry in the 1990s, with opportunities for adaptable residential developers.

Meanwhile, the nation's housing stock continues to age; thus, the supply of buildings available for rehabilitation will continue to grow. While the tax benefits that encouraged much of the rehabilitation and adaptive use between 1976 and 1986 will be limited, rehabilitation projects will continue by those companies whose investors are not bound by putting equity in projects only for the benefit of a tax shelter. Rehabilitation will also continue in areas where state and local government incentives have been increased to help counteract federal cutbacks. Advocates for historic preservation and other proponents for the

reuse of older buildings will find a more cautious, but settled, rehabilitation industry intent largely on specialized markets in the 1990s.

Development Organization

A developer's organization and method of operation can be expected to change in response to these factors and forces. Council member Anthony J. Trella suggests, "The 1990s will see a new residential development industry; the notion of business-as-usual is out the door." The 1990s will bring a decline in the number of development companies as a result of several certainties: a more complex and lengthy development process, difficulty in finding financing, the increased cost of doing business, the slackening of demand, more fragmented and highly specialized markets, and increasing financial risks. "The bigger, geographically diversified, better capitalized developers should be able to survive—if not prosper," says council member J. Ronald Terwilliger. "At the other end of the spectrum, smaller developers who carry less overhead and are more flexible, more in tune with local market conditions, should also survive. Everybody else might to a certain extent get squeezed out."

Council member D. Michael Crow agrees: "Residential development is an increasingly *local* business." Small, flexible, well-capitalized development organizations working within familiar geographic areas will have a better chance for success because they will be able to respond more quickly to new markets, new opportunities, and new constraints. Future residential development must be highly specialized and sophisticated, leaving less room for error.

Given the growing complexity of the real estate development industry, the developer's team will probably need to be expanded to include more disciplines. Residential development is increasingly less a "seat-of-the-pants" business and more a sophisticated science. And with the increased sophistication will come the realization that more experts will be needed, particularly related to financial, regulatory, market analysis, and environmental issues. Council member William E. Becker believes that development companies will need to organize on the basis of a "key person": "Building a team will be essential to success in the 1990s, and developers must begin now to assemble the strengths they might lack within the organization." Smaller development organizations that cannot retain these experts on staff should align themselves with qualified consultants.

---

[11] *Development Digest*, Winter 1989, p. 2.

The 1990s will probably also see fewer residential developers engaged in large-scale development projects (over 1,000 acres). Only the largest and strongest companies will be able to carry the costs required to complete such ventures. Economies of scale generated by large projects were advantageous when development was easier, when a mass market existed for conventional housing products, when land and housing prices were escalating rapidly, and when hard costs accounted for a larger percentage of total development costs than they do today. The soft costs of development—financing, processing costs, and development fees—will continue to garner a greater percentage of total development costs.

The lack of ready finance capital (already coined the "credit crunch") will limit the ability of new residential development companies to enter the market. Council member Gordon E. Tippell notes, "There will be less money and fewer lenders in the 1990s. And those lenders active in real estate finance will be reluctant to gamble on new companies without an established track record."

Summary

Housing demand in the 1990s will be a natural progression of that established in the 1980s, modified by age. The overall demand will decline from the peaks reached in the 1970s and 1980s—to 1.1 to 1.2 million households per year. The nation's economic focus has shifted, however, with a corresponding shift in the location of demand.

America's economy will be far more metropolitan, far more suburban, and far more dominated by services than at any time in history. The suburban periphery in general, and existing suburban growth corridors in particular, will define areas of probable demand for housing.

A wide variety of configurations of dwelling units will be required. Household age can be anticipated with certainty, implying a shelter for raising a family. Precise composition of households is more indefinite, however. While the primary demand group—maturing baby boomers—will be at the traditional family-raising stage of the life cycle (which establishes more income-potent demand), they may well decide to maintain their nontraditional past (which produces more income-constrained demand). Overall, demand promises to be more complex and fragmented than ever before, and residential developers will need to make astute marketing decisions.

The United States is entering a period of scarce labor, particularly in the suburbs. The nation's economy can be hindered by shortages of workers. Suburban labor shortages coupled with an inadequate transportation system can negatively affect national economic productivity. Thus, the demand for affordable housing in suburban centers (near job growth centers) seems not only apparent—but also increasingly urgent.

Appendices
and
Index

APPENDIX A
Sources of Market Data

Information that is relevant to decisions involving residential development is available from a variety of public and private sources. These sources can provide useful data on a wide range of factors—market area economic and development trends, growth in population, income, and employment, and construction activity and costs—or they can direct a developer to more specific information. Consideration of these factors helps developers to make informed decisions about the feasibility and marketability of a residential development project.

In the following citations, publications marked "GPO" are available from the Superintendent of Documents, U.S. Government Printing Office, Washington, D.C. 20402-9325 (202-783-3238). Sources listed under "U.S. Bureau of the Census" are available from U.S. Bureau of the Census, Data User Services Division, Customer Services Branch, Washington, D.C. 20233 (202-763-4100). The geographic designation Metropolitan Statistical Area is abbreviated "MSA."

General

- *How to Conduct and Analyze Real Estate Market and Feasibility Studies*
  Introduction to market analysis, including a detailed description of how to perform a residential market analysis. St. Vincent Barnett and John P. Blair (New York: Van Nostrand Reinhold, 1988) (800-926-2665).

Market Area, Economic, and Growth Trends

- State and Local Governments
  Departments and agencies of metropolitan, county, state, and regional governments produce or sponsor reports on current conditions and trends in a wide variety of subjects: population, income, housing, zoning, community planning, patterns of growth and development (planning departments); transportation networks, access, infrastructure planning (highway departments); employment data, lists of major employers (economic research departments). Several organizations publish useful directories of governmental agencies:
  1. *Regional Council Directory* (annual)
     National Association of Regional Councils
     1700 K Street, N.W.
     Washington, D.C. 20006
     800-783-0710
  2. National Association of State Development Agencies
     Membership Directory ($75)
     444 North Capitol Street, N.W.
     Washington, D.C. 20001
     202-624-5411
  3. *Municipal Yearbook* (annual)
     International City Management Association
     777 North Capitol Street, N.E.
     Washington, D.C. 20002
     202-289-4262
  4. *Book of the States* (biennial)
     Council of State Governments
     P.O. Box 11910
     Lexington, Kentucky 40578
     606-252-2291

- *County and City Data Book*
  Nearly 200 statistical items for counties, MSAs, cities, urbanized areas, and unincorporated places. Available every four or five years from GPO (latest edition 1988).

- *Statistical Abstract of the United States*
  A list of state statistical abstracts. Available annually from GPO.

- Federal Reserve District Banks
  Information on regional economic activity and trends.

- Trade Associations, Chambers of Commerce, and Real Estate Boards
  Local economic statistics or referrals to a reliable source.

- Major Financial Institutions and Public Utilities
  Areawide data on demographic and business conditions and trends.

- Universities
  Market-oriented studies from university departments of business, real estate, or planning.

Employment

- State Labor Departments and Employment Security Commissions

- *Employment and Earnings*
  Current data by nation, state, and 200 local areas on number of employed, earnings, hours, rates of turnover, and unemployment rates. Available monthly from the U.S. Department of Labor, Bureau of Labor Statistics, GPO.

- *County Business Patterns*
  First-quarter employment and payroll statistics for states, counties, and MSAs by industry. Available annually from the U.S. Bureau of the Census (latest edition 1987).

- *County and City Data Book* (see above)

Demographics

- *Insider's Guide to Demographic Know-How*
  Comprehensive list of public and private sources of demographic data, what each source offers, and an explanation of how to use demographic data (Ithaca, N.Y.: American Demographic Press, latest edition 1990) (800-828-1133).

- U.S. Bureau of the Census
  Detailed demographic information in numerous publications:
  1. *Census Population* (decennial, latest edition 1980)
     Detailed demographic, social, and economic characteristics of the population for different geographic units.
  2. *Census of Population and Housing 1980*
     Data from the 1980 population census and the 1980 housing census, including population and housing characteristics for census tracts within MSAs and a comparison of characteristics between 1970 and 1980 for metropolitan areas.
  3. *Current Population Reports*
     Illustrative reports, special studies, and special censuses (produced irregularly) covering such topics as mobility of the population, population projections, educational attainment, marital status, ethnic origin, and so on.

- *Editor and Publisher Market Guide*
  Current estimates of population and households for newspaper markets. Available annually from Editor and Publisher Company, 11 West 19th Street, New York, New York 10011 (212-675-4380).
- *The Statistical Bulletin*
  Demographic and health care statistics from Census Bureau figures and from the Statistical Bureau of Metropolitan Life. Available quarterly from Metropolitan Life Insurance Company, One Madison Avenue, New York, New York 10010 (212-578-2211).
- *Survey of Buying Power*
  Data on population and income by state, county, and city. Available annually from Sales and Marketing Management, 633 Third Avenue, New York, New York 10017 (800-825-8508).

Income

- *County and City Data Book* (see above)
- *Survey of Buying Power* (see above)
- Bureau of Economic Analysis, Regional Economic Measurement Division
  Estimates of personal incomes for states, counties, and metropolitan areas. Published annually in the April and August issues of the Department of Commerce's *Survey of Current Business,* GPO.
- *Consumer Buying Indicators* (Current Population Reports, Series P60)
  Statistics on spending for selected major durables by selected household characteristics. Available annually from the U.S. Bureau of the Census.

Absorption

- *Market Absorption of Apartments* (Current Housing Reports, Series H130)
  U.S. data on apartment rental rates, including characteristics of the units. Available quarterly and annually from the U.S. Bureau of the Census.
- Local Associations of Homebuilders
- Local Real Estate Boards
- Local Appraisers

Construction Activity

- National Association of Home Builders
  Several publications containing a variety of data on the homebuilding industry: *Current Housing Situations* (monthly); *Housing Economics* (monthly); *Forecast of Housing Activity* (biannual). Available from NAHB, 15th & M Streets, N.W., Washington, D.C. 20005 (800-368-5242).
- Municipal Building Departments
  Data on the number of dwelling units authorized by permit and/or on the value of authorized construction. In areas where permits are not issued or where permit data are unreliable, utility companies' data on new services or hookups can indicate construction activity.
- *Construction Review*
  Statistical series covering construction put in place, housing, building permits, contract awards, costs and prices, construction materials, and contract construction employment.

Available bimonthly from the U.S. Department of Commerce, GPO.

- U.S. Bureau of the Census
  Numerous publications providing detailed information on residential construction:
  1. *Housing Starts* (Current Construction Reports, Series C20) (monthly)
     Data on new housing units started for the nation, regions, and inside/outside MSAs.
  2. *Housing Completions* (Current Construction Reports, Series C22) (monthly)
     Data on new housing completed for the nation, regions, and inside/outside MSAs.
  3. *Value of New Construction Put in Place* (Current Construction Reports, Series C30) (monthly)
     Nationwide data by type of owner.
  4. *Housing Units Authorized by Building Permits* (Current Construction Reports, Series C40) (monthly and annual)
     Statistics on new housing units authorized for regions, divisions, states, and 132 selected MSAs. Data from 17,000 permit-issuing places account for approximately 85 percent of all new residential construction in the United States. Also contains data on the number of new housing units and single-family structures authorized in 4,700 selected places, which account for a major portion of all residential buildings authorized by permit in the United States, and separate data on all publicly owned housing units for which construction contracts are awarded.
  5. *Expenditures for Residential Upkeep and Improvements* (Current Construction Reports, Series C50) (quarterly and annual)
     Nationwide estimates of expenditures for residential additions, alterations, and repairs.
- CENDATA
  The Census Bureau's on-line data system, providing excerpts and information from the Census. Information about CENDATA is available through CompuServe (800-848-8199) and DIALOG Information Services (800-334-2564).

Housing Inventory

- *U.S. Housing Markets*
  Tracks the housing markets in 53 cities and MSAs, with information on housing starts, permits, vacancy rates, apartment completions, and employment. Available quarterly by subscription from Lomas Nettleton (313-963-9441).
- U.S. Bureau of the Census
  Several reports providing detailed information on characteristics of the housing stock:
  1. *Census of Housing* (decennial, latest edition 1980)
     General and detailed housing characteristics for different geographic units.
  2. *New One-Family Houses Sold and For Sale* (Current Construction Reports, Series C25) (monthly and annual)
     Nationwide data on new single-family houses sold, their sale price, number, and physical characteristics.
  3. *Annual Housing Survey* (Current Housing Reports, Series H150) (annual)
     Data on general housing characteristics, housing and neighborhood quality, financial characteristics, and urban and rural housing characteristics.

Vacancies

- U.S. Bureau of the Census
  Housing Vacancies and Homeownership (Current Housing Reports, Series H111) (quarterly and annual)
  Vacancy rates and characteristics of vacant units for the United States, regions, inside/outside MSAs, and central cities.
- Local Real Estate Boards
- Local Appraisers

Marketability

- Local Real Estate Boards
- Local Associations of Homebuilders
- Newspapers

Prices and Rents

- U.S. Bureau of the Census
  Price Index of New One-Family Houses Sold (Current Construction Reports, Series C27) (quarterly)
  Price indexes and average movements in sale prices of houses for the United States and regions.
- *Existing Home Sales*
  Median price of resales of single-family houses in different regions. Available monthly from National Association of Realtors, 1777 14th Street, N.W., Washington, D.C. 20005 (202-383-1000).
- *IREM Expense Analysis: Apartments and Condominiums, Cooperatives, and Planned Unit Developments*
  Survey of income and operating expenses for different types of apartments and for condominiums, cooperatives, and PUDs in over 100 cities. Available annually from the Institute of Real Estate Management, 430 North Michigan Avenue, Chicago, Illinois 60611 (312-661-1930).

Building Costs

- *Residential Cost Data Book* and *Means Construction Cost Indexes*
  Industry cost data for materials and labor unit pricing for residential construction and cost factors for 19 divisions of work for over 200 cities, respectively. Both available annually from R.S. Means Co., Inc., 110 Construction Plaza, P.O. Box 800, Kingston, Massachusetts 02364 (800-448-8182).
- *Boeckh Building Valuation Manual* (volume 2)
  Detailed construction cost information for residential builders.
- *Boeckh Cost Modifier* and *Boeckh Building Cost Index Numbers* (both bimonthly)
  Changes in construction costs for 10 types of buildings in over 200 cities.
- Boeckh's *1990 Residential Building Cost Guide*
  General construction cost estimates for replacement of residential units.
  Available from American Appraisal Company, Boeckh Customer Service, 525 East Michigan Street, Milwaukee, Wisconsin 53201 (800-558-8650).
- *Producer Price Indexes* (monthly)
  Price movements of selected construction materials. Available from the U.S. Department of Labor, Bureau of Labor Statistics, GPO.

- *Residential Cost Handbook* (quarterly)
  Replacement cost estimates for residential development. Available from Marshall & Swift, 1200 Route 22, Bridgewater, New Jersey 08807 (800-533-7650).

Periodicals and Newsletters

- *American Demographics*
  Dow Jones & Company, Inc., for American Demographics, Inc.
  108 North Cayuga Street
  Ithaca, New York 14850
  800-828-1133
- *Apartment Resources*
  The Danter Company
  40 West Spruce Street
  Columbus, Ohio 43215
  614-221-9096
- *Builder*
  Hanley-Wood, Inc., for National Association of Home Builders
  655 15th Street, N.W., Suite 475
  Washington, D.C. 20005
  202-737-0717
- *Housing Affairs Letter*
  CD Publications
  8555 16th Street
  Silver Spring, Maryland 20910
  301-588-6380
- *Housing Law Bulletin*
  National Housing Law Project
  1950 Addison Street
  Berkeley, California 94704
  415-548-9400
- *Housing Market Report*
  CD Publications
  8555 16th Street
  Silver Spring, Maryland 20910
  301-588-6380
- *Journal of Housing*
  National Association of Housing and Redevelopment Officials
  1320 18th Street, N.W.
  Washington, D.C. 20036
  202-429-2960
- *Managing Housing Letter*
  CD Publications
  8555 16th Street
  Silver Spring, Maryland 20910
  301-588-6380
- *Multi-Housing News*
  Gralla Publications
  1515 Broadway, 34th Floor
  New York, New York 10036
  212-869-1300
- *Professional Builder*
  Cahners Publishing Company
  1350 East Touhy Avenue
  Des Plaines, Illinois 60017
  708-635-8800

- *Real Estate Finance*
  Federal Research Press
  210 Lincoln Street
  Boston, Massachusetts 02111
  617-423-0978

- *Real Estate Finance Journal*
  Warren, Gorham & Lamont, Inc.
  210 South Street
  Boston, Massachusetts 02111
  617-423-2020

- *Real Estate Forum*
  Real Estate Forum, Inc.
  12 West 37th Street
  New York, New York 10018
  212-563-6460

- *Real Estate Review*
  Warren, Gorham & Lamont, Inc.
  210 South Street
  Boston, Massachusetts 02111
  617-423-2020

- *The States and Housing*
  Council of State Community Affairs Agencies
  Hall of the States
  444 North Capitol Street, Suite 251
  Washington, D.C. 20001
  202-393-6435

- *Urban Land*
  ULI–the Urban Land Institute
  625 Indiana Avenue, N.W.
  Washington, D.C. 20004
  202-624-7000

APPENDIX B
Directory of Housing-Related Associations

Community and Neighborhood Development

Center for Community Change
Assists community organizations and community development groups with federal programs for the urban and rural poor, such as Community Development Block Grants, use of the Community Reinvestment Act, and subsidized housing.
1000 Wisconsin Avenue, N.W.
Washington, D.C. 20007
202-342-0519

Community Development Society
Concerned with the promotion of citizens' participation in community development as well as with providing a forum for the exchange of ideas and advocacy of excellence in community programs.
c/o Robert Anderson
Resource Development Department
302 National Resources Building
Michigan State University
East Lansing, Michigan 48824
517-355-0100

Housing Action Council
A nonprofit, nonmembership organization that provides technical assistance to all levels of government and all types of developers concerned with housing and community development.
18 Hamilton Place
Tarrytown, New York 10591
914-332-4144

National Association of Neighborhoods
Acts as a national policy vehicle for neighborhood organizations, provides training and information for them, and works toward public awareness of the neighborhood movement.
1651 Fuller Street, N.W.
Washington, D.C. 20009
202-332-7766

National Community Development Association
An organization of directors of community development programs that supports the interests of Community Development Block Grant programs as well as other community and economic development issues.
522 21st Street, N.W., Suite 120
Washington, D.C. 20006
202-293-7587

National Congress for Community Economic Development
Provides a national program of promotion, partnership, and assistance for organizations in community-based economic development.
1612 K Street, N.W., Suite 510
Washington, D.C. 20006
202-659-8411

National Neighborhood Coalition
A coalition of national organizations that work with inner-city neighborhood groups, serving as a clearinghouse for information and education on policies and programs that affect low- and moderate-income neighborhoods and covering such issues as housing, community reinvestment, and economic development.
810 First Street, N.E., Suite 300
Washington, D.C. 20002
202-289-1551

National People's Action
A group of organizations concerned with investment in and revitalization of individual neighborhoods. Lobbies on issues concerning housing and community development funds and was instrumental in passage of the Home Mortgage Disclosure Act and the Community Reinvestment Act.
810 Milwaukee Avenue
Chicago, Illinois 60622
312-243-3038

National Urban Coalition
Promotes action and service, advocacy, and information to improve the quality of life and opportunities in urban areas.
8601 Georgia Avenue, Suite 500
Silver Spring, Maryland 20910
301-495-4999

National Urban League
A service organization that works to achieve equal opportunity for blacks and other minorities and to provide direct service to minorities in areas such as housing and community development.
500 East 62nd Street
New York, New York 10021
212-644-6500

Partners for Livable Places
An alliance of organizations and individuals working to improve community environments through the combined efforts of public, private, and governmental sectors.
1429 21st Street, N.W.
Washington, D.C. 20036
202-887-5990

Financial and Legal Issues

American Bankers Association
Membership organization that seeks to enhance the role of commercial banks as providers of financial services to housing and community development organizations and individuals.
1120 Connecticut Avenue, N.W.
Washington, D.C. 20036
202-467-4000

American Land Title Association
The national organization for the majority of abstractors, title insurance companies, and attorneys specializing in real property law.
1828 L Street, N.W., Suite 705
Washington, D.C. 20036
202-296-3671

Association for Local Housing Finance Agencies
An organization of professionals in housing finance concerned with issues affecting affordable housing.
1101 Connecticut Avenue, N.W., Suite 700
Washington, D.C. 20036
202-857-1197

Mortgage Bankers Association of America
The trade organization for the nation's mortgage banking industry, which seeks to improve methods of originating, servicing, and marketing loans for residential and income-producing properties.
1125 15th Street, N.W.
Washington, D.C. 20005
202-861-6500

Mortgage Insurance Companies of America
The trade association of mortgage insurance companies, which represents their interests before governmental agencies that review housing-related legislation.
805 15th Street, N.W., Suite 1110
Washington, D.C. 20005
202-371-2899

National Association of Real Estate Brokers
Serves members of the real estate industry, providing research, educational, and certification programs.
1629 K Street, N.W., Suite 605
Washington, D.C. 20006
202-785-4477

National Association of Real Estate Investment Trusts
The trade association for REITs, which provides government representation and public relations services for members that manage real estate under multiple ownership.
1129 20th Street, N.W., Suite 705
Washington, D.C. 20036
202-785-8717

National Economic Development and Law Center
Offers assistance on legal and tax issues to community development corporations and other entities working in the field of community and economic development.
1950 Addison Street, Suite 200
Berkeley, California 94704
415-548-2600

National Housing Law Project

Provides assistance, including research and litigation, to local legal services programs in such areas of housing law as landlord-tenant law, displacement, rural housing, and single-family housing.

> 1950 Addison Street
> Berkeley, California 94704
> 415-548-9400

National Realty Committee

Represents owners, developers, and financiers of income-producing property and their interests concerning tax laws and real estate development.

> 1250 Connecticut Avenue, N.W., Suite 630
> Washington, D.C. 20036
> 202-785-0808

United Mortgage Bankers of America

An organization of minority mortgage brokers and mortgage bankers that seeks to channel mortgage money to all and provides training and education for new mortgage bankers.

> 800 Ivy Hill Road
> Philadelphia, Pennsylvania 19150
> 215-242-6061

United States League of Savings Institutions

A trade association for savings institutions that provides information, liaison, management workshops, and analysis of issues pertaining to taxation and housing legislation.

> 1709 New York Avenue, N.W.
> Washington, D.C. 20006
> 202-637-8900

Low- and Moderate-Income Housing

Cooperative Housing Foundation

A nonprofit, nonmembership organization that promotes the development of housing and housing-related community services for low- and moderate-income families in the United States and internationally.

> 1010 Wayne Avenue, Suite 240
> Silver Spring, Maryland 20910
> 301-587-4700

Council of Large Public Housing Authorities

Represents authorities of large public housing facilities, with the purpose of supporting public housing by securing adequate federal funding for the operation, development, and improvement of housing for low-income persons.

> 122 C Street, N.W., Suite 865
> Washington, D.C. 20001
> 202-638-1300

Housing Assistance Council

Provides technical assistance, seed money loans, program and policy assistance, and training and information services to organizations devoted to providing low-income housing in rural areas.

> 1025 Vermont Avenue, N.W., Suite 606
> Washington, D.C. 20005
> 202-842-8600

National Leased Housing Association

Provides assistance and information to public and private organizations concerned and involved with government-assisted housing programs and represents members' interests before Congress and HUD.

> 2300 M Street, N.W., Suite 260
> Washington, D.C. 20037
> 202-955-9636

National Low-Income Housing Coalition

Carries out a program of education, organization, and advocacy designed to improve and expand low-income housing programs, monitors low-income housing needs and programs, and develops advocacy and action positions.

> 1012 14th Street, N.W., Suite 1500
> Washington, D.C. 20005
> 202-662-1530

Public Housing Authorities Directors Association

Provides information to directors of public housing authorities about HUD and federal actions and activities related to public housing agencies.

> 511 Capitol Court, N.E., Suite 200
> Washington, D.C. 20002
> 202-546-5445

Multifamily Housing

Apartment Owners and Managers Association of America

Represents builders who also manage the multifamily housing they construct and publishes a newsletter with pertinent information for builders, developers, and apartment owners and managers.

> 65 Cherry Avenue
> Watertown, Connecticut 06795
> 203-274-2589

Community Associations Institute

Assists builders, developers, property managers, public officials, and homeowners with the creation, financing, operation, and management of condominiums and homeowners associations.

> 1423 Powhatan Street
> Alexandria, Virginia 22314
> 703-548-8600

Multifamily Housing Association

Works to advance the interests of those involved in the development and financing of multifamily housing.

> 1055 Thomas Jefferson Street, N.W., Suite 501
> Washington, D.C. 20007
> 202-293-3306

National Apartment Association

The trade organization for managers, investors, developers, owners, and suppliers of apartment houses and other rental property.

> 1111 14th Street, N.W., Suite 900
> Washington, D.C. 20005
> 202-842-4050

National Association of Housing Cooperatives

Assists nonprofit housing cooperatives through technical research, training, and advisory aid to groups interested in forming housing cooperatives.

> 1614 King Street
> Alexandria, Virginia 22314
> 703-549-5201

National Cooperative Business Association

A federation of all types of cooperative business organizations, including housing, to provide education and training for the formation and operation of cooperatives.

> 1401 New York Avenue, N.W., Suite 1100
> Washington, D.C. 20005
> 202-638-6222

National Multihousing Council

Represents developers and owners of multifamily housing, seeks to promote multifamily housing by monitoring policies and programs at the federal, state, and local levels, and undertakes special projects, such as fighting rent control and promoting the conversion of apartments to condominiums.

> 1250 Connecticut Avenue, N.W., Suite 620
> Washington, D.C. 20036
> 202-659-3381

Municipal Management

Council of State Community Affairs Agencies

A national organization of directors and staffs of state community affairs agencies that provides a forum for discussion of and action on national issues and agencies' programs related to the area of comprehensive community development.

> 444 North Capitol Street, N.W., Suite 251
> Washington, D.C. 20001
> 202-393-6435

Council of State Governments

A joint agency of all state governments that researches and disseminates information on such topics as housing programs and problems, promotes intergovernmental cooperation, and assists in the liaison between federal and state governments.

> Iron Works Pike, P.O. Box 11910
> Lexington, Kentucky 40578
> 606-252-2291

Council of State Policy and Planning Agencies

Promotes mutual assistance and improved planning between state policy and planning agencies and conducts policy and technical research and economic development policy.

> 444 North Capitol Street, N.W., Suite 285
> Washington, D.C. 20001
> 202-624-5386

International City Management Association

A professional and educational organization for executives of municipal governments that seeks to increase the effectiveness and quality of local governments through, among other things, operating training programs for municipal employees in various fields of administration.

> 777 North Capitol Street, N.E., Suite 500
> Washington, D.C. 20002
> 202-289-4262

National Association of Counties

Represents local county officials at the national level. Provides research and reference services in management or policy for elected and appointed county governing officials in areas such as community development.

> 440 First Street, N.W., 8th Floor
> Washington, D.C. 20001
> 202-393-6226

National Association of Development Organizations

An organization of multicounty planning and development organizations and government agencies concerned with economic, community, and business development whose principal aim is to promote economic development in rural areas and small towns.

> 444 North Capitol Street, N.W., Suite 628
> Washington, D.C. 20001
> 202-624-7806

National Association of Housing and Redevelopment Officials

Promotes communication and action for individuals and public agencies engaged in community development, public housing, housing rehabilitation, and neighborhood conservation.

> 1320 18th Street, N.W., 5th Floor
> Washington, D.C. 20036
> 202-429-2960

National Association of Regional Councils

Serves the interests of members who use a regional approach of pooled resources to solve regional problems, such as housing, community development, and rural development. Provides legislative representation in Washington and technical assistance.

> 1700 K Street, N.W., Suite 1300
> Washington, D.C. 20006
> 202-457-0710

National Association of Towns and Townships

Provides technical assistance, educational services, research, and public policy recommendations to help local officials improve the quality of life in small communities.

> 1522 K Street, N.W., Suite 730
> Washington, D.C. 20005
> 202-737-5200

National Conference of State Legislatures

Works to improve the quality and effectiveness of state legislatures, to represent the states' interest at the federal level, and to foster interstate communication and cooperation.

> 1050 17th Street, Suite 2100
> Denver, Colorado 80265
> 303-623-7800

National Council of State Housing Agencies

National association of state housing finance agencies and affiliated members that finance, develop, and manage low- and moderate-income single and multifamily housing.

> 444 North Capitol Street, N.W., Suite 118
> Washington, D.C. 20001
> 202-624-7710

National Council for Urban Economic Development

Provides information on urban economic development and conducts workshops and training institutes to give technical assistance to public officials on economic development strategies.

> 1730 K Street, N.W.
> Washington, D.C. 20006
> 202-223-4735

National Governors' Association

Serves as the vehicle through which governors of the 50 states and all territories influence the development and implementation of national policy and apply creative leadership to state problems.

> 444 North Capitol Street, N.W., Suite 250
> Washington, D.C. 20001
> 202-624-5300

National League of Cities

A federation of state leagues and cities that focuses its national policy analysis on solutions to urban problems and improvement of urban life. Conducts comprehensive analysis of national policies and related programs and represents municipalities before Congress and federal agencies.

> 1301 Pennsylvania Avenue, N.W.
> Washington, D.C. 20004
> 202-626-3000

United States Conference of Mayors

Association of mayors of cities with populations over 30,000 that works to improve municipal government by cooperation between city and federal governments. Works to promote the interests of large cities.

> 1620 I Street, N.W.
> Washington, D.C. 20006
> 202-293-7330

Production and Management

American Institute of Architects

Through the National Committee on Housing, sponsors and offers programs and seminars and publishes research reports on housing issues aimed at improving the quality of the living environment.

> 1735 New York Avenue, N.W.
> Washington, D.C. 20006
> 202-626-7300

American Institute of Real Estate Appraisers

An organization of appraisers of real property that supports stricter standards for appraisal, sponsors training courses in all aspects of real estate appraising, offers professional designations for appraisers, and publishes literature for the industry.

> 430 North Michigan Avenue
> Chicago, Illinois 60611
> 312-329-8559

American Planning Association

Provides extensive professional services and publications to professionals and laymen in planning and related fields and serves the entire planning community with its research, information, and advisory services.

> 1776 Massachusetts Avenue, N.W., Suite 704
> Washington, D.C. 20036
> 202-872-0611

American Society of Consulting Planners

A professional society for private planning firms that conducts research and specialized educational programs on issues involving planning and public welfare.

> 1015 15th Street, N.W., Suite 600
> Washington, D.C. 20005
> 202-789-0220

Associated General Contractors of America

A leading voice for the construction industry, representing construction contractors for highways, buildings, heavy industries, and municipal utilities.

> 1957 E Street, N.W.
> Washington, D.C. 20006
> 202-393-2040

Building Officials and Code Administrators International, Inc.

An organization of governmental officials and agencies responsible for the administration or formulation of building, zoning, or housing regulations.

> 4051 West Flossmore Road
> Country Club Hills, Illinois 60447
> 708-799-2300

Council for American Building Officials

A group of three model code organizations that represents building officials at all levels of government and works to promote public health, safety, and general welfare through the acceptance of new products and adoption of uniform regulations and model codes.

> 5203 Leesburg Pike, Suite 708
> Falls Church, Virginia 22041
> 703-931-4533

Home Owners Warranty Corporation

Offers an insured protection plan to homeowners through registered and screened builders and informal procedures to settle disputes.

> 1110 North Glebe Road, Suite 800
> Arlington, Virginia 22201
> 703-516-4100

Institute for Real Estate Management
A professional organization of real property managers that offers management and training courses and awards professional designations to qualifying individuals and managing firms.
> 430 North Michigan Avenue
> Chicago, Illinois 60611
> 312-661-1930

International Conference of Building Officials
Represents those in local, regional, and state governments who deal with the Uniform Building Code and related documents, conducts research into the principles underlying safety to life and property in the construction, use, and location of buildings, and seeks to promote safety in building codes through uniform regulations and guidelines for building inspections.
> 5360 South Workman Mill Road
> Whittier, California 90601
> 213-699-0541

Manufactured Housing Institute
A trade organization for the manufacturers of manufactured houses and the suppliers of equipment, components, furnishings, and services for such houses.
> 1745 Jefferson Davis Highway, Suite 511
> Arlington, Virginia 22202
> 703-979-6620

National Association of Home Builders
The trade organization of the homebuilding industry, which acts on behalf of the building industry and conducts research and activities to increase the public's understanding of housing and the economy.
> 15th & M Streets, N.W.
> Washington, D.C. 20005
> 202-822-0200

National Association of Realtors
An association of local real estate boards whose membership includes brokers, managers, appraisers, and sales persons involved in all types of property. Services include educational programs and research in various real estate specialties, legislation, and numerous publications dealing with residential real estate statistics and issues.
> 430 North Michigan Avenue
> Chicago, Illinois 60611
> 312-329-8200

National Center for Housing Management, Inc.
Serves the housing management industry by providing training for all levels of housing management, research, technical assistance, accreditation of housing management firms, and certification for occupancy specialists and maintenance managers.
> 1275 K Street, N.W., Suite 700
> Washington, D.C. 20005
> 202-872-1717

National Conference of States on Building Codes and Standards, Inc.
Assists members in improving building programs and regulations, encourages cooperation among officials involved in the building regulatory system, and promotes the adoption of uniform building codes.
> 481 Carlisle Drive
> Herndon, Virginia 22070
> 703-437-0100

National Forest Products Association
Represents the forest industries on national issues concerning the growing of timber and the manufacture, distribution, marketing, and use of wood products.
> 1250 Connecticut Avenue, N.W., Suite 200
> Washington, D.C. 20036
> 202-463-2700

National Housing and Rehabilitation Association
A trade association representing the interests of members in development, finance, construction, and property management who work in the areas of housing rehabilitation and new construction.
> 1726 18th Street, N.W.
> Washington, D.C. 20009
> 202-328-9171

National Manufactured Housing Federation, Inc.
Represents all segments of the manufactured housing industry before Congress and federal regulatory agencies.
> 1701 K Street, N.W., Suite 400
> Washington, D.C. 20006
> 202-822-6470

National Parking Association
A trade organization representing owners and operators of off-street parking facilities that provides education programs, research, compilation of statistics, and a speakers bureau.
> 1112 16th Street, N.W., Suite 300
> Washington, D.C. 20036
> 202-296-4336

Society of Real Estate Appraisers
A professional, educational, and accreditation association for appraisal professionals that awards professional designations based on education and experience.
> 225 North Michigan Avenue
> Chicago, Illinois 60601
> 312-819-2400

Southern Building Code Congress International, Inc.
An organization that provides a wide range of technical, educational, and research services on building codes to municipal governments and their building code departments. Seeks to develop and promote the adoption of uniform standard codes.
> 900 Montclair Road
> Birmingham, Alabama 35213
> 215-591-1853

Recreation

American Resort and Residential Development Association
Trade association for developers of residential retirement, resort, and vacation communities.
> 1220 L Street, N.W., Suite 510
> Washington, D.C. 20005
> 202-371-6700

Club Managers Association of America
An association for professional managers and assistant managers of private golf, yacht, athletic, city, country, luncheon, university, and military clubs. Conducts seminars, workshops, conferences, and exhibitions.
> 1733 King Street
> Alexandria, Virginia 22314
> 703-739-9500

National Golf Foundation
A foundation for golf-oriented businesses that sponsors research and educational programs, offers consultant services pertaining to instructional aspects of the game, develops feasibility studies for golf facilities, conducts operational analyses, and compiles statistics.
> 1150 S. U.S. Highway One
> Jupiter, Florida 33477
> 407-744-6006

National Recreation and Park Association
Public interest organization concerned with improving opportunities for recreation and leisure.
> 3101 Park Center Drive, 12th Floor
> Alexandria, Virginia 22302
> 703-820-4940

United States Golf Association
Association of organized golf clubs and courses that serves as the governing body for golf and provides data on regulations.
> P.O. Box 708
> Far Hills, New Jersey 07931
> 201-234-2300

United States Tennis Association, Inc.
Federation of tennis clubs, education institutions, recreation departments, and other groups interested in the promotion of tennis for recreation and physical fitness.
> 1212 Avenue of the Americas
> New York, New York 10036
> 212-302-3322

Research and Education

Conservation Foundation
Works to encourage conservation worldwide through research and sharing information on land conservation, including community development in revitalized urban areas.
> 1250 Connecticut Avenue, N.W., Suite 500
> Washington, D.C. 20037
> 202-293-4800

Development Training Institute, Inc.
Offers training programs in housing and community economic development to community-based development groups.

4806 Seton Drive
Baltimore, Maryland 21215
301-764-0780

National Housing Conference, Inc.
Provides information and support for effective programs in housing and community development and adequate housing for people of all income levels.

1126 16th Street, N.W.
Washington, D.C. 20036
202-223-4844

National Housing Institute
A resource center dealing with issues like housing, tenants' rights, tenant/landlord relations, and rent control. Serves as information clearinghouse and technical advisory.

439 Main Street
Orange, New Jersey 07050
201-678-3110

National Trust for Historic Preservation
National private organization chartered by the U.S. Congress to facilitate public participation in the preservation of buildings, sites, and objects significant in American history and culture.

1785 Massachusetts Avenue, N.W.
Washington, D.C. 20036
202-673-4000

ULI–the Urban Land Institute
A nonprofit research and educational organization dedicated to encouraging intelligent use of land resources.

625 Indiana Avenue, N.W., Suite 400
Washington, D.C. 20004
202-624-7000

Rural Development

Community Transportation Association of America
Assists local governments and organizations in small towns and rural areas in meeting service and developmental needs in housing, community organization, and rural transportation. Administers the Rural Development Fund, which provides seed money for low-income rural housing.

725 15th Street, N.W., Suite 900
Washington, D.C. 20005
202-628-1480

Council for Rural Housing and Development
Represents developers, syndicators, managers, architects, and others involved in rural rental housing and the Farmers Home Administration Section 515 program.

2300 M Street, N.W.
Washington, D.C. 20037
202-955-9600

National Rural Housing Coalition
Lobbies for low-income rural housing and community facilities and supports improved government and private housing programs for rural areas.

122 C Street, N.W., Suite 875
Washington, D.C. 20001
202-393-5229

Senior Living

American Association of Homes for the Aging
Represents sponsors of housing and health-related facilities and services for seniors.

1129 20th Street, N.W., Suite 400
Washington, D.C. 20036
202-296-5960

National Association for Senior Living Industries
Provides networking opportunities for providers of services to seniors. Members include developers, architects, and owners of housing for seniors, product suppliers, and financial institutions involved in funding the construction of housing for seniors.

184 Duke of Gloucester Street
Annapolis, Maryland 21401
301-263-0991

National Council of Senior Citizens: Housing Management Corporation
Serves the interests of senior citizens and works on issues and programs affecting them. The Housing Management Corporation sponsors and manages housing for seniors.

117 C Street, S.E.
Washington, D.C. 20003
202-546-4374

National Institute of Senior Housing
Concerned with the special housing needs of older adults. Provides a forum for the exchange of information and experience in the development and management of housing facilities for the elderly.

c/o National Council on the Aging
600 Maryland Avenue, S.W., West Wing 100
Washington, D.C. 20024
202-479-1200

Source: Encyclopedia of Associations (Detroit: Gale Research, Inc., 1989).

Appendix C
Sample Site Analysis Checklist

Mapping

— Boundary survey/acreage
— Legal description
— Patterns of Ownership
— Easements (by type and location)
— Rights-of-way
— Topography
— Aerial photography
— Regional/site location

Topography

— Slopes (mapped by percentage categories)
— Elevations (high and low points)
— Ridges
— Drainageways
— Special features (e.g., rock outcroppings)
— Views (on- and off-site)

Soils

— Types and characteristics
— Depth of topsoil
— Subsoil conditions
— Potential "borrow" sites for construction materials
— Depth to bedrock/groundwater

Drainage

— Surface drainage features
— Groundwater table
— Floodplain boundaries
— Wetlands/marshes
— Location of wells
— Depth to groundwater
— Sources of on- and off-site pollution
— Tide data

Vegetation

— Species present on site
— Woodlands/fencerows/vegetation masses
— Location/size of specimen trees
— Special features/habitats

Land Use

— Existing on-site uses (structures and activities)
— Historical site uses (potential for contamination)
— Surrounding uses (note any objectionable uses or activities)
— Adjacent plats
— Open space/vacant land
— Qualitative assessment of neighborhood
— Growth/development patterns in area

Regulations

— Governmental authorities (city, county, school district, park district, utility districts, other)
— Master/general plan policies
— Existing zoning (for site and adjacent parcels)
— Subdivision ordinance
— Applicable development/impact fees
— Special assessments
— Other applicable municipal, regional, and state regulations affecting the site

Transportation/Circulation

— Existing traffic patterns
— Access points/entries
— Proximity to regional transportation system
— Planned/proposed transportation system improvements
— Trails/paths (existing and planned)
— Accessibility to transit

Utilities

For each, describe location, design, purveyor, availability, tie-in distance from site, costs borne by utility company, and developer fee structures. Note any potential for moratoriums or other factors that could delay or prohibit development.

— Sanitary sewer
— Water
— Stormwater
— Electricity
— Natural gas
— Cable television
— Telephone

Public Services/Conveniences

— Schools
— Location/proximity to site
— Capacity
— Reputation of school district
— Parks and recreational facilities
— Emergency services
— Fire
— Police
— Ambulance/paramedic
— Public transportation/transit
— Commercial services/shopping
— Employment services

Other Features

— Prevailing wind direction
— Climatic conditions
— Archaeological sites
— Wildlife (species and habitats)
— Sources of Noise
— Aesthetic quality of site and environs

APPENDIX D
Intercompatibility of Lake and Pond Functions

SECONDARY USE (rows) × PRIMARY USE (columns)

SECONDARY USE	FLOOD CONTROL	SEDIMENT CONTROL	RUNOFF POLLUTION CONTROL	STORAGE OF STORM WATER FOR REUSE
FLOOD CONTROL		Ponds of sufficient size for sediment control will have flood control benefits.	Ponds for runoff pollution control afford some control of smaller floods.	Only feasible with very clean runoff for on-channel impoundments. Reuse rate will determine flood control effectiveness.
SEDIMENT CONTROL	Pond built only for flood control may not be large enough for sediment control.		Pond for runoff pollution control will rarely be large enough for sediment control.	Storage ponds will have value for sediment control only if on-channel and if runoff requires no treatment other than sediment removal.
RUNOFF POLLUTION CONTROL	Flood control pond will usually have sufficient capacity for pollution control use, but rate of release may be too fast for treatment unit.	Sediment control pond will normally accommodate enough runoff for pollution control.		Stored storm water is usually already treated. Pollution control pond may be installed upstream but almost never in same facility except where only minimum treatment (such as chlorination and settlement) is given.
STORAGE OF STORM WATER FOR REUSE	Flood control ponds will be empty within a short period following storms and therefore cannot be used for storage.	Sediment control pond will normally be nearly empty and will have no value for storage of storm water.	Runoff pollution control ponds are rarely used to store water but may be used for minimum treatment or to feed treatment plant at constant rate.	
RECREATIONAL USES	Flood control pond has no value for water recreation use. May be safety hazard.	Sediment control pond will have no recreational benefits and may even be a safety hazard.	Runoff pollution control pond will have little or no recreational benefits; normally its drawdown will be too great.	Ponds for the storage of storm water for reuse will have little recreational or aesthetic value; drawdown is too great.
WILDLIFE	Flood control pond has little or no wildlife value except as a feeding ground for brief periods after flood abatement.	Sediment control pond has no wildlife value except as a feeding ground for waders for a brief period following drawdown.	Runoff pollution control ponds will have little benefit for wildlife other than as an occasional feeding ground for waders.	Storage ponds may have some value for wildlife, but wildlife may be undesirable on impoundments for potable water.
WATER TREATMENT (OXIDATION PONDS)	Flood control pond has no water treatment benefits.	Sediment control ponds have no value for water treatment by oxidation process.	Runoff pollution control ponds are rarely used for oxidation but may be used to feed treatment plant at constant rate.	Where clean water is being stored for reuse, the growth of water plants and organisms is usually discouraged.
AQUIFER RECHARGE	Flood control pond rarely permits substantial aquifer recharge, as the permeability of the base is usually reduced by sediment deposits.	Sediment control pond almost never has any aquifer recharge benefits, because of the impermeability of precipitated sediment.	Runoff pollution control pond should be lined if the runoff is badly polluted. Aquifer recharge will be minimal because of precipitated solids.	Pond where water is stored for reuse may also be managed so that some of the water infiltrates. With fairly heavily polluted water, reuse may include irrigation for aquifer recharge.

KEY

- ☐ Primary and secondary uses are compatible, with only slight loss of efficiency of secondary use.
- ■ No conflict between primary and secondary uses, but slight modifications may be required.
- ◯ Multi-use may cause some conflict or may require major modifications.

Source: Joachim Tourbier and Richard Westmacott, *Lakes and Ponds,* Technical Bulletin 72 (Washington, D.C.: ULI–the Urban Land Institute, 1976).

RECREATIONAL USES	WILDLIFE	WATER TREATMENT (OXIDATION PONDS)	AQUIFER RECHARGE
(○) Recreational pond may have some flood control benefits if designed with large freeboard, floodable periphery, and provision for rapid drawdown to original level.	(○) Wildlife pond may have some flood control benefits, but drawdown will make nesting hazardous except in floating boxes.	(▲) Water treatment pond has no flood control benefits.	(△) Aquifer recharge pond rarely has any flood control benefits unless fed by large supply pond.
(○) Ponds for recreational use will precipitate sediment if on-channel, but this may reduce recreational value. Install small pond upstream to precipitate larger sediment and reduce drawdown.	(○) On-channel wildlife pond will precipitate sediment, which will tend to smother bottom vegetation.	(▲) Water treatment ponds are intended primarily for removing nutrients. Sediments will smother life on bottom and reduce available oxygen.	(▲) Aquifer recharge ponds will become clogged if water contains sediment.
(●) Ponds for recreational use will have considerable settling and even some nutrient removal by oxidation. Water may also be dormated.	(●) Wildlife ponds can serve for some types of pollution control (settling, and some nutrient removal) but should generally be fed with stream runoff.	(□) Oxidation ponds may be used for runoff pollution control where small discharges of badly polluted runoff are to be treated.	(▲) Aquifer recharge ponds should not be used for runoff pollution control, as runoff should be free of solids when entering recharge basins.
(△) Recreational ponds which are also used to store storm water for reuse will have their recreational and aesthetic value reduced by drawdown of storm waters for reuse.	(●) Wildlife ponds may occasionally be used for water supply if drawdown is small.	(●) Effluent from oxidation ponds can often be reused but usually only for irrigation. Public acceptance is necessary.	(△) Aquifer recharge pond will have little use as a storage reservoir; the aim will be to empty pond quickly by maximizing the rate of recharge.
	Recreational uses and wildlife are compatible if wildlife are species which tolerate disturbance. This may impose minimum size restrictions for shy species or may make quiet areas necessary.	(○) Oxidation ponds may support considerable fish life and may be aesthetically pleasing if properly landscaped. Some management requirements (such as algae harvesting) may reduce amenity value.	(▲) Aquifer recharge pond will have no recreational value and is likely to be very difficult to make aesthetically pleasing.
(○) Recreational ponds may have some value for tolerant wildlife species if wildlife density is kept fairly low. Water's edge treatment might present conflicts.		(□) Water treatment/oxidation pond is attractive to wildlife usually only in ponds used for advanced stages of treatment.	(△) Aquifer recharge ponds will have little value for wildlife.
(○) Recreation ponds (not for primary contact) may have a modified management program, including aeration and algae harvest, which could improve water quality.	Wildlife pond could easily be managed to improve quality of drinking water. Sufficient period of impoundment, occasional algae harvesting, and a selective intake system are required.		(▲) Aquifer recharge pond will have no value for oxidation water treatment.
(□) Water from a recreation pond may be allowed to infiltrate the aquifer provided that supply is sufficient to offset loss and that quality of water is sufficient for aquifer recharge.	If water supply is great enough to keep wildlife constant and is of sufficient quality, there is no need to prevent infiltration to the aquifer. Otherwise the pond should be lined.	(△) Infiltration of water from oxidation ponds into aquifer recharge areas should be kept to a minimum.	

 In other than exceptional circumstances, pond will have very little value for secondary use.

(△) No real conflict, but little or no value for secondary use.

 Any concession to secondary use would severely affect primary use.

APPENDIX E
Methods to Reduce Levels of Radon in New Construction

Construction Techniques

Some of the radon prevention techniques discussed below are common building practices in many areas and, in any case, are less costly if accomplished during construction. Costs to retrofit existing houses with the same features would be significantly higher. Although these construction techniques do not require any fundamental changes in building design, the need continues for quality control, supervision, and more careful attention to certain construction details. Construction techniques for minimizing radon entry can be grouped into two basic categories:

- Methods to reduce pathways for radon entry.
- Methods to reduce the vacuum effect of a house on surrounding and underlying soil.

Typically, the techniques in both categories are used in conjunction with each other.

Methods to Reduce Pathways for Radon Entry

In Basement and Slab-on-Grade Construction:

- Place a six-mil polyethylene vapor barrier under the slab. Overlap joints in the barrier 12 inches. Penetrations of the barrier by plumbing should be sealed or taped, and care should be taken to avoid puncturing the barrier when pouring slab.
- To minimize shrinkage and cracks in slabs, use recommended water content in concrete mix and keep the slab covered and damp for several days after the pour.
- To help reduce major floor cracks, ensure that steel reinforcing mesh, if used, is imbedded in (and not under) the slab. Reducing major cracks in footings, block foundations, and poured-concrete walls will reduce the rate of radon entry. Radon can, however, enter houses through even the smallest of cracks in concrete slabs and walls if a driving pressure is applied to those surfaces.

E-1 METHODS TO REDUCE PATHWAYS FOR RADON ENTRY

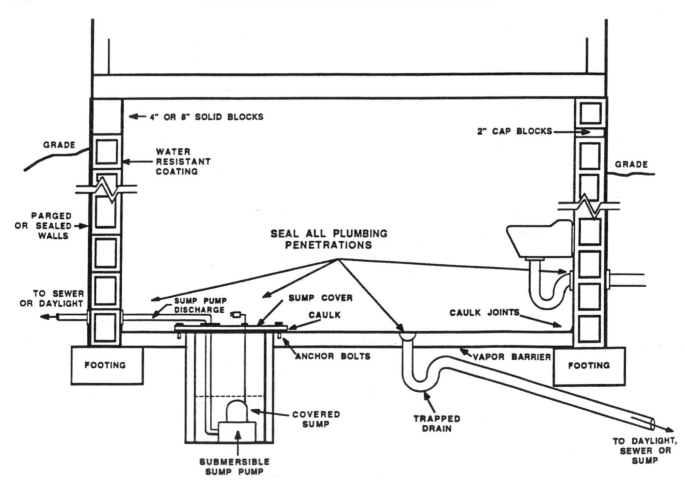

Source: U.S. Environmental Protection Agency, *Radon Reduction in New Construction: An Interim Guide* (OPA-87-009), August 1987.

- The most common pathways of radon entry are inside perimeter floor/wall joints and any control joints between separately poured slab sections. To reduce radon entry through these joints, install a common flexible expansion joint material around the perimeter of the slab and between any slab sections. After the slab has cured for several days, remove or depress the top one-half inch or so of this material and fill the gap with a good quality, noncracking polyurethane or similar caulk. Similar techniques for sealing these joints may also be used.

- In some areas, basement slabs are poured with a French drain channel around the slab perimeter. To be effective, this

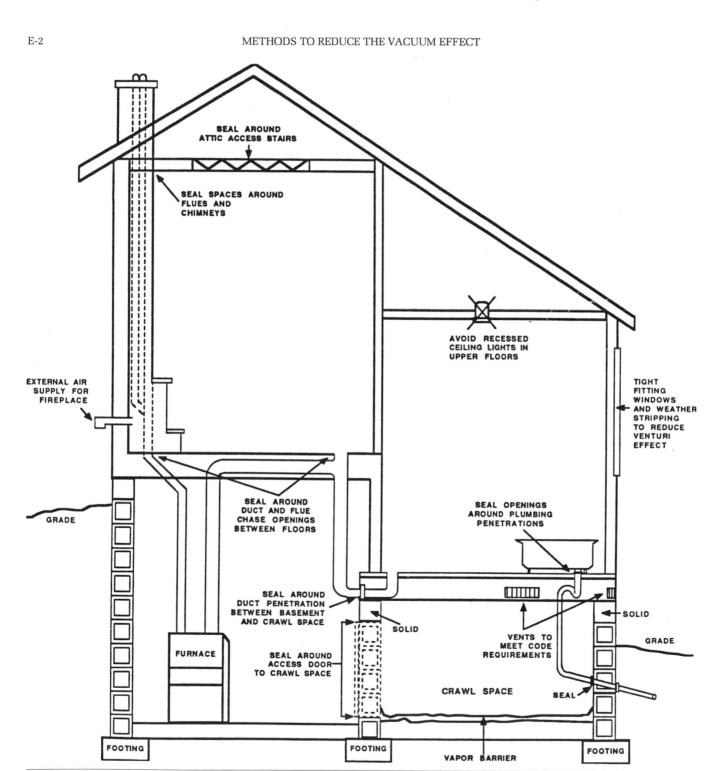

Source: U.S. Environmental Protection Agency, *Radon Reduction in New Construction: An Interim Guide* (OPA-87-009), August 1987.

moisture control technique requires that the floor/wall joint be open to permit water to seep out into the subslab area. To reduce radon entry through such open joints, it may be necessary to install a perforated drain pipe loop under the slab, adjacent to the footing and imbedded in aggregate, and to tie this pipe into a subslab ventilation system to draw radon gas away from the French drain joint. For additional information on water control techniques, refer to the NAHB publication, *Basement Water Leakage: Causes, Prevention, and Correction*.

- When building slab-on-grade houses in warm climates, pour the foundation and slab as a single (monolithic) unit. If properly insulated below grade level, shallow foundations and slabs can also be poured as a single unit in cold climates.
- Remove all grade stakes and screed boards and fill the holes as the slab is being finished. Doing so will prevent future radon pathways through the slab, which might otherwise be created as imbedded wood eventually deteriorates.
- Carefully seal around all pipes and wires penetrating the slab, paying particular attention to bathtub, shower, and toilet openings around traps.
- Floor drains, if installed, should drain to daylight, a sewer, or to a sump with pump discharge. Floor drains should not be drained into a sump if such a pit will be used as part of a subslab ventilation system. Suction on the sump could be defeated by an open line to the floor drain.
- Sumps should be sealed at the top. In closed sumps used for subslab ventilation systems, the continuous flow of moist air through the sump can cause rapid corrosion of exposed sump pump motors. For this reason, submersible-type sump pumps are recommended for closed-sump applications.

In Basement and Crawl Space Construction:

- Seal or cap the tops of hollow-block foundation walls using one of the techniques shown in "Methods to Reduce Pathways for Radon Entry."
- Carefully seal around any pipe or wire penetrations of below-grade walls.
- Exterior block walls should be parged and coated with high-quality vapor/water sealants or polyethylene films. For additional information on wall sealing, refer to the NAHB publication, *Basement Water Leakage: Causes, Prevention, and Correction*. Several new products for use on exterior walls are designed to provide an airway for soil gas to reach the surface outside the wall rather than being drawn through the wall. Similar materials may also be used in subslab ventilation applications.
- Interior surfaces of masonry foundations may be covered with a high-quality, water-resistant coating.
- Heating or air-conditioning ductwork that must be routed through a crawl space or beneath a slab should be properly taped or sealed, particularly for return air ducting, which is under negative pressure. Because of the difficulty in achieving permanent sealing of such ductwork, it may be advisable to redesign heating and ventilating systems to avoid ducting through subslab or crawl space areas, particularly in areas where elevated soil radon levels have been confirmed.
- Install air-tight seals on any doors or other openings between basements and adjoining crawl spaces.
- Seal around any ducting, pipe, or wire penetrations of walls between basements and adjoining crawl spaces and close any openings between floor joists over the dividing wall.
- Place a six-mil polyethylene vapor barrier on the soil in the crawl space. Use a 12-inch overlap and seal the seams between barrier sections. Seal edges to foundation walls.

Methods to Reduce the Vacuum Effect

- Ensure that vents are installed in crawl space walls and are sized and located in accordance with local building practices. Adequate ventilation of crawl spaces is the best defense against radon entry in crawl space–type houses.
- Reduce air flow from the crawl space into living areas by closing and sealing any openings and penetrations of the floor over the crawl space.
- To reduce the stack effect, close thermal bypasses, such as spaces around chimney flues and plumbing chases. Attic access stairs should also be closed and sealed. (Note: Because of potential heat buildup, most codes prohibit insulating around recessed ceiling lights. Such lights should therefore be avoided in top-floor ceilings. As an alternative, use recessed ceiling lights designed to permit insulation or "hi-hat" covers and seal to minimize air leakage.)
- Install ducting to provide an external air supply for fireplace combustion.
- In areas frequently exposed to above-average winds, install extra weather sealing above the soil line to reduce depressurization caused by the Venturi effect. Such sealing will also save energy and reduce the stack effect.
- Air-to-air heat exchange systems are designed to increase ventilation and improve indoor air quality. They may also be adjusted to help neutralize any imbalance between indoor and outdoor air pressure and thus reduce the stack effect of the house. They should not, however, be relied upon as a stand-alone solution to radon reduction in new construction. (A slightly positive pressure, in the basement, may contribute to reducing radon flow into a house.)

Source: U.S. Environmental Protection Agency, *Radon Reduction in New Construction: An Interim Guide* (OPA-87-009), August 1987.

APPENDIX F
Building Code Abbreviations and
Standards-Writing Organizations

Most of the building codes in the United States are based on model codes or other nationally recognized standards. Many building departments offer code books for sale or they are available from the organizations that publish the standards. A partial list of the codes, abbreviations used in this handbook, and where to order follows.

ANSI
American National Standards Institute
1430 Broadway
New York, New York 10018
212-354-3300

ANSI A17.1 Elevators, Escalators, and Moving Walks
ANSI A117.1 Making Buildings and Facilities Accessible to and
  Usable by Physically Handicapped People
ANSI A225.1 Manufactured Home Installations (order from NCSBCS)

ASHRAE
American Society of Heating,
  Refrigerating, and Air-Conditioning
  Engineers, Inc.
1791 Tullie Circle, N.E.
Atlanta, Georgia 30329
404-636-8400

ASHRAE 90-75, 90A-80 Energy Conservation in New Buildings
MCEC Model Code for Energy Conservation in New Building
  Construction

ASME
American Society of Mechanical
  Engineers
2029 K Street, N.W.
Room 605
Washington, D.C. 20006
202-785-3756

ANSI/ASME A17.1 Elevators, Escalators, and Moving Walks

ASTM
American Society of Testing and
  Materials
1916 Race Street
Philadelphia, Pennsylvania 19103
215-299-5400

ATBCB
Architectural and Transportation
  Barriers Compliance Board
330 C Street, S.W.
Washington, D.C. 20202
202-653-7834

UFAS Uniform Federal Accessibility Standards

BOCA
Building Officials and Code
  Administrators International
4051 West Flossmoor Road
Country Club Hills, Illinois 60477
312-799-2300

NBC National Building Code (or Basic Building Code)
NFC National Fire Prevention Code (or Basic Fire Prevention Code)
NMC National Mechanical Code (or Basic Mechanical Code)
NPC National Plumbing Code (or Basic Plumbing Code)
NECC National Energy Conservation Code

CABO
Council of American Building Officials
5203 Leesburg Pike, Suite 708
Falls Church, Virginia 22041
703-931-4533

MEC Model Energy Code
CABO One- and Two-Family Dwelling Code

IAPMO	International Association of Plumbing and Mechanical Officials 5032 Alhambra Avenue Los Angeles, California 90032 213-223-1471	UPC Uniform Plumbing Code UMC Uniform Mechanical Code Uniform Solar Energy Code Uniform Swimming Pool Code
ICBO	International Conference of Building Officials 5360 South Workman Mill Road Whittier, California 90601 213-699-0541	UBC Uniform Building Code UFC Uniform Fire Code UHC Uniform Housing Code UMC Uniform Mechanical Code UPC Uniform Plumbing Code
NCSBCS	National Conference of States on Building Codes and Standards, Inc. 505 Huntmar Park Drive, Suite 210 Herndon, Virginia 22070 703-437-0100	ANSI/NCSBCS A225.1 Manufactured Home Installations Directory of Building Codes and Regulations
NFPA	National Fire Protection Association Batterymarch Park Quincy, Massachusetts 02269 617-770-3000	NEC National Electrical Code NFPA 101 Life Safety Code NFPA 501A Fire Safety Criteria for Manufactured Home Installations, Sites, and Communities
SBCCI	Southern Building Code Congress International 900 Montclair Road Birmingham, Alabama 35213 205-591-1853	SBC Standard Building Code SFC Standard Fire Prevention Code SHC Standard Housing Code SMC Standard Mechanical Code SPC Standard Plumbing Code

Source: National Conference of States on Building Codes and Standards, *Directory of Building Codes and Regulations*, Volume II—State Residential Codes, July 1989. Reprinted with permission.

APPENDIX G
Sample Information Brochure for a Community Association

Commonly Asked Questions about the Cedar Creek Community
June 1989
Subject to Revision

This brochure is intended merely as an overview of the Cedar Creek Community and is not to be read as a substitute for the Declaration of Covenants for the Cedar Creek Community or the Declaration of Covenants, Conditions, and Restrictions for the Village Associations.

Who Is the Developer?

Cedar Creek Properties, Inc., is the owner of this 3,300-acre master-planned community, which is currently under development. Cedar Creek Properties, Inc., is a wholly owned subsidiary of Ash Grove Cement Company. Ash Grove Cement Company is a privately held company that has achieved distinction over the past 109 years for its quality products and services. The company has a proven commitment to Kansas City and strives to be a partner in its growth.

What Is the Cedar Creek Community Services Corporation?

Cedar Creek will be a mixed-use community with various land uses, some private and some public. To create a vehicle to maintain and operate the "public" areas of Cedar Creek, a not-for-profit corporation has been formed. This corporation is called the Cedar Creek Community Services Corporation (CCCSC).

For ease of operations and keeping the Community Services Corporation to a workable number of people, the CCCSC members will be the three Village Associations and the Nonresidential Association (commercial areas). They will be represented by elected or appointed directors of each Village Association and the Nonresidential Association.

As the Cedar Creek Community is developed, the CCCSC will serve the Community in a role similar to a Parks and Recreation Department.

What Are the Primary Responsibilities of the Cedar Creek Community Services Corporation?

The first and most obvious role of CCCSC will be that of a service-oriented "cooperative" business. It will provide a means for the Owners to work together in a privately owned and operated vehicle of service to Cedar Creek.

The CCCSC will enforce use restrictions on the property that it owns (common properties), as more fully specified in the Declaration of Covenants for the Cedar Creek Community, and any Supplemental Declarations.

What Is the Cedar Creek Village I Association, Inc.?

Cedar Creek Properties is comprised of geographic areas of contiguous land that are planned around three Village areas. Each Village will have a "master homeowners' association," referred to as a Village Association. Cedar Creek Village I Association, Inc., is the homeowners' association that is responsible for its respective Areas of Common Responsibility and enforcement of architectural control and rules and regulations within Village I.

What Is the Village Association?

The Village Association is a Kansas not-for-profit corporation in which all property owners in the Village automatically are Members. With that membership, homeowners will have certain rights and obligations. Through this association, homeowners will share in the enjoyment and ownership of common facilities and other amenities. The Village Association also provides a vehicle through which the homeowners can voice their opinions on community-related issues.

What Does the Village Association Do?

The major responsibility of the Village Association is to protect the investment and the value of the property within the Village. It is accomplished by providing the physical maintenance and operation of the common facilities, such as landscape and irrigation maintenance.

Other additional responsibilities of the Village Association will be enforcing the rules and regulations and architectural control guidelines, planning recreational programs, and setting up effective communication among members.

What Are the Primary Responsibilities of the Village Association?

The role of the Village Association will also be that of a service-oriented "cooperative" business, providing a means for the Owners to work together in a privately owned and operated vehicle of service to Cedar Creek.

The Village Association will be responsible for preparing and maintaining accurate budgets, for assessing and collecting each Member's share of the common Expenses, and maintaining a reserve fund sufficient to repair and restore depreciable assets that are part of the Village Common Areas.

How Does the Village Association Work?

The daily operations of the Village Association are the responsibility of the Board of Directors. The Board of Directors is elected by Voting Members, who in turn are elected by the homeowners (Members). It is through these Voting Members, who are your representatives, not unlike those in our governmental system, that the concerns of the homeowners are communicated.

What Is a Neighborhood?

For purposes of voting, providing services, and keeping the association's meetings to a workable number, Village Associations will be comprised of Neighborhoods. A Neighborhood is a separately developed or designated residential area in which the Owners have a common interest other than those common to all Members of the Village Association, e.g., private streets, maintenance concerns, or entry features for the exclusive use of those Owners.

What Is a Neighborhood Association?

If the maintenance requirements of a Neighborhood are elaborate, such as in an area with attached housing, a Neighborhood Association may be formed. Neighborhood Associations will be formed by the Developer and governed by their own elected Board of Directors.

Owners in a Neighborhood without a Neighborhood Association will annually elect a Neighborhood Committee. This committee will consist of three to five people and will act as a liaison to the Village Association.

How Can I Participate in My Association?

As a homeowner in Cedar Creek, you are automatically a Member of a Village Association and a Member of the Neighborhood in which your home is located. You are encouraged to become as involved in your Association's activities as you would like to be, through service on your Neighborhood Committee or other such committees. However, you must observe the Covenants, Conditions, and Restrictions, and your maintenance assessments must be current.

Can I Serve on Any Committee?

Homeowners like yourself will serve on many committees that work with your Village Association. Committees are vital in making your Association a success, and you are encouraged to become involved. You will also find that your committee experience is an asset, should you consider running for a position on the Board of Directors.

How Do I Participate in the Voting Process?

All Owners within each Village Association will exercise their voting rights through a representative form of government. The Owners will all be Members of the Village Association, but their voting rights will be vested in a Voting Member, elected by the Owners within each Neighborhood, thus allowing the Village Association to function with a minimal number of people. Each Voting Member will be entitled to cast one vote for each unit within the Neighborhood that he or she represents.

All operational decisions for the Village Associations will be made by their respective Boards of Directors, which are comprised of directors elected by the Voting Members from each of the different Neighborhoods within the Village Associations.

Will I Have to Pay Assessments?

All Owners will be responsible to pay two levels of assessments to their Village Association: base assessments and neighborhood assessments. Base assessments will be paid equally by all Owners within a particular Village to fund common expenses, such as administrative and maintenance costs associated with the common area facilities in that Village. Base assessments may differ from Village to Village. Base assessments paid to each Village Association will also include assessments to cover that Village's share of the common expenses of that CCCSC.

Neighborhood assessments will be paid to the Village Association by those Owners residing within Neighborhoods that receive special services benefiting only homes within that Neighborhood. An Owner who is also a member of a Neighborhood Association will pay an additional assessment to such Neighborhood Association to cover his share of the expenses of such Neighborhood Association.

Your assessments are critical to the financing of operations and services provided by the Cedar Creek Community Services Corporation, the Village Association, and your Neighborhood Association, if any. Each year, the Board of Directors establishes the assessment rate through the preparation of a budget. Homeowners are then billed monthly or quarterly as determined by the Board of Directors. Prompt payment of your assessments is necessary to maintain the Association's various operations.

What Will the Village Association Maintain?

Each Village Association will own and maintain common areas that are for the use of all residents of that Village. These maintenance functions will be funded through payment of your assessments to the respective Village Association. Maintenance may include landscaping and irrigation of common areas, maintenance of entry features, snow removal, and general repairs, among other things.

What Will the Cedar Creek Community Services Corporation Maintain?

The CCCSC will maintain common areas that are for the benefit of all Owners within Cedar Creek (residential and commercial). Some of these areas will include lakes and ponds, lakeside parks, major entry monuments, irrigation systems for the landscaped common areas, storm drainage systems, the Shadow Lake dam and related features, the main entry water features and related pumps, and all pedestrian trails located within Cedar Creek Valley. CCCSC may also maintain some common areas and facilities that are primarily for the benefit of the residential owners and occupants in all three Villages.

What Amenities Are Available to All Residents?

Cedar Creek offers a variety of leisure-time activities designed to appeal to many lifestyles. Planned amenities may include a 65-acre sailing and fishing lake, the Cedar Creek Swim and Racquet Club, tennis courts, jogging and walking trails, neighborhood parks, picnic areas, a lakeside park, and cycling paths.

What Is the Shadow Glen Golf Club?

Shadow Glen Golf Club is a private club offering 365 memberships to both residents and nonresidents. Membership in the club is achieved through application and selection governed by the procedures established and administered by the board of directors of the club. Only members of the club will be entitled to use of the club's golf course, clubhouse, and any other related facilities. Anyone interested in obtaining a membership in the Shadow Glen Golf Club is encouraged to contact the club office for further information.

Are There Rules and Regulations That I Must Adhere To?

A variety of rules and covenants are set forth in the Declaration of Covenants for the Cedar Creek Community and the Conditions and Restrictions for your Village. These documents should be reviewed by all Owners within the Cedar Creek Community.

In addition, the Village Association may adopt rules and regulations from time to time to help maintain the lifestyle and property values within your Village. You will receive a notice of such rules and regulations as they are adopted.

How Will the Village Association Protect the Value of My Home?

Architectural control is a key element for the protection of all Owners. Two committees have been established to be responsible for architectural control. The New Construction Committee (NCC) is responsible for approving all building and landscape plans for new homes. All Featured Builders and homesite purchasers must receive NCC approval before construction. The NCC has published guidelines and criteria in an "Architectural Review Manual" for assistance in the approval process.

The Modifications Committee (MC) will be established to review and approve any changes, additions, or modifications made to existing houses. The MC will also publish guidelines and criteria to expedite the approval process.

These architectural standards are designed to enhance the appearance of your community and preserve the value of your home. Your commitment and careful attention to these standards will ensure the preservation of the superior living environment of Cedar Creek.

Who Are the Featured Builders?

To achieve these architectural standards, Cedar Creek has established a Featured Builders Program through which various builders have been selected to participate in the development of Cedar Creek. All Featured Builders have been chosen after an extensive study of local builders, their customer satisfaction, quality of construction, and many other factors. These Builders must meet the same high standards of excellence in construction as the developer has established in the development of Cedar Creek.

What Types of Houses Are Available at Cedar Creek?

In the first phase of development, you may purchase through one of the Featured Builders a single-family house, a lake villa, a golf villa, or an attached townhouse. Naturally, price ranges vary depending on location, square footage, and architectural design. Future phases of the development may include these and other types of houses.

How Do I Buy a House in Cedar Creek?

Buying a house within Cedar Creek is a simple process. To make this process easy to understand, we have broken it down into a series of steps, including time limitations, dollar amount needed, and buyer/builder procedures:

1. Day 1 - You select and reserve the lot upon which you would like to build your house. At this time you will make a deposit of 10 percent of the total lot price.

2. By Day 30 - You select the Featured Builder that you would like to build your house and sign a preliminary Home Purchase Agreement with that Featured Builder.

3. By Day 60 - Your Featured Builder will have developed preliminary plans, specifications, and prices for your house. He will then submit these items to the New Construction Committee

for preliminary approval. At this point, you will need to make an additional deposit of 10 percent of the total lot price.

4. On Day 60 - Lot reservations will expire unless an extension has been granted. Extensions will be granted only if all of the above requirements have been completed.

5. Over the Next 60 Days - Your Featured Builder must now prepare the final plans, specifications, and prices. He must also receive final approval from the NCC.

6. By Day 120 - You must sign a Home Purchase Agreement with your Featured Builder, who will then close on the purchase of the lot from the Developer. At this point, you will need to deposit 10 percent of the total purchase price of your lot and home.

7. Your Builder is required to begin construction on your home within 45 days after he has closed on the purchase of the lot from the developer.

8. Your home must be completed by your Featured Builder within one year, at which time you will close with your Builder on your new home in Cedar Creek.

The accompanying flowchart visually represents these steps.

G-1   HOME PURCHASE PROCESS

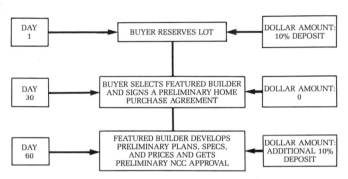

LOT RESERVATION EXPIRES UNLESS EXTENDED

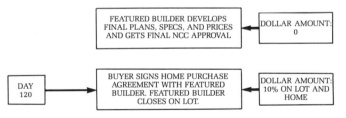

EXTENDED LOT RESERVATION EXPIRES

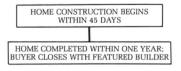

Source: Judith H. Reagan, Community Consultants, Inc., Deerfield Beach, Florida, and Cedar Creek Properties, Inc.

APPENDIX H
Sample Operating Budget Deficit for a Community Association

Provided on these two pages is one developer's projected budget deficit for operating a community association during the estimated period of development (1986 through 1995). In this example, the project consists of a hotel, clubhouse, limited retail and commercial uses, and 1,200 residential units. This sample budget is intended to illustrate the substantial costs that developers can incur to maintain a community association during development phasing. In this case, the developer's estimated deficit is about $11.7 million.

PERIOD OF OPERATION	FIRST YEAR		SECOND YEAR		THIRD YEAR		FOURTH YEAR		FIFTH YEAR	
	JUN 1986	DEC 1986	JUN 1987	DEC 1987	JUN 1988	DEC 1988	JUN 1989	DEC 1989	JUN 1990	DEC 1990
ESTIMATED UNITS SOLD	15	45	50	50	75	75	75	75	75	75
ADD'L ASSESSMENT UNITS										
CLUB	15									
RETAIL/COMMERCIAL	49					26				
HOTEL					120					
TOTAL ASSESSMENT UNITS	79	45	50	50	195	101	75	75	75	75
CUMULATIVE ASSESSMENT UNITS	79	124	174	224	419	520	595	670	745	820
PROJECTED INCOME										
MAINTENANCE FEES-$1302/6MTH	102858	161448	226548	291648	545538	677040	774690	872340	969990	1067640
PROJECTED EXPENSES										
ADMINISTRATIVE EXPENSES										
PROPERTY MANAGEMENT	3318	5208	7308	9408	17598	21840	24990	28140	31290	34440
LEGAL FEES	1000	1000	1000	1000	1000	1000	1000	1000	1000	1000
ACCOUNTING FEES			2500		2500		2500		2500	
INSURANCE	6000		6000		6000		6000		6000	
ADMINISTRATIVE EXPENSES	15	60	110	160	235	310	385	460	535	610
TOTAL ADMINISTRATIVE EXP.	10333	6268	16918	10568	27333	23150	34875	29600	41325	36050
OPERATING EXPENSES										
LANDSCAPE MAINTENANCE	215500	215500	215500	215500	215500	215500	215500	215500	215500	215500
IRRIGATION MAINTENANCE	33000	33000	33000	33000	33000	33000	33000	33000	33000	33000
JANITORIAL SERVICE	29400	29400	29400	29400	29400	29400	29400	29400	29400	29400
REPAIRS AND MAINTENANCE	6000	6000	6000	6000	6000	6000	6000	6000	6000	6000
UTILITIES-ELECTRICITY	10000	10000	10000	10000	10000	10000	10000	10000	10000	10000
WATER & SEWER	87500	87500	87500	87500	87500	87500	87500	87500	87500	87500
TOTAL OPERATING EXPENSES	381400	381400	381400	381400	381400	381400	381400	381400	381400	381400
RESERVES										
ROADWAYS	109	171	240	309	578	718	821	925	1028	1132
CONTINGENCY	133	208	292	376	704	874	1000	1126	1252	1378
TOTAL RESERVES	242	379	532	685	1282	1591	1821	2050	2280	2509
TRANSPORTATION EXPENSES	652455	652456	893449	893449	894055	894056	1416041	1416041	1451402	1451402
TOTAL EXPENSES	1044430	1040503	1292299	1286102	1304070	1300197	1834137	1829091	1876407	1871361
PROJECTED DEFICIT	-941572	-879055	-1065751	-994454	-758532	-623157	-1059447	-956751	-906417	-803721
CUMULATIVE PROJ. DEFICIT	-941572	-1820627	-2886379	-3880833	-4639365	-5262523	-6321969	-7278721	-8185137	-8988858

PERIOD OF OPERATION	SIXTH YEAR		SEVENTH YEAR		EIGHTH YEAR		NINTH YEAR		TENTH YEAR		
	JUN 1991	DEC 1991	JUN 1992	DEC 1992	JUN 1993	DEC 1993	JUN 1994	DEC 1994	JUN 1995	DEC 1995	TOTAL
ESTIMATED UNITS SOLD	75	75	60	65	60	65	50	50	45	45	1200
ADD'L ASSESSMENT UNITS											0
CLUB											15
RETAIL/COMMERCIAL											75
HOTEL		80									200
TOTAL ASSESSMENT UNITS	75	155	60	65	60	65	50	50	45	45	1490
CUMULATIVE ASSESSMENT UNITS	895	1050	1110	1175	1235	1300	1350	1400	1445	1490	1490
PROJECTED INCOME											
MAINTENANCE FEES-$1302/6MTH	1165290	1367100	1445220	1529850	1607970	1692600	1757700	1822800	1881390	1939980	21899640
PROJECTED EXPENSES											
ADMINISTRATIVE EXPENSES											
PROPERTY MANAGEMENT	37590	44100	46620	49350	51870	54600	56700	58800	60690	62580	706440
LEGAL FEES	1000	1000	1000	1000	1000	1000	1000	1000	1000	1000	20000
ACCOUNTING FEES	2500		2500		2500		2500		2500		22500
INSURANCE	6000		6000		6000		6000		6000		60000
ADMINISTRATIVE EXPENSES	685	760	820	885	945	1010	1060	1110	1145	1200	12500
TOTAL ADMINISTRATIVE EXP.	47775	45860	56940	51235	62315	56610	67260	60910	71335	64780	821440
OPERATING EXPENSES											
LANDSCAPE MAINTENANCE	215500	215500	215500	215500	215500	215500	215500	215500	215500	215500	4310000
IRRIGATION MAINTENANCE	33000	33000	33000	33000	33000	33000	33000	33000	33000	33000	660000
JANITORIAL SERVICE	29400	29400	29400	29400	29400	29400	29400	29400	29400	29400	588000
REPAIRS AND MAINTENANCE	6000	6000	6000	6000	6000	6000	6000	6000	6000	6000	120000
UTILITIES-ELECTRICITY	10000	10000	10000	10000	10000	10000	10000	10000	10000	10000	200000
WATER & SEWER	87500	87500	87500	87500	87500	87500	87500	87500	87500	87500	1750000
TOTAL OPERATING EXPENSES	381400	381400	381400	381400	381400	381400	381400	381400	381400	381400	7628000
RESERVES											
ROADWAYS	1235	1449	1532	1621	1704	1794	1863	1932	1994	2056	23212
CONTINGENCY	1504	1764	1865	1974	2075	2184	2268	2352	2428	2503	28258
TOTAL RESERVES	2739	3213	3397	3596	3779	3978	4131	4284	4422	4559	51469
TRANSPORTATION EXPENSES	1451402	1451402	1451402	1451402	1451402	1451402	1451402	1451402	1451402	1451402	25128826
TOTAL EXPENSES	1883316	1881875	1893139	1887632	1898896	1893390	1904193	1897996	1908559	1902141	33629735
PROJECTED DEFICIT	-718026	-514775	-447919	-357782	290926	-200790	-146493	-75196	-27169	37839	-11730095
CUMULATIVE PROJ. DEFICIT	-9706884	-10221659	-10669578	-11027360	-11318286	-11519076	-11665569	-11740765	-11767934		

397

APPENDIX I
Sample Operational Plan for a Community Association
Willoughby Golf Club—Stuart, Florida

Willoughby Golf Club is a 659-acre planned unit development in Stuart, Florida, approved by the Board of County Commissioners through Development Orders 84-12.13 and 87-12.30 on December 22, 1987. The development orders approved 1,421 residential housing units and 45,000 square feet of commercial use. Certain requirements of the development orders will be assigned to the Willoughby Community Association's responsibility, as more fully detailed later in this operational plan. The east side of the property contains 16 parcels, which have currently been master planned for 421 units. The west side contains three residential parcels, which are planned for construction of 1,000 units and one mixed-use parcel planned to contain 48 units and 45,000 square feet of commercial space. The west side of the property is not part of the Willoughby Community Association, and at this time the developer has not determined what form of association, if any, will be imposed on those properties.

The developer intends to construct all units within the multi-family parcels on the east side and offer lots for sale to the public and selected builders within the single-family parcels.

The community will contain a 180-acre golf course and a site for a clubhouse. The club is proposed as an equity-membership facility designed to serve exclusively the property owners on the east side. Other planned amenities include neighborhood recreational features, a pedestrian path system, private roads, custom signs and lighting, and limited-access gates manned 24 hours a day. The west side of the community contains an environmentally protected area of approximately 40 acres, which will be subject to a Shared Costs Agreement between the community association and the property owners on the west side.

The Association

The developer intends to encumber the Willoughby PUD with a master homeowners' association called the Willoughby Community Association. The association will share the responsibility with the west side owners for the costs of maintaining 1) the stormwater management and drainage systems, 2) landscaping in the median and right-of-way along Waterford Boulevard, and 3) the scrub preserve (see Figure I-1) (hereinafter called "Areas of Shared Costs").

The association will be structured using the concepts of neighborhoods and voting members. It will be able to provide specialized services within a neighborhood without the need to form a subassociation. Property owners will all be members of the association, but their voting rights will be vested in a voting member, thus allowing the association to function with a minimal number of people (see Figure I-2).

The Association's Role and Formation

Willoughby was approved for development as a singular PUD; therefore, many ongoing activities and requirements as detailed in the development order must be assigned to the association for perpetual maintenance. Specifically, the habitat management plan for the 40.8-acre scrub preserve must be created and implemented by the developer, and the ongoing maintenance for roads, streets, streetlighting, rights-of-way, irrigation systems, the master drainage system, wetlands and preserves, bike paths, and common areas is the responsibility of the association.

Because products and lifestyle on the east and west sides will be so diverse, the interaction between the two sides will be limited. The developer will initially establish expenses for the Areas of Shared Costs, and the documents should contain protective measures to ensure fair representation for both communities.

The association's first and most obvious role is a service-oriented cooperative business, which will provide a means for the owners to work together in a privately owned and operated vehicle to service the Willoughby PUD. The association will be responsible for preparing and maintaining accurate budgets, assessing and collecting each member's share of the common expenses, and maintaining a reserve fund sufficient to repair and restore depreciable assets.

The community association will have the authority to make rules, enforcing general and neighborhood use restrictions under a cohesive plan of development as more fully specified in the Declaration of CCRs and supplemental declarations as applicable. It will develop communitywide maintenance standards and architectural codes for the various product types and land uses and implement those standards as published in an architectural review and maintenance manual. The developer will enforce architectural and design control over initial construction within the properties.

The association is a not-for-profit corporation formed when the Articles of Incorporation are filed with the Secretary of the state. The property to be initially encumbered is described in two exhibits attached to the Declaration of CCRs, one describing the total property that could eventually be brought into the association, the other describing the initial phases of development (parcels A, B, and D).

For purposes of voting, providing services, and keeping the association's meetings to a workable number, the association will be formed into neighborhoods. The initial formation of neighborhoods will require a supplemental declaration to the Declaration of CCRs. The supplemental declaration must contain any deed restrictions applicable to the particular neighborhood and product type. For neighborhoods of single-family detached housing where the community association does not maintain the properties on behalf of the neighborhood, the supplemental declaration must still contain certain basic information—a legal description of the property along with a sketch of a survey, minimum square footage (if applicable), requirements for architectural control, specifications for materials, and so on. All plats must clearly delineate the common areas, including exclusive common areas that the association will own but where the units in the particular neighborhood will share maintenance costs (see Figure I-3).

All supplemental declarations must be reviewed to ensure that they conform to the community association declaration and do not conflict with any of its provisions. The maintenance requirements should also be reviewed, especially those for multifamily products, to ascertain that the community association can perform the required maintenance. If maintenance requirements are too elaborate, a separate neighborhood association should be considered. If

MASTER DEVELOPMENT PLAN AND AREAS OF
SHARED RESPONSIBILITY FOR MAINTENANCE

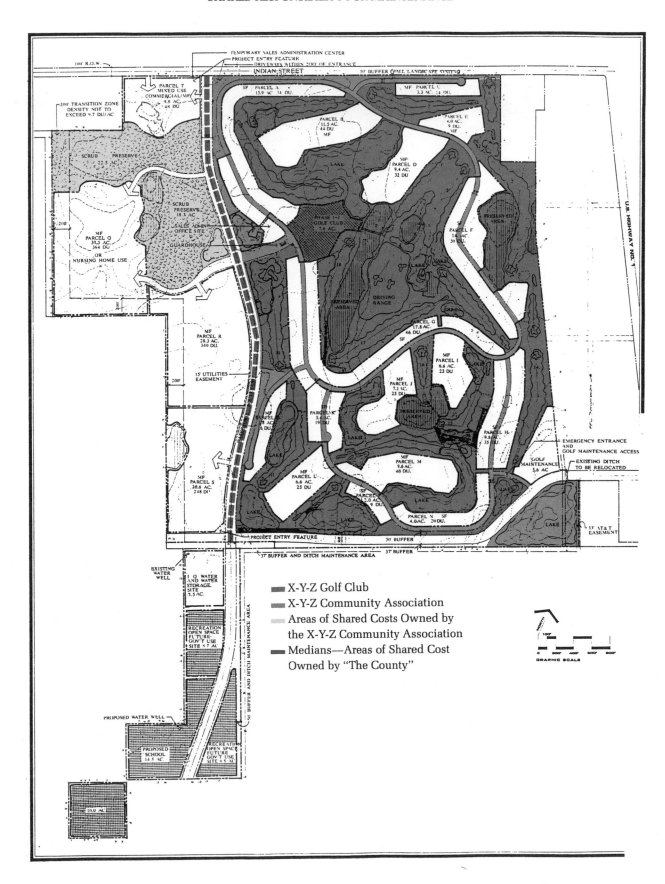

X-Y-Z Golf Club

X-Y-Z Community Association

Areas of Shared Costs Owned by
the X-Y-Z Community Association

Medians—Areas of Shared Cost
Owned by "The County"

STRUCTURE OF COMMUNITY ASSOCIATION
AFTER TURNOVER TO RESIDENTS

Voting

The purpose of forming neighborhoods is to provide a vehicle for the election of directors who represent the total community, to eliminate the need for a meeting involving *all* the homeowners, which in turn minimizes the problem of the lack of a quorum, and to provide the developer-controlled board of directors with a forum for discussing issues affecting the owners. Once a year, the board of directors must convene neighborhood meetings, which might include all neighborhoods of like products. The owners will meet and elect their neighborhood committee and one voting member from their neighborhood, who will proportionally represent the collective votes of that neighborhood at all meetings of the community association.

Before the community association is turned over to the residents, the developer will assign each neighborhood to a voting group, which should include neighborhoods of like product and density. After the turnover, the voting members from each neighborhood cast their collective votes to elect a director to the community association board representing their group, thus ensuring a balanced board that represents all owners and products. Figure I-4 illustrates the five voting groups that could be formed if the current planning for each parcel is implemented.

The boards of directors will make all policy decisions for the association. The association's initial board of directors will be comprised of three individuals appointed by the developer. The developer will have the right to appoint a majority of the board

special or new covenants are created for the neighborhood, the board must adopt and publish appropriate rules and regulations for the owners. For purposes of simplicity, each parcel (A through P) as designated on the master plan may be considered a separate neighborhood.

PLAT NO. 3, SHOWING COMMON AREAS

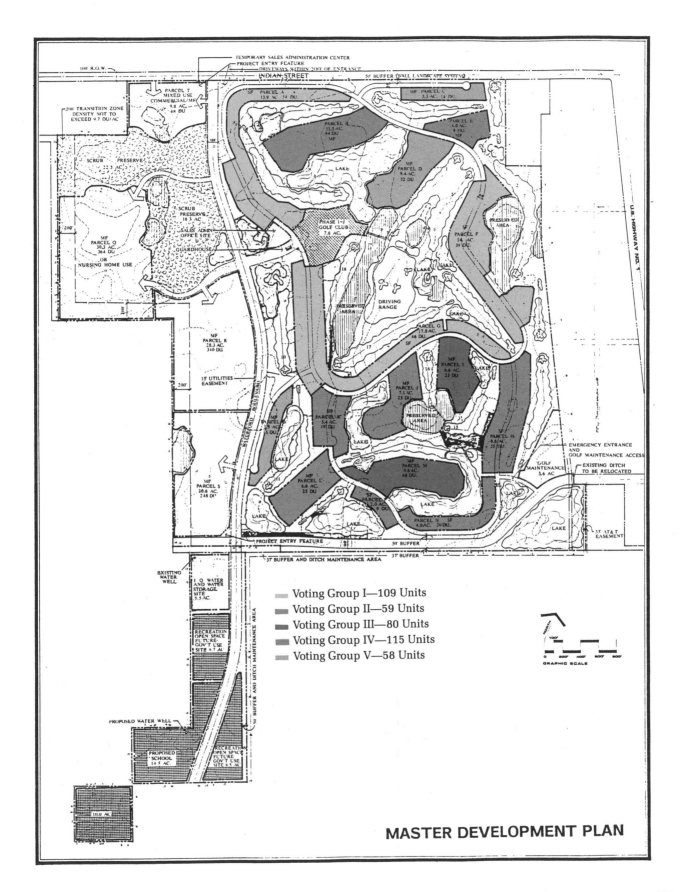

Voting Group I—109 Units
Voting Group II—59 Units
Voting Group III—80 Units
Voting Group IV—115 Units
Voting Group V—58 Units

MASTER DEVELOPMENT PLAN

I-5 BREAKDOWN OF ASSOCIATION BUDGET BY MAJOR LINE ITEM

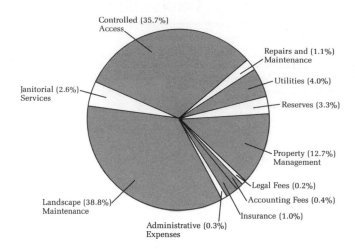

Controlled (35.7%) Access

Repairs and (1.1%) Maintenance

Utilities (4.0%)

Janitorial (2.6%) Services

Reserves (3.3%)

Property (12.7%) Management

Legal Fees (0.2%)

Accounting Fees (0.4%)

Insurance (1.0%)

Landscape (38.8%) Maintenance

Administrative (0.3%) Expenses

I-6 BREAKDOWN OF ASSOCIATION BUDGET PER UNIT

| | PER UNIT | | |
	ANNUALLY	QUARTERLY	MONTHLY
ADMINISTRATIVE EXPENSES			
Property Management	$91.14	$22.79	$7.60
Legal Fees	1.27	0.32	0.11
Accounting Fees	3.16	0.79	0.26
Insurance	7.09	1.77	0.59
Administrative Expenses	1.90	0.48	0.16
Total Administrative Expenses	$104.56	$26.14	$8.71
OPERATING EXPENSES			
Landscape Maintenance	$235.44	$58.86	$19.62
Landscape Extras	30.38	7.60	2.53
Irrigation Maintenance	13.29	3.32	1.11
Janitorial Services	18.99	4.75	1.58
Controlled Access	256.96	64.24	21.41
Repairs and Maintenance	7.59	1.90	0.63
Utilities			
Electricity	27.59	6.90	2.30
Water and Sewer	1.14	0.29	0.10
Total Operating Expenses	$591.38	$147.85	$49.28
RESERVES			
Resurfacing	$20.25	$5.06	$1.69
Contingency	3.80	0.95	0.32
Total Reserves	$24.05	$6.01	$2.01
TOTAL EXPENSES	$720.00	$180.00	$60.00

Note: The expenses shown in this schedule have been rounded to the nearest one cent, which accounts for minor differences between the amounts in the annual, quarterly, and monthly columns.

until 75 percent of the units in the association have been conveyed to owners.

When 25 percent of the units in the community are closed to owners, one member of the board will be replaced with a member elected from the community at large. When 50 percent of the units are closed, an additional director will be elected from the community at large and another one appointed by the developer, thus increasing the board to five members. Only homeowners can vote for these at-large seats. Within 60 days of the closing of 75 percent of the *total* number of units in the association or 10 years of the formation of the community association, whichever occurs first, the neighborhoods will elect a five-member board comprised of one director from each voting group. The board will be elected by the voting members, who will each have one equal vote for the purpose of electing directors. The individuals receiving the majority of votes for each voting group will become directors.

Sales Budget

Figure I-5 shows the percentage of each item in the total budget, and Figure I-6 breaks down the association's budget per unit.

- *Property management.* Fee for a management company, which will bill and collect assessments, pay invoices, prepare correspondence and financial statements, and attend the community association's meetings.
- *Legal fees.* Fees for changing documents and collecting delinquent maintenance fees.
- *Accounting fees.* Fee for an annual review of financial statements by a CPA and preparation of required tax returns.
- *Insurance.* Liability and property damage coverage for the community association's property.
- *Administrative expenses.* Office supplies and mailing costs for the community association.

- *Landscape and irrigation system maintenance.* Maintenance of the community association's landscaping, including cutting grass, applying fertilizer and mulch, and pruning trees.
- *Janitorial services.* Cleaning and maintaining the community association's property in first-class condition.
- *Controlled access.* Gate attendants and roving patrols for the community.
- *Repairs and maintenance.* Cost of minor repairs to and maintenance of the community association's property.
- *Utilities–electricity.* Cost of electricity for the community association's properties, including street lights.
- *Utilities–water and sewer.* Water and sewer for the gatehouse.
- *Reserves–resurfacing.* For resurfacing private roads.
- *Reserves–contingency.* Includes costs of repairs to the gatehouse, entry features, and so on.

APPENDIX J
Sample Chart of Accounts for a Community Association

The following sample chart of accounts is one example of a chart of accounts for a community association. Because of the various conditions that exist within community associations in different parts of the country, the chart of accounts must be tailored to meet the needs of the particular community. Grouping the various accounts into subcategories should be considered to facilitate the reading of financial statements if someone is interested only in totals for categories rather than details. These categories might include administrative expenses, landscape maintenance, controlled access, operational expenses, utilities, reserves, and so on.

Current Assets

Cash - Operating Account
Cash - Special Assessment
Cash - Reserve Account
Cash - Working Capital
Cash - Payroll Account
Cash - Money Market
Cash - Petty Cash
Certificate of Deposit
Accounts Receivable - Homeowner
    Assessments
Accounts Receivable - Special
    Assessments
Accounts Receivable - Commercial
    Association Assessments
Accounts Receivable - Developer
    Assessments
Accounts Receivable - Residential
    Association Assessments
Accounts Receivable - Base Assessment
Accounts Receivable - Neighborhood
    Assessments
Accounts Receivable - Late Fees
Accounts Receivable - Other
Allowance for Bad Debts

Other Assets

Prepaid Insurance
Prepaid Taxes
Other Prepaid Expenses
Furniture & Fixtures
Maintenance Equipment
Recreation Equipment
Vehicles
Accumulated Depreciation
Deposits - Gas
Deposits - Electric
Deposits - Telephone
Deposits - Water
Deposits - Other

Current Liabilities

Accounts Payable
Due to Developer
Due to Community Association
Accrued Payroll Expenses
Taxes - Federal Withholding Tax
Taxes - FICA Payable
Taxes - Federal Unemployment Insurance
Taxes - State Unemployment Insurance

Taxes - State Withholding Tax
Taxes - Federal Income Tax
Taxes - State Income Tax
Taxes - Personal Property Tax
Taxes Payable
Accrued Expenses
Deferred Homeowner Assessments
Deferred Residential Assessments
Deferred Commercial Assessments

Long-Term Liabilities

Reserves
Reserves - Painting
Reserves - Paving/Resurfacing
Reserves - Roof
Reserves - Contingency

Members' Equity

Capital Contribution - Homeowners
Capital Contribution - Developer
Members' Equity
Current Year - Income/Loss
Prior Year - Income/Loss

Income

Homeowner Assessments
Developer Assessments
Developer Contribution
Residential Association Assessments
Commercial Association Assessments
Base Assessments
Neighborhood Assessments
Special Assessments
Entry Cards
Clubhouse Rentals
Vending Machine Income
Interest Income
Late Fee Income
Architectural Review Fees
Screening Fees
Other Income
Insurance - Refund
Rental Income

General and Administrative Expenses

Accounting Fees
Administration Expenses
Bank Charges

Bookkeeping Fees
Dues & Subscriptions
Engineering Expenses
Employee Benefits
Education Expense
Income Tax
Insurance - Fire & Casualty
Insurance - Liability
Insurance - Multiperil
Insurance - Directors & Officers
Insurance - Fidelity Bond
Insurance - Workers' Compensation
Insurance - Group Health
Insurance - Flood
Insurance (all insurance included in one
    account)
Interest Expense
Legal Fees
Licenses & Fees
Management Fees
Miscellaneous
Newsletter
Office Rental
Office Expenses
Payroll Computer Service
Payroll Tax
Postage
Printing Expense
Professional Service
Property Taxes
Salaries
Sales Tax
Screening Fees

Operating Expenses

Telephone
Air Conditioning Repair
Building Maintenance
Cabana Maintenance
Carpet Cleaning
Elevator Maintenance
Entry Features
Equipment Replacement
Fence Repairs
Fountain Maintenance
Janitorial Service
Janitorial Supplies
Lake Maintenance
Lighting Repairs
Miscellaneous
Operating Supplies
Painting

Pedestrian Paths
Perimeter Walls
Pest Control - Exterior
Pest Control - Interior
Repairs & Maintenance
Roadway and Parking Repairs &
    Maintenance
Roof Repairs
Sidewalks
Sign Maintenance
Street Sweeping
Trash Removal
Uniforms
Water Management System
Window Cleaning

Controlled Access

Alarm System
Entry Cards
Gate Repairs
Gatehouse Maintenance
Guard Service
Payroll Expenses
Payroll Taxes
Personnel - Salaries
Radio Leasing
Security Supplies
Telephone - Gatehouse
Uniforms - Gatehouse Staff
Vehicle - Gas
Vehicle Repairs & Maintenance

Landscape Maintenance

Annuals (Flowers)
Fertilizing
Irrigation Maintenance
Irrigation Supplies
Landscape Extras
Lawn Care
Mulch Replacement
Pest Control - Lawn
Shrub Replacement
Tree Pruning

Pool Maintenance

Pool Chemicals
Pool Equipment
Pool Filters
Pool Furniture
Pool Repairs
Pool Service
Pool Supplies
Pump Repairs
Spa Repairs & Maintenance

Utilities

Electric
Gas
Water & Sewer

Reserves

Painting
Paving/Resurfacing
Roof Maintenance
Perimeter Wall
Contingency

Master Association Fees

Commercial Association Fees
Residential Association Fees

Service Fees

Cable TV
Monitoring System Fees

Source: Judith H. Reagan, Community Consultants, Inc., Deerfield Beach, Florida. For a more detailed chart of accounts, see *Financial Management of Condominium and Homeowners' Associations*, 2d rev. ed. (Washington, D.C./Alexandria, Va.: ULI–the Urban Land Institute and CAI–Community Associations Institute, 1985), pp. 31–40.

APPENDIX K
Market Analysis Checklist

1. Description of Market Area
   a. Size (total population)
   b. Topographical features
   c. Transportation arteries, ease of access
   d. Direction of recent growth
   e. Special features, characteristics, and considerations
   f. Community developments planned or in process
   g. Map of area

2. Economics of Market Area
   a. Brief history of growth and development
   b. Analysis of office and retail markets, strengths and weaknesses
   c. Employment: types and trends
   d. Principal employers
   e. Unemployment: current levels and trends
   f. Average family income: current levels and trends

3. Demographics of Market Area
   a. Distribution by age
   b. Distribution by education
   c. Distribution by household size
   d. Special features, for example, military-connected households
   e. Current estimate and future trends

4. Conditions of Market Area
   a. Housing supply: characteristics by type and structural condition
   b. Residential building activity: current and planned
   c. Description of comparable competitive projects: number of units, size, rents
   d. Absorption of comparable projects (by month, by year)
   e. Tenure of occupancy: current estimate and past trends
   f. Vacancy rates: owners and renters
   g. Mortgage market: activity and source of funds
   h. Sales market: volume, prices, inventory, and outlook
   i. Rental market: existing/new, prices and outlook, volume

5. Demand for Housing
   a. Projected increase in types of households
   b. Locations favorable for market absorption
   c. Occupancy potential for subsidized/nonsubsidized single-family units
   d. Occupancy potential for subsidized/nonsubsidized multifamily units

---

Source: Adapted from U.S. Department of Housing and Urban Development, "How to Design a Rental Rehabilitation Program" (Washington, D.C.: Author, 1985).

INDEX